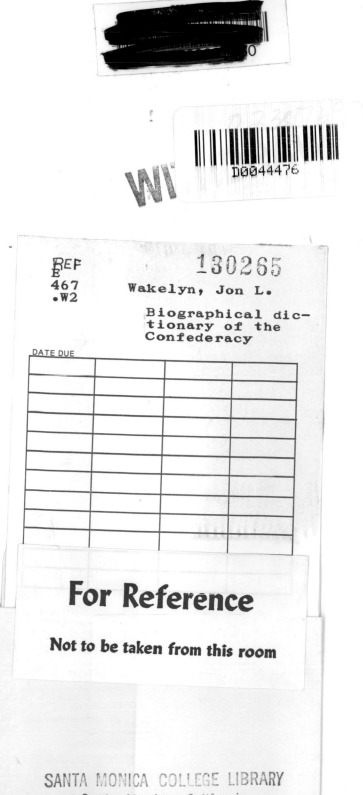

D0044476

REF
E
467
.W2   130265

Wakelyn, Jon L.

Biographical dic-
tionary of the
Confederacy

DATE DUE

For Reference

Not to be taken from this room

SANTA MONICA COLLEGE LIBRARY
Santa Monica, California

*Biographical
Dictionary
of the
Confederacy*

BIOGRAPHICAL DICTIONARY OF THE CONFEDERACY

JON L. WAKELYN

Frank E. Vandiver, *ADVISORY EDITOR*

(G P) *GREENWOOD PRESS*

WESTPORT, CONNECTICUT • LONDON, ENGLAND

SANTA MONICA COLLEGE LIBRARY
Santa Monica, California

Library of Congress Cataloging in Publication Data

Wakelyn, Jon L
  Biographical dictionary of the Confederacy.

  Bibliography: p.
  Includes index.
  1. Confederate States of America—Biography.
2. United States—History—Civil War, 1861-1865—
Biography. I. Title.
E467.W2   973.7'13'03   72-13870
ISBN 0-8371-6124-X

Copyright © 1977 by Jon L. Wakelyn

All rights reserved. No portion of this book may be
reproduced, by any process or technique, without
the express written consent of the publisher.

Library of Congress Catalog Card Number: 72-13870
ISBN: 0-8371-6124-X

First published in 1977

Greenwood Press, Inc.
51 Riverside Avenue, Westport, Connecticut 06880

Printed in the United States of America

To the memory of
ARTHUR THOMAS WAKELYN
1906-1972

130265

Contents

Prefatory Note

Despite the surfeit of books dealing with Confederate affairs, there is a scarcity of biographical information on Southern wartime leaders. This is odd because the Civil War, especially the Confederate's war, was so personal. The formidable *War of the Rebellion: A Compilation of the Official Records of the Union and Confederate Armies*, the recollective *Battles and Leaders of the Civil War*, and the legions of memoirs illustrate the personal focus of the war. But the great compendia, and even most reminiscences, tend to emphasize events rather than careers. Especially forgotten are the political, business, and intellectual figures of Rebel society.

Jon Wakelyn's interest in certain Southern intellectual leaders of the nineteenth century led him, in time, to the Confederate establishment. The paucity of information on this particular social element spurred him to a general survey of Confederate biographical sources. The survey revealed a peculiar gap in personal data, and so it was that he launched into this *Dictionary* project. As he progressed, he became increasingly intrigued with "Collective Biography" and employed computational techniques in comparative analyses of lives and careers. The result is a remarkably useful historical tool—a biographical directory that is also an analytical dictionary of attitudes, occupations, and power structures. Here may be found sketches of soldiers, politicians, women, editors, clergymen and many other kinds of leaders. Here, too, are prewar parallels in background, education, and politics along with postwar careers. From these varieties of information come glimpses of a class, insights into an elite, which provide new indexes to leadership.

Some readers may quibble about people included, some will want additions, but all will be grateful for so useful a book—one which is both a solid reference and a methodological primer.

Frank E. Vandiver

Preface

Study of Confederate leaders has been largely approached through individual biographies. Thus, anyone seeking to establish the interrelationships between the military, political, and business leaders, relationships which are vital to any understanding of individual and collective performance, would have to consult a multitude of sources. The few scholars who have studied collective leadership have only analyzed specific groups, such as the Army of Northern Virginia, the Davis cabinet, or the Confederate Congress. This *Dictionary* chronicles the career patterns of the most important Confederate leaders in one volume, so as to provide a corrective to the specific group and the individual biographical study of Confederate leadership. A reference work based on such an approach should be of value to both the scholar and general reader.

Full evaluation of collective action among wartime careers is a task beyond the scope of this project, although some judgments of that nature were attempted. The problems of selectivity and information from careers placed severe limitations on final judgments of the leaders' performances. Criteria for analyzing collective performance simply do not transfer from military to civilian political personnel. However, when the various duties of the groups selected for study are compared, it is hoped that the relative success of some leadership groups may lend themselves to comparative analysis.

To that end, the introductory chapters that follow are designed to complement the individual biographical sketches and the appendices contained in the *Dictionary*. The first chapter treats the uses of collective biography for historical analysis, the criteria used for leadership selection, the factual information included in each biography necessary to an evaluation of performance, the sources from which the data were drawn, and the processes by which the lives were analyzed and the careers compared. The second chapter attempts to study the prewar career patterns of the wartime leaders in terms of their preparation for the war effort. Some special attention has been given to the questions of generational patterns of family political and material power as well as detailed analysis of secessionist/unionist positions of the leaders. The third chapter discusses and compares the wartime activities of the leaders, points out the problems of coordination and continuity, and makes tentative judgments on the quality of performance and the obstacles to effective performance. The fourth chapter carries the question of the continuity of leadership into the postwar years in order to test the effectiveness of wartime leaders in creating a "New South." The conclusions drawn, largely quantitative in nature, may serve as a beginning for collective analysis of Southern leadership in the era of Civil War and Reconstruction.

There is always pleasure in thanking those people and institutions who not only made the project possible but also share none of the blame for its contents. The staffs of the Library of Congress, the Jefferson Davis Papers at Rice University, the Southern Historical Collection at the University of North Carolina, the Duke Library, and the South Caroliniana Library at the University of South Carolina have been helpful and patient. Bob Hagelstein and Jim Sabin of Greenwood Press have been understanding. Frank E. Vandiver not only served in the thankless role of advisor to one who takes little advice, but also finally convinced me that the Civil War is worth studying. My colleagues at Catholic University, Guy Lytle and Tom Henderson, spent much time listening to my plans for how the project would evolve. Friends in the profession, John T. Hubbell and Thomas L. Connelly, have encouraged the project. Roland Parenteau put in yeoman effort on the quantitative aspects of this study. Lastly, my wife, Catherine Carl Wakelyn, as always turned my stilted prose into readable sentences, revised many of the individual biographical sketches, and is responsible for most of the appendices.

July 1975
Washington, D.C.

Introduction

1 / *The Study of Leadership*

Lawrence Stone has described collective biography as "the investigation of the common background characteristics of a group of actors in history by means of a collective study of their lives."[1] In the case of the Confederate leaders, contributions to the war effort define the group for study. But exactly which individuals and occupations within that group deserve inclusion in an analysis of leadership? Also, what aspects of their lives or their career patterns require discussion for an understanding of their wartime behavior? Since the continuity of leadership also reflects on the values the society placed on positions of public trust, the total career pattern calls for study. In order to evaluate that performance, the entire period of the Civil War and Reconstruction (1830-1877) must be considered.

Once the group and the chronological perimeters are established, many questions remain. For example, what background characteristics deserve study? Since each future leader led a somewhat different life from that of his peers, what patterns of similarity of background should be included in this study? Given the many questions of status and class, what values should be placed on the conditions of opportunity, growth, and mobility as factors in the prewar careers of the future leaders? How does one accurately judge the relationship of the career patterns to the preparation for the leadership thrust upon these individuals? Above all, once the data for study are selected, where can that information be found? Fortunately, there exists a body of works on collective biography which should at least assist in determining how the above questions may be approached.[2]

Perhaps the first systematic attempt at collective biography in this country was Orin Grant Libby's *Distribution of the Vote of the Federal Constitution* (1894), which compared the lives of the delegates to the Constitutional Convention in order to determine why they supported or opposed the Constitution. Charles Beard's monumental *Economic Interpretation of the Constitution* (1913) was also an attempt to understand the vote of each delegate to the Convention and to analyze state support or opposition to ratification of the Constitution. Since other scholars have studied these works so thoroughly, let it simply be stated here that both Libby and Beard brought a single deterministic view to the study of human behavior. Libby believed that the jealousy of states based on their geographical location determined how each delegate voted, while Beard insisted that the single desire for material gain determined human behavior.[3] Neither work really studied the dynamics of group pressure on the individual decisionmaker. Both books teach one to guard against predetermined and unicausal conclusions on individual and group behavior.

Libby and Beard remained alone among American scholars in their studies of collective behavior until the 1930s, when Frank Lawrence Owsley and his students formed the Vanderbilt school of social historians.[4] Owsley's most important work, *Plain Folk of the Old South*, is the culmination of years of study of the middle class and the democratic nature of the Old South. His imaginative use of manuscript census returns influenced the studies of Barnes Lathrop and his students at the University of Texas.[5] Both men emphasized the importance of studying class structure and undoubtedly influenced the best modern work on social history, as most recently exemplified by Stephen Thernstrom's *Poverty and Progress* (1964).[6] Thernstrom's use of census returns and local records, including probate and marriage records, in analyzing the social composition of Irish immigrants in a New England town over a forty-year period has become a model study of the common people. Although Owsley, Lathrop, and Thernstrom have not dealt with the problems of an elite leadership class, their use of new materials has provided needed information on the middle-class background of nineteenth-century political and business leaders. They have also elucidated the expectations and social values of much of that society.

Other spinoffs from the study of collective action have revealed some of the restrictions on the decisionmaking practices of the elite, as well as the ideals and issues to which the leadership must subscribe. After the publication of Lee Benson's *The Concept of Jacksonian Democracy* in 1961, historians finally acknowledged the revolutionary impact of collective voting behavior analysis on the study of political history.[7] Benson's use of county records and census returns showed the multiple factors in voter decisions and directed scholars to an appreciation of local and regional issues and issues which transcended narrow material interests. Benson's book and the works of Paul Kleppner and Richard Jensen have shown the importance of ethnic and religious ties in influencing behavior. In doing so, they have pointed to the meaning of bloc pressure voting on a local community. Employing the concept of negative reference group theory, they have revealed lasting hostilities among groups which continue to influence political behavior long after the issues which caused the disagreement have been forgotten.[8] These studies have further refined analysis of collective behavior by showing the implications of voter power over the decisionmakers. Their work has had major implications for understanding the qualities of leadership the people desired.[9]

Several recent studies of elites have also influenced the methodology of this present work. For example, Thomas Cochran's *Railroad Leaders* (1953) analyzed the leading railroad executives between 1845 and 1890, in order to understand how they rose to power and how they maintained that power. Cochran collected data on the lives of the railroad men, classified the data, and then compared those lives.[10] Edward Digby Baltzell in *Philadelphia Gentlemen* (1958) has described the continuity and the power of an upper class over long periods of time. Using *Who's Who in America* and the Philadelphia *Social Register*, Baltzell has shown the importance of family and kinship ties as well as church membership in sustaining the social connections of the upper classes. The flexibility of that elite is also demonstrated in its willingness to admit the best political and business talent from the middle classes into its group.[11]

A significant recent study in collective biography is Sidney Aronson's *Status and Kinship in the Higher Civil Service* (1964), a work that finally puts to rest the notion that the Age of Jackson ended elite politics in the United States.[12] Aronson studied the many facets of the relationship between social class and political power over forty years of government service. He used occupation to understand the meaning of status, because it often dictated wealth and demonstrated what public service the leadership class would enter. His use of the *Dictionary of American Biography*, family histories, and county histories reveals an understanding of the need to collect personal data for collective analysis. His comparison of educational levels calls attention to the generational status upheaval resulting from changes in patterns of attendance at prestigious universities. Both the kinds of questions posed and the methods of categorizing the data for collective comparison over generations make Aronson's work almost a model for collective biography.

The most important works on leadership and collective action in the antebellum South are Ralph Wooster's *The Secession Conventions of the South* (1962) and *The People in Power* (1969), studies which have been largely ignored by the qualitative historians of the period.[13] Tired of the loose judgments on who led the South to secession, Wooster used the pioneering work of Barnes Lathrop in the manuscript census reports and found significant data on the lives of those men who served in the secession conventions. Using schedule number two of the 1860 census, which listed slaveholding and property worth, Wooster established a correlation between secession vote and slaveownership in the Upper South. But his evidence also revealed no correlation between radical action and slaveownership in the Lower South. Wooster's first book also included some analysis of occupation as a factor in the support of or opposition to secession. One wishes that Wooster had compared age groupings to public office and political experience to the intensity of initial secession sentiment in order to get a set of multiple reasons for a delegate's position on secession.

In *The People in Power*, Wooster amended his previous conclusion "that the leaders of these heavily slave-populated areas were convinced that secession was necessary to protect their economic-social order from destruction. . . ." He analyzed both the sources and the positions of political power in the antebellum South and described how leaders exercised their power.[14] His sources included county histories and the laws and procedures of the county court system. He studied the career patterns of state legislators, governors, judges, and county officials. By looking at the relationship between officeholding and family connections, Wooster demonstrated the dramatic shifts in personnel in public office and established that turnover kept any single political faction from consolidating its power in a state or dictating a state's response to the secession crisis. The biographical data in this dictionary, when combined with Wooster's work, should provide additional information on leadership behavior and change in the years before and during the Civil War.

Thomas P. Alexander and Richard E. Beringer in *The Anatomy of the Confederate Congress* (1972) have asked penetrating questions about the collective behavior of the Congress in terms of its support or rejection of the Davis administration.[15] Their roll call analysis of congressional votes shows that biographical information on each congressman assists in determining political actions. For example, through collective analysis of the career patterns of the Confederate Congress, they have shown how prewar political support for secession and the state from which each congressman came influenced his performance during the war. Additional biographical information included in this dictionary should serve to affirm, and perhaps even sharpen, their major conclusions on congressional behavior.

The Politics of Command (1973) by Thomas L. Connelly and Archer Jones is the most recent study of collective military behavior in the Confederacy.[16] The authors have asked questions about the political decisions related to troop movements, troop allocations, and military strategy. Through an analysis of family connections, old school ties, state loyalties, and political cliques, they have attempted to understand the most sensitive relations between the military and the Congress and the bureaucracy. Connelly and Jones have discovered what they call a "western concentration bloc." This group remained loyal to President Davis throughout most of the war but opposed him on the issues of the excessive use of manpower to defend Virginia and the second-rate commanders sent to the western theatre of military operations. Their knowledge of the role of the military in the war effort, together with their original analysis of collective kinship ties as factors in decisionmaking, make this the most original book on the reasons why the Confederate leadership failed.

The above studies not only reveal the impossibility of fully determining human action, but they also offer some insights into the leadership of the Civil War and Reconstruction era. The interaction between class and status and the politics of republican government show that the leaders had only limited control over their own activities.[17] Wartime often calls for qualities of leadership which are sublimated during peacetime, but the reader still gathers from these studies the qualities of leadership, obstacles to wartime success, and the aspects of a career which contribute to an understanding of the meaning of success or failure.

Scholars and buffs will no doubt quarrel with the personnel included in this dictionary as Confederate leaders, but when the criteria for selection are fully explored, it is hoped that the people included, the facts about their lives, and the sources used to derive those facts will be accepted as one means of answering the difficult questions of collective analysis of the Confederate war effort.

Those who fought the war have long been regarded as the most important leaders of the Confederacy. Hence, of the 651 men and women in this study, 265 are generals and naval officers.[18] Many young men made up the cadres of officers and enlisted personnel who actually did the fighting and most of the dying. Unfortunately, they cannot be considered for a study of leadership, since few of them made the decisions of where, when, and how to fight. Likewise, the judgments of success and failure cannot be laid at the feet of all of the 425 general officers. The generals who are included in this dictionary were selected on the basis of their time in positions of major command, their participation in major battles, and their duties during the war. Staff officers who planned the strategy of war and generally made key decisions as to when to fight, and officers who directed supplies and ordnance are included because of their roles in warmaking.

Congressmen were uneven in their contributions to the war effort. Many served only for a few months, spoke little, and left no significant record of votes. But they all voted, and those votes directly affected President Davis's and the cabinet's direction of the war. The congressmen's general reflection of constituent opinion also makes them important as political representatives. Some congressmen, like James L. Orr and Robert M. T. Hunter, actually made policy; others became so disruptive of political continuity in Richmond that they deserve inclusion for their negative contributions. Because Congress influenced military policy by their votes, all Confederate congressmen have been included in this study.[19]

The president, vice-president, and cabinet made policy decisions and sought to implement them. Clearly, their relations with Congress and the military require their inclusion in this dictionary.[20] Not so obvious are the subcabinet leaders who defy categorization but made important contributions to the war effort. Some of them held line offices and important staff positions in the military, while others came to represent the new breed of professional government employees, the forerunners of the modern American bureaucracy. They were responsible for raising, supplying, and even moving troops. Many served the cabinet as liaison officers with the Congress, others actually directed various government departments, while some served in the diplomatic corps. Few of them have been recognized for their contributions, and even fewer have had biographers. It is hoped that the sketches in this dictionary will be of use to those scholars who are at last taking a serious look at these leaders.[21]

The state governors, except for the state rights heroes such as Joseph E. Brown of Georgia and Zebulon B. Vance of North Carolina, have not been carefully studied for their roles in the war effort.[22] Yet, they made state war policy, controlled the state militias, and so affected the war effort that some of them were accused of sabotage. The governors influenced Confederate congressmen, reflected their states' support for the war, and even shared with the Richmond government the formation of policy. Their state legislatures did have a few men who so influenced state policy that they must be included in this work. An example is Linton Stephens of Georgia, who worked closely with his brother, the vice-president.

Because there was no Confederate Supreme Court, the state courts assumed all of the judicial burdens. A few judges served as bulwarks to protect the individual and state rights and often hindered Confederate government policy. These state leaders must have a place in any attempt to analyze the performance of the collective leadership of the Confederacy.

With so much interest in the economics of war and in the controversies over the role of war in speeding industrialism, one would expect that the business leaders of the Confederacy would already have been carefully studied. But, aside from the recent biography of Joseph Anderson of the Tredegar Iron Works, only the unsung heroines of the ersatz war have been closely examined.[23] The government relied heavily on private business, from blockade runners to ironmakers to powdermak-ers. Individual businessmen, farmers, and scientists made contributions vital to the total coordination of the personnel of the war. They too are included in this dictionary.

A most subjective decision has been that of including only those cultural leaders who served as wartime propagandists. Loyalists such as William Gilmore Simms and men who would develop their literary talent during the war, such as Henry Timrod and Sidney Lanier, made little contribution to the war.[24] On the other hand, "Bill Arp" and Augusta Jane Evans, author of *Macaria*, influenced troop performance through their humor and their patriotism, and they emerged as important wartime cultural leaders. Some educational leaders also belong in this study, especially those like David Swain, president of the University of North Carolina, who kept his school open throughout the war and made plans for the New South. Most importantly, those cultural leaders who played a political propagan-distic role deserve inclusion in this study. The ministers who preached in favor of continuing the war effort made immeasurable contributions to citizen morale. Members of the press also have a place because their continued coverage of the battles served to sustain public support for the war. Editors such as Edward A. Pollard, who turned against the Davis administration, are important for their negative contributions. Although one must be careful in making claims for the cultural leaders, their role cannot be underestimated.

As contribution to the total war effort defined the rationale for selecting the leaders in this work, so the events in their prewar lives which may have influenced their wartime behavior provided the rationale for selecting the information used in the individual biographies. The facts of the Confederate leaders' lives included in this study follow the general pattern of short biographical sketches contained in works such as the *Dictionary of American Biography*. However, some material is unique to this study because both the prewar and the postwar periods have been examined to sharpen an understanding of wartime contributions. One must also remember that the subjective choice of biographical material determines both the types and the quality of questions which may be asked about collective behavior.

Birth and death dates are obvious background material to assess the impact of age on participation in critical events. The birthplace of each leader, how often he moved, where he lived in 1860, and whether he remained in the South after the war are important for understanding the impact of geography, mobility, and state pride on the actions of the Confederate leaders. To test the continuity of leadership and the idea of an hereditary Southern aristocracy, family background in terms of father's occupation, father's political affiliation, family relationships from both sides, and relationship to another war leader have been included in this study. Educational level and professional training, rank in class, attendance at a military school, and religious affiliation, long a neglected area for analysis, have also been noted.

Out of career background material evolves the second category of prewar activities. Prewar and postwar party affiliation, along with presidential support in 1860, are important when one realizes the place of lasting political allegiances and hostilities in the Old South. Private career patterns based on years in each business or professional career and public offices in terms of years in each position and the importance of the office are included because they relate directly to the kind of experience brought to the war. Attendance at various conventions, including the Nashville convention of 1850, the Charleston national Democratic convention of 1860, and state secession conventions, reveals prewar political attitudes and exposure to other leaders. For the military personnel and the many civilians who served in the army, experience in the Black Hawk War, the Seminole wars, and the Mexican War has been noted. The position of Confederate leaders on secession in 1860-1861 concludes the prewar information.[25]

President Jefferson Davis's Richmond government coordinated the war effort, and the president served as the chief decision and policymaker. But Davis was only a success as his subordinates remained able and willing to carry out his dictates. Support or antagonism to the peace movement, votes in favor of or against executive policy, and turnover in political office are key factors in understanding Confederate congressional behavior. For the generals, rank achieved, types of duties, numbers of promotions, and theatres of operation are included. For all leaders who resigned from office, their reasons for resignation are examined. Qualitative information, such as letters and diaries, supplement the quantitative data questions for studying the activities of the Confederate leaders. In this manner, the actual performance, as well as the many physical obstacles to performance, have been related to a tentative evaluation of the quality of leadership.

In order to conclude the investigation of performance, generational change, and leadership upheaval, the postwar years were also studied. Many myths have arisen over the role of wartime leaders in directing both the political resistance to Reconstruction and the restoration of the antebellum plantation aristocracy in the

New South.[26] Information was gathered on postwar private occupations and public career patterns, changes in postwar party affiliation, mobility in terms of times moved and final location, and obstacles to public service.

Information analyzed in earlier literature as determinants of behavior was omitted from this study. For example, slaveholding was so common and had so little effect on wartime activities that it was not included. Moreover, most of the leaders owned property and Alexander and Beringer found no correlation between ownership and congressional position on secession or support for the Confederacy. But the reader is advised to peruse for himself the many earlier studies of material possessions and political and military behavior.[27]

The data included in the sketches and used to analyze the career patterns of the Confederate leadership are no better than the sources from which they are derived.[28] Some of the individuals studied have had multiple biographies. For the most famous of them, letters, wills, and obituaries are easily available for verifying the biographical material. With regard to those whose reputations have been exaggerated over the years, the generals chronicled in laudatory journals such as the *Confederate Veteran*, information from West Point records and from the *Official Record of the Union and Confederate Armies* has hopefully put these men in proper perspective. On the other hand, other military men and a large number of congressmen who dropped out of public sight when the war ended have been difficult to trace. The search for material on most of them required digging into old files and county studies.

The *Dictionary of American Biography*, the nineteenth-century *Cyclopedia of American Biography*, and *Appleton's Encyclopedia of American Biography* served as the initial sources for biographical information. However, these collections are elitist, omit many of the Confederate leaders, and sometimes have faulty and misleading information. Still, they have been indispensable to this study. Key information on prewar activities, names of friends and business associates, and even religious affiliation were obtained from the filiopietistic state and county biographical directories. Most of these books were compiled in the late nineteenth century and, except for the bias against former Confederates in the biographical studies of Tennessee and Kentucky, generally contained helpful information. Owen's *History of Alabama and Dictionary of Alabama Biography*, although a carefully researched study, sometimes distorted the importance of native Alabama leaders. Those biographical studies compiled in large urban areas or in the economic boom days around World War I were contracted by subscription and are suspect because they contain only the praiseworthy information which the powerful and rich wanted included about themselves or their ancestors.[29]

Amateur scholars who knew virtually nothing about social history usually wrote the county and town histories. Though often distorted, these works contain biographical information on positions held and family connections which cannot be obtained elsewhere. The biographies of its nineteenth-century legislators collected by the State Historical Society of Tennessee were indispensable to this work. But the best information on the individual lives was found in the county and city courthouses, which house wills, marriage records, city directories, church membership rolls, birth rolls, and county census returns. When possible, they were used to corroborate facts in the secondary material which was used to create these biographical sketches.[30]

Once gathered, how is it possible to analyze the factual information, amounting to some seventy-two variables, on the lives of so many Confederate leaders? Since collective performance and analysis of that performance are the intent of this study, the large number of leaders' lives can only be compared by use of the computer. The computer enabled me to ask questions about these collective lives which greatly enhanced this study, and at the same time served as an unprecedented educational tool.[31]

Even with the use of the computer for quantifiable accuracy, however, this effort must remain subjective. If questions about a leader's life are faulty and if the amount and accuracy of information available are limited, any study will be distorted to some degree. Data such as previous evaluations of an individual leader's place in the war effort have been taken largely from the best of the secondary works. My understanding of class and the governmental system is based on both primary and secondary material. Prewar career information on each leader was available in unequal amounts. Finally, I have been able to use only a minimal amount of comparative analysis with the Northern counterparts of these Southern leaders. Thus, the actual judgment of actions, or even the atypicality of the Confederate leaders' career patterns in the entire era of Civil War and Reconstruction, cannot as yet be fully understood. Yet, it is hoped that the questions posed and the tentative answers ventured may enable future scholars to build upon this study of collective behavior.

2 / Background and Preparation / of the Confederate Leaders

What effect did the Confederate leaders' prewar careers have on their behavior during the Civil War? Though the level of preparedness for wartime service surely cannot be used as a single criterion for evaluating performance, it should give an indicator of what to expect from the Confederacy's leadership. The information extant on family background, class and status loyalties, and job opportunities is incomplete. Yet, their actual career patterns, public and private, military and civilian, should give some idea of how they were prepared for positions of leadership during the war.[1] The various arguments relating positions on secession to willingness to fight and to give moral support to the government are areas for analysis which can determine the characteristics of leadership as well as the values and loyalties of those who would lead the Confederacy.[2]

Despite limitations of data, family background remains the best means of evaluating the relationship between class sentiment and opportunities for advancement in antebellum society. The occupations of 320 of the 651 leaders are known. Sixty-four of them served in political life, half of whom were also prominent professional men or owned large plantations. Seventy-six were planters and men of importance in their communities. Only 9 were lawyers, 39 were doctors, 40 were businessmen, 1 was in the newspaper business, and 15 were ministers or teachers. Forty-two, or 13 percent, of them had fathers who had important military careers, some of which, such as that of "Light Horse Harry" Lee, dated back to the Revolutionary War. Only 6 were common laborers, and 28 were small nonslaveholding farmers. Certainly, as a group the future Confederate leaders came from the more professional and affluent sectors of private life; but fathers' careers did not necessarily influence their advantaged sons.[3]

Fifty percent of the future Confederate leaders had important relatives on either their mothers' or fathers' sides, and many of that group married well. They were related to 50 men who had military careers, while 74 future leaders had family connections with at least one professional person. Fifty-two were related to prominent politicians, 50 had family connections with wealth and politics, and 99 were from families of wealth by early antebellum standards. It is difficult to tell whether poor boys married well or whether wealth married into more wealth.[4] All that can be discovered is that 30 married into wealth and 32 married into wealth and political power. Thirteen of the wives came from political families, while 12 had relatives who had some professional status in their communities. In short, family connections not only gave many of the leaders a start in professional life but also may well have influenced the politics and future loyalties of the Confederate leaders.

Evidence exists on the relationship between the future leaders' patterns and family professional connections. Nineteen fathers were politicians, and they had 10 sons who held political office, only 1 of whom held national office. Of the 41 fathers who were wealthy planters, only 19 of the sons held political office. The 20 businessmen fathers had only 3 sons in public life, and 29 career military fathers had only 14 sons in public office and only a handful of career military officer sons. Except for those from planter families, the future military leaders seemed to have derived little political power from their fathers.[5]

Analysis of family connections shows that fully 166 Confederate military leaders were related to families of importance. Yet, only 53 future leaders received assistance from their families which enabled them to enter public life. Future military leaders also married into families of some importance. But of the 47 who married into powerful families, only 14 had prewar political careers. The test of military hierarchy and continuity reveals that future military leaders were related either directly or by marriage to 47 men who had had military careers in an earlier generation. Specifically, the 102 career military men who served in the Civil War were related to 27 men who had been career military officers in an earlier generation. One can conclude that family connections hardly seemed a major factor in aiding prewar public careers or in influencing prewar military careers.

Family connections of the future Confederate congressmen also reflect the extent of family and generational control of antebellum political life. Of the 245 congressmen, 94 had fathers with important careers, of whom 25 were planters, 18 farmers, 10 doctors, 10 businessmen, and only 2 lawyers. They may have helped 73 of their sons who held prewar public office. Seventy-eight family relatives of importance seemed to have had an effect on 61 future congressmen. Nineteen careers may have been influenced by the 28 family connections made by marrying into prominent families. Clearly, family political power was not as important as family wealth and professional training in influencing the public careers of the future Confederate congressmen.

Forty-two fathers of the future Confederate cabinet and bureau chiefs had important positions in their communities. They may have helped the prewar public careers of 15 sons. Eleven future bureaucrats may have benefited by family wealth and position in their prewar careers. Jefferson Davis is a conspicuous example of one who came from a poor family where a successful brother was able to provide for his education and to assist in the early stages of his political career. In the case of the 39 men who served in important state government positions during the Civil War, 16 fathers may have helped their careers, including 3 who became state governors. Yet, 2 of those governors came from stable but small farming families. Nineteen future state leaders were related to men of importance, of whom 6 were wealthy farmers. Three men married into wealth and power.

The one future cultural leader who became governor of his state came from a family of small farmers, while only 1 of the 3 legislators had a father who was a wealthy planter. There were important professional legacies, since 7 fathers were doctors, 5 educators, and 4 businessmen. But with 30 important relatives, only 5 future cultural leaders managed to attain public office. One future cultural leader married into wealth, and his public life was spent in the state legislature. It seems clear that in the cases of both the cabinet and bureau chiefs and the cultural leaders, family background had a mixed effect on their careers.

Family connections in relation to secession or wartime leaders may reveal both hierarchical continuity and family pressures for conformity. Thirty percent, or 78, of the future military leaders had such connections. Forty-three of the future congressmen were related to secession leaders. The wartime executives, bureaucrats, and diplomats had 21 relatives who were secession or wartime leaders. Yet, of the 39 state leaders, only 6 were related to other wartime leaders. Of those who became the professional and intellectual elite of the Confederacy, 12, or 21 percent, were related to other leaders. For all of the family assistance given these future leaders, only 150 leaders were actually related to the men of power in 1860 and after.

It is hardly correct to claim planter control, political legacies, or professional influence from the families of the wartime leaders. There were aristocratic legacies, but there were many more parvenues or middle-class, self-made Confederate leaders. If most of the family connections were wealthy planters, it is because status and power in the early antebellum period were largely related to agricultural holdings. Therefore, any assertion of the continuity of leadership from one generation to another cannot account for the prewar career patterns. This hardly makes claim that an aristocracy did not exist; it only shows that the future leaders did not come from the aristocratic classes.[6]

Patterns of activity in the future leaders' formative years, such as mobility and education, might extend analysis of family status and power. More particularly, geographical mobility and change reveal both the stability and the wanderlust of men following their careers. Higher education supposedly became less important to material and professional success in the careers of late antebellum leaders. Yet, old school ties do reveal personal connections and even a sense of what may have been important symbols of status for the future leaders.

The inventory of the Confederate military leaders' states of birth shows 64 were born in Virginia, 25 in South Carolina, 37 in Georgia, and 27 in Tennessee.[7] Full information exists on the mobility patterns of 174 future military leaders, of whom 40 did not move at all, 51 once, 31 twice, 21 three times, 16 four times, and 15 from five to eight times before the war. If more than two moves reveals an ambitious and rootless society, then (even conceding that career officers were transferred often) the future military leaders were an obviously mobile and ambitious lot. In 1860, only 39 men who would become military leaders did not reside in the South. Virginia led with 43 residing there (a loss of 21 from those born there), followed by Georgia with 29, Alabama with 23, and South Carolina and Tennessee with 18 apiece. The obvious pattern of westward migration should be even more pronounced when the mobility of political leaders is considered.

The future Confederate military leaders were well educated, with 83 percent having attended college or professional school. Fifty-six went to Southern universities, 12 to Northern universities, 4 to universities in both the North and the South, 87 to West Point, and 12 to both West Point and another Southern college. Seventeen graduated from another military school, 4 more attended both military school and college, 25 went to law school, and 3 to medical school. Of the total 425 general officers included in Ezra Warner's *Generals in Gray*, 156 attended West Point and 23 went to other military schools. Of the 265 military leaders studied in this dictionary, 99 graduated from West Point and 21 attended other military schools. The level of education for military leaders was high by any standard in the South. Nine future generals also ranked first in their college class, 27 finished in the top 25 percent at West Point, while 26 finished in the bottom quartile of their West Point class. In short, attendance at institutions of higher learning reveals something of the status, ambition, and exposure to other future military leaders among the Confederate generals.

The future Confederate congressmen for the most part held political office either in their community or in state politics. Their mobility patterns, although individual, do reveal something about their prewar ambitions. To understand the motivations for mobility is not only to grasp a persistent pattern, but also to perceive the importance of mobility and state pride in the lives of the Confederate political leaders. To observe also the disastrous loss of talent by the eastern seaboard South is to understand the internal sectionalism and squabbles which militated against complete harmony in the Confederacy.[8]

Fully two-thirds of the Confederate congressmen were born on the East Coast. Four were born in Maryland, 60 in Virginia, 35 in North Carolina, 27 in South Carolina, and 35 in Georgia. In the West, 28 were born in Kentucky, 1 in Missouri, and 26 in Tennessee. After 1830, the Gulf Coast states began to swell with people, but only 9 of the leaders were born in Alabama, 3 in Mississippi, and 4 in Louisiana. Fifty future congressmen remained in the county in which they were born. But 85 moved once, 30 twice, 28 at least three times, 7 four times, 4 at least five times, and one hardy individual, six times before 1860. Clearly, the future politicians were a mobile breed who probably moved for a better business or political opportunity. It is known that some men traversed between Alabama and Tennessee looking for constituents, and one future leader actually served as congressman in two states. One wonders just how many of those congressmen continued to hold some loyalty to their native states during the war.

Certainly, many politicians saw education merely as a means to learn a trade, and many young men had neither the time nor the patience for the classroom. But a self-made man like the ubiquitous Joseph Brown of Georgia worked his way through school and later borrowed money from a friend to read law at the Yale Law School. Alexander Stephens, whose father was a laborer, went to Franklin College (later the University of Georgia) on loans, promises of future tutoring, and summer teaching jobs. Most of the ambitious considered the status, polish, and contacts made for future work too important to pass up.[9] Only 41 future congressmen did not attend college, while 84 went to college in the South, 13 to college in the North, and 7 attended universities in both the North and South. Four went to West Point, 2 to another military school, 30 only to law school, and 5 studied medicine. Twenty-one of the future congressmen ranked first in their college class, while 1 West Point graduate finished in the top quartile of his class. Like the military leaders, the future congressmen were well educated and should have compared favorably in education to any sitting political body in the nation.[10]

The future Confederate government executives—cabinet, subcabinet, and bureaucrats—were also largely from the East Coast. Maryland had 2 executives, Virginia 16, North Carolina 6, South Carolina 10, and Georgia 5. Kentucky led the West with 8 (most of whom were descended from Virginia families), and Tennessee had 4. Alabama had 3 and Mississippi 1 leader. Nineteen were either born in the North or the territories, or their births have not been recorded. Nine did not move at all, 13 moved once, 11 moved twice, and 8 moved three times—all ordinary patterns of men looking for success. But 9 future bureaucrats moved 4 times, 2 moved five times, 1 moved six times, and 3 men moved at least eight times before 1860. A look at where those men lived in 1860 will show further patterns of mobility and will provide some clues into hopes of bureaucratic favoritism for some states. Again the East Coast dominated, with 15 residing in Virginia in 1860, 2 in North Carolina, 7 in South Carolina, 8 in Georgia, and 1 in Maryland. The West was represented by 4 from Kentucky, 3 from Tennessee, 2 from Arkansas, and 3 from Texas. Florida had 1, Alabama 8, Mississippi 4, and Louisiana 5.

The level of education which the executives and bureaucrats received relates to their preparation for future professional and public careers and even for wartime decisionmaking. Nineteen, or 26.3 percent, did not attend college. Thirteen went to college in the South, 3 in the North, and 2 in both the North and South. Eight went to West Point, 11 to law school, 4 to medical school, 3 to college and to West Point, and 2 to military school and to college. Thus, 13 future leaders in government had some form of military training to influence their prewar career patterns and their wartime decisionmaking. For those who have found fault with Jefferson Davis's excessive interference with the military, his military training may well have been a mixed blessing. Seven executives and bureaucrats ranked first in their college class, while 6 ranked in the top quarter at West Point.

Thirty-nine Confederate governors, judges, and state legislators had significant roles in the war effort. Their mobility patterns register prewar drive, and they also indicate wartime loyalties and interests in more than one state. Again, the East Coast dominated the known birthplaces of the state leaders. Eight were born in Virginia, 5 in North Carolina, 9 in South Carolina, and 4 in Georgia. Three were born in Kentucky and 5 in Tennessee, and one each in the Gulf states of Alabama and Mississippi. In terms of movement, 5 did not move at all, 7 moved only once, 11 twice, and 9 three times before 1860. Two moved four times, and only one moved five times. Those who held important state positions seemed the least mobile of any political group in the war. They were widely dispersed in 1860, with all states having 2 leaders except for Virginia, Georgia, Alabama, and Tennessee with 3, North Carolina, Louisiana, and Texas with 4, and Mississippi with 5. Clearly, the Southeast lost leaders of importance to the Gulf Coast.

Eight state leaders went only to secondary school, 15 went to college in the South, 2 to college in the North, 3 to colleges in both the North and South, 4 to law school, and only one attended military school. Two of the wartime state leaders graduated first in their college class. With 21 college graduates in the group, one could expect the poise and training needed to coordinate plans with the Confederate government. But if any military decisions were necessary, the governors, judges, and state legislators certainly lacked the training to make them.

Since the cultural and business leaders made important wartime propaganda and financial decisions, and since their patterns of ambition and experience are important to gauge performance, their mobility patterns have also been included here. Of the 57 people included, 15 were born outside the South. Of the remainder, Virginia produced 12, Georgia 10, South Carolina 9, and North Carolina 5. Many of these men were born into business and professional families which thrived in the Southeast in the early 1800s. Seven did not move, 6 moved once, 11 twice, 11 three times, 5 four times, 4 five times, 2 six times, and 1 eight times before 1860. Perhaps professional training and early success kept them close to home and therefore made them one of the least mobile groups included in this dictionary. By 1860, the East Coast retained 9 cultural and business leaders in Virginia, 3 in North Carolina, 8 in South Carolina, and 9 in Georgia. But hustling business- and professional-oriented Alabama had 11 of the best cultural and business leaders of the war period included in this volume. Tennessee had 4, while Louisiana had 3. The pattern of mobility and place of residence in 1860 seemed to show an excessive supply of talent in some states.

Sixteen of the future cultural and business leaders went to college in the South, only 2 in the North, and 3 in both the North and the South. One went to law school, and 9 to medical school. The medical training of the future army doctors was impressive, but the paucity of legal training among the businessmen suggests the unimportance of that field for business in the Old South. Ten of them ranked first in their college class, making for an extremely intelligent and well-trained set of professional leaders.

Preparation of the future Confederate leaders for their prewar careers reveals that most of them came from families of position in their communities, but not of political and social power. The idea that an aristocracy of family power based on agricultural and commercial wealth dictated the political leadership of the antebellum South simply does not hold for the group of Confederate leaders included in this study. The implication is that either the old ideas of a class power structure never really extended into the nineteenth century, or that the Confederate leaders were not in the mainstream of the best family tradition. Too much opportunity for the bright and the ambitious existed in this semi-frontier society. Education and mobility became the equalizers for most of the future leaders. Yet, what did they make of their opportunities and what did they accomplish in their public and private careers in the late antebellum South? Like family background, the careers served as preparation for leadership in the war and suggest what to expect from their wartime performances.[11]

Information on private career patterns is available for most of the 265 men in this study who served in the Confederate military. Only 104 of them had continuous prewar military careers. Even some of the West Point graduates resigned their commissions to enter private business or to become government engineers. Examples are the careers of the brilliant Hébert cousins from Louisiana. Paul Octave Hébert left the army in 1854 to become a planter and soon became governor, while Louis resigned in 1856 to become an engineer and was instrumental in widening the ship channel near New Orleans. Twenty men either left the military to manage family plantations, marry into planter families, or seek the status and political future open to men of ambition. Seventy-three of the wartime military leaders practiced law before the war. Seventeen were lawyer-politicians, men who devoted their careers to party politics. Three became ministers, the most famous of whom was Bishop Leonidas Polk. Eight became educators, 3 scientists, 1 a newspaper editor, and 16 successful businessmen. The professional training, financial success, and status in their communities gave these men important experience in the handling of responsibility and personnel.

While a planting career was considered the most prestigious stepping stone to public life in the early antebellum South, lawyers who advanced from county solicitor to positions in state government demonstrated the most common pattern of political success.[12] Many future military leaders made successful careers in private business, but only 33 percent, or 89 men, held important prewar public office. Seven were mayors of their towns, 10 county solicitors, 6 judges, 47 state legislators, 12 U.S. congressmen, 2 U.S. senators, and 4 governors of their states. Eighteen served only one term in the state legislature, 6 one term in the U.S. Congress, and one governor served one term. A glance at secondary public office shows few years of actual public service, and only 15 future military leaders managed to hold at least three different public offices. These men were the young men of the 1850s whose political future lay in their accomplishments during the war. But the paucity of public experience in these men, "Extra Billy" Smith, Robert Toombs, and Howell Cobb being exceptions, would be a disadvantage in the understanding of politics required of all military personnel.

While prewar military experience will be developed more fully in connection with actual wartime performance, it is worth noting that service in one's state militia was not only a sign of social acceptance but also an opportunity to rise in the state's political hierarchy.[13] Of the future military leaders, one man fought in the Black Hawk War, 4 in various engagements against the Seminole Indians, 87 exclusively in the Mexican War, 2 in both the Black Hawk and the Mexican wars, and 16 in both the Seminole and Mexican wars. On the whole, the future military leaders of the Confederacy had significant line duties during the Mexican War; few of them held positions of command. But only one future congressman served in the Black Hawk War, while 6 participated in the Seminole campaigns and 12 fought in the Mexican War. A large number belonged to their state militias. Two of the wartime state leaders served in the Black Hawk War, and 2 others in the Seminole campaigns. Clearly, the future congressional leaders may have had militia experience, but their actual prewar military experience was minimal.

The business and political experience of the future Congress indicates some of the political expertise which they would contribute to the war.[14] Their private career experience tends to confirm that the Confederate leaders came from the professional ranks and that only a handful were of the planter elite. One preacher, 3 educators, 5 newspapermen, 1 scientist, and 5 physicians lent their various expertise to the politics of war. There were 118 lawyers, 33 lawyer-planters, and 27 lawyer-politicians. Thus, 178 out of 245 Confederate congressmen had been lawyers before the war. Thirteen men listed their professional occupation as politician. Twenty-nine were planters and 7 businessmen.

The years in public office should give some idea of the political experience which the future congressmen would bring to the politics of war. Information on the primary public careers reveals 3 city officials, 8 county solicitors, 15 judges, 80 state legislators, 55 members of the national House of Representatives, 11 U.S. senators, and 6 governors. Eight state legislators served at least 12 years each, and one served 20 years. Fourteen served two terms in the U.S. House, 10 served three terms, and 5 served as many as 16 years each in the House. Three men served two terms in the U.S. Senate, and one man three terms. The pattern of second public political offices held shows 46 future leaders who served in their state legislatures. There were 8 who held second offices in the U.S. House, with two men serving four terms and one man six terms. Six U.S. senators served a total of 30 years, and two governors served 6 years each. Some future congressmen held three political offices during their prewar careers. That included 9 men who served a total of 52 years in their state legislatures. Four men in that group of third offices served a total of 20 years in the U.S. House, 1 man 6 years in the U.S. Senate, and 1 governor served one term. Clearly, the future Confederate congressmen held impressive prewar public positions. Yet, there is some indication that a few of the older leaders held the many multiple duties in politics and had the most important offices.

The wartime executives and bureaucrats also had prewar private careers that could have given them experience for their wartime positions. Two were educators, 24 lawyers, 5 professional politicians, 4 doctors, 1 a planter, 3 lawyer-planters, 11 career military, 5 businessmen, 2 scientists, and 8 editors. One would have expected efficiency, political acumen, an ability to deal with the press, and the general professional decisionmaking gained from years of business experience. Their pattern also reveals a highly trained and worldly group which obviously possessed significant power and wealth in their local communities.

Surprisingly, only 29 of the future executives and bureaucrats held major public offices before the war. Prewar military careers may partially explain this low percentage, which nevertheless says something about the ability of these men to transfer private profession into public political power. From a group which included such political figures as Jefferson Davis and Alexander Stephens, more public experience should have been expected. Four were local judges, 1 held local office, 1 was a county solicitor, 2 state supreme court judges, 9 state legislators, 5 congressmen, 6 senators, and one a governor of his state. Only 7 men served a total of 30 years in a second public office. In other words, the collective experience in public life of the men who would make the executive office decisions compares unfavorably with that of the years in prewar service of the future Confederate congressmen.[15] All their years of professional experience would not help in pressure politics without similar experience in public service. This information also suggests that many of the wartime political appointees were not prewar leaders.

The wartime state leaders, men with crucial liaison and cooperative responsibility during the war, have already been shown to have been less mobile than their fellow political leaders. What kind of experience did they bring to the war and what kind of power did they have in the prewar South? Their private careers showed much experience. Twenty-two were lawyers, 3 politicians, 4 planters (the pattern of prewar power in private and public life seems to work against any idea of planter dominance), 3 lawyer-planters, 6 lawyer-politicians, and 1 an editor. All 39 made important private professional careers for themselves.

The future state leaders also held important prewar public offices. Six had been governors, and many would also serve in a state executive capacity during the war. Four had served in the U.S. House, 20 in their state legislatures, 3 as state supreme court justices, 1 as a lower court judge, and 1 as district attorney. Their years in service were also impressive: 3 men served 6 years each in the legislature, and 3 others served from 10 to 14 years each in the legislature. Three state supreme court judges served between 12 and 15 years each on the bench, 4 governors served two terms each, and 1 governor served three terms. Their secondary public careers also showed years of public service on the state level, and the total number of years served was impressive. The future state leaders had much experience in the government of their own states, but they had only minimal contact with leaders from other Southern states. When the time came to run a united war effort, would their preoccupation with state affairs and their years in state and local positions be helpful in the negotiations necessary to a united war effort?

The Confederacy's cultural and business leaders brought outstanding credentials of private professional experience to the war. Twelve were ministers, 5 educators, 2 lawyers, 9 doctors, 2 lawyer-politicians, 10 important businessmen with years of experience, and 10 newspapermen. They made policy, affected opinion, and generally held much of the private wartime power, even if their numbers hardly speak for the many private citizens of talent who were excluded from the war effort.[16]

However, the cultural and business leaders were not important public servants. They seemed to have dedicated their lives to their private careers and not to have taken an interest in politics. One man was a lower court judge, 5 were state legislators, and 1 was a governor of his state. Only 1 man held three public offices before the war, a fact showing that power seemed to circulate among the same people. Journalism and political office did not mix, even though politics was the trade of both professions. The future cultural leaders simply did not make public policy in their local communities, and they virtually held no offices outside of their states. There was some danger in the parochial nature of those men who would make propaganda for the Confederacy; the ministers and newspapermen probably learned from each other and subsequently did not focus on issues of importance to the entire Confederacy.

Party affiliation of the future Confederate leaders also contributes to an understanding of their roles in prewar public life. Of the 220 future Confederate generals, 112 were Democrats, 2 were Democrat-Americans, 12 were Whigs who became Democrats in 1860, and 24 remained Whigs until after the South had seceded. Of the 245 future Congressmen, 130 were prewar Democrats, 2 Democrat-Americans, 13 Whig-Americans, 23 Whigs who became Democrats, and 50 diehard Whigs, even after the South had seceded. Forty of the more than 50 future executives and bureaucrats were Democrats, 1 a Whig-American, 5 Whigs who became Democrats, and 5 remained Whigs. Of the 39 wartime state leaders, 23 were Democrats, 3 Whigs who became Democrats, and 4 remained Whig through 1860. Even a large number of the more than 35 cultural leaders had party affiliations, including 24 Democrats, 3 Whigs who became Democrats, and 6 Whigs. Party affiliation obviously meant something to the unconverted Whigs, but the overwhelming number of wartime leaders had been Democrats.[17]

The role of the future generals in the presidential election of 1860 shows that they were hardly involved in political activities, since only 28 supported Breckinridge, 5 supported Bell, and 1 backed Douglas. Of the future congressmen, 49 were known to have supported Breckinridge, 15 Bell, and 15 Douglas. The cultural leaders also stayed out of the presidential battles, with only 5 for Breckinridge and 3 for Douglas. As one might expect, the future congressmen were the most concerned with national issues, and the overwhelming majority of all groups supported Breckinridge.[18]

Participation in the antebellum commercial and political conventions gave future leaders the opportunity to meet their peers from other states and, in the case of the secession conventions, revealed something of their actual leadership roles in the Old South. Only 1 future congressman attended the Nashville convention in 1850, 8 future congressmen were delegates to the Charleston national Democratic convention in 1860, and 80 attended their states' secession conventions. The future executives and bureaucrats sent 1 man to Nashville, 4 to Charleston in 1860, and only 12 to their states' secession conventions. The state leaders sent 1 man to Nashville, 1 to Charleston, and 8 to their states' secession conventions. Various other wartime groups added at least 29 more to the number of delegates to the secession conventions. When one realizes that only 129 out of 651 Confederate leaders included here actually participated in making the Civil War, it becomes obvious that these men were not the prime movers in the secession movement, nor were they the major political figures in the antebellum South.[19] Further analysis of the secession conventions and of the secession positions of each of the future leaders should affirm or deny the conclusions suggested here.

In order to understand how support for or against secession was to affect the war effort, one should consult Alexander and Beringer, *The Anatomy of the Confederate Congress*. Wooster's *Secession Conventions of the South* also analyzes the composition of the conventions and by inference comments on both the quality of the prewar leadership and the problem of generational turnover. Yet, a look at the conventions' actual debates, the final votes on secession, and the secession position of many of these future leaders of the war shows that the additional biographical information from this dictionary calls for some analysis beyond those two seminal studies in collective biography.[20]

Information is available on 315 of the secessionists and 99 of the unionists who became wartime leaders. Not all of the secessionists were "fire-eaters" of the William Lowndes Yancey type, nor were all of the unionists Yankee sympathizers such as Thomas C. Fuller of North Carolina. Even staunch secessionists had some fear of the implications of secession, while many unionists, except in some of the border states, became loyal to the Southern cause after the firing on Fort Sumter. Study of the actual secession debates reveals hesitation to act without assurances that other states would follow or the certainty that a conservative constitution would be written to govern the new nation. Most of the delegates to the conventions seemed fearful of past secession failure, yet committed to a united Southern defense of its way of life.[21]

A comparison of known party affiliation shows that the secessionists included 218 Democrats, 3 Democrat-Americans, 21 Whigs, 8 Whig-Americans, and 30 Whigs who turned Democrat by 1860. Ninety-one supported Breckinridge in 1860, 8 supported Bell, and 12 remained with Douglas. One hundred fifteen secessionists attended one or more of the important antebellum conventions. Three went to Nashville, 8 were at the Democratic convention of 1860 in Charleston, 89 attended their state secession conventions, and 14 attended at least two conventions, including their states' secession conventions. Not surprisingly, the unionists' party affiliation revealed only 16 Democrats, 51 Whigs, 6 Whig-Americans, and 7 Whigs who became Democrats by 1860. In the presidential race of 1860, 5 unionists supported Breckinridge, 15 supported Bell, and 3 supported Douglas. Figures are scanty on the unionists' attendance at prewar conventions. Only 3 are known to have attended the Charleston Democratic convention, but 29 were delegates to their states' secession conventions. There are hardly any surprises surrounding the politics and political affiliations of the opposing forces until one comes to the secession conventions. Thirty percent of the unionists and 32 percent of the secessionists were active participants in the secession debates. These figures reveal a unionist force in wartime public life to reckon with and confirm the influence of the unionists in the secession movement.

There are other factors in an individual's development, factors which have been largely ignored or at least have not been compared, that might shed some light on the makeup of the secessionists and unionists. Of the 174 secessionists whose religious affiliations are known, 21 were Catholics, 2 Jewish, 23 Baptists, 49 Presbyterians, 18 Methodists, 4 Methodist-Episcopalians, and 57 Episcopalians. The prewar private career patterns of the secessionists show 11 ministers, 8 educators, 5 doctors, 9 career military men, 2 military-planters, 11 businessmen, and 14 editors. One hundred thirty-one were lawyers, 18 political leaders, 30 planters, 29 lawyer-planters, and 36 lawyer-politicians.[22] The educational pattern of the secessionists reveals that at least 51 did not go to college, 106 went to college in the South, 19 went to college in the North, 11 attended college in both the North and South, 13 went to West Point, 7 to another military school, 40 to law school, 8 to medical school, 4 to college and West Point, and 1 attended college and military school. Five of the secessionists were born in Maryland, 67 in Virginia, 28 in North Carolina, 60 in South Carolina, and 41 in Georgia; the West had 32 from Kentucky, 1 from Missouri, and 31 from Tennessee; and the unsettled Gulf had 14 from Alabama, 5 from Mississippi, and 6 from Louisiana. Mobility patterns show that 58 did not leave their home counties, 98 moved only once, 47 twice, 40 three times, and 72 at least four times. By 1860, the Southeast still retained 38 who lived in Virginia, 18 in North Carolina, 37 in South Carolina, and 31 in Georgia, while the West had 16 in Kentucky, 15 in Missouri, 19 in Texas, 11 in Arkansas, and 22 in Tennessee, and the Gulf swelled to 12 in Florida, 38 in Alabama, 30 in Mississippi, and 20 in Louisiana.

The unionists included 23 Presbyterians, 15 Episcopalians, 2 Catholics, 5 Baptists, 6 Methodists, and 5 Methodist-Episcopalians. Fifty-three of them were lawyers, 7 career military men, 8 planters, 2 businessmen, 7 lawyer-planters, and 5 lawyer-politicians. Again, law led the professions. The unionist educational pattern shows 21 did not go to college, 33 went to college in the South, 4 to college in the North, 1 to college in both the North and South, 9 to West Point, 8 to law school, 2 to medical school, 1 to college and West Point, and 2 to college and another military school. In terms of mobility, the unionists were clustered, with 23 born in Virginia, 16 in Georgia, 24 in North Carolina, 9 in Tennessee, and 10 in Kentucky. The unionists were not mobile. Fifteen never left their home county, 33 moved only once, 16 twice, and 11 three times. By 1860, only 15 lived in Virginia, 19 in North Carolina, 13 in Georgia, 9 in Alabama, 5 in Mississippi, 2 in Louisiana, 2 in Texas, 9 in Tennessee, 4 in Kentucky, and 2 in Arkansas.

Religious affiliation shows that both groups were dominated by Presbyterians and Episcopalians, with the secessionists leading 32 percent to 27 percent in number of Episcopalians and having an overwhelming lead in the number of Catholics. Not surprisingly, the lawyers led both groups, although the unionists had a larger percentage of them. Both groups were planter-poor and were filled with professionals. The secessionists had a larger percentage with higher education, but the unionists had a larger percentage of military-trained. The secessionists had a larger percentage of law school graduates, despite their trailing in numbers in that profession. Only in North Carolina did the percentage of unionists surpass that of the secessionists born there, while Virginia was the birthplace of the largest number of secessionists. The secessionists were more mobile, and a larger percentage of them moved three times or more. If one discounts South Carolina, the unionists had greater percentages of leaders living in the Southeast in 1860, and the Gulf Coast and Southwest, except for Tennessee, were overwhelmingly secessionist.[23]

Whether the Confederate leaders were also the leaders of the antebellum South relates to the secession movement in terms of the age level and the prewar public careers of those who took a stand on secession or union in 1860. Almost two-thirds of the secessionists were born in the prime wartime leadership years between 1811 and 1825, while 49, or slightly less than half of the unionists, were born in those years. In 1860, 20 percent of the secessionists and 32 percent of the unionists were over the age of fifty. The unionists were older than the secessionists, but did they have comparatively more public experience?

Of the 90 secessionists whose primary prewar public service was in the state legislature, 61 were between thirty-five and fifty years old during the secession crisis. Of the 56 U.S. congressmen, 42 were between thirty-five and fifty, and of the 14 U.S. senators, 7 were between thirty-five and fifty. Of the 13 governors, 8 were between thirty-five and fifty. By comparison, the unionists' leaders between thirty-five and fifty included 21 of 37 state legislators, 6 of 10 U.S. congressmen, 2 of 3 U.S. senators, and no governors. Approximately 34 percent of the primary public offices among both the unionists and the secessionists were held by men between the ages of thirty-five and fifty. But the unionists also had a sizable number of leaders in public office over the age of fifty, while the secessionists had almost none in that age group. Fifty-two percent of the unionists had held at least one public office, as opposed to less than 48 percent of the secessionists. If the unionists among the future Confederate leaders had more public experience, neither group seemed to have dominated antebellum political life.[24]

Age and attendance at the secession conventions show that the secessionists had only one man born before 1800 at his state convention, compared to 9 unionists who attended their conventions. Fifty-nine of the 89 secessionists who attended secession conventions were born between 1811 and 1825, while 13 were born after 1826. Seventeen unionists who went to secession conventions were born between 1811 and 1825, while only 3 were born after 1826. The unionist state leaders who made an impact at their secession conventions were growing old, while the secessionists were in the prime of life. Confederate leadership, then, was composed of a relatively youthful group of staunch secessionists.

Wartime career patterns are also reflected in the leaders' positions on secession. One hundred and eighty-five secessionists would serve in the Confederate government: 14 in the cabinet, 23 as bureaucrats, 22 as senators, and 136 as congressmen. Eighteen secessionists became governors of their states, and 6 became important judges. By comparison, the unionists held 64 government posts: 1 cabinet member, 5 bureaucrats, 8 senators, and 50 members of the Confederate House. Three became judges and 2 became governors. The unionists were older and tended to come from the eastern seaboard South. Four businessmen, 10 clergymen, 2 educators, 8 editors, and 80 generals were secessionists. The unionists contributed only 29 generals and only a handful of the members of the professional class to the war effort. The extent to which secession support came to influence the behavior of the Confederate leadership remains to be seen.

Clearly, the future Confederate leaders came from the middle class and made a financial success of their lives. Most held some form of private professional career, which should have prepared them for the serious business of administrative conduct of the war effort. Some held important prewar public offices. Taken collectively, their experience in public life was short, and perhaps they would pay for that when the war called for the political poise of statesmen. Also, the future military leaders seemed to know as much about politics as soldiering. Few of their Northern counterparts had more military experience, although the Northern government had a larger population from which to draw its leaders. As a group, the future Confederate leaders neither made secession nor constructed the Confederacy. Still, the vast majority of them supported secession and were committed to the New South. In short, the Civil War hastened the creation of a new leadership class which was just coming into political prominence in the 1850s.[25] What that enthusiasm and inexperience meant for the wartime performance of those leaders remains a question for further study.

3 / Confederate Leadership

Previous studies of the Confederate leaders have usually concentrated on individual acts of heroism and the material and emotional obstacles to their efforts to fight a successful war. The generals have been praised for keeping the war going despite the fact that they were outmanned, outgunned, and sabotaged by their own political leaders. The politicians have generally been evaluated as blunderers who were often disloyal to the military. Few studies exist on the business or cultural leaders, though they have been given some credit for their contributions. Only a handful of state leaders have had biographers, and those studied were the most disruptive states'-rights-oriented leaders. In short, no systematic attempt has been made to examine all of the various groups of Confederate leaders.[1]

Even authors of collective biographies have in part attributed the Confederacy's military losses to the South's material and emotional dilemmas rather than to the collective behavior of the leaders. For example, one author maintains that President Jefferson Davis and his executive department were unable to gain their people's support because they knew their cause was morally wrong.[2] Another claims that the South died of states' rights, the reason for that death being that the civilian leaders in Richmond were unable to understand the needs of the rank and file behind the battle lines. Others simply show that the bureaucracy never coordinated the delivery of goods to the front lines with the splendid performance of the individual generals. Lastly, the generals are criticized for individual rather than collective blunders.[3]

Yet, these studies actually uncovered at least one valid explanation of the Confederacy's problems, namely, that the Confederate leaders were under-manned. Underpopulation and the necessity to defend a large expanse of territory surely were important determinants of the Confederate leaders' actions. That their talents and experience were spread too thin affected their stability in office. Loss of personnel influenced the Congress's ability to garner support for the executive department's decisions and, in turn, the executives' ability to deal with the sensitivities of the Congress. Turnover in office compounded the problems of the competitive, often divisive military leaders. A comparison of the collective activities, as they relate to numbers and stability, should provide some means of evaluating the Confederate leadership.

The statistics on turnover elucidate why cooperation and support were not forthcoming from the leadership. Of the 651 leaders studied, 76 died during the war. The deaths of 10 generals in 1863 and 20 generals in 1864 certainly obstructed command leadership in these critical years of the war.[4] In addition, 33 political leaders died in office during the war. The problem of replenishing the leadership with men and women of similar qualities, at a time when many of the South's ablest men were on the front lines, was overwhelming.[5]

Leaders often served in multiple capacities, not only dissipating their energies and narrowing the pool of talent, but also requiring the retraining of other personnel. For example, of the 265 men whose primary role was military, 29 also served in Congress or in a bureaucratic post, 5 became governors of their states during the war, 7 were either businessmen or blockade runners, 1 practiced medicine, and 3 were also clergymen. Of those who served primarily in the Confederate government, 15 held more than one government post, 26 also served in their state governments, 6 were businessmen, 3 were editors, and 107 also served in the military. Some congressmen actually held two important positions simultaneously. Of the state leaders, 11 governors were also in military service. In sum, at least 263 leaders held at least two wartime positions.[6]

With the pool of leadership drawn repeatedly from the same group, any dissipation of that element must surely have caused discontinuity. The same can also be said of turnover in office. Of the total 361 men who at one time served in political or appointive governmental office, fully 109 no longer held a government position in 1865. Five of the original Confederate senators held no office in 1865, while 79 men who had served in the Confederate House were also out of Confederate service in 1865. During the war, Judah P. Benjamin held three different cabinet posts, a fact that must have impaired his efficiency. John H. Reagan, postmaster general, and Stephen Mallory, secretary of navy, were the only cabinet officers who managed to hold onto their jobs throughout the war. Of the 53 subcabinet and bureaucratic figures studied, 19 left office between 1863 and 1865. The same problem affected the state governors: 17 out of a total of 24 were new to their office in 1864-1865, the most crucial years for relations between the state and national governments.

Overextension and attrition among the cabinet, bureaucrats, state leaders, and business and cultural leaders (the Congress and the military will have separate studies) resulted in an unstable, discontinuous leadership which led to many resignations from office.[7] Five cabinet members resigned to take another office, 1 resigned out of resentment toward his superior, 2 because of old age or disability, and 1 to take a military post; only 9 held executive positions throughout the war. Of the bureaucrats and the diplomatic corps, 11 men resigned to take another office, 3 resigned to enter the military, 2 left office out of resentment toward their superiors, 1 was too sick to carry on, 2 died in office, and 2 were fired; only 27 of 53 men considered held some kind of continuous bureaucratic position. On the state level, the almost powerless judges were the most stable leaders, with 9 out of 15 holding office throughout the war. But even in that position, 1 judge resigned to take another office, 2 entered the military, the enemy captured 2, and 1 man died in office. For the governors, including the powerless positions in Kentucky and Missouri, 2 resigned, 3 left office to take another job, 1 resigned to join the army, 3 were too old to continue in office, 7 refused to stand for reelection, and 1 was defeated in 1863; only 6 out of 24 governors managed to remain in office throughout the war.

Chaos among the lower hierarchy undoubtedly contributed to difficulties in the other government branches and the military, who also squabbled among themselves. The heads of the various agencies competed for goods with each other, thereby creating divided loyalties and confusion over duties. Richard D. Goff concludes his study of the *Confederate Supply*: "At the end, Richmond had abdicated responsibility for the supply effort amid a welter of recrimination and intrigue."[8] Lack of cooperation may well have resulted from the bureaucrats' multiple tasks as well as from the large personnel turnover. Certainly, the cabinet turnover must have aggravated the problems caused by the absence of qualified leadership in supply management.

Although Congress had full access to the cabinet for information, cabinet turnover constantly disrupted policy. The president was left with confused advice, the Congress with constant political and policy changes, and branches of the government without any consistent policies from Richmond.[9] With the turnover in gubernatorial offices, the president and his cabinet lacked sufficient input from the states to decide on proper state policies, let alone create the stability necessary to deal with governors preoccupied with the defense of their own states.[10] It is little wonder that the cabinet and state governments rarely coordinated their governmental duties with the most political branch of all, the Congress. What happened when the most important groups of Confederate leaders, the military and the Congress, also suffered from turnover in office? Turnover in office and the ensuing change in composition of those bodies created other problems for those groups, problems that directly affected their abilities to perform.

The problems of coordinating the military and civilian branches of the government were reflected in the questions of stability in office and the levels of cooperation of the Confederate Congress with the executive branch of government. The two most important studies of the Confederate Congress both conclude that the extent to which a congressman's state came under siege from the enemy determined his wartime support for the administration. But the authors both point out that loyalty to the Confederate cause waned among those elected to the second Confederate Congress.[11] Therefore, the issue of stability in office and the reasons for turnover in office, as well as a comparison of the individual performances in the several Congresses, remain part of any final verdict on the role of the Congress in coordinating the war effort.[12]

According to their biographer, the 66 men who served only in the provisional Congress were the most intelligent and the most diligent of the congressmen.[13] Since they organized the government in terms of its structure and its laws, they were responsible for whatever powers the legislative branch was to have in the government. Provisional congressmen were a mature group: 18 were born before 1810, 26 were between the ages of forty and fifty, and 12 were between the ages of thirty and forty when the war began. By comparison, those who served only in the first Congress included 10 men past the age of fifty, 17 who were between forty and fifty, 8 between thirty and forty, and at least 2 under thirty in 1861. The age pattern for those who held office only in the second Congress showed 10 men over the age of fifty, 15 between forty and fifty, 18 between thirty and forty, and 4 under thirty in 1861. Of those who served in all three Congresses, only one was born before 1800, while 7 were over fifty, 15 between forty and fifty, 10 between thirty and forty, and 1 under thirty in 1861. The new men in the second Congress made up the youngest age group. Only the multiple-term servers kept the pattern middle-aged and gave it some experience and training.

A comparison of the educational patterns of Confederate congressmen in each of the Congresses also relates to expectations of their capacity for service. Educational information is available on 45 of those who served exclusively in the provisional Congress. Five did not attend college, 27, or 60 percent, of those known went to college in the South, 2 to college in the North, 1 to West Point, 1 to another military school, 7 to law school, and 2 to medical school. Of those who served exclusively in the first Congress, 25 attended college, but 8 did not. Of the 34 men who attended only the second Congress and whose education is known, 13 did not go to college. Thirty-one college graduates and 8 law school graduates served in both the first and second congresses. Clearly, educational level declined from the first to the second Confederate Congress.

Prewar private career patterns also reveal the level of business and professional experience available in each Congress. One hundred sixty-eight of the congressmen studied were lawyers, 27 were lawyer-politicians, and 33 were planter-lawyers. Thirty-nine lawyers served only in the provisional Congress, whereas 28 served only in the first, 35 only in the second, 38 in both the first and second, and 25 in all three. Of the 29 congressmen who called themselves planters, 10 served only in the provisional, 2 only in the first, 6 only in the second, 6 in both the first and second, and 3 in all three Congresses. The level of prewar professional specialization also declined with the changes in Congress.

Party labels have been said to have had little effect on congressional loyalty to the war effort and to the Davis administration; yet, an interesting pattern of party support may be seen in the various Congresses.[14] The overall pattern of party affiliation in the Confederate Congress reveals that fully 59 percent of the total had been consistently Democratic in the antebellum period. Of those who attended only the provisional Congress, 50 party affiliations are known: 31 were Democrats, 2 Democrat-Americans, 2 Whig-Americans, 5 Whigs who became Democrats by 1860, and only 10 remained Whig even on into the Civil War. Of the 33 known party designations of those who served only in the first Congress, 21 were Democrats, 3 Whigs, 4 Whig-Americans, and 5 Whigs who became Democrats. Among those who served only in the second Congress, 17 were Democrats, 18 remained Whig after the war had begun, 3 were Whig-Americans, and 2 were Democrats who had been Whigs. The Democrats still outnumbered the Whigs in the second Congress 52 to 34. In each Congress, the Democrats could dominate if they were united. But the new delegates to the second Congress revealed the growing political power of the Whigs, and that Congress was least supportive of the Davis administration policies.

Support or opposition to secession supposedly had little effect on the question of congressional loyalty to the administration.[15] Still, a look at secessionists and unionists in each Congress might reveal patterns helpful to an understanding of the relationship of turnover in office and change in the composition of Congress to congressional achievements. For those men who served only in the provisional Congress, the available figures show 42 secessionists and 10 unionists. The first Congress reveals 30 secessionists and only 5 unionists. But of those elected in 1863 to serve only in the second Congress, 20 had been unionists and 20 had been secessionists. The second Congress alone had 40 percent of the total number of unionists who served in the Congress. In the second Congress, the secessionists led the unionists 56 to 27.

The relationship of years in prewar public service to terms in Congress could illustrate some patterns of expectations of performance from the Confederate politicians. The provisional Congress had 33 percent with no prewar public service, as compared to 44 percent for the first Congress and 56 percent for those who served only in the second Congress. Fifty-eight percent of those who served only in the provisional Congress had between three and ten years of primary public service, compared to 46 percent of those who served only in the first Congress and 38 percent of those who served only in the second, who had similar service. Only 20 percent of those who served in all three Congresses had no prewar public service, while 33 percent of those who served in the first and second Congresses had no prewar public service. Again, the decline of years of prewar experience increased as the war continued. Although the hard core of leadership in the Congress had held at least two important prewar public positions and had served for many years in elective office, it is significant that a large number of congressmen, especially in the second Congress, were new to political life.

If the ranks of experienced men diminished as the war progressed, where did the best congressmen go, what other tasks did they assume, and of what importance was turnover in Congress to the stability of the political decisionmaking process? Of the 66 provisional congressmen, 15 held second positions in the national government, 5 served in the state governments, 2 entered business, 17 joined the military, and one became a newspaperman. This list included men of the stature of Robert Toombs, Howell Cobb, Alexander A. Stephens, and James Chesnut, who went on to other important service in the Confederacy. Of the 26 who left public life, brilliant men like Walker Brooke of Mississippi were lost completely to the Confederacy.[16] Of the 41 men studied who served only in the first Congress, 5 remained in the national government, 2 served in state government, 1 entered business, and 11 joined the military, while 22 left public life altogether. Of the 50 studied who served only in the second Congress, 4 had held other national government positions, 6 had served in the state government, 1 had entered business, 26 had served in the military (many of those one-term congressmen were elected to Congress by the troops in the field), and 13 seemed to have had no previous wartime experience. Of the 17 men who served in both the provisional and the first Congress, 3 held other offices in the national government, 2 served in their state governments, 6 served in the military, and 6 dropped out of Confederate service. Only 3 men held office in both the provisional and the second Congresses, of whom 2 also served in the military and the other dropped out of public life. Of those 51 important men who served as the stabilizing factor in both the first and the second Congresses, 5 had served in state government and 21 had served in the military. Of the 35 who served in all three Congresses, 2 also had national government posts, 2 held state posts, and 10 fought in the military. Even some of those who devoted almost their entire efforts to the Confederate Congress found time to serve simultaneously in the military. In fact, 93 congressmen served in the Confederate military at some time during the war.

It is apparent that the level of expectations of loyalty to the Confederacy and support for the Davis administration declined in each succeeding Congress. The loss did irreparable damage to any hopes of continuity of political efforts. The reasons for the congressmen's leaving office might provide further information on governmental instability.[17] Resignation to assume other offices often disrupted the continuity of proceedings during the middle of a congressional session. Fifteen men resigned to enter the military, at least 18 to take a bureaucratic position, 3 because of personal resentments, 9 because of old age or disability, and 13 died during the war. Fourteen provisional congressmen, 9 from the first Congress and 5 who served in both the provisional and first Congresses, refused to stand for reelection. Five provisional congressmen were refused reelection, as were 9 from the first Congress and 3 who served in both the provisional and first Congresses.

A study of those who left office during their terms or lost their bids for reelection reveals a pattern of quality which may have affected the overall performance of the Congress. Age groupings show that those from the prime years of experience, the ages of forty to fifty, represented the largest group of those who left office. Fully 76 percent of those who resigned or were not reelected had some form of college training. The lawyers made up the largest numbers of professionals to leave office. Percentages show that the Whigs and Democrats left office for similar reasons.

The most damaging departures were of those who held the longest and most important prewar public careers; these represented the largest number of resignations. Some of them also lost bids for reelection as the citizenry seemed to recriminate against those political figures most known to them. When combined with the study of just who served in each Congress, the matter of resignation and loss of reelection reflects clearly the meaning of turnover for coordinating efforts, supporting the war, and remaining loyal to the Southern cause.

The stability factor cannot be isolated from willingness to promote the Confederate cause back home and to support the Davis administration.[18] For example, of those who served exclusively in the provisional Congress, 19 supported and 6 opposed the Davis administration. For those who served only in the first Congress, 19 supported, 10 opposed, and 2 were neutral on the administration. For those who served only in the second Congress, 16 supported, 21 opposed the administration on more than one-half of the crucial votes, and 2 were either divided or neutral. Ten of those who served only in the second Congress supported the congressional peace movement, and 14 opposed it. Of those who served in both the first and the second Congresses, 26 supported, only 9 opposed, and 10 were divided in loyalty to President Davis. Had there been no such stabilizing influence, the administration would have lost the support of the second Congress.

Turnover affected support for the administration. Only 47 strong supporters served continuously throughout the Congresses. One supporter resigned, 2 left out of resentment, 5 were lost from old age or disability, 6 died in office, 15 resigned to take other governmental positions, 5 entered the army, 14 refused to stand for reelection, and 9 were defeated for reelection. The opponents of the administration included 6 who refused reelection and 5 who were defeated for reelection; 1 left for the military, and 14 resigned to enter the government. On balance the president lost more supporters than opponents.[19] With the problems of economic survival in Richmond, consistent constituent requests, and the pressures for political conformity, clearly, Congress had great difficulties in concentrating on the legislation vital to coordinating the war effort.

Although there was never a formal peace organization, the pressures of the congressional peace movement affected support for administration policies. Seventy-five congressmen registered their opinions on peace, of whom 3 who supported the Davis administration also supported peace, while 40 who supported the administration vigorously opposed the congressional peace movement. Eleven opponents of the administration supported the movement, while 13 opponents of the administration also opposed the peace movement. Since the supporters of peace were not always the opponents of the administration, their desires for peace may have been based on practical considerations. Also, some opposition to the administration, like that of the "fire-eaters" Robert Barnwell Rhett and William Lowndes Yancey, may have been based on the fact that Davis's policy was not considered strong enough to carry on a successful war. In addition to the importance of turnover in office, factors in the prewar career patterns of the Congress require comparison in order to analyze the relative support for the Davis administration as well as the meaning of the peace movement.

In terms of age patterns, the supporters of the administration appeared to have been younger than their opponents. Of the 105 known supporters and the 54 known opponents, 4 percent of each group were over sixty, but 16, or 28 percent, of the administration opponents were between the ages of fifty and sixty, as were 19, or 18 percent, of the administration supporters. Forty-seven supporters and 22 opponents were between forty and fifty, and 32 supporters and 12 opponents were between thirty and forty. The figures for support or opposition to the congressional peace movement seem to follow the same pattern. Of the 20 who openly supported the movement, 7 were over fifty, 9 were between forty and fifty, while only 4 were between thirty and forty. For those who registered formal opposition to the congressional peace movement, 11 were over fifty, 21 between forty and fifty, 22 between thirty and forty, and 3 under thirty. Eighty-five percent of the peace congressmen were over forty, while 57 percent of the opponents of congressional peace were over forty. Attachment to the old Union may have had a lingering effect on the older congressmen, and they may have been less ambitious and more politically realistic than their younger colleagues.

Current theory on congressional support or opposition for the administration asserts that states under siege tended to support the administration, while states which were relatively free from enemy threat produced some opposition to the administration.[20] The theory seems to hold for states in which the congressmen lived in 1860. For example, over the course of the war congressmen in states under Union domination such as Kentucky were 12 to 2 in favor of the administration, Missouri 8 to 1, Tennessee 13 to 5, Arkansas 5 to 1, Virginia 10 to 5, Texas 7 to 3, and the Gulf Coast states over 2 to 1 in favor of the administration. North Carolina was 6 to 14 against the administration, South Carolina split 4 to 4, and Georgia 11 to 6 for the administration. Besides the occupation/free from occupation pattern, the above figures reveal that the western states (except for Alabama) tended to support the administration, while the eastern states tended to oppose it, although for different reasons. The support and opposition for congressional peace seem also to have split as much along East-West lines as along occupational lines. Every western state except Tennessee, which went 2 for peace and 5 against, was overwhelmingly against peace, while every state connected to the Atlantic Coast except South Carolina gave some support to the peace movement. Although the figures are by no means conclusive, Virginia went 4 to 3 for peace, North Carolina supported peace 9 to 2, while Georgia registered 3 for peace and 6 against.

A further look at the birthplaces of congressmen reveals that again the East showed a close vote in opposition to the Davis administration, with the Virginia-born congressmen supporting the administration 27 to 11, North Carolinians opposing 13 to 15, South Carolinians opposing 8 to 9, and Georgians supporting 14 to 8. Congressmen from occupied and southwestern states registered over-whelming support for the administration except for those who were born in

Tennessee, who still supported the administration 12 to 5. In terms of peace stand by state of birth, the pattern again goes East-West. Virginia-born congressmen went 10 to 5 against peace, native North Carolinians 9 to 3 for peace, native Georgians 10 to 3 against peace, and even native South Carolinians only 12 to 2 against peace. In short, the East-West pattern of support or opposition to the Davis administration in terms of historical loyalties deserves further analysis.

In the Confederate Congress, party affiliation was too weak to show distinctions between points of view, but when one traces party loyalty in 1860, party affiliation does have some small significance. Of the congressmen who supported the administration in 1860, 66 were Democrats, 18 Whigs, 4 Whig-Americans, and 5 Whigs who became Democrats. Six hardline Whigs of 1860 remained neutral toward the administration. Thus, 41 percent of the hardline Whigs and only 22 percent of the Democrats opposed the administration. The Whigs of 1860 also showed a propensity to support peace in larger numbers than the Whigs who had become Democrats before the war, particularly in the second Congress.

A closer look at the position of congressmen on the final vote for secession in 1860 reveals an interesting pattern of wartime political behavior. Seventeen unionists opposed the Davis administration while they were in office, 24 gave support and 5 remained neutral. Eighty-one secessionists supported Davis, 25 opposed him, and 57 remained neutral or switched sides. Thirteen unionists supported the congressional peace movement, while 10 opposed it. Seven secessionists gave open support to the 1864 peace movement, and 43 registered their opposition. The secessionists largely favored the administration throughout the course of the war. Some of the more cautious men from 1860 seemed to understand that the administration had no chance of permanent separation from the Union.

If the pattern of maturity and experience is to hold, educational level should have some bearing on the question of administration loyalty. Twenty-four of the known supporters of the administration left no record of their education, and 23 did not attend college. Of those who opposed the administration, 9 left no record of college attendance and 13 did not attend college. Thirty-seven administration supporters, 19 opponents, and 9 neutrals went to a Southern college; 9 supporters, 6 opponents, and 6 neutrals were law school graduates. Of the 20 congressmen who supported peace, 3 did not attend college and 3 are unknown. Of the 58 who vigorously opposed the peace movement, 13 did not go to college and 10 left no record of school attendance. Twenty-three percent of the peace congressmen and 27 percent of their opponents were not college-trained. The peace leaders also had a larger percentage of trained lawyers, but the opponents of peace led 7 to 0 in Northern college attendance. Thus, the Davis administration opponents, the neutral congressmen, and the peace congressmen held a slight edge in education over administration supporters.

The breakdown on administration support by prewar professional occupation reveals that 59 percent of the lawyers in Congress supported the administration, that is, 56 supported, 28 opposed, and 11 remained neutral. Five professional politicians supported, 3 opposed, and 2 were neutral, while the lawyer-politicians were overwhelmingly in support of the administration, 17 to 5, with 2 neutral. On the other hand, the planters supported Davis only 10 to 5, with 2 neutral. The businessmen who served in Congress were 2 in support, 3 opposed, and 2 neutral. The lawyer-planters were 4 to 2 in favor of the peace movement. This contrasted with the lawyers, who opposed the peace movement 38 to 7; the politicians, who opposed 3 to 1; and the planters, who opposed 5 to 2. All of the physicians and educators who served in Congress were supporters of the peace movement. Although prewar occupation reveals no clear pattern, these statistics indicate that the Davis administration men got more support from professional men than from those with little prewar professional prominence.

Prewar public political experience also gives some pattern of support or opposition for the administration. Thirty-seven percent of those who supported the Davis administration, 38 percent of those in opposition, and 40 percent of those who were neutral seemed to have had no prewar public careers. Sixty congressmen, or 55 percent of the administration supporters, had from three to ten years of public service. Twenty percent of the known supporters of peace and 38 percent of those opposed had no prewar public positions. Fifteen, or 75 percent, of the known supporters of peace had from three to ten years in public life. In comparison, only 31, or 53 percent, of the opponents of peace had no prewar public service. Although the figures are small, the peace supporters seem to have had more political experience than those who spoke out against the congressional peace movement, while the administration's supporters and opponents seemed evenly divided as regards their political background.

Stability in office and experience emerge as factors in an understanding of the Confederate congressional behavior during the Civil War. The congressional leadership was torn over what it considered best for the South. Subregional differences, then, were compounded by the instability of officeholding. The congressional role in advising constituents on their actions was obviously interrupted when their homes were occupied by the enemy. In short, a combination of the political inexperience of the new men in public life, growing public hostility to an inability to deliver military victory, and the resulting turnover in office left the Congress without the information it needed to decide what was indeed best for the Confederacy.

The celebrated early combat successes of the military leaders made them the most popular men of the war period. But the performance of the generals, especially when those early victories turned to later losses, also requires study in terms of the collective war efforts of the various groups involved. Turnover in office and the deaths of famous generals are most important in understanding the performance of the military. Many have claimed that the deaths of the celebrated Barnard Bee and the brilliant Albert Sidney Johnston early in the war led to ultimate defeat. The "if-only school of scholars" says that, after "Stonewall" Jackson was killed by his own men, the military lost the heart of its leadership corps. But 425 men held the rank of general officer (of whom over 260 are studied here), and the meaning of attrition at that rank can only be understood by studying their collective efforts. Likewise, collective behavior calls for an analysis of how the general staff was rated by its own leadership. Promotion, duties held, and field of service relate directly to an evaluation of the collective performance of the general officers.

Turnover in office continuously influenced the performance of the general officers. Lack of promotion seemed to have been a prime determinant of resignation. Two brigadiers and 3 major generals were fired, 3 of whom were promoted just once. Two were infantry generals, and of the remaining 3, one each held staff, artillery, and multiple commands. Of the 6 brigadiers and 2 major generals who resigned out of resentment for lack of recognition, only the two major generals had received promotions in the general rank. The one man who resigned because of resentment toward a superior officer was commissioned a major general but was never promoted. Of the 16 who resigned ostensibly for old age, 11 were never promoted. Most of those who resigned or were lost to further combat were not old, and 8 of the 11 men who were captured and forced to sit out the duration of the war were under the age of thirty-five. Eight of the generals lost because of disability were younger than thirty-five. Of the 34 generals who were either killed in action or died of wartime wounds, 16 were between the ages of thirty and forty, and 10 were between the ages of twenty and thirty in 1860.

Other factors influenced the turnover in office among the general officers. Education, level of competence, and ambition revealed that 3 of the generals who resigned were from West Point, as were 3 of the 8 who resigned to take government office, while 3 others were law school graduates. The one man who resigned out of resentment toward a superior was also a West Point graduate. Twenty of the 34 men who died in action were West Point graduates, and 3 of the 5 men whose resignations were requested were military school graduates. The one general who resigned out of resentment was a career officer before the war, as were 13 of the 34 who died in the war and 6 of the 11 who were captured.

A pattern of resignation also emerges in terms of the theatre in which the generals served. Three generals from Virginia and 1 from Tennessee resigned from the military to take a government post. The one man who resigned out of resentment toward a superior also fought exclusively in Virginia. Virginia led 7 to 5 in resignation for old age or disability but lost 16 from death in action while Tennessee lost 7. One Virginia general and 2 Tennessee generals were relieved permanently from command.

Instability in office because of death, capture, old age, and even transfer of office, while disruptive of quality military contribution, is understandable. But the loss of general officers for what appear to be political and personality reasons relates to a larger question of collective performance. For example, the Virginia army seems to have had a politically ambitious group of generals who left office, while Tennessee's losses seem to have been based on both military and defeatist attitudes. The military not only lost youthful and brave fighting men, but it also lost young men unwilling to accept being passed over for promotion. The number of well-educated and well-trained generals who resigned from office reveals further political problems. Clearly, the level of instability in militarily important offices calls for evaluation of the relationship between the reasons for those losses and the level of performance of the general officers.[21]

Therefore, any attempt to understand the performance of the military leaders must transcend the romantic hero-worship which the postwar period heaped upon them. Only a subjective judgment could determine who was a good individual fighter, especially in light of so many factors which may have influenced their orders, their fighting, and the personnel and materiel at their command. However, there are objective quantifiable facts about the actions and conditions of those general officers which might allow some evaluation of their performance. Their fighting experience, based on what they brought to the war effort, the duties performed, and the rank achieved when collectively compared, could reveal something of the quality of performance. The theatres in which they fought could help to explain the key question of cooperation and coordination of the war effort across such a wide expanse of territory. The stability factor as it related to achievement, theatre of action, and turnover in office also contributes to an evaluation of the military and their place in the war effort.

Factors such as age, prewar military experience, military education, prewar civilian profession and politics, and wartime theatre of operation may well have influenced rank achieved and duties performed during the war. Merit, based on where one fought, what kind of command held, and important duties, is reducible to quantifiable terms. Factors such as demands for specific generals, the shrewdness of political generals, and nepotism surely influenced the types of duties and commands, the theatres of action, and the promotions from the ranks. Pressures on President Davis from important military leaders and Congress, as well as personal whims, often decided promotions. With the president as recommending agent, the Congress as ratifying agent, and public opinion as pressure agent, performance in the lines was sometimes secondary to the politics of promotion.[22]

Age was naturally a factor in rank held. Of the 157 brigadier generals studied, 12 were born between 1801 and 1810, and 37 between 1811 and 1820. Thirty-seven were in the prime fighting years between thirty-five and forty, 30 were between thirty and thirty-five, 31 under thirty, and 10 under twenty-five years of age. Of the 68 major generals, 3 were born before 1810 and 18 were born between 1811 and 1820. Sixteen were in the prime years thirty-five to forty, 15 between thirty and thirty-five, 10 under thirty, and 6 under twenty-five. Of 18 lieutenant generals, 2 were born before 1810 and 5 were born between 1811 and 1820. Eight were in the prime years thirty-five to forty, and one each was born in the periods 1826-1830, 1831-1835, and 1836-1840. Most of the full generals were old by military standards, with only two, Braxton Bragg and P.G.T. Beauregard, under forty-five in 1861. The provisional full generals who were never confirmed were

John Bell Hood, who was twenty-nine in 1861, and Edmund Kirby Smith, who was thirty-six.

The generals' duties also reflected the factor of age. For example, of the 18 men who were primarily staff officers, 2 were born before 1810 and 11 were between forty and fifty, while only one staff general was younger than thirty in 1861. As one would expect, many of the line or infantry officers belonged to the prime years, with 6 over fifty, 21 between the ages of forty and fifty, 43 between the ages of thirty and forty, 16 under thirty, and 5 under twenty-five in 1861. Of the 32 cavalry officers considered, 28 were under forty in 1861. Eight artillery experts became generals, 6 of whom were under forty in 1861. Of the 101 generals who held more than one duty, only 11 were born before 1810. Twenty-five were under fifty, while 44 were between thirty and forty, and 21 were under thirty. Age seems to have been as much a factor in promotion in rank as in duties held. For example, of the 159 generals with only one promotion, 40 were under thirty, 68 were under forty, 36 were under fifty, while 15 were over fifty. Seventy generals had at least two promotions in rank, 4 of whom were over fifty, 17 of whom were under thirty, and 49 of whom were between thirty and fifty in 1861. Of the 18 men who had at least three promotions, only one was born before 1810, while 5 were between the ages of forty and fifty, 9 were in the prime years of thirty-five to forty, and 3 were under thirty-five. Age seemed a factor in determining rank achieved and the responsibilities a general had during the war.

Educational achievement may have influenced promotion and duties performed during the war. For example, 58, or 37 percent, of the brigadier generals in this study attended West Point or another military school, of whom 44 were West Point graduates. Sixteen were in the top quarter of their class at the academy, 12 in the second quarter, 4 in the third quarter, and 12 in the last quarter. Thirty-nine, or 57 percent, of the major generals went to West Point or another military school, all but 4 of whom went to West Point. Six were in the top quarter of their class at the academy, 12 in the second, 5 in the third, 10 in the last, and 2 did not graduate. Fourteen of the 18 lieutenant generals went to West Point, and 1 went to another military academy. Two were in the top quarter, 6 in the second, 3 in the third, and 3 in the last. All the full generals went to West Point, 3 of whom were in the top quarter of their class. West Point graduates controlled the Confederate high command, and the higher one graduated in his class, the more opportunity he had for high command.[23]

These assertions are corroborated by examining the duties the West Point graduates held during the war. Of the 18 staff officers, 11 were West Point-trained and only 1 did not attend college. Nine had been in the top quarter of their classes at West Point. Only 18 of the line or infantry officers went to West Point, while another 7 went to another military school. Of the West Point graduates, 2 were in the top quarter, 4 in the second, 2 in the third, and 10 in the last. Twelve cavalry officers went to West Point, and another went to military school. Only 1 was in the top quarter, while 3 were in the second quarter, 1 in the third, and 5 in the last quarter. Of the 8 artillery generals, 3 of 4 were in the top quarter of their West Point class, and 3 others went to military school. Fifty-four of the 101 men who held multiple military duties attended West Point, while 8 went to another military school. Twelve were in the top quarter of their class, 22 in the second, and 10 each were in the third and fourth quarters. The Confederacy's military strategists were well-educated, while the line officers tended to place low in their class and to have the least professional military education.

West Point attendance seems also to have influenced promotion for the general officers. Of the 159 generals promoted only once, 18 attended no college, 5 did not record their education, but 61 went either to West Point or to another military school. Of the 47 who went to West Point, 21 were in the top quarter, 12 in the second, 2 in the third, and 12 in the fourth. Forty-two of the men who had two promotions in the general rank went to a military academy or to West Point. Of those who went to West Point, 5 were in the top quarter, 12 in the second, 6 in the third, and 10 in the fourth quarter. Of those who had three promotions, 15 went to some military school and one attended college. One finished in the top quarter at West Point, 6 in the second, 4 in the third, and 3 in the bottom quarter.

No wartime general held high command in prewar military engagements, but prewar military experience influenced rank achieved and duties held during the war. For example, 46 of the brigadiers fought in the Mexican War, 3 in the Seminole wars, and 5 in the Seminole and Mexican wars, while 102 had had no prewar experience. Twenty-six major generals fought in Mexico, 5 in both the Seminole and Mexican wars, and 36 had no prewar experience. Five lieutenant generals fought in Mexico, 5 were in both the Mexican and Seminole wars, and only 5 had no prewar action. Of the 6 full generals, only Samuel Cooper had no prewar fighting experience. Of the staff generals, 9 saw no prewar action, while 55 line officers, 28 cavalry officers, and 47 generals who held multiple duties had had no prewar action. Wartime promotion seemed in part to follow prewar military action. This was because of personal contacts made with other officers during the Mexican War.[24]

Officers were supposedly promoted on the basis of their wartime performance. But prewar career patterns may also have been an influence. Of the 93 prewar career military officers who became generals, 42 served only as brigadiers, 33 became major generals, 12 attained the rank of lieutenant general, and 6 held the position of full general. Twelve out of the 18 who had three promotions in general grade were career officers, while the 2 men who had provisional appointments to full general also were career men. Fifty-two, or 33 percent, of the brigadiers considered in this study, 17 of the major generals, and 1 lieutenant general had been lawyers before the war. By contrast, only 18 brigadiers had been planters, 5 of whom were lawyer-planters. Four major generals and 2 lieutenant generals had been planters. Civilian politics and ambitions undoubtedly affected those promotions. But most promotions seemed to have been based on whether one had been a career officer before the war.

Even the important duties held during the war reflected the influence of West Point and prewar military careers. Staff offices were held by 10 career military, 1 planter, and 5 lawyer-politicians. Eleven career officers, along with 9 lawyers, became generals of cavalry. The 8 artillery generals included 1 prewar editor, 1 lawyer, 1 clergyman, and 2 educators who had at one time been career officers. The generals who held more than one type of command, ostensibly the most important officers, included 48 prewar career military officers, 25 lawyers, and 6 planters. Only among the line or infantry generals does one find a preponderance of prewar civilians. Twenty career military officers became line generals, while 11 prewar planters, 32 lawyers, 2 politicians, and 9 lawyer-politicians were line officers. In effect, the career officers made the decisions to fight, planned the strategy, and directed the battles, but they let the civilian talent lead the charges and actually do the fighting. Thus, to equate excellence of performance with duties held and numbers of promotions is a mistake.

If promotion and type of command relate to evaluation of military leaders by their peers, where the generals fought is important to an understanding of the problems of coordinating the war effort. Davis's plan of an offensive-defensive strategy called for the concentration of troops with the best leaders in the geographical areas under most severe attack. Certain key locations such as the capital and the Tredegar Works at Richmond, Atlanta and the Selma Works, Vicksburg and the lower Mississippi River, and the port of Galveston called for such extensive defenses that the theory of concentration hardly had an opportunity to succeed. Two recent studies of department and theatre command and of the deployment of troops in the most vital spots question the proper utilization of the important military leaders, especially in the two major theatres of the Army of Northern Virginia and the Army of Tennessee.[25]

The celebrated dispute between Braxton Bragg and his general staff over the western command illustrates the jealousies over promotion and the quarrels over the need for transferring key military leaders to fight where the enemy concentrated its troops. The Army of Northern Virginia and the Virginia theatre had 60 brigadiers, 26 major generals, 6 lieutenant generals, and 2 full generals, with 2 more full generals at one time serving there. By comparison, the Tennessee command had only 30 brigadiers, 12 major generals, 4 lieutenant generals, and 1 full general, with 2 other full generals also serving there at one time. Of the entire list of 68 major generals studied, 54 at one time fought in Virginia, while only 32 served in Tennessee. Virginia led Tennessee 6 to 2 in staff officers, 12 to 10 in cavalry, and 35 to 15 in generals who held multiple war duties. In the important areas of favored promotions, Virginia had 27 men promoted at least once from brigadier, while Tennessee had only 13. For those who had two promotions from brigadier, Virginia led 6 to 3. In terms of the elite military personnel, Virginia outstaffed, outmanned, and outranked the Tennessee generals. Yet, who would say that the western theatre was less important or required fewer troops for its defense than did the eastern theatre? Perhaps the proximity to the Congress assisted in promotions, since that body promoted the Virginia generals more often and faster than the Tennessee generals.

In order to illustrate further the seeming lack of cooperation between East and West, the background and experience of the generals who served in the various theatres should be compared collectively. Of the 252 generals studied who were assigned to various commands, 95, or 37 percent, served exclusively in the Army of Northern Virginia. Forty-eight, or 19 percent, of the generals served exclusively in the Army of Tennessee. Age groupings show only that the prime ages were most represented in Virginia. Of the Virginia generals, 43 were in the prime thirty to forty age group and 25 were under thirty in 1861. The pattern by age holds for all the theatres, but the numbers by age show overwhelming general participation in Virginia. Fully 150 of the important generals at one time served in the Army of Northern Virginia, while only 88 spent any time in Tennessee. With age groups being equal, the numbers are all-important. The charge that the rest of the war was sacrificed to the threat on Richmond seems to have some meaning in light of where the generals served in their prime fighting years.

Subregional loyalties often influenced behavior in the Old South. A look at where the generals were born might reveal attachments and might also help explain their behavior in regard to the total war effort. For example, of the 95 generals who fought only in the Army of Northern Virginia, 37 were born in Virginia, 4 in Maryland, 18 in North Carolina, and 11 in South Carolina. Ten others who at one time fought in Virginia were born there. Of the 48 generals who fought exclusively in the Army of Tennessee, 6 were born in Kentucky, 1 in Missouri, 7 in Georgia, 4 in Alabama, and 15 in Tennessee. Only 5 men born in Virginia fought exclusively in Tennessee, while 2 born in Tennessee fought only in Virginia. Birth loyalty was important, but so was the general's residence in 1860. Again, of the 95 generals who fought exclusively in Virginia, 30 lived in Virginia in 1860, 3 in Maryland, 13 in North Carolina, and 11 in South Carolina. One man who lived in Tennessee in 1860 fought only in Virginia. Seven other Virginians fought at one time in the Army of Northern Virginia. Of the 48 generals who fought exclusively in Tennessee, none lived in Virginia or North Carolina, 3 in Kentucky, 2 in Georgia, 8 in Alabama, 3 in Mississippi, 2 in Louisiana, and 13 in Tennessee. Georgia was in the peculiar situation of having 19 of its generals fight in Virginia and 14 in Tennessee. Residence in 1860 and birthplace created loyalties which no doubt affected the high command's flexibility in deploying its personnel.

Further examination of the best and the brightest of the generals reveals that the Richmond-controlled high command may not have wanted to distribute the talent evenly. In terms of education, 33, or 38 percent, of the generals who graduated from West Point fought exclusively in Virginia. Fifty-eight West Point graduates served at one time in Virginia. In comparison, 12 of the generals who served exclusively in the Army of Tennessee were West Point graduates. The Army of Northern Virginia also had 27 college graduates and 11 law school graduates, while the Army of Tennessee had 15 college graduates and 5 who went to law school. Rank in class at West Point showed that 10 in the top quarter, 15 in the second, 2 in the third, and 9 in the last fought exclusively in the Army of Northern Virginia. In contrast, the Army of Tennessee had 5 in the first quarter, 3 in the second, 1 in the third, and 4 in the last quarter of their class at West Point. In terms of military education and brainpower, the Virginia army far surpassed any other army in the Confederacy.

If education does not explain fighting ability, prewar military experience certainly gives some idea of wartime expectation in terms of the most experienced fighters for each theatre. The one general who served in the Seminole, Black Hawk, and Mexican wars fought in both Tennessee and Virginia. But of the generals with Mexican War service alone, 25 served only in Virginia and only 10 served exclusively in Tennessee. Of the 80 generals who had served in the Mexican War, 50 at one time served in Virginia and 41 served in Tennessee. Again, Virginia led in prewar experience.

Of those generals who had professional military careers, 33 fought only in Virginia and 12 only in Tennessee. The Army of Northern Virginia also had more lawyers (29 to Tennessee's 14), businessmen (7 to Tennessee's 5), journalists (3 and none in Tennessee), and educators (4 to Tennessee's 1). The suggestion that Tennessee was discriminated against in terms of expertise with which to fight the war seems valid so far as the generals discussed in this dictionary are concerned.[26]

Although no attempt has been made to evaluate individual or collective performance of the general officers, given the pool of talent and experience from which to choose, any loss of personnel was a severe blow to the war effort. Aside from the normal military attrition rate of death in action, retirement because of wounds, or capture, the Confederacy lost a number of general officers through resignation from office. A close look at the process of promotion, duties held, and use of personnel in the various theatres has revealed some of the problems associated with a limited number of leaders. It is true that many men exhibited great bravery during the war and that generals were often made on the battlefield. But it is also true that both the promotion system and the duties held reflect a reliance on expected performance based on prewar career rather than actual performance. Too, the generals' seeming reluctance to cooperate on the various needs of the theatres of battle created a weakness that no doubt contributed to the dissension and turnover among the general officers.

If the military and political and bureaucratic leaders seemed unable to cooperate on strategy and war aims, then how could the state leaders succeed in their roles of support for the central war effort? They too suffered from attrition and disruption in office. Yet, heroic feats of cooperation from such governors as Henry Watkins Allen and Francis Lubbock in providing goods and men to the central government marked most of the state leaders' performances. Even the recalcitrant behavior of Governor Joseph E. Brown of Georgia, who willingly sacrificed the Confederate cause to the protection of Georgia, requires rationalization based on the preferred localistic behavior of most of the leaders in Richmond. Without effective leadership from above, Brown had to take the war into his own hands.[27]

Other secondary leaders, including the cultural and business leaders, performed quite adequately. The business community continued to provide needed goods and services to the front lines until either their mills or factories were overrun by the enemy or the central government could no longer transport these goods. The ministers, writers, and pressmen generally supported the war effort and worked to convince the Southern people to continue to sacrifice for the Confederacy. Those who turned against the Richmond government usually attacked it on the basis of its futile pursuit of the war effort. Edward A. Pollard turned on President Davis over Davis's refusal to fight a concentrated offensive war. Again, when those leaders began to oppose the cause, the reasons stemmed from Richmond's inability to provide the enthusiasm necessary for a propaganda effort.

But no final judgment of performance exists beyond the collective analysis of all the leaders involved in the war effort. If one is finally to blame one or more branches of leadership for the Confederate defeat then those branches require collective condemnation. The Confederacy simply never had the numbers available to pursue a long and drawn-out war of attrition. One can hardly blame President Davis or the cabinet for either their lack of coordination or emotional support of the war effort.[28] Congress represented the democratic spirit of the times, and the members usually did what they thought best for the Southern people. That Congress clashed with the president and the bureaucracy over policy reflects a true division on objectives.[29] The military leaders were only in part the victims of an inexperienced Congress and a stubborn executive. Many of the generals had little prewar experience, and they were called upon to perform sustained duties which their numbers simply would not allow. To some extent, they actually did expend themselves whipping the enemy.[30] The fanatical states' righters such as Alexander Stephens merely reflected the larger problems of cooperation and coordination which were revealed in the dissension over theatre of concentration and subregional loyalties. Finally, aside from the military, perhaps the best men from the Old South simply were not part of the Confederate leadership. The new men who led the Confederacy lacked the experience for the sustained effort. How they performed in the politics of Reconstruction remains the final test of Southern leadership in the era under study.

4 / Confederate Leadership in the Postwar Era

The question of continuity of leadership during the era of the Civil War and Reconstruction remains important to a clearer understanding of the career patterns of those who rose to prominence in the Confederate cause. Did the Civil War create a leadership class which became the power elite of the New South? Or were the postwar Southern leaders a continuation of the prewar leadership class, unlike the leaders of the war? Or, is it possible that a new leadership emerged out of the war which had led neither the Old South nor the Confederacy? Since wartime leadership experience should have been important to the postwar period, both to assist in reviving the financial and business structure of the Old South and to restore union, the extent of participation and nonparticipation in public and private life remains essential to an understanding of Reconstruction.[1]

But obstacles to service, such as old age and the attrition of war, tired and recalcitrant men, restrictive laws on officeholding, and a vindictive Southern people, require analysis. For those who did emerge from the Civil War as the leadership class, what experience did they bring to the task of reconstructing the Union? Without making full judgment on the success or failure of those who created a New South, this study should reflect what could be expected from the postwar leaders, based on their previous experience before the war and their role in making the Confederate nation function, both materially and spiritually.[2]

Of the 651 leaders included in this dictionary, 76 died during the war, 33 of whom had held executive or legislative offices during the war, 39 had been generals, 2 had been journalists, and 2 had held miscellaneous wartime positions. During Reconstruction, another 124 died, of whom 61 had served in wartime executive or legislative positions, 13 had been governors or judges, 36 generals, 4 businessmen, 1 a doctor, 4 clergymen, 1 an educator, and 4 journalists during the war. Although some of these men had short postwar public careers and quite a few held significant positions in private life, their deaths broke the continuity of leadership from Reconstruction to home rule in the New South. Another 41 died during the crucial transition years between 1877 and 1881. And only a small number of the ex-Confederate leaders who lived past 1881 participated in public life after 1882.[3]

A look at those who remained to participate in public life after the war ended reveals that many of them kept out of postwar politics. Of the 321 leaders who served in the national or state governments during the war, 221 of those who survived into Reconstruction held no known public office. One who served in the U.S. House and 1 who was on the state supreme court eventually left the South. Of the 265 former generals, 167 held no postwar public office. Nineteen other ex-generals left the South permanently, 2 of whom had held major postwar appointive offices. Of the ex-professional leaders, 51 of 63 studied held no postwar public office. Seven wartime professionals left the South permanently after the war. If some of the wartime leaders managed to have major professional careers after the war, the diverse and experienced political and professional leadership left approximately 206 individuals for public leadership in the New South.[4]

The loss of leaders in terms of prewar public positions shows an attrition of political talent of irreparable dimension. Sixty-five former state legislators who had held important government positions during the war either died in the war or held no postwar public office. Ten state supreme court judges, 7 lower court judges, 32 U.S. congressmen, 16 U.S. senators, and 9 governors—all important prewar public figures who had served in the Confederate government in some capacity—either died during the war or held no postwar public offices. A total of 119 important generals from the war who held no postwar public office also had no prewar public careers. But 6 mayors, 4 district attorneys, 5 judges, 23 state legislators, 5 congressmen, 2 senators, and 2 governors who were important wartime military figures held no postwar public office. Thus, 48 generals who held prewar public office were lost to the postwar political world. Some, like Howell Cobb and Robert Toombs, were hardly missed, but others who had achieved the steadiness gained only in combat were lost to public life, perhaps when they were most needed.

A similar correlation of prewar to postwar private profession reveals the tragic numbers of talented lawyers, cultural leaders, and businessmen lost to the New South. For example, of the most important civilian group during the war, the members of the national and state governments and the Congress, 83 died during the war or had no known postwar private career. Thirty-seven lawyers, 3 doctors, 10 planters, 15 lawyer-planters, and 3 newspapermen did not resume their professions after the war. Of the wartime military, 39 died during the war and 6 others held no known postwar private careers. Only 20 of them had been career military officers before the war. The generals lost to postwar private service included 1 preacher, 2 educators, 6 lawyers, 1 political officeholder, 1 military-planter, 4 businessmen, and 1 scientist. Seven of those who had held major professional wartime jobs had no postwar private careers. Two had been preachers, 1 was a planter, 1 a lawyer-politician, 1 a businessman, and 1 a newspaperman. Those 125 wartime leaders created a great vacuum in business experience in postwar private life.

Seventeen military leaders, 16 government leaders (6 of whom had been congressmen), and 7 wartime professionals left the South after the war. Mobility and residence patterns proved to have been factors influencing the wartime leaders' lack of participation in postwar public life. Of the military, 44 moved once, 17 twice, 14 three times, 2 four times, and 2 five times. Of the ex-government leaders including Congress, 38 moved once, 16 twice, 6 three times, 3 four times, and 2 five times. Of the wartime professionals, 17 moved once, 4 twice, 1 three times, and 1 four times. No doubt, this group of men was seeking occupational opportunities and simply had no time to give to public life. There is some evidence that wartime congressmen from the Southwest fared worse in their search for work than did their counterparts in the Southeast.[5]

Federal government obstacles to postwar public service delayed some state leaders from re-entering public life longer than others. Of the ex-military leaders from Kentucky, 4 were barred from office until they took the loyalty oath, and 3 had no obstacles to public service. Of those from Virginia, 15 were barred until their state rejoined the Union, 1 was barred until 1876, and 4 seemed to have had no restrictions on their public service. In terms of ex-congressmen, only Missouri with 4 of 12, Georgia with 9 of 28, Mississippi with 6 of 18, and Texas with 5 of 13 had more than 33 percent of their leaders barred from public service until the states returned to the Union or until the ex-leaders signed the loyalty oath. In Mississippi 4, or 22 percent, of its wartime congressmen were barred from public service until after 1876. Obstacles to public service seemed an important factor in the relative absence of wartime congressional leaders in postwar public leadership positions.[6]

Age also had a major effect on postwar service, and it obviously explains why many wartime leaders had no postwar careers. Twenty-two of the 27 ex-military leaders born before 1810 held no postwar public office. (Some of that number died during the war.) Of the 64 born between 1811 and 1820, 45 held no postwar public office. Of the wartime government leaders, including the Congress, 99 who did not serve in public life were over fifty, and 77 were over forty in 1865. Of the wartime professionals, 23 of the 45 who did not serve in postwar public life were over forty-five in 1865. When restrictions combined with age of the wartime leaders, many did not have the stamina for a return to public life.

Thus, many wartime leaders were lost to postwar political leadership. Some who might have had a viable role did become involved in presidential Reconstruction, only to find that the Northern Congress would not accept their credentials. Their disillusionment led them to forsake politics altogether.[7] Others were too old, too poor, or too tired to try to mold a New South. Some left the South because they could no longer see a future there for their old way of life; many of these men hoped to set up a replica of the South elsewhere. Others knew nothing other than how to fight and were simply not useful to the peacetime efforts. In short, years of prewar experience and the knowledge gained from the wartime efforts of those men were lost to the New South.[8]

Those wartime leaders who went into vital private business in order to restore their financial losses or to serve the South as best they could, given the restrictions placed on them by the Northern government, were in many ways a loss to the political world of the New South.[9] Many leaders who had served in important prewar public careers held no postwar public careers but did have significant private careers. Of the wartime military leaders, 89 had held important prewar public offices, whereas of those who survived only 39 held postwar private positions. Of the total government leaders from the war, 255 had held important prewar public offices. Ninety-five held no postwar public office but did have postwar private careers of some importance. Of those who had important professional positions during the war, only 8 had prewar public careers, 6 of whom had important postwar private careers.

The great majority of all the Confederate leaders who lived into the postwar period went into private rather than public positions after the war. Of those men who led the wartime military effort, 220 had only private careers after the war. Five became ministers, 19 either educators or writers (most of the military leaders who became educators taught the practical sciences), 36 professional politicians, 42 lawyers, 1 a doctor, 43 planters, 7 planter-lawyers, 1 a planter and a member of a foreign army, 49 businessmen, 9 scientists, 2 newspapermen, and 5 served in a foreign military capacity. Most of them had served in private life, usually in some professional capacity, before the war. But the war experience did redirect some of their postwar professions. For example, of the 82 career military officers who survived the war, 13 became educators, 11 professional politicians, and only 3 lawyers, while 23 became planters or farmers, 1 a lawyer-planter, 3 foreign military officers, 20 businessmen, 6 engineers, and 1 an editor. Of the 17 generals who had been planters, 11 returned to planting, 1 became an educator, 2 career politicians, 1 a businessman, and 1 a scientist. Nine of the generals who had been businessmen returned to business, while 1 became a lawyer and 2 planters. Thirty-four generals returned to their law practices, while 11 of them took up business, 2 became planters, 3 planter-lawyers, and 2 educators.[10]

The wartime government and congressional leaders also took an active part in the professional life of rebuilding the tattered South. Of those left to participate in private life, 17 turned to education, 95 practiced law, 59 became part of the new breed of professional politicians, 2 practiced medicine, 24 turned to planting or farming, 4 became lawyer-planters, 1 went to work for a foreign potentate, 30 entered business, 2 became scientists, and 3 entered the newspaper business. Twenty-one had been planters before the war, of whom 10 returned to planting, 4 entered business, 3 became professional politicians, 2 became lawyers, and 1 entered teaching. Of 9 prewar businessmen who had held wartime public office, 5 returned to their businesses and 1 became an educator. Sixty-seven men returned to their law practices, 29 became professional politicians, 4 educators, 4 planters, and 10 businessmen. Among the government and political leaders of the war, many of the planters and the lawyers changed their careers, while the postwar period produced a new group of business leaders.

For the ex-Confederate congressmen, the figures show that 1 became a minister, 10 educators, 71 lawyers, 2 doctors, 20 planters or farmers, 3 planter-lawyers, 1 a member of a foreign military service, 20 businessmen, 2 editors, and 48 remained professional politicians. Nine men returned to their plantations, while 4 became businessmen, 2 lawyers, and 3 professional politicians. Of the prewar business-men who had served in the Confederate Congress, 1 became an educator, 1 a planter, and 2 returned to business. Eight professional politicians returned to political life. Forty-nine of the 118 prewar lawyers who had been congressmen returned to the law, while 20 turned to professional politics, 4 to education, 4 to planting, and 8 to business. Even in this specific group, the numbers of lawyers and planters declined, while that of businessmen grew.[11]

The wartime professionals, including the businessmen, scientists, ministers, and editors, if they did not contribute to postwar public life, did return to important professional jobs in the postwar era. Eight prewar ministers and 1 doctor became ministers after the war. Thirteen became educators, 2 professional politicians, and 4 lawyers. Six doctors returned to prewar practice, but some soon left the South for Northern appointments. One prewar physician became a planter, 10 businessmen, and 5 either writers or newspaper editors. All 5 of the prewar newspapermen and 84 of the prewar businessmen continued their careers. The expertise which the wartime professionals had gained during the war became useful to the New South, since most of them returned to their prewar professional careers.[12]

Analysis of postwar private professions shows that a large number of the prewar professional elite returned to important positions in the financial and professional life of their communities. Surprisingly, many changed professions, the planter world declined among the ex-Confederate leaders (although planters had led neither the secession movement nor the war effort), and the business world gained importance in the New South. That all the generals did not become wealthy postwar businessmen and that the powerful prewar lawyers found themselves competing with the emerging legal class is not unexpected, however. Neverthe-less, the ex-Confederate leaders who survived the war had an important role in the private life of the New South. Some evidence suggests that even those who did not become insurance or railroad magnates also managed to influence the public life of the New South. They were part of a new business elite whose impact on politics requires further study.

What of those who did have postwar public careers? Who were they and what could be expected of them? The prewar private career experience could indicate the interests, allegiances, and even the performance of these leaders. The wartime military remains an important area for study because of the impact of the military mystique on the Southern electorate.[13] Two generals who had been educators in the antebellum period went on to hold important appointive offices as college presidents after the war. Prewar career military officers held 5 town offices, 1 U.S. House seat, 4 governorships, and 14 major appointive offices in postwar public life. Prewar lawyers won 3 city positions, 2 county solicitorships, 3 lower court judgeships, 1 seat on the state supreme court, 9 seats in state legislatures, 5 seats in the U.S. House, 8 seats in the U.S. Senate, 5 governorships, and 5 major public appointments. Planters were not so successful. They included 2 town positions, 1 seat in the state legislature, 1 seat in the U.S. Senate, 1 governorship, and 2 major public appointments. The prewar lawyer-planters produced 1 state legislator, 2 U.S. senators, and 2 governors in the postwar period. The prewar businessmen held 1 county solicitorship, 2 congressional seats, and 2 seats in the U.S. Senate. Clearly, the prewar planters and businessmen did not fare as well in postwar public life as the prewar lawyers who had become important political-military leaders during the war. In terms of continuity of power by profession and postwar political leadership, those lawyer-generals merit further study.[14]

Of the wartime political and government leaders who held prewar private positions, only 98 held postwar public offices and were able to use that experience in postwar public life. It is obvious that either Northern restrictions were harsh or that the people of the South no longer trusted them. For example, of the prewar lawyer pool, which produced the largest number of postwar leaders, 1 held town office, 5 became lower court judges, 11 members of their state supreme courts, 13 state legislators, 7 U.S. congressmen, 6 U.S. senators, 6 governors, and 8 holders of major public appointments. The prewar planters held 1 city office, 1 seat each in the state legislature, the U.S. Congress, and the U.S. Senate, and 2 important public appointments. The lawyer-planters included 1 town official, 2 county attorneys, 1 state supreme court judge, 4 state legislators, 1 congressman, 1 senator, and 1 major public appointment in the postwar period. The lawyer-politicians held 2 lower court judgeships, 2 state supreme court judgeships, 2 seats in the state legislature, and 1 seat each in the U.S. House and the U.S. Senate. In other words, the prewar lawyers who had led the Confederacy's politics and bureaucracy held a total of 76 postwar public positions.

A glance at those who served in the Confederate Congress and had important prewar private offices also reveals that the lawyers managed to grab the major postwar public offices. For example, of the 83 congressmen who managed to hold postwar public office, 43 were lawyers. Four became lower court judges, 9 state supreme court justices, 10 state legislators, 7 U.S. congressmen, 3 U.S. senators, 3 governors, and 7 others managed important appointive offices. The lawyer-planters in the Confederate Congress contributed 10 leaders, and the lawyer-politicians 8 more postwar public leaders. The prewar planters who served in the Confederate Congress contributed only 6 public offices to the postwar period, including 1 U.S. congressman and 1 U.S. senator. None of the businessmen who had served in the Confederate Congress managed postwar public careers. The lawyer class in the Old South provided what continuity there was in the New South's leadership.

Since the wartime professional leaders brought so much business experience to the war effort, their positions in postwar public life require some analysis. Only 8 of that group held postwar public office, including 1 lawyer and 1 newspaperman who became mayors of their towns. Two prewar ministers, 1 educator, and 1 physician held major postwar appointive office. One became a U.S. congressman, and another was elected governor of his state. It is clear that the professional prewar elite, including the prestigious business leaders, held few postwar public offices. The administrative ability and experience lost was incalculable.

Any test of the continuity of political power or any judgment on expectation of postwar performance must also include a comparison of prewar and postwar major public office. The wartime military leaders present an excellent picture of the rise and decline in political power. Of the 167 generals who held no postwar office, 119 had held no office in the antebellum South. But of the 12 ex-military who held postwar positions in their towns, 2 had been state legislators, 2 had served in the U.S. Congress, and 8 had held no prewar public office. Of the 3 generals who became postwar county solicitors, 1 had been in the state legislature and 2 had held no previous public office. All of the 3 generals who became lower court judges after the war had served in their state legislatures before the war, as had the 1 military leader who became a state supreme court judge in the postwar period. Of the 13 military men who entered their state legislatures after the war, 1 had been a mayor, 1 a county solicitor, 4 state legislators, 2 congressmen, 1 governor, and 4 had no prewar public experience. Thirteen military leaders entered the U.S. House, of whom 2 had been county solicitors, 3 state legislators, 2 members of the prewar U.S. House, and 6 without previous public careers. Of the 15 generals who became U.S. senators, 3 had been county solicitors, 1 a lower court judge, 5 state legislators, and 6 without prewar public office. Of the 12 generals who became governors, 1 had been a mayor, 3 state legislators, 1 a prewar U.S. congressman, and 7 without prewar public experience. Twenty-six held important postwar appointive offices, such as college presidencies or ambassadorial posts. Two of these men had served in their state legislatures, but the remaining 24 had held no political office in the antebellum South. Thus, military service was a means to postwar public office. Fifty-seven of the 98 generals who held postwar public office had held no office before the war. Of the 24 ex-state legislators who held public office in the postwar period, 18 attained better elected offices in the postwar period.[15]

The wartime congressional and bureaucratic leaders are also important for their prewar and postwar public careers. They were not as popular as the generals with the postwar electorate. Less than 100 of these important government leaders obtained postwar public positions compared with 225 who had held prewar office. Death and old age seemed factors in this attrition, but resentment against wartime political failures may also have contributed to their decline in numbers. The continuity of leadership also broke down. For example, of the 3 postwar mayors, only 1 had served in the prewar state legislature. Of the 2 county solicitors, 1 had been in the U.S. House and the other had held no office. The 9 lower court judges included 1 prewar county solicitor, 3 state legislators, 2 U.S. congressmen, 1 governor, and 2 with no previous experience. Of the 17 state supreme court justices, 1 had been a county solicitor, 2 lower court judges, 7 state legislators, 4 U.S. congressmen, and 3 without prewar office. Of the 27 who served in their postwar state legislatures, 2 had been county solicitors, 1 had been a lower court judge, 14 state legislators, 7 U.S. congressmen, and 3 without office. Of the 11 postwar U.S. congressmen, 2 had been county solicitors, 1 a lower court judge, 3 state legislators, 2 prewar U.S. congressmen, and 3 without office. Of the 10 postwar U.S. senators, 4 had been state legislators, 3 U.S. congressmen, 2 governors, and 1 without office. Six wartime politicians became state governors after the war, 2 of whom had been state legislators, 1 a U.S. congressman, 1 a county solicitor, and 2 without prewar public office. Fifteen government leaders received important postwar public appointments, of whom 5 had been state legislators, 7 U.S. congressmen, and 3 without prewar office. So much for any theory that there was continuity of experience throughout the entire era of Civil War and Reconstruction.

A short look at the Confederate congressmen, supposedly the most political individuals in the South, should also confirm the absence of continuity in the political leadership of the New South. Eighty-two of 245 wartime congressmen held postwar public office, of whom only 65 had also served in antebellum political life. The war made 17 public careers. Twenty-two became judges, of whom 1 had been a judge, 9 state legislators, 5 U.S. congressmen, and 1 a governor of his state. Twenty-two entered the state legislature, of whom 13 had been state legislators and 6 had served in the prewar Congress. Twelve entered the U.S. Congress, of whom 2 had been legislators and 3 had also been members of the U.S. House. Six became U.S. senators, of whom 4 had been legislators and 1 a U.S. congressman. Of the 3 congressmen who became postwar governors, 1 had been a U.S. congressman before the war. Of the 12 ex-Confederate congressmen who received postwar appointive office, 4 had been legislators and 6 had served in the prewar U.S. House.

Little postwar political service should have been expected from men and women who had private professional duties during the war. Only 8 of the 57 individuals studied held postwar political office, and only 1 of these 8 had held political office before the war. This individual had been governor of his state, and he held a postwar political appointment. Two became mayors, 1 entered the U.S. House, 1 became governor, and 4 held appointive offices such as college presidencies.

In sum, of the Confederate leaders analyzed for continuous public experience, 206 held postwar public office, 122 of whom also held public office before the war. Thus, there was no real continuity of leadership except for what the war provided. Even considering those who died during the war or were too old for service, one cannot claim that the wartime leaders were the major leaders of the postwar South's politics.

The 206 men who held important postwar public office are subject to analysis for their contributions to postwar life. Factors such as when they were able to take office, their party loyalties, their performance during the war (meaning their reputations), and especially the relationship between their postwar public and private career patterns might provide some further knowledge of what those Confederate leaders did for the New South. Again, wartime occupation will serve to delineate the groups for analysis.

The private postwar career patterns of the wartime military leaders who served in postwar public life could tell something of the interests of that group. Those who served as postwar mayors included 4 professional politicians, 1 lawyer, 2 planters, and 5 businessmen in their postwar private careers. Two postwar lawyers and 1 postwar planter served as county solicitors. Three postwar lawyers also became county judges. The one state supreme court justice was a lawyer in private practice. The wartime military leaders who became state legislators included 4 professional politicians, 5 lawyers, 2 planters, and 2 businessmen in private life. The U.S. congressmen included 7 professional politicians (no doubt many of these men also had business and legal careers), 3 lawyers, 1 planter, and 2 businessmen. The military men who became U.S. senators were in private life 7 professional politicians, 3 lawyers, 2 planters, 1 lawyer-planter, and 2 businessmen. Of the governors, 4 were also professional politicians, 2 lawyers, 2 planters, 1 a lawyer-planter, and 3 businessmen. Of those ex-generals who held important appointive positions, 5 were also educators, 7 professional politicians, 1 a lawyer, 1 a doctor, 3 planters, 2 lawyer-planters, and 7 business executives. Fully 23 of the generals who had postwar public careers became professional politicians, while the lawyers, businessmen, and planters shared the remaining private positions about equally.[16]

Postwar political affiliation may well reveal something about the political performance of the ex-generals, especially when it is compared to prewar party support.[17] Sixty-five of the postwar public officials who had been generals either joined or returned to the Democrats. That number included 11 of 13 state legislators, 11 of 13 U.S. congressmen, 12 of 15 U.S. senators, and 9 of 12 governors. One governor called himself a Conservative, 1 was a Democrat who turned Populist, and 1 was of unknown affiliation.[18] The Republicans, who included men like William Mahone of Virginia, managed 1 state legislator, 2 U.S. congressmen, 1 U.S. senator, and 2 public appointees. One senator called himself a Democrat-Populist, and another a Republican-Populist. Thirteen men who held important postwar appointive office professed no party affiliation. Clearly, the wartime generals were overwhelmingly Democrat in their postwar politics.

The mobility pattern of the ex-generals shows that they did not often stray far from home if they were going to participate in postwar public life. It is known that 37 did not move at all. Only 23 moved one time. Twelve moved twice, 4 three times, 2 four times, and only 2 five or more times. Only 2 generals who held postwar public office permanently left the South, and they both held appointive office.[19]

Ex-military leaders who finally held office encountered obstacles which help to explain their nonparticipation in making a just peace and their lateness in directing a New South. Forty-four of those who would eventually hold public office were barred from office until they either took a loyalty oath or their states reentered the Union. Fifteen were barred from any public service until after 1876. Still, 30 public leaders experienced no noticeable hindrance to postwar participation. Party affiliation may have been a factor in barring them from public life. Forty-two Democrats were barred until their states returned to the Union and 18 until at least 1876; only 15 Democrats had no restrictions. Only 4 Republicans were barred until their states returned to the Union, while 3 had no restrictions at all.[20]

So much has been written about the influence of the ex-Whigs in the South's postwar political behavior that a test of the continuity of party as it related to wartime leadership groups who held postwar public office could reveal something more about the activities of those leaders. The wartime military leaders who held postwar office consisted of 65 Democrats, of whom 42 had been Democrats before the war, 1 a Democrat-American, 9 Whigs, and 6 Whig-Democrats. There were 7 postwar Republicans, of whom 2 had been Democrats and 3 Whigs. Of the 97 ex-generals whose postwar party affiliations are known, 50 had been Democrats before the war, 1 a Democrat-American, 7 Whig-Democrats, and 14 diehard Whigs. As far as the military was concerned, there were few hidden Whigs in postwar public life.

Other factors affected the ex-military leaders in New South politics. Thirty-five had been secessionists, while only 15 had been unionists. The unionists led in number of postwar governors, 5 to 2, but trailed in all other postwar public offices. The extent to which their holding postwar office depended upon their position in 1860 is not as important as the fact that unionists and secessionists seemed to cooperate in postwar politics.

The question of family connections has been tested in terms of prewar rise in politics and wartime duties held. To complete the study, the ex-military leaders also need some analysis of the continuity of leadership over the years. Of the 98 who served in postwar public life, 38 had no connection with important prewar families. That included 10 who held appointive office, 5 governors, 5 U.S. senators, 6 U.S. congressmen, and 5 state legislators. But both the wartime and postwar leadership had about the same number, 38 percent, of the total leadership who had come from important families. The postwar leadership from families of politics and wealth showed 8 legislators, 7 U.S. congressmen, 10 U.S. senators, 7 governors, and 14 public appointees. The little that is known about marriages into families of importance shows that 18 had important relatives from their wives' families. Considering that 36 who held military careers during the war had family connections by marriage, there was a slight decline in family status after the war.[21]

Age patterns may also tell something about what might have been expected from the postwar public performance of those who held important wartime military office. One state legislator was over sixty-five in 1865. One legislator, 1 governor, and 2 appointed officials were born before 1810. Only 1 U.S. congressman was born before 1815. Fully 27 public officials were over forty-five in 1865, while another 44 were over thirty-five. When added to the restrictions on public service of those who finally served, 43 men over thirty-five in 1865 could not participate in public life until after 1872, and another 21 of the same age group could not serve until after 1876. Thus, age limited the number of productive years a political leader could serve in postwar life. Only 20 ex-military leaders who were over thirty-five in 1865 seemed to have had no restrictions on their postwar public service. The number actually able to participate in Reconstruction politics was 32, hardly enough to allow the wartime leaders to make a major impact on political life and policy in the crucial early postwar years.

Some of the wartime government and political figures who participated in postwar public life also had important postwar private careers. Of the 3 mayors, 1 was a professional politician, 1 a lawyer, and 1 a planter. One of the county solicitors was a professional politician; the other was a businessman. Of the lower court judges, 5 were professional politicians and 4 lawyers. Of the state supreme court judges, 8 were professional politicians, 6 lawyers, and 2 businessmen. Of the congressmen, 6 were professional politicians and 4 lawyers. The senators included 1 educator, 8 professional politicians, and 1 businessman. The governors included 1 professional politician, 4 lawyers, and 1 lawyer-planter. Those who held major appointive office included 1 educator, 8 professional politicians, 3 lawyers, 1 planter, and 2 businessmen. Unlike the military, which had a sizable number of planters in public life, the government and political figures only had 2 planters in public life, as compared to 8 businessmen and 31 who made their livings as lawyers. If there was conflict of interest involved when some men held political office and were also under the influence of business, the pattern does not seem large.

Again, Democrats held the overwhelming number of postwar public offices. Sixty-three who held public office from the wartime politician corps were Democrats; for another 23, of whom 11 served in the state legislature, their postwar political affiliations were unavailable. Only 9 were Republicans, of whom 3 were state supreme court judges, 2 state legislators, 1 a governor, and 3 appointive officials. The governor was Joseph Brown of Georgia, who again became a Democrat in 1872. Most of the Republicans were from North Carolina, and they would not survive long in politics after 1876.

The mobility pattern of wartime political figures shows that those who became postwar political leaders, unlike their ex-military counterparts, did not move often. Forty-six did not move at all, 28 moved once, 3 twice, 5 three times, and only 2 four times. Only 2 ex-government and political leaders who held political office after the war eventually left the South. One was a state supreme court justice and 1 had served in the U.S. House.[22]

On the other hand, restrictions on the postwar political activities of these leaders severely limited their contributions to Reconstruction. Most had to wait until after 1876 to enter public life. Only 1 mayor was not restricted in reentering public life. (Some of these leaders held political office early after the war and were denied office once congressional Reconstruction began. Some never returned to office.) One county solicitor was kept from office until his state returned to the Union. A total of 35 had no restrictions, including 14 state legislators, 3 congressmen, 7 senators, 5 governors, and 7 who did not have to stand for election. Eight leaders had to wait until 1876 before they could serve in a public office, including 2 congressmen and 1 senator. Those restrictions probably accounted for the permanent loss of many leaders of political ability and statesmanship.[23]

The figures on restrictions on ex-government and political leaders show a prejudice against Democrats. Fifty Democrats were barred from public service until their states rejoined the Union, as opposed to only 2 Republicans. Twelve Democrats were barred from public office until 1876, while no Republicans seemed to have been so restricted. The Democrats had 14 and the Republicans 7 who faced no such obstacles. However, in most ex-Confederate states, being a Republican was tantamount to disbarment from public office after 1876.[24]

An isolated look at those who served in the Confederate Congress and also held postwar office should corroborate the figures found on the combined congressional and governmental leaders of the war. Of the 98 ex-congressmen who held postwar public office, 43 were professional politicians, 24 lawyers, 2 planters, and 8 businessmen. The planters produced only 1 appointed official and 1 mayor, thereby demonstrating that postwar planter-political influence was negligible in terms of political offices held. The mobility pattern shows that 34 did not move at all, 24 moved once, 5 twice, 3 three times, and 2 four times. No one who held elective office moved more than twice after the war. Only 3 left the South permanently. Fifty were Democrats, 8 Republicans, and 2 Republicans who turned Democrat. Only 33 of the ex-congressmen had no apparent restrictions on their movements. But 39 were kept from political office until their states returned to the Union, and 7 were barred until after 1876. Wartime congressional experience undoubtedly was invaluable for those who participated in postwar politics. But there was a large number whose talents remained beyond the use of the New South.

A further test of the idea of persistent Whig influence in the New South is found in an analysis of wartime government officials who held postwar public office. Of the 63 postwar Democrats, 41 had been Democrats before the war, 1 a Democrat-American, 7 Whigs, 4 Whig-Americans, 7 Whig-Democrats, and 3 had unknown party affiliations. Of the 9 postwar Republicans, 3 had been Democrats, 4 Whigs, and 2 Whig-Americans. Of the 2 Republicans who turned Democrat, 1 had been a Whig and the other a Whig-Democrat. Twelve without postwar party affiliation had been prewar Democrats, and 5 Whigs. Within that group of politicians, the ex-Confederate congressmen were the most political. Of the 50 postwar Democrats, 31 had been Democrats, 1 a Democrat-American, 6 Whigs, 3 Whig-Americans, and 6 Whig-Democrats. The 8 postwar Republicans included 3 Democrats, 3 Whigs, and 2 Whig-Americans. The 2 Conservatives had both been Whigs. The 2 Republicans who turned Democrat had also been prewar Whigs. Ten without postwar party affiliation had been prewar Democrats, whereas 5 had been prewar Whigs. As far as the total government group is concerned, the Whigs had little say in postwar political life. However, among the ex-Confederate congressmen a total of 45 had been Democrats and 81 had served in various forms of the Whig party in the prewar years. The Whigs no longer had their old party and had become loyal Democrats; nevertheless, they played a sizable role in postwar public life.[25]

Secession position may also reveal something of the political expectations for the postwar public leaders. Sixty-three had been secessionists and 24 had been unionists. Surprisingly, the unionists led 6 to 5 in men who served in the U.S. House and trailed only 7 to 8 among those who held postwar state supreme court judgeships. Among the ex-Confederate congressmen who held postwar public office, the secessionists led the unionists 53 to 21. The unionists led 2 to 0 in postwar governors, tied 6 to 6 in the U.S. House, and trailed 6 to 7 in state supreme court officials. Clearly, the ex-unionists had a place in postwar public life far beyond their power in Congress during the war or in late antebellum politics.

Among the postwar political leaders who had served in the Confederate government, family connection was not as important as it had been among the ex-military leaders. Yet, approximately one-third of each group had some significant family connections. Sixty-five men rose to postwar power because of their wartime reputations rather than their family names. Thirty-four came from families with wealth and political power. The difference is that 10 of 16 state supreme court judges rose from no family background, as did 19 of 27 state legislators, 8 of 11 U.S. congressmen, 8 of 10 senators, and 5 of 6 governors. Only 8 postwar leaders were known to have married into families who had been politically and economically powerful before the war. The same pattern seems to hold for the Confederate congressmen, except that 54 had no family connections, while 27 had such connections. Only 6 seemed to have married into prestigious families. Continuity of family influence was most sharply observed among the ex-Confederate congressmen. Thirty-four percent of them may have benefited from important family connections in their prewar public careers. The idea of overwhelming aristocratic continuity does not hold for any period of leadership studied here.[26]

The age factor is important to an understanding of postwar performance of the wartime government leaders. For example, only 36 men served in postwar politics who were over the age of fifty in 1865. Important age groups were kept from public service until after Reconstruction. Of those restricted until their states returned to the Union, 24 were over fifty in 1865, and another 43 were over thirty-five in 1865. Thus, they probably had to delay entering public service until their mid-forties at least. Six of those who could not serve until after 1876 were over fifty in 1865, and another 6 were over thirty-five. The same pattern holds for the ex-congressmen. They were denied power in the postwar period until they were old men.

The wartime leaders were also hampered by state restrictions. In only Georgia and Texas did as many as half of the wartime government and political leaders enter postwar politics. Eleven of 41 Virginians participated, as did 13 of 34 North Carolinians, 8 of 21 South Carolinians, 9 of 30 Alabamians, 7 of 27 Mississippians, and 5 of 26 Tennesseans. The same pattern holds for the ex-congressmen, with some apparent correlation between wartime peace leaders and postwar political leaders. The loss of trained leadership by the Confederate states provided for almost uniform lack of that expertise in postwar public life. The government and political leaders were no help to their states until they were almost too old for public life. The obstacles to public service were similar, with Georgia having 11 restrictions and Mississippi 13. The fewest restrictions on wartime politicians were in Virginia with 5 of 12, North Carolina with 8 of 15, and Georgia with 6 of 17 participating in postwar politics.

The ex-Confederate congressmen who finally held postwar political positions provide an interesting test of political restrictions and party affiliation by state in the postwar period. For obviously different reasons, the North placed fewer restrictions on the ex-congressmen of the southeastern states than on those of the southwestern states. In Virginia, 6 of 11 ex-congressmen faced restrictions of some sort on postwar service. Similar figures for other states include North Carolina with 5 of 10, South Carolina with 4 of 8, Florida with 1 of 3, and Arkansas with 3 of 7 who were restricted. In the West, Georgia had 10 of 15, Alabama 6 of 9, Mississippi 10 of 11, Louisiana 3 of 3, Texas 5 of 5, and Tennessee 5 of 7. Restrictions on ex-congressmen were fewest in states with larger numbers of Republican ex-congressmen. Virginia had 9 Democrats, 1 Republican, and 2 Conservatives who flirted with both parties.[27] North Carolina had 4 Democrats, 5 Republicans, and 2 Conservatives. South Carolina, Alabama, Tennessee, and Arkansas had 1 Republican apiece. The pattern followed along the lines of where wartime loyalty to the Confederacy had been greatest, if Georgia is excluded. Restrictions also seemed to have been imposed most often in states whose wartime loyalty to the Confederacy had been greatest.

It is already known that few wartime professional leaders held postwar elective public office. Of the 2 mayors, 1 was a lawyer and 1 an editor. The one congressman was also an editor. The governor was a professional politician. Of the appointed officeholders, 3 were educators and one was a minister who became a bishop. The congressman and the 2 mayors were Democrats. The governor was a Republican, while the 4 appointed officials had no political affiliation. Two did not move, 3 moved once, 1 appointed officeholder twice, and the congressman three times. They were not a mobile group, as none of the professional wartime leaders who became postwar politicians moved from the South. Obstacles to their officeholding showed that there was little recrimination against professional figures. Only the one man who became a congressman was kept from public office until after 1876, and he was a partisan Democrat. But their small numbers meant that those men were unable to make a significant contribution to postwar public life.[28]

The 3 wartime professionals who were Democrats after the war were also Democrats before the war, while the single Republican was a Whig-Democrat. Two had also been secessionists. Four were men who had made their careers during the war, while 3 had family connections. Only 1 had powerful family ties by marriage. Only 2 professionals with postwar public careers were over fifty in 1865, and 1 of them held a public appointment. Four were between forty-five and fifty-five in 1865. Only 2 were barred from postwar public service, and they were comparatively young men in 1865. Two were from Virginia, of whom 1 became governor. The only other important officeholder was a Tennessee congressman. A Virginian and a Georgian were restricted. One of these wartime professionals was a North Carolina Republican; the rest were Democrats. Although they were hardly political men, study of wartime professionals reveals a pattern similar to that of the other groups.

The Confederate leaders who served in public life in the New South were men of position and prominence. Those who returned to private life served in important and successful capacities in their states and communities. But the overall contribution was diminished by the small number of participants in public life. There is some truth to the notions that good military and bureaucratic leaders do not make good civilian leaders and that their wartime positions may have hindered their postwar careers. In addition, those Confederate leaders who desired a New South did not seem able to change the direction of their section. But it is certain that the top echelon of the Confederate leaders was not the dominant political force in the New South. Age, weariness, defeatism, and popular recrimination may have kept them out of public life. The postwar leadership that had wartime experience was probably made up largely of those with minor roles in the Civil War.

Considering the entire pattern of leadership continuity during the Civil War and Reconstruction, it is evident that the Confederate leaders came to prominence in the 1850s. Many of them were either radicals or hesitant political trimmers who combined ambition with a sense of duty, but they did not have the political experience to sustain a major war effort. Whatever experience they gained during the war was largely lost to the New South. Just as the great men of the antebellum period did not lead either a secession movement or the Confederacy, the great men of the Confederacy did not lead the New South. The fame of the Confederate leaders belongs to the war; their wartime performances belong to history.

NOTES TO INTRODUCTION

Chapter 1

1. Lawrence Stone, "Prosopography," *Daedalus*, Winter 1971.
2. Stone, "Prosopography"; Richard Jensen, "Quantitative Collective Biography: An Application to Metropolitan Elites," in Robert P. Swierenga (ed.), *Quantification in American History* (New York, 1970).
3. Charles Beard, *An Economic Interpretation of the Constitution* (New York, 1913).
4. Frank L. Owsley, *Plain Folk of the Old South* (Baton Rouge, La., 1949).
5. Barnes Lathrop, *Migration into East Texas 1835-1860: A Study from the United States Census* (Austin, Tex., 1949); Barnes Lathrop, "History from the Census Returns," *The Southwestern Historical Quarterly LI*.
6. Stephen Thernstrom, *Poverty and Progress* (Boston, 1964). Thernstrom was one of a number of students who studied social history under Oscar Handlin at Harvard University during the mid-1950s. See also Anselm L. Strauss, *The Contexts of Social Mobility* (Chicago, 1971).
7. Lee Benson, *The Concept of Jacksonian Democracy* (New York, 1961); for the counter to Benson see Frank Otto Gatell, "Money and Party in Jacksonian America," *Political Science Quarterly LXXXII*.
8. Paul Kleppner, *The Cross of Culture* (New York, 1970); Richard Jensen, *The Winning of the Middle West* (Chicago, 1971).
9. Robert Dahl, *Who Governs?* (New Haven, Conn., 1961).
10. Thomas Cochran, *Railroad Leaders* (Cambridge, Mass., 1953).
11. E. Digby Baltzell, *Philadelphia Gentlemen* (Glencoe, Ill., 1958); also see Jack P. Greene, "Foundation of Political Power in the Virginia House of Burgesses, 1720-1776," *William and Mary Quarterly* (1959).
12. Sidney H. Aronson, *Status and Kinship in the Higher Civil Service* (Cambridge, Mass., 1964).
13. Ralph Wooster, *The Secession Conventions of the South* (Princeton, N. J., 1962). For voter analysis at its most sophisticated see Thomas P. Alexander, *Sectional Stress and Party Strength* (Nashville, Tenn., 1967), and Joel H. Silbey and Samuel T. McSeveney, *Voters, Parties, and Elections* (Lexington, Mass., 1972).
14. Ralph Wooster, *The People in Power* (Knoxville, Tenn., 1969).
15. Thomas P. Alexander and Richard E. Beringer, *The Anatomy of the Confederate Congress* (Nashville, Tenn., 1972).
16. Thomas L. Connelly and Archer Jones, *The Politics of Command* (Baton Rouge, La., 1973).
17. Stone, "Prosopography"; Neil Smelser, *Theory of Collective Behavior* (New York, 1963).

18. Ezra Warner, *Generals in Gray* (Baton Rouge, La., 1959).

19. Wilfred B. Yearns, *The Confederate Congress* (Athens, Ga., 1960). Ezra Warner and Wilfred Buck Yearns, *Biographical Register of the Confederate Congress* (Baton Rouge, La., 1975) has provided valuable information on the births and deaths of the more obscure congressmen. However, the essays in the dictionary contain more information on family and career than does the work of Warner and Yearns.

20. Rembert Patrick, *Jefferson Davis and His Cabinet* (Baton, Rouge, La., 1944).

21. Frank E. Vandiver, *Ploughshares into Swords* (Austin, Tex., 1952); June I. Gow, "Military Administration in the Confederate Army of Tennessee," *Journal of Southern History* XL (1974): 182-195.

22. For example, see Louise B. Hill, *Joseph E. Brown and the Confederacy* (Westport, Conn., 1972).

23. Charles W. Ramsdell, *Behind the Lines in the Southern Confederacy* (Baton Rouge, La., 1944); Mary E. Massey, *Ersatz in the Confederacy* (Columbia, S.C., 1952); for additional information on Confederate women whose lives were of great importance but whose contributions to the war effort were minimal, see Bell I. Wiley, *Confederate Women* (Westport, Conn., 1975).

24. Jon L. Wakelyn, *The Politics of a Literary Man* (Westport, Conn., 1973); James Silver, *Confederate Morale and Church Propaganda* (Tuscaloosa, Ala., 1957).

25. I have attempted a more precise determination of secession stand by looking at the actual debates in the secession conventions.

26. In most cases the factual information comes from secondary source material.

27. Otto H. Olsen, "Historians and the Extent of Slave Ownership in the Southern United States," *Civil War History*, 1972; Leonard P. Curry, "Urbanization and Urbanism in the Old South: A Comparative View," *Journal of Southern History* XL (1974): 43-60.

28. Jensen, "Quantitative Collective Biography."

29. Thomas M. Owen, *History of Alabama and Dictionary of Alabama Biography* (Chicago, 1905). Also consult William F. Amann (ed.), *Personnel of the Civil War* (2 vols., New York, 1961).

30. For an exception, see Thomas H. Pope, *The History of Newberry County, South Carolina, 1749-1860* (Columbia, S.C., 1973).

31. Roderick Floud, *An Introduction to Quantitative Methods for Historians* (Princeton, N.J., 1973).

Chapter 2

1. All data for this and the following chapters are stored in the Computer Center at the Catholic University of America, Washington, D.C.

2. Charles S. Sydnor, *Gentlemen Freeholders* (Chapel Hill, N.C., 1952).

3. P.G.M. Harris, "The Social Origins of American Leaders: The Demographic Foundations," in *Perspectives in American History* III (Cambridge, Mass., 1969).

4. Wives' relatives are important, but facts about their lives were difficult to obtain.

5. Marcus Cunliffe, *Soldiers and Civilians: The Martial Spirit in America, 1775-1865* (New York, 1973).

6. Robert M. Ireland, "Aristocrats All," *The Review of Politics*; P.G.M. Harris, "The Social Origins of American Leaders," *Perspectives in American History* III (1969): 159-343.

7. See Appendices for further information on mobility.

8. Alvy King, *Louis Wigfall* (Baton Rouge, La., 1971).

9. The most comprehensive study of higher education in the antebellum South is Edgar W. Knight (ed.), *A Documentary History of Education in the South Before 1860* (4 vols., Chapel Hill, N.C., 1949-1953). The author is also at work on education in the South in connection with a study of antebellum historical writing.

10. Owsley, *Plain Folk of the Old South*.

11. Wooster, *People in Power*; Clement Eaton, *The Mind of the Old South* (Baton Rouge, La., 1964).

12. For one side of the status decline question, see Robert William Fogel and Stanley L. Engerman, *Time on the Cross* (Boston, 1974).

13. John Hope Franklin, *The Militant South* (Cambridge, Mass., 1956).

14. Age as a factor in capacity for public service will be analyzed later in this study.

15. Patrick, *Jefferson Davis and His Cabinet*.

16. The impact of prewar propaganda on the secession movement is difficult to gauge.

17. Carl Degler, *The Other South* (New York, 1973); Richard Hofstadter, *The Idea of Party* (Berkeley, Calif., 1969); Max Williams, "Foundations of the Whig Party in North Carolina," *North Carolina Historical Review* XLVII (1970): 115-129.

18. Ollinger Crenshaw, *The Slave States in the Presidential Election of 1860* (Baltimore, 1945).

19. Wooster, *The Secession Conventions of the South*; William J. Donnelly, "Conspiracy or Popular Movement; The Historiography of the Southern Support for Secession," *North Carolina Historical Review* XLII (1965): 70-84.

20. Alexander and Beringer, *Anatomy of the Confederate Congress*.

21. For example, see William Russell Smith, *History and Debates of the Convention of the People of Alabama* (Atlanta, 1861).

22. Eugene G. Genovese, *The Political Economy of Slavery* (New York, 1965).

23. William L. Barney, *The Secessionist Impulse* (Princeton, N.J., 1974).

24. Leadership qualities have not been studied for the antebellum period; see Charles S. Sydnor, *Gentlemen Freeholders* (Durham, N.C., 1952).

25. David T. Gilchrist and W. David Lewis (eds.), *Economic Change in the Civil War Era* (Greenville, Del., 1965).

Chapter 3

1. For a systematic bibliography on the problem of studying leaders in time of war, see Randall and Donald, *The Civil War and Reconstruction* (New York, 1971).
2. Allan Nevins, *The Statesmen of the Civil War* (New York, 1954).
3. Frank L. Owsley, *State Rights in the Confederacy* (Chicago, 1925); Charles W. Ramsdell, *Behind the Lines in the Southern Confederacy*.
4. For the total number of generals lost, see Warner, *Generals in Gray*.
5. William Y. Thompson, *Robert Toombs of Georgia* (Baton Rouge, La., 1966).
6. Patrick, *Jefferson Davis and His Cabinet*.
7. Frank E. Vandiver, *Rebel Brass* (Baton Rouge, La., 1956).
8. Richard Goff, *Confederate Supply* (Durham, N.C., 1973).
9. Patrick, *Jefferson Davis and His Cabinet*.
10. Amos E. Simpson and Vincent Cassiday, "The Wartime Administration of Governor Henry Watkins Allen," *Louisiana History* V (1964) 257-270.
11. Yearns, *The Confederate Congress*; Alexander and Beringer, *The Anatomy of the Confederate Congress*.
12. Vandiver, *Rebel Brass*; Curtis A. Amlund, *Federalism in the Southern Confederacy* (Washington, D.C., 1966); Georgia Lee Tatum, *Disloyalty in the Confederacy* (Chapel Hill, N.C., 1940).
13. Charles Lee, *Confederate Constitutions* (Chapel Hill, N.C., 1963).
14. Richard E. Beringer, "The Unconscious 'Spirit of Party' in the Confederate Congress," *Civil War History* XVIII (1970); 312-333.
15. Wooster, *Secession Conventions of the South*; Alexander and Beringer, *Anatomy of the Confederate Congress*.
16. See the biographical sketches of Walker Brooke and others in this dictionary.
17. Yearns, *The Confederate Congress*.
18. Alexander and Beringer, *Anatomy of the Confederate Congress*.
19. Beringer, "Unconscious 'Spirit of Party'."
20. Neither Yearns nor Alexander and Beringer has looked at the subregions which existed in the Confederacy.
21. Warner, *Generals in Gray*.
22. Connelly and Jones, *The Politics of Command*.
23. Ellsworth Eliot, *West Point in the Confederacy* (New Haven, Conn., 1905).
24. Grady McWhiney, *Southerners and Other Americans* (New York, 1973); Connelly and Jones, *The Politics of Command*.
25. Archer Jones, *Confederate Strategy from Shiloh to Vicksburg* (Baton Rouge, La., 1961); Thomas L. Connelly, *Autumn of Glory* (Baton Rouge, La., 1971).
26. Connelly and Jones, *The Politics of Command*.
27. Simpson and Cassiday, "The Wartime Administration of Governor Henry Watkins Allen."
28. William J. Cooper, "A Reassessment of Jefferson Davis as War Leader," *Journal of Southern History* XXXVI (1970): 189-204.

29. Amlund, *Federalism in the Southern Confederacy*; Bell I. Wiley (ed.), *Letters of Warren Aiken, Confederate Congressman* (Athens, Ga., 1959).

30. Grady McWhiney, "Who Whipped Whom? Confederate Defeat Reexamined," *Civil War History* XI (1965): 5-26.

Chapter 4

1. C. Vann Woodward, *The Burden of Southern History* (New York, 1961); William B. Hesseltine, *Confederate Leaders in the New South* (Westport, Conn., 1970).

2. Hesseltine, *Confederate Leaders in the New South*; Richard L. Curry (ed.), *Radicalism, Racism, and Party Realignment* (Baltimore, Md., 1969).

3. Thomas L. Livermore, *Numbers and Losses in the Civil War in America* (New York, 1901).

4. It is possible that some of those leaders held local power and gave up the efforts for national office to hold onto that power.

5. Thomas P. Alexander, *Political Reconstruction in Tennessee* (Nashville, Tenn., 1950).

6. Jonathan T. Dorris, *Pardon and Amnesty Under Lincoln and Johnson* (Chapel Hill, N.C., 1953).

7. Michael Perman, *Reunion Without Compromise* (Cambridge, England, 1973); Dorris, *Pardon and Amnesty Under Lincoln and Johnson*.

8. See Chapter 3 for a study of experience and war effort.

9. Hesseltine, *Confederate Leaders in the New South*.

10. Some leaders held multiple postwar private careers; see the sketches in this dictionary.

11. The businessmen also tended to change corporations, especially those who had been active in wartime politics. See C. Vann Woodward, *Origins of the New South* (Baton Rouge, La., 1951).

12. Joseph F. Wall, *Henry Watterson: Reconstructed Rebel* (New York, 1956); Paul M. Gaston, *The New South Creed* (New York, 1970).

13. Hesseltine, *Confederate Leaders in the New South*.

14. Woodward, *Origins of the New South*.

15. See the biographical sketches in this dictionary for the public offices which the generals held.

16. C. Vann Woodward, *Reunion and Reaction* (Baton Rouge, La., 1950).

17. Thomas B. Alexander has written most perceptively on the question of persistent Whig power. See his "Persistent Whiggery in the Confederate South, 1860-1877," *Journal of Southern History*, XXVII (1961): 305-329.

18. Jack P. Maddex, *The Virginia Conservatives, 1867-1879* (Chapel Hill, N.C., 1970).

19. See appendices for postwar mobility patterns.

20. Dorris, *Pardon and Amnesty Under Lincoln and Johnson*; James A. Rawley, "The General Amnesty Act of 1872," *Mississippi Valley Historical Review* XLVII (1960): 480-484.

21. P.G.M. Harris, "The Social Origins of American Leaders."
22. See appendices for postwar mobility patterns.
23. Dorris, *Amnesty and Pardon Under Lincoln and Johnson*.
24. Stanley Hirschorn, *Farewell to the Bloody Shirt* (Baltimore, Md., 1959). For an ability to shift parties with success, see Derrell C. Roberts, *Joseph E. Brown and the Politics of Reconstruction* (Tuscaloosa, Ala., 1973).
25. See Thomas B. Alexander, "Persistent Whiggery in the Confederate South."
26. See Milton M. Gordon, *Social Class in American Sociology* (New York, 1963).
27. Dorris, *Amnesty and Pardon Under Lincoln and Johnson*.
28. Hesseltine, *Confederate Leaders in the New South*.

Biographical Sketches

A

ADAMS, Daniel Weisiger (*General*), was born to George Adams, a federal judge, and his wife Anna (Weisiger) on May 1, 1821, in Frankfort, Kentucky. An older brother, William Wirt Adams (*q.v.*), also became a Confederate general. In 1825, the family moved to Natchez, Mississippi. From 1838 to 1842, the younger Adams attended the University of Virginia. After reading law, he was admitted to the Mississippi bar. He was married twice and had four children. In 1843, Adams killed in a duel a Vicksburg newspaper editor who had publicly criticized his father's politics. Adams was elected as the state senator from Jackson and served in the 1852 session. Shortly thereafter he moved to New Orleans, Louisiana, to practice law. Although he opposed the early moves toward secession, he was appointed by Governor Thomas O. Moore (*q.v.*) to raise troops and help prepare Louisiana for war. As a colonel in the 1st Louisiana Infantry, he was stationed at Pensacola and Mobile in 1861. After losing his right eye at the battle of Shiloh, he was promoted to brigadier general on May 23, 1862. During the Kentucky campaign, he fought at the battle of Perryville and served under General Braxton Bragg (*q.v.*) at the battles of Corinth and Murfreesboro in late 1862. He was wounded and captured at Chickamauga in 1863. After being exchanged, he commanded a cavalry brigade in north Alabama in 1864 and was appointed district commander for Alabama in late 1864. During the last month of the war, he commanded all Confederate forces in Alabama north of the Department of the Gulf. After the war, Adams traveled in England before returning to New Orleans where he continued his career as a lawyer and businessman. He died in New Orleans on June 14, 1872. Evans, *Confederate Military History*, X; Fortier, *A History of Louisiana*, I; New Orleans *National Republican*, June 14, 1872.

ADAMS, John (*General*), son of Thomas P. Adams, was born on July 1, 1825, in Nashville, Tennessee. His family later moved to Pulaski, Tennessee. Adams graduated twenty-fifth in a class of fifty-nine from the U.S. Military Academy in 1846. On May 3, 1854, he married Georgia McDougal, the daughter of a distinguished U.S. Army surgeon; they had four sons and two daughters. Adams served as a first lieutenant brevet in the Mexican War. He was promoted to first lieutenant in 1851 and served for two years in New Mexico Territory before going to Minnesota, where he was promoted to captain in 1856. Adams resigned his commission in May 1861 and entered the Confederate Army as a captain of cavalry. He was promoted to colonel in 1862 and to brigadier general on December 29 of that year. He earned distinction in the west with the Army of Tennessee. In 1863, he participated in the relief of Vicksburg, and in 1864, he fought at the battles of Jackson and Resaca under General Leonidas K. Polk (*q.v.*). He served with distinction under General John B. Hood (*q.v.*) during the Atlanta campaign and was a hero at the battle of Dalton. He was killed during an assault on Franklin, Tennessee, on November 30, 1864. *Confederate Veteran*, V.

ADAMS, William Wirt (*General*), son of Judge George Adams and his wife Anna (Weisiger) and brother of the future Confederate General Daniel W. Adams (*q.v.*), was born on March 22, 1819, in Frankfort, Kentucky. He attended school in Bardstown, Kentucky, fought in the Mexican War, and lived in Texas until his father died. Adams was probably a Whig. He married Sallie Huger Mayrant in 1850. In 1846, he was a sugar planter in Iberville, Louisiana, but after his marriage he became a banker and planter in Jackson and Vicksburg, Mississippi. In 1858 and 1860, he was elected to the Mississippi legislature. After Mississippi seceded, Adams was appointed a commissioner to encourage Louisiana's secession. He also recruited soldiers for the Confederate Army. In 1861, President Davis (*q.v.*) offered him the cabinet post of postmaster general, which Adams refused because of his business interests. He organized the 1st Mississippi Regiment in May 1861, and in the winter of 1861-1862, he held outpost duty in Tennessee. He fought at the battle of Shiloh and was in the rear guard of the retreat from Bowling Green, Kentucky, in the spring of 1862. At the battles of Iuka and Corinth in the fall of 1862, he was colonel in charge of artillery under General Earl Van Dorn (*q.v.*). He served with the cavalry in western Tennessee and participated in the defense of Vicksburg, after which he was promoted to brigadier general on September 18, 1863. After his promotion, he was stationed at Natchez, Mississippi, and, in 1864, at Baton Rouge, Louisiana. He met Sherman's advance on Meridian, Mississippi, in February 1864. Throughout the remainder of the war, he served with Nathan B. Forrest (*q.v.*) in north Alabama. He surrendered in May 1865 and soon after gained his parole. After the war, he retired from public life and was active in the business revival of Vicksburg. He was a state revenue agent in 1880 and postmaster in Jackson, Mississippi, in 1885. He died in a duel with John Martin, a Jackson newspaper editor, on May 1, 1888, in Jackson. Evans, *Confederate Military History*, VII; Roland (ed.), *Mississippi*, I.

AKIN, Warren (*Congressman*), was born to Thomas and Catherine (Beall) Akin on October 9 or 11, 1811, in Elbert County, Georgia. He received his education in the ordinary schools of Elbert and Walton counties. He married Eliza Hooper on May 5, 1845, and after her death, he married Mary Verdery on October 12, 1848. His first marriage produced one daughter and his second, thirteen children, only six of whom survived to maturity. In 1836, Akin was admitted to the Bartow (Cass County) bar, where he became a leading lawyer of the Cherokee District. At this time he also became a local Methodist preacher and trustee of Emory University. A Whig since 1840, Akin lost the 1859 gubernatorial race to his Democratic opponent, Joseph E. Brown (*q.v.*). In 1861, he served as speaker of the lower house of the Georgia state legislature, where he opposed secession and successfully changed the name of Cass County to Bartow County. As he was physically unfit for military service, he served in Congress instead. He filled an unexpired term in the Tenth District of Georgia in the Confederate Congress for eighteen weeks in 1863. Akin was an advisor and friend of President Davis (*q.v.*) and served on the House Committee on Claims, where he introduced twenty-four measures during his brief term in office. He supported such administration measures as the curbing of speculation and the discontinuation of military exemptions for slaveowners, and defended Davis's constitutional prerogatives. He also preached to Georgia soldiers during the war. After the war, he had to abandon his home in Cassville, Georgia, where he had resided during the war. He returned to Bartow County to practice law and retired from public life. Akin died on December 17, 1877, in Cartersville. Cunyus, *History of Bartow County*; Wiley (ed.), *Letters of Warren Akin*.

ALCORN, James Lusk (*General*), the eldest of eight children of James and Louisa (Lusk) Alcorn, was born on November 4, 1816, in Golconda, Illinois Territory, where his father operated trading boats on the Mississippi River. Alcorn was a Presbyterian. He was raised in Kentucky and attended Cumberland College there. In 1839, he married Mary C. Stewart, by whom he had three children prior to her death. His second marriage, in 1850, to Amelia Walton Glover produced five children. Alcorn taught school in Jackson, Arkansas, and served as deputy sheriff and member of the state legislature in Livingston County, Kentucky, from 1839 to 1843 before moving to Delta, Coshoma County, Mississippi. He owned a small plantation, founded the Mississippi levee system, practiced law, and served as a Whig member of the Mississippi state legislature for fifteen years (1846-1860) prior to secession. He was also a delegate to the state constitutional conventions of 1851 and 1861. Alcorn was an unsuccessful candidate for the U.S. House in 1856. He personally opposed secession, but in the Mississippi secession convention he described himself as "Southern" and was part of the Whig faction that voted consistently with the secessionists. The secession convention elected him brigadier general of state troops in 1861. During the war, he turned down an opportunity to serve in the Confederate Congress, electing to remain in the army. Alcorn was taken prisoner in Arkansas in 1862; upon his parole later in the year, he became a colonel of a Confederate force operating along the Mississippi River. His military service was undistinguished. He opposed President Davis (*q.v.*) and played partisan politics but gave generously of his considerable wealth to the Confederate cause. When Mississippi was overrun by Union forces, Alcorn urged the arming of black troops and the freeing of slaves once the fighting had ended. Congress would not allow him to take his seat in the U.S. Senate, to which the Mississippi legislature had elected him in May 1865. He served as governor of Mississippi from 1870 to 1871 and as U.S. senator from 1871 to 1877, in both instances as a Republican. As governor, he resisted all federal efforts to enforce social equality for the blacks. After his Senate term, Alcorn resumed the practice of law in Friar Point, Mississippi. He served as a member of the Mississippi constitutional convention of 1890 and supported the disfranchising clause. He died on December 20, 1894, in Eagles Nest, Mississippi. Pereya, *James Lusk Alcorn*.

ALEXANDER, Edward Porter (*General*), was born on May 26, 1835, in Washington, Wilkes County, Georgia, to Adam Leopold and Sarah (Gilbert) Alexander. He graduated third in a class of thirty-eight from the U.S. Military Academy in 1857. Alexander, who married Bettie Mason in 1860 and her sister Mary L. Mason in 1901, had three sons and two daughters. He was a member of the Presbyterian church. From 1858 to 1860, he was an assistant instructor of practical military engineering at West Point, where he became an expert in military signaling. In 1858, he participated in the Utah expedition against the Mormons. Although he was not a strong secessionist, he entered the Confederate Army on April 3, 1861, as a captain of engineers. During the battle of First Manassas, he served on the staff of P.G.T. Beauregard (*q.v.*) as an engineer in charge of the Signal Service. He was made chief of ordnance for the Army of Northern Virginia and was promoted to lieutenant colonel in December 1861 and to colonel in December 1862. From November 8, 1862, to February 26, 1864, he was a battalion commander under General James Longstreet (*q.v.*). After serving as artillery commander at Fredericksburg in 1862 and at Chancellorsville in 1863, his battery prepared the way for Pickett's charge during the battle of Gettysburg. He became chief of artillery in the Knoxville campaign during the summer of 1863. In September 1863, he accompanied Longstreet to Georgia and Tennessee. Promoted to brigadier general on February 26, 1865, he commanded all artillery in Longstreet's Corps and participated in the defense of Richmond. He was in the retreat from Petersburg and surrendered on April 9, 1865. He had a distinguished educational and business career after the war. From 1866 to 1869, Alexander was a professor of mathematics and civil and military engineering at the University of South Carolina. From 1869 to 1871, he was president of the Columbia Oil Company, and in 1871, he became superintendent of the Columbia and Augusta Railroad. He lived in Savannah from 1871 to 1875 as president of the Savannah and Memphis Railroad. From 1883 to 1888, he was a member of the Capitol Commission of the state of Georgia. Alexander was the author of *Military Memoirs of a Confederate* (1907) and a treatise entitled *Railway Practice* (1887). He retired to Savannah, where he died on April 28, 1910. Klein, *Edward Porter Alexander*.

ALEXANDER, Peter Wellington (*Reporter*), was born in Elberton, Georgia, on March 21, 1824. Little is known about his family or his early life. He graduated second in the class of 1844 at the University of Georgia as a student in English composition. He studied law and was admitted to the Thomaston, Georgia, bar in 1845. He married Maria Theresa Shorter on September 27, 1870. Alexander, a Whig, did editorial writing for the *Savannah Republican*, the leading Whig organ in Georgia, before becoming its editor-in-chief in 1853. In 1857, he returned to Thomaston to practice law. Throughout the Georgia secession convention, in which he was a delegate, Alexander held steadfast to his unionist beliefs. Writing under the initials P.W.A. during the war, he reported for the *Savannah Republican* and later the *Atlanta Confederacy*, *Columbus Sun*, *Mobile Advertiser and Register*, and other Confederate newspapers. His articles were read and copied throughout the South, and he was idolized by soldiers and civilians alike. In 1861, he provided on-the-scene reports of the battle of First Manassas. Although he was a reporter, at First Manassas he was made an acting colonel for his work as a forward observer. A close friend of General Robert Toombs (*q.v.*), Alexander was sharply critical of incompetence and injustice in Confederate civilian and military life. Alexander no doubt influenced the states' rights movement in Georgia during the last stages of the war. After the war, he settled in Columbus, Georgia, where he practiced law with James Milton Smith (*q.v.*). When Smith became governor in 1872, he named Alexander his private secretary. In 1877, he moved to Marietta, Georgia, where he lived until his death on September 23, 1886. Andrews, *The South Reports the Civil War*; Myers, *The Children of Pride*.

ALLEN, Henry Watkins (*General, Governor*), was born on April 29, 1820, in Prince Edward County, Virginia, to Dr. Thomas Allen and his wife Ann (Watkins). He moved to Kay County, Missouri, in 1833 with his parents and attended Marion College and Marionville Collegiate Institute there from 1835 to 1837. The Presbyterian Allen taught school, studied law, and was admitted to the Mississippi bar in 1841. In 1840, he established a school in Grand Gulf, Mississippi, and in 1842, he served in Texas with President Sam Houston. His marriage on July 4, 1844, in Rodney, Mississippi, to Salome Anne Crane, a planter's daughter, ended with her death in 1850; they had no children. Meanwhile, he had become a prominent planter in Mississippi. He represented Claiborne County in the Mississippi state legislature of 1846. During the 1850s, Allen became a sugar planter in West Baton Rouge, Louisiana, and he wrote a book on his experiences, *Travels of a Sugar Planter* (1861). He also served in the Louisiana legislature in 1853 and became a prominent politician. Allen attended Harvard Law School during 1854. He traveled to Italy in 1859 to enlist with Garibaldi, only to discover that the war had ended. He returned to Louisiana and enlisted as a private in the Confederate cause. During the Civil War, Allen served in the army as lieutenant colonel and later as colonel of the 4th Louisiana Regiment. He was wounded at Shiloh and at

Baton Rouge in August 1862 and was made military governor at Jackson, Mississippi, at the end of the year. In 1863, he was appointed brigadier general under Edmund Kirby Smith (*q.v.*), and later that same year he was elected governor of Louisiana. During his term as governor, Allen organized a trade route to the Mexican border, exchanged cotton for supplies and food, established state stores for civilians, built a cloth factory and an iron foundry, and secured for planters the right to pay the cotton tax in kind. He rebuilt the industry of western Louisiana. Allen negotiated the surrender of the Trans-Mississippi Army and prepared the way for an orderly peace in the Southwest. To escape punishment he removed to Mexico City, where he helped establish the *Mexican Times* and where he died on April 22, 1867. Dorsey, *Recollections of Henry Watkins Allen*; Simpson and Cassiday, *Henry Watkins Allen*.

ALLEN, William Wirt (*General*), son of Wade Hampton and Eliza (Sayre) Allen, was born in New York City in 1835. His father, a planter, mail contractor, and successful steamship company owner, had many business contacts in the South. The younger Allen attended schools in Montgomery, Alabama, before graduating from Princeton College in 1854. Allen, a Methodist, abandoned his study of law to become a planter. On August 13, 1857, he married Susan Claiborne (Bell?), by whom he had eleven children. Allen's prewar career was uneventful as he devoted himself to turning a profit on his plantation. Although he did not particularly support the war, he entered the Confederate Army in 1862 as major and later colonel in the 1st Alabama Cavalry. He served with distinction at the battle of Shiloh. Wounded at the battles of Perryville and Murfreesboro, he was promoted to brigadier general on February 26, 1864, and served in the Army of Tennessee during the Atlanta campaign. In March 1865, he was promoted to major general in charge of Crew's and Anderson's Brigades in the Carolinas. He surrendered at Salisbury, North Carolina, in May 1865 and was paroled at Charlotte before the end of the year. After the war, he returned to planting. He was appointed adjutant general of Alabama in 1870 and served as a U.S. marshal in the Cleveland administration. Allen died on November 24, 1894, in Sheffield, Alabama. *Confederate Veteran*, II. Owen, *History of Alabama and Dictionary of Alabama Biography*, III.

ANDERSON, Clifford (*Congressman*), was born in Nottoway County, Virginia, on March 23, 1833. He was orphaned at the age of twelve, and at sixteen he moved to Macon, Georgia, where he studied law with his brother and was admitted to the bar in 1852. He had no secondary education, and his early life seemed uneventful. He was a Presbyterian. In January 1857, he married Anna Le Conte, by whom he had thirteen children. After her death, he married Sarah Nisbet, widow of the Confederate General Martin L. Smith (*q.v.*) and daughter of a prominent political leader in Georgia. In 1856, he was a judge in the city court of Macon, and in 1857, he was elected to the city council. A Whig, he served in the Georgia House of

Representatives in 1859, where he opposed secession, but after South Carolina seceded in 1860, he advocated secession for Georgia too. Early in 1861, he enlisted in the Confederate Army as a private. Later he was elected captain in the Adjutant General's Department and served as brigade inspector on the staff of Ambrose Ransom Wright (q.v.). In 1863, he was elected to the House of Representatives in the second Confederate Congress, where he was a loyal supporter of President Davis (q.v.). He served on the Conference, Joint, and Ways and Means Committees.. After the war, he returned to his law practice, served as attorney general for the state of Georgia from 1880 to 1890, and helped to draw up a new law code for the state in 1893-1895. Little is known about his private life. He died in 1899. Northen (ed.), *Men of Mark in Georgia*, I.

ANDERSON, George Thomas (*General*), was born to Joseph Stewart and Lucy (Cunningham) Anderson on February 3, 1824, in Covington, Georgia. He attended Emory College, married, and had a family. Anderson, a Methodist, was a man of considerable property before the Civil War. He served in the Georgia Cavalry during the Mexican War, and in 1855, he was commissioned into the regular service of the U.S. Army. Three years later he resigned his commission as a captain in the 1st Cavalry. He joined the 11th Georgia Infantry when the war began and was made its colonel. A close friend of Robert Toombs (q.v.), Anderson accompanied Toombs' 11th Georgia Regiment to Virginia, where in 1862 he served as brigade commander during the battles of the Seven Days, Second Manassas, and Sharpsburg. Promoted to brigadier general on November 1, 1862, he fought at Fredericksburg under Longstreet (q.v.), at Chancellorsville and in the Suffolk expedition in the spring of 1863. On July 2, 1863, he was severely wounded at Round Top at the battle of Gettysburg. After his recovery, he saw action at Chickamauga, and in September 1863, he accompanied Longstreet to aid Bragg (q.v.) in northern Georgia. He saw action during the siege of Knoxville in east Tennessee, and he fought heroically in the Virginia Wilderness campaign of 1864 at Spotsylvania and Cold Harbor. He surrendered with Lee (q.v.) at Appomattox. After the war, Anderson served as freight agent for the Georgia Railroad, a local railroad in Atlanta. Although details of his postwar private career are sketchy, it appears that he lost much of his prewar wealth. It is known that he served for a time as police chief of Atlanta. Anderson retired to Alabama but became chief of police and county tax collector in Anniston, Alabama, prior to his death in that city on April 4, 1901. *Confederate Veteran*, IX; Wright, *General Officers of the Confederate Army*.

ANDERSON, James Patton (*Congressman, General*), son of William Preston and Margaret L. (Adair) Anderson, was born on February 16, 1822, in Winchester, Franklin County, Tennessee. Anderson, reared by a grandfather (his father had died in 1831), attended country schools and was a student at Jefferson College in Canonsburg, Pennsylvania, from 1836 to 1840. He alternately traveled and worked at odd jobs until 1843, when he began to practice medicine, although not specifically trained, in Hernando County, Mississippi. He married a cousin, Henriette Buford Adair, on April 30, 1853, by whom he had children. From 1843 to 1846, Anderson was sheriff of DeSoto County, Mississippi, pausing during the summers of 1844 and 1845 to study law at Montrose Law School. In 1847, he became a law partner of R. B. Mayes, and in the same year he raised a company for the Mexican War, where he served as a colonel at Tampico. A Democrat who later blamed the disruption of the Union on the Republicans, he was elected to the Mississippi House in 1850, where he was an ally of Jefferson Davis (*q.v.*). He opposed the Compromise of 1850 and lost his bid for reelection the following year. In 1853, he was U.S. marshal of the Washington Territory, where he compiled the territorial census. From 1855 to 1857, he served as a Democrat in the U.S. House from the Washington Territory. He declined an offer to become governor of the territory in 1857 because he thought that secession was imminent. Instead, he moved to Florida to supervise his aunt's plantation, "Casablanca," in Monticello, Jefferson County. A secessionist delegate to the Florida convention, he also served on the Military Affairs and Public Lands Committees in the provisional Confederate Congress before he resigned to enter the Confederate Army. Anderson enlisted in the Jefferson County Volunteers of the 1st Florida Regiment in the summer of 1861 and served under Braxton Bragg (*q.v.*) at Pensacola. Promoted to brigadier general on February 10, 1862, he fought at Shiloh, Corinth, and Murfreesboro and commanded a division at Perryville, Kentucky, in 1862. In 1863, he distinguished himself at Chickamauga and served as a division commander at Chattanooga. He was promoted to major general on February 17, 1864. During the last part of the Atlanta campaign, he commanded the District of Florida and saw some action around Jacksonville. After succeeding John B. Hood (*q.v.*) as commander of the Army of Tennessee, he fought battles at Ezra Church and at Jonesboro, Georgia, where he was wounded and was forced to give up active service in August 1864. During the final days of the war, he rejoined his army in North Carolina despite his surgeon's warning. He opposed the end of the war and never sought parole. After the war he sold life insurance, edited an agricultural magazine, and was a tax collector in Memphis, Tennessee, where he died on September 20, 1872. "Autobiography of General Patton Anderson," *Southern Historical Society Papers*, XXIV.

ANDERSON, Joseph Reid (*General, Businessman*), was born to William and Anne (Thomas) Anderson on February 6, 1813, in Fincastle, Botetourt County, Virginia. He attended the academy of Daniel Stephens in Fincastle and graduated fourth in a class of forty-nine from the U.S. Military Academy in 1836. Anderson was a vestryman of St. Paul's Episcopal Church in Richmond, Virginia, from 1844 until 1892. He married Sally Archer on May 12, 1837, and, following her death, Mary Pegram. Anderson had two sons and four daughters. He was commissioned into the 3rd Artillery but in 1837 was transferred to the Corps of Engineers.

He served in the Engineering Bureau in Washington and helped build Fort Pulaski on the Savannah River before resigning on September 30, 1837, to become assistant engineer for the state of Virginia. From 1838 to 1841, he was chief engineer for the Valley Turnpike Company, and from 1841 to 1861, he headed the firm of Joseph R. Anderson and Company, which owned the Tredegar Iron Works. Anderson was a Whig member of the Virginia House of Delegates from 1852 to 1855, and in 1857, he joined the Democratic party. He lost a contest for election to the House of Delegates in 1859. Anderson was active in the Southern commercial convention movement. While he was cautious on the issue of secession, he ultimately supported secession, and, when the war began, he contracted to supply arms and ammunition to the Confederacy. In September 1861, he joined the army and became brigadier general in command of Confederate forces at Wilmington, North Carolina. He fought in the Virginia Peninsular campaign in June 1862 under General Joseph E. Johnston (q.v.) and commanded a division under Ambrose P. Hill (q.v.) during the Seven Days' battles, where he was wounded at Frayser's Farm on June 30, 1862. He resigned from the army on July 19, 1862, and spent the rest of the war managing the Tredegar Iron Works. He became the mainstay of the Confederate ammunition supply. He also produced heavy guns at his foundry and rolling mills. He was forced to suspend operations in April 1865, but upon his parole he reopened the Tredegar Iron Works in 1867. Anderson also served in various civic organizations in Richmond such as the Chamber of Commerce. He devoted his postwar life to rebuilding industry in the South. He died at Isle of Shoals, New Hampshire, on September 7, 1892. Dew, *Ironmaker to the Confederacy*.

ANDERSON, Richard Heron (*General*), grandson of a Revolutionary War hero and son of Dr. William Wallace Anderson and his wife, Mary Jane (Mackenzie), was born on October 7, 1821, in Hill Crest, Sumter County, South Carolina. He graduated fortieth in a class of fifty-six from the U.S. Military Academy in 1842. Anderson was a vestryman at St. Helena Episcopal Church. He had a son and a daughter by his 1850 marriage to Sarah Gibson. She died and he married Martha Mellette on December 24, 1874. In 1842, he attended cavalry school at Carlisle, Pennsylvania, and was breveted a second lieutenant in the 1st Dragoons. He spent the years 1843-1845 in frontier service and fought under William Hardee (q.v.) during the Mexican War, where he saw action at Vera Cruz, Contreras, and Churubusco. He was breveted a first lieutenant at San Augustine. He returned to cavalry school at Carlisle in 1849-1850 and again served on the frontier in 1852-1856, where he was a captain of dragoons in 1855. He was stationed in Kansas in 1856 and participated in the Utah expedition of 1858-1859. From 1859 to 1861, he was stationed at Fort Kearney, Nebraska. Upon the secession of South Carolina he resigned his commission. Anderson entered the Confederate Army as a major in the Department of South Carolina and Florida. Promoted to brigadier general on July 18, 1861, he succeeded P.G.T. Beauregard (q.v.) as commander in Charleston, South Carolina. In the spring and early summer of 1862, he fought at the battles of Seven Pines, Cold Harbor, and Malvern Hill during the Peninsular campaign in Virginia. He was promoted to major general on July 14, 1862. Anderson subsequently fought in the battles of Second Manassas, Sharpsburg, and Fredericksburg in 1862 and at the battles of Chancellorsville and Gettysburg in 1863. He distinguished himself throughout and became one of Lee's (*q.v.*) trusted lieutenants. Promoted to lieutenant general under General James Longstreet (*q.v.*) on May 31, 1864, he commanded Longstreet's Corps at Spotsylvania and Cold Harbor. Anderson was vindicated from Fitzhugh Lee's (*q.v.*) accusation of incompetence after the battle of Five Forks in April 1865. He was nevertheless relieved of command and did not surrender with Lee's army at Appomattox. After the war, he tried planting at his ancestral home in Hill Crest, South Carolina, but he knew nothing about agriculture and went bankrupt. He was a state phosphate agent at Beaufort, South Carolina, and a day laborer in a railroad yard before being made a railroad agent, a job from which he was fired. Anderson died on June 26, 1879, in Beaufort, South Carolina. Walker, *The Life of Lieutenant General Richard Heron Anderson*.

ANDERSON, Robert Houstoun (*General*), was born to John Wayne and Sarah Ann (Houstoun) Anderson on October 1, 1835, in Savannah, Georgia. He attended the Savannah common schools and graduated thirty-fifth in a class of thirty-eight from the U.S. Military Academy in 1857. His marriage to Sarah Clitz on December 3, 1857, produced one son. He was commissioned into the infantry and saw frontier duty in the Washington Territory from 1858 to 1861. Upon his resignation from the U.S. Army in late 1861, Anderson was appointed a first lieutenant of artillery in the Confederate Army and spent the early part of the war as acting adjutant general of troops on the Georgia coast and as aide-de-camp to General William H. T. Walker (*q.v.*). In January 1863, Anderson gained a line assignment, and he participated in the successful defense of Fort McAllister, Georgia. Later, he was transferred to the Army of Tennessee, where he participated in the Atlanta campaign and was promoted to brigadier general of cavalry on July 26, 1864. Anderson commanded one of the best divisions of General Joseph Wheeler's (*q.v.*) Cavalry Corps. He surrendered in North Carolina in May 1865. After the war, he ran his father's commission business and owned his own insurance firm. He also served as an advisor to the U.S. Military Academy. From 1867 until his death on February 8, 1888, he was chief of police for Savannah, Georgia. Northen (ed.), *Men of Mark in Georgia*, I.

ARCHER, James Jay (*General*), son of Dr. John Archer and his wife Ann (Stump), was born on December 19, 1817, in Stafford, Harford County, Maryland, into an old and distinguished Maryland family. He attended Princeton College in 1835 and studied civil engineering at Bacon College in Georgetown,

Kentucky, in 1838 before studying law with his brother, Henry. He was a bachelor and a member of the Presbyterian church. Archer practiced law in Maryland but had no important prewar civilian career. A captain during the Mexican War, he was breveted major at Chapultepec. He reentered civilian life but joined the army again in 1855 as a captain in the Pacific Coast service. He resigned his commission in 1861 and volunteered for the Confederate Army. At the battle of Seven Pines in June 1862, he was part of the "light division" under Ambrose P. Hill (*q.v.*); he was promoted to brigadier general on June 3, 1862. Archer fought at Mechanicsville and Gaines' Mill during the Seven Days' battles, at Cedar Mountain, Second Manassas, Ox Hill (Maryland), Antietam, and Fredericksburg in 1862, and at the battle of Chancellorsville in May 1863. He served as a distinguished officer in Longstreet's (*q.v.*) corps. At the battle of Gettysburg he was captured, and his brigade was largely dispersed. Held in Northern Pines for a year, he was exchanged in the summer of 1864. Archer was given his old brigade in the Army of Northern Virginia, but he never recovered from his confinement. He died in Richmond on October 24, 1864. *The Biographical Cyclopedia of Representative Men of Maryland and D.C.*; Evans, *Confederate Military History*, II.

ARMISTEAD, Lewis Addison (*General*), was born to General Walker Keith Armistead, a veteran of the War of 1812, and his wife Elizabeth (Stanley) on February 18, 1816, in New Bern, North Carolina. He entered the U.S. Military Academy in 1834 but was unable to finish his studies because of poor preparation. Armistead gained an appointment to the infantry in 1839, where he was promoted to first lieutenant in 1844. He was an Episcopalian and was married to Cecelia Lee Love. Armistead was a career officer in the U.S. Army before the Civil War and was breveted captain at Contreras and Churubusco and major at Molino del Rey during the Mexican War. After being promoted to captain in 1855, he was sent to the frontier. Upon the outbreak of the Civil War, he resigned his commission and came east with Albert Sidney Johnston (*q.v.*). He entered the Confederate Army in late 1861 and served as major and, later, as colonel of the 57th North Carolina Regiment. He was promoted to brigadier general on April 1, 1862, and was subsequently cited for personal bravery at the battle of Seven Pines. At the battle of Malvern Hill he led the initial charge under Fitzhugh Lee (*q.v.*). He also participated in the battles of Second Manassas, Harper's Ferry, and Sharpsburg during August and September 1862. On September 6, 1862, he was named provost marshal general of the Confederate Army, and he was in the rear of the army as it advanced into Maryland. His brigade led Pickett's charge at the battle of Gettysburg, during which Armistead was mortally wounded, on July 4, 1863. It is said that he made the farthest advance into the Union lines of any Confederate. Armistead's actions became a symbol for later Confederate bravery. Johnson and Buel, eds., *Battles and Leaders of the Civil War*; Evans, *Confederate Military History*, III.

ARMSTRONG, Frank Crawford (*General*), was born on November 22, 1835, in the Choctaw Agency, Indian Territory, to Frank W. and Anne (Millard) Armstrong. His stepfather was General Persifer Smith, a hero of the Mexican War. He was educated at Holy Cross Academy and College in Massachusetts, and he entered the cavalry as a second lieutenant in 1855. He accompanied Albert Sidney Johnston (*q.v.*) on the Utah expedition in 1858-1859 and was promoted to captain in June 1861. Armstrong was married twice, to Maria Polk Walker and to Charlotte McSherry. He fought on the Union side at First Manassas but resigned his commission to join the Confederate Army in August 1861. He accompanied Colonel James Z. McIntosh to the Indian Territory and fought with Ben McCulloch at Wilson's Creek, Arkansas, in August 1861. In March 1862, he served as assistant adjutant general at the battle of Elkhorn, and in June of that year, General Sterling Price (*q.v.*) appointed him acting brigadier general in command of all cavalry in the west. Armstrong achieved recognition for his attack on Courtland, Alabama, and he was the hero of the battle of Britton's Lane in western Tennessee in July 1862. After participating in the battles of Iuka and Corinth, Mississippi, he was promoted to brigadier general on January 30, 1863, after which he was victorious at Spring Hill in western Tennessee. His cavalry division participated in the evacuation of Chattanooga and fought at Chicamauga. During the winter of 1863-1864, he was with Longstreet (*q.v.*) and in the spring of 1864, he accompanied General Leonidas Polk's (*q.v.*) army during the Atlanta campaign from Resaca to Jonesboro. He fought in the battle of Franklin, Tennessee, in November 1864, accompanied Hood (*q.v.*) in the campaign against Murfreesboro, and engaged the enemy in a heroic rear guard action during the retreat from Nashville in December 1864. His last battle was in Selma, Alabama, where he surrendered. After the war, he worked for the Overland Mail Service in Texas for a time and was unsuccessful in private business. Armstrong spent most of his postwar career in government service on the western frontier. He was assistant commissioner of Indian Affairs from 1893 to 1895. He died on September 8, 1909, in Bar Harbor, Maine. *New York Times*, September 9, 1909; *Who's Who in America*, 1908-1909.

ARRINGTON, Archibald Hunter (*Congressman*), son of John and Elizabeth (Mann) Arrington, was born on November 13, 1809, in Nashville, Nash County, North Carolina. Little is known about his early family life. He attended the local academy at Hilliardston and Louisburg Male Academy. Prior to the Civil War, he was a lawyer and planter with large landholdings. From 1841 to 1845, he served as a Democrat from North Carolina in the U.S. House of Representatives. He lost a bid for reelection in 1844. Arrington, a secessionist, voted for secession as a delegate to the state convention in 1861. In a vicious campaign he defeated Josiah Turner (*q.v.*) for the first Confederate Congress. As a congressman he opposed a majority of the Davis legislation. He served on the Indian Affairs and Special Committees and was frequently absent from Richmond. He lost a bid for reelection in 1863. Arrington managed to continue planting and produced food for the North Carolina army. He retired to private life and his political career seems to have stopped in 1863. He was one of the earliest North Carolinians to request pardon from President Andrew Johnson. In 1866, he was a delegate to the Union national convention in Philadelphia. Little else is known of his postwar public life, except for his flirtation with the Republican party. Arrington was also a county commissioner in 1868 and chairman of the Court of Common Pleas for Nash County. He had saved his large estate and spent much of his private life managing his holdings. He died at his country home near Nashville, North Carolina, on July 20, 1872. Ashe, *Cyclopedia of Eminent and Representative Men of the Carolinas* . . . ; Hamilton, *Reconstruction in North Carolina*.

ASHBY, Turner (*General*), was born to Colonel Turner Ashby and his wife, Dorothy (Green), on October 23, 1828, in Fauquier County, Virginia. His grandfather, Captain John Ashby, had fought in the Revolutionary War. He was educated at Major Ambler's private school and by private tutors, and he became a wealthy grain dealer, planter, and local politician in the Shenandoah Valley before the war. He never married. Although he opposed secession, he had ridden to defend his state from John Brown's raid at Harper's Ferry in 1859. When Virginia seceded, he again raised a private army and went to the defense of Harper's Ferry. His private command was incorporated into the 7th Virginia Cavalry in 1861. Ashby served as a cavalry commander in the Valley District. He was an idol of the troops at Harper's Ferry and achieved a legendary reputation for his daring trip in disguise to Chambersburg, Pennsylvania, to obtain information in the early spring of 1862. As commander of "Stonewall" Jackson's (*q.v.*) Cavalry in the Valley campaign during the late spring of 1862, Ashby enjoyed a semi-autonomous command and was noted for his disregard of traditional military discipline. He was promoted to brigadier general on May 23, 1862. He fought at the battles of Kernstown, McDowell, and Middletown before being killed during a skirmish at Harrisonburg, Pennsylvania, on June 6, 1862. Ashby became a symbol of courage to the troops, with Jackson himself invoking his memory to stir his troops to greater effort. Avirett, *Memoirs of General Turner Ashby and His Compeers*; Freeman, *Lee's Lieutenants*, I.

ASHCRAFT, Thomas (*Businessman*), son of John Ashcraft, was born in Sampson County, North Carolina, on August 6, 1786. He was a Baptist and a Whig until he became a Democrat in 1860. He spent his youth in South Carolina. He married Catherine Abel on March 15, 1815, by whom he had nine children. He moved to Georgia in 1818 and to Randolph County, Alabama, in 1836. In 1852, he moved to Talladega (now Clay) County, Alabama, where he was a farmer and an inventor of machinery. He patented a threshing machine, a house cotton press, and a torpedo. He became an important manufacturer and had connections with the Selma Iron Works in Alabama. Ashcraft supported the Confederate cause and manufactured spinning reels and looms for processing cotton clothing for the troops. He also developed a torpedo and gave the plans to the Confederate War Department. The Davis government considered him an important scientist-businessman and made him an advisor to the War Department. An old, broken, and disappointed man after the fall of the Confederacy, he died in Clay County, Alabama, on December 18, 1866. Owen, *History of Alabama and Dictionary of Alabama Biography*, III.

ASHE, Thomas Samuel (*Congressman*), son of Pasquale Paoli and Elizabeth (Strudwick) Ashe, was born on July 19 or 21, 1812, in Hawfield, North Carolina. A member of an old and venerated North Carolina family of Revolutionary heroes, the younger Ashe was raised as an aristocrat. For a brief interlude his father emigrated with his family to Alabama but soon returned to live in New Hanover County, North Carolina. Ashe received his primary education at the exclusive Bingham School in Orange County. He graduated third in the class of 1832 at the University of North Carolina and studied law under the celebrated antebellum political leader Thomas Ruffin (*q.v.*) before being admitted to the bar in 1834. Ashe practiced law in Wadesboro, North Carolina, where he also became a vestryman in the Episcopal church. Married to Caroline Burgwin in June 1837, he became the father of three daughters. A cousin of William Sheppard Ashe (*q.v.*), he served as a delegate from Anson County in the North Carolina House of Commons in 1842, as a solicitor for the Fifth Judicial District from 1847 to 1851, and as a member of the North Carolina Senate in 1854. Ashe was a Clay Whig and a unionist until 1861, when Lincoln called for North Carolina troops to assist in putting down the Confederate insurrection. He became a secessionist. As a member of the Confederate House of Representatives from 1861 to 1864, he strongly supported the war effort but opposed the Davis administration. He served on both the Conference and Judiciary Committees. In 1864, Ashe soured on the war, and he ran as a peace candidate for the Confederate Senate against the avowed administration loyalist, William Dortch (*q.v.*), and defeated him. But the war ended before he could take his seat. Ashe initially supported conciliation with the North, but he soon joined the conservative or anti-Holden party and resisted Reconstruction. In 1866, he served as a state councilor, and in 1868 he lost the North Carolina gubernatorial race to William W. Holden (*q.v.*). He served as a Democrat in the U.S. House of Representatives from 1873 to 1877 where he gained a reputation as a watchdog of corrupt Republican party practices. As associate justice of the state Supreme Court from 1878 to 1887, he became involved in landmark civil rights cases. Ashe also managed to practice law when he was not in public office. He died in Wadesboro on February 4, 1887. Ashe (ed.), *Cyclopedia of Eminent and Representative Men of the Carolinas . . .*; Yearns, *The Confederate Congress*.

ASHE, William Sheppard (*Bureaucrat*), son of Colonel Samuel and Elizabeth (Shepherd) Ashe, was born in Rocky Point, North Carolina, on August 12, 1813.

(Note: His son later claimed his birth date to be September 14, 1814.) His parents came from distinguished North Carolina families. He attended school in Fayetteville, North Carolina, and at Trinity College in Hartford, Connecticut. He was a deeply religious Episcopalian. He and his wife, the former Sarah Ann Green, had four sons. Ashe became a rice planter and also studied law, being admitted to the North Carolina bar in 1836. Unlike most people who lived in the Cape Fear area, he was an ardent supporter of Andrew Jackson, and in 1844 he was a presidential elector on the Polk ticket. He represented New Hanover in 1846-1848 in the North Carolina Senate, and from 1849 to 1855, he served in the U.S. House of Representatives, where he was known as an ultra-Southern Democrat and a supporter of internal improvements. But Ashe was perhaps best known as the "father of the North Carolina railroad," who from 1854 to 1862 was president of the Wilmington and Weldon Railroad Company. He returned to the state Senate in 1859-1861 and was a delegate to the Democratic national convention in 1860 and to the North Carolina constitutional convention in 1861. Ashe was a committed secessionist. He entered the government in 1861 as a major in the Confederate Army. He was put in charge of all government transportation from South Carolina to Virginia, and President Davis (*q.v.*) nominated him to supervise all government transportation from the Mississippi River to Virginia. He was also assistant quartermaster general of the Confederate Army in 1861-1862 and started the salt works at Wrightsville, North Carolina. Ashe was killed in a railroad accident in Wilmington, North Carolina, on September 14, 1862. His death was also a deathblow to the Confederate transportation system. Ashe, *Cyclopedia of Eminent and Representative Men of the Carolinas* . . . ; Black, *The Railroads of the Confederacy*; McCormick, "Personnel of the Convention of 1861".

ATKINS, John DeWitt Clinton (*Congressman*), was born on June 4, 1825, in Manly's Chapel, Henry County, Tennessee, to John and Sarah (Manly) Atkins. Educated privately at Paris Male Academy and at East Tennessee University, Atkins graduated first in the class of 1846 at the University of Knoxville. He studied law before he inherited his wealthy father's farm. His marriage to Elizabeth Bacon Porter on November 23, 1847, produced five children. A Methodist and a Democrat, Atkins served in the state House of Representatives in 1849-1851, in the state Senate from 1855 to 1857, and as a representative of the Ninth District of Tennessee in the U.S. House of Representatives from 1857 to 1859. He sought reelection to Congress but lost. In 1860, he was a delegate to the Democratic national convention in Charleston and to the moderate second convention in Baltimore, from which he withdrew. When the Civil War began, he was appointed a lieutenant colonel in the 5th Tennessee Regiment. Atkins served in both the provisional and the first and second Confederate Congresses, where he was a member of the Post Office, Post Roads, Army, and Foreign Affairs Committees. He was especially active in trying to regulate impressment payments. Atkins generally supported President Davis's (*q.v.*) legislation. The end of the war found him broke, and he returned to his farm, where he raised stock and cultivated grass for feeding purposes. He founded the *Paris Intelligencer* in 1867. Atkins returned to public life in 1873 as a Democratic member of the U.S. House of Representatives, where he served until 1883. He was U.S. commissioner of Indian Affairs from 1885 to 1888. In 1888, he lost his bid for the U.S. Senate. He retired to his farm, where he died in Paris, Tennessee, on June 2, 1908. Temple, *Notable Men of Tennessee from 1833 to 1875*; Yearns, *The Confederate Congress*.

AVERY, William Waightstill (*Congressman*), was born to Colonel Isaac Thomas and Harriet (Erwin) Avery in Burke County, North Carolina, on May 25, 1816. His father was a rich planter and his mother came from a famous North Carolina political family. He studied law and graduated first in his class at the University of North Carolina in 1837. In May 1846, he married the daughter of Governor John Motley Morehead (*q.v.*), Corrinna M. Morehead, who bore him five children. Avery was a Presbyterian and a states' rights Democrat. He was admitted to the bar in 1839 and became a successful lawyer. He was elected to the North Carolina House of Representatives in 1842, 1850, and 1852 and to the state Senate in 1856. As chairman of the North Carolina delegation to the Democratic national convention in Charleston in 1860, Avery seceded with the Southern wing, and he subsequently urged the calling of the North Carolina secession convention. He served in the provisional Confederate Congress until 1862, where he was the chairman of the Committee on Military Affairs. A staunch supporter of the administration, he lost his bid for the Confederate Senate. President Davis (*q.v.*) wanted him to raise a regiment, but his family urged him to stay home. He served in the state militia and participated in many engagements in North Carolina. Avery fought in a battle against the Union Army in Tennessee, where he was killed at Morgantown on July 3, 1864. Barrett, *The Civil War in North Carolina*; Yearns, *The Confederate Congress*.

AYER, Lewis Malone, Jr. (*Congressman*), was born on November 12, 1821, in Barnwell District, South Carolina, to Lewis Malone and Rebecca (Ervin) Ayer. After studying at Edgefield and Mount Zion Institute, he attended South Carolina College in 1838-1839 and studied law at the University of Virginia in 1841 and at Harvard University in 1842. Ayer was a Baptist and a Democrat. He was first married to Anna Elizabeth Patterson, who died in 1862, and subsequently to Lilly Moore. He was admitted to the bar in Barnwell in 1842 and became a planter in 1846. From 1848 to 1852, he served in the South Carolina House of Representatives. In 1853, he was made a brigadier general in the 3rd Brigade of the South Carolina Militia, but he later resigned his commission. He was elected to the U.S. House of Representatives in 1860 but never took his seat. A delegate to the South Carolina secession convention, Ayer defeated David F. Jamison for election to the Confederate House of Representatives in 1861. He was reelected in 1863, defeating the obstructionist Robert Barnwell Rhett (*q.v.*). Consistently in opposition to the Davis administration, he served on the War Tax, Quartermaster and Commissary Departments, Commerce, Ordnance and Ordnance Stores Committees and the special committee on conscription. Ayer especially opposed forced funding of the war effort. After the war, with his plantation destroyed, Ayer became a Charleston cotton merchant. He returned to his plantation in 1868 and became the first planter in South Carolina to rent land to ex-slaves. He was a Baptist minister from 1872 to 1875 in South Carolina and from 1876 to 1879 in Tennessee. He returned to South Carolina and taught at the Anderson Female Academy from 1879 to 1887 and was a professor at Patrick Military Academy in 1890. He died on March 8, 1895, in Anderson, South Carolina. Faunt and May, *South Carolina Secedes*.

B

BAGBY, George William (*Editor*), son of George and Virginia Young (Evans) Bagby, was born on August 13, 1828, in Buckingham County, Virginia. The son of a Lynchburg merchant, he attended Dr. Page's boarding school, Edgehill School in Princeton, and Delaware College. He graduated from the University of Pennsylvania Medical School in 1849 and briefly practiced medicine before beginning a long journalistic career. Bagby and his wife Lucy Parke Chamberlayne, whom he married on February 16, 1863, had ten children. In the 1850s he helped to edit the Lynchburg *Virginian*, edited the Lynchburg *Express*, and was Washington correspondent for several Southern newspapers until 1859. He wrote for the *Southern Literary Messenger*, which he edited from 1860 to 1864. During his wartime career on the *Messenger*, he created the character of Mozis Adduma, a crackerbarrel philosopher and wit. He also joined the army at the outbreak of the war, but ill health kept him from the front lines. Bagby was at the battle of First Manassas, where he served as a clerk to P.G.T. Beauregard's (*q.v.*) chief of staff; he was discharged in 1864 and spent the remainder of the war as associate editor of the Richmond *Whig* and as Richmond correspondent for other newspapers. A strong Confederate patriot, he was nevertheless very critical of Davis. At the end of the war in 1865, Bagby moved to New York, but failing eyesight brought him back to Virginia where he lectured, edited the *Native Virginian* in 1868, and served as librarian of the state library at Richmond from 1870 to 1878. A prolific writer, he authored *Daniel's Latch Key* (1868), the popular *What I Did with My Millions* (1874), and *Meekins's Twinses* (1877). He also was the author of the

Writings of Dr. Bagby, which was published posthumously in three volumes in 1884-1886. Active in politics throughout the postwar period, he became a vigorous foe of the Virginia reformers known as Readjusters. He died in Richmond on November 29, 1883. Alderman, *Library of Southern Literature*, I; Bagby, *The Old Virginia Gentleman*; King, *Dr. William Bagby*.

BAKER, Alpheus (*General*), son of Alpheus and Elizabeth (Courtney) Baker, was born on March 23, 1828, at Abbeville Courthouse, South Carolina. He was educated in the law by his father and taught school at the age of sixteen before being admitted to the Eufaula, Alabama, bar in 1849. He was a Democrat and a Catholic. He married Louise Garvin on January 7, 1851, and Pheribee M. Ricks on December 4, 1866; he had six children by his second wife. In 1856, Baker traveled to Kansas, which he wanted to make a slave state. In 1861, he represented Barbour County, Alabama, in the state legislature before becoming a captain of the Eufaula Rifles in the Confederate Army. First stationed as a colonel in Pensacola, he commanded the 54th Alabama Regiment in the siege of New Madrid, Missouri, where he was captured in April 1862. Exchanged in September 1862, he fought at Fort Pemberton and was wounded at the battle of Baker's Creek, Mississippi, on May 16, 1863. After being promoted to brigadier general on March 5, 1864, he was again wounded at the battle of Ezra Church, Georgia, on July 28, 1864. In January 1865, he went to the Carolinas, where he fought at the battle of Bentonville. He surrendered with his troops in North Carolina. Baker returned to Alabama and practiced law in Eufaula from 1865 until he moved to Louisville, Kentucky, in 1878 when he probably retired, though little is known about the remainder of his life. He died in Louisville on October 22, 1891. Levin, *Lawyers and Lawmakers of Kentucky*; Owen, *History of Alabama and Dictionary of Alabama Biography*, III.

BAKER, James McNair (*Congressman*), was born to Archibald and Katherine Baker on July 20, 1822, in Robeson County, North Carolina. After graduating from Davidson College in 1844, he practiced law in Lumberton, North Carolina. Around 1850, he removed to Florida to practice law in Old Columbus and Lake City, where he became an elder in the Presbyterian church. He also planted. In 1859, he married Fanny Gilchrist, by whom he had three sons and two daughters. He served the Suwannee circuit in Florida as state's attorney in 1852 and as judge in 1859. In 1856, he ran unsuccessfully as a Whig for the U.S. House of Representatives from Florida. Baker supported the constitutional unionist John Bell for president in 1860. When the war broke out, he became a loyal Confederate, serving in the Confederate Senate from 1861 to 1865. He supported the Davis administration in the first Senate but opposed it in the second Senate. A respected and hardworking senator, Baker served on the Claims, Commerce, Naval Affairs, Post Office and Post Roads, Public Lands, Buildings, and Engrossment and Enrollment Committees. When Richmond surrendered, he returned to Florida to his law practice. In 1866, he was named associate justice of the Florida Supreme Court. Because of restrictions on officeholding by ex-Confederates, he returned to his private practice and worked on an internal improvements fund. A Democrat redemptionist, he returned to public life after Reconstruction and served in 1881 as judge of the Fourth Circuit Court. He died in Jacksonville, Florida, on June 20, 1892. Rerick, *Memories of Florida*, I.

BAKER, Laurence Simmons (*General*), was born into the old and honorable family of Dr. John Burgess Baker and his wife Mary Wynn on May 15, 1830, in Gates County, North Carolina. He attended Norfolk Academy and graduated last in his class at the U.S. Military Academy in 1851. Baker had a son and two daughters by his marriage to Elizabeth Earl Henderson in March 1855. He entered the service as a second lieutenant of cavalry, served on the frontier, and by 1860, had been promoted to captain. He opposed secession but when the war began, he resigned his commission. He entered the Confederate Army in May 1861 as a lieutenant colonel in command of the 9th North Carolina Cavalry, served under General J.E.B. Stuart (*q.v.*), and was promoted to colonel in March 1862. During the Seven Days' battles, he commanded the Confederate cavalry at Charles City Road on June 29, and he served under General Wade Hampton (*q.v.*) at Second Manassas, Sharpsburg, and Frederick City, Maryland, in defense of the southern mountain passes. Baker also fought at Fredericksburg and Chancellorsville and distinguished himself at the battle of Upperville. He was promoted to brigadier general for his bravery at the battle of Brandy Station, where he was seriously wounded in June 1863. Hampton wanted to appoint him as his division commander at Gettysburg, but since Baker's health was poor, Baker protected the Confederate Army's retreat at Hagerstown and Falling Waters. He was assigned to the War Department of the Second Military District of South Carolina in 1864, where he had the duties of a major general. He protected the Weldon Railroad and confronted Sherman at Savannah and Augusta in late 1864. He was given department command in North Carolina and took part in the battle of Bentonville in the spring of 1865. He surrendered after Richmond fell, and he was paroled in May 1865. After the war, he sold life insurance and farmed for a while in New Bern, North Carolina, until 1877, when he became agent of the Seaboard Air Line Railroad in Suffolk, Virginia. He was also in the trucking business in Norfolk before his death on April 10, 1907, in Suffolk. Evans, *Confederate Military History*, IV.

BALDWIN, John Brown (*Congressman*), son of Judge Briscoe G. Baldwin and his wife Martha (Brown), was born in Spring Farm, Augusta County, Virginia, on January 11, 1820. Baldwin's father was a judge of the Supreme Court of Appeals in Virginia. The younger Baldwin graduated from Staunton Military Academy in 1836 and from the University of Virginia in 1839. He then studied law and was admitted to the Staunton bar in 1841. On September 20, 1842, he married Susan Madison Peyton. He served as a Whig in the Virginia House of Delegates in 1845 but lost a subsequent bid for reelection in 1847. A practicing attorney, he ran unsuccessfully for judge of the court of appeals in 1859. After supporting John Bell for the presidency in 1860, Baldwin was a unionist delegate from Augusta County to the Virginia secession convention in 1861, and he was sent to confer with President Lincoln. The firing on Fort Sumter ended all compromise, and Baldwin reluctantly joined the Virginia secessionists. He immediately volunteered for service in the Army of Virginia, and Governor John Letcher (*q.v.*) appointed him inspector general of the Virginia State Volunteers in August 1861. He then served as colonel of the 52nd Virginia Regiment, but his military career was terminated by illness in West Virginia at the end of 1861. He was elected to the Confederate Congress from Augusta County, and he served in both the first and second Confederate Congresses. Baldwin supported the Davis administration in the first Congress and opposed it in the second. Consistently in opposition to the suspension of *habeas corpus*, Baldwin served on the Conference, Impressments, Joint, Ways and Means, and Currency Committees. When the war ended, he returned to his law practice. Baldwin joined the Conservative party and served as speaker of the Virginia House of Delegates in 1865. He also was president of the Virginia Conservative convention in 1868 and rejoined national political life as a delegate to the national Democratic convention in 1868. In 1870, he was involved in a scheme to extend the Chesapeake and Ohio Railroad to the Ohio River. Soon after, Baldwin became seriously ill and retired to private life. He died on September 30, 1873, probably in Staunton, Virginia. McGregor, *The Disruption of Virginia*; Tyler, *Encyclopedia of Virginia Biography*, I.

BARKSDALE, Ethelbert (*Congressman*), son of William and Nancy Hervey (Lester) Barksdale, and brother of William E. Barksdale (*q.v.*), was born on January 4, 1824, in Smyrna, Rutherford County, Tennessee. Little is known about his early education. He was a Methodist (the family was Baptist) and a unionist Democrat, and he was regarded as antebellum Mississippi's greatest newspaperman. He married Alice Harris in 1843. Barksdale wrote for the Yazoo *Democrat* in 1845 and for the Jackson *Mississippian* from 1850 to 1861. From 1854 to 1861, the *Mississippian* was the official organ of the state. In 1859, he was an ally of Jehu Orr (*q.v.*) as a delegate to the state Democratic convention. The following year, he served on the Platform Committee of the Charleston Democratic convention, and he later wrote a justification of the Mississippi delegation's walkout to the people back home. He supported John C. Breckinridge (*q.v.*) for the presidency in 1860 and said that he would favor secession if Lincoln were elected. In the fall of 1861, he was elected to the Confederate Congress, and he continued to represent the Seventh Congressional District in the Confederate House throughout the war. He served on the Foreign Affairs, Printing, and Ways and Means Committees and headed the committee to report the proceedings of Congress.

Barksdale was consistently a Jefferson Davis (*q.v.*) spokesman in the House. In 1862, he helped pass the suspension of the writ of *habeas corpus* as a part of the war effort, and he sponsored a mild retaliatory bill following the issuance of Lincoln's preliminary Emancipation Proclamation. He directed the movement to expel Henry S. Foote (*q.v.*) from the House. In May 1864, he led the move to extend the funding bill for the Confederate States, and in November 1864 he spoke for the president when he claimed that a peace initiative could not originate in the Congress. In 1865, he opposed the exemption of overseers from military service, and he and Williamson S. Oldham (*q.v.*) introduced a bill to arm the slaves. After the war, Barksdale returned to private life in Mississippi where he became a farmer. He contributed to the Mississippi political revolution of 1875 by supporting the drive to impeach Governor Adelbert Ames. In 1876, he farmed in Yazoo County and served as presidential elector on the Benjamin Tilden Democratic ticket. He also edited the Jackson *Clarion*, which was the Democratic party organ from 1876 to 1883. From 1877 to 1879, he was chairman of the Democratic Executive Committee, and from 1882 to 1887, he served in the U.S. House. In 1890, he was the Alliance (Populist) candidate for Congress, and in 1892, he supported the subtreasury plan. Barksdale died on February 17, 1893, in Jackson, Mississippi. Barksdale, *Barksdale Family History and Genealogy*; Rainwater, *Mississippi, Storm Center of Secession, 1856-1861*.

BARKSDALE, William E. (*General*), son of William and Nancy Hervey (Lester) Barksdale, was born in Smyrna, Rutherford County, Tennessee, on August 21, 1821, where his grandfather had moved from Virginia in 1808. He was a brother of Ethelbert Barksdale (*q.v.*). After attending the University of Nashville in 1839, he studied law at Columbus, Mississippi. He abandoned his practice to become editor of the strongly proslavery Columbus *Democrat* in 1842. During the Mexican War, he was a captain in the 2nd Mississippi Regiment and its assistant commissary in 1847-1848. He was a Baptist and was married. In 1851, he was a unionist and lived in Lowndes County, Mississippi. Elected Democratic congressman-at-large from Mississippi in 1853, Barksdale served until his resignation on January 12, 1861. While in the House, he was a filibusterer (one who favored expansion of slavery into South America) and a close friend of the radical Preston Brooks of South Carolina. Having become a radical in Congress, he favored secession. Barksdale joined the Confederate Army in March 1861, and he became quartermaster general for the Mississippi army. He was promoted to colonel in the 13th Mississippi Regiment. He fought at the battle of First Manassas in July 1861 and distinguished himself at the battle of Edward's Ferry during the Virginia Peninsular campaign and at Malvern Hill during the Seven Days' battles in the spring of 1862. Promoted to brigadier general on August 12, 1862, he fought at the battles of Sharpsburg and Chancellorsville and was a hero of the battle of Fredericksburg. Barksdale served in Longstreet's (*q.v.*) Corps in the Army of Northern Virginia. He died within the Union lines during the second day of the battle of Peach Orchard at Gettysburg, Pennsylvania, on July 2, 1863. Barksdale, *Barksdale Family History and Genealogy*; Freeman, *Lee's Lieutenants*, II.

BARNWELL, Robert Woodward (*Congressman*), was born near Beaufort, South Carolina, on August 10, 1801, to Robert and Elizabeth Wigg (Hayne) Barnwell. His father was a Revolutionary War veteran and U.S. congressman. He graduated with high honors from Harvard College in 1821 and received his M.A. from South Carolina College in 1823, which awarded him an honorary L.L.B. in 1842. He read law and was admitted to the South Carolina bar in 1822. On August 9, 1827, he married his second cousin, Eliza Barnwell. He was an Episcopal vestryman, planter, and lifelong Democrat. Barnwell served in the South Carolina House of Representatives from 1826 to 1829 and in the U.S. House of Representatives from 1829 to 1833. He was a delegate to the South Carolina nullification convention in 1832, and he signed the Ordinance of Nullification. He became president of South Carolina College in 1835 and served until 1841, when he retired because of poor health. Barnwell became a U.S. senator in 1850 and served at the Southern rights convention in 1852 where he favored cooperation among the Southern states. After 1852, he retired to his family plantation and wrote often in defense of slavery. A cautious secessionist, he was a delegate to the South Carolina secession convention in 1860, where he served on the committee to write the Declaration of Immediate Causes of Secession. He went to Washington, D.C., as a secession delegate in December 1860 to try to convince Southern congressmen to urge their states to secede. In 1861, he served as temporary chairman of the provisional Confederate Congress in Montgomery, Alabama, and helped to draft the Confederate Constitution. He was a signer of the Confederate Constitution. Barnwell was offered the post of secretary of state in the Confederacy by President Davis (*q.v.*), but he refused it, considering himself unworthy of the post. He remained a loyal Confederate and a Davis supporter throughout the war, serving in the first and second Confederate Senates. He held posts on the Conference, Impressments, Territories, and Finance Committees. An active member of the Finance Committee, Barnwell was a staunch defender of Secretary Christopher G. Memminger's (*q.v.*) policies. He opposed the peace movement in Congress in 1864. Since his property was destroyed during the war, Barnwell moved to Greenville, South Carolina, in 1865. He never again sought public office. From 1865 to 1873, he was chairman of the faculty of the University of South Carolina. He operated a school for girls in Columbia from 1873 to 1877 and was librarian of the University of South Carolina from 1877 until his death on November 24, 1882, in Columbia. Davidson, *The Last Foray*; Lee, *The Confederate Constitutions; South Carolina Historical and Genealogical Magazine*, II.

BARRINGER, Rufus (*General*), son of General Paul Barringer and his wife Elizabeth (Brandon), was born on December 2, 1821, in Poplar Grove, North Carolina. He attended Sugar Creek Academy, graduated from the University of

North Carolina in 1842, and studied law with Richmond Hill. He settled in Concord, Cabarrus County, North Carolina, in 1844, where he became a famous lawyer and a member of the Whig party. Barringer was a Presbyterian and a temperance worker. He married Eugenia Morrison, a sister of the wife of General Thomas J. Jackson (*q.v.*) in 1854; following her death, he married Rosalie Chunn and, later, Margaret Long. Barringer had three sons, the best known of whom was Dr. Paul B. Barringer. Elected to the state assembly in 1848, he joined William S. Ashe (*q.v.*) in the state Senate in 1851 to attempt to obtain a railroad charter. He retired from political life in 1852 after serving one Senate term. He was a unionist and a Whig elector for John Bell in the presidential election of 1860. Though he opposed secession, he joined the Confederate Army after the war began. During the Civil War, he refused to go to Congress, preferring to stay with the army. He raised a cavalry company of which he was captain, and he served ably in the Army of Northern Virginia. In June 1864, he was promoted to brigadier general. In all, he fought in seventy-six engagements during the war. He was a conspicuous participant at Willis Church and was wounded at Brandy Station in June 1863. At Reams' Station in August 1864, he was a division commander, and at Chamberlin Run he distinguished himself in battle. He covered the withdrawal from Richmond in April 1865, and his brigade was destroyed. Captured by Northern troops, he was imprisoned in Delaware until June 1865, when he took the oath of allegiance to the Union. After the war, he joined the Republican party and began an active political career. He advocated acceptance of the Reconstruction Act of 1867. In 1880, he ran unsuccessfully for lieutenant-governor of North Carolina. Barringer also practiced law in Charlotte, North Carolina, from 1865 to 1884. He retired in 1884 and took up the life of a gentleman farmer and became a historian of the Civil War. He died on February 3, 1895, in Charlotte. Dowd, *Sketches of Prominent Living North Carolinians*; Evans, *Confederate Military History*, IV.

BARRON, Samuel (*Naval Commander*), was born into the seafaring family of Commodore Samuel and Jane (Sawyer) Barron at Hampton, Virginia, on November 28, 1809. He made his first cruise at the age of eleven. On October 31, 1832, he married Imogen Wright by whom he had three sons and three daughters. His entire prewar career was devoted to the navy. From 1849 to 1853, Barron commanded the *John Adams* off the African coast. He was made a captain in September 1855 and commanded the *Wabash* in the Mediterranean in 1858-1859. He resigned from the navy on April 22, 1861, and immediately offered his services to the Confederate Navy. During the Civil War, Barron served as a captain in the Confederate Navy, where he organized naval defense and supervised the distribution of ordnance. From April through July 1861, he was chief of the Bureau of Orders and Detail, and in July he was put in charge of naval defenses in Virginia and North Carolina. In August of that year, he assumed command of Fort Hatteras. When the fort was surrendered, he became a prisoner for eleven months until he was exchanged. In November 1862, he commanded naval forces in all of Virginia.

Barron was sent to England in the summer of 1863 to bring back two ironclads for the Confederacy. He seized the ships and went to Paris, where he became the flag officer commanding Confederate naval forces in Europe. He resigned from that duty in February 1865. For the remainder of the war, he directed operations of commerce destroyers in Europe, including the *Stonewall* and the *Georgia*. After the war, he settled into retirement in Essex County, Virginia, where he died on February 26, 1888. *Army and Navy Journal*, March 3, 1888; Scharf, *History of the Confederate Navy*.

BARRY, William Taylor Sullivan (*Congressman*), son of Richard and Mary (Sullivan) Barry, was born in Columbus, Mississippi, on December 10, 1821. He was a nominal Presbyterian. Barry graduated from Yale College in 1841 and studied law, which he practiced in Columbus until he became a planter in 1847 in Oktibbeha County, Mississippi. He married Sally Fearn, daughter of Confederate Congressman Thomas Fearn (*q.v.*), on December 20, 1851. Barry was elected to the Mississippi state legislature in 1850 and 1852 and to the U.S. House of Representatives in 1853 as a Democrat. In Congress, he vigorously opposed the Know-Nothings and delivered a speech on "Civil and Religious Toleration." He was again elected to the state legislature in 1854, 1856, and 1858 and served as speaker of the state House of Representatives in 1855. Barry was one of the delegates who walked out of the Charleston Democratic convention in 1860, and he subsequently served as delegate from Lowndes County to the Mississippi secession convention where he voted for secession. He served as president of his state's constitutional convention in 1861 and as a member of the provisional Confederate Congresses at both Montgomery and Richmond. He served on the Finance, Constitutional, and Inauguration Committees of the provisional Confederate Congress and resigned to organize a regiment in Mississippi in 1862. As colonel of the 35th Regiment Mississippi Infantry, he took part in the battle of Corinth and the defense of Vicksburg. He was wounded in the Atlanta campaign and was captured at Mobile in April 1865. Upon his release, he led a secluded life, grew despondent, and yielded to disease. He practiced law in Columbus, Mississippi, where he died on January 29, 1868. *Biographical and Historical Memoirs of Mississippi*, I; Lynch, *The Bench and Bar of Mississippi*.

BARTOW, Francis Stebbins (*Congressman*), son of Dr. Theodosius and Frances Lloyd (Stebbins) Bartow, was born on September 6, 1816, in Savannah, Georgia. After graduating first in the class of 1835 at Franklin College (later the University of Georgia), he attended Yale Law School and studied law under John M. Berrien in 1837. He married Berrien's daughter, Louisa Greene Berrien, on April 18, 1844; they had no children. A prominent Savannah lawyer, Bartow served as a Whig in both houses of the Georgia state legislature before running unsuccessfully as a Know-Nothing for the U.S. House of Representatives in 1857. He supported secession at the Georgia convention. As chairman of the Military

Affairs Committee of the provisional and first Confederate Congresses, he was responsible for selecting the gray uniform of the Confederate Army. Bartow also served ably on the Flag and Seal and Engrossment Committees. He left Congress in 1861 to join the military as colonel of the 8th Georgia Regiment. Early in the war, he seized Fort McAllister for the Confederacy. Bartow broke with Governor Joseph Brown (*q.v.*) of Georgia over placement of the Georgia militia in the Confederate government's hands. He went to Virginia as brigade commander of the 7th, 8th, 9th, and 11th Georgia and the 1st Kentucky Regiments. He died during General Barnard Bee's charge at the battle of First Manassas on July 21, 1861. Freeman, *Lee's Lieutenants*, I; Northen (ed.), *Men of Mark in Georgia*, III.

BASS, Nathan (*Congressman*), was born October 1, 1808, in Putnam County, Georgia. In 1840 he moved to the frontier of Floyd County, Georgia. He and his wife, Carolina, had three children. Bass became a successful planter and in 1850 moved to Macon, Georgia, where he became active in Southern business expansion. Bass, who supported Stephen A. Douglas for the presidency in 1860, was a member of the unionist minority in the state delegation to the Charleston Democratic convention. Along with Herschel V. Johnson (*q.v.*) and Eugenius A. Nisbet (*q.v.*), he was appointed to address the people of Georgia on the alternative courses of action for Democrats in the state following the breakup of the Charleston convention. Bass himself refused to recognize the Richmond Democratic convention which nominated John C. Breckinridge (*q.v.*) for president in 1860. But in 1861, he supported secession and called for a Confederate cotton planters' convention in the hopes of directing the planting powers to support the war effort. He served in the provisional Confederate Congress in 1861, and he nominally supported the administration. He refused to stand for election to the first Confederate Congress; instead he returned to Macon and served the state government as an advisor on the international cotton market. After the war, having lost his wealth, he became a farmer in Rome, Floyd County, Georgia. He died in Rome on September 2, 1890. Battey, *A History of Rome and Floyd County*.

BATE, William Brimage (*General*), son of James Henry and Amanda (Weathered) Bate, was born in Bledsoe's Lick, Sumner County, Tennessee, on October 7, 1826. He attended a rural academy and clerked on a steamboat from 1842 until 1847. During the Mexican War, he served as a private and, later, as a first lieutenant in the 3rd Tennessee Volunteer Infantry from 1847 to 1849. He edited the Democratic newspaper, *The Tenth Legion*, in Gallatin, Tennessee, in 1849. A Democrat, he was a member of the Tennessee House from 1849 to 1851. After receiving his law degree from Lebanon University of Tennessee in 1852, he practiced law in Nashville until 1854. In 1856, he married Julia Peete. From 1854 to 1860, he was attorney general for the Nashville District. Bate, a staunch secessionist, served as a presidential elector on the Breckinridge ticket in 1860.

Upon the outbreak of war, he entered the Confederate Army as a private and later fought with the Army of Tennessee as a colonel of the 2nd Tennessee Regiment. Wounded at Shiloh in the spring of 1862, he had garrison duty at Huntsville, Alabama, later that year and was promoted to brigadier general on October 3, 1862. In 1863, he fought in the Tullahoma campaign and was a prominent participant at Chickamauga and a division commander at Missionary Ridge. Promoted to major general on February 23, 1864, he was a hero at Resaca, fought under Hood (*q.v.*) during the Atlanta campaign, and was cited for heroism during the battle of Franklin, Tennessee. In December 1864, he also participated in the defense of Nashville. He refused the office of governor of Tennessee in 1863 in order to remain in the field. He surrendered at Greensboro, North Carolina, in April 1865. Upon returning home to Nashville, he was disfranchised by the William J. Brownlow administration and retired to private life to practice law. Even so, he worked for the state Democratic party while he was disfranchised. After his restrictions were lifted, Bate was elected governor of Tennessee in 1882 and served a second term until 1886, when he was elected to the U.S. Senate and became an influential politician. Bate authored the act of 1893 which removed restrictions on local elections and thus effectively ended Reconstruction. He served continuously in the Senate until his death in Washington, D.C., on March 9, 1905. *Biographical Directory of the American Congress*; Marshall, *William B. Bate*.

BATSON, Felix Ives (*Congressman*), was born in Dickson County, Tennessee, on September 6, 1819. He was a lawyer; he was married and had a daughter, Emma. Little is known about his early career or education. From 1853 to 1858, Batson, who lived in Clarksville, Johnson County, Arkansas, was a circuit judge for the Fourth Judicial Circuit of Arkansas. In 1858, he was a state Supreme Court judge, a position which he resigned in 1860. At the state secession convention in 1861, he voted for secession. He represented the First Congressional District of northwest Arkansas in the first and second Confederate House of Representatives. In the first Congress, he was a member of the Inauguration, Military Affairs, and Territories and Public Lands Committees. In the second Congress, he served on the Judiciary Committee and on select committees to inform state governors to lessen the granting of exemptions and to increase the number of troops in each state. He was a loyal supporter of the Davis administration, and he opposed General Edmund Kirby Smith's (*q.v.*) desire to remove state troops from Arkansas. Batson volunteered as a private in the state militia at the beginning of the war, but his company disbanded after two weeks of service. He lost an estimated 75 percent of his fortune during the war years. Batson practiced law in Clarksville, Arkansas, after the war. He died in Clarksville on March 11, 1871, never having recouped his wartime losses. Hempstead, *Historical Review of Arkansas*; Thomas, *Arkansas in War and Reconstruction, 1861-1874*.

BATTLE, Cullen Andrews (*General*), was born to the physician and planter Cullen Battle and his wife Jane Andrews (Lamon) on June 1, 1829, in Powelton, Georgia. In 1836, his family moved to Eufaula, Alabama. He attended Brownwood Institute in Georgia and graduated from the University of Alabama in 1851. Battle studied law in the office of Governor John Shorter (*q.v.*) and was admitted to the Alabama bar in 1852. Before the war he practiced law in Tuskegee with William P. Chilton (*q.v.*). He was a Baptist and a Democrat, and he had a son and a daughter by his 1851 marriage to Georgia Florida Williams. He was a secessionist and an ally of William L. Yancey (*q.v.*) and supported John C. Breckinridge (*q.v.*) for president in 1860. When the war began, he enlisted as a private but was later elected a major of the 3rd Alabama Regiment. After he was wounded in the battle of Seven Pines in June 1862, he was promoted to colonel. He participated in the battles of Sharpsburg and Fredericksburg before being made a brigadier general on the field at Gettysburg. He won praise for his action at Spotsylvania during the Wilderness campaign, and he was promoted to major general following his heroism at the battle of Winchester in September 1864. Because of serious wounds at the battle of Cedar Creek in October of the same year, he never took the field again. After the war, he practiced law in Tuskegee, Alabama. He was elected to the U.S. House in 1868, although the test oath prevented him from taking his seat. In 1874, he served as a delegate to the Alabama constitutional convention. In 1880, he moved to New Bern, North Carolina, where he edited the *New Bern Journal* and served as mayor of New Bern. In 1903, he retired and moved to his son's home in Greensboro. Battle died on April 8, 1905, in Greensboro, North Carolina. Owen, *History of Alabama and Dictionary of Alabama Biography*, III.

BAYLOR, John Robert (*Governor, Congressman*), was born in Paris, Kentucky, on July 20, 1822. He was married and had two sons. A lawyer, he emigrated to Texas in 1839 and fought in the Comanche campaign the following year. He served in the Texas legislature in 1853-1854. In 1860-1861, he edited a Democratic paper called *The White Man* in Weatherford, Texas. As a delegate from Weatherford to the Texas secession convention in January 1861, he voted for secession. Baylor became lieutenant colonel of the 2nd Texas Cavalry in 1861, and he commanded the surrender of U.S. forces at San Antonio. He also commanded the second line of defense on the western frontier in mid-1861. In June 1861, he occupied Marsilla, New Mexico, and in July 1861, he captured Fort Fillmore. On August 1, 1861, he took command of the Arizona Territory, of which Davis (*q.v.*) made him governor on February 14, 1862. Baylor actively protected white settlers in Arizona from Indian forays. His too vigorous attempts to quell Indian unrest finally forced his removal as governor. He was elected to the second Confederate House from Texas by a large majority, having conducted a harsh campaign in which he attacked incompetence and accused the opposition of disloyalty. As a pro-administration congressman from 1863 to 1865, he served on the Indian Affairs and Patents Committees and on special committees concerning army pay and additional taxation. After the war, he lived in San Antonio and practiced law before moving to Montell, Texas, where he died on February 6, 1894. Lubbock, *Six Decades in Texas: The Memoirs of Francis R. Lubbock*.

BEALE, Richard Lee Turbeville (*General*), was born to Robert and Martha Felicia (Turbeville) Beale on May 22, 1819, at Hickory Hill, Westmoreland County, Virginia. After attending Northumberland and Rappahannock Academies and Dickinson College, he graduated from the University of Virginia Law School in 1838 and was admitted to the bar the following year. He was an Episcopalian and a Democrat. He was married and had at least one son who also fought in the Confederate Army. Beale practiced law at Hague in Westmoreland County, Virginia, before the war and served a term in the U.S. House from 1847 to 1849 but declined to seek reelection. He was a delegate to the state reform convention in 1850 and to the constitutional convention the following year. From 1858 to 1860, he served in the state Senate. He entered the Confederate Army as a first lieutenant in the 9th Virginia Cavalry, and during the war he served in all campaigns of the cavalry division of the Army of Northern Virginia. As a colonel, he commanded Camp Lee, captured Leeds Garrison, and served as a bridge builder. In December 1862, he was part of Stuart's expedition into Rappahannock County. His unexplained resignation from military service in 1862 and 1863 was never accepted. Beale repelled Stoneman's cavalry raid in April 1863, participated in the battles of Brandy Station, Gettysburg, and Culpeper Court House and in Stuart's raid into Maryland in 1863. In March 1864, he intercepted Dahlgren, capturing Union plans for the burning of Richmond and the assassination of President Davis (*q. v.*). In the campaign from the Rapidan to the James, he distinguished himself at the battle of Stony Creek. In August 1864, he was promoted to brigadier general, but the appointment did not come through until February 1865. Beale took Dinwiddie Court House in March 1865. After the surrender, he farmed and practiced law in Hague, Virginia. Restrictions kept him from public life until the end of Reconstruction in Virginia. From 1879 to 1881, he served as a Democrat in the U.S. House, after which he retired to his law practice. He wrote the history of the 9th Virginia Cavalry prior to his death on April 21, 1893, in Hague. Beale, *History of the Ninth Virginia Cavalry*; Tyler, *Encyclopedia of Virginia*, III.

BEAUREGARD, Pierre Gustave Toutant (*General*), son of Jacques Toutant and Helen Judith (de Reggio) Beauregard, was born on May 28, 1818, in St. Bernard Parish, Louisiana. He was a member of an old and aristocratic Creole family. For a time he was educated in a private school in New York City. He graduated second in a class of forty-five from the U.S. Military Academy in 1838. He was a Catholic. He married Laure Marie Villère, sister of Charles Villère (*q. v.*) in 1841, and Caroline Deslonde in 1860. Beauregard entered the U.S. Army as a second lieutenant of engineers and served chiefly in Louisiana until 1846. In 1847, he supervised the construction of defenses at Tampico. He also participated in the siege of Vera Cruz and Mexico City and was breveted a major during the Mexican War. From 1853 to 1861, he was a captain of engineers on the Gulf Coast of Louisiana. In January 1861, he was named superintendent of the U.S. Military Academy, a position which he resigned to become the first brigadier general in the Confederate Army. He was commander of Confederate forces at the battles of Fort Sumter and First Manassas. He also designed the Confederate battle flag in September 1861. In the spring of 1862, he assumed Confederate command at Shiloh following the death of General Albert Sidney Johnston (*q.v.*), but he was forced to give up the battle. After the battle of Corinth in October 1862, he was accused of overly elaborate battle plans. Ill health forced his temporary retirement from active military service in late 1862, after which he was a commander of Confederate forces at Charleston, South Carolina, a city which he held for two years. In April 1864, he defeated the Union general Benjamin Butler at the battle of Petersburg, and from October 1864 until he was relieved by General Joseph E. Johnston (*q.v.*) in February 1865, he commanded the Army of the West. Beauregard, who published *Maxima of Art of War* in 1863, was also a prolific correspondent and military theoretician. He was the symbolic leader of the "Western concentration bloc" of anti-Davis forces. His wartime career was marred by petty jealousies against his early successes. He served the final few months of the war with Joseph Johnston in North Carolina. After the surrender he returned to Louisiana, having declined an offer to command the Rumanian army. From 1865 to 1870, he was president of the New Orleans, Jackson, and Mississippi Railroad. He became manager of the Louisiana lottery from which he recouped the family losses from the war. In 1888, he served as the commander of public works in New Orleans. An excellent writer, he became an important historian of Civil War battles in the last years of his life. Beauregard died in New Orleans on February 20, 1893. Fortier, *A History of Louisiana*, I; Williams, *Napoleon in Gray*.

BEE, Hamilton Prioleau (*General*), was born to Colonel Barnard E. and his wife —————— (Faysoux) Bee on July 22, 1822, in Charleston, South Carolina. His father moved to Galveston, Texas, in 1835 and later served as secretary of state for the Republic of Texas. Hamilton Bee's younger brother, Barnard, also became a Confederate general. The younger Bee had five sons and a daughter by his 1854 marriage to Mildred Tarver. He was a Democrat and a member of the Episcopal church. Little is known of his early education. In 1839, he served as secretary to the commission which established the boundaries between Texas and the United States. In 1846, he became the secretary of the first Texas Senate. Bee was subsequently a clerk to Governor Francis Lubbock (*q.v.*) and speaker of the third Texas House in the 1850s. He enlisted as a private in the Mexican War and was later promoted to first lieutenant in 1847. He enlisted in the Texas Militia in 1861 and commanded Texas coastal troops. In March 1862, he was promoted to brigadier general and was given command of Brownsville, Texas, where he ran cotton through the Union blockade and bought munitions from Europe. In 1863, he was made a coastal commander, and the following year he commanded a cavalry division in the Red River campaign, where he participated in the battle of Mansfield, Louisiana, and was wounded at Pleasant Hill. He also commanded a cavalry division in the Indian Territory with General Samuel B. Maxey (*q.v.*) and was promoted to major general by Edmund Kirby Smith (*q.v.*). He surrendered with the trans-Mississippi troops and was paroled in June 1865. After the war, he lived in Mexico until 1876. He then moved to San Antonio, Texas, engaged in various businesses, retired, and died on October 2, 1897. *Confederate Veteran*, V; Evans, *Confederate Military History*, XI.

BELL, Casper Wister (*Congressman*), was born in Prince Edward County, Virginia, on February 2, 1819. Little is known of his youth except that he graduated from William and Mary in 1837, and studied law at the University of Virginia. In 1843 he emigrated to Brunswick, Chariton County, Missouri. He was a lawyer, a Whig, and eventually became a judge. He also owned a newspaper in Brunswick. Bell, an early unionist, became a Democrat in 1854 and soon became a moderate supporter of secession. He was elected to the provisional Confederate Congress and to the first Confederate Congress from Brunswick. In the first Congress, he served on the Medical Department and Military Affairs Committees, and was chairman of the Patents Committee. He was a stickler for hospital efficiency and constantly introduced bills of inspection. A close associate of Henry Foote (*q.v.*), he was staunchly anti-Davis. Also an associate of Governor Thomas Reynolds (*q.v.*), Bell allowed John B. Clark (*q.v.*) to replace him in the second House. After the war he returned to Missouri to his law practice. He practiced law in Brunswick with John Venable. He died in Brunswick on October 27, 1898. Kirkpatrick, "Missouri's Delegation to the Confederate Congress," *Civil War History*, V.

BELL, Hiram Parks (*Congressman*), was born into the poor farmer family of Joseph Scott and Rachael (Phinezee) Bell in Jackson County, Georgia, on January 19, 1827. Having received his education at the village academy of Cumming, Forsyth County, Georgia, in 1847, he taught at the Ellijay Academy, read law, and was admitted to the bar in 1849. He practiced law in Cumming. He was a member of the Methodist Episcopal church and a trustee of Emory University. Bell's first marriage, to Virginia M. Lester on January 22, 1850, produced six children. After his first wife died, he married Anna Adelaide Jordan on June 11, 1890. A Whig cooperationist (one who believed in a united Southern effort) who opposed secession, Bell was a candidate on the Georgia presidential electoral ticket of John Bell (no relation) in 1860. While a delegate to the Georgia secession convention in 1861, he opposed secession, yet served on the committee to solicit the cooperation of the state of Tennessee. He was a member of the state Senate in 1861. In 1862, he joined the Confederate Army and served as a captain in the battle of Second Manassas and as a colonel at Chickasau Bayou, Mississippi, where he was wounded. A second and more severe wound at Vicksburg in 1863 disabled him for further military service, and he spent the years 1864-1865 as a member of the second Confederate House, where he was on the Post Office and Post Roads and the Privileges and Elections Committees. Bell was an opponent of the Davis administration and supported the movement to suspend taxes in Georgia. After the war, he returned to his law practice at Cumming. From 1868 to 1871, he was a member of the state Democratic Executive Committee; later, he served on the Democratic National Committee. In 1872 and 1876, he was elected as a Democrat to the U.S. House of Representatives but lost his bid for reelection in 1878. He then returned to the practice of law. Bell was elected to the state House of Representatives in 1898 and to the state Senate in 1900. He retired and on August 16 or 17, 1907, Bell died in Atlanta, Georgia. Avery, *History of the State of Georgia*; Northen (ed.), *Men of Mark in Georgia*, I.

BENJAMIN, Judah Philip (*Cabinet Member*), was born on August 6, 1811, in St. Croix, Danish West Indies, to Sephardic Jewish parents, Philip and Rebecca (de Mendes) Benjamin. His family later settled in Savannah, where he was educated in the common schools. He attended Fayetteville Academy and Yale College from 1825 to 1827. In 1831, he moved to New Orleans, where he taught school, studied law, and was admitted to the bar in 1832. The following year he married Natalie St. Martin. A self-made man, he became a planter as well as a lawyer, equally reputed for his intellect and his substantial wealth. In 1842, he entered public life and was elected to the Louisiana legislature. In 1845, Benjamin was a delegate to the Louisiana state constitutional convention. He served in the U.S. Senate as a Whig from 1853 and as a Democrat from 1859 to 1861. After Lincoln's election, he advocated secession and he resigned from the Senate in February 1861. Jeffsrson Davis (*q.v.*) named him attorney general of the Confederacy on February 21, 1861. He filled this post with distinction, achieving stability in his department and proving himself a good manager. Of the Confederate cabinet he was perhaps the closest to Davis, who chose him to succeed Leroy P. Walker (*q.v.*) as secretary of war on September 17, 1861. Being almost wholly ignorant of the military aspect of the war, Benjamin was less successful in his second cabinet post. Although he cut bureaucratic red tape in his department, he drew congressional censure for the Confederate losses at Forts Henry and Donelson and at Roanoke Island. But as an insult to Congress, President Davis made Benjamin secretary of state on March 24, 1862. He held that post with distinction for the remainder of the war. He was responsible for many of the European loans to the Confederacy. But he could never coordinate the Confederate diplomatic effort, which he felt was the reason the Confederate government failed to achieve European recognition. At the war's end, he offered President Davis the plan of allowing each Confederate state to negotiate its own terms of readmission to the

Union. During the retreat from Richmond, he left the presidential party, made his way to the coast, and escaped to England. He became a law student at Lincoln's Inn in January 1866. He wrote for newspapers and magazines to earn an income, and he was allowed to practice law in June 1866. Benjamin practiced law in Liverpool, England, and soon recouped his finances through the cotton trade. He wrote a *Treatise on the Law of Sale of Personal Property* (1868). He was appointed to the Queen's Council in 1872 and continued to practice law until 1882. Benjamin maintained a residence for his family in Paris, France, and he died there on May 8, 1884. Meade, *Judah P. Benjamin*; Patrick, *Jefferson Davis and His Cabinet*.

BENNING, Henry Lewis (*General*), son of the part Cherokee Pleasant Moon and Matilda Meriwether (White) Benning, was born on April 2, 1814, in Columbus, Georgia. He graduated first in the class of 1834 from Franklin College (later the University of Georgia), studied law, and was admitted to the Columbus bar the following year. On September 12, 1839, he married Mary Howard Jones, the daughter of his law partner; they had a son and five daughters. In 1837, Benning was solicitor general for the Chattahoochee Circuit, which included Columbus. He was a states' rights Democrat who served as a delegate to the Nashville convention in 1850. He lost a bid for Congress in 1851, and from 1853 to 1859, he was a judge of the state Supreme Court. An earnest advocate of secession, he was sent by the state secession convention in early 1861 as a commissioner to influence the secession of Virginia. In August 1861, he became a colonel of the 17th Georgia Regiment. He served under Robert Toombs (*q.v.*) in Virginia and frequently commanded Hood's Division. Benning (for whom Fort Benning, Georgia, was later named) participated in the battles of Malvern Hill, Second Manassas, Sharpsburg, Fredericksburg, Chickamauga, Wilderness, Knoxville, Petersburg, and Farmville. He was severely wounded in the arm during the second day of the Wilderness campaign, on May 6, 1864, and was incapacitated until the final days at Appomattox. He surrendered with Lee (*q.v.*) and was paroled on April 9, 1865. Benning was impoverished at the end of the war. He held no postwar public office but instead rebuilt his large, lucrative law practice. He died on his way to court in Columbus, Georgia, on July 10, 1875. Standard, *Columbus, Georgia in the Confederacy*.

BLANDFORD, Mark Hardin (*Congressman*), was born to the wealthy Judge Mark A. Blandford and his wife on July 13, 1826, in Warren County, Georgia. He attended Mercer University and was admitted to the Hamilton, Georgia, bar in 1844 at the age of eighteen. Blandford's marriage to Sarah C. Daniel on December 12, 1852, was childless. In 1846, he served in the Mexican War as a sergeant in the Georgia Light Infantry, after which he became a successful businessman and lawyer in Buena Vista, Marion County, Georgia. At the outbreak of the war, he joined the Georgia state army. As a member of the 12th Georgia Regiment, he lost an arm at the battle of McDowell, Virginia, in May 1862. President Davis (*q. v.*) subsequently made him a judge in the military court, with the rank of lieutenant colonel of cavalry. Elected to the second Confederate House in 1864, Blandford cast over half of his votes against the administration, although he supported President Davis's efforts to end class exemptions from military service. He served on the Judiciary, Pay and Mileage Committees, and on the special committee to investigate Stewart Hospital. When the war ended, he returned to his law practice. In 1869, he moved to Columbus, Georgia. From 1872 to 1880, he was an associate justice of the Georgia Supreme Court. He died in Columbus in retirement on January 31, 1902. Knight, *A Standard History of Georgia and Georgians*; Northen (ed.), *Men of Mark in Georgia*, II.

BLEDSOE, Albert Taylor (*Bureaucrat*), son of Moses Ousley and Sophia Childress (Taylor) Bledsoe, was born on November 9, 1809, in Frankfort, Kentucky, where his father edited the Frankfort *Commonwealth*. He was graduated from the U.S. Military Academy in 1830, was commissioned a second lieutenant, and served for two years on the plains as an Indian fighter before resigning his commission. He studied theology at Kenyon Theological Seminary in Ohio and was ordained in the Episcopal clergy in 1833. He was at one time an assistant to the Episcopal Bishop of Kentucky. Bledsoe also studied law, which he practiced in Springfield, Illinois, and later in Washington, D.C., in the early 1840s. His marriage to Harriet Coxe in 1836 produced one daughter. As an educator, Bledsoe had a varied career. He tutored in mathematics at Kenyon College from 1833 to 1834 and was a professor of mathematics at Miami University, Ohio, in 1835-1836. He also held chairs in mathematics and astronomy at the University of Mississippi from 1848 to 1854 and in mathematics at the University of Virginia from 1854 to 1861. In 1856, he published an *Essay on Liberty and Slavery*. A strong unionist, Bledsoe nevertheless traveled to England at the outset of the war to gather materials for the constitutional argument for secession. During the war, he joined the army and held the rank of colonel. Bledsoe also was a blockade runner. From 1861 to 1865, he served as an assistant secretary of war in the Davis cabinet. In 1864, he was sent to London to influence English public opinion. He returned to Virginia as the war ended, and he devoted 1866 to writing a vindication of President Davis in his famous book *Is Davis a Traitor?* In 1867, he founded and edited the *Southern Review* in Baltimore. The magazine, which he edited until 1877, became the platform of the romantic lost cause. Increasingly bitter in his old age, Bledsoe died in Alexandria, Virginia, on December 8, 1877. *Library of Southern Literature*, I.

BOCOCK, Thomas Stanley (*Congressman*), was born to John Thomas and Mary (Flood) Bocock on May 18, 1815, in Buckingham (later Appomattox) County, Virginia. He was educated by private tutors, graduated first in the class of 1838 at Hampden-Sidney College, studied law with his brother Willis Bocock, and was admitted to the Virginia bar in 1840. He was a Presbyterian. He was married twice, first to Sarah P. Flood, and, upon her death, to Annie Faulkner. He was a member of the Virginia House of Delegates from 1842 to 1844 and was state's attorney for Appomattox County in 1845-1846. A Democrat, Bocock served in the U.S. House of Representatives from 1847 until 1861, when he made an unsuccessful contest for speaker against John Sherman. A secessionist, he joined the provisional Confederate Congress in May 1861. He was speaker of the House of both permanent Confederate Congresses. Generally a supporter of the administration, he broke with the president in 1865 after the Virginia delegation lost confidence in the cabinet. Still, he had steered much legislation through Congress and had served as liaison officer between the government and the Army of Northern Virginia. After the war he returned home, became an active Democrat, and served in the Virginia House of Delegates in 1869-1870 and 1877-1878. He also was a railroad attorney and a member of the board of Hampden-Sidney College in the 1880s. Bocock died in Appomattox County on August 5, 1891. Goode, *Recollections of a Lifetime*; Tyler, *Encyclopedia of Virginia*, I.

BOGGS, William Robertson (*General*), was born to the Augusta, Georgia, merchant Archibald Boggs and his wife Mary Ann (Robertson) on March 18, 1829. He attended Augusta Academy and graduated fourth in a class of fifty-two from the U.S. Military Academy in 1853. He was an Episcopalian. He married Mary Sophia Symington on December 19, 1855; they had three sons and two daughters. Boggs accepted a commission in the Corps of Engineers, and joined the Topographical Bureau of the Pacific Railroad survey in 1853. The following year he was made a second lieutenant of the Ordnance Corps and was stationed in New York; in 1856, he was promoted to first lieutenant. He was named inspector of ordnance at Port Isabel, Texas, in 1859. At the beginning of the Civil War, Boggs was a captain in the Corps of Engineers stationed at Charleston. In February 1861, he resigned his commission and was appointed captain of ordnance in the Confederate Army. A staff rather than a line officer, he designed guns, secured fortifications, and purchased supplies for the Confederacy in 1861. In December 1861, he became chief engineer for the state of Georgia, on the staff of Governor Joseph Brown (*q.v.*). As superintendent of the Louisiana State Seminary in 1862, he was favored by General Braxton Bragg (*q.v.*), but he later broke with Bragg at Pensacola, when Boggs felt himself unjustly bypassed for promotion. From August 1862 to 1864, Boggs served as chief of staff for the Trans-Mississippi Department under General Edmund Kirby Smith (*q.v.*). He was promoted to brigadier general following the Kentucky campaign, on November 4, 1862. After the Red River campaign of 1864, Boggs broke with Kirby Smith and resigned his commission. He was made commander of the Louisiana District, and early in 1865 he enlisted but later withdrew from a military expedition into Mexico. He never surrendered. After the war, he became a Savannah architect in 1866. He moved to

St. Louis in the late 1860s and served as chief engineer of the Lexington and St. Louis Railroad. From 1875 until his retirement in 1881, he taught mechanics at Virginia Polytechnic Institute. Boggs spent the last years of his life writing military reminiscences. He died on September 11, 1911, in Winston-Salem, North Carolina. Boggs, *Military Reminiscences of General William R. Boggs*.

BONHAM, Milledge Luke (*General, Congressman, Governor*), son of James and Sophia (Smith) Bonham, was born in Edgefield District, South Carolina, on December 25, 1813. (Some sources claim he was born on May 6, 1815.) He attended private schools, graduated second in the class of 1834 at South Carolina college, studied law, and was admitted to the Edgefield bar in 1837. He had a successful law practice. He and his wife, the former Ann Patience Griffin, were married on November 13, 1845; they had fourteen children, the most important of whom was Bonham's namesake, who later became governor of South Carolina. Bonham fought in the Seminole Wars as a major and adjutant general of a South Carolina brigade in 1836. During the Mexican War of 1847-1848, he served as a lieutenant colonel and major general in the South Carolina Militia and in the 12th Regiment of the U.S. Infantry. He was a member of the state House of Representatives from 1840 to 1844 and was solicitor for the Southern Circuit of South Carolina from 1848 to 1857. A states' rights Democrat, he served in the U.S. House of Representatives from 1857 to 1860. During the secession winter of 1860-1861, Bonham was a commissioner sent by the South Carolina legislature to secure the cooperative secession of Mississippi. He was appointed major general and commander of the Army of South Carolina in February 1861. When the war began, he volunteered for service under Beauregard (*q.v.*), and as a brigadier general he commanded the center of the Confederate line at the battle of First Manassas. He resigned his military commission on January 27, 1862, in protest over loss of seniority. He was elected to the first Confederate House, served on the important Ways and Means Committee, and voted against the administration's legislation. From 1862 to 1864, he was governor of South Carolina, where his primary concern was the prosecution of the war. As governor, he supported the administration on conscription, raised troops, took a strong position against deserters, and used slave labor for building defenses. In February 1865, he was made brigadier general in the Confederate Cavalry, and he served with Joseph E. Johnston (*q.v.*) in the last campaigns in North Carolina. He surrendered with Johnston's army. When the war ended, Bonham returned to Edgefield District to run his plantation and to practice law. He was a member of the South Carolina legislature in 1865-1867 and a delegate to the South Carolina taxpayers' conventions in 1871 and 1874. In 1876, he assisted Governor Wade Hampton (*q.v.*) in restoring white supremacy in South Carolina. He also served as state railroad commissioner from 1878 until his death on August 27, 1890, in White Sulphur Springs, North Carolina. Cauthen, *South Carolina Goes to War, 1861-1865*.

BOTELER, Alexander Robinson (*Congressman*), was born on May 16, 1815, in Shepherdstown, Virginia, to Dr. Henry Boteler and his wife Priscilla (Robinson). The elder Boteler was a physician and a prominent Baltimore merchant and shipowner. After he graduated from Princeton College in 1835, the younger Boteler turned to farming and to writing in Shepherdstown, Virginia. He married Helen Macomb Stockton in 1836. A Whig and a Presbyterian who later joined the American party, he served from 1859 until his resignation in 1861 in the U.S. House of Representatives. He lost a bid for the House speakership to James L. Orr (*q.v.*). He was a unionist who strongly supported the Crittenden compromise on secession. Upon his resignation from Congress, he was elected to the Virginia Assembly in 1861. During the war, he served in the provisional and first Confederate Houses. He also was on the staff of Thomas J. Jackson (*q.v.*), who used Boteler as his congressional spokesman. A supporter of the Davis administration, Boteler represented the interests of the Shenandoah Valley. He served on the Buildings, Indian Affairs, Printing and Ordnance, and Ordnance Stores Committees. He was also an aide to James E. B. Stuart (*q.v.*), and he left the Confederate House to advise Governors William Smith (*q.v.*) and John Letcher (*q.v.*) of Virginia. He also served on the military courts-martial in 1864. After the war, he returned to his farm in what had become West Virginia. In 1876, he was a member of the U.S. Centennial Commission, and President Chester Alan Arthur appointed him to the Tariff Commission in 1881. In the Department of Justice, he was a Republican assistant attorney in 1882-1883 and a pardon clerk from 1884 to 1889, after which he retired to his family home to write articles on the war. Boteler died on May 8, 1892, in Shepherdstown, West Virginia. Tyler, *Encyclopedia of Virginia*, II.

BOUDINOT, Elias Cornelius (*Congressman*), was born to Elias and Harriet Ruggles (Gold) Boudinot on August 1, 1835, in Rome, Georgia. His father, the Cherokee Chief Killa-kee-nah, had taken the name of Elias Boudinot as a student in Connecticut. The younger Boudinot studied civil engineering in Vermont in 1854 and law in Fayetteville, Arkansas. He was admitted to the Arkansas bar in 1856. He and his wife, the former Clara Minear, had no children. Boudinot, a Mason, was associate editor of the *Arkansian* and editor of the *True Democrat* in the late 1850s. In 1860, he was chairman of the Arkansas Central Committee of the Democratic party and attended the Democratic state convention. The following year, he was secretary of the Arkansas secession convention and a staunch secessionist. When the war began, Boudinot helped his uncle, Stand Watie (*q.v.*), raise a regiment for the Confederacy from the Cherokee Nation. He fought at Oak Hills and at Elkhorn as a lieutenant colonel. From 1863 to the end of the war, he served in the Confederate Congress as a delegate from the Indian Territory. When the war ended, he returned to the Indian Territory. In September 1865, he defended the Cherokee Nation's role in the war before a congressional committee. In 1867, he operated a tobacco factory, and the following year he negotiated an

Indian treaty with the United States. He lived in Washington, D.C., from 1868 until 1885, and he vigorously pursued Indian claims. He returned to a farm in the Indian Territory, practiced law, and died on September 27, 1890. Dale and Litton, *Cherokee Cavaliers*.

BOWEN, John Stevens (*General*), was born in Savannah, Georgia, on October 30, 1830. He was probably the son of William Parker Bowen, an unsuccessful merchant, and his wife, Ann Elizabeth (Wilkins). The younger Bowen attended Milledgeville Academy and graduated thirteenth in a class of fifty-one from the U.S. Military Academy in 1853. He was a Presbyterian. He was married and had a daughter. After attending the Carlisle Cavalry School, Bowen was commissioned a second lieutenant and served on the frontier from 1854 to 1856. He resigned his commission and returned to Savannah in 1856, where he was an architect and a lieutenant colonel in the Georgia Militia before moving to St. Louis, Missouri, in 1857. From 1859 to 1861, he was a captain in the Missouri Militia. At the outbreak of war, he joined the Confederate Army and commanded the 2nd Regiment of Frost's Brigade. Bowen served as acting chief of staff to General Daniel M. Frost in early 1861. In Memphis he raised the 1st Regiment of Missouri infantry, of which he was colonel, and he served under General Leonidas Polk (*q.v.*) at Columbus, Kentucky. After being wounded during the battle of Shiloh, where he served under General John C. Breckinridge (*q.v.*), he was promoted to the rank of brigadier general on March 14, 1862. In 1863, he resisted Grant at Bruinsburg during the Vicksburg campaign. Distinguished for his bravery at Port Gibson, Mississippi, he attained the rank of major general on May 25, 1863. During the siege of Vicksburg, he contracted dysentery and surrendered with his troops. He was shortly thereafter paroled and died on July 13, 1863, at Raymond, Mississippi. *Confederate Veteran*, XXII.

BOYCE, William Waters (*Congressman*), son of Robert and Lydia (Waters) Boyce, was born in Charleston, South Carolina, on October 24, 1818. He attended South Carolina College and the University of Virginia, studied law, and was admitted to the bar in 1839. During the 1840s, he practiced law and was a planter in Winnsboro, South Carolina. He was an Episcopalian, and he married a daughter of Dr. George Butler Pearson. Boyce was elected as a states' rights Democrat to the state House of Representatives in 1850 and to the U.S. House, where he served from 1853 until his resignation in 1860. He was considered a cooperationist and a moderate, but he spoke strongly in favor of secession in 1860. As a delegate to the Montgomery provisional convention, he supported Howell Cobb (*q.v.*) for president of the Confederacy. Boyce argued in favor of a constitution identical to that of the United States, except for his resolution that would permit a state to secede from the Confederacy. In the provisional Congress, he served on the Postal Affairs and Inauguration Committees and on the committee which organized the Executive Department. He also served in both permanent Confederate Congresses where he turned against the Davis administration. An active congressman, Boyce served on the Naval Affairs, Currency, and Ways and Means Committees, opposed conscription, and offered a deflationary currency plan in the second Congress. In 1863, he joined the peace movement, for which he was condemned in South Carolina as a submissionist. Boyce believed that the Davis government had created a military despotism; accordingly, he supported George McClellan for president in 1864 and advocated peace without reconstruction. For that, his political career was doomed in South Carolina. After the war he moved to Washington, D.C., and practiced law there. Boyce never again entered public life. He died on February 3, 1890, in Fairfax County, Virginia. Cauthen, *South Carolina Goes to War, 1861-1865*; Lee, *The Confederate Constitutions*.

BRADFORD, Alexander Blackburn (*Congressman*), was born in Jefferson County, Tennessee, on June 2, 1799. He read law in Nashville and began his practice in Jackson, Tennessee. He married Darthula Miller in 1821 and they had one son. He served as attorney general for the Fourteenth Judicial District in southwest Tennessee in 1823. He was elected as a Whig to the Tennessee Senate in 1837. He was also a major general in the state militia during the Seminole War of 1836. In 1839, Bradford moved to Holly Springs, Mississippi, where he became a close associate of Alexander M. Clayton (*q.v.*). He also owned a small railroad in Mississippi. In 1841, he was elected to the state legislature from Marshall County, Mississippi. He was a delegate to the Memphis commercial convention in 1846. In the Mexican War, he was cited for bravery at Monterrey. He was captain of the marshall guards and was made colonel of the 1st Mississippi Regiment in 1847 but resigned in order for Jefferson Davis (*q.v.*) to become colonel. He was the Whig candidate for governor in 1847 but lost. He served again in the state legislature during the late 1840s but was defeated in his try for the U.S. House in 1852. He attended the Memphis commercial convention in 1853. Bradford supported secession and actively supported the formation of the Confederacy. He served on the Committee on Public Lands in the provisional Congress. He remained a close friend and advisor to Mississippi leaders, but advancing age forced his retirement from public life. He continued to practice law during the war. When the war ended, he was impoverished. Bradford managed to recoup some of his losses by practicing law during the late 1860s in Boliver County, Mississippi. He died in Boliver on July 10, 1873. Clayton, *History of Marshall County*; Sillers (comp.), *History of Boliver County*.

BRADLEY, Benjamin Franklin (*Congressman*), was born in Scott County, Kentucky, on October 5, 1825. He graduated from Georgetown College of Kentucky in 1843 and received his law degree from Transylvania University in Kentucky in 1849. In 1851, he married Mrs. Emily (Sanders) Stuart, by whom he had four children. He served with the Kentucky Volunteer Infantry in 1847 during the Mexican War. Bradley, an ally of Kentucky Governor George W. Johnson (*q.v.*), farmed and practiced law prior to the Civil War. After the firing on Fort Sumter, he volunteered for service in the Confederate Army. For a few months in 1861, he served as assistant adjutant general on the staff of General Humphrey Marshall (*q.v.*). During 1862, he was commandant of the 1st Battalion of Kentucky Mounted Rifles. After resigning from the army in 1863 because of ill health, Bradley was elected to the second Confederate House, where he served until the end of the war. He was a member of the Ordnance and Ordnance Stores and Post Office and Post Roads Committees. As a member of the Confederate Congress, he favored vigorous prosecution of the war, but he opposed harsh treatment of prisoners. When the war ended, he returned to his law practice in Georgetown. From 1868 to 1880, Bradley was clerk of the circuit court for Scott County. As a Democratic member of the Kentucky Senate in 1889, he was chairman of the Railroads Committee. He died on January 22, 1897, in Georgetown, Kentucky. Collins, *Historical Sketches of Kentucky*, II.

BRAGG, Braxton (*General*), was born to the contractor Thomas Bragg and his wife, Margaret (Crossland), on March 22, 1817, in Warren County, North Carolina. He was a brother of Confederate Attorney General Thomas Bragg (*q.v.*). After attending Warrenton Academy, he graduated fifth in a class of fifty from the U.S. Military Academy in 1837. Commissioned a second lieutenant in the regular army, he was stationed at Fort Monroe in 1837-1838. He served as a first lieutenant during the Indian wars in Florida from 1838 to 1845. During the Mexican War, he was breveted captain at Fort Brown, major at Monterrey, and lieutenant colonel at Buena Vista. He was stationed at Jefferson Barracks, Missouri, from 1849 until he resigned from the army in 1856 to become a sugar planter in Lafourche Parish, Louisiana. He was an Episcopalian and a teetotaler, and he married Elisa Brooks Ellis on June 7, 1849. From 1859 to 1861, he was commissioner of public works for the Second District of Louisiana, in charge of drainage and levees. At the outbreak of war, he volunteered for service in the Confederate provisional army. Bragg was put in command of the Confederate forces at Pensacola, Florida, in mid-1861. In January 1862, he was promoted to lieutenant general in command of the Department of Alabama and West Florida. At the battle of Shiloh he commanded the 2nd Army Corps. Upon the death of General Albert S. Johnston (*q.v.*), he was promoted to full general and was given command of the Army of Tennessee, succeeding P.G.T. Beauregard (q.v.). Bragg planned the invasion of Kentucky in mid-1862. Although he experienced success at Munfordville, he failed to take the offensive and was defeated at Perryville in October 1862. He subsequently checked the Northern General Rosecrans at Murfreesboro and was victorious at Chickamauga in September 1863. But he failed to take advantage of his superiority of numbers, and in November he was forced to yield his command at Chattanooga to General Joseph E. Johnston (*q.v.*). Bragg, a close friend of President Davis (*q.v.*) and a constant squabbler with subordinates, was assigned to duty at Richmond in February 1864. A victim of his own indecisiveness and of the pettiness of subordinates while in Richmond, Bragg assisted in coordinating the final Confederate defense in the east. In November of the same year, he was given a command at Wilmington, North Carolina, and he participated in the Confederate victory at Bentonville, North Carolina, in March 1865. He served with President Davis on the final retreat into Georgia where he was captured in early May. After the war, he was a civil engineer in New Orleans and later superintendent of harbor improvements in Mobile, Alabama. In the 1870s, he became commissioner of public works for the state of Alabama and chief engineer for the Gulf, Colorado, and Santa Fe Railroad. He moved to Galveston, Texas, and remained in the railroad business; he died there on September 27, 1876. McWhiney, *Braxton Bragg and Confederate Defeat*; Seitz, *Braxton Bragg General of the Confederacy*.

BRAGG, Thomas (*Cabinet Member*), brother of Braxton Bragg (*q.v.*), was born to the skilled carpenter and contractor Thomas and his wife Margaret (Crossland) Bragg in Warrenton, North Carolina, on November 9 or 10, 1810. After attending Warrenton Academy and the military academy of Middletown, Connecticut, he was admitted to the bar in 1833. In the same year, he began the practice of law in Jackson, North Carolina. He married Isabelle M. Cuthbert in October 1837. A lifelong Democrat and staunch Presbyterian, Bragg was elected to the state legislature in 1842 and 1844. In 1845, he served as prosecuting attorney for Northampton County. As governor of his state from 1855 to 1859 and as U.S. senator from 1859 to 1861, he was a conservative secessionist who believed that the South could not establish its independence. He resigned from the Senate after North Carolina seceded. Bragg was appointed aide to the governor of North Carolina after war broke out. As attorney general in the Confederate cabinet from November 21, 1861, to March 18, 1862, he was close to President Davis (*q.v.*). He defended civilian rights and held that the Confederate government was financially liable for all materials used by the army. A diligent and meticulous man, he carefully reorganized the department to make it more responsive to state needs. He also favored the establishment of a Confederate supreme court. Bragg resigned his office on March 18, 1862, to return to North Carolina, where he sought to stop the peace movement which had begun during 1862. Bragg also attempted to effect a reconciliation between President Davis and Governor Zebulon Vance (*q.v.*). He helped edit the once unionist *State Journal* during 1864. Bragg ably served the Confederate interests at the end of the war and effected a just settlement of federal properties in the hands of Southerners. In 1865, when the war had ended, he returned to his law practice in Raleigh. Bragg helped to reorganize the state government during the late 1860s. He also was a lawyer for the prosecution in the trial of Governor William W. Holden (*q.v.*) in 1870. He died in Raleigh on January 21, 1872. Ashe, *Cyclopedia of Eminent and Representative Men of the Carolinas* . . . ; Patrick, *Jefferson Davis and His Cabinet*; Peele (comp.), *Lives of Distinguished North Carolinians*.

BRANCH, Anthony Martin (*Congressman*), was born in Buckingham County, Virginia, on July 16, 1823. Nothing is known of his early life or his parents. He graduated from Hampden-Sidney College in 1842 and moved to Huntsville, Texas, in 1847, where he practiced law with Henderson Yoakum and became a good friend of Sam Houston. (Branch was executor of Houston's will.) A unionist Democrat, he was elected district attorney for the Seventh Judicial District in 1850. He served in the Texas House in 1859 and in the state Senate in 1861. He resigned from the Senate when the war began, and he joined the Confederate provisional army where he was made captain of the 21st Texas Cavalry. In August 1863, he was elected from the Third District of Texas to the second Confederate House, where he served for the rest of the war. Branch, a member of the Committees on Elections, Military Affairs, and Territories and Public Lands, assisted in transporting trans-Mississippi cotton to the ports for shipment to Europe. He was a staunch defender of the Davis administration. When the Richmond government surrendered, Branch returned to Texas. After the war, the federal authorities denied him the seat in the U.S. House to which he had been elected in 1866. He subsequently practiced law in Huntsville, Texas, where he died during a yellow fever epidemic on October 3, 1867. Lynch, *The Bench and Bar of Texas*.

BRATTON, John (*General*), was born on March 7, 1831, in Winnsboro, Fairfield County, South Carolina, to the prominent physician William Bratton and his wife Isabella (Means). He attended Mount Zion College and graduated from South Carolina College in 1850 and from the Medical College of Charleston in 1853. He was an Episcopalian and a Democrat. He had three children by his marriage to Elizabeth P. Du Bose in 1859. From 1853 until 1861, he was a planter and physician in Winnsboro. When his state seceded, he enlisted in the Confederate Army as a private. Bratton held the rank of captain at the battle of Fort Sumter, and he was wounded and captured at the battle of Seven Pines. Exchanged in 1863, he was promoted to colonel. He was made a brigadier general on the battlefield during the Wilderness campaign in May 1864. At the time of the surrender at Appomattox, he commanded the largest brigade in the Confederate Army, which he surrendered to the Union Army. Soon after, he was paroled and he returned to Winnsboro to become a farmer. In 1865, Bratton was a delegate to the state constitutional convention. He represented Fairfield County in the South Carolina Senate from 1865 to 1866. A confirmed Democrat, he remained active in Reconstruction politics. In 1881, he was elected comptroller of South Carolina, and in 1884, he was elected to the U.S. House where he served one term. Bratton lost a bid for the governorship of South Carolina in 1890 to the Populist Benjamin Tillman, after which he returned to planting and retired from politics. He continued as a planter until his death on January 12, 1898, in Winnsboro. McGrady, *Cyclopedia of Eminent and Representative Men of the Carolinas. . .*, II; Williamson, *After Slavery*.

BRECKINRIDGE, John Cabell (*General*, *Cabinet Member*), was born on January 21, 1821, near Lexington, Kentucky, to the Honorable Joseph Cabell and Mary Clay (Smith) Breckinridge. The younger Breckinridge was descended from a powerful political family; his grandfather had been attorney general under Thomas Jefferson. He attended Pisgah Academy, and after graduating from Centre College, Kentucky, in 1839, he left Kentucky to study law at Princeton College. He also studied law at Transylvania University in Lexington, Kentucky, during 1840 and 1841. In 1841, he began a law practice at Burlington, Iowa. He returned to Kentucky in 1843 and moved to Lexington in 1845, where he practiced and taught law at Transylvania University. He was a Presbyterian. In December 1843, he married Mary C. Burch. During the Mexican War, he served as a major of the 3rd Regiment Kentucky Volunteers in 1847. A Democrat, he represented Fayette County in the state House of Representatives in 1849 and served in the U.S. House of Representatives from 1851 to 1855. In 1856, he became the youngest vice-president the United States ever had, but four years later he lost his bid for the presidency. The Kentucky legislature had meanwhile elected him to the U.S. Senate in which he served from March to September 1861. He worked for the Crittenden compromise in hopes of avoiding war. He returned to Kentucky in September 1861 and helped to organize the provisional Confederate government there. Breckinridge was expelled from the U.S. Senate in December 1861 because he had left Washington to join the Confederacy. In November 1861, he was appointed a general in the Confederate Army under Albert S. Johnston (*q.v.*). Breckinridge distinguished himself at the battles of Bowling Green and Shiloh. He was made a division commander in June 1862 at Vicksburg, stormed Baton Rouge, and served under Joseph E. Johnston (*q.v.*) at Jackson and under Braxton Bragg (*q.v.*) at Chickamauga. He was a corps engineer at Missionary Ridge and at Winchester. In 1864, he was named commander of the Department of West Virginia. On February 6, 1865, he became the last Confederate secretary of war. He left Richmond with the cabinet in April 1865 and eventually escaped to Cuba. After the war he traveled in Europe before returning to Lexington in 1868 to practice law, after having been given permission by the federal government to return. But restrictions on his officeholding remained, and he was unable to participate in postwar political life. He was made vice-president of the Elizabethtown, Lexington, and Big Sandy Railroad Company in 1869. He died in Lexington on May 17, 1875. *Biographical Encyclopedia of Kentucky of Dead and Living Men of the Nineteenth Century*; Connelly and Coulter (eds.), *History of Kentucky*, III; Davis, *Breckinridge*.

BRECKINRIDGE, Robert Jefferson (*Congressman*), son of the Presbyterian clergyman Dr. Robert J. Breckinridge and his wife Sophonisba (Preston) and a nephew of John C. Breckinridge (*q.v.*), was born in Baltimore, Maryland, on September 14, 1834. He attended Centre College in Kentucky and graduated from the University of Virginia in 1852. His marriage to Kate Morrison in 1856 produced two children. A Democrat, Breckinridge served for three years in the U.S. Coastal Survey before resigning in 1854 to practice law in Danville and later in Lexington, Kentucky. In 1856, he taught law at Transylvania University. Despite the fact that his father remained loyal to the Union, the younger Breckinridge volunteered for service in the Confederate Army when the war broke out. During 1861, he served in the 2nd Kentucky Infantry. He was elected to the first Confederate House of Representatives in 1862 but soon resigned to become a colonel of cavalry. In the House, he served on the Committee on Foreign Affairs and generally opposed Davis administration legislation. Little is known of his wartime career, save that he was captured in the spring of 1864. He was paroled when the war ended. After the war, he farmed and practiced law in Lincoln County, Kentucky. In 1873, he moved to New York City, but he later returned to Danville to practice law. His postwar public career is not known except that he served as a judge of the Court of Common Pleas in 1876. Thereafter, Breckinridge apparently sank into obscurity. Alexander and Beringer, *Anatomy of the Confederate Congress*; *Biographical Encyclopedia of Kentucky*.

BRIDGERS, Robert Rufus (*Congressman*), was born in Edgecombe County, North Carolina, on November 28, 1819, to John and Elizabeth Kettlewells (Routh) Bridgers. Although he was poor and received most of his early education behind a plow, he attended Stony Hill Academy and graduated first in his class at the University of North Carolina in 1841. In that same year, he passed the bar examination and began practice in Edgecombe County. He married Margaret Elizabeth Johnston on December 12, 1849. In 1844, he was elected as a Democrat to the state legislature and served on the Judiciary Committee. He returned to private life and farmed his Strabane Plantation and practiced law. He became a great cotton producer and was known not only as a progressive farmer but as an able financier, who at one time ran a branch of the state bank and was a railroad director. Bridgers served in the state legislature again from 1858 to 1861, where he was a moderate but a strong states' rights advocate. He converted to secessionism at his state's secession convention. He served in both Confederate Houses. Bridgers was a strong supporter of President Davis (*q.v.*) in the first Congress but turned against him in the second. He advocated financial policies based on sound business principles and urged that the Confederacy raise cotton and exchange it for gold on the world market. He served on the Currency, Military Affairs, and Conference Committees. Many of his colleagues wanted him to be named secretary of the treasury. The end of the war found him bankrupt, but he struggled to regain his wealth. He never returned to public life. He was a banker, managed the Navassa Guano Company, and earned a national reputation as the developer of the Atlantic Coast Line Railroad. Bridgers was most respected as president of the Wilmington and Weldon Railroad Company from 1865 until his death in Columbia, South Carolina, on December 10, 1888. Ashe, *Cyclopedia of Eminent and Representative Men of the Carolinas*, I; McCormick, "Personnel of the Convention of 1861."

BROCKENBROUGH, John White (*Judge, Congressman*), son of William Brockenbrough, was born in Hanover County, Virginia, on December 23, 1806. After graduating from the College of William and Mary in 1825, he attended the University of Virginia in 1826. He also read law in Winchester, Virginia, under the distinguished lawyer Henry St. George Tucker. In 1834, he married Mary C. Boyer; they had one son. Brockenbrough was admitted to the bar in 1827. He also served as commonwealth attorney for Hanover County in the late 1820s. In 1834, he moved to Lexington, Rockbridge County, Virginia, where he practiced law and founded a law school in 1849. He also wrote *Reports of the Decisions of Justice Marshall*. From 1845 to 1861, he held the appointed post of judge of the U.S. Court for the Western District of Virginia. A Democrat, he supported the secession movement in Virginia. He was a delegate to the peace convention in Washington, D.C., in February 1861. Brockenbrough was also elected a member of the provisional Confederate Congress at Richmond, where he served on the Judiciary Committee. His most distinguished service to the Confederacy was as judge for Virginia's Western District from 1861 to 1865. He consistently upheld the claims of the administration. After the war, he became a professor of law at Washington and Lee University in Lexington, a post he held for the rest of his life. He also practiced law until his death there on February 20, 1877. Tyler, *Encyclopedia of Virginia Biography*, II.

BROOKE, John Mercer (*Naval Commander, Scientist*), was born to General George Mercer and Lucy (Thomas) Brooke on December 18, 1826, in Tampa, Florida. After early tutoring, he joined the U.S. Navy in March 1841 and served on the *Delaware*. In 1845, he entered the U.S. Naval Academy from which he graduated in 1847. He was an Episcopalian. He was married twice, first to Elizabeth Selden Garnett and then to Kate Corbin Pendleton. In 1849 and 1850, he served on the U.S. Coastal Survey. Affiliated with the U.S. Naval Observatory from 1851 to 1853, he surveyed the route between California and China, tested the use of deep sea sounding apparatus, and made marine surveys of Japan. He received the Gold Science Medal of Berlin from King William I of Prussia. Brooke resigned his navy commission in April 1861 and entered the Confederate Navy. He spent the Civil War in service around Richmond, Virginia, where his inventive genius strengthened the otherwise weak naval resources of the Confederacy. He received a Confederate patent in 1861 for his submerged bow type of ship construction, which was used in building the ironclad ram, the *Virginia*. In 1863, he was made a captain in charge of ordnance and hydrography; later, he was promoted to the rank of commander. He also was the first to place the firing charge of the naval gun in front of the chamber, which lessened the initial tension of gases.

His invention was called the "Brooke" gun. After the war ended, he became a professor at Virginia Military Institute, where he taught from 1865 until his retirement in 1899. He died in Virginia in 1904. Scharf, *History of the Confederate Navy*; Tyler, *Encyclopedia of Virginia*, II.

BROOKE, Walker (*Congressman*), was born in Winchester, Clarke County, Virginia, on December 25, 1813. He graduated from the University of Virginia in 1835, studied law under Henry St. George Tucker, and was admitted to the Virginia bar in 1838. In 1840, he married Jane L. Eskridge. Brooke was a Whig who did not join the Democratic party until 1861. He taught school in Kentucky before moving to Lexington, Holmes County, Mississippi, in the 1840s where he built up a large law practice. He was elected to the lower house of the Mississippi legislature in 1848 and to the upper house in 1850 and 1852. In 1852-1853, he served as a member of the Mississippi Union party in the U.S. Senate. As a cooperationist member of the Mississippi constitutional convention of 1861, he was a cautious member of the Committee of 15 which drew up the Ordinance of Secession. He voted for secession and was the only Whig in the Mississippi delegation elected to the provisional Congress at Montgomery. In the provisional Congress, he was a member of the committee to organize the Executive Department and served on the Inauguration and the Patents Committees. Brooke became a Democrat but was defeated for the Confederate Senate by James Phelan (*q.v.*) in late 1861. In 1862, President Davis (*q.v.*) appointed him to the Board of Commissioners under the Sequestration Act. There he dealt with the confiscated estates of alien enemies. In late 1863, he was provost marshal of Vicksburg. Although he had much experience and ability, Brooke did little during the remainder of the war. He might have fallen out of sympathy with the Confederate cause and merely retired to private life. Little is known of his postwar career, save that his law practice declined and that he lost the will to participate in the reconstruction of his state. He died in poverty in Vicksburg, Mississippi, on February 19, 1869. *Biographical and Historical Memoirs of Mississippi*; Woods, "A Sketch of the Mississippi Secession Convention of 1861,—Its Membership and Work," *Publications of the Mississippi Historical Society*, VI.

BROWN, Albert Gallatin (*Congressman*), was born in Chester District, South Carolina, on May 31, 1813. His father, Joseph Brown, was a poor farmer and an old-school Federalist who moved his family to Mississippi in 1823 and became a well-to-do planter. The younger Brown attended Mississippi College from 1829 to 1832 and Jefferson College in Mississippi in 1832, studied law, and was admitted to the bar in 1833. In October 1835, he married Elizabeth Frances Taliaferro, who died soon after their marriage. He had two sons by his second marriage to Roberta Young on January 12, 1841. He began the practice of law in 1833 at Gallatin, Mississippi. As a Democratic representative from Copiah County in the Mississippi state legislature in 1835, where he was speaker *pro tem*, and again in 1838,

Brown opposed the national bank and supported Martin Van Buren for president. He served one term in the U.S. House of Representatives from 1839 to 1841 and was elected a circuit court judge in 1842. He resigned his judgeship in 1843 to run for governor. In 1844 and 1846, he was elected governor of Mississippi, where he worked to harmonize the state's Democratic factions and to reform the educational system, repudiated bank bonds, and debated the issue of slavery in the territories with Jefferson Davis (*q.v.*) and Thomas Quitman. He returned to the U.S. House in 1848, where he remained until 1854. He was elected to the U.S. Senate in 1854 and was reelected in 1859 on an extension of slavery platform. He resigned his Senate seat on January 14, 1861. Although an opponent of separate state secession, Brown supported Southern nationalist secession when it was proposed in the Mississippi secession convention. He gave money to help arm Mississippi troops. When the war began, he formed his own company and fought in the 18th Mississippi Regiment at the battle of First Manassus and was a captain in the infantry at Leesburg. He served in both permanent Confederate Senates; he supported the Davis administration in the first Senate and turned against it in the second. Brown was on the Conference, Inauguration, Naval Affairs, and Territorial Committees. He advocated extending conscription, limiting cotton production, and arming slaves, and was a watchdog of the military, vehemently opposing promotions of western generals he believed unworthy of command. He accepted the South's defeat, and after the war led an uneventful life as a farmer. His advocacy of peace with the Northern government proved unpopular, and he never again participated in politics. On June 12, 1880, he died in Terry, Hinds County, Mississippi. Ranck, *Albert Gallatin Brown: Radical Southern Nationalist*.

BROWN, John Calvin (*General*), son of Duncan and Margaret (Smith) Brown, was born on January 6, 1827, in Giles County, Tennessee. (A brother, Neill S. Brown, was governor of Tennessee from 1847 to 1849.) He graduated from Jackson College, Tennessee, in 1846 and was admitted to the Pulaski bar two years later. He developed an excellent law practice in Pulaski during the 1850s. He was first married to Ann Pointer and then to Elizabeth Childress in 1864 by whom he had four children. He was a Presbyterian and a Whig. He remained out of politics until 1860 when he became an elector on the John Bell Constitutional Unionist party ticket. While a moderate in politics, when his state seceded Brown enlisted in the Confederate Army as a private. At the battle of Fort Donelson in February 1862, he commanded the 3rd Tennessee Infantry. Wounded at Perryville during the Kentucky campaign of October 1862 and again at Chickamauga in September 1863, he was a hero at Missionary Ridge in 1863 and in the Dalton-Atlanta campaign of 1864. Brown was promoted to brigadier general on August 30, 1862, and to major general on August 4, 1846. He served under General John B. Hood (*q.v.*) as commander of Cheatham's Division. Brown was severely wounded during the charge at Franklin, Tennessee, in November 1864 and saw no further military duty. After the war, he returned to his Pulaski law practice. He was disfranchised until 1869 when he was elected to the state legislature. He was defeated in an 1875 U.S. Senate race by former President Andrew Johnson. He then returned to his law practice. After 1876, Brown worked for New York financier Jay Gould as president of the Texas and Pacific Railroad, and he lived at various times in Washington, D.C., and in Texas. In 1889, he returned to Tennessee as president of the Tennessee Coal, Iron, and Railroad Company. He died on August 17, 1889, in Red Boiling Springs, Tennessee. Evans, *Confederate Military History*, VIII.

BROWN, Joseph Emerson (*Governor*), son of Mackey and Sallie (Rice) Brown, was born in Pickens District, South Carolina, on April 15, 1821. His father, a poor farmer, moved to Georgia in the 1830s. The younger Brown attended Calhoun Academy in Anderson District, South Carolina, in 1840-1842, taught school at Canton, Georgia, in 1843, read for the law in 1844, and was admitted to the Georgia bar in 1845. After graduating from Yale Law School (a benefactor had paid his way), he began the practice of law in Canton in 1846. The following year he married Elizabeth Gresham. He was a staunch Baptist and a Democrat. Brown was elected to the state Senate in 1849 as a candidate of the people and served one term. He was appointed judge of the Superior Court of the Blue Ridge Circuit in 1855; he resigned in 1857 to run for governor and was elected. He was reelected each term until his resignation in late 1865. He remained a radical states' rights secessionist throughout his tenure in office. In late 1860, even before the war began, Brown captured Fort Pulaski. During the war, he generally opposed President Davis (*q.v.*), tried to control the disposition of all Georgia troops, and opposed all attempts at conscription. But he also attempted to get Georgia planters to reduce their cotton crops and to grow food for the Confederate Army. Brown's distrust of President Davis led to his alliance with Vice-President Alexander H. Stephens (*q.v.*) in an effort to achieve a negotiated peace settlement in late 1864. When the war ended, Brown was imprisoned in Washington but soon was pardoned by President Andrew Johnson. He returned to his law practice and removed to Atlanta. By 1868, Brown had joined the Republican party and had become an advocate of congressional Reconstruction. He was appointed chief justice of the Georgia Supreme Court in 1868 and served until 1870. In 1871, perhaps because of a sense that the party had no future in Georgia or because of charges of corruption leveled against the party, Brown returned to the Democratic party. He supported Horace Greeley for president in 1872. He also became quite successful in private business, attaining the presidency of the Western and Atlantic Railroad Company in 1870. Brown made a fortune speculating in real estate in the growing city of Atlanta. In 1880, Georgia's governor appointed him to the U.S. Senate, and in late 1880 he was elected in his own right. He served until 1891 when he went into semi-retirement in Atlanta. Brown also became a vigorous member of the Georgia Populist party. He died on November 30, 1894, in Atlanta. Bryan, *Confederate Georgia*; Hill, *Joseph E. Brown and the Confederacy*.

BROWNE, William Montague (*General, Cabinet Member*), was born on July 7, 1827, in Dublin, County Mayo, Ireland, to the Right Honorable D. Geoffrey Browne, a member of Parliament, and his wife. He attended Rugby Preparatory School, Trinity College, Dublin, and the Irish National University before seeing diplomatic service during the Crimean War. Browne was married but was childless. In 1853, he moved to New York, where he was political editor for the *Journal of Commerce*. In 1857, the Democrat Browne moved to Washington to edit the *Constitution*, a Buchanan organ. Four years later, he accompanied his intimate friend Howell Cobb (*q.v.*) to Athens, Georgia. While attending the Montgomery Confederate convention, he met and became a fast friend of Jefferson Davis (*q.v.*). He volunteered for service in the Confederate Army, but Davis appointed him to his personal staff. As a member of Davis's Department of Organization, he was a valuable aide. In the early months of 1862, he was also *ad interim* secretary of state. Although Browne participated in little actual fighting during the war, he was promoted to brigadier general in November 1864 and was sent to Savannah to serve under General Hugh Mercer during Sherman's siege. However, the Confederate Senate refused to confirm his promotion. He surrendered in North Carolina in mid-1865 and he was subsequently paroled. After the war, Browne settled near Athens, where he failed as a planter but edited a paper called *Farm and Home* and authored a biography of Alexander Stephens (*q.v.*) during the 1860s. Through his connections with Howell Cobb, Browne obtained a professorship of law, history, and political economy at the University of Georgia, which he held from 1866 until his death in Athens on April 28, 1883. Lonn, *Foreigners in the Confederacy*; Myers, *The Children of Pride*.

BRUCE, Eli Metcalfe (*Congressman*), was born in Flemingsburg, Kentucky, on February 22, 1828. He attended local schools, moved to Maysville, Kentucky, in 1846, and became a clerk in a dry goods store. He entered the commission merchant business and became a Democrat, but was too busy in business to enter politics. Bruce manufactured pig iron in Terre Haute, Indiana, from 1854 to 1859, and then entered the pork-packing business in St. Louis, Missouri. In 1861, he moved to Chattanooga, Tennessee, and became a source of supplies for the Confederacy. After First Manassas, he donated $1,000 to the Kentucky soldiers' relief fund; the Confederate government of Kentucky elected him to the first Confederate Congress. An opponent of the Davis administration, he supported the Confederate privateers and invested in the Erlanger Loan. His plan was to dispose of his cotton in France, but he was admonished by Congress for his actions. Reelected to the second Congress in 1864, he served ably on the Ways and Means Committee, and he became a supporter of the administration. He hoped to stop inflation by reducing the currency in circulation, but his fellow congressmen refused to support his plan. He also spoke often on the safety and care of prisoners of war. When the war ended, he went to Washington and received a pardon from

President Johnson. In late 1865, he moved to New York City and entered the hotel business. He died there on December 15, 1866. Warner and Yearns, *Biographical Register of the Confederate Congress*.

BRUCE, Horatio Washington (*Congressman*), was born into the Virginia family of Alexander and Amanda (Bragg) Bruce near Vanceburg in Lewis County, Kentucky, on February 22, 1830. Educated in the private schools of Lewis County during the 1840s, he married Elizabeth Barbour Helm on June 12, 1856. They had five children. Bruce was a salesman and bookkeeper at a general store in Vanceburg, a postmaster, and a schoolteacher in 1849 before being admitted to the bar in 1851. Originally a Whig, he joined the American party and represented Fleming County in the Kentucky legislature in 1855-1856. In 1858, he moved to Louisville to practice law, where he spent the rest of his life. He was commonwealth attorney for the Tenth Judicial District from 1856 until his resignation in 1859. In 1860, he supported John Bell for president and was a states' rights candidate for the U.S. House of Representatives. He was a delegate to the state convention in Russellville in October 1861 and to the Kentucky sovereignty convention, where he served on the legislative council and advocated secession. In 1862, he was elected to the Confederate House, where he supported the Davis administration. In Congress, he served on the Foreign Affairs, Patents, Commerce, Enrolled Bills, and Inauguration Committees. After the war, he returned to Louisville to practice law. He was named circuit judge for the Ninth Judicial District in 1868, and from 1873 to 1880 he was chancellor of the University of Louisville. In 1880, he was attorney for the Louisville and Nashville Railroad. He died in Louisville on January 22, 1903. Levin (ed.), *The Lawyers and Lawmakers of Kentucky*.

BRYAN, Goode (*General*), son of Joseph and Anne (Goode) Bryan, was born on August 31, 1811, in Hancock County, Georgia. He graduated twenty-fifth in a class of thirty-six from the U.S. Military Academy in 1834. He was first married to Frances Maria Myers in July 1849; he had a son and three daughters by his second marriage to Anna E. Twiggs, daughter of General David E. Twiggs. Bryan was garrisoned at the Augusta arsenal in 1834-1835, resigning his military commission in 1836 to become a civil engineer for the Augusta and Athens Railroad until 1839. He then moved to Alabama and became a planter. A Democrat, Bryan served in the Alabama House in 1843-1844. From 1842 to 1846, he was a colonel in the state militia. During the Mexican War, he was a major in the 1st Alabama Volunteers. In 1849, he returned to Georgia and became a planter, residing in Jefferson County until 1853 and in Richmond County from 1853 to 1861. As a Lee County delegate to the secession convention, he voted for secession. When the war began, Bryan entered the Confederate Army as a captain in the 16th Georgia Regiment. Promoted to colonel in February 1862, he served under General Thomas R. R. Cobb (*q.v.*) in Magruder's Division. He saw action during the Seven Days' battles, at Fredericksburg, Chancellorsville, and Gettysburg. Promoted to brigadier general on August 29, 1863, he accompanied James Longstreet (*q. v.*), under whom he served during the East Tennessee campaign, in the siege of Knoxville and the attack on Fort Saunders. In Virginia during the spring of 1864, he fought at Spotsylvania, Cold Harbor, in the Wilderness, and at Richmond and Petersburg. Failing health prompted his retirement from military service in September 1864. After the war, he returned to planting around Augusta and had no part in public life. He soon became semi-retired. Bryan died on August 16, 1885, in Augusta. Northen (ed.), *Men of Mark in Georgia*, II.

BUCHANAN, Franklin (*Naval Commander*), son of Dr. George and Laetitia (McKean) Buchanan, was born in Baltimore, Maryland, on September 11, 1800. He was an Episcopalian. He married Ann Catherine Lloyd, daughter of Governor Edward Lloyd of Maryland, in 1835. He entered the U.S. Navy as a midshipman in January 1815. Buchanan served five years in the Mediterranean and six years suppressing piracy in the Caribbean. He was promoted to lieutenant in January 1825 and to master commander in September 1841. In 1845, Buchanan organized the U.S. Naval Academy at Annapolis, where he was the first superintendent from 1845 to 1847. During the Mexican War, he commanded the *Germantown*, which landed troops at Vera Cruz and captured San Juan d'Ulloa. He commanded the flagship *Susquehanna* during Commodore Matthew Perry's expedition to Japan in 1852-1855. In 1855, he was promoted to captain, and in 1859, he was made commander of the Washington Navy Yard. Loyal to the South, he resigned from the navy on April 22, 1861. Buchanan enlisted as a captain in the Confederate Navy in September 1861 and was made chief of the Bureau of Orders and Details, serving in that capacity until February 1, 1862. He commanded the ironclad *Virginia* in 1861 and was wounded at Hampton Roads. On August 21, 1862, he was promoted to the rank of admiral and had assumed command at Mobile Harbor. Buchanan cooperated with General Dabney H. Maury (*q. v.*) to hold Mobile. In command of the ram *Tennessee*, he was defeated by Admiral David Farragut in the battle of Mobile Bay, where his leg was broken and he was taken prisoner in August 1864. He was exchanged in February 1865. Buchanan then returned to his family home in Talbot County, Maryland, and saw no further service. He was named president of the Maryland Agricultural College in 1866 and resigned that post in June 1869. He moved to Mobile in 1869 and became secretary of the Life Insurance Company of America. He returned to his home in Talbot County and died in retirement there on May 11, 1874. Tilghman, *History of Talbot County, Maryland*, I.

BUCKNER, Simon Bolivar (*General*), was born to Aylett Hartswell and Elizabeth Ann (Morehead) Buckner on April 21, 1823, in Hart County, Kentucky, where his father was a financially unsuccessful manufacturer. After attending the academy at Hopkinsville, Kentucky, he graduated eleventh in a class of twenty-five from the U.S. Military Academy in 1844. Bucker was an Episcopalian and a Democrat. He married Mary Kingsbury on May 2, 1850, and Delia Claiborne on June 10, 1885. By his second marriage, he had a son who died in childhood and a daughter. Buckner was an assistant professor of ethics at West Point in 1845-1846 and an assistant instructor in tactics from 1848 to 1850. A quartermaster at the beginning of the Mexican War, he was breveted first lieutenant for gallantry at Churubusco and was breveted captain at Molino del Rey. He was promoted to first lieutenant in 1851 and to captain the following year, but he resigned his commission in 1855 to deal in real estate in Chicago. In 1860, he returned to Hart County, Kentucky, to become inspector general of state guards. Although he owned no slaves and opposed secession, Buckner offered his services to the Confederacy and was commissioned a brigadier general commanding all Confederate troops in Kentucky on September 14, 1861. In February 1862, he surrendered Fort Donelson, was captured, and was later exchanged. He led a division at the Kentucky battles of Munfordville and Perryville in the fall of 1862, after which he spent several months as commander of the Department of South Alabama, working on the engineering of the Mobile defenses. In May 1863, he commanded the Department of East Tennessee and West Virginia, and later the same year he was a corps commander at Chickamauga. In the spring of 1864, he joined the Army of Northern Virginia, where he was promoted to lieutenant general. In late 1864, he was made corps commander of the Trans-Mississippi Department but saw little action. During the war, he was a member of the Kentucky faction in the army which opposed Braxton Bragg (*q.v.*) and President Davis (*q.v.*). He surrendered his army after Lee surrendered. Since his terms of surrender denied him the right to return to Kentucky, Buckner lived in New Orleans for three years and was in the insurance business. In 1868, he returned to Kentucky and became editor of the Louisville *Courier* for the next twenty years. From 1887 to 1892, he was Democratic governor of Kentucky. He then farmed on his estate near Munfordville, Kentucky. In 1896, he bolted the party to run for vice-president on the National Gold Standard ticket. Buckner went into retirement but became a noted platform speaker. He had the distinction of being a pallbearer at the funeral of U. S. Grant. He outlived all other Confederate veterans of his military rank, dying on January 8, 1914, in Hart County, Kentucky. Johnson, *Three Representative Kentuckians*; Stickles, *Simon Bolivar Buckner*.

BULLOCH, James Dunwoody (*Diplomat*), was born in Savannah, Georgia, on June 25, 1823, to Major James Stephens and Hester Amarinthia (Elliott) Bulloch, daughter of U.S. Senator John Elliott. He was married twice, to Elizabeth Euphemia Caskie on November 19, 1851, who died in 1854, and to Mrs. Harriett Cross Foster in January 1857. Bullock enlisted as a midshipman in the U.S. Navy in 1839, sailed on the *United States*, and was stationed off the coast of Brazil on the *Potomac*. In 1842, he cruised the Mediterranean on the battleship *Delaware*. He attended naval school at Philadelphia in 1844-1845, graduating second in his class. During the Mexican War, he saw duty on the Pacific Coast. He later commanded the *Georgia*, the first subsidized mail steamer to California. From 1849 to 1851, he served on the U.S. Coastal Survey. Bullock joined the Confederate Navy as a commander in Georgia. Although he had requested a line job, his talents were considered too valuable and instead the Confederate government sent him as a naval agent to England where he was to buy or build naval vessels. After furnishing the Confederacy with the English cruisers *Florida*, *Alabama*, and *Shenandoah* and the French ram *Stonewall*, Bulloch aided in Confederate diplomatic negotiations. After the war, he was excluded from pardon and so resided in Liverpool, England, where he entered the mercantile business and became a scholar and master of maritime and international law. He published *The Secret Service of the Confederate States in Europe* in 1884. Bulloch died in retirement in Liverpool on January 7, 1901. Northen (ed.), *Men of Mark in Georgia*, II; Owsley, *King Cotton Diplomacy*.

BURNETT, Henry Cornelius (*Congressman*), was born on November 25, 1825, in Essex County, Virginia. His parents, Dr. Isaac and Martha (Garnett) Burnett, brought him to Kentucky as a child, where he was educated in the academy at Hopkinsville, studied law, and was admitted to the bar in Cadiz in 1847. He was a member of the Christian church. His marriage on April 13, 1847, to Mary A. Terry produced three children. From 1850 to 1852, he was a clerk of the circuit court. He was a Democratic candidate for Congress in 1854 but dropped out of the race after making a deal with his opponent, Linn Boyd, who agreed not to seek another term. Burnett was elected to the U.S. House of Representatives in 1855, where he served until his resignation in 1861. He originally opposed, but later supported, Kentucky's secession in 1861. Burnett volunteered for duty in the Confederate Army, fighting at Fort Donelson as a colonel in the 8th Kentucky Infantry. He was elected to the Confederate state legislature of Kentucky and served in the provisional and first and second Confederate Senates from 1861 to 1865. He supported the Davis administration throughout the war. A severe critic of Braxton Bragg (*q.v.*), Burnett belonged to that western clique of congressmen who urged the administration to invade Kentucky. He served on the Finance, Building, Claims, Commerce, Conference, Judiciary, Naval Affairs, and many special committees while in the Senate. After the war, he returned to his law practice. He died of cholera at Cadiz, Kentucky on September 28, 1866. Connelly and Jones, *The Politics of Command*; Levin (ed.), *Lawyers and Lawmakers of Kentucky*.

BURNETT, Theodore Legrand (*Congressman*), was born on November 14, 1829, in Spencer County, Kentucky. His parents died when he was young. He attended Transylvania University and studied law with the eminent Kentucky judge Mark Houston in 1846. A Whig, he practiced law in nearby Taylorsville and became county attorney for Spencer County in 1847. He served in the Mexican

War during 1847. He was an Episcopalian. He married Elizabeth S. Gilbert on January 29, 1852; they had five children. He was a Whig unionist in 1860, but when Lincoln called for an invasion of Kentucky, he volunteered for service in the Confederate Army. He served in the Army of Tennessee as a major on the staff of General John S. Williams (*q.v.*). Burnett was elected to both Confederate Congresses and generally supported the Davis administration. When the war ended he was destitute. He returned to his law practice at Taylorsville but moved to Louisville in 1866. In 1870, he became city attorney of Louisville, and later he served as a city judge for many years. He died in Louisville on October 30, 1917. *Encyclopedia of Kentucky*; Levin (ed.), *The Lawyers and Lawmakers of Kentucky*.

BURTON, James H. (*Bureaucrat*), was born in Virginia. He married and had at least one daughter who lived in Winchester, Virginia. Little else is known of his early life. When the war started, he joined the Virginia Ordnance Department. His talents were noted by Josiah Gorgas (*q.v.*), and he served admirably under him. However, Burton incurred the wrath of Congressman James L. Orr (*q.v.*) for allegedly dealing with private gunmakers. He was reprimanded by Gorgas. Burton built the Macon, Georgia, armory in 1862 and became the superintendent of small-arms production in 1863. He also purchased machinery for the Confederacy in England. In 1864, he commanded the Macon, Atlanta, Columbus, and Tallahassee armories. In June 1864, he was named inspector of all armories of the Confederate states, and proved an extremely important administrator. Burton disappeared into obscurity when the war ended. Unsubstantiated rumors claim that he emigrated to the West Coast. Vandiver, *Ploughshares into Swords*.

BUTLER, Matthew Calbraith (*General*), was born to Dr. William Butler and his wife Jane Tweedy (Perry) on March 8, 1836, in Greenville, South Carolina. His grandfather had been a Revolutionary War hero, and his father was a U.S. Army surgeon. Although he accompanied his father to Arkansas in 1848, he returned to South Carolina in 1851 to live with his uncle, U.S. Senator Andrew P. Butler of Edgefield. Butler attended Edgefield Academy and South Carolina College in 1856, studied law, and was admitted to the bar in 1857. He practiced law in Edgefield. In 1858, he married Maria Calhoun Pickens, daughter of Governor Francis W. Pickens. In 1906, his first wife having died, Butler married Mrs. Nannie Whitman. He was a secessionist Democrat and served in the state legislature in 1860-1861. He resigned from the legislature and became captain of the Edgefield volunteers to the Confederate Army. At the battle of First Manassas he was a captain in the Hampton Legion. Promoted to major, he fought gallantly at the battle of Williamsburg in May 1862. As colonel of the 2nd Regiment South Carolina Cavalry, he participated in the battle of Second Manassas, in the Maryland campaigns, and in the Chambersburg raid of 1862. In June 1863 at the battle of Brandy Station, he lost his right foot. When he returned to duty on September 1,

1863, he was promoted to brigadier general. Butler attained the rank of major general of cavalry on September 27, 1864, having displayed heroism at Spotsylvania and in the Wilderness. He also participated in the 1864 battles of Howe's Shop, Cold Harbor, and Trevilian Station, and in the spring of 1865, he tried to stop Sherman in the Carolinas. He surrendered to the Union Army in April 1865 and was soon paroled. Financially ruined by the war, he again practiced law in Edgefield. Butler returned to the state legislature in 1866 and lost a bid for lieutenant governor of South Carolina in 1870. From 1876 until his defeat by Ben Tillman in 1894, Butler was a Democratic U.S. senator from South Carolina. He practiced law in Washington, D.C., in 1895 but later returned to Edgefield. In 1898, President McKinley made him a major general in the Spanish-American War. Butler was elected vice-president of the Southern Historical Association in 1903. The following year he moved to Mexico, where he was president of a mining company. He died on April 14, 1909, in semi-retirement in Washington, D.C. Brooks, *Butler and His Cavalry in the War of Secession*.

C

CABELL, William Lewis (*General*), son of General Benjamin W. S. Cabell and Sarah Eppes (Doswell), was born in Danville, Virginia, on January 1, 1827. He graduated thirty-third in a class of forty-four from the U.S. Military Academy in 1850 and began his military career as a second lieutenant in the U.S. Army. He was an Episcopalian. He had five sons and a daughter by his July 22, 1856, marriage to Harriet A. Rector, daughter of Governor Henry Massey Rector (*q.v.*) of Arkansas. Cabell was promoted to first lieutenant and regimental quartermaster in 1855 and to captain in the Quartermaster Corps in 1858. He participated in the Utah expedition in 1858. He resigned his commission in 1861 and volunteered for the Confederate Army. As a major during the early days of the war, he assisted in organizing the Quartermaster, Commissary, and Ordnance Departments. At the battle of First Manassas he was the chief quartermaster of the Army of the Potomac under P.G.T. Beauregard (*q.v.*). He was transferred to the Trans-Mississippi Department early in 1862 and offered invaluable assistance at the battle of Elkhorn Tavern and commanded all troops on the White River in Arkansas. In late 1862, he saw action at Iuka, Saltillo, Corinth, and Hatchie Bridge, where he was wounded while commanding the rear of the army as it retreated from Corinth, Mississippi. In February 1863, upon his recovery, he organized a cavalry brigade in northwest Arkansas, and he sanctioned the recruitment of soldiers from that western state. After promotion to the rank of brigadier general on April 23, 1863, he fought in the battles of Poison Spring, Marks' Mill, and Jenkins' Ferry in Arkansas during the spring of 1864. In October of that year, he was captured during General Sterling Price's (*q.v.*) raid into Missouri and was not released until August 1865. After the war, Cabell moved to Fort Smith, Arkansas, where he studied law and was admitted to the bar in 1866. In December 1872, he moved to Dallas, Texas, to practice law. He served four terms as mayor of Dallas between 1874 and 1882. Cabell, a well-known Democratic politician in the state, was also vice-president and general manager for Texas Trunk Railway during the 1880s. From 1885 to 1889, he served as U.S. marshal for the northern district of Texas. When he retired from public life and business, Cabell became active in Confederate veteran organizations. He died in Dallas on February 22, 1911. Evans, *Confederate Military History*, X.

CALLAHAN, Samuel B. (*Congressman*), was born in 1834 in Eufaula, Alabama. His parentage is unknown. At the age of three he was taken to the Indian Territory, where his father subsequently died of exposure. He was married and had at least six children. He became a wealthy rancher near Okmulgee and owned a large number of slaves. During the 1850s, though not an Indian, Callahan was elected a member of the Creek tribal council and was later elected chief justice of the Indian court system. An ardent states' rights supporter, he joined the Confederate Army immediately after war was declared. He had been the Creek Nation's delegate to the Washington government and had come to believe that the Confederacy offered more stability to the Creeks. During the war, he organized a company of Creeks, became its captain, and joined Sterling Price's (*q.v.*) army in Missouri. In 1862, he was elected to the first Confederate House as the representative of the Creek and Seminole Nations. A nonvoting member, he served well in an advisory capacity to the Committee on Military Affairs. When his term ended, he continued in Richmond as an advisor on Indian affairs. He lost all his property during the war and the Union army forced him and his wife and children to leave the Indian Territory. Callahan settled in Texas and farmed for twenty years. In 1885, he was able to return to the Indian Territory where he rebuilt his ranch. But the "blackleg" epidemic of 1887 destroyed his cattle herd, and he was once more impoverished. He spent the last years of his life as a poor farmer. He died on February 17, 1911, in Muskogee, Oklahoma. Abel, *The American Indian as Slaveholder and Secessionist*, II; *Confederate Veteran*, XIX.

CAMPBELL, Alexander William (*General*), was born to the banker William Campbell and his wife Jane E. (Porter) on June 4, 1828, in Nashville, Tennessee. He attended Jackson Male Academy and West Tennessee College before studying law at Cumberland University in 1848. Campbell began a law practice in Jackson,

Tennessee. On January 13, 1852, he married Ann Dixon Allen, by whom he had three sons and three daughters. A Democrat, he was elected mayor of Jackson in 1856. From 1854 to 1860, he was a U.S. district attorney for the western district of Tennessee. After enlisting as a private in the Confederate Army early in 1861, he was promoted first to major and later to colonel in the 33rd Regiment of Tennessee Infantry, serving with distinction in the battle of Shiloh, during which he was also wounded in the arm. In addition, Campbell participated in the battles of Perryville and Murfreesboro in 1862. In 1862-1863, he was assistant adjutant and inspector general on the staff of General Leonidas Polk (*q.v.*). Later, he was attached to the Volunteer and Conscript Bureau under General Gideon J. Pillow, and in 1863, Governor Isham Harris (*q.v.*) made him inspector general of the provisional army of Tennessee. Captured the same year, Campbell was held a prisoner for over a year. Upon his release, he was promoted to brigadier general in March 1865. He served during the last part of the war as a commander of cavalry under General Nathan B. Forrest (*q.v.*), and surrendered in May 1865 with Forrest's troops. After the war, he returned to his law practice in Jackson. Restrictions seem to have kept him from public life for some years. He was later a bank president, and in 1880, he tried unsuccessfully for the Democratic gubernatorial nomination of Tennessee. Campbell died on June 13, 1893, in Jackson. Speer, *Sketches of Prominent Tennesseans*.

CAMPBELL, John Archibald (*Bureaucrat*), son of the distinguished lawyer Duncan Greene Campbell and Mary (Williamson), was born on June 24, 1811, at Washington, Wilkes County, Georgia. He was a cousin of Lucius Q. C. Lamar (*q.v.*). After graduating first in his class at Franklin College (later the University of Georgia) in 1826, he received an appointment to the U.S. Military Academy but resigned upon his father's death in 1828 after three years of study. He was a Presbyterian and a Democrat. He married Anne Esther Goldthwaite in 1830 and had several children. He moved to Montgomery, Alabama, where he studied law and was admitted to the bar in 1830. In 1836, he was elected to the state legislature. Campbell moved to Mobile, Alabama, in 1837, where he continued his law practice. In 1842, he served as a district judge and was elected to the state legislature, where he served until 1846. In 1850, he was a moderate delegate to the Southern rights convention at Nashville. From 1853 until May 1860, when he resigned, he was an associate justice of the U.S. Supreme Court. He followed Alabama in its secession movement. In March and April 1861, he was a mediator between the Confederate peace commissioners and federal authorities in Washington, D.C. Because he was distrusted in the South for seeming Unionist sympathies, he remained in private life until the fall of 1862. Campbell was appointed assistant secretary of war in the Davis cabinet in October 1862 and served throughout the remainder of the war. He was the chief administrator of the conscript law. In late 1864, Campbell, realizing that the Confederacy was exhausted, promoted the Hampton Roads Peace Conference and was a member of it in February 1865. At the end of the war, he was confined to Fort Pulaski for six months. He was released but never pardoned. He moved to New Orleans in 1866, where he developed a large law practice. In 1877, he was Samuel J. Tilden's legal counsel for the contested presidential election. Campbell died in Baltimore, Maryland, on March 12 or 13, 1889. Conner, *John Archibald Campbell*; Kirkland, *The Peacemakers of 1864*.

CAMPBELL, Josiah Abigal Patterson (*Congressman*), was born on March 2, 1830, in Abeville District, South Carolina, to the Presbyterian minister Robert B. Campbell and his wife Mary (Patterson). Educated at Camden Academy and Davidson College in North Carolina, he studied law in Madison County, Mississippi, where his father had moved in 1845. In 1847, he began his law practice in Kosciusko, Mississippi. He married Eugenie E. Nash on May 23, 1850. The following year he entered the state legislature as a Democrat, where he served until 1853. He returned to private practice and was elected speaker of the lower house in 1859. As a secessionist delegate to the Montgomery convention in 1861, he helped to write the Confederate Constitution. He was a member of the provisional Confederate Congress, served on the Accounts and Territories Committees and was a president pro tempore. In 1862, he entered the Confederate Army, where he fought as a regimental commander, attaining the rank of lieutenant colonel, at Iuka and Corinth, Mississippi, and was wounded. He also served under General Leonidas Polk (*q.v.*) at Vicksburg and was a member of Polk's Corps' military court. He served in that capacity until the end of the war when he returned to his home. After the war, he was elected a circuit court judge in 1865 but was forced to retire in 1870 when he refused to take the test oath. He was offered, but declined, a professorship of law at the University of Mississippi in 1871 and was named chief justice of the state Supreme Court in 1876. In 1880, he served on the commission which revised the state legal code. He served on the state supreme court until 1894 when he retired. After his retirement from public life, he practiced law in Canton, Mississippi, for a few years. He died on January 10, 1917, in Canton. *Biographical and Historical Memoirs of Mississippi*; Lynch, *The Bench and Bar of Mississippi*.

CANTEY, James (*General*), was born on December 30, 1818, in Camden, Kershaw County, South Carolina, to the planter John Cantey and his wife Emma Susanna (Richardson). He attended Hatfield's School in Camden and graduated from South Carolina College in 1833, after which he studied law under Henry De Saussure in Charleston. Cantey was a Democrat, a Mason, and an Episcopalian. He was married to Martha Elizabeth Benton on April 14, 1858; they had two sons and a daughter. He practiced law in Camden and served in the South Carolina legislature during the 1840s. During the Mexican War, he was a second lieutenant and later a captain in the Palmetto Regiment. In 1849, he settled in Russell County, Alabama, where he became a planter. A secessionist, he volunteered for service in the Confederate Army when the war began. As a colonel of the 15th Alabama Infantry, he served with General Thomas J. Jackson (*q.v.*) during the Valley campaign and was credited with the Confederate victory at Cross Keys, Virginia, on June 8, 1862. He was promoted to brigadier general on January 8, 1863, and spent much of the last part of the war as a commander stationed at Mobile, where he was responsible for the defense of that port city. He also took part in the Atlanta campaign and surrendered at Greensboro, North Carolina. Upon his release he returned to his plantation. He seemed to have never requested pardon. Cantey died at Fort Mitchell, Russell County, Alabama, on June 30, 1874. Owen, *History of Alabama and Dictionary of Alabama Biography*, III.

CAPERS, Ellison (*General*), son of Methodist Bishop William Capers and his wife Susan (McGill), was born on October 14, 1837, in Charleston, South Carolina. Capers attended Charleston High School and graduated from South Carolina Military Academy in 1857. He taught mathematics and rhetoric at the Citadel in Charleston in 1858 and attained the rank of professor in 1860. Although Capers was also a lawyer, he never practiced. On February 24, 1859, he married Charlotte Rebecca Palmer, by whom he had five sons and two daughters. He was a member of the Democratic party. At the beginning of the Civil War, he enlisted in the South Carolina Rifles, and during the early bombardment of Fort Sumter, he commanded the light artillery at nearby Sullivan's Island. Later a colonel in the 24th South Carolina Volunteers, he was stationed in Wilmington, North Carolina, in 1862. In 1863, he was wounded twice, the first time in May, during the relief of Vicksburg, and the second in late summer, during the battle of Chickamauga. He recovered sufficiently to command Gist's Brigade in the seige of Atlanta and Jonesville in 1864, but he was severely wounded during the battle of Franklin, Tennessee, in November of that year. Promoted to brigadier general on March 1, 1865, Capers served during the last days of the war under General Joseph E. Johnston (*q.v.*) in North Carolina. At the conclusion of the war he returned to Charleston. From 1866 to 1868, he was secretary of state for South Carolina. Capers became an Episcopal minister after the war, serving in Greenville from 1867 to 1887 and in Columbia from 1887 to 1893. In July 1893, he was named Episcopal bishop of South Carolina, and in 1904, he became chancellor of the University of the South in Sewanee, Tennessee. A member of the Southern Historical Association, he also edited the South Carolina volume of *Confederate Military History* in 1899. Capers died in Columbia, South Carolina, on April 22, 1908. Capers, *The Soldier-Bishop Ellison Capers*.

CAPERTON, Allen Taylor (*Congressman*), was born into the wealthy planting family of Hugh and Jane (Erskine) Caperton on November 21, 1810, in Union,

Monroe County, Virginia. He attended schools in Huntsville, Alabama, and the University of Virginia before graduating seventh in the class of 1832 at Yale College and studying law in a Staunton, Virginia, law office. In 1832, he married Harriet Echois. He began a law practice in Staunton in 1833 but soon abandoned it for politics and business. Caperton served as a Whig in the Virginia House of Delegates in 1841-1842 and again from 1857 to 1859. From 1844 to 1848 and in 1859-1860, he represented Monroe County in the state Senate. He also was a director of the James River and Kanawha Canal Company and became a well-to-do financier. As a delegate to the Virginia constitutional convention of 1850, he sided with the western counties and argued for a white basis of voter representation. While no secessionist, he nevertheless voted for secession at the state convention because he believed that it would bring peace. The members of the Virginia state legislature elected him to the Confederate Senate in late 1861, where he served throughout the war. An opponent of the Davis administration in both Senates, Caperton served on the Accounts, Conference, Engrossment and Enrollment, Foreign Relations, and Judiciary Committees. After the war, he removed to his family home in Union, and he counseled moderation. Caperton at first went back to private life; when his restrictions ended, he entered political life. As a Democratic U.S. senator from West Virginia in 1875-1876, he served on the Railroad and Claims Committees, and he helped to bring the coal and timber wealth of West Virginia to the knowledge of investors. He died in Washington, D.C., on July 26, 1876. Atkinson (ed.), *Bench and Bar of West Virginia*; Oren, *A History of Monroe County, West Virginia*.

CARROLL, David Williamson (*Congressman*), son of Henry Carroll, was born in Baltimore, Maryland, on March 11, 1816. A Catholic, he attended St. Mary's College in Baltimore in the mid-1830s and moved to Pine Bluff, Arkansas, in 1836. He was an Arkansas surveyor until 1839, when he returned to Maryland for five more years. In 1844, Carroll returned to Pine Bluff to teach school. Two years later, he was deputy clerk of the U.S. district court, and in 1848, he was admitted to the bar. Carroll, a staunch Democrat, represented Pulaski County in the Arkansas legislature of 1850. In 1853, he was a land agent for a Pine Bluff land office. He was a secessionist. When the Civil War began, he volunteered for duty in the Confederacy and was appointed a colonel in the 18th Arkansas Regiment. He participated in the battle of DeVall's Bluff and served in the army throughout most of the war. When Augustus H. Garland (*q.v.*) went to the Confederate Senate, Carroll was elected to his House seat on January 11, 1865. While in Congress, Carroll advocated changing the Cotton Bureau and making it responsible to the planters; he also served on the Commerce Committee and the special committee to levy additional taxes. After the war he returned to Arkansas to practice law. From 1866 to 1868, he was probate and county judge of Jefferson County, Arkansas. From 1868 to 1878, he practiced law, and from 1878 to 1887, he was a judge holding the rank of chancellor of the state. Carroll lived in retirement in Little Rock, Arkansas and died there on June 24, 1905. Thomas, *Arkansas in War and Reconstruction*; *Arkansas Gazette*, June 24, 1905.

CARTER, John Carpenter (*General*), was born in Waynesboro, Georgia, on December 19, 1837. He attended the University of Virginia from 1854 to 1856 and later studied law at Cumberland University in Lebanon, Tennessee, under Judge Abram Caruthers, whose daughter he married. Carter was an Episcopalian. He taught law at Cumberland Law School before moving to Memphis in 1860 to practice law. He was commissioned in the Confederate Army as a captain in the 38th Tennessee Infantry and was distinguished for his performance during the battle of Shiloh in the spring of 1862. Carter also fought heroically in the battles of Perryville and Murfreesboro. He was appointed regimental commander during the battle of Chickamauga in the summer of 1863 and participated in the battle of Missionary Ridge before attaining the rank of brigadier general on July 7, 1864, during the Atlanta campaign. At Jonesboro, Georgia, he served as temporary division commander of Benjamin F. Cheatham's (*q.v.*) Division. Carter's last assignment was under Hood (*q.v.*) in Tennessee, where he was mortally wounded while leading the assault on the federal works at Franklin. He died on December 10, 1864. Connelly, *Autumn of Glory*; Warner, *Generals in Gray*.

CARUTHERS, Robert Looney (*Congressman, Governor*), was born on July 31, 1800, in Smith County, Tennessee. He was educated at Woodward's Academy and Greenville College and studied law. He was admitted to the bar in Carthage, Tennessee, in 1823. Caruthers removed to Lebanon, Tennessee, and became clerk of the state House of Representatives in 1824. For a time he was editor of the *Tennessee Republican*. A Presbyterian and a member of the Sons of Temperance, he became a Whig leader in state politics. He was states' attorney from 1827 to 1832, became brigadier general of the Tennessee State militia in 1834, and served in the state House of Representatives in 1835. He served in the U.S. House from 1841 to 1843. In 1844, he became a Democrat. He helped to found Cumberland University in Lebanon in 1842 and headed its law department in 1847. He also served as judge of the Supreme Court of Tennessee from 1852 until 1861. Throughout, he was a staunch secessionist. However, he was a member of the Washington Peace Conference in 1861 and tried to avoid war between the states. He was elected to the provisional Confederate Congress and served ably on the Judiciary Committee. The Tennessee secessionists elected him governor in 1862, but he was unable to take office because of Union occupation. He served in various minor governmental posts throughout the rest of the war. After the war, he moved to Wilson County, Tennessee, where he formed a law partnership with John C. Gant in 1865. He was indicted for treason but was never brought to trial. In the 1870s, he became a professor of law at Cumberland

University, a position he held for the remainder of his life. Caruthers died in Lebanon, Tennessee, on October 2, 1882. Connelly, *Army of the Heartland*; Robinson, *Justice in Grey*.

CHALMERS, James Ronald (*General*), son of Joseph Williams and Fannie (Henderson) Chalmers, was born on January 11, 1831, in Halifax County, Virginia. His father moved the family to Tennessee in 1835 and to Mississippi in 1839, where the elder Chalmers later served in the U.S. Senate and the younger Chalmers attended St. Thomas Hall in Holly Springs. After graduating second in the class of 1851 from South Carolina College, he was admitted to the bar in 1853 and began his practice in Holly Springs. In 1858, he became district attorney for the Seventh Judicial District of Mississippi. Chalmers, a states' rights Democrat and a staunch secessionist, was a delegate to the Mississippi secession convention of 1861, where he was chairman of the Military Affairs Committee. He entered the Confederate Army as a colonel in the 9th Mississippi Regiment and was sent to Pensacola. Promoted to brigadier general on February 13, 1862, he was a brigade commander whose splendid performance during the battle of Shiloh was widely recognized in the spring of 1862. Chalmers, who was considered a brilliant general of cavalry and who responded well under great pressure, served in the Kentucky campaign with Bragg (*q.v.*) in 1862 and distinguished himself at the battle of Murfreesboro. In April 1863 he was given command of the military district of Mississippi and eastern Louisiana under General Nathan B. Forrest (*q.v.*). During 1864 as a cavalry brigade commander under Forrest and later John B. Hood (*q.v.*), he participated in all military operations in northern Mississippi, Kentucky, and west Tennessee. By February 1865, he commanded all Mississippi cavalry. He surrendered in May 1865 and was soon paroled. After the war, he returned to his law practice before serving in the state Senate from 1875 to 1877. From 1877 to 1881, he was a Democratic U.S. congressman from Mississippi, and in 1884, he was elected to a final term in the U.S. House on the Independent Republican and Greenback ticket. He lost his bid for reelection in 1886. Although he maintained a home in Vicksburg, Mississippi, for the rest of his life, he spent his final years practicing law in Memphis, Tennessee, where he died on April 9, 1898. Evans, *Confederate Military History*, VII; Mathes, *The Old Guard in Gray*.

CHAMBERS, Henry Cousins (*Congressman*), was born in Limestone County, Alabama, on July 26, 1823, to Henry H. and ——— (Smith) Chambers. His father practiced medicine in Alabama and also served that state as a Democrat in the U.S. Senate. All that is known of the younger Chambers' early life is that his father died in 1826 and that his mother raised him. He was a Presbyterian and a graduate of Princeton College in 1844. Chambers settled in Robson Landing, Mississippi, and became a successful planter. He married Susan Alyda Young, by whom he had three children. It is not known whether he had a prewar public career, although he was recorded as a secessionist. When the Civil War began, he joined the Mississippi army and eventually rose to the rank of colonel. He saw action in northern Mississippi and Alabama, but the extent of that action is not known. In late 1861, he killed William A. Lake in a duel over the campaign for election to the Confederate House. Chambers was elected to the Congress in the Fourth Mississippi Congressional District and was reelected in 1864. He was a Davis administration supporter, and he held positions on the Conference, Flag and Seal, Impressments, Military Affairs, and Commerce Committees. While in Congress he proposed a plan to supervise impressments, the question of illegal impressments having caused much trouble in his own state. When the war ended, Chambers returned to Mississippi where he attempted to plant on his ruined lands. In late 1865, he was elected to the U.S. House of Representatives, but the national Congress refused to seat him. Under political restrictions, Chambers never really recovered from the hardships of the war; he retired to his plantation in Bolivar County. He died in Carson, Mississippi, on May 1, 1871. Stubbs, *Early Settlers in Alabama*; Yearns, *The Confederate Congress*.

CHAMBLISS, John Randolph, Sr. (*Congressman*), was born on March 4, 1809, in Sussex County, Virginia, to Lewis H. Chambliss. He attended local public schools and taught public school before studying law in Winchester, Virginia, from 1828 to 1829. A lawyer who also planted, Chambliss resided in Hicksford, Greensville County, Virginia. A Baptist, he was a Whig and a unionist, elected commonwealth attorney for the county in 1849. He opposed secession at the Virginia secession convention. He married Tilly Woodruff and they had one son, John Randolph Chambliss, Jr., who was a colonel in the 13th Virginia Cavalry Regiment. Chambliss, Sr., was elected to the first Confederate Congress, where he served on the Committee on Naval Affairs from 1862 until 1864. He was a vigorous supporter of the Davis administration and its policies on building gunboats for the protection of the Virginia coastline. Chambliss also served on the special committee on the veterans' home for wounded soldiers of the Army of Virginia. He refused to run for reelection. A man with little political experience, Chambliss spent the rest of his life in paying off debts incurred during the war. He died near Hicksford on April 3, 1875. Alexander and Beringer, *Anatomy of the Confederate Congress*; Warner and Yearns, *Biographical Register of the Confederate Congress*.

CHEATHAM, Benjamin Franklin (*General*), son of Leonard Pope and Elizabeth (Robertson) Cheatham, was born in Nashville, Tennessee, on October 20, 1820. Like his father before him, he was a farmer. In 1866, he married Anna Bell, by whom he had three sons and two daughters. Cheatham was a captain and later a colonel of Tennessee Volunteers during the Mexican War. He participated in the California gold rush of 1849 but returned to Tennessee four years later.

Before the war, he was a major general in the state militia, a Democrat, and a close friend of Tennessee Governor Isham Harris (*q.v.*). In the early days of the Civil War, he volunteered for the army, and the governor made him a brigadier and later major general of the provisional army of Tennessee. Named a brigadier general in the Confederate Army on July 9, 1861, he earned a reputation for brilliance in battle, and on March 10, 1862, he was promoted to major general during the battle of Shiloh, where he commanded the second division of the 1st Corps under General Leonidas Polk (*q.v.*). He also saw major action at the battles of Perryville, Murfreesboro, Chickamauga, Missionary Ridge, Kenesaw Mountain, and Atlanta. Always a controversial figure, Cheatham was accused by General John B. Hood (*q.v.*) of errors at Spring Hill, Tennessee, in the fall of 1864 which led to Confederate defeat at the battle of Franklin. A military court cleared Cheatham of all charges. He joined Joseph E. Johnston's (*q.v.*) army in North Carolina and surrendered there in April 1865. Upon obtaining parole, he returned to Tennessee to farm. In 1872, Cheatham ran unsuccessfully for the U.S. House. For four years he was superintendent of the state prison, and from 1885 until his death on September 4, 1886, he was postmaster at Nashville. Burt, *Nashville: Its Life and Times*; Connelly, *Army of the Heartland*.

CHESNUT, James, Jr. (*Congressman, General*), son of the planter James Chesnut and his wife Mary (Cox), was born at Camden, South Carolina, on January 18, 1815. A graduate of Princeton College in 1835, he studied law in 1837, was admitted to the bar in 1838, and began his practice in Camden. On April 23, 1840, he married Mary Boykin Miller, a daughter of Governor Stephen N. Miller of South Carolina; they had no children. Chesnut, a states' rights Democrat and a Presbyterian, served in the lower house of the South Carolina legislature in 1840-1846 and 1850-1852 and in the upper house from 1854 to 1858, where he was president of the Senate from 1856 to 1858. In 1858, upon the death of Senator Josiah J. Evans, he was named to the U.S. Senate, and he resigned on November 10, 1860. As a delegate to the South Carolina secession convention from Kershaw District, he helped to draft the Ordinance of Secession. As a delegate to the provisional Confederate Congress in 1861, he helped to draft the permanent Confederate Constitution. Chesnut also tried to force the reopening of the African slave trade in 1861. In the provisional Congress, he was a member of the Committees on Naval Affairs and the Territories and was a supporter of the Davis administration. He was commissioned a colonel in the Confederate Army and served as an aide to P.G.T. Beauregard (*q.v.*) at the battle of First Manassas and as an aide-de-camp on President Davis's military staff during the remainder of 1861. In 1862, the governor of South Carolina appointed him chief of militia on the South Carolina Executive Council, a position he resigned that November. Chesnut, a trusted friend of President Davis (*q.v.*), again served in a military staff position in Richmond from 1862 to 1864. He was promoted to brigadier general in

1864 and was put in charge of all reserve forces on the South Carolina coast. He served in that post until the war's end. After the war, he returned to his law practice in Camden and was a delegate to the Democratic national convention of 1868 and to the state taxpayers' conventions of 1871 and 1874. He served as president of the state convention of 1867 which protested military rule, and though disfranchised, he took un active role in the movement during the 1870s to end Reconstruction. After Reconstruction, he practiced law once again. He died on February 1, 1885, on his plantation near Camden, South Carolina. Cauthen, *South Carolina Goes to War, 1861-1865*; Davidson, *The Last Foray*.

CHEVES, Langdon (*Engineer*), was born to Langdon and Mary Elizabeth (Dulles) Cheves on June 17, 1814, in Philadelphia. He was educated in the Philadelphia schools, graduated from South Carolina College in 1833, attended the U.S. Military Academy from 1833 to 1835 but took no degree, and was admitted to the Columbia bar in 1836. His wife was the former Charlotte Lorain McCord, a sister of David J. McCord, a wealthy South Carolina planter. In 1841, Cheves abandoned his law practice and moved to Savannah, Georgia, where he ran a business and also became a rice planter in St. Peter's Parish, Beaufort District, South Carolina. He was a Democrat and an Episcopalian. He was a delegate to the Southern rights convention at Nashville in 1852 and to the Georgia secession convention in 1860. He voted for secession. As a captain of engineers during the war, he repaired and built the forts at Savannah and at Hilton Head, South Carolina, and designed and constructed the first war balloon, which was used for observation in Virginia. In 1862, he constructed the works at Morris Island, Cummings Point, and Battery Wagner. His service in the Corps of Engineers was invaluable. He was mortally wounded at Battery Wagner on July 10, 1863. Davidson, *The Last Foray*; Freeman, *Lee's Lieutenants*, II.

CHILTON, Robert Hall (*General*), son of William and Sarah (Powell) Chilton, was born on February 25, 1814, in Loudon County, Virginia. After graduating forty-eighth in a class of fifty from the U.S. Military Academy in 1837, he began a U.S. Army career as a second lieutenant in the 1st Dragoons and saw frontier duty in Kansas and the Indian Territory. He was married and had a family. Chilton was sent to Texas in 1844 and served in the Mexican War, where he was breveted a major for his performance at Buena Vista. In 1854, he was transferred to a staff assignment, and until he resigned his commission on April 29, 1861, he was a major and paymaster in the U.S. Army and stationed in Washington, D.C. He entered the Confederate Army as a lieutenant colonel in the Adjutant General Department and served as Robert E. Lee's (*q.v.*) chief of staff during 1861. He was promoted to brigadier general on October 20, 1862, but was not confirmed in this position by the Senate until February 16, 1864, because of clashes with General John B. Magruder (*q.v.*). In April 1864, he was relieved of field duty and was assigned to Richmond as inspector general for the Army of Northern Virginia until the end of the war. After the war, he was president of a manufacturing company in Columbus, Georgia, where he died on February 18, 1879. Freeman, *Lee's Lieutenants*, II, III; Tyler, *Encyclopedia of Virginia*, II.

CHILTON, William Parish (*Congressman*), was born to Thomas John and Margaret (Bledsoe) Chilton in Adair County, Kentucky, on August 10, 1810. Orphaned at the age of seventeen, he taught school in Kentucky and moved to Nashville, Tennessee, in 1828. He studied law there until 1831 when he moved to Talladega County, Alabama, and opened a law office. Chilton's father had been a Baptist minister in Virginia, and Chilton himself was a deacon in the Baptist church. In 1829, he married Mary C. Morgan, by whom he had five children. After his first wife's death, he married her sister, Elivia France Morgan, by whom he had seven children. Chilton, an old-line Whig who became a Democrat during the Civil War, represented Talladega County in the Alabama legislature from 1839 until 1843. He was named a judge to the state Supreme Court in 1847 and served as chief justice from 1852 to 1856, when he retired to resume his law practice in Macon County. In 1859, he was elected to the state Senate from Macon County. He resigned in 1860 and moved to Montgomery, Alabama. Although Chilton opposed secession, he accepted election to the provisional Confederate Congress in 1861, where he served on the Printing and Postal Affairs Committees. He was elected to the Confederate House of Representatives and served throughout the war. An able member of the Flag and Seal, Impressments, Judiciary, Patents, and Post Office Committees, he voted with the Davis administration. In 1865, he proposed a congressional committee to oversee the conduct of the war. At the end of the war he was a poor man, but he retrieved his losses and practiced law until his death on January 21, 1871, in Montgomery. Owen, *History of Alabama and Dictionary of Alabama Biography*, III.

CHISOLM, John Julian (*Physician*), son of the surgeon Dr. Robert Trail and Harriet Emily Chisolm, was born in Charleston, South Carolina, on April 16, 1830. After graduating from the South Carolina Medical College in 1850, he traveled to Europe, where he studied medicine in London and Paris. Chisolm was married twice, to Mary Edings on February 3, 1852, and to Elizabeth Steel on January 14, 1894. He returned to Charleston in 1852 and soon established a lucrative medical practice. In 1858, he was named a professor of surgery at the South Carolina Medical College. When the Civil War began, he received a commission as a medical officer. During the war, he attended the wounded at Fort Sumter, directed a plant for the manufacture of medicines at Charleston, and was chief surgeon of the military hospital at Richmond. He also wrote the *Manual of Military Surgery* (1861) which served as a textbook for doctors in the field. After the war, he returned to teach at the medical school and was dean of the South Carolina Medical College until 1869. He then left Charleston for Baltimore, where he taught surgery at the University of Maryland Medical School. He founded

Presbyterian Eye, Ear and Throat Hospital in Baltimore in 1877. In 1895, he was dean of the University of Maryland Medical School. Chisolm continued to teach until his death on November 2, 1903, in Petersburg, Virginia. Cunningham, *Doctors in Gray*; Kelly and Burrage (eds.), *American Medical Biographies*.

CHRISMAN, James Stone (*Congressman*), was born to John and Sally (Stone) Chrisman at Monticello, Wayne County, Kentucky, on September 14, 1818. He obtained his education in the common schools, studied law, and was admitted to the bar in 1849. He practiced law in Wayne County until the outbreak of the Civil War. On December 10, 1845, he married Lucy Nelson Bell. Chrisman, a secessionist Democrat, served in the U.S. House of Representatives from 1853 to 1855 but lost his attempt for reelection. He was a delegate to the Kentucky convention at Russellville in 1861, where he was made a member of the Executive Council. Chrisman also represented his state in both permanent Confederate Houses. A supporter of the Davis administration, he served on the Elections, Indian Affairs, Territories and Public Lands, War Tax, and Medical Department Committees of the House. He also urged the Confederate invasion of Kentucky. During the last years of the war, he believed that an invasion of Kentucky would divide the Union army and deliver additional troops to the Confederate cause. After the war, he returned to his law practice in Wayne County. He served in the lower house of the Kentucky legislature from 1869 to 1871, returned to his law practice from 1871 to 1873, and later was a delegate to the state constitutional convention of 1876. He continued his law practice until he died on July 29, 1881, in Monticello. Johnson, *A Century of Wayne County, Kentucky*.

CHURCHILL, Thomas James (*General*), was born to Samuel and Abby (Odham) Churchill on March 10, 1824, near Louisville in Jefferson County, Kentucky. He graduated from St. Mary's College, Kentucky in 1844 and studied law at Transylvania University during 1845. Churchill, who was probably a Whig, married Anne Sevier, daughter of Arkansas Senator Ambrose H. Sevier, on July 31, 1849; they had one son and three daughters. During the Mexican War, he served as a lieutenant in the 1st Kentucky Mounted Rifles. In 1848, he moved to Little Rock, Arkansas, to become a planter. He was postmaster of Little Rock from 1857 to 1861. Early in the Civil War, he raised a regiment and was made a colonel in the 1st Arkansas Mounted Rifles. After displaying gallantry at the battles of Wilson's Creek and Elkhorn, he was promoted to brigadier general on March 4, 1862. He participated in the Kentucky campaign, particularly in the Confederate victory at Richmond, Kentucky, in August 1862. Late in 1862, he was sent to the defense of the Arkansas Post, where he was forced to surrender in January 1863. He was exchanged shortly thereafter. Churchill later served with Braxton Bragg (*q. v.*) in Tennessee and fought in the Red River campaign at the battles of Pleasant Hill and Jenkins' Ferry, for which he was promoted to major general on March 18, 1865. He went to Texas with General Edmund Kirby Smith (*q. v.*) and surrendered there in June 1865. After he was paroled, Churchill retired to his farm in Pulaski County, Arkansas. Elected lieutenant governor in 1866, he was denied the office by the Union authorities, but he continued to be active in Democratic politics. From 1874 to 1880, he was treasurer of the state, and in 1880, he was elected governor by a large margin. After his term as governor, he retired to Little Rock, where he died on May 14, 1905. Evans, *Confederate Military History*, X; Hempstead, *Historical Review of Arkansas*, I.

CLANTON, James Holt (*General*), was born on January 8, 1827, in Columbia County, Georgia, to Nathaniel Holt and Mary (Clayton) Clanton. He attended the county schools of Macon County and the University of Georgia, leaving school to fight in the Mexican War. He later studied law under Judge Robert Chilton (*q.v.*) in Alabama, and in 1850, he was admitted to the Alabama bar. Clanton had two sons and a daughter by his marriage to Parthenia Abercrombie. A Democrat, he represented Montgomery County in the Alabama legislature in 1855. Clanton opposed secession and was a John Bell elector in 1860. However, he joined the Confederate Army immediately after the war began and was sent to Florida as aide-de-camp to General Braxton Bragg (*q.v.*). He fought in the battle of Shiloh and also participated in the battles of Booneville and Farmington, Mississippi, in May 1862. While on the staff of General Leonidas Polk (*q.v.*) during 1863, he harassed the Union Army in Alabama. He was promoted to brigadier general on November 16, 1863. He served in the Atlanta campaign. On March 25, 1865, he was seriously wounded and captured at Bluffton Spring, Florida. Clanton was paroled in Mobile in May 1865. After the war, he resumed his Alabama law practice and became a leader in the Democratic party. He was state's attorney during the late 1860s. An ex-Union officer shot Clanton to death in Knoxville, Tennessee, on September 26, 1871. Owen, *History of Alabama and Dictionary of Alabama Biography*, III.

CLAPP, Jeremiah Watkins (*Congressman*), was born in Abingdon, Washington County, Virginia, on September 24, 1814, to Dr. Earl B. Clapp and his wife Elizabeth (Craig). Educated at Abingdon Academy, he graduated from Hampden-Sidney College in 1835, was admitted to the bar in 1839, and practiced law in Abingdon until 1841. He then went to Holly Springs, Mississippi, where he became a planter and continued his law practice. He had eight children by his marriage in May 1843 to Evelina D. Lucas. Clapp was a Whig who joined the Union and States' Rights party of Mississippi in 1850. He was elected to the Mississippi legislature in 1856, and two years later he helped to draw up the state's legal code. Clapp served in the legislature through 1860. He became a Democrat and voted for secession at his state's convention in 1861. He was elected to the first Confederate House, where he served on the Claims, Elections, Ordnance and Ordnance Stores, and on numerous special committees. After his term ended, Secretary of the Treasury Christopher G. Memminger (*q.v.*) appointed him supervisor of the transportation of Confederate cotton in the west; he held that position until the end of the war. After the war, having lost most of his wealth, he moved to Memphis to practice law. In 1876, he was active in Democratic politics, and two years later he was elected to the Tennessee Senate. He died in Memphis on September 5, 1898. *Biographical and Historical Memoirs of Mississippi.*

CLARK, Charles (*Governor, General*), was born on May 24, 1811, in Lebanon, Warren County, Ohio, where his family had moved from Maryland. After receiving a college education in either Cincinnati or Kentucky, he came to Mississippi in 1831. Clark taught and read law in Jefferson County before moving to Bolivar County, Mississippi, where he was a planter. He had a son and three daughters by his marriage to Ann Eliza Darden. A Clay Whig until he became a secessionist Democrat in 1856, he served in the state legislature from 1838 to 1844. During the Mexican War, he held the rank of captain but never saw action. At the state secession convention of 1851, he supported the unionists. He moved to a plantation in Boliver County the next year. In 1856, he was again elected to the state legislature, where he served until 1861. In 1860, he was a radical delegate to the Democratic convention in Charleston. He ran unsuccessfully for a seat at the Mississippi secession convention, losing to Miles H. McGeehee, a cooperationist. At the beginning of the Civil War, Clark was chosen to be a brigadier general and later a major general of state troops, and he became a brigadier general in the Confederate Army on May 22, 1861. As a division commander at Shiloh under General A. S. Johnston (*q.v.*), he was wounded in the hip. After his recovery, he served under General Earl Van Dorn (*q.v.*) in Mississippi, and he led a division under Breckinridge (*q.v.*) during the Confederate attack on Baton Rouge, where he was again wounded and was taken prisoner in August 1862. Released in February 1863, Clark spent the rest of his life on crutches. He resigned his commission on October 31, 1863. He served as governor of his state from 1863 to 1865, and at the end of the war he advised acquiescence and obedience to federal law. After the war, he resumed his law practice and took an active part in state redemptionist politics. In 1876, he was chancellor for his district. Clark was also a trustee of the University of Mississippi prior to his death on December 17, 1877, in Bolivar County. Bettersworth, *Mississippi in the Confederacy.*

CLARK, Henry Toole (*Governor*), was born in Tarboro, North Carolina, in 1808. He received his B.A. and M.A. degrees from the University of North Carolina in 1826 and 1832, respectively. Clark was admitted to the bar in 1833, became a planter, married, and had a family. From 1858 to 1861, he served in the North Carolina Senate, where he was also speaker. As speaker of the Senate, he succeeded to the office of governor upon the death of John W. Ellis (*q.v.*) on July 7, 1861. During his term in office, Clark was unjustly criticized for not doing more to protect the North Carolina coastline, and the Confederate Congress investigated him after the loss of Roanoke Island. In turn, Clark felt that Richmond did not send sufficient troops to North Carolina, and he personally worked to recruit state troops and tried to protect the railroads in the eastern part of the state. He also opposed William Ashe's (*q.v.*) attempts to seize arms in North Carolina. In 1862, his policies in the state were attacked by William W. Holden (*q.v.*). Holden attempted to remove Clark from office but failed. Although a strong supporter of states' rights, the moderate forces of the state did not consider Clark to be effective. He was not a candidate for reelection and was replaced in 1863 by Zebulon Vance (*q.v.*). Clark had no further duties during the Civil War. After the war, he was elected to the state legislature of 1865 but was unable to serve because Governor Holden refused to pardon him. He was a man without means, but he repaid all of his debts after the war. Clark died on February 21 or April 14, 1874, in Tarboro. Barrett, *The Civil War in North Carolina*.

CLARK, John Bullock (*Congressman*), son of Bennett and Martha (Bullock) Clark, was born on April 17, 1802, in Madison County, Kentucky. His family moved to Missouri in 1818, where the younger Clark attended country schools and studied law. He was admitted to the Fayette, Missouri, bar in 1824. He married Eleanor Turner; one of their sons, John B. Clark, Jr., became a brigadier general in the Confederate Army. Though without formal higher education, Clark nevertheless became a successful lawyer, known for his common sense and his grasp of human nature. He served as clerk of the Howard County courts from 1824 to 1835. In 1830, he was appointed a brigadier general in the state militia, and two years later as a colonel in the Missouri Mounted Volunteers, he fought in the Black Hawk War. He was promoted to major general in the state militia in 1848. Clark served in the state House of Representatives in 1850-1851. He was elected as a Democrat to the U.S. House of Representatives in 1857 and served until his expulsion for joining the Confederacy in 1861. He was a strong secessionist and a leader of the Missouri secession movement. During the Civil War, Clark became a brigadier of Missouri state troops and fought at the battle of Springfield, where he was wounded in August 1861. He also served in the provisional Confederate Congress, the first Confederate Senate, and the second Confederate House, and supported the Davis administration throughout the war. Clark's talk of counter-revolution in Missouri produced a falling out with Governor Thomas C. Reynolds (*q.v.*) and, subsequently, a loss of support for reelection to the second Senate. An irascible man, Clark wanted the Confederate government to direct the Missouri Militia, defended martial law, and advocated that all Northern officers who commanded Negro troops be shot. After the war, he returned to his law practice in Fayette, Missouri. He remained out of public life and died in Fayette on October 29, 1885. Ryle, *Missouri: Union or Secession*; Stewart (ed.), *The History of the Bench and Bar of Missouri*.

CLARK, William White (*Congressman*), was born in Augusta, Georgia, on September 23, 1819. He attended college and was a lawyer and planter in

Covington, Newton County, Georgia, during most of his adult life. He served one term in the state legislature in 1841, but took no further interest in public life before the Civil War. Clark was married and had four children. As representative of the Sixth District of Georgia in the first Confederate House of Representatives, he was quite active and supported the Davis administration. He was a member of the Post Office and Post Roads, Quartermaster's and Commissary Department, War Tax, and Medical Department Committees. Clark was interested in the economics of war factories and pushed for hospital reform, yet he refused to support the first conscript law. After his term ended, Clark was a tax assessor in Covington in 1864. He returned to his law practice and for a time served as a director of the Georgia Railroad and Banking Company. He died in Baltimore, Maryland, on August 6, 1883. Yearns, *The Confederate Congress*; Warner and Yearns, *Biographical Register of the Confederate Congress*.

CLARK, Willis Gaylord (*Editor*), was born in the western part of New York on October 27, 1827, to Dr. Willis Fish and Charity (Barnard) Clark. After attending Collegiate Institute at Quincy, Illinois, he studied law in 1848 and traveled South, where he settled at Mobile, Alabama, and began a law practice in 1849. His marriage to Caroline Erwin Scott was childless. Clark, a Democrat, edited the *Southern Magazine* and, from 1852 to 1861, the Mobile *Daily Advertiser*. During the Civil War, his paper merged with the Mobile *Register*, and Clark served with John Forsyth (*q.v.*) as co-editor of the staunchly Confederate organ. He was an outstanding war correspondent and reported from the front lines to the people on the Gulf Coast. When the war ended, he resettled in Mobile. In 1867, Clark began a paper manufacturing company, and he later served as president of the Washington Avenue Railroad Company. In 1885, he was named collector of the port of Mobile. He published his *History of Education in Alabama* in 1888 and lived for ten more years in semi-retirement before dying on September 10, 1898, in Roanoke, Virginia. Andrews, *The South Reports the Civil War*; Owen, *History of Alabama and Dictionary of Alabama Biography*, III.

CLAY, Clement Claiborne (*Congressman, Diplomat*) was born on December 13, 1816, in Huntsville, Alabama, the son of Clement Comer and Susanna Claiborne (Withers) Clay. His father, a self-made man, was governor of Alabama from 1835 to 1837. The younger Clay received his B.A. in 1834 and his M.A. in 1837 from the University of Alabama. While his father was governor, he served as his private secretary. In 1839, he graduated from the University of Virginia Law School, was admitted to the bar, and joined his father's law firm in Huntsville. His marriage to Virginia Caroline Tunstall on February 1, 1843, was childless. Always a religious man, he joined the Episcopal church in 1867. Clay, a Democrat, edited the Huntsville *Democrat* from 1840 until he was elected to the state legislature in 1842. He served in the legislature from 1842 until 1846. From 1846 to 1848, he was judge of the County Court of Madison County. He was elected to the U.S. Senate in 1852 and was reelected in 1858 on a state sovereignty platform. A secessionist and close friend of Jefferson Davis (*q.v.*), Clay remained loyal to the administration throughout the war. He was elected to the first Confederate Senate but lost his bid for reelection in 1863 to Richard W. Walker (*q.v.*), ostensibly because Clay was too loyal to the Davis administration. In the Senate he opposed the formation of a Confederate Supreme Court, and proposed a bill to draft foreigners into the Confederate Army. He served on the Commerce, Conference, and Military Affairs Committees. In 1864, he was sent as a Confederate diplomatic agent to Canada; he had previously served as a foreign policy advisor to the president. At the end of the war, he was charged with complicity in the murder of President Lincoln but was released in 1866. Clay settled on his plantation "Wildwood" near Huntsville and practiced law. The ordeal of the war left him in ill health, and permanent restrictions kept him from public service in the postwar years. He died in Madison County, Alabama, on January 3, 1882. Nuermberger, *The Clays of Alabama*.

CLAYTON, Alexander Mosby (*Congressman, Judge*), son of William and Clarissa (Mosby) Clayton, was born in Campbell County, Virginia, on January 15, 1801. After studying law in Fredericksburg, he was admitted to the Virginia bar in 1823 and practiced in Louisa. He was a Democrat and an Episcopalian. He was married twice, to Mary Talker Thomas in 1826 and to Barbara A. Barker in 1839. Clayton moved to Clarksville, Tennessee, in the late 1820s. From 1832 to 1834, he served as federal judge of the Arkansas Territory. In 1837, he moved to Mississippi, where he became a planter and lawyer in Lamar, Marshall (later Benton) County. He served on the state Supreme Court from 1842 to 1851 but lost his reelection bid in 1851. In 1850, he espoused the causes of states' rights and secession. President Franklin Pierce appointed him consul to Havana in 1853, but he resigned in 1854 and returned to Mississippi. He was a delegate to the Charleston Democratic convention in 1860 and to the Mississippi secession convention in 1861, where he wrote the Secession Ordinance. Clayton also served on the Judiciary and Permanent Constitution Committees of the provisional Confederate Congress. He wrote the provisions making the state governments equal to the federal government, asked for quick ratification of the Constitution, and was instrumental in securing the presidency for Jefferson Davis (*q.v.*). After his service in the provisional Congress, President Davis appointed Clayton judge of the Confederate States court of Mississippi, a position which he retained throughout the Civil War. When the war ended, the Reconstruction government removed him from office. He never again took part in public life. Clayton subsequently became a promoter of the Mississippi Central Railroad. He died in Lamar, Mississippi, on September 30, 1889. *Biographical and Historical Memoirs of Mississippi*; Lee, *The Confederate Constitutions*; Rowland, *Courts, Judges, and Lawyers of Mississippi, 1798-1835*.

CLAYTON, Henry Delamar (*General*), was born to the farmer and Georgia legislator Nelson Clayton and his wife Sara (Carruthers) on March 7, 1827, in Pulaski County, Georgia. He attended Vineville Academy near Macon and graduated from Emory and Henry College in 1848. Clayton studied law under John Shorter (*q.v.*) in Eufaula, Alabama, and was admitted to the Clayton, Alabama, bar in 1849. He was an Episcopalian and a secessionist Democrat. He had eight sons and four daughters by his 1850 marriage to Victoria Virginia Hunter. He was elected to the state legislature in 1857 and again in 1859. At the beginning of the war, Clayton enlisted as a private in the Clayton Guards and went to Pensacola. He later was a colonel in the 1st Alabama Regiment. Wounded at the battle of Murfreesboro in 1862, he was promoted to brigadier general on April 22, 1863, and fought at the battle of Chickamauga. On July 7, 1864, he was promoted to major general. He took over Alexander P. Stewart's (*q.v.*) Division of the Army of Tennessee, which played a prominent part in the action around Atlanta and Jonesboro, Georgia, and which formed the rear guard of the Confederate Army as it retreated from Nashville late in 1864. He subsequently saw service with Joseph Johnston (*q.v.*) in North Carolina and surrendered there in April 1865. After the war, Clayton farmed and practiced law near Clayton, Alabama. He was elected judge of the Third Circuit Court of Alabama and served almost continuously from 1866 until he resigned in 1886 to become president of the University of Alabama. Clayton died in Tuscaloosa on October 3, 1889. Connelly, *Autumn of Glory*; Owen, *History of Alabama and Dictionary of Alabama Biography*, III.

CLAYTON, Philip (*Bureaucrat*), was born in Athens, Georgia, on March 19, 1815, to Judge Augustus Smith Clayton and his wife Julia (Carnes). His father, a distinguished jurist and statesman, at one time served in the U.S. House of Representatives as a Democrat. The younger Clayton, also a Democrat, was trained in the law, graduated first in his class of 1833 at Franklin College (later the University of Georgia), and was admitted to the bar in 1836. He had a son by his marriage in 1836 to Leonora Harper. Clayton ran his father's plantation in Mississippi before returning to Georgia in 1839, where he edited the *Southern Banner* at Athens until 1849. From 1849 to 1857, Clayton was second auditor in the U.S. Treasury. Howell Cobb (*q.v.*) appointed him assistant secretary of the treasury in the Buchanan administration, where he served from 1857 to 1861. When the Civil War began, he was named assistant secretary of the treasury of the Confederate government under Christopher G. Memminger (*q.v.*). His duties were to examine letters, contracts, and warrants and to advise the secretary. He also helped to organize the Treasury Department. Clayton soon dissented from what he believed was the authoritarian nature of the secretary, and he resigned from office in 1863. His resignation illustrates a case of years of previous experience being lost to the Confederacy over the problems of personality. Clayton returned to Georgia and held no further office in the Confederacy. After the war, he became a Republican and served as a teller in a savings bank in

Augusta, Georgia. In 1874, President Grant made him consul to Peru. Clayton died of yellow fever near Callao, Peru, on March 22, 1877. Northen (ed.), *Men of Mark in Georgia*, III; Todd, *Confederate Finance*.

CLEBURNE, Patrick Ronayne (*General*), son of Joseph and Mary Ann (Ronayne) Cleburne, was born on March 17, 1828, in County Cork, Ireland. He was apprenticed as a druggist in Ireland and served in the British army before emigrating to New Orleans in November 1849. Cleburne was a Whig who became a Democrat in reaction to the Know-Nothing movement. He was a vestryman in the Episcopal church and a Mason. He never married. (At the time of his death, he was engaged to Miss Sue Tarleton of Mobile, Alabama.) Cleburne moved to Arkansas in 1850 and became a druggist. In 1856, he was admitted to the bar and soon developed a successful property law practice in Helena, Arkansas. Even before the war began, he helped to form a company of volunteers for the Confederacy. In 1861, he was a captain in the Yellow Rifles and later a colonel in the 15th Arkansas Regiment. Cleburne, who was later known as the "Jackson of the West," felt that slaves should be freed and used as soldiers. After serving in Missouri under General William Hardee (*q.v.*) and in Bowling Green, Kentucky, Cleburne was promoted to brigadier general on March 4, 1862, during the battle of Shiloh, where he achieved a reputation for discipline and efficiency. He was wounded while a division commander at Richmond, Kentucky, in August 1862. When he recovered, he fought at the battle of Perryville and was promoted to major general on December 20, 1862. At the battle of Murfreesboro, he attacked the right flank of the Union Army. In 1863, he fought at Chickamauga, defeated Sherman at Missionary Ridge, and saved Braxton Bragg's (*q.v.*) artillery and wagons at Ringgold Gap. During the Atlanta campaign of 1864, he was victorious at Pickett's Mill. Cleburne was killed in action on November 30, 1864, at Franklin, Tennessee. Purdue, *Pat Cleburne Confederate General*; *Southern Historical Society Papers*, XXXI.

CLINGMAN, Thomas Lanier (*General*), was born into the German family of Jacob and Jane (Poindexter) Clingman on June 27, 1812, in Huntersville County (now Yadkin County), North Carolina. Although his father died when Thomas was four years old, the younger Clingman completed his education, graduating first in the class of 1832 from the University of North Carolina. He studied law at Hillsboro under William A. Graham (*q.v.*). Clingman was a Presbyterian and a lifelong bachelor. The Whig Clingman was elected to represent Surry County in the state legislature in 1835. He moved to Asheville, Buncombe County, the following year and was elected to the state Senate in 1840. From 1843 to 1845 and from 1847 to 1858, he was one of the moderate Southern leaders in the U.S. House of Representatives. In 1845, he fought a duel with William Lowndes Yancey (*q.v.*) and in 1850, he joined the Democratic party. Clingman served in the U.S. Senate from 1858 to 1861. In May 1861, he was selected by the secession convention to give assurance to the Confederate Congress that North Carolina would enter the Confederacy. In late 1861, he was expelled from the U.S. Senate for anti-Union activities. He then volunteered as a colonel of the 25th North Carolina Infantry, and on May 17, 1862, he was promoted to brigadier general in command of the defense of Goldsboro, North Carolina. Clingman continued to serve there and in Charleston, South Carolina, until the spring of 1864, when his brigade was ordered to Virginia. He defeated General Benjamin F. Butler at Drewry's Bluff in May of that year. He was wounded at Cold Harbor but recovered sufficiently to participate in the defense of Petersburg before being so seriously wounded in the battle on the Weldon Railroad in August that he did not rejoin his troops until just before the surrender in 1865. After the war, he remained a power in the North Carolina Democratic party, but he was never able to hold public office. Clingman lost his wealth during the war and attempted to recoup it by practicing law and mining for mica in western North Carolina. He died in Morgantown, North Carolina, on November 3, 1897. Evans, *Confederate Military History*, IV; Hamilton, *Reconstruction in North Carolina*.

CLOPTON, David (*Congressman*) was born to Dr. Alfred Clopton and his wife Sarah (Kendrick) on September 29, 1820, in Putnam County, Georgia. His father was a physician, a bank president, and a member of the Georgia legislature. Clopton attended Eatonton Academy in Georgia and graduated first in his class at Randolph-Macon College in 1840. He studied law and was admitted to the bar in 1841. In 1844, he moved to Tuskegee, Alabama, where he began the practice of law. He was a Democrat and a member of the Methodist Episcopal church. He had one son, Edward Hunter, by his marriage to Martha E. Ligon; she died in November 1867. He subsequently married Mary F. Chambers; his third wife was Virginia Tunstall Clay, the widow of Clemont Claiborne Clay (*q.v.*). Little is known of his political activities or his business practice except that he was a successful lawyer. In 1859, he was elected to the U.S. House of Representatives from Alabama as a secessionist and a states' rights Democrat. He retired from the House in January 1861. Clopton enlisted in the Civil War as a private in the 12th Alabama Infantry at the outbreak of hostilities and served as quartermaster of his regiment. He also was elected to both permanent Confederate Houses. He served on the Claims, Naval Affairs, Illegal Seizures, and Medical Department Committees. Clopton supported the Davis administration. After the war, he made his home in Montgomery, where he practiced law and participated in the redemptionist movement in Alabama. In 1878, he was named speaker of the lower house of the Alabama legislature. He declined reelection. Clopton also organized both the First National Bank of Sheffield and the Sheffield Iron and Coal Company during the 1870s. In 1884, he was appointed associate justice of the state Supreme Court, a position which he held until his death on February 5, 1892, at Montgomery. Garrett, *Reminiscences of Public Men in Alabama*; Owen, *History of Alabama and Dictionary of Alabama Biography*, III.

CLUSKY, Michael Walsh (*Congressman*), was born to Irish parents in May 1832, in Savannah, Georgia, where his father was a surveyor and an architect. His marriage to Mrs. W. R. Jacob (Hall) was childless. From 1851 to 1859, Clusky was postmaster of the U.S. House of Representatives. In 1859, he moved to Memphis, Tennessee, where he edited the *Avalanche*. During Buchanan's administration, he was secretary of the Democratic National Committee, and he published *Clusky's Political Text-book*. He supported secession. When the war began, he was commissioned as a captain in the 2nd Tennessee Regiment and fought with the Army of Tennessee in Virginia and at Shiloh. He was adjutant general on the staff of Preston Smith and attained the rank of major. He was severely wounded at Atlanta in the Georgia campaign. The soldiers of the Army of Tennessee elected him to the Confederate House in 1864. Upon his recovery, he served on the Conference and Naval Affairs Committees and was generally a Davis administration supporter. After the war, he returned to Memphis to resume editorship of the *Avalanche*. In the late 1860s, he moved to Louisville, Kentucky, where he edited the *Ledger*, a Democratic party paper. Clusky died on January 13, 1873, in Louisville. *Biographical Encyclopedia of Kentucky of Dead and Living Men of the Nineteenth Century.*

COBB, Howell (*Congressman, General*), son of the wealthy planter Colonel John Addison Cobb and his wife Sarah Robinson (Rootes), was born on September 17, 1815, in Jefferson County, Georgia. He graduated from Franklin College (later the University of Georgia) in 1834, was admitted to the bar in 1836, and began a practice in Athens, Georgia. Cobb, brother of Thomas R. R. Cobb (*q.v.*), was a Presbyterian and a Jacksonian Democrat. In 1834, he married Mary Ann Lamar, by whom he had four sons and two daughters. From 1837 to 1841, he was solicitor general of the Western Judicial Circuit. As a Democrat in the U.S. House from the Sixth Congressional District of Georgia from 1843 to 1851, he supported free trade and compromise over slavery. He was speaker of the House during the Thirty-First Congress. As governor of Georgia from 1851 to 1853, he was considered a staunch unionist, but later, along with his brother, he became an ardent secessionist. Cobb practiced law for two years before returning to the U.S. House in 1855-1857, where he was chairman of the Ways and Means Committee. From 1857 to 1860, he was secretary of the treasury under Buchanan. In 1860, he supported the Southern walkout from the Democratic convention at Charleston. Later, he was chairman of the Montgomery convention and president of the provisional Confederate Congress. He entered the Confederate Army at the beginning of the war as a colonel of the 16th Georgia Infantry and had both civil and military duties until February 13, 1862, when he was promoted to brigadier general. After participating in the 1862 battle of Seven Pines, the Seven Days, Second Manassas, and Sharpsburg, he was promoted to major general on September 9, 1863. As commander of the District of Georgia in 1863, he was responsible for resolving differences between Governor Joseph Brown (*q.v.*) and

President Davis (*q.v.*) and between Congress and the generals. In 1864, he was credited with the defeat of General George Stoneman at Macon. At the war's end he surrendered at Macon. After the war, he opened a law office in Macon with James Jackson and was a successful lawyer as well as planter. His "Bush Arbor Speech" in support of Robert Toombs (*q.v.*) and Benjamin H. Hill (*q.v.*) as candidates for office stood as a direct attack on the Union ideas of Reconstruction. Reconstruction kept him from entering public office. Cobb died in New York City during a business trip on October 9, 1868. Montgomery, *Howell Cobb's Confederate Career*; Northen (ed.), *Men of Mark in Georgia*, III.

COBB, Thomas Reade Rootes (*Congressman, General*), brother of Howell Cobb (*q.v.*) and son of John Addison and Sarah Robinson (Rootes) Cobb, was born in Jefferson County, Georgia, on April 10, 1823. He graduated first in the class of 1841 from the University of Georgia and was admitted to the Athens bar the following year. Like his brother, he was a Presbyterian and a Democrat. On January 9, 1844, he married Marion Lumpkin, by whom he had one daughter. Cobb, whose father had lost all of his money during the depression of the late 1830s, was assistant secretary to the Georgia Senate during the late 1840s and later vice-president of a temperance society. From 1849 to 1857, he was a reporter for the state Supreme Court, and he codified the state's legal statutes prior to the Civil War. Cobb codified the laws of the state of Georgia in 1851. He was also the author of *An Inquiry into the Law of Negro Slavery* (1858), a most influential defense of slavery. As a delegate to the Georgia secession convention, he favored immediate secession and opposed compromise. At the meeting of the provisional Confederate Congress in Montgomery, Cobb was assigned to the committee to write a permanent constitution, and he was in part responsible for writing that document. Cobb refused civil office; he joined the Confederate Army in August 1861, feeling that his duty lay in the field. His "Cobb's Legion" won the praise of General John B. Magruder (*q.v.*). Promoted to brigadier general on November 1, 1862, he was a brigade commander at the battle of Fredericksburg and held his position despite six attacks from the federal forces. Cobb's thigh was shattered and he bled to death in Fredericksburg, Virginia, on December 13, 1862. "The Correspondence of Thomas Reade Rootes Cobb, 1860-1862," *Southern Historical Association Publications*, XI; Northen (ed.), *Men of Mark in Georgia*, III.

COCKRELL, Francis Marion (*General*), son of Joseph and Nancy (Ellis) Cockrell and a brother of the U.S. senator from Missouri, Jeremiah Vardaman Cockrell, was born on October 1, 1834, in Warrensburg, Johnson County, Missouri. He graduated with honors from Chapel Hill College, Lafayette County, Missouri, in 1853, studied law, and was admitted to the Warrensburg bar in 1855. Cockrell married Arethusa D. Stapp in 1853, Anna E. Mann in 1866, and later Anna Ewing. He had seven sons and two daughters. A lifelong Democrat, he held no public office before the war. He enlisted in the state militia when the war began. Cockrell served under General Sterling Price (*q.v.*) in the battles of Carthage and Wilson's Creek in 1861 and at the battle of Elkhorn Tavern in March 1862, after which he was promoted to colonel in the Confederate Army. Wounded during the battle of Corinth, Mississippi, in October 1862, when he recovered he was considered the hero of Hatchie Bridge. With his promotion to brigadier general on July 18, 1863, he took over command of the Missouri Brigade at Vicksburg and Port Gibson. He was captured and paroled during the seige of Vicksburg and commanded all Missouri troops in the Army of Mississippi in 1864. In that year, he fought at Lost Mountain and Jonesboro and was wounded twice, at Atlanta and severely at the battle of Franklin, Tennessee. In the spring of 1865, he was made a division commander, and he was captured at the fall of Mobile. At the end of the war, he practiced law with Thomas T. Crittenden in Warrensburg, Missouri. Although there were restrictions on his participation in public life until after 1872, he became active in Democratic party politics. In 1874, he succeeded Carl Schurz as U.S. senator from Missouri, serving ably until his defeat in 1905. Cockrell was then appointed to the Interstate Commerce Commission and remained there until 1910. In 1911, he was a member of the U.S. commission to determine the boundary line between Texas and Mexico. Cockrell was also a civilian member of the Board of Ordnance of the Army Department prior to his death on December 13, 1915, in Washington, D.C. *Confederate Veteran*, XXIII; St. Louis *Globe Democrat*, December 14, 1915.

COLLIER, Charles Fenton (*Congressman*), was born in Petersburg, Virginia, on September 27, 1817. He was an Episcopalian. He married Mrs. Elizabeth Amos on April 18, 1843. Collier attended the University of Virginia and studied law at Harvard from 1847 to 1848. Before the Civil War, he was a slaveholding farmer of relative affluence, a law partner of Joseph S. Budd in Petersburg, Virginia, and a member of the unionist wing of the Democratic party. Collier sat in the lower house of the Virginia legislature from 1857 to 1862. In May 1860, while presiding over a Petersburg meeting, he disapproved of a Southern walkout from the Charleston Democratic convention on the grounds of party harmony. He supported Stephen A. Douglas for president in 1860. However, in rallying secession feelings for the Richmond convention he could be labeled a secessionist. In 1862, he replaced Roger Pryor (*q.v.*) as congressman from Virginia's Fourth Congressional District. He served on the Naval Affairs, Commerce, and War Tax Committees. He was a candidate for the second Confederate House in 1863 but lost to Thomas S. Gholson (*q.v.*), a states' rights Democrat and ally of James A. Seddon (*q.v.*), by a margin of twenty-seven votes. He returned to Petersburg and participated in local government affairs during the remainder of the war. In 1865, he offered the surrender of Petersburg to Northern troops; he had been a member of the Common Council of the city. He returned to his law practice and was elected mayor of Petersburg in 1866; the Reconstruction Congress removed him from office in 1868. He was again elected mayor in 1888, and served until his death in Petersburg on June 29, 1899. *Dinwiddie County*; McGregor, *The Disruption of Virginia*.

COLQUITT, Alfred Holt (*General*), son of Walter Terry and Nancy H. (Lane) Colquitt, was born on April 20, 1824, in Monroe, Walton County, Georgia. His father was a Democratic U.S. senator from Georgia and an ardent secessionist in 1850. The younger Colquitt attended the schools of Monroe, Georgia, and graduated with honors from Princeton College in 1844. In 1846, he was admitted to the Monroe bar. Like his father, Colquitt was a Democrat, a Methodist minister, and a temperance advocate. He married Dorothy Tarver in 1848, and her sister Sarah Tarver in the 1850s. He served as a staff major during the Mexican War. Before the Civil War, he also farmed a plantation in Baker County in southwest Georgia. He became assistant secretary of the state Senate in 1849. Colquitt served a term as a Democrat in the U.S. House from 1853 to 1855, but did not stand for reelection. He entered the state legislature in 1859, supported John C. Breckinridge (*q.v.*) for president in 1860, and was a pro-secessionist delegate to the state secession convention. When the war began, he enlisted in the army and was made captain and later a colonel in the 6th Georgia Infantry, participating in the Peninsular campaign, and the battles of Seven Days, Sharpsburg, Fredericksburg, and Chancellorsville. On September 1, 1862, he was promoted to brigadier general. In 1864, he won the battle of Olustee, Florida, and was thus credited for stopping the invasion of that state. He surrendered during the siege of Petersburg and was paroled in North Carolina in May 1865. Colquitt returned to his farm and his law practice. Restrictions prevented him from holding office, but he became a political opponent of Joseph E. Brown (*q.v.*). He was president of the Georgia Argricultural Society from 1870 to 1876, and from 1876 to 1882, he was governor of Georgia. From 1882 until his death on March 26, 1894, in Washington, D.C., he served in the U.S. Senate. Felton, *My Memoirs of Georgia Politics*; Northen (ed.), *Men of Mark in Georgia*, III.

COLSTON, Raleigh Edward (*General*), the adopted son of Raleigh Edward and Elizabeth (Marshall) Colston, was born on October 31, 1825, in Paris, France. He emigrated to the United States at the age of seventeen and graduated from the Virginia Military Institute in 1846. Colston taught French at Virginia Military Institute from 1846 until 1861. In 1854 he was promoted to full professor. Colston was married to the former Louise Meriwether Gardiner. At the beginning of the war, he took the cadets from Virginia Military Institute to Richmond, where he entered the Confederate Army as a colonel in the 16th Virginia Regiment. Promoted to brigadier general on December 24, 1861, he commanded a brigade in the 1862 battles of Yorktown, Williamsburg, and Seven Pines. He was a division commander at Fredericksburg in 1862 and at Chancellorsville in 1863. In May

1863, he was transferred to staff duty in Richmond, and in October of that year, he was assigned to a command at Savannah. In 1864, he served under P.G.T. Beauregard (q.v.) at the defense of Petersburg and commanded at Lynchburg. He surrendered in April 1865. After the war, he operated a military academy in Wilmington, North Carolina. From 1873 to 1879, he was a colonel in the Egyptian army, where he was paralyzed from injuries received in the Sudan. In 1879, Colston returned to the United States and later served as a clerk in the War Department in Washington, D.C., from 1883 to 1894. He died poverty-stricken on July 29, 1896, in the Confederate Soldier's Home at Richmond, Virginia. Tyler, *Encyclopedia of Virginia Biography*, III; Warner, *Generals in Gray*.

COLYAR, Arthur St. Clair (*Congressman*), son of Alexander and ——— (Sherill) Colyar, was born on June 23, 1818, in Washington County, Tennessee. He came from a poor family which eventually moved to Franklin, Tennessee. He was self-educated and studied law. He maintained a law office in Nashville but did not live in that city until 1866. (His son, John B. Colyar, wrote *A Boy's Opinion of General Lee*.) A Whig, he became a Constitutional Unionist and opposed immediate secession. In 1863, he risked his life by defending Tennessee Unionists who had been unlawfully arrested. He was elected to the second House in May 1864. He served on the Ways and Means Committee, generally supported the administration, and favored extending the tax-in-kind. He was a staunch opponent of any special privileges for Southern corporations. Along with John B. Baldwin (q.v.) of Virginia, he tried to pressure Congress into negotiations with the North even before the Hampton Roads meeting. After the war, Colyar became an important Democratic party leader but lost the race for governor in 1878. Colyar was an active lawyer who wrote for the *Confederate Veteran*. He also reorganized the Tennessee Coal and Railroad Company and became its president. He was considered a conservative because of his 1867 appeal to allow the freedman the vote. From 1881 to 1884, he edited the *Nashville American*. He also wrote the *Life and Times of Andrew Jackson*. He died in Nashville December 13, 1907. Alexander and Beringer, *Anatomy of the Confederate Congress*; Patton, *Unionism and Reconstruction in Tennessee*, *Tennessee Historical Quarterly*, XII.

CONNER, James (*General*), was born to Henry Workman and Juliana (Courtney) Conner on September 1, 1829, in Charleston, South Carolina. He graduated from South Carolina College in 1849 and read law under James L. Petigru before being admitted to the Charleston bar in 1851. Conner was an Episcopalian and a Democrat and married Sallie Enders on October 10, 1866. He built up a large law practice, and his writings on legal matters included *The History of a Suit at Law* (1857). While he was U.S. district attorney for South Carolina in 1856, Conner prosecuted the famous case of the slave ship *Echo*. He resigned this position in December 1860 but later served the Confederacy in the same capacity. Although

Conner urged the convening of the South Carolina secession convention and was himself a delegate, he did not vote on the issue. He entered the Confederate Army when the war began and was made captain of the Washington Light Infantry. He was promoted to major following the battle of First Manassas. He was a colonel of the 22nd North Carolina Regiment from the battle of Seven Pines until he was promoted to brigadier general on June 1, 1864. Seriously wounded in the leg at the battle of Gaines' Mill during the Seven Days' battles in June 1862, when he recovered Conner served as acting major general in command of McGowan's Brigade and Kershaw's Brigade before he finally lost his leg at the battle of Cedar Creek on October 13, 1864. He held no further military duty. After the war, he returned to his law practice, serving as solicitor for the South Carolina Railroad and for the Bank of Charleston. He was also a delegate to the state constitutional convention of 1870. Conner was elected state attorney general in 1876 but resigned in December 1877 after establishing the legality of the Wade Hampton (*q.v.*) government. His health deteriorated rapidly and he went into semi-retirement. He died in Richmond, Virginia, on June 26, 1883. *Confederate Veteran*, VII; O'Neal, *Biographical Sketches of the Bench and Bar of South Carolina*, I.

CONRAD, Charles Magill (*Congressman*), was born in Winchester, Frederick County, Virginia, on December 24, 1804. His parents, Frederick Conner and Frances (Thruston) Conrad, first moved to Mississippi and then to New Iberia, Louisiana. The younger Conrad attended private schools in New Orleans and read law there in 1827 before being admitted to the bar and beginning a practice in 1828. He was an Episcopalian and a Jacksonian Democrat and became a Whig over the bank issue. His wife was the former M. W. Angela Lewis. After serving in the state House of Representatives for several terms in the 1830s, Conrad was appointed as a Whig to the U.S. Senate in 1842. Defeated for election to the Senate in 1843, he retired from office. In 1844, he was a delegate to the Louisiana constitutional convention. He was elected to the U.S. House in 1849, where he opposed the Compromise of 1850 before resigning in 1850 to become President Millard Fillmore's secretary of war, a post which he held until 1853. He retired to a lucrative New Orleans law practice. Conrad also owned a profitable plantation. As a member of the Constitutional Union party in 1860, he supported John Bell for president. A leader of the cooperationist movement in Louisiana, he ultimately supported secession. He represented his state in the provisional Confederate Congress and was elected to both Confederate Houses. In the provisional Congress, he served on the Naval Affairs Committee and the committee to organize the Executive Department, and he contributed to the debate over the permanent Constitution as well as supported a plan for economic stability. He served on the Impressments, Public Buildings, Ways and Means, Naval Affairs, and Currency Committees in the House and was generally considered a Davis administration supporter. He also served as a brigadier general in the state militia toward the end of the war. Conrad's estate was confiscated when New Orleans fell in April 1862. After the war, he returned to New Orleans, where he practiced law until his death on February 11, 1878. Bragg, *Louisiana in the Confederacy*; Lee, *The Confederate Constitutions*; *The South in the Building of the Nation*, VII.

CONROW, Aaron H. (*Congressman*), was born on June 9, 1824, in Cincinnati, Ohio. His parents moved to Illinois and, in 1840, to Ray County, Missouri, where eventually he was to practice law in Richmond. Conrow was married to Mary Ann Quesenberry on May 17, 1848; they had four children. Conrow was judge of the first probate court in Ray County during the early 1850s and spent the years 1857-1861 as circuit attorney for the Fifth Judicial Circuit. In 1860, he was elected as a Democrat to the state legislature. A secessionist, he resigned from the state House and enlisted in the Confederate Army when the war began. He was a colonel in the Missouri State Guards. Conrow was elected by Missouri state troops to serve in the provisional Confederate Congress; the citizens of the Fourth Congressional District elected him to both the first and the second Confederate House of Representatives. He served on the Finance, War Tax, Currency, Naval Affairs, Ordnance and Ordnance Stores, and Public Buildings Committees. He was considered a capable and hard-working congressman and was one of the administration's strongest supporters in the House. After the war, he accompanied General M. M. Parsons (*q.v.*) to Mexico, where he was massacred by Mexican liberalists on August 14, 1865, in Camarzo, Mexico. *History of Ray County, Missouri*.

COOKE, John Esten (*Bureaucrat*), son of Dr. John Rogers and Maria (Pendleton) Cooke, was born on November 3, 1830, in Winchester, Frederick County, Virginia. Nine years later, his family moved to Richmond, where he studied law with his father before being admitted to the bar in 1851. He married Mary Francis Page on September 18, 1867; they had three children. He published historical works, such as the *Youth of Jefferson*, and six novels, including *Virginia Comedians* and *Last of the Frontier*, before the war. An extreme secessionist, Cooke used his pen to assist in creating a climate for secession. He served in the Confederate Army on the staff of J.E.B. Stuart (*q.v.*) when the war began and took an active part in the early Virginia engagements. He was also inspector general of horse artillery for the Army of Northern Virginia. Cooke published a biography of "Stonewall" Jackson (*q.v.*) in 1863. He surrendered with Lee (*q.v.*) at Appomattox. After the war, he published *Surrey of Eagle's Nest* (1866) and a biography of Lee (1871). Cooke used the Civil War as a setting for his postwar novels. He was a planter in Clark County, Virginia, when he died on September 20, 1886. Beaty, *John Esten Cooke, Virginian*.

COOKE, John Rogers (*General*), was born on June 9, 1833, in Jefferson Barracks, Missouri. His father, Philip St. George Cooke, was a career officer in the U.S. Army and remained loyal to the United States during the Civil War. A sister was married to General J.E.B. Stuart (*q.v.*). The younger Cooke graduated from the University of Missouri in 1849 and received a degree in civil engineering from Harvard College in 1854. On January 5, 1864, he married Nannie G. Patton, by whom he had eight children. Cooke worked on railroad construction in Missouri before entering the U.S. Army as a second lieutenant in 1855. Before the war he served in Texas, New Mexico, and Arizona. At the beginning of the Civil War, he resigned his commission and raised a company of light artillery which saw service along the Potomac. In February 1862, he became a major and chief of artillery to the Department of North Carolina, and in April 1862, he was promoted to colonel. He fought at the battle of Seven Pines, and for his performance at the battle of Sharpsburg he was promoted to brigadier general on November 1, 1862. He later fought in the battle of Fredericksburg and distinguished himself in the Wilderness campaign. He surrendered in North Carolina at the war's end. After the war, he was in the mercantile business in Richmond, Virginia, and while active in Democratic politics, he held no public office. He founded the Old Soldier's Home in Richmond during the 1880s. Cooke died in Richmond on April 10, 1891. Freeman, *Lee's Lieutenants*, II, III; Tyler, *Encyclopedia of Virginia Biography*, III.

COOKE, William Mordecai (*Congressman*), whose father's family had settled in Virginia in 1650, was born in Portsmouth, Virginia, on December 11, 1823, to Mordecai and Margaret (Kearns) Cooke. After attending the University of Virginia, he moved to St. Louis in 1843 and studied law. He was a Roman Catholic. He had seven children by his marriage in 1846 to Eliza Von Puhl. In 1849, he moved to Hannibal, where he was judge of the Court of Common Pleas. He returned to St. Louis in 1854. In a state where party lines had been blurred since 1845, as a result of Thomas Hart Benton's change of attitude toward slavery, Cooke joined the anti-Benton forces which were trying to break the political hold of Francis P. Blair, Jr. A secessionist, he sided with the South during the Civil War. In March 1861, he was sent by Governor Claiborne Jackson (*q.v.*) as a commissioner to President Davis (*q.v.*). He served in the provisional Confederate Congress and was elected to the first Confederate House, where he became one of Davis's trusted friends and advisors. He was a member of the Accounts, Commerce, Naval Affairs, Inauguration, and Ordnance and Ordnance Stores Committees of the Congress. He did not stand for reelection. As an aide on the staff of Claiborne Jackson, he also saw military service in the battles of Booneville, Carthage, and Oak Hill. He died of battle wounds on April 14, 1863, at Petersburg, Virginia. Scharf, *History of St. Louis . . . Including Biographical Sketches of Representative Men*, I.

COOPER, Charles Philip (*Bureaucrat*), was born in Cuba on August 13, 1827, to Charles Merien and Annie F. (Garnier) Cooper. There is evidence that he was raised in south Georgia. He had three sons by his first marriage to Hessie Mildred Jackson. After her death, he married Julia Dozier. Little is known of his education or training for the law. Cooper, a Democrat, practiced law in Athens, Georgia, before moving to Duval County, Florida. He later returned to Georgia. As a general agent in the U.S. Treasury Department from 1857 to 1861, Cooper supervised all customs from North Carolina to New Mexico. He resigned his position when the war began, and he went to Richmond to volunteer for service. During the Civil War, he helped to organize the Confederate Treasury Department and was a trusted aide to Christopher G. Memminger (*q.v.*) throughout the war. When the war ended, he practiced law in Duval County. He also represented Duval County in the state legislature in 1866. Little is known of Cooper's postwar life except that he attained prominence as a lawyer in Jacksonville, Florida. He died on January 9, 1895, in Jacksonville. Todd, *Confederate Finance*.

COOPER, Douglas Hancock (*General*), son of the physician Hugh W. Cooper and his wife Mary A. (McClendhan), was born on November 1, 1815, in Amite County, Mississippi. He attended the University of Virginia from 1832 to 1834 but took no degree. He returned to Mississippi and became a planter in Wilkinson County. He was a Baptist and a Democrat. Cooper was married and had a family. He served as a captain of the 1st Mississippi Rifles during the Mexican war. In 1853, President Franklin Pierce appointed him U.S. agent to the Choctaw Nation. There is evidence that he remained in the west until the war began. Pro-Southern, he volunteered for duty in the Confederacy. The Confederate government sent him to secure the allegiance of the Indians at the beginning of the Civil War, and Cooper was commissioned a colonel of the 1st Choctaw and Chickasaw Regiment of Mounted Rifles. In November and December 1861, he fought the battles of Chusro-Talasah and Chustenabla. He commanded Indian troops in the battles of Elkhorn Tavern, Arkansas, and Newtonia, Missouri. In May 1862, he recommended that Indians be used as guerrilla fighters. Although he had helped General Albert Pike to raise a regiment, he ordered Pike's arrest for dereliction of duty in August 1862. In October 1862, he was defeated and temporarily disgraced in the battle of Fort Wayne. For further services rendered in Missouri, he was promoted to brigadier general on May 2, 1863. In August of that year, he allied with Elias Boudinot (*q.v.*) and Stand Watie (*q.v.*) to defeat pro-Union Indian troops. In 1864, he redeemed some of his reputation by commanding an Indian brigade during General Sterling Price's (*q.v.*) second invasion of Missouri. During the last part of the war, Cooper commanded all-Indian troops in the Trans-Mississippi West. There is no evidence of his surrender or parole. After the war, he resided in the Indian Territory, and he prosecuted the Choctaw and Chickasaw claims for lands against the federal government. He died on April 29, 1879, at Old Fort Washita, Indian Nation (now Bryan County, Oklahoma). Abel, *The American Indian as Participant in the Civil War*.

COOPER, Samuel (*General*), son of Major Samuel and Mary (Horton) Cooper, was born on June 12, 1798, in Hackensack, New Jersey. He graduated thirty-sixth in his class of forty at the U.S. Military Academy in 1815 and was commissioned a second lieutenant in the light artillery. From 1818 to 1825, he served in the adjutant general's office in Washington. In 1827, he married a granddaughter of George Mason and sister of James M. Mason (*q.v.*). He became thoroughly Southern after his marriage into this aristocratic Virginia family. He was a nominal Democrat and an Episcopalian. In 1836, he was promoted to captain of the 4th Artillery and wrote *Concise History of Instruction and Regulation for the Militia and Volunteers of the United States*. During the Florida Seminole War of 1841-1842, he was chief of staff to General William J. Worth. As a lieutenant colonel, he served in the War Department from 1842 to 1852 as an assistant adjutant general. He was made a brevet colonel during the Mexican War. In 1852, he became adjutant general of the army, a position he held until his resignation from the army in March 1861. During the Civil War, he served as adjutant and inspector general of the Confederate Army, and on May 16, 1861, he was named a full general, the highest ranking officer in the Confederacy. Too old for field command, he was an organizational genius who was most responsible for controlling the uncoordinated maneuvers of the early troops. Much of the success at First Manassas was attributable to him. A close friend of President Jefferson Davis (*q.v.*), he was involved in major strategy decisions throughout the war. He left Richmond with the cabinet at the end of the war and surrendered in April 1865. He was soon paroled and allowed to return to his home near Alexandria, Virginia. Cooper retired to private life and died in Alexandria on December 14, 1876. *Southern Historical Society Papers*, III; Wright, *General Officers of the Confederate Army*.

CORSE, Montgomery Dent (*General*), was born on March 14, 1816, in Alexandria, Virginia. He received an academic and business education. He was an Episcopalian. Corse was a captain of the 1st Virginia Regiment during the Mexican War. He seems to have served as a bank clerk in Alexandria during the 1840s. After seeking gold in California, he became an Alexandria banker in 1856. In 1860, he organized the Old Dominion Rifles, and he entered the Confederate Army as colonel of the 17th Virginia Regiment. Corse served in James Longstreet's (*q.v.*) Brigade during the battle of First Manassas in July 1861 and in the battles of Yorktown, Williamsburg, Seven Pines, and the Seven Days in 1862, winning the praise of both Longstreet and Lee (*q.v.*). In August and September of that year, he was wounded at Second Manassas and again at South Mountain. Upon his recovery, he was promoted to brigadier general on November 1, 1862. He was given a brigade in Pickett's Division and later served in the Pennsylvania campaigns of 1863-1864, in southwest Virginia, and in eastern Tennessee. In 1864, he opposed General Benjamin F. Butler on the James River, and he participated in the Virginia battles of Petersburg, Richmond, Dinwiddie Court

House, and Five Forks. He was captured on April 6, 1865, during the battle of Sailor's Creek and was confined until August 1865. After his parole, he returned to banking in Alexandria. He died there in retirement on February 11, 1895. Freeman, *Lee's Lieutenants*, II, III.

COX, William Ruffin (*General*), son of Thomas and Olivia (Norfleet) Cox, was born on March 11, 1832, in Scotland Neck, Halifax County, North Carolina, where his father was a merchant. He attended Vine Hill Academy in North Carolina before moving with his mother to Tennessee, where he graduated from Franklin College in 1851 and the Lebanon College Law School in 1853. Admitted to the bar in 1853, he practiced in Nashville from 1853 to 1857. He was an Episcopalian and a Democrat. Cox was married three times: to Penelope B. Battle in 1857, Fannie Augusta Lyman in 1883, and Mrs. Herbert A. Claiborne in 1905. He had two sons by his second wife. Soon after his first marriage, Cox returned to North Carolina to become a planter in Edgecombe County. He was a firm secessionist. When the war began, Cox enlisted in the Confederate Army and was made a major in the 2nd North Carolina Regiment. He participated in the Virginia battles of Mechanicsville, Malvern Hill, and Sharpsburg in 1862. In 1863, he fought at the battle of Chancellorsville, and on May 31, 1864, he was promoted to brigadier general, after participating in the battle of Spotsylvania. Cox also served with General Jubal A. Early (*q.v.*) in the Valley and with Robert E. Lee (*q.v.*) at Petersburg, and he led the last charge before the surrender at Appomattox. He was paroled soon after. He then returned to practice law and to serve as president of the Chatham Coal Fields Railroad in Raleigh during the late 1860s. From 1868 to 1874, he was solicitor for the Sixth District of North Carolina, and he helped to restore the power of the Democratic party in the state. After a term as superior court judge in 1877-1878, he was elected three times to the U.S. House, from 1881 to 1887. In the House, he was a member of the Foreign Affairs Committee and served as chairman of the congressional committee on civil service reform. He was defeated in a bid for reelection. From 1893 to 1900, he was secretary of the U.S. Senate. Cox then returned to his farm near Raleigh. He was president of the North Carolina Agricultural Society in 1900-1901 and a member of the Board of Trustees of the University of the South prior to his death on December 26, 1919, in Richmond, Virginia. *Biographical Directory of the American Congress*; Evans, *Confederate Military History*, II.

CRAIGE, Francis Burton (*Congressman*), was born into the farming family of David and Mary (Foster) Craige on March 13, 1811, in Rowan County, North Carolina. He received a classical education in the schools of Salisbury before graduating in 1829 from the University of North Carolina. He also received his M.A. there in 1847. His marriage to Elizabeth Phifer Erwin produced three sons. From 1829 to 1831, Craige edited the *Western Carolinian* in Salisbury. He studied law and was admitted to the Salisbury bar in 1832. A Democrat, he represented Salisbury in the state legislature from 1832 to 1834. Active in local politics, he held no further public office until he was elected to the U.S. House in 1853. He served continuously in the House until his state seceded, at which time he resigned. As a delegate to the North Carolina secession convention in 1861, Craige, a secessionist, offered the Ordinance of Secession. He also served in the provisional Confederate Congress at Richmond but retired because he thought himself too old. In Richmond, he served on special committees and was a supporter of the Davis administration. There is no evidence that he gave further service in the Confederate government. Craige practiced law when the war ended. There is no record that he remained in public life. He died in Concord, North Carolina, on December 30, 1875. Ashe, *Cyclopedia of Eminent and Representative Men of the Carolinas. . . . Century*, I.

CRAIGMILES, John H. (*Bureaucrat*), was born on July 7, 1825, to Joseph Craigmiles and was raised in Cleveland, Tennessee. He was an Episcopal church warden and became a banker in Cleveland sometime in the 1840s. Nothing is known of his prewar public career. He voted against secession in the Tennessee convention but volunteered for service in the Confederate government after the war began. As chief commissary agent under Secretary of War Judah P. Benjamin (*q.v.*), his task was to gather and transport food to the troops in the field. He ably coordinated the movement of all goods to the front lines. When the war ended, he returned to banking in Cleveland. Because of the severe internal dissension in Tennessee left over from the war, Craigmiles was never able to participate in public life after the war. At one time the Brownlow government accused him of treason to the Union because of his dedication to the Confederate cause. He married Adelia Thompson in 1866 and they had two daughters. Craigmiles became president of the First National Bank of Cleveland during the late 1860s and served in that capacity until his death there on January 7, 1899. Goff, *Confederate Supply*.

CRAWFORD, Martin Jenkins (*Congressman*), was born into the well-known planting family of Major Hardy and Betsy Roberts (Jenkins) Crawford in Jasper County, Georgia, on March 17, 1820. Educated at Brownwood Institute and Mercer University, he studied law and was admitted to the bar in 1839 in Hamilton, Harris County, Georgia. Crawford was a farmer and a Baptist like his father. He married Amanda J. Reese on December 29, 1842; they had five children. He served in the state House of Representatives from 1845 to 1847. In 1849, he moved to Columbus, Muscogee County, where he was a member of the law firm of Ingram and Porter. In 1850, he was a delegate to the Southern rights convention in Nashville, and in 1854, he was named judge of the Superior Court of the Chattahoochee Circuit. He served as a Democrat in the U.S. House of Representatives from 1855 to 1861, where he opposed the Know-Nothing party and was a moderate secessionist who strongly advocated states' rights. He withdrew from Washington and the Congress when Georgia seceded. In the provisional Confederate Congress, he was a member of the Commercial Affairs and Accounts Committees and supported Howell Cobb (*q.v.*) for the presidency of the Confederacy. President Davis (*q.v.*) appointed him a special peace commissioner to the United States in 1861. Crawford also organized the 3rd Regiment of Georgia Cavalry and served in 1862-1863 as a colonel on the staff of Howell Cobb. He served mainly in Georgia. The war ruined him financially. Crawford resumed his law practice in Columbus. He served as judge of the Superior Court of the Chattahoochee Circuit again from 1875 to 1880 and as an associate justice of the Georgia Supreme Court from 1880 until his death on July 23, 1883, in Columbus. Candler and Evans (eds.), *Cyclopedia of Georgia*, II; Northen (ed.), *Men of Mark in Georgia*, III.

CRENSHAW, William Graves (*Businessman, Diplomat*), was from Richmond, Virginia. Little is known of his family or his upbringing. He was an Episcopalian and a Democrat, and he was married to Fanny Elizabeth Graves, a cousin. Crenshaw was senior member of the Richmond firm of Crenshaw and Company, importers and exporters, in the years before the Civil War. He supported secession and used his business talents in the employ of the Confederate government. He organized and equipped the Crenshaw battery of artillery and was its commander from 1861 to 1863. In 1863, he was a special Confederate agent to England, procuring war vessels and supplies and attempting to persuade the English government to support the Confederacy. After the war, he remained in England until 1868, when he returned to Richmond. In the 1880s, he made a fortune in mining pyrites for the manufacture of sulphuric acid. It is not known when he died. Goff, *Confederate Supply*; *National Cyclopedia of American Biography*; Owsley, *King Cotton Diplomacy*.

CRITTENDEN, George Bibb (*General*), son of John Jordan and Sally (Lee) Crittenden, was born in Russellville, Logan County, Kentucky, on March 20, 1812. His brother, Thomas L. Crittenden, was a Union general during the Civil War. He graduated twenty-sixth in a class of forty-five from the U.S. Military Academy in 1832 and resigned from the army the following year to study law at Transylvania University. Crittenden was a member of the Whig party. In 1835, he went to Texas, where he was held prisoner by the Mexicans for a year. He returned to Kentucky in 1837 and practiced law for ten years before serving as a captain of Kentucky Mounted Rifles during the Mexican War. Breveted major for his gallantry at Contreras and Churubusco, he remained in the regular army on frontier duty, becoming a full major in 1848 and a lieutenant colonel in 1856. At the beginning of the Civil War, Crittenden went against his father's wishes, resigned his commission, and joined the Confederate Army, becoming a colonel of infantry. In June 1861, he commanded the Trans-Allegheny Department. Promoted to brigadier general on August 15, 1861, and to major general on November 9, 1861, he commanded the District of East Tennessee and had charge of military operations in Kentucky. At the battles of Mill Springs and Logan's Crossroads, Kentucky, on January 19-20, 1862, he was badly defeated and was subsequently censured and placed under arrest. He resigned his commission on October 23, 1862, and served without rank on the staff of General John S. Williams (*q.v.*) for the rest of the war. After the war, he moved to Frankfort, Kentucky, where he was state librarian from 1867 to 1874. Crittenden died in retirement on November 27, 1880, in Danville, Kentucky. Kirwin, *John J. Crittenden: The Struggle for the Union*; Warner, *Generals in Gray*.

CROCKETT, John Watkins (*Congressman*), son of John W. and Louisa (Bullock) Crockett, was born on May 17, 1818, in Jessamine County, Kentucky, where his father was a farmer. Educated in the common schools, he practiced law in Paducah before moving to Henderson, Kentucky, prior to the Civil War. He had two children by his first marriage to a Mrs. Smedley, and a son by his second marriage to Louisa Ingram. Crockett, though a Whig politician and a unionist, supported secession after Fort Sumter. He was a delegate to the Kentucky convention at Bowling Green, where he was elected to represent the Second Congressional District in the first Confederate House of Representatives. He served on the Committee on elections in the House and when he was not on leave of absence, generally recorded his vote with the Davis administration. Crockett did not stand for reelection; instead he practiced law in Henderson. He took no further part in the war effort. After the war, Crockett returned to his law practice and refrained from all political life. He died in Madisonville, Kentucky, on June 20, 1874. *Centennial of Henderson County, Kentucky*; Levin, *Lawyers and Lawmakers of Kentucky*.

CRUIKSHANK, Marcus Henderson (*Congressman*), was born on December 12, 1826, in Autauga County, Alabama. He studied law in Talladega under Alexander White, whose firm he joined in 1847. He was a Whig ally of William P. Chilton (*q.v.*) and a Presbyterian. Cruikshank married Matilda Washington Chrisman, by whom he had one son. Before the war, he was registrar in chancery and mayor of Talladega during the 1850s. He was also editor and owner of the Talladega *Reporter*. He continued as mayor during the early part of the war, when his fear of Negro uprisings prompted him to begin a patrol system in the town. Even though he was considered a unionist, if not a reconstructionist, he defeated Jabez L. M. Curry (*q.v.*) for election to the second Confederate House in 1863. Curry's support of the Davis administration was a strong factor in his defeat. Though Cruikshank voted mostly against administration legislation, he loyally performed many tasks for the Confederacy. In 1864, he was involved in purchasing and delivering food to Confederate soldiers. He served on the Enrolled Bills, Printing, and Ordnance Stores Committees, and he was a vigorous opponent of the writ of *habeas corpus*. Earlier in the war he had directed a salt works for the government. After the war, he worked with the Reconstruction governor of Alabama on a committee to relieve the destitute of Alàbama. In 1873, he was owner and editor of the *Reporter and Watchtower* in Talladega, which he continued to edit until he died on October 10, 1881. Jemison, *Historic Tales of Talladega*.

CRUMP, William Wood (*Bureaucrat*), son of Sterling Jamieson and Elizabeth (Wood) Crump, was born on November 25, 1819, in Henrico County, Virginia. His father was an importer-merchant in Richmond, where the younger Crump attended Dr. Gwathmey's school before going to Amherst Institute in Massachusetts. He graduated from the College of William and Mary in 1838, where he read law under Beverly Tucker. In 1840, he was admitted to the Richmond bar, practicing in that city for some years. He was a staunch states' rights Democrat and an Episcopalian. He had four children by his marriage to Mary S. Tabb. Crump was a judge of the circuit court of Richmond in 1851-1852 and a member of the Richmond city council in the late 1850s. During the Civil War, he was an ardent Confederate and he was appointed assistant secretary of the treasury to George Trenholm (*q.v.*). He opposed the congressional movement to remove from office all government employees under forty years of age, and he formulated a plan for continuing the employment of those minor bureaucrats. After the war, he returned to his law practice, assisted in the legal defense of former President Davis (*q.v.*), and served in the state legislature. Little else is known of his postwar career. He died in Richmond on February 27, 1897. Todd, *Confederate Finance*; Tyler, *Encyclopedia of Virginia Biography*, II.

CUMMING, Alfred (*General*), was born to Henry H. and Julia (Bryan) Cumming on January 30, 1829, in Augusta, Georgia, a city which his family had helped to make a cotton manufacturing center. He graduated thirty-fifth in a class of forty-three from the U.S. Military Academy in 1849. Cumming was an Episcopalian and had three children by his marriage to Sarah M. Davis. He was a career officer in the U.S. Army, and from 1851 to 1853, he was an aide to General David Twiggs in New Orleans. Promoted to first lieutenant in 1855 and to captain the following year, he participated in the Utah expedition of 1859-1860. He resigned from the army in January 1861 and entered the service of the Confederate government. At the beginning of the Civil War, he commanded a Georgia arsenal, but, craving action, he was commissioned a lieutenant colonel in the 10th Georgia Regiment. After being promoted to colonel in October 1861, he was twice wounded while commanding an Alabama brigade during the battles of Malvern Hill and Sharpsburg. He was promoted to brigadier general on October 29, 1862. Captured during the siege of Vicksburg, upon his exchange he served in the battle of Missionary Ridge in 1863 and during the Atlanta campaign at Chickamauga, Dalton, Allatoona, New Hope Church, and Kenesaw Mountain. He was disabled on August 3, 1864, at Jonesboro and gave no further service to the Confederacy. After the war, he farmed in Floyd County, Georgia, for some years. He lived in Rome, Georgia, from 1880 to 1896, when he moved to Augusta and retired. Cumming died on December 5, 1910, in Rome, Georgia. Northen (ed.), *Men of Mark in Georgia*, III.

CURRIN, David Maney (*Congressman*), was born in Murfreesboro, Tennessee, on November 11, 1817. He graduated from Nashville University in 1834 and he practiced law in Memphis. His law partner was Howell Edmunds Jackson, who became one of Tennessee's most eminent attorneys and who was a brother of General William Hicks Jackson (*q.v.*). A Democrat, he served in the state legislature in 1851. At the outbreak of war, the law partnership was dissolved. Currin was a secessionist. He served in the provisional Congress on the Commercial Affairs Committee. In the first Confederate House, he served on the Buildings and Naval Affairs Committees. He generally supported the Davis administration, and he earned a reputation as a conscientious congressman. Currin was elected to the second Congress but died in Richmond on March 25, 1864. *National Cyclopedia of American Biography*.

CURRY, Jabez Lamar Monroe (*Congressman*), was born to William and Susan (Winn) Curry in Lincoln County, Georgia, on June 5, 1825. His family moved to Talladega County, Alabama, in 1837, and he was educated in private schools in Georgia and South Carolina, including Moses Waddell's School of Law. He graduated from the University of Georgia in 1843 and attended the Dane Law School at Harvard University in 1845. He was admitted to the Talladega bar in 1846. He was also a Baptist minister. Curry had four children by his March 4, 1847, marriage to Ann Alexander Bowie. Following her death, he married Mary Wortham on June 25, 1867. He served briefly in the Texas Rangers during the Mexican War before serving terms in the Alabama legislature in 1847, 1853, and 1855. As a states' right Democrat, he was elected to the U.S. House of Representatives in 1857 and 1859. He was a secessionist and a member of the provisional Congress and the first Confederate House but was defeated for reelection to the second. In the provisional Congress, he was active in the constitutional debates. In the House, he served on the Commerce, Elections, Rules, and Conference Committees. Generally an administration supporter, in 1863 he became critical of President Davis's (*q.v.*) conduct of the war. After he left the Confederate Congress in 1864, he was made lieutenant colonel of the 5th Alabama Regiment. He saw no major action. After the war, he was a historian, Baptist minister, educator, and redemptionist politician. He was named president of Alabama's Howard College in 1865. As president of Richmond College from 1868 to 1881, he helped to transform that small Baptist college into a good university. From 1885 to 1888, he was American envoy extraordinary and minister plenipotentiary to Spain, and in 1891, he published a biography of William Gladstone. He became an active Democrat. From 1881 until his death, he was also an agent for the Peabody Fund for aid to Southern education. He died on February 12, 1903, in Asheville, North Carolina. Alderman and Gordon, *Jabez L. M. Curry*.

D

DABNEY, Robert Lewis (*Minister*), was born to Charles Dabney, Jr., and his wife Elizabeth R. (Price) on March 5, 1820, in Louisa County, Virginia. He attended Hampden-Sidney College from 1836 to 1837 and received his M.A. from the University of Virginia in 1842. After teaching school, he entered Union Theological Seminary at Richmond and graduated first in his class in 1846. He was licensed to preach in the Presbyterian church the same year and became a missionary in Louisa County. On March 28, 1848, he married Lavinia Morrison; they had children. From 1847 to 1853, Dabney held a pastorate in Augusta County, Virginia. In 1853, he became a professor of church history at Union Theological Seminary, a position which he kept for thirty years. He was the editor and founder of the *Presbyterian Critic* and the co-editor of the *Southern Presbyterian Review*. Dabney opposed the Civil War, but in 1861, he became a chaplain for the 18th Virginia Regiment. He also served as chief of staff, adjutant general, and confidant of his friend, General Thomas J. Jackson (*q.v.*), whose biography he published in 1864. When the war ended, he returned to teach at Union Theological Seminary. In 1868, Dabney published *Defense of Virginia and the South*. He became one of the great spokesmen for a return to the romantic Old South. From 1883 to 1894, he held a chair of moral philosophy at the University of Texas. He was also a founder of Austin Theological Seminary in Texas in the late 1880s. Dabney died in retirement in Victoria, Texas, on January 3, 1898. Johnson, *Life and Letters of Robert Lewis Dabney*.

DANIEL, John Moncure (*Editor*), was born to the physician John Moncure Daniel and his wife Azia (Mitchell) on October 24, 1825, in Stafford County,

Virginia. Largely self-educated, he attended school in Richmond and studied law in Fredericksburg. He was a Democrat, an Episcopalian, and a bachelor. In 1846, he was librarian of the Patrick Henry Society. He edited the *Southern Planter* and later the Richmond *Examiner* (1848-1861), a Democratic party organ, before the Civil War. He also held two diplomatic posts: as charge d'affairs at the court of Tunis in 1853 and as minister resident to Sardinia in 1856. Daniel was not a secessionist, yet he helped the secessionist movement in Virginia. By the time of the state secession convention, he believed that secession was the only solution to the South's dilemma. When the war began, he volunteered for the staff of General John B. Floyd; later he served on the staff of Ambrose P. Hill (*q.v.*). But his major contribution to the war effort was as editor of the Richmond *Examiner*. He reported the Seven Days' battles and was wounded at Mechanicsville. He soon became contemptuous of the Davis administration's attempt to conduct the war, and he turned the *Examiner* into an anti-administration organ. His articles revealed an interest in the civil as well as military operations of the war. He was a newspaper genius who covered the war from the front, and his articles influenced military policy. For example, his criticism of Braxton Bragg (*q.v.*) permanently affected that general's career, and he leveled withering attacks on other generals. He also objected to the Davis administration's crude attempt to plant favorable stories in the press, and he argued for a free press in the Confederacy. In 1864, he fought a duel with Edward A. Elmore, the treasurer of the Confederate States. He died on March 30, 1865, in Richmond. Andrews, *The South Reports the Civil War*; Hughs, *Editors of the Past*.

DANIEL, Junius (*General*), son of John Reeve Jones Daniel, was born on June 27, 1828, in Halifax, North Carolina. His father was a North Carolina congressman and attorney general. The younger Daniel received a presidential appointment from James Knox Polk to the U.S. Military Academy, where he graduated thirty-third in a class of forty-two in 1851. In October 1860, he married Ellen Long. Daniel was a second lieutenant in the army in Kentucky in 1851. The following year he was promoted to first lieutenant, and he served in New Mexico before resigning in 1858 to run his father's plantation in Shreveport, Caddo Parish, Louisiana. When the Civil War began, he was elected colonel of the 14th North Carolina Infantry; he also helped to organize troops at the beginning of the Civil War. He was a brigade commander during the Seven Days' battles and served with particular gallantry at the battle of Malvern Hill. Promoted to brigadier general on September 1, 1862, he was a hero on the first day of the battle of Gettysburg in July 1863. Daniel continued service with the Army of Northern Virginia and fought in the battle of Drewry's Bluff in May 1864. Lee (*q.v.*) himself recommended his promotion to major general. Daniel was mortally wounded at the "Bloody Angle" of Spotsylvania Court House while trying to recapture the Confederate works. He died there on May 13, 1864. Evans, *Confederate Military History*, IV.

DARDEN, Stephen Heard (*Congressman*), was born on November 19, 1816, in Fayette, Mississippi, to Washington Lee and Ann (Sharkey) Darden. He was a Mason and was twice married, the second time in 1862. Little is known of his early training. In 1836, Darden came to Texas, where he fought in the Texas army during the war for independence. He moved to Madison County, Mississippi, in the early 1840s but returned to Texas in 1846 to farm in Gonzales County. Before the Civil War, he represented Gonzales County three times in the state House and once in the state Senate. He was a Democrat, and he was elected to the Texas secession convention. He was a unionist when secession was initially proposed but finally voted for the Secession Ordinance because the majority of the delegates supported it. When the war began, he volunteered for the army. As a first lieutenant and later captain in Key's Infantry, Hood's Regiment of the 4th Texas Brigade, Darden fought in engagements from Yorktown to Sharpsburg until he was discharged because of ill health. He subsequently joined the state militia as major and later as colonel. In 1864, he was elected to fill the unexpired term of John Wilcox (*q.v.*) in the Confederate House. He served on the Committee on Naval Affairs and generally opposed the Davis administration. After the war he was broke. There is some evidence that he returned to his farm in Gonzales County. In 1874, he was Democratic state comptroller of public accounts. He died in retirement on May 16, 1902, in Wharton, Texas. *Confederate Veteran*, XI.

DARGAN, Edmund Strother (Spann) (*Congressman*), was born on April 15, 1805, in Wadesboro, North Carolina, to a Baptist preacher and farmer and his wife Lilly. His father died while he was young, and Dargan subsequently earned his living as a farm laborer. Largely self-educated, he studied law and was admitted to the Wadesboro bar in 1829. Dargan had one daughter by his marriage to Roxana Brock. He moved to Alabama in 1829 and taught school and served as a justice of the peace in Washington, Alabama. He began a law practice in Montgomery in 1833. He was a circuit court judge in Mobile in 1841-1842 and took up residence there. He served simultaneously as state senator and mayor of Mobile in 1844. In 1845, he was elected as a Democrat to the U.S. House of Representatives, but two years later he refused renomination. From 1847 to 1849, he was associate justice of the state Supreme Court; he became chief justice in 1849 and resigned three years later to resume his law practice in Mobile. In 1861, he voted for secession at the state convention. The Mobile district elected him to the first Confederate Congress where he was a Davis supporter. Dargan declined reelection to a second term in 1864, returned to his law practice, and never reentered public life. While in Congress, he assisted the trading center of Mobile by opposing the impressment of farm produce. He actively supported conscription. Dargan once attacked Henry S. Foote (*q.v.*) with a knife on the floor of the Confederate House. His service on the Judiciary Committee was considered important, and he was instrumental in writing major Confederate legislation. After the war, he practiced law in Mobile, where he lived at the time of his death on November 22, 1879. *Confederate Veteran*, XXXI; Garrett, *Reminiscences of Public Men in Alabama*.

DAVIDSON, Allen Turner (*Congressman*), son of William Mitchell and Elizabeth (Vance) Davidson, was born in Haywood County, North Carolina, on May 9, 1819. He attended Waynesville Academy, clerked in his father's Waynesville store, and served as clerk and master in equity of Haywood County in 1843. He was admitted to the North Carolina bar in 1845. By his marriage in 1842 to Elizabeth A. Howell, Davidson had three daughters and three sons. A Whig and a member of the Methodist Episcopal church, he was also one of the leading lawyers in his part of the state. From 1846 to 1862, he was solicitor (district attorney) for Cherokee County, North Carolina. In 1860, he became president of the Merchants and Miners Bank. Davidson opposed secession until Lincoln sent troops into the South. During the war, he represented Macon County in the provisional Congress and the first Confederate House, where he lost his bid for reelection in 1864. He voted against a majority of the Davis administration's legislation, following his constituents' antagonism to the war effort. A conservative, Davidson resented arbitrary conscription laws. He served on the Post Office and Post Roads, the Commissary, and the Military Transportation Committees. In 1864-1865, he served as a member of Governor Zebulon Vance's (*q.v.*) Council of the State of North Carolina. As agent of the Commissary Department of North Carolina, he also provided supplies for the families of North Carolina soldiers. After the war, Davidson mostly avoided politics, although he did serve on the Conservative party nominating committee and was an opponent of the Republican William W. Holden (*q.v.*). In 1865, he settled in Franklin, Macon County, and practiced law. He moved to Asheville, North Carolina, in 1869, where he became a leader of the Asheville bar until his retirement in 1885. He died in Asheville on January 24, 1905. Ashe, *Cyclopedia of Eminent and Representative Men of the Carolinas*. . . .

DAVIS, George (*Congressman, Cabinet Member*), whose aristocratic family had lived in the Cape Fear District for a century, was born on his father's plantation in New Hanover County, North Carolina, on March 1, 1820, to Thomas Frederick and Sarah Isabella (Eagles) Davis. He graduated first in his class of 1838 at the University of North Carolina and two years later began a law practice in Wilmington, North Carolina. He had a son by his first marriage on November 17, 1842, to Mary A. Polk. After her death, he married Monimia Fairfax on May 9, 1866. A brother was an Episcopal bishop of North Carolina. Before the war, Davis was a staunch Whig in a Democratic section and refused to run for office. He initially opposed secession and was a delegate to the Washington peace conference early in 1861. But on March 2 of that year he pushed for secession, and he helped to unite the Cape Fear District behind the war effort. As a member of the provisional Confederate Congress, he supported measures which would protect property interests. He also served in the first Confederate Senate, where he achieved a reputation as a legal genius and a supporter of the Davis administration. In Congress he served on the Buildings, Claims, Finance, Naval Affairs, and Conference Committees. Because he had become a Democrat and a supporter of secession, he was defeated for reelection to the Senate by William A. Graham (*q.v.*), a unionist Whig. President Jefferson Davis (*q.v.*) made Davis attorney general of the Confederacy on January 4, 1864, a position which he held for the remainder of the war. He performed well as attorney general, although much of his time was spent as an advisor to the president and the other cabinet members. Davis seldom wrote opinions in favor of individual states' claims; he had become a thoroughgoing Southern nationalist. He often sided with the president against Congress. At the end of the war, he attempted to escape to Europe but was captured and imprisoned in Fort Hamilton and later released. He returned to his law practice in Wilmington, where he served as legal counsel to the Atlantic Coast Line Railroad. He shunned public office, maintaining a successful law practice and also lecturing widely on the merits of the Confederate war effort. In 1878, he turned down an appointment as chief justice of the North Carolina Supreme Court. He died in Wilmington, North Carolina, on February 23, 1896. Ashe, *George Davis, Attorney General of the Confederate States*; Patrick, *Jefferson Davis and His Cabinet*.

DAVIS, Jefferson (*President*), was born on June 3, 1808, in Christian (now Todd) County, Kentucky. The son of the farmer Samuel Davis and his wife Jane (Cook), the younger Davis was raised a Baptist, but converted to the Episcopal church during the Civil War. He grew up on a small farm in Wilkinson County, Mississippi. He was educated at the Roman Catholic Seminary in Washington County, Kentucky, and attended Transylvania University from 1821 to 1824. His older brother Joseph had become a successful planter, and he sent Jefferson to West Point, from where he graduated in 1828. Davis held frontier posts, participated in the Black Hawk War in 1832, and resigned his commission in 1835. In July 1835, he married Sarah Knox Taylor, daughter of Zachary Taylor. She died of malaria on September 15, 1835. Heartbroken, Davis drifted back to Mississippi, where his brother Joseph gave him a plantation to run. On February 26, 1845, he married Varina Howell (*q.v.*), the daughter of a wealthy planter. They had six children. Davis had entered politics as a Democrat and was elected to the U.S. House of Representatives, where he served from 1845 to 1847. The state legislature appointed him to the U.S. Senate in 1847. During the Mexican War he served as colonel of the "Mississippi Rifles" and was wounded at the battle of Buena Vista. Davis was a successful military commander and formed many lasting friendships with his fellow officers. When the war ended, he returned to the Senate but resigned to make an unsuccessful bid for governor of Mississippi in 1850..An ardent expansionist and opponent of California's entrance into the Union as a free state, he nonetheless advocated cooperation and moderation in the Compromise of

1850. This stand may have been responsible for his loss in the gubernatorial race. He remained active in Democratic politics and, as President Franklin Pierce's secretary of war from 1853 to 1857, he gained a reputation as an excellent administrator. In 1857, he returned to the U.S. Senate and became a staunch opponent of interference with slavery in the territories. Although a moderate on secession and a supporter of the Crittenden Compromise, he favored the secession of Mississippi. When the state seceded, he resigned from the Senate and was made major general of Mississippi state troops. The provisional Confederate Congress elected him president of the Confederacy, and he was made permanent president in October 1861. Davis believed that his task was to mount a defensive war effort, to serve as commander in chief of the Confederate Army, and to organize support from the many conflicting political interests in the South. But he also believed in the self-determination of the state governments, and he refused to force central authority on the Southern governors. Because he discouraged disagreement and often chose cabinet members who supported his views, the dialogue which was needed to insure a successful central coordination of the war effort never materialized. Although he was a man of utmost personal integrity, he could never inspire the Southern people to make sacrifices for the war effort. Davis found that the Confederate Congress reflected that lack of unity in its refusal to give his plans wholehearted support. He also lacked the political acumen to manipulate the varied interests in the Congress. Lacking that support and given his reputation for poor judgment in selecting his subordinates, the president fell victim to the overly strong military personality of Robert E. Lee (*q.v.*) and his friendship for Braxton Bragg (*q.v.*). As a result, he made commitments to protect the eastern front, remained loyal to inferior officers for too long, and found his plans for a defensive war evaporating in the need for a decisive offensive action. He was also afflicted with migraine headaches and subject to periodic fits of depression which diminished his capacity to lead. Yet historians claim Davis was the most qualified man in the South for that impossible task of governing the Confederacy. As the war drew to a close, Davis left Richmond, went south, and considered the formation of a government in exile. But Federal troops captured him near Irwinville, Georgia, on May 10, 1865, and on May 24, he was indicted for treason against the United States. He was made a prisoner in Fort Monroe, Virginia, where he suffered extreme hardship until his release on May 14, 1867. Davis was never brought to trial and never sought restoration of his citizenship. He retired to his home Beauvoir, near Biloxi, Mississippi, entered into several unsuccessful business ventures, and wrote his version of the secession crisis, *The Rise and Fall of the Confederate Government* (2 vols., 1878-1881), in which he claimed the South had seceded to protect the rights of states. He died in New Orleans on December 6, 1889. Cooper, "A Reassessment of Jefferson Davis as War Leader: The Case from Atlanta to Nashville"; Nevins, *Statesmanship of the Civil War*; Strode, *Jefferson Davis*, I-III.

DAVIS, Joseph Robert (*General*), was born to Isaac Davis, a brother of Jefferson Davis (*q.v.*), and his wife, Susan (Gartley) on January 12, 1825, in Woodville, Wilkinson County, Mississippi. He attended school in Nashville, Tennessee, and Miami University in Ohio before practicing law in Canton, Madison County, Mississippi. He developed a large and successful practice.He was first married to Frances Peyton in 1848; he had a son and two daughters by his second marriage to Margaret Cary Green in 1879. Davis, who was also a farmer, served as a secessionist Democrat in the state Senate in 1860. In April 1861, he resigned and became a lieutenant colonel of the 10th Mississippi Infantry. He served as aide-de-camp to Jefferson Davis and was promoted to colonel in August 1861. After becoming brigadier general on September 15, 1862, he served with distinction at the battle of Gettysburg in 1863 and in the Wilderness, at Spotsylvania, and at Cold Harbor in 1864. Davis fought in nearly all battles of the Army of Northern Virginia under General Henry Heth (*q.v.*). He surrendered at Appomattox and was paroled in April 1865. After the war, he was a lawyer and farmer in Biloxi, Mississippi, where he died on September 15, 1896. Davis held no postwar public office. Evans, *Confederate Military History*, VII; Morrison (ed.), *Memoirs of Henry Heth*.

DAVIS, Nicholas, Jr. (*Congressman*), son of Nicholas and Martha (Hargrave) Davis, was born in Athens, Georgia, on January 14, 1825. He attended the University of Virginia before becoming a planter like his father. He had four children by his marriage to Sophia Lowe. Davis served under Colonel Jere Clemens in the Mexican War. He was a conservative delegate to the Nashville Convention of 1850. In 1851, he represented Limestone County in the lower House of the Alabama legislature as a Whig. He was a presidential elector on the Winfield Scott ticket in 1852 and on the Stephen Douglas ticket in 1860. In 1855, he became solicitor for the city of Huntsville. Davis was a cooperationist delegate and an ally of Jere Clemens in the Alabama secession convention in 1861. When he was certain that other Southern states would follow Alabama, he supported secession. Later, he completed Thomas Fearn's (*q.v.*) term in the provisional Congress, where he served on the Public Lands, Territories, and Pay and Mileage Committees. He also commanded a battalion in the Confederate Army during 1862, as lieutenant colonel of the 19th Alabama Infantry. He became dissatisfied with the war and fled behind the Union lines into north Alabama, but in no way assisted the Union cause. He held no further duties in the Confederacy, devoting himself to farming. After the war, Davis joined the Union party in hopes of being a leader in Alabama's reconstruction, but soon left the party because of his opposition to carpetbaggers and Negro politicians. He practiced criminal law in Huntsville, Alabama, where he died on November 3, 1874. Fleming, *Civil War and Reconstruction in Alabama*; Owen, *History of Alabama and Dictionary of Alabama Biography*, III.

DAVIS, Reuben (*Congressman*), was born in Winchester, Tennessee, on January 18, 1813, where his father, the Reverend John Davis, was a Baptist minister and farmer. The family moved to northern Alabama five years later, where the younger Davis studied medicine and read for the law. In 1831, he married Mary Halbert; after her death he married a niece of Joseph G. Baldwin. In 1832, he practiced law and served as district attorney for the Sixth Judicial District in Athens, Monroe County, Mississippi. Davis moved to Aberdeen to practice law, and he received the Whig nomination for Congress in 1838. He held conservative views on bank legislation and supported the Whigs in 1840 but joined the Democratic party after the 1840 election. In 1842, he was named associate justice of the state Supreme Court. During the Mexican War, Davis was colonel of the 2nd Mississippi Regiment and almost died from diarrhea in 1847. The following year he ran for Congress as an independent but withdrew from the race. He opposed Calhoun's Address to the Southern People. After he had fallen one vote short of being elected to Congress as a Union Democrat candidate in 1851, he became an attorney for the New Orleans, Jackson, and Great Northern Railroad. In 1855, he was elected to the state legislature, where he opposed the Know-Nothings and decried the secession movement as a step toward bloody revolution. He was finally elected to the U.S. House of Representatives from Mississippi in 1857 and reelected in 1859. In Congress, he became an ultra fire-eater who aligned himself with John J. Pettus (*q.v.*) and William Barksdale (*q.v.*), but in 1860-1861 he joined the Congressional Committee of Thirty-three, which sought to avert war. The election of Lincoln confirmed his views on the necessity for secession, and he urged Mississippi to action. Davis resigned from Congress early in 1861. He held the ranks of brigadier and major general of Mississippi state troops and served in the Kentucky invasion of 1861. He was also elected to the Confederate House, where he continuously criticized war policy and fell out of favor with the Davis administration. He urged an offensive war, opposed the suspension of *habeas corpus*, and usually opposed administration legislation. He served on the Military Affairs Committee, was often absent from sessions, and finally resigned from Congress in 1864 to run for governor. But his unpopularity with the troops and his connections with the unpopular Governor Pettus hurt his chances for election. After his defeat for governor, he provided no further service to the Confederacy. After the war, he practiced law in Huntsville and soon became one of the leading criminal lawyers in the state. In 1878, he ran unsuccessfully for the U.S. House of Representatives on the Greenback party ticket. He published his *Recollections of Mississippi and Mississippians* in 1880. He died on October 14, 1890, in Huntsville. Bettersworth, *Mississippi in the Confederacy*; Davis, *Recollections of Mississippi and Mississippians*.

DAVIS, Varina Howell (*Confederate First Lady*), was born in Natchez, Mississippi, on May 7, 1826. She was the daughter of William Burr and Margaret (Kempe) Howell. Educated at Madame Grelaude's School in Philadelphia and by private tutors at home, she became an excellent student of literature. She was a member of the Episcopal church. On February 26, 1845, she became the second wife of Jefferson Davis (*q.v.*); they had four sons and two daughters. Mrs. Davis ran her husband's plantation while he was in Washington. During the Civil War, she served as the official hostess of the Confederacy. She was a constant comfort to her husband and a major source of information about the politics of Richmond. If, as some historians claim, she clashed with other leaders' wives, she apparently at no time attempted to influence her husband's decisions on personnel. After the war, she was in England from 1867 to 1870 before settling in Memphis from 1870 to 1878. She spent the remaining days of the ex-president's life with him at Beauvoir Station, Mississippi, assisting him in the editing of *The Rise and Fall of the Confederate Government* (1881). She also wrote for many newspapers and magazines and wrote *Memoir of Jefferson Davis* (1890). She died in retirement in New York City on October 16, 1906. Ross, *First Lady of the South*.

DAVIS, William George Mackey (*General*), was born to George and Margaret (Mackey) Davis on May 9, 1812, in Portsmouth, Virginia. His father, an officer in the U.S. Navy, died while the younger Davis was a child, and William ran away to sea at the age of seventeen. On November 14, 1837, he married Mary Elizabeth Mills, by whom he had two sons. Davis was a Whig and an Episcopalian. After his youthful adventure at sea, he edited a newspaper in Eufaula, Alabama, and was a lawyer and cotton speculator in Apalachicola, Franklin County, Florida. In 1844, he was elected county judge of Franklin County. Two years later, he moved to St. Joseph and in 1848 to Tallahassee, Florida. He represented Leon County at the Florida secession convention. He was a secessionist. In 1861, he contributed $50,000 to the Confederate cause and recruited and equipped the 1st Florida Cavalry, of which he was colonel. Although he was chosen for the Confederate Congress, he preferred military service. He was promoted to brigadier general on November 4, 1862, and commanded the Department of East Tennessee before resigning his commission on May 6, 1863. He was a close friend of Jefferson Davis (*q.v.*). He moved to Richmond, where he operated a fleet of blockade runners to Nassau for the remainder of the war. After the war, he practiced law in Jacksonville and later in Washington, D.C. Around 1880, he purchased a plantation near Norfolk. Davis died in Alexandria, Virginia, on March 11, 1898. *Florida Law Journal*, XXIII; Warner, *Generals in Gray*.

DAWKINS, James Baird (*Congressman, Judge*), son of Elijah Dawkins, was born in Union District, South Carolina, on November 14, 1820. The younger Dawkins graduated from the University of South Carolina in 1840, studied law, and began practice in Union District. In the 1840s he moved to Gainesville, Florida, and practiced law. From 1856 to 1861 he was solicitor for the Sewanee Judicial Circuit. A delegate to the Florida secession convention, he supported secession. He was the delegate from east Florida to the first Confederate Congress where he served on the Elections, Naval Affairs, and Military Transportation Committees. He proposed that a military railroad be built in Florida, and he generally supported the Davis administration. Dawkins was appointed a circuit judge in Florida in late 1862 just prior to the expiration of his congressional term. He served in that capacity throughout the remainder of the war. After the war Dawkins practiced law near Gainesville. He held no office during Reconstruction; from 1877 until 1883 he served as judge of the Fifth Judicial Circuit. Dawkins died in Gainesville on February 12, 1883. Alexander and Beringer, *The Anatomy of the Confederate Congress*; Warner and Yearns, *Biographical Register of the Confederate Congress*.

DEAS, Zachariah Cantey (*General*), son of Colonel James Sutherland and Margaret (Chesnut) Deas, was born on October 25, 1819, in Camden, South Carolina. He was a nephew of James Chesnut, Jr. (*q. v.*). He was raised in Mobile, Alabama, and educated in Columbia, South Carolina, and at Caudebec in Calvados, France. He married Helen Gaines Lyon on May 16, 1853; they had no children. Deas was a Democrat and an Episcopalian. He served in the Mexican War during 1847 and 1848. At the outbreak of the Civil War, he was a successful cotton broker in Mobile. In 1861, he enlisted in the Alabama Volunteers and was on the staff of General J. E. Johnston (*q. v.*) at the battle of First Manassas. In October 1861, he became a colonel of the 22nd Alabama Infantry. In 1862, he was a brigade commander at Shiloh and participated in Bragg's (*q. v.*) Kentucky campaign. After his promotion to brigadier general on December 13, 1862, he served under General Leonidas Polk (*q. v.*) at the battle of Murfreesboro. He also fought in the battles of Chickamauga and Missionary Ridge in 1863 and in the campaign from Dalton to Atlanta to Jonesboro and Resaca in 1864. In December 1864, he commanded Johnston's Division at Nashville. He continued to serve with the Army of Tennessee in the Carolinas until he was felled by illness in the spring of 1865. After the war, he moved to New York City, where he was a cotton broker and a member of the stock exchange. He died in New York City on March 6, 1882. Owen, *History of Alabama and Dictionary of Alabama Biography*, III.

DeBOW, James Dunwoody Brownson (*Editor*), son of Garret and Mary Bridget (Norton) DeBow, was born in Charleston, South Carolina, on July 10, 1820. He attended public schools in Charleston and clerked in a grocery store before graduating first in his class from the College of Charleston in 1843 and being admitted to the bar the following year. He was a secretary of the Memphis Commercial Convention in 1845. He was an Episcopalian. DeBow had a daughter and a son by his marriage on August 5, 1854, to Caroline Poe. After her death, he married Martha E. Johns in 1860; they had four children. Unsuccessful as a lawyer, he went to work for the *Southern Quarterly Review* in 1844. DeBow moved to New Orleans in 1845 and soon thereafter founded *DeBow's Review*.

Although he was a nominal Democrat, he tried to keep the *Review* above politics. In 1848, he was named professor of political economy at the University of Louisiana; he held that post, though he seldom taught, throughout the remainder of the antebellum period. In 1850, he helped to found the Louisiana Historical Society and also headed the Louisiana Census Bureau. He served as President Franklin Pierce's superintendent of the Census Bureau from 1853 to 1855. His *Statistical View of the United States* was published in 1854. DeBow, a secessionist, supported John C. Breckinridge (*q.v.*) for president in 1860. During the war, he supported President Davis (*q.v.*) and used the *Review* to build confidence in the future of the Confederacy and to encourage Southern manufacturing. He was forced to suspend publication in 1864 because of financial troubles. He also served in the Confederate Department of the Treasury, where he tried to devise a means to establish credit with foreign countries. In 1862, he was named general agent for the Produce Loan, an arrangement by which the Confederate government would obtain surplus cotton in return for Confederate bonds. After the war, he revived the *Review* in Nashville and in 1866, testified before the Joint Congressional Committee on Reconstruction. He also served as president of the Tennessee Pacific Railroad Company. DeBow died of pleurisy at Elizabeth, New Jersey, on February 27, 1867. Skipper, *J.D.B. DeBow, Magazinist of the Old South*.

DeCLOUET, Alexander (*Congressman*), was born on June 9, 1812, in St. Martin's Parish, Louisiana to ———— (Fuselier) DeClouet. His mother died when he was quite young. He attended school in Bardstown, Kentucky, and graduated with high honors from Georgetown College, D.C. He also made an extended tour of Europe and studied law in the office of Judge Edward Simon in Bardstown before abandoning his practice to become a sugar planter, amassing a large fortune. DeClouet was a Roman Catholic. He had six sons and seven daughters by his marriage to Marie Louise de St. Clair. In 1837, he was elected as a Whig to the Louisiana legislature, serving for several years. In 1849, he ran as a Whig for governor, losing to General Joseph Walker. When the Whig party collapsed, he became a Democrat. He was a delegate to the Louisiana constitutional convention in 1852 and to the state secession convention of 1861, where he voted for secession. DeClouet was a member of the committee to draw up the Confederate Constitution and a member of the Commercial Affairs and Accounts Committees of the provisional Congress. He actually wrote Article V of the Confederate Constitution dealing with the calling of conventions. DeClouet had no other office in the Confederacy, but he helped to outfit Louisiana troopers. After the war, he began to recoup his financial losses. He retired from public life when the Reconstructionist Francis T. Nicholls became governor of Louisiana. DeClouet died in retirement on June 26, 1890, in Lafayette Parish, Louisiana. *Biographical and Historical Memoirs of Mississippi*; Perrin (ed.), *Southwest Louisiana Biographical and Historical*.

DE FONTAINE, Felix Gregory (*Editor*), son of Louis Antoine and ——— (Allen) de Fontaine, was born in 1834 in Boston. His father, a French nobleman, had followed Charles X into exile. De Fontaine was educated by private tutors and was Roman Catholic. He married Georgia Vigneron Moore, daughter of the Charleston minister George Moore, in 1860. He was a congressional reporter in Washington and a member of the New York press before he moved to Charleston in 1860. In the early days of the war, he provided the New York *Herald* with news of the attack on Fort Sumter. In May 1861, he went (with the rank of major) as a military correspondent to Richmond with the 1st South Carolina Regiment, where he depicted the various aspects of Confederate camp life for the readers of the Charleston *Courier*. He was a close friend of General P.G.T. Beauregard (*q.v.*) and often received information for his stories from him. De Fontaine founded the Columbia *Daily South Carolinian* in 1862, turning that paper into a propaganda instrument of the Confederate cause. His press was burned by Sherman's destruction of Columbia in 1864. In 1864, he published *Marginalia*, a collection of his articles, which praised the sacrifices of the Southern people during the war and urged them to continue to defend their values. After the war, De Fontaine opposed the carpetbaggers; he also wrote against Reconstruction in South Carolina. He moved to New York, where in 1868 he became managing editor of the *Telegram*. He later served as financial editor of the New York *Herald*, a position he held for the rest of his life. De Fontaine was preparing a book on the missing records of the Confederate cabinet when he died on December 11, 1896, in Columbia, South Carolina. Andrews, *The South Reports the Civil War*.

DE JARNETTE, Daniel Coleman (*Congressman*), son of Joseph De Jarnette and a relative of the Hamptons of Virginia, was born at Bowling Green, Caroline County, Virginia, on October 18, 1822. He attended Bethany College in Bethany, Virginia (now West Virginia). De Jarnette was married and had a son. He was a wealthy farmer and slaveholder prior to the Civil War. He served in the Virginia House from 1853 to 1858 and was a Democratic member of the U.S. House of Representatives from 1859 to 1861, where he opposed the Buchanan administration and favored secession. He was elected to the Thirty-Seventh Congress but did not serve. During the war, he represented the Eighth Congressional District of Virginia in the first and second Confederate Houses. As a congressman, De Jarnette opposed the conscription of foreigners. A Davis administration supporter, he served on the Foreign Affairs, Medical Department, and Conference Committees. When the war ended, he returned to Caroline County and farmed; he never again held public office. De Jarnette arbitrated the boundary between Maryland and Virginia in 1871. He died at While Sulphur Springs, Virginia, on August 20, 1881. Wingfield, *A History of Caroline County, Virginia*.

DE LEON, David Camden (*Surgeon General*), was born in 1813 in Camden, South Carolina, to Dr. Mardici Heimrich and Rebecca (Lopez-y-Numez) De

Leon. A brother of the writer Thomas Cooper and Edwin De Leon (*q.v.*), he graduated from South Carolina College in 1833 and from the Medical Department of the University of Pennsylvania in 1836. He was raised in the Jewish faith. De Leon became an assistant surgeon in the army and had a command in Florida during the Seminole War. During the Mexican War, he was attached to the staffs of Generals Zachary Taylor and Winfield Scott. It was here that De Leon earned the sobriquet "The Fighting Doctor," for he led charges at Chapultepec and Molino del Rey in 1847. He served on the southwestern frontier until 1860, when he traveled in the Orient. De Leon resigned his army commission in the spring of 1861. President Davis (*q.v.*) named him acting surgeon general of the Confederacy in 1861; he held the post for one year. He organized the Medical Department, served in the field in the Peninsula and Richmond campaigns, and later was transferred to the Trans-Mississippi Department. After the war, he went to Mexico with Magruder (*q.v.*). He moved to Albuquerque, New Mexico, in 1866 to practice medicine and died there on September 3, 1872. Cunningham, *Doctors in Gray*.

DE LEON, Edwin (*Diplomat*), son of Dr. Mardici Heimrich and Rebecca (Lopez-y-Numez) De Leon and brother of Thomas Cooper and David Camden De Leon (*q.v.*), was born on May 4, 1818, in Columbia, South Carolina. He was of the Jewish faith. He graduated from South Carolina College in 1837 and was admitted to the bar in 1840. In 1841, he became editor of the *Republican* in Savannah, but he returned to Columbia as editor of the *Telegraph* in the late 1840s. From 1850 to 1854, he was part of the southern wing of the Democratic party, and during that period he edited *The Southern Press* in Washington, D.C. In 1854, he was appointed consul general and diplomatic agent to Egypt. When the war began, he returned to the South and volunteered for service in the Confederate government. In 1862, he went to Europe as a diplomatic agent of the Confederacy. He spent his entire fortune for the Confederacy, made many trips through the blockade, and used large amounts of Confederate funds for propaganda in the foreign press. He served with Henry Hotze (*q.v.*) as propaganda agent. His primary location was Paris, where he planted stories in the newspaper about Confederate military successes. An intimate friend of President Davis (*q.v.*), he quarreled with John Slidell (*q.v.*) over how to better Confederate relations with France. His formal career ended in February 1864 when he publicly criticized the French government. De Leon remained in Europe throughout the rest of the war. After the war, he lived in Egypt and Europe and did not return to the United States until 1879. In 1881, he returned to Egypt for a short time and introduced the telephone there. He was author of *The Khedive's Egypt* (1872), *Under the Stars and Crescent* (1879), and *Thirty Years of Life in Three Continents* (1886). He died on December 1, 1891, in New York City. Callahan, *Diplomatic History of the Confederacy*; Owsley, *King Cotton Diplomacy*.

DEVINE, Thomas Jefferson (*Diplomat*), was born to William and Catherine (Maxwell) Devine on February 28, 1820, in Halifax, Nova Scotia. At the age of fifteen he emigrated to Tallahassee, Florida, where he clerked for a merchant. He studied law in Mississippi in 1838 and received a law degree from Transylvania University in Kentucky in 1843. Devine was a Roman Catholic and a Democrat. He had ten children by his marriage to Helen Ann Elder on October 31, 1844. In 1843, he emigrated to Texas where he lived first in La Grange and then in San Antonio, where he practiced law. He became city attorney of San Antonio in 1850. He achieved a brilliant reputation as district judge for the Bexar District, a position which he received in 1851. He served as district judge until the outbreak of the Civil War. Devine was a leading secessionist delegate to the Texas secession convention in 1861, and as a member of a committee of public safety, he worked to remove U.S. troops from Texas. He also served on a Confederate committee to receive all U.S. property seized in Texas. During the war, as judge for the Western District of Texas he assisted in developing the machinery of the Confederate court system. In 1861, he was named an associate justice of the state Supreme Court. He traveled to Mexico City in 1863 to attempt to solve trade problems between Mexico and the Confederacy; he also was a commissioner to Monterrey. The following year he solved problems of conscription and embargo in Texas. When the war ended, he went to Mexico and then returned to Texas, where he was arrested. He was twice indicted, though never brought to trial, by the United States for high treason, the only Confederate besides Davis to have received this dubious distinction. Devine also practiced law in San Antonio after the war. He was named an associate justice of the Texas Supreme Court in 1873 but resigned two years later. In 1878, he lost a race for the governorship. He died in San Antonio, Texas, on March 16, 1890. Johnson, *Texans Who Wore the Gray*; Lonn, *Foreigners in the Confederacy*.

DeWITT, William Henry (*Congressman*), son of the Reverend Samuel and (McWhirter) DeWitt, was born on October 24, 1827, in Smith County, Tennessee, where his father was a preacher and small farmer. A self-made man, the younger DeWitt received his education at Berea Academy in Chapel Hill, Tennessee, where he studied under John M. Barnes. He was a Mason and a member of the Methodist Episcopal church. By his marriage to Emilia Price on May 30, 1847, he had five children; he had two more children by his marriage on May 30, 1867, to Bettie Wilson. DeWitt taught at Montpelier Academy in Gainesborough, Tennessee, in 1847-1848; in 1849-1850, he taught in Jackson County, Tennessee. Admitted to the Smith County, Tennessee, bar in 1850, he practiced in Lafayette from 1850 to 1856, in Lebanon from 1856 to 1858, and in Carthage from 1858 to 1875. In the state House of 1855-1856, he was the Whig representative from Smith, Sumner, and Macon counties; he refused to run for reelection in 1857. As a unionist delegate to the constitutional convention of 1861, he opposed the convention, but he later was elected to the provisional Confederate Congress. He served until early 1862 on the Printing and Territories Committees. As he represented a unionist district in Tennessee, DeWitt came under much attack and was forced to retire from public life for the duration of the war. After the war, DeWitt became a conservative Democrat and returned to his law practice. In 1872, he was named special chancellor in the Fifth Chancery Division. In 1875, he settled in Chattanooga, where he practiced law and from 1888 to 1890 was chancellor of the state of Tennessee. He died in Chattanooga on April 11, 1896. *East Tennessee, Historical and Biographical*.

DIBRELL, George Gibbs (*General*), was born on April 12, 1822, in Sparta, White County, Tennessee, to Anthony and Mildred (Carter) Dibrell. His father, a local politician, was a state treasurer and a member of the legislature of Tennessee; he went broke from security debts. The younger Dibrell attended public schools and spent one year at the University of Tennessee in 1838 before going to work as a schoolteacher. From 1840 to 1846, he was clerk of the Bank of Tennessee at Sparta. In 1843, he graduated from East Tennessee University at Knoxville and was admitted to the bar in 1846. Dibrell was a Whig and a Methodist. He married Mary E. Leftwich on January 13, 1842; and they had seven sons and one daughter. From 1846 to 1860, he was also a county clerk. In 1861, he was a union candidate to the state convention, which never met, but he was elected to the Tennessee legislature that same year. Dibrell enlisted as a private in the Confederate Army when the war began. He became a lieutenant colonel in the 25th Tennessee Infantry and served in Tennessee and Kentucky under General Felix Zollicoffer. He participated in the battles of Mill Springs, Kentucky, in January 1862 and Farmington, Mississippi, in May 1862. The 8th Tennessee Cavalry Regiment which Dibrell raised served under Nathan B. Forrest (*q.v.*) from Kentucky to Virginia in battles including Neely's Bend, Sparta, Chickamauga, Philadelphia, Maryville, Lone Mountain; Franklin, Tennessee; Florence, Alabama; and in the siege of Knoxville, all in 1863. From July 1863 to January 1864, Dibrell commanded Forrest's Brigade around Atlanta. He served with General Joseph Wheeler (*q.v.*) in mid-Tennessee in July 1864 and later harassed Sherman at Forsyth, Georgia. Promoted to brigadier general on January 28, 1865, he fought in North and South Carolina in the final months of the war. When his brigade was disbanded, Dibrell went home to Tennessee. From 1865 to 1875, he was a merchant. In 1866, he became a director of the Southwestern Railroad, of which he became president in 1869. In 1870, he helped to write the new state constitution. From 1874 until he declined reelection in 1885, he served as a Democrat in the U.S. House. He also farmed and raised livestock, and in 1872, he joined the Granger movement. Dibrell died on May 9, 1888, in Sparta, Tennessee. Lindsley, *Military History of Tennessee*; Pryor, *History of Forrest's Campaign*; Spear (comp.), *Biographical Directory of the Tennessee General Assembly*.

DICKINSON, James Shelton (*Congressman*), was born in Spotsylvania County, Virginia, on January 18, 1818, the son of Richard and ———— (Crawford) Dickinson. After graduating from the University of Virginia Law School in 1844, he opened a law office at Grove Hill, Alabama, in 1845. In 1844, he married his first cousin, Mary F. Dickinson, by whom he had fourteen children. He married Alice A. Savage in June 1868 after the death of his first wife. Dickinson was a Baptist, a Mason, and a member of the Sons of Temperance. He served in the Alabama Senate as a Democrat from 1853 to 1855. He was a presidential elector in the John C. Breckinridge (*q.v.*) ticket in 1860 and supported secession. When the Civil War began, he raised and equipped a company, but he saw little military service. Dickinson served in the second Confederate House, defeating Charles C. Langdon in 1864. Generally a Davis administration supporter, he held positions on the Claims, Commerce, and Conference Committees. After the war, he returned home and became president of the Board of Trustees of the Grove Hill Academy. He also resumed his law practice. He died on July 23, 1882, in Grove Hill. Owen, *History of Alabama and Dictionary of Alabama Biography*, III.

DOLES, George Pierce (*General*), was born to the tailor Josiah Doles and his wife Martha (Pierce) on May 14, 1830, in Milledgeville, Georgia. He attended schools in Milledgeville. He was married to Sarah Williams in 1852 and had a daughter. Doles was in the mercantile business before the war. When the war began, he entered the Confederate Army as colonel of the 4th Georgia Regiment, having previously formed a militia company known as the "Baldwin Blues." He won laurels for his part in the battle of Seven Pines and fought well during the Seven Days in 1862. Promoted to brigadier general on November 1, 1862, Doles was a brigade commander with the Army of Northern Virginia during the battles of Sharpsburg, Gettysburg, Chancellorsville, and Cold Harbor. He was considered one of the best brigadiers in the Confederate Army. Doles was killed by a sharpshooter near Bethesda Church at Cold Harbor, Virginia, on June 2, 1864. Evans, *Confederate Military History*, VI; Thomas, *A History of the Doles-Cook Brigade*.

DONELSON, Daniel Smith (*General*), son of Samuel and Mary Ann (Smith) Donelson, was born on June 23, 1801, in Sumner County, Tennessse. His father was a law partner and brother-in-law of Andrew Jackson and his brother was the Tennessee political leader Andrew Jackson Donelson. The younger Donelson attended Dr. Priestley's boarding school in Nashville and graduated fifth in a class of thirty-seven from the U.S. Military Academy in 1825. Donelson was a Presbyterian and a Democrat. He married Margaret Branch, daughter of Governor John Branch of North Carolina, in 1830; they had eleven children. He was commissioned a second lieutenant of the 3rd Artillery in 1825 but resigned the following year. He served in the Tennessee Militia as a major from 1827 to 1829 and as a general from 1829 to 1834. From 1826 to 1834, he was a planter in

Sumner County. He was a planter in the Florida Territory for the next two years but returned home to become a successful planter in Sumner County. From 1841 to 1843 and from 1855 to 1861, he was a member of the state House, where he was also speaker during the latter period. Donelson, a power in the state Democratic party during the 1850s, was a secessionist and a vehement opponent of the Know-Nothings. He built Fort Donelson on the Cumberland River while serving as a colonel in the provisional army of Tennessee. He joined the Confederacy in 1861 as a brigadier general of state forces and was appointed a brigadier general in the Confederate Army on July 9, 1861. After fighting in the Cheat Mountain campaign in West Virginia in 1861, he accompanied Robert E. Lee (*q.v.*) to Charleston the following year, and he served with General Braxton Bragg (*q.v.*) in the Kentucky campaign at Perryville, Murfreesboro, and Shelbyville. In January 1863, illness forced his transfer to the command of the Department of East Tennessee. He was killed by bushwhackers at Byhalia, Mississippi, on April 17, 1863. Clayton, *History of Davidson County, Tennessee*; Durham, *The Great Leap Westward*.

DORTCH, William Theophilus (*Congressman*), was born to William and Drusilla Dortch on August 23, 1824, in Nash County, North Carolina. He attended Bingham School, studied law under B. F. Moore, and became a wealthy lawyer and planter before the Civil War. Dortch was married and had six children. A Democrat, he was elected county attorney of Nash County in 1844 and served until 1848. In 1849, he moved to Goldsboro, North Carolina, where he was elected county attorney for Wayne County and, in 1852, was elected to the lower house of the North Carolina legislature. With the exception of 1856-1857, Dortch served in the legislature from 1852 until 1861; for the last ten months of his final term he was speaker of the House. He supported Stephen A. Douglas for the presidency, but voted for John C. Breckinridge (*q.v.*) when he thought that Douglas could not win. Dortch claimed that he opposed secession; he did not attend the state secession convention. He defeated four opponents for election to the Confederate Senate in 1861, and he contended that he remained in the Senate throughout the war to avoid conscription. Dortch was a supporter of the Davis administration. He is said to have persuaded President Davis (*q.v.*) not to arrest W. W. Holden (*q.v.*) for treason. He served on the Acounts, Commerce, Naval Affairs, Engrossment and Enrollment, and Special Committees. Dortch supported revisions in the conscription laws, served in the most important role of explaining the president's actions to Governor Zebulon Vance (*q.v.*), and tried unsuccessfully to persuade President Davis to propose some plan for peace negotiations in order to gather moderate support from North Carolina for the final efforts of the Confederacy. In late 1864, Governor Vance helped elect Thomas S. Ashe (*q.v.*), a moderate, over Dortch. The war ended before Dortch's term expired. After the war he farmed and practiced law. By 1866, he was negotiating for the purchase of river land to build a cotton factory, and he aspired for a gubernatorial appointment to a railroad board, which he never received. In 1879, he was elected to the state Senate, where he was chairman of the Judiciary Committee for two years. He served in the state Senate from 1879 until 1885. In 1881, he was a member of the Code Commission. He continued his law practice and dropped from public view. Dortch died in Goldsboro on November 29, 1889. Dowd, *Sketches of Prominent Living North Carolinians*; Yearns, *The Confederate Congress*.

DUKE, Basil C. (*Physician*), was born on March 31, 1815, in Orangeburg, Mason County, Kentucky, to Dr. Alexander and Mary M. (Broome) Duke, who had moved to Kentucky from Maryland in 1810. He attended private schools in Mason County and studied medicine in Baltimore in 1831 under Professor N. R. Smith. He was an Episcopalian and a Clay Whig. He married L. M. Mitchell on November 13, 1835. He was a member of the Medical Department of the University of Maryland in 1834 and some years later had a large practice in Mayslick, Kentucky. In 1860, he supported John Bell for the presidency. When the war began, he enlisted in the Confederate Army as a private in the 5th Kentucky Volunteers. Duke was made a regimental surgeon in late 1861 and later was promoted to brigadier general, though the position was never confirmed. In 1862, he served under Humphrey Marshall (*q. v.*) as medical director of southwest Virginia, east Tennessee, and east Kentucky. He also fought in various engagements in Virginia and Tennessee. After the war, he became a Democrat and moved his medical practice to Memphis. It is not known when he died. Cunningham, *Doctors in Gray*.

DUKE, Basil Wilson (*General*), was born to Nathaniel Wilson Duke, a naval officer, and his wife Mary (Currie) on May 28, 1838 in Scott County, Kentucky. He attended a private secondary school in Maysville and Georgetown, Kentucky, and later went to Centre College in Kentucky. He studied law at Transylvania University. In 1858, Duke moved to Missouri and was admitted to the St. Louis bar. He was an Episcopalian. He married Henrietta Hunt Morgan, the sister of the Civil War General John H. Morgan (*q. v.*), on June 19, 1861; they had three sons and three daughters. Duke was a secessionist who worked secretly for the secession of Missouri. At the beginning of the Civil War, he enlisted as a private in his brother-in-law's company, the Lexington Rifles, and when this company became part of the 2nd Kentucky Cavalry he was appointed lieutenant colonel and, later, colonel. Wounded at the battle of Shiloh in March 1862, he escaped to Kentucky. He fought in all of Morgan's engagements in the Kentucky- Missouri border area. Duke was promoted to brigadier general on September 15, 1864, after Morgan had been killed, and he assumed command of Morgan's Brigade. Because of his constant movements into enemy territory, he was almost hanged as a spy by both sides. In the final days of the war, his brigade provided a military escort for the fugitive Confederate government. He surrendered in Georgia and was soon paroled. After the war, he settled in Louisville, Kentucky. A lawyer, he was also a tobacco inspector in 1866-1867. Duke served as a member of the state legislature in 1869-1870 and as commonwealth's attorney for the Louisville District from 1875 to 1880. He was counsel for the Louisville and Nashville Railroad from 1882 to 1894. Duke's historical publications included his *Reminiscences* (1911), *Morgan's Cavalry* (1867), and *A History of the Bank of Kentucky* (1895). He died on September 16, 1916, in New York City. Duke, *Reminiscences of Basil W. Duke*.

DUPRE, Lucius Jacques (*Congressman*), whose grandfather was governor of Louisiana in 1830, was born in St. Landry Parish, Louisiana, on April 18, 1822. He attended the University of Virginia and studied law there under Henry St. George Tucker and at the University of Louisiana. He practiced law in Opelousas. Dupré, a secessionist Whig, was married and had one son. Before the war, he served as judge of the Fifteenth Judicial District and was one of the most prominent lawyers in Louisiana. He was a delegate to the state secession convention in 1861, where he supported secession. In the early days of the war, Dupré enlisted as a private in the 18th Louisiana Regiment. He was also elected as a pro-administration member of both the first and the second Confederate House. He served on the Judiciary, Printing, and Indian Affairs Committees. An opponent of conscription, Dupré claimed that Louisiana was left without sufficient troops to save New Orleans from falling into federal hands. He spent much of his Confederate congressional career advocating a Confederate land invasion of New Orleans. Disillusioned and probably bankrupt by the war, he returned to Louisiana when the war ended and resumed his law practice. He died in Opelousas on March 5, 1869. Perrin (ed.), *Southwest Louisiana Biographical and Historical*; Yearns, *The Confederate Congress*.

E

EARLY, Jubal Anderson (*General*), was born to the farmer and lawyer Joab Early and his wife Ruth (Hairston) on November 3, 1816, in Franklin County, Virginia. He attended Danville Male Academy and graduated eighteenth in a class of fifty from the U.S. Military Academy in 1837. Early was a Whig and an Episcopalian and a lifelong bachelor. He was commissioned second lieutenant in the army in 1837. In 1838, he served in the Seminole War as a first lieutenant of artillery. He resigned his commission in 1839 to study law under Norbonne Taliaferro in Rocky Mount, Virginia. Early was admitted to the Franklin County bar in 1840. He represented Franklin County in the Virginia House of Delegates in 1841-1842 and was commonwealth's attorney from 1842 to 1852. During the Mexican War, he was a major of volunteers in 1847-1848. He resumed his law practice and lost a race for the state legislature in 1853. At the Virginia secession convention, he was a unionist delegate from Franklin County and opposed secession. However, when the war began he entered the Confederate Army as a colonel of the 24th Virginia Regiment and commanded a brigade at the battle of First Manassas, following which he was promoted to brigadier general on July 21, 1861. He was wounded at Williamsburg on May 5, 1862. He was a brigade commander at the battle of Second Manassas and a division commander at the battles of Sharpsburg and Fredericksburg in late 1862. Promoted to major general on January 17, 1863, he distinguished himself at the battle of Gettysburg in July of that year. At the Wilderness in May 1864, he protected Lee's (*q.v.*) flank, and at Spotsylvania he defeated General Ambrose Burnside. Following his promotion to lieutenant general on May 31, 1864, he defeated General David Hunter at Lynchburg and executed a daring raid on Washington, D.C., before being defeated in the Virginia battles of Winchester and Fisher's Hill in September 1864. Early was relieved from command a few days before Appomattox because his troops lost confidence in him. When the Civil War ended, Early refused to surrender and escaped to Mexico. He sought other wars to fight—in Texas, Mexico, and Canada—but found no use for his talents. In 1869, he returned to Virginia and resumed his law practice, wrote his memoirs, and was the first president of the Southern Historical Society. He remained unreconstructed. Late in his life he moved to New Orleans, where he supervised the Louisiana lottery. He returned to Virginia and died on March 2, 1894, in Lynchburg. Bushong, *Old Jube*; Vandiver, *Jubal's Raid*.

ECHOLS, John (*General*), was born to Joseph and Elizabeth F. (Lambeth) Echols on March 20, 1823, in Lynchburg, Virginia. He attended Virginia Military Institute and Washington College in Virginia, studied law at Harvard, and was admitted to the Rockbridge County, Virginia, bar in 1843. He was a Democrat and an Episcopalian. He married Mary Jane Caperton, a sister of Senator Allen T. Caperton (*q.v.*), and, following her death, Mrs. Mary Cochrane Reid. A son, Edward, later was a Virginia state senator. Echols moved in the mid-1840s to Monroe County, Virginia (now West Virginia), and developed a law practice there. He held minor political posts and was a member of the Virginia General Assembly during the 1850s. Echols was a secessionist delegate to the state convention in 1861, and he recruited for the Confederate Army in Staunton. As lieutenant colonel, he commanded the 27th Virginia Regiment of the Stonewall Brigade in the battle of First Manassas and served as a colonel under General Thomas J. Jackson (*q.v.*) in the Shenandoah Valley. He was wounded at the battle of Kernstown in March 1862, and upon his recovery he was promoted to brigadier general on April 16, 1862. He served as commander of the Department of West Virginia until the spring of 1863. He had duty on a court of inquiry following the surrender of Vicksburg. In May 1864, he was successful in the battle of New Market on the Cold Harbor line, and, in August 1864, he took charge of the District of Southwest Virginia. During the last days of the war, he accompanied Davis southward. He surrendered in Greensboro, North Carolina, and was soon paroled. After the war, he resumed his law practice and became a successful businessman in Staunton. He was president of the Staunton National Valley Bank and helped to organize the Chesapeake and Ohio Railroad, for which he was receiver and general manager. He also served in the Virginia House. Echols moved to Louisville, Kentucky, in 1886, where he spent most of the remaining years of his life in the railroad business. He died while visiting his son in Staunton on May 24, 1896. Gordon, *Men of Mark in Virginia.*

ECHOLS, Joseph Hubbard (*Congressman*), was born in Washington, Georgia, on December 25, 1816, to John and Isabella (Moon) Echols. He had two daughters by his marriage to Martha E. Smith on February 1, 1844. Echols was a minister, an extensive planter, and a lawyer in Oglethorpe, Georgia, before the Civil War. He served as president of the female college in Madison, Georgia, and was considered an ardent patriot, although he did not vote for secession. Echols nevertheless served actively in the Georgia Senate from 1861 to 1863, where he supported Governor Joseph Brown's (*q.v.*) attack on the Confederate government. He was also elected by the Sixth Congressional District of Georgia to the second Confederate House in 1864. An anti-administration man, he served on the Indian Affairs, the Medical Department, and Pay and Mileage Committees. He favored the annual sale of government cotton to provide funds for payment on the Confederate debt, and he wanted to protect cotton brokers by allowing cotton to be sold cheaply only to the government. In May 1864, he advocated an increase in army pay. Echols took many leaves of absence from the House. He returned to his law practice and became a Methodist minister in Oglethorpe when the war ended, and he never again held public office. He died in Lexington, Georgia, on September 23, 1885. Smith, *The History of Oglethorpe County, Georgia.*

ECTOR, Matthew Duncan (*General*), was born in Putnam County, Georgia, on February 28, 1822. Educated in LaGrange, Georgia, and at Centre College, Kentucky, he was admitted to the Georgia bar in 1844. He practiced law and served a term, 1845-1847, in the Georgia legislature. Ector was married to Louisa Phillips from 1842 to 1848, to Letitia M. Graham from 1851 to 1859, and to Sallie P. Chew in 1864. He had three children by his first two marriages. Ector served in a Georgia regiment during the Mexican War. In 1849, he moved to Henderson, Texas, which he represented in the Texas legislature in 1855. When the war began, he left the legislature, enlisted as a private in the Confederate Army, and served as adjutant to General Joseph L. Hogg at Corinth, Mississippi. He was later elected colonel of the 14th Texas Cavalry, and he was promoted to brigadier general on August 23, 1862. He fought in the battles of Richmond, Kentucky; Murfreesboro, Tennessee; and Chickamauga, Georgia; and in the Atlanta campaign, where he lost his leg as a result of wounds on July 27, 1864. Forced to retire from active military service, he spent the last part of the war in command of the Department of Alabama, Mississippi, and East Louisiana in Mobile. Ector participated in the defense of Mobile at the end of the war, surrendered, and was soon paroled. He returned to Texas and practiced law. From 1866 until he was deposed the following year, Ector was judge of the Sixth Judicial District of Texas. Restrictions kept him from public office until after Reconstruction. In 1867, he practiced law in Marshall, Texas. He was elected judge of the Seventh Judicial District in 1874 and served as a judge of the Court of Appeals from 1876 until his death on October 29, 1879 in Tyler, Texas. Evans, *Confederate Military History*, XI; Johnson, *Texans Who Wore the Gray*.

ELLIOTT, John Milton (*Congressman*), son of John Lloyd and Jane (Ritchie) Elliott, was born on May 20, 1820, in Scott County, Virginia. His family later moved to Kentucky, where his father was a Lawrence County politician and farmer. Educated in the Kentucky common schools, he graduated from Emory and Henry College of Georgia in 1841, studied law, and was admitted to the Kentucky bar in 1843. He married Susan J. Smith in 1848. In 1847, he represented Floyd County, Kentucky, in the lower house of the state legislature. He served in the U.S. House as a Democrat from 1853 to 1859 but did not run for reelection in 1858. After returning to his law practice, he again represented Floyd County in the state House in 1861 but was expelled in December of that year for his Southern sympathies. A secessionist, he served in the provisional Congress and in both permanent Confederate Houses. He held assignments on the Enrolled Bills, Indian Affairs, and special committees and was generally a Davis administration supporter. He practiced law after the war. Elliott was a circuit judge at Owingsburg, Kentucky, from 1868 to 1874 and a judge of the Court of Appeals from 1876 until his assassination by an irate defendant over a land deed on March 26, 1879, in Frankfort, Kentucky. Levin (ed.), *The Lawyers and Lawmakers of Kentucky*.

ELLIOTT, Stephen (*Minister*), the first Episcopal bishop of Georgia, was born on August 31, 1806, in Beaufort, South Carolina, to Stephen Elliott, founder of the *Southern Review*, and his wife Esther (Habersham). He attended private schools in Charleston and went to Harvard College before graduating third in the class of 1825 at South Carolina College in Columbia. He studied law under James L. Petigru, was admitted to the South Carolina bar in 1827, and began a law practice in Charleston before moving to Beaufort and a law practice there. In 1832, in Beaufort he caught the challenge of new religious awakening and entered the ministry. Elliott had two children by his first marriage to Mary Barnwell and six children by his second marriage to Charlotte Buell Barnwell; the Barnwell sisters were sisters of Robert Woodward Barnwell (*q.v.*). Elliott became a deacon in 1835 and was ordained the following year. From 1835 to 1840, he served as chaplain and professor of sacred literature and Christian evidences at South Carolina College. After he was named bishop of Savannah in 1840, he attempted to redevelop the Episcopal church in Georgia. In 1841, he began the Georgia Episcopal Institute in Monroe County, and, in 1852, he was named rector of the Christ Church in Savannah. In 1860, along with Bishop Leonidas Polk (*q.v.*) of Louisiana and Bishop James Harvey Otey of Tennessee, he helped to found the University of the South at Sewanee, Tennessee. He also was a founder of the Georgia Historical Society. He was an ardent secessionist and turned his pen and sermons to the service of the Confederacy. During the war, he served as senior bishop of the South. Although he was one of the religious leaders of the Confederacy, he managed to remain on good terms with the Northern branch of the church, which facilitated the reunion of the church after the war. His heroic work in behalf of the spiritual and emotional mood of the soldiers was of great importance to the war effort. Elliott died on December 31, 1866, in Savannah, Georgia. *Men Who Made Sewanee*; Owens, *Georgia's Planting Prelate*; Silver, *Confederate Morale and Church Propaganda*.

ELLIS, John Willis (*Governor*), was born to Anderson and Judith (Bailey) Ellis in July 1820 in Rowan (now Davidson) County, North Carolina. He attended the academy at Beattie's Ford, North Carolina, and Randolph-Macon College in Virginia before graduating from the University of North Carolina in 1841. He studied law and was admitted to the Salisbury, North Carolina, bar, where he began a law practice in 1842. He was an Episcopalian. Ellis married Mary White on August 25, 1844; by his second marriage to Mary McKinley Daves on August 11, 1858, he had two daughters. Ellis, a Democrat, was elected to the state House of Representatives in 1844, 1846, and 1848, where he favored internal improvements. He was judge of the Superior Court of North Carolina from 1848 to 1858. In 1858, he was elected governor of the state, and he was reelected in 1860 as a secessionist. His proclamation calling for a convention was instrumental in bringing North Carolina into the Confederacy. Although he opposed violent action, Ellis reorganized the militia, forbade Northern garrisons at North Carolina forts, and turned over all forts in the state to the Confederate government. While governor, he kept North Carolina in almost complete support of the Confederacy. He died on July 7, 1861, in Red Sulphur Springs, Virginia, from strain and overwork. His death was a blow for Confederate loyalty in the "Old North" state. Ashe, *Cyclopedia of Eminent and Representative Men of the Carolinas*, I; Barrett, *The Civil War in North Carolina*; Garrard, "John W. Ellis."

ELZEY, Arnold (Jones) (*General*), was born on December 18, 1816, in Somerset County, Maryland. His father, Colonel Arnold Elzey Jones, represented

Somerset County in the state House, and his mother, Anne Wilson (Jackson), was from a wealthy Maryland family. In 1837, he graduated thirty-third in a class of fifty from the U.S. Military Academy, at which time he dropped his patronymic for his middle name. He had one son by his 1845 marriage to Ellen Irwin. Elzey, a career military officer, served in the artillery during the Seminole War and fired the first gun of the Mexican War, where he was breveted twice. In 1860, he was a captain of artillery in command of the U.S. arsenal at Augusta, Georgia. In April 1861, he resigned his army commission and entered the Confederate Army as a lieutenant colonel. After helping to turn the tide of the battle at First Manassas, he was promoted on the field by President Davis (*q.v.*) himself on July 21, 1861. In 1862, he served with Thomas J. Jackson (*q.v.*) in the Valley campaign and during the Seven Days. He was wounded at the battle of Port Republic in June 1862 and saw no further field service after a second wound at Cold Harbor in June 1864. He was promoted to major general on December 4, 1862, and commanded the Department of Richmond until the fall of 1864, when he joined the Army of Tennessee as Hood's (*q.v.*) chief of artillery. He surrendered at the war's end and was paroled in Washington, Georgia, in May 1865. After the war, he returned to a small farm in Anne Arundel County, Maryland. He died on February 21, 1871, in Baltimore. Evans, *Confederate Military History*, II.

EVANS, Augusta Jane (*Writer*), daughter of Matthew Ryon and Sarah Skrine (Howard) Evans, was born in Columbus, Georgia, on May 18, 1835. Her parents moved to San Antonio, Texas, in 1846 and in 1848 to Mobile, Alabama, where she was educated by her mother. She was a Methodist and a Democrat. She married Lorenzo Madison Wilson on December 3, 1868. Before the war, she published two novels, *Inez* (1855) and *Beulah* (1859). In 1861, she organized a hospital for Confederate soldiers in Mobile, where she nursed the wounded. A staunch secessionist, she was a political advisor to Confederate Congressman J.L.M. Curry (*q.v.*). Her most important novel, *Macaria* (1863) was a favorite among the Confederate troops. Because of its inflammatory commentary upon the potential effects of emancipation on the nation, the novel created insubordination among Northern troops; Northern General George Thomas had it banned from Union lines. She also wrote many articles about the war effort and generally attacked President Davis (*q.v.*) for his performance. A member of the anti-Bragg group, she wanted P.G.T. Beauregard (*q.v.*) to command the troops in the west. After the war, she published *St. Elmo* (1866), *Vashti* (1869), *Infelice* (1875), *A Speckled Bird* (1902), and *Devota* (1907). She died on May 9, 1909, in Mobile. Fidler, *Augusta Jane Evans Wilson, 1835-1900*; Sterkx, *Partners in Rebellion: Alabama Women in the Civil War*.

EVANS, Clement Anselm (*General*), was born to Anselm Lynch and Sarah Hinton (Bryan) Evans on February 25, 1833, in Stewart County, Georgia. He attended the schools of Lumpkin, Georgia, and studied law under William Tracy

Gould at the Georgia School of Law in Augusta in 1852. He was admitted to the bar the same year and practiced in Lumpkin. Evans was a Democrat and a Methodist. He married Allie Walton on February 8, 1854, and upon her death, Mrs. Sarah Avary Howard on October 14, 1885. In 1854-1855, he was a judge of the Stewart County court, and in 1859-1860, he was a state senator. He supported Breckinridge (q.v.) for president in 1860. Evans entered the Confederate Army in the spring of 1861 as a major of the 31st Georgia Regiment and was promoted to colonel in April 1862. He was attached to Lawton's Brigade in Jackson's Corps of the Army of Northern Virginia with which he fought in every engagement from the Peninsular campaign in the spring of 1862 to Appomattox. He was promoted to brigadier general on May 19, 1864, and participated in the retreat from Petersburg and in Jubal Early's (q.v.) raid on Washington in July 1864, having been slightly wounded at Monocacy only days before. In November 1864, he became a division commander and acting major general in John B. Gordon's (q.v.) Corps. He was wounded a total of five times during the war. Evans surrendered in North Carolina in mid-1865 and was soon paroled. After the war, he was a Methodist Episcopal minister for twenty-five years. He organized the Educational Loan Fund Association, published *Military History of Georgia* (1895), and edited the twelve-volume *Confederate Military History* (1899). He was also on the state board of prison commissioners. Evans retired from the ministry in 1892 and made his home in Atlanta, where he died on July 2, 1911. Northen (ed.), *Men of Mark in Georgia*, IV.

EWELL, Richard Stoddert (*General*), son of Dr. Thomas Ewell and his wife Elizabeth (Stoddert), was born on February 8, 1817, in Georgetown, D.C. His father died in 1826, and young Ewell was educated at home in Prince William County, Virginia. In 1840, he graduated thirteenth in a class of forty-two from the U.S. Military Academy and began a military career in the Dragoons. He was assigned to frontier service. On May 24, 1863, he married Mrs. Lizinka (Campbell) Brown; they had no children. Breveted captain at Vera Cruz, he fought in the Mexican War battles of Cerro Gordo, Contreras, Churubusco, and Chapultepec. His prewar service continued on the frontier, and he was active against the Apaches in New Mexico in 1857. A strong unionist, he nevertheless resigned his commission in May 1861 and offered his services to Virginia. Ewell was appointed brigadier general in the Confederate Army on June 17, 1861, and commanded the second brigade at the battle of First Manassas. Promoted to major general, he served under Jackson (q.v.) in the Valley, defeated Banks at Winchester and Fremont at Cross Keys before he lost his leg at Groveton, Virginia, in August 1862. Upon his recovery, he was promoted to lieutenant general on May 23, 1863, and he succeeded General Thomas J. Jackson as commander of the 2nd Corps of the Army of Northern Virginia. He served with distinction at the battle of Gettysburg, where, though wounded, he fought strapped into his saddle. Ewell also participated in the battles of the Wilderness and Spotsylvania in May 1864.

During the last part of the war, he commanded the Department of Henrico in the defense of Richmond. He was confined for four months at the end of the war after being captured during the battle of Sayler's Creek in April 1865. After the war, he lived on a farm near Nashville, Tennessee, where he died on January 25, 1872. Hamlin, *"Old Bald Head."*

EWING, George Washington (*Congressman*), son of Robert Ewing and a relative of Judge Ephraim M. Ewing, was born in Logan County, Kentucky, on November 29, 1808. He married Nannie L. Williams, daughter of General Sam L. Williams, on August 28, 1846. A son, Henry Clay Ewing, became a prominent figure in Kentucky politics. Ewing, a Whig lawyer and planter who lived in Russellville, Logan County, Kentucky, served in the Kentucky legislature from 1862 to 1865. He also represented the Fourth District of Kentucky for a few days in the provisional Confederate Congress and served in both the first and the second Confederate House of Representatives, where he supported the administration. His service simultaneously in the Kentucky and the Confederate legislatures kept him primarily in his home state. In the first Confederate House, he served on the Committees on Territories and Public Lands and the Special Committee for Clerks' Raises; in the second, he served on the Committees on Claims and Territories and Public Lands. In January 1865, he urged that the Confederacy launch an invasion into Kentucky to overthrow the Yankee government there. As with so many Kentuckians, he was allied with the Preston family in the western congressional bloc. After the war, he lived briefly in Greensboro, North Carolina, until he could return to his home. He held no public office, but was content to farm near Adairville, Kentucky, for the rest of his life. He died there on May 20, 1888. Collins, *Historical Sketches of Kentucky*, II; *Kentucky Marriages*.

F

FAGAN, James Fleming (*General*), was born to Steven and Catherine A. (Stevens) Fagan on March 1, 1828, in Louisville, Clark County, Kentucky. When he was ten, his family moved to Arkansas, where his father was the contractor for the state house. His father died two years later, and his mother married Samuel Adams, a governor of Alabama. Fagan was a Whig. He had three daughters by his marriage to Mura Ellisiff Beall, a sister of U.S. General W.N.R. Beall, and five children by his later marriage to Lizzie Repley. He farmed on the family plantation in Arkansas. Before the Civil War, Fagan represented Saline County in the Arkansas legislature for one term in the 1840s and was a lieutenant in Archibald Yell's Regiment during the Mexican War. From 1856 to 1858, he was a receiver for the State Bank of Arkansas. When his state seceded, he entered the Confederate Army as colonel of the 1st Arkansas Regiment. Fagan distinguished himself at the battle of Shiloh. Promoted to brigadier general on September 12, 1862, he was attached to the Trans-Mississippi Department, and he participated in the siege of Helena, Arkansas, and raised troops for the defense of his state in 1863. In the spring of 1864, his cavalry division was victorious in the Arkansas battles of Camden and Marks' Mills. After his promotion to major general on April 25, 1864, he accompanied General Sterling Price (*q.v.*) on his last expedition into Missouri. At the end of the war, Fagan commanded the District of Arkansas. When Lee surrendered, he refused to follow suit; he finally surrendered in June 1865 and was soon paroled. After the war, he was a farmer and a politician, joining the Republican party. In 1875, President Grant appointed him U.S. marshal for the Western District of Arkansas. Two years later, he was named receiver for the Land Office in Little Rock, where he died on September 1, 1893. Kerby, *Kirby Smith's Confederacy: The Trans-Mississippi South, 1863-1865*; Warner, *Generals in Gray*.

FARROW, James (*Congressman*), was born in Laurens, South Carolina, on April 3, 1827, to Samuel Farrow, lieutenant governor and, later, state legislator from Spartanburg District. The younger Farrow studied law with William D. Simpson (*q.v.*), practiced law, and edited a secessionist paper in South Carolina. Farrow, who said that he had been an "extreme disunionist" for all of his adult life, was a member of the Bluffton Movement in the mid-1840s and defended the radical students of South Carolina College in the 1850s. In summer of 1861, along with Simpson Bobo and Reverend N. P. Walker, President Davis (*q.v.*) appointed him to sell Confederate bonds. Farrow also represented South Carolina's Fifth Congressional District in the Confederate Congress. He was elected to the first Confederate House, and in 1863, he defeated James P. Boyce for reelection to that body. He served on the Claims and Medical Department Committees during both House terms. In addition, he served on the Accounts, Commerce, and Deceased Soldiers' Claims Committees during his second term. Only he and William D. Simpson (*q.v.*) of the South Carolina delegation voted to arm the slaves in February 1865. Farrow was also a lieutenant colonel in the South Carolina Militia during the war but saw little service. When the war ended, he returned to Spartanburg to practice law. He was a delegate to the state convention in 1865, the same year in which the Fourth District elected him to the state legislature, where he was an ally of James L. Orr (*q.v.*). In 1866, he was a delegate to the National Unionist party convention, where he made a speech entitled "The State of Public Affairs," in which he justified his attempts to counter the inhibiting influence of the radical Reconstructionists on Southern politics. In 1870 he moved to Kansas City, Missouri, and served as a county judge. He returned to South Carolina in 1875 and became president of Laurens Female College. He died in Laurens on July 2, 1892. *A History of Spartanburg County*.

FEARN, Thomas (*Congressman*), was born in Danville, Virginia, on November 15, 1789, to Thomas and Mary (Burton) Fearn. He attended Washington College in Lexington, Virginia, and was graduated from the Old Medical College in Philadelphia in 1810. Fearn, who was connected by marriage to Leroy Pope Walker (*q.v.*), married Sallie Bledsoe Shelby on February 26, 1822; they had seven daughters. Fearn settled in Huntsville, Alabama, in 1810 to practice medicine. He traveled to Europe in 1818 to study surgery and was made a member of the Royal College of Surgeons in London. From 1820 to 1837, he practiced in Huntsville. He was a member of the State Board of Medical Examiners from 1823 to 1829. He practiced medicine for fifty years, owned a plantation, and ran a bank in Huntsville. Although a unionist, Fearn was elected to the Montgomery Convention. In the provisional Confederate Congress, he served on the Public Lands and Territories Committees and spoke out for Southern unity. He was a Democrat. At seventy-two, he was the oldest delegate to the Congress, and he soon retired in favor of a younger and more vigorous candidate. He held no further office in the Confederacy. Fearn died in Huntsville on January 16, 1868. Owen, *History of Alabama and Dictionary of Alabama Biography*, III.

FEATHERSTON, Winfield Scott (*General*), son of Charles and Lucy (Pitts) Featherston, was born on August 8, 1820, in Rutherford County, Tennessee, where his parents had settled after leaving Virginia. He was married to Mary Hold Harris in 1848 and, when she died, to Elizabeth M. McEwen in 1858. Featherston fought in the Creek War in 1836. He was in business with his brother in Memphis before he studied law and moved to Houston, Mississippi, in 1840. He served as a Democrat in the U.S. House of Representatives from 1847 until he lost a second bid for reelection in 1851. In 1857, he moved to Holly Springs, Mississippi, and, in December 1860, he was a commissioner to Kentucky for the Mississippi secessionists. When the war began, he became a colonel in the 17th Mississippi Regiment. Featherston fought at the battle of First Manassas and served with distinction at the engagement at Leesburg, as a result of which he was promoted to brigadier general on March 4, 1862. He was wounded during the Seven Days in the summer of 1862 but recovered sufficiently to fight in the battles of Second Manassas, Sharpsburg, and Fredericksburg later that same year. Late in 1862, he asked to go to Mississippi to fight General Grant, and he served with distinction in the Yazoo Delta and in the defense of Vicksburg. At the battles of Atlanta and Nashville, he commanded William W. Loring's (*q.v.*) Division, and he participated in the Carolina campaign of 1865. He surrendered at Greensboro, North Carolina, and was paroled there in May 1865. After the war, he practiced law at

Holly Springs. He was elected to the state legislature in 1876 after helping to overthrow the carpetbag regime of Governor Adelbert Ames, and he was reelected and served as chairman of the Judiciary Committee until 1882. In 1882, he became a judge for the Second Circuit, and, in 1889, he was the unsuccessful Democratic candidate for governor. Featherston was a delegate to the state constitutional convention in 1890 and died on May 28, 1891, in Holly Springs. Evans, *Confederate Military History*, VII; *Biographical and Historical Memoirs of Mississippi*.

FERGUSON, Samuel Wragg (*General*), was born to James and Abby Ann (Barker) Ferguson on November 3, 1834, in Charleston, South Carolina. His father, a planter and state legislator, had fought in the War of 1812. Ferguson attended the private school of Christopher Coates in Charleston and graduated nineteenth in a class of thirty-eight from the U.S. Military Academy in 1857. He was commissioned a second lieutenant in the army; he was a member of the Mormon expedition and also served on the Pacific Coast prior to the Civil War. He was an Episcopalian. He married Kate Lee, whose father was a cousin of Robert E. Lee (*q.v.*), on August 28, 1862; they had three sons and two daughters. He resigned his commission in March 1861. As a captain in the South Carolina army, Ferguson aided P.G.T. Beauregard (*q.v.*) at the battles of Fort Sumter, First Manassas, Shiloh, Farmington, and in the siege of Corinth. Promoted to colonel in 1862, he gained a reputation for his attacks on federal shipping along the Mississippi River. In 1863, he fought a Union expedition in the Mississippi Delta, and on July 23, 1863, he was promoted to the rank of brigadier general. As commander of cavalry for the Army of Mississippi, he opposed William T. Sherman's march to Chattanooga and participated in the Atlanta campaign. General Joseph Wheeler (*q.v.*), who considered Ferguson a troublemaker, opposed his nomination to the rank of major general in August 1864. Toward the end of the war, Ferguson was part of President Davis's (*q.v.*) escort in the flight from Richmond. He surrendered in Georgia and was soon paroled. After the war, he practiced law in Greenville, Mississippi. He was a member of the State Levee Commission in 1876 and of the U.S. Rivers Commission in 1883. In 1894, he returned to Charleston, where he became a civil engineer. In 1898, he volunteered for duty in the Spanish-American War. Ferguson died on February 3, 1917, in Jackson, Mississippi. *Biographical and Historical Memoirs of Mississippi*; Evans, *Confederate Military History*, V.

FIELD, Charles William (*General*), was born on April 6, 1828, in Woodford County, Kentucky, to Willis and Isabella Miriam (Buck) Field. He graduated twenty-seventh in a class of forty-three from the U.S. Military Academy in 1849. He had two sons by his marriage to Monimia Mason in 1857. Field, a career officer in the U.S. Army, fought the Indians in Texas and New Mexico from 1849 to 1854. He was promoted to second lieutenant in 1851 and to first lieutenant in 1855.

From 1856 to 1861, he was chief of cavalry and an assistant instructor of cavalry tactics at West Point. He was promoted to captain in the army in January 1861 and resigned his commission in May 1861 to become a captain of cavalry in the Confederate Army. After being promoted to brigadier general on March 9, 1862, he participated in the 1862 battles of the Seven Days and Cedar Mountain before a hip wound at the battle of Second Manassas forced his retirement from active combat for a year. During this interlude, he was superintendent of the Conscription Bureau in Richmond. Promoted to major general on February 12, 1864, he led Hood's (*q.v.*) Texas division and saved Lee's (*q.v.*) right wing at the battle of the Wilderness in May, retook the Bermuda Hundred line, and fought in August of that year from Chapin's Bluff to New Market Heights. He surrendered at Appomattox and was soon paroled. After the war, he was a businessman in Baltimore and Georgia for ten years. From 1875 to 1877, he was colonel of engineers in the Egyptian army. Upon his return to the United States, he was named doorkeeper of the U.S. House of Representatives and held that post from 1878 to 1881. He served as a civil engineer for the U.S. government from 1881 to 1885 and as superintendent of the Indian reservation at Hot Springs, Arkansas, from 1885 to 1889. Field died on April 2, 1892, in Washington, D.C. Freeman, *Lee's Lieutenants*, III; Heitman, *Historical Register and Dictionary of the United States Army*; *Southern Historical Society Papers*, XV.

FINLEY, Jesse Johnson (*General, Judge*), was born to the planter Obadiah Gaines Finley and his wife Mary Lewis (Johnson), on November 18, 1812, in Lebanon, Wilson County, Tennessee. He attended Campbell Academy, read law in Nashville, and began his law practice in Lebanon. He was a Presbyterian and a Whig. He had two sons by his first marriage to Amanda Catherine Yerger. After her death, he married Eliza Holland Lamb in 1839; they had a son and two daughters. After her death in 1845, he married Margaret Harris Martin, by whom he had a son and a daughter. Finley was a captain in the Seminole War in 1836. He represented Wilson County in the Tennessee Senate in 1837. In 1840, he moved to Mississippi County, Arkansas, and the following year he was elected to the Arkansas Senate from Little Rock. He subsequently moved to Memphis, where he practiced law and was elected mayor in 1845. In November 1846, he moved to Marianna, Florida, and from 1850 to 1854, he served as a Whig in the Florida Senate. Finley, who advocated the popular election of judges, also served as judge for the Western Circuit of Florida from 1853 to 1861. At the beginning of the Civil War, he was made judge for the Confederate court of the Florida District. He resigned this post in March 1862 to enter the Confederate Army as a private. Later a colonel in the 6th Florida Regiment, he served under General Edmund Kirby Smith (*q.v.*) in east Tennessee during the Kentucky campaign of 1862. He served with distinction at Chickamauga and at Missionary Ridge. Promoted to brigadier general on November 16, 1863, he commanded the Florida Infantry in the Army of Tennessee. He led a brigade during the Atlanta campaign, where he was wounded at Resaca and at Jonesboro and was incapacitated for further military duty. In November and December 1864, he was president of the courts-martial at Knoxville for his department. He held no further office in the Confederacy. From 1865 to 1871, Finley practiced law in Lake City, Florida. He moved to Jacksonville in 1871. From 1875 to 1879 and in 1881-1882, he served as a Democrat in the U.S. House of Representatives. He lost a race for governor in 1882 but was elected to the U.S. Senate in 1867. The fact that he never had an official parole, however, prevented him from ever taking his seat. He was elected a judge of the Florida Fifth Judicial Circuit in 1887 and served until 1903. Finley died on November 6, 1904, in Lake City, Florida. Evans, *Confederate Military History*, XI; *Florida Law Journal*, XXIII.

FLANAGIN, Harris (*Governor*), son of James and Mary Flanigan, was born on November 3, 1817, in Roadstown, New Jersey. He was educated at a Quaker school in New Jersey and taught in a seminary at Clermont, Pennsylvania, before moving to Arkansas in 1837 and being admitted to the Clark County bar. He had three children by his marriage to Martha E. Nash on July 3, 1851. Flanagin lived first in Greenville and then in Arkadelphia. He represented Clark County as a Democrat in the 1842 state legislature. He was a unionist delegate to the secession convention in 1861 but became a secessionist after the firing on Fort Sumter. He entered the Civil War as a captain in the 2nd Regiment of Arkansas Mounted Rifles and served as a colonel of his regiment in Tennessee. By special election, he was chosen to succeed Henry Rector (*q. v.*) as governor of Arkansas on November 15, 1862. Aligned with the R. H. Johnson clique, Flanagin defeated Rector by a margin of two to one, and he remained governor until the war ended. He was instrumental in keeping Arkansas troops home and in getting the Confederacy to fight in Arkansas. As governor, he helped Kirby Smith (*q. v.*) to raise troops for the Confederacy, encouraged manufacturing, and raised money for relief. As the end of the war approached, he tried to devise a way for the southwestern states to cooperate with the Union. After the war, he practiced law in Arkadelphia. He was elected to the state constitutional convention in 1874. Flanagin died in Arkadelphia on October 23, 1874. Hempstead, *Historical Review of Arkansas*; Thomas, *Arkansas in War and Reconstruction, 1861-1874*.

FOOTE, Henry Stuart (*Congressman*), was born in Fauquier County, Virginia, on September 20, 1800, to Richard Helm and Jane (Stuart) Foote. He graduated from Washington College in Lexington, Virginia, in 1819 and was admitted to the Richmond bar in 1822. He moved to Alabama in 1823 and began his law practice. Foote was an Episcopalian. He was married twice—to Elizabeth Winters, whose family was from Virginia, and, upon her death, to Mrs. Rachel D. Smiley. He moved to Mississippi after a duel and there he set up his law practice and became a planter. He edited *The Mississippian* in Jackson in 1832. He served at least one term in the Mississippi legislature during the 1840s. Interested in Texas affairs, he wrote a history of *Texas and the Texans* in 1841. He was elected to the U.S. Senate in 1847 and was a pronounced unionist who defended slavery and supported the Compromise of 1850. In 1851, as a Whig he won the gubernatorial election over Jefferson Davis (*q.v.*) and served until 1854. He moved to California in 1854 but returned to Vicksburg in 1858. Shortly thereafter he moved to Tennessee. In 1859, he opposed secession as a member of the Southern convention in Knoxville, Tennessee. During the war, he represented Tennessee in both Confederate Houses where he opposed conscription, wanted to draft foreigners, supported a curb on speculation, condemned martial law, and criticized the Davis administration for not pursuing a vigorous war effort in the west. He served on the Foreign Affairs, Illegal Seizures, and Special Committees. He was censured in Congress for consorting with the Union troops and was expelled from that body in 1864. In 1865, he called for peace and was called a traitor to the Confederacy. Foote ran to Montreal after the war and later moved back to Tennessee. He also practiced law in Washington, D.C., and became a Republican during the 1870s. From 1878 to 1880, he was superintendent of the U.S. mint in New Orleans. He died on May 20, 1880, in Nashville. Foote, *War of the Rebellion*; Gonzales, "Henry Stuart Foote: Confederate Congressman and Exile," *Civil War History*, XI.

FORD, Samuel Howard (*Congressman, Minister*), was born on February 19, 1819, in London, England, where his father was a minister. His parents, Thomas Howard and Ann (Buck) Ford, later emigrated to the United States, where they lived in Illinois and Missouri. The younger Ford graduated from Missouri State University in 1843 and was ordained a Baptist minister the same year. His wife was the former Sallie Rochester. Ford was a pastor in Jefferson City in 1844, in St. Louis in 1846, and in Cape Girardeau in 1846-1847. From 1853 to 1860, he was minister of the East Baptist Church in Louisville, Kentucky. In 1860, he edited the Missouri *Baptist* and wrote *Origin of Baptists*. Ford was elected to the provisional Confederate Congress from Kentucky in 1861 where he served on the Committee on Inauguration. He held pastorates in Memphis in 1861 and in Mobile from 1863 to 1865. Ford was loyal to the Confederacy and he stirred his congregations to contribute to the war effort. After the war, he again held a pastorate in Memphis from 1865 to 1871. He moved to St. Louis, Missouri, where he wrote books on ecclesiastical history. He died in St. Louis on July 5, 1905. Alexander and Beringer, *The Anatomy of the Confederate Congress*; Spencer, *A History of Kentucky Baptists from 1769 to 1885*.

FORMAN, Thomas Marsh (*Congressman*), was born to Joseph Bryan and Delia Forman near Savannah, Georgia, on January 4, 1809. He was educated at St. Mary's College in Maryland. He married Florida Troup, daughter of Georgia Governor George M. Troup, and she died in 1854. Forman, a wealthy farmer from Glynn County, Georgia, served as a Democrat in the state Senate in 1847. In

1860 he resided in Savannah. Forman served in the Provisional Confederate Congress from August 1861 until February 1862. He had an active congressional career, serving on the Inauguration Committee and advocating the opening of Confederate ports to trade. During the remainder of the war, he raised funds for the Georgia State Navy. After the war, Forman returned to farming. He died on September 27, 1875, near Brunswick, Georgia. Knight, *A Standard History of Georgia and Georgians*.

FORNEY, John Horace (*General*), was born to Peter and Sabina Swope (Hoke) Forney on August 12, 1829, in Batley Forge, Lincoln County, North Carolina. His father, a planter, moved the family to Alabama in 1835, settling in Jacksonville, where the younger Forney was educated by private tutors. Forney graduated twenty-second in a class of forty-three from the U.S. Military Academy in 1852. He was an Episcopalian and a Democrat. He married Septinia Sexta Middleton on February 5, 1863; they had two sons and five daughters. Before the war, he was a career officer in the army, attaining the rank of second lieutenant in 1853 and first lieutenant in 1855. After serving garrison duty in Kentucky, he was a member of the Utah expedition, and in 1860, he became an instructor in tactics at West Point. He resigned from the federal army when the war began. He volunteered for the Confederate Army and was made colonel of Alabama state troops at the beginning of the war. Forney was sent to Pensacola, where General Braxton Bragg (*q.v.*) made him acting inspector general. He went as colonel of the 10th Alabama Regiment under General Edmund Kirby Smith (*q.v.*) to Virginia. He was wounded at the battle of Dranesville in the winter of 1861. Upon his recovery he was promoted to brigadier general on March 10, 1862 and was sent to Mobile to command the District of the Gulf. On October 27, 1862, he was promoted to major general in the Department of South Alabama and West Florida. In May 1863, he became commander of the Second Military District of Vicksburg, and in July 1864, he was assigned to the Trans-Mississippi Department. At the close of the war, he served under General John B. Magruder (*q.v.*). It is not known when he surrendered. After the war he was a planter and engineer in Alabama. Forney died on September 13, 1902, in Jacksonville, Alabama. Owen, *History of Alabama and Dictionary of Alabama Biography*, III.

FORREST, Nathan Bedford (*General*), was born to William and Mariam (Beck) Forrest on July 13, 1821, in Chapel Hill, Bedford County, Tennessee. The family moved to Tippah County, Mississippi, in 1834. Young Forrest received little education himself, although he helped to educate his brother. He was a Presbyterian and a Democrat. He had a son and a daughter by his marriage to Mary Ann Montgomery on September 25, 1845. He was a blacksmith and a hill farmer, and by 1840 he began to prosper. In 1842, he moved to Hernando, Mississippi, where he became a planter, dealing in horses and slaves. In 1851, he went into the real estate business in Memphis, where he was also a town alderman from 1858 to 1860. By 1859, he had returned to planting. When the war began, Forrest enlisted as a private in the Tennessee Cavalry. As lieutenant colonel of his own battalion, he defended Fort Donelson, and he was colonel of the 3rd Tennessee Cavalry at the battle of Shiloh, where he also covered the Confederate retreat in the spring of 1862. Forrest, who has been called a born military genius, was promoted to brigadier general on July 21, 1862. In 1862-1863, he was engaged in west Tennessee, where he captured the Union garrison at Murfreesboro. He was shot by a subordinate during one of his raids, and upon his recovery he clashed with Braxton Bragg (*q.v.*) after the battle of Chickamauga. President Davis (*q.v.*) later gave him an independent command in north Mississippi and west Tennessee. Promoted to major general on December 4, 1863, he participated in the Fort Pillow Massacre in April 1864, and in June of that year, he won his greatest military victory against overwhelming odds at Brice's Crossroads, Mississippi. He became a lieutenant general on February 28, 1865. Although Forrest's forces were finally overwhelmed at Selma, Alabama, in April 1865, he had the distinction of winning all the major engagements which he led. He surrendered in May and was soon paroled. Impoverished after the war, he returned to planting in Tennessee. Forrest was also an employee of the Selma and Memphis Railroad during the 1870s. He was the first Grand Wizard of the Ku Klux Klan. Forrest died in Memphis on October 24, 1877. Henry, *"First with the Most" Forrest*.

FORSYTH, John (*Editor*), son of the U.S. Senator and Georgia Governor John Forsyth and his wife Clara (Meigs), was born on October 31, 1812, in Augusta, Georgia. He received his secondary education abroad and was valedictorian of his class at Princeton in 1832. In 1834, he was admitted to the Georgia bar. He had two sons by his marriage to a Miss Hull. His sister was married to the prominent prewar Georgia and Confederate General Alfred Iverson (*q.v.*). Forsyth moved to Alabama to practice law and became U.S. attorney for the Southern District. He returned to Georgia in the 1840s to edit the Columbus *Times*. He also saw service in the Mexican War. Forsyth moved to Mobile in 1853 where he built lumber mills and edited the *Register*. President Buchanan named him minister to Mexico in 1856, and he served in that capacity for three years. In 1859, he was elected to the Alabama legislature, and in 1860, he was elected mayor of Mobile. As a delegate to the Democratic national convention at Charleston in 1860, he supported Stephen A. Douglas for the presidency. After the Confederacy was formed, President Jefferson Davis (*q.v.*) made him a peace commissioner to Washington; Forsyth, concluding that no just peace could be made with the Union government, urged Davis to prepare for war. During the war, he continued as mayor of Mobile and planned that city's defense. He also served for a time as Braxton Bragg's (*q.v.*) staff officer. Forsyth edited the *Register* throughout the war, making that paper a propaganda organ for the Confederate war effort. He continued as mayor until 1866, and he remained as editor of the *Register*. He used his paper to oppose federal Reconstruction legislation. Forsyth died in Mobile on May 2, 1879. Andrews, *The South Reports the Civil War*; Owen, *History of Alabama and Dictionary of Alabama Biography*, III.

FOSTER, Thomas Jefferson (*Congressman*), was born in Nashville, Tennessee, on July 11, 1809, to Robert Coleman and Ann (Hubbard) Foster, who had moved westward, first to Kentucky and then to Tennessee, from their native state of Virginia. The family moved to Lawrence County, Alabama, in 1830, where the younger Foster soon became a large slaveholding planter and manufacturer. He was first married to Virginia Prudence on October 30, 1836; he had three children by his second marriage to Ann Hood. His third wife was a Mrs. Wray. Although he held no prewar political office, Foster voted as a Whig and was considered a unionist. Foster volunteered for service in the Confederate Army and was named colonel of the 27th Alabama Infantry (known as Foster's Regiment). He helped to construct Fort Henry. He also served in both permanent Confederate Houses. He supported conscription and stood with the Davis administration in the first Congress, but turned against it in the second. He served on the Conference, Indian Affairs, Territories and Public Lands, and Accounts and other committees in his long political service to the Confederacy. When the war ended, he returned to his plantation in Lawrence County. He was elected to the U.S. House of Representatives in 1865 but was not seated because of restrictions on his public service. He moved to Kentucky in 1867 and died there in obscurity on February 24, 1887. Owen, *History of Alabama and Dictionary of Alabama Biography*, III.

FREEMAN, Thomas W. (*Congressman*), was born in Anderson County, Kentucky, in 1824. Little is known of his family or his upbringing. He was admitted to the Anderson County bar in 1847. In 1851 he moved to Boliver, Polk County, Missouri, and was a Democrat and a successful lawyer. In 1860, he was a John C. Breckinridge (*q.v.*) presidential elector and a secessionist. He also was elected to the Missouri General Assembly in 1860. In the provisional Confederate Congress, he served on the Postal Affairs Committee. In the first Confederate House, he held duties on the Territorial and Public Lands, Enrolled Bills, and Naval Affairs Committees. He was absent much of the time, but generally was a Davis administration supporter. Peter S. Wilkes (*q.v.*) defeated him for election to the Second Congress. He seems to have held no further office in the Confederacy. Freeman died in St. Louis on October 24, 1865. Kirkpatrick, ''Missouri's Delegation in the Confederate Congress,'' *Civil War History*, V.

FRENCH, Samuel Gibbs (*General*), son of Samuel and Rebecca (Clark) French, was born on November 22, 1818, in Gloucester County, New Jersey. His family had been among the founders of New Jersey. He attended the academy in Burlington, New Jersey, and graduated fourteenth in a class of thirty-nine from the U.S. Military Academy in 1843. French had one daughter by his marriage to E.

Matilda Roberts on April 26, 1853; after his first wife died, he had two sons and a daughter by his marriage to Mary Fontaine Abercrombie on January 12, 1865. He accepted a commission into the U.S. Army as an artillery officer. During the Mexican War, he served under Zachary Taylor as an artillery officer. Promoted to second lieutenant for his action at Monterrey, he was breveted captain the following year. He also participated in the battles of Palo Alto and Resaca de la Palma. In 1856, he resigned his military commission to operate a plantation near Greenville, Mississippi. When his state seceded from the Union in February 1861, he was made chief of ordnance in the Mississippi army. He entered the Confederate Army as a major of artillery, and in the early months of the war he fortified Wilmington, North Carolina, and Petersburg, Virginia, blockaded the Potomac River, and built Fort Fisher, North Carolina. After promotion to brigadier general on October 23, 1861, he commanded the Department of Southern Virginia and North Carolina. In July 1862, he attacked McClellan at the battle of Malvern Hill during the Seven Days. He was promoted to major general on October 22, 1862, and, in May 1863, he was sent to Mississippi, where he served with General Joseph E. Johnston (*q.v.*) in the Army of Tennessee. During 1864, his division fought in the Atlanta and Tennessee campaigns, participating most conspicuously at the battles of New Hope Church, Kenesaw Mountain, Franklin, and Nashville. During the last part of the war, he was almost blind from an eye infection, and he was on inactive service in Mobile when the war ended. He returned to his Greenville plantation, where he planted cotton, and he helped to rebuild the Mississippi levees in the postwar period. In 1876, he moved to Columbus, Georgia, and in 1881, he became a planter of orange groves in Winter Park, Florida. French published his autobiography, *Two Wars*, prior to his death in retirement in Florala, Alabama, on April 20, 1910. Evans, *Confederate Military History, VII; French, Two Wars: An Autobiography.*

FRY, Birkett Davenport (*General*), was born on June 24, 1822, in Kanawha County, Virginia, to Thornton and Eliza R. (Thompson) Fry. He attended Washington College in Pennsylvania and Virginia Military Institute. He also attended the U.S. Military Academy from 1842 to 1844 but dropped out before finishing his degree. In 1846, he was admitted to the Virginia bar. Fry was an Episcopalian and married Martha (Micou) Baker. He distinguished himself as a first lieutenant during the Mexican War, after which he practiced law in Sacramento, California, in 1849. In 1856, he was a brigadier in William Walker's filibuster army in a scheme to take over the government of Nicaragua. In 1859, he moved to Tallassee, Alabama, where he managed a cotton mill. When the war began, he entered the Confederate Army as a colonel of the 13th Alabama Infantry. He was severely wounded at the battle of Seven Pines in the late spring of 1862, and upon his recovery his arm was shattered during the battle of Sharpsburg. He recovered and participated in the battle of Chancellorsville and served as a brigade commander at Gettysburg, where he was yet again wounded and captured during Pickett's charge. Fry was exchanged in April 1864, and he returned to the Army of Northern Virginia. He also commanded a brigade at the battle of Drewry's Bluff, after which he was promoted to brigadier general on May 24, 1864. Fry subsequently fought in the battle of Cold Harbor before being chosen by General Braxton Bragg (*q.v.*) to command the military district of Augusta. He was in Augusta at the close of the war. He lived in Cuba from 1865 to 1868, when he returned to Tallassee to the cotton mill. In 1881, he became a cotton buyer in Richmond, Virginia, and, from 1886 to 1891, he was president of the Marshall Manufacturing Company. Fry died in Richmond on January 21 or February 5, 1891. Freeman, *Lee's Lieutenants*, III; Owen, *History of Alabama and Dictionary of Alabama Biography*, III.

FULLER, Thomas Charles (*Congressman*), son of the merchant Thomas Charles Fuller and his wife Catherine (Raboteau), was born in Fayetteville, North Carolina, on February 27, 1832. His father died young. The younger Fuller attended the University of North Carolina from 1849 until 1851 but left school to become a merchant in Fayetteville. He studied law under Judge Richmond M. Pearson (*q.v.*) in 1855 and began his Fayetteville practice in 1856. Fuller was a Presbyterian. He married Caroline Douglas Whitehead on November 5, 1857, and had two sons. He held no prewar political office. An ardent Whig, he opposed secession until Lincoln called for troops to invade the Confederacy. He joined the Lafayette Light Infantry in 1861 and fought at Bethel, attaining the rank of first lieutenant. In 1863, he became the youngest member to be elected to the Confederate House and was known among his colleagues for his military expertise. He was also the poorest member of the second House, to which he was elected by the North Carolina "Conservative" party. He served on the Commerce, Patents, and Enrolled Bills Committees and generally opposed the centralizing measures of the Davis administration. Following the war, Fuller returned to his law practice. He became a Democrat and was elected to the U.S. House in 1865 but was never seated. In 1870, he defended the actions of the Ku Klux Klan, but as chairman of the Democratic state convention in 1871 he condemned the Klan's excesses. In 1873, he moved to Raleigh, where he was a partner in the law firm of Merriman, Fuller, and Ashe. President Benjamin Harrison appointed him judge of the Court of Private Land Claims established to rule on Mexican lands in 1891. He died in that office on October 20, 1901, in Raleigh. Alexander and Beringer, *The Anatomy of the Confederate Congress*; *Amnesty Petitions*; Ashe, *Cyclopedia of Eminent and Representative Men of the Carolinas*. . . .

FUNSTEN, David (*Congressman*), was born in Clarke County, Virginia, on October 14, 1819. He attended boarding school in Alexandria and graduated from Princeton in 1838. He was a lawyer in Alexandria for nearly twenty years prior to the Civil War. Funsten served one term in the Virginia House of Delegates in 1844. When the war began, he enlisted as a captain of the infantry in the 11th

Virginia Regiment. Promoted to colonel in the spring of 1862, he left the army the same year after receiving a wound at Seven Pines which permanently disabled him. Funsten spent the remainder of the war as a member of the first and second Confederate House of Representatives. He was elected from the Ninth Virginia Confederate Congressional District. In the first House, he served on the Printing Committee and the special committee to inquire into illegal arrests. In the second House, he was a member of the Committees on Compensation for Patents, Flag and Seal, and Illegal Seizures, as well as the Joint Committee of Naval Affairs. In December 1864, he sponsored a measure to consolidate regiments and companies to facilitate the development of the troops. He was a protector of local interests but supported the Davis administration. He practiced law again in Alexandria when the war ended. He died there on April 6, 1866. Evans, *Confederate Military History*, III.

FURMAN, James Clement (*Minister*), was born to the Reverend Richard and Dorothea Maria (Burn) Furman on December 5, 1809, in Charleston, South Carolina. He graduated from the College of Charleston in 1826 and attended Furman Theological Institute prior to his ordination as a Baptist minister in 1832. Furman married Harriet E. Davis in 1833 and, upon her death, her sister Mary Glenn Davis in 1855. He served as pastor of the Baptist Church of Society Hill, South Carolina, from 1833 to 1844, when he became president of Furman Theological Institute in Charleston, South Carolina. In 1852, he moved the school to Greenville, South Carolina, and he served as president of Furman University until 1879. An ardent secessionist, he represented Greenville District at the South Carolina secession convention. During the war, while Furman University was closed, he taught at Greenville Female College and served as a wartime spiritual leader. He represented the idea of continuing education throughout the war and through his sermons and his life symbolized both the spiritual and cultural leadership of the Confederacy. His school reopened in 1866 and he again became its president. Furman was a bitter foe of Reconstruction. He died in Greenville, South Carolina, in retirement on March 3, 1891. Cook, *The Life and Work of James Clement Furman*; Haynesworth, *Haynesworth, Furman and Allied Families*.

G

GAITHER, Burgess Sidney (*Congressman*), was born in Iredell County, North Carolina, on March 16, 1807. His father, Burgess Gaither, was a politician who died in 1819, leaving ten children. The younger Gaither attended Hull's High School and Franklin College (later the University of Georgia) before being admitted to the North Carolina bar in 1829. He married Elizabeth Sharpe Erwin on July 3, 1830, and Sarah F. Corpening in 1871. A Whig, he served as a clerk of the Burke County, North Carolina, Superior Court and was a delegate to the state constitutional convention of 1835 before being named that same year superintendent of the federal mint at Charlotte, North Carolina. He was elected to the state Senate in 1840 and reelected in 1844, when he served as president of the Senate. From 1844 to 1848, he was solicitor of the Seventh Judicial District. A unionist Whig in 1851, Gaither campaigned for John Bell in 1860 in western North Carolina. Yet, he was a strong supporter of the South during the war and he ably represented the Ninth Confederate Congressional District in both permanent Confederate Houses, where he generally voted against the Davis administration. However, he supported congressional war measures and opposed the North Carolina unionists. While he was a personal friend of President Davis (*q. v.*), he disliked Davis's secretiveness. He opposed extending conscription and served on the Conference, Impressments, Judiciary, Naval Affairs and special committees. After the war, he returned to his law practice and held no further public office. Gaither died in Morgantown, North Carolina, on February 23, 1892. Ashe, *Cyclopedia of Eminent and Representative Men of the Carolinas. . .* , I.

GARDENHIRE, Erasmus Lee (*Congressman*), was the son of the small farmer Adam Gardenhire and Ailsey (Tippett). He was born on November 12, 1815, in Overton County, Tennessee. Educated at Clinton College in Tennessee, in 1839 he began the practice of law. He married Mary McMillan on December 5, 1839; they had seven children. Gardenhire was a Mason, a member of the Christian Church (his family was Methodist), and a Democrat. For a time he taught school at Livingston Academy and he also had a small farm. He practiced law in Livingston but moved to Sparta, Tennessee, in 1851. He served in the state Senate during the 1850s, edited the Sparta *Mountain Democrat* in 1856-1857, and was elected judge of the Fifth Judicial District in 1858. He resigned his judgeship in 1861. A secessionist, he was elected to the first Confederate Congress and was pro-administration. He held positions on the Claims, Elections, and Enrolled Bills Committees. In 1862, he converted all his real estate into cash in hopes of speculating in cotton; he was soon wiped out. Gardenhire declined reelection to the second Congress in an effort to recoup his losses. He served in no further capacity in the war. Governor William G. Brownlow described him as a bitter rebel. In 1875, he represented White and Putnam Counties in the Tennessee legislature and was chairman of the Judiciary Committee. In 1876, he moved to Carthage, Tennessee, and, in 1883, he was judge of the Court of Referees of west Tennessee. He died in Carthage on April 4, 1899. Speer, *Sketches of Prominent Tennesseans*; Warner and Yearns, *Biographical Register of the Confederate Congress*.

GARDNER, Franklin (*General*), was born in New York City on January 29, 1823, to Colonel Charles K. and Ann Eliza (McLean) Gardner. His father was a career officer in the U.S. Army. Gardner, whose parents moved to Iowa in the 1830s, graduated seventeenth in a class of thirty-nine from the U.S. Military Academy in 1843. He began his military career at Pensacola harbor and later served on the frontier. He was a Catholic and a Democrat. He married into the Mouton family of Louisiana. Breveted captain during the Mexican War, he participated in the battles of Monterrey, Vera Cruz, Cerro Gordo, Contreras, Churubusco, and Molino del Rey. He then saw frontier duty in Florida, Louisiana, and Arkansas and served as captain of the 10th Infantry in the Utah Territory during the 1850s. Against the wishes of his father and his brother, both of whom remained loyal to the Union, Gardner entered the Confederate Army as a lieutenant colonel in 1861. He did not bother to resign from the federal army. He helped to organize the cavalry at the battle of Shiloh and was promoted to brigadier general on April 11, 1862. He served with Polk's Corps during Bragg's invasion of Kentucky in 1862 and on December 13 of that year he was promoted to major general. Gardner commanded Port Hudson, Louisiana, from December 1862 until July 8, 1863. He was taken prisoner after the fall of Vicksburg and was exchanged in August 1864. Afterwards, he served under General Richard Taylor (*q.v.*) in Mississippi, but the Confederates distrusted him because of his Northern background and he was given no further line duty. After the war, Gardner lived the quiet life of a planter until his death on April 29, 1873, in Vermilionville, Louisiana. Fortier, *A History of Louisiana*, I.

GARLAND, Augustus Hill (*Congressman*), was born to Rufus and Barbara (Hill) Garland on June 11, 1832, in Tipton County, Tennessee. His family moved to Hempstead County, Arkansas, in 1833. He attended St. Mary's College, Kentucky, graduated from St. Joseph's College, Kentucky, in 1849, and was admitted to the Hempstead County bar in 1853. He married Sarah Virginia Sanders the same year; they had three children. Garland practiced law in Washington, Arkansas, until he moved to Little Rock in 1856. He was a unionist and a Whig who supported John Bell for president in 1860. After the election, he became a Democrat and represented Pulaski County as a unionist delegate to the state convention. In 1861, Garland, an anti-Johnsonite in Arkansas politics, voted to submit the secession issue to popular referendum, but he voted to support secession after the firing on Fort Sumter. He served in the provisional Confederate Congress, where he had a part in framing the Confederate Constitution, and he was elected from Arkansas' Third Congressional District to the first Confederate House of Representatives. He was elected to the Confederate Senate in 1864, and he served on many of the key committees. A staunch supporter of the Davis administration throughout the war, Garland opposed martial law. He left Richmond in March 1865 and returned to Arkansas, where he attempted to bargain for easy peace terms with the federal government. Garland was elected to the U.S. Senate in 1867 but was unable to take his seat because of restrictions. He resumed his law practice in Little Rock before returning to public life, first as governor of Arkansas from 1874 to 1876 and later as a Democrat in the U.S. Senate from 1876 to 1885. He was also attorney general in the Cleveland administration from 1885 to 1889. Late in life, Garland was involved in a scandal concerning fictitious bank capital which was supposedly issued while he was affiliated with the Pan Electric Telephone Company, but he was never prosecuted. He died while arguing a case before the Supreme Court in Washington, D.C., on January 26, 1899. Newberry, *A Life of Mr. Garland of Arkansas*; Thomas, *Arkansas and Its People, A History, 1541-1930*, III.

GARLAND, Landon Cabell (*Educator*), whose father was a lawyer and clerk of court, was born on March 21, 1810, in Nelson County, Virginia, to Spotswood and Lucinda (Rose) Garland. His brother was Rufus King Garland. After attending prep school, he graduated first in his class at Hampden-Sidney College in 1829. He was a Methodist. He married Mary Burwell in 1831, who died a few years later. On December 29, 1835, he married Louisa Frances Garland, a third cousin, by whom he had ten children. In 1830, Garland tutored in chemistry at Washington College in Virginia. In 1833, he received the chair of natural history and chemistry at Randolph-Macon College; he was also president of the college from 1837 until his resignation ten years later. He declined the presidency of the College of William and Mary and occupied the chair of English literature, rhetoric, and history at the University of Alabama from 1847 until he became its president in 1854. He remained on as president during the Civil War, keeping the university open and establishing a fund to rebuild the school. In 1867, he held the chair of physics and astronomy at the University of Mississippi, and, in 1875, he became chancellor of Vanderbilt University. He retired from the chancellorship in 1893 and remained at the university as an instructor. Garland died on February 13, 1895, in Nashville. Owens, *History of Alabama and Dictionary of Alabama Biography*, III.

GARLAND, Rufus King, Jr. (*Congressman*), son of Rufus King and Barbara (Hill) Garland and brother of Augustus Hill Garland (*q. v.*), was born in Tipton County, Tennessee, on May 22, 1830. He married Isabelle Walker, daughter of a wealthy farmer in Hempstead County, Arkansas; they had no children. Garland, a lawyer and a farmer, was a Whig who became a Democrat in 1860. He was also a Methodist preacher during the 1850s. He was a unionist in the Arkansas secession convention of 1861, but he shifted to secession when he became convinced that equal rights were no longer protected in Washington. He represented Arkansas in the second Confederate House, being elected by a military vote. He volunteered for duty when the war began and served in the Army of Tennessee. He was a colonel in the Arkansas campaigns of 1863. When Arkansas was overrun by Union troops and government almost disappeared, Garland was the only congressman in the Confederate Congress during 1864 who consistently opposed the Davis Administration. He was an active member of the Committee on Ways and Means. After the war, he returned to his law practice, continued as an itinerant preacher, and lost a bid for governor as a Greenback candidate in 1882. He died on December 12, 1886, in Prescott, Arkansas. Thomas, *Arkansas in War and Reconstruction, 1861-1874*.

GARNETT, Muscoe Russell Hunter (*Congressman*), was born to James Mercer Garnett, Jr., and his wife Maria (Hunter), sister of Robert M. T. Hunter (*q. v.*), in Essex County, Virginia, on July 25, 1821. He graduated from the University of Virginia in 1839, studied law there in 1841, and was admitted to the bar in Loretto, Essex County, in 1842. He was an Episcopalian. Garnett married Mary Picton Stevens on July 26, 1860. He was a Democratic delegate to the state constitutional convention in 1850-1851 and supported the equalizing of the western vote. In 1850, he wrote *The Union, Past and Future*, a pamphlet which expressed fear over government centralization. As a member of the Board of Visitors of the University of Virginia from 1855 to 1859, he was responsible for the establishment of the chair of history there. Garnett also served in the Virginia House of Burgesses from 1853 to 1856 and in the U.S. House of Representatives from 1856 to 1861. Garnett, a man of keen intellect, also ran a successful plantation. As a delegate to the state secession convention and to the state constitutional convention in 1861, he was a strong secessionist. His historical articles served as useful propaganda in the secession movement. Garnett resigned from Congress after the war began. The citizens of Virginia's First Congressional District elected him to the first Confederate House, but he was defeated for reelection by Robert L. Montague (*q. v.*). Generally a Davis administration opponent, he served on the Conference, Military

Affairs, and the Ways and Means Committees. Before his term ran out, he died on February 14, 1864, of typhoid fever in Essex County. Garnett, ''Biographical Sketch of Honorable Muscoe Russell Hunter Garnett,'' *William and Mary Quarterly*, XVIII.

GARTRELL, Lucius Jeremiah (*General, Congressman*), son of the planter and merchant Joseph Gartrell and his wife——— (Boswell), was born on January 7, 1821, in Wilkes County, Georgia. He attended private schools in Wilkes County and also attended Randolph-Macon College in 1841; he attended Franklin College (later the University of Georgia) from 1842 to 1843. Gartrell studied law in the office of Robert Toombs (*q.v.*) and was admitted to the Lincoln County, Georgia, bar in 1842. He had six children by his marriage in 1841 to Louisiana O. Gideon and, after her death, five children by his marriage in 1855 to Antoinette T. Burke. After her death, he married Maud Condon in 1888. From 1843 to 1847, he served as solicitor general for the Northern Judicial Circuit. After moving back to Wilkes County, Gartrell, an extreme states' rights Whig, served in the House of Representatives from 1847 to 1850, where he offered a Southern rights resolution in 1850. In 1854, he moved to Atlanta and subsequently beat a Know-Nothing candidate for election to the U.S. House of Representatives, where he served as a Democrat from 1857 to 1861. He resigned when Georgia seceded from the Union. A strong secessionist, when the war began he organized the 7th Regiment Georgia Volunteer Infantry, where he served as a colonel and distinguished himself at the battle of First Manassas. Gartrell left military service from 1862 until 1864 in order to take his seat in the Confederate House, to which he was elected from Georgia's Eighth Congressional District. A supporter of the Davis administration, Gartrell urged price ceilings in order to curb inflation and also proposed the suspension of *habeas corpus*. He served on the Committee on the Judiciary and many conference committees. He returned to the field and was commissioned brigadier general on August 22, 1864. Gartrell fought largely in South Carolina. He made a celebrated stand against William T. Sherman at Coosawatchie, South Carolina, toward the end of 1864. He was wounded in that engagement and saw no further field service. When the war ended, he returned to his law practice and became a famous criminal lawyer. In 1877, he was a delegate to the Georgia constitutional convention, and, in 1882, he lost a race for governor to Alexander Stephens (*q.v.*). He died in Atlanta on April 7, 1891. Knight, *A Standard History of Georgia and Georgians*; Northen, *Men of Mark in Georgia*, IV.

GENTRY, Meredith Poindexter (*Congressman*), was born to the wealthy planter Watson and his wife Theodesia (Poindexter) Gentry in Rockingham County, North Carolina, on September 15, 1809. In 1813 his parents moved to Williamson County, Tennessee, where he later studied law. He never attended college, and although he was admitted to the bar in 1830, he practiced law only briefly in Franklin, Williamson County. Instead, he became a successful planter in

College Grove, Tennessee. Gentry had two daughters, Mary and Emily, by his marriage in 1837 to Emily Saunders. After she died, he married Caledonia Brown in 1846. Gentry, a Whig, served in the Tennessee House of Representatives from 1835 to 1839 and in the U.S. House during 1839-1843 and 1845-1853. While in the U.S. House, he opposed the Mexican War and refused to support Winfield Scott for president in 1852. In 1855, he was the unsuccessful American party candidate for governor of Tennessee, losing to Andrew Johnson. He retired to his plantation from 1855 to 1861. Gentry was a unionist until friends and family persuaded him to support secession. He was elected to the first Confederate House, where he made only one speech but disagreed with Davis (*q.v.*) over the conduct of the war. He served on special committees and, like many congressmen from occupied states, he was often absent without leave. In 1864, he was captured by federal troops while home in Tennessee. Impoverished after the war, he settled on his farm at College Grove. He died on November 2, 1866, in Nashville. Temple, *Notable Men of Tennessee from 1833 to 1875*.

GHOLSON, Samuel James (*General*), was born on May 19, 1808, in Madison County, Kentucky. His father's name is unknown, and his mother died while he was a child. Gholson moved with his family to Alabama at the age of nine; he attended the common schools, studied law in Russellville, and began to practice in 1829. He was a Democrat and a member of the Odd Fellows. In 1838, he married a Miss Ragsdale; they had children. Gholson moved to Athens, Monroe County, Mississippi, in 1830, and he served as a Democrat to the state legislature in 1835-1836 and 1839. From 1836 to 1838, he served parts of terms in the U.S. House of Representatives; he was defeated for reelection in 1838. From 1839 until his resignation in 1861, he was a federal court judge in Mississippi. A secessionist, he was president of the state Democratic convention in 1860. After his resignation as judge, he enlisted as a private in the Confederate Army and was named a brigadier general of state troops in 1861. In February 1862, he was wounded, captured, and exchanged at the battle of Fort Donelson, Kentucky. He was wounded a second time at the battle of Corinth in October 1862; upon recovery he was promoted to major general of state troops and placed in charge of all railroads in Mississippi in 1863. In 1864, he commanded a cavalry brigade in Alabama and Mississippi, and on May 6 of that year he was promoted to brigadier general in the Confederate Army. Later the same month, he was wounded at Jackson, Mississippi. He stopped Grierson's Raid at Egypt, Mississippi, on December 28, 1864, losing an arm in the process. He saw no further military service in the Confederacy. After the war, Gholson set up a law practice in Aberdeen, Mississippi. He served terms in the Mississippi House from 1865 to 1867 and in 1878, when he was elected speaker of that body. He also helped to restore home rule to Mississippi in the 1870s. He continued his law practice in Aberdeen and died there on October 16, 1883. Lynch, *The Bench and Bar of Mississippi*; Natchez *Democrat*, October 24, 1883.

GHOLSON, Thomas Saunders (*Congressman*), was born in Gholsonville, Brunswick County, Virginia, on December 9, 1809, to Major William and Mary (Saunders) Gholson. He attended school in Oxford, North Carolina, graduated from the University of Virginia in 1827, and began his law practice in Brunswick County. On May 14, 1829, he married a first cousin, Cary Ann Gholson, who gave him two children. Gholson was a vestryman in the Episcopal church. He moved to Petersburg, Virginia, in 1840 and to Richmond in 1848, practicing law in both places. He also served as president of the Bank of Petersburg and as president of a railroad company prior to the Civil War. A Whig, he supported the secession movement in Virginia. From 1859 to 1863, he was judge of the State Circuit Court for the Fifth Circuit. He was elected a member of the second Confederate House where he favored a vigorous military policy and conscription for all able-bodied men. He served on the Conference, Judiciary, and special committees. After the war, he established a cotton and tobacco commission house in Liverpool, England. In 1868, he returned to Petersburg. He died on December 13, 1868, in Savannah, Georgia. Slaughter, *History of Bristol Parish*; Tyler, *Encyclopedia of Virginia Biography*, III.

GIBSON, Randall Lee (*General*), was born on September 10, 1832, in Versailles, Woodford County, Kentucky, to Tobias and Louisiana (Hart) Gibson. His father was a prominent sugar planter in Terrebonne Parish, Louisiana. Young Gibson graduated first in the class of 1853 from Yale College, studied law at the University of Louisiana in 1855, and traveled in Europe before becoming a planter in Lafourche Parish, Louisiana, in 1858. He had three sons by his marriage to Mary Montgomery on January 25, 1868. At the outbreak of the war, Gibson, a Democrat, became aide-de-camp to Governor Thomas O. Moore (*q.v.*) of Louisiana. In August 1861, he became colonel of the 13th Louisiana Regiment and soon became known for his discipline. He performed well while commanding a Louisiana brigade at the battle of Shiloh, and he distinguished himself at Perryville in 1862. In 1863, Gibson also participated in the Tennessee battles of Murfreesboro and Missionary Ridge and commanded a brigade at Chickamauga. On January 11, 1864, he was promoted to brigadier general. He subsequently fought with distinction in the Atlanta and Nashville campaigns of 1864. In the spring of 1865, he held the Spanish Fort at Mobile. He surrendered and was later paroled in May 1865. After the war, Gibson returned to planting and practiced law in New Orleans. He was elected (but not seated) as a Democrat in the U.S. House of Representatives in 1872; he was reelected and seated two years later and served continuously until 1882. From 1883 to 1892, he served in the U.S. Senate. In 1879, he helped to establish the Mississippi River Commission. A regent of the Smithsonian Institution, Gibson was also agent for Paul Tulane in founding Tulane University, of which Gibson was the first president of the board in 1885. He died on December 15, 1892, on vacation in Hot Springs, Arkansas. Eliot, *Yale in the Civil War*; Fortier, *A History of Louisiana*, I.

GILMER, Francis Meriwether (*Businessman*), son of Nicholas Meriwether and Amelia (Clark) Gilmer, was born in Oglethorpe County, Georgia, on June 8, 1810. He received his education in common schools in Kentucky. He was a Democrat and a Methodist, and he had five children by his marriage in May 1838 to Sara Eleanor Taylor. A son, James Nicholas Gilmer, was adjutant general of Alabama during the Civil War. His wife died, and he was later married to Martha Ann Gratten; after her death he was married a third time, to Callie McKeithen. In about 1830, Gilmer moved to Alabama where he clerked in a store, taught school in Haynesville, and ran a cotton warehouse. He became a cotton broker during the late 1830s. He was a founder of the Central Bank of Alabama in Montgomery in the 1840s and of the Red Mountain Iron and Coal Company. During the 1850s, he also built the Southern and Northern Alabama Railroad, of which he was the first president. Gilmer supported secession. In 1861, he was appointed by Governor Thomas O. Moore (*q.v.*) to serve on the committee which was sent to urge Virginia to secede. He supported Jefferson Davis's (*q.v.*) bid for the presidency of the Confederacy and served him as a financial advisor. Gilmer also gave much of his fortune to help the war effort. The Confederacy was never able to make good use of his business expertise. Gilmer, who also owned several plantations, was president of the Central Bank of Alabama, which became a deposit bank for the Confederate government during the war. When the war ended, he continued as bank president and farmed for a time. Little is known of his postwar career. He died in Montgomery on January 9, 1892. Owen, *History of Alabama and Dictionary of Alabama Biography*, III.

GILMER, Jeremy Francis (*Forbes*) (*General, Bureaucrat*), was born on February 23, 1818, in Guilford County, North Carolina, to Captain Robert Shaw Gilmer, a career officer in the U.S. Army, and his wife Anna (Forbis). He was a brother of John Adams Gilmer (*q.v.*) who became a Confederate congressman. Gilmer graduated fourth in a class of thirty-one from the U.S. Military Academy in 1839 and entered the Engineering Corps of the army as a second lieutenant. He was married to Louisa Alexander, daughter of Confederate General Edward P. Alexander (*q.v.*). Gilmer was an assistant professor of engineering at West Point in 1840 and assisted in the construction of Fort Schuyler, New York, in 1840-1844. From 1844 to 1846, he was assistant chief of engineers in Washington, D.C. Promoted to first lieutenant in 1845, he was chief engineer for the Army of the West in New Mexico during the Mexican War. In 1853, he was promoted to captain, and, from 1853 to 1858, he was engaged in the improvement of rivers and fortifications throughout the South. From 1858 to 1861, he supervised the construction of defenses at the entrance to San Francisco Bay. He submitted his resignation to the federal army in June 1861 and entered the Confederate Army as a lieutenant colonel of engineers. He was severely wounded at the battle of Shiloh in the spring of 1862. He was promoted to brigadier general on October 4, 1862, and became chief of the Engineering Bureau for the Confederate War Department. In 1863, he was promoted to major general and was named second in command of the Department of South Carolina, Georgia, and Florida. He helped to fortify Atlanta. One of the outstanding military engineers in the Confederacy, his active service ended in early 1865. After the war, Gilmer had railroad and engineering enterprises in Savannah, where he was also president and chief engineer for the Gas Light Company from 1867 to 1883. He died in Savannah on December 1, 1883. Evans, *Confederate Military History*, IV; Stockard, *History of Guilford County, North Carolina*.

GILMER, John Adams (*Congressman*), brother to Jeremy Francis Gilmer (*q.v.*), was born in Greensboro, Guilford County, North Carolina, on November 4, 1805, to Captain Robert Shaw and Anne (Forbes) Gilmer. After attending grammar school and the academy in Greensboro, he taught at the Mount Vernon Grammar School in South Carolina. He was admitted to the Greensboro bar in 1832 and had a long and active practice. He was a Presbyterian. He had a son by his 1832 marriage to Julianna Paisley. Gilmer served as county solicitor during the late 1830s and as state senator from Guilford County from 1846 to 1856. In 1856, he was unsuccessful as the Whig candidate for governor. Gilmer was elected as a member of the American party to the U.S. House in 1857 and served until 1861. He opposed the Lecompton Constitution for Kansas. He was offered the post of secretary of the interior in President Lincoln's cabinet; he refused. Gilmer was an outstanding Southern unionist, and he sent 100,000 copies of his anti-secession speeches to North Carolina before being elected to the state secession convention as a conservative. After Lincoln called for troops, however, Gilmer supported secession. He served in various local capacities during the early years of the war. In 1864, he was elected to the second Confederate Congress and became chairman of the Committee on Elections and a member of the Ways and Means Committee. In Congress he protested government impressment practices and supported increasing taxes but generally voted against Davis administration measures. He made peace overtures to Washington late in 1864. After the war, he supported President Johnson and served as a delegate to the Union national convention of conservatives at Philadelphia in 1866. He also returned to his law practice in Guilford County. He died on May 14, 1868, in Greensboro. Stockard, *History of Guilford County, North Carolina*.

GIST, States Rights (*General*), was born on September 3, 1831, in Union District, South Carolina, to the wealthy planter William Henry and Mary Elizabeth (Rice) Gist. His father was governor of South Carolina in 1860. Young Gist attended preparatory school in Winnsboro, South Carolina, and graduated from South Carolina College in 1852 and from Harvard Law School in 1854. Before the war, he practiced law in Union District. He never married. He was a Democrat and a Methodist. Gist, who was a brigadier in the South Carolina state militia in 1859, was an adjutant and inspector general on the staff of General R. S. Ripley (*q.v.*)

prior to the battle of Fort Sumter. At the battle of First Manassas, he held the rank of colonel and was aide to General Barnard Bee. Gist organized South Carolina troops for the war and saw duty along the South Carolina coast and in the relief of Wilmington, North Carolina, in 1862. On March 20, 1862, he was promoted to brigadier general. In May 1863, he was assigned to the Army of Tennessee under General John L. Pemberton (*q.v.*) in Mississippi, and he served under General Joseph E. Johnston (*q.v.*) in Vicksburg. Gist participated in the battles of Jackson, Chickamauga, Chattanooga, and Missionary Ridge in 1863 and in the Atlanta campaign of 1863-1864. He accompanied General John B. Hood (*q.v.*) west and was killed on November 30, 1864, during the battle of Franklin, Tennessee. Cauthen, *South Carolina Goes to War, 1861-1865*; Evans, *Confederate Military History*, V.

GOODE, John, Jr. (*Congressman*), was born to John and Ann M. (Leftwich) Goode on May 27, 1829, in Bedford County, Virginia, where his father was a farmer. He attended New London Academy in Connecticut, graduated from Emory and Henry College in Virginia in 1848, attended law school in Lexington, Virginia, in 1849-1850, and was admitted to the bar in 1851. He began his practice in Liberty, Virginia. On July 10, 1855, he married Sallie Urquhart, by whom he had five children. He was an Episcopalian. A Democrat, Goode represented Bedford County in the State House in 1852. He was also a secessionist, and as a delegate to the state constitutional convention of 1860, he voted for the Ordinance of Secession. He enlisted as a private and served as a colonel in the Confederate Army on the staff of Jubal Early (*q.v.*) at First Manassas, where he was wounded. Goode was elected from Bedford District, South Carolina, to two terms in the Confederate House and served for the remainder of the war. A Davis administration supporter, he served on the Commerce, Printing, Enrolled Bills, Indian Affairs, Medical Department, and special committees. He gained a reputation for attacking the bureaucracy, accusing the cabinet of misunderstanding popular feelings. After the war, he practiced law in Norfolk, Virginia. He was a member of the lower house of the state legislature in 1866-1867 and a member of the Democratic National Executive Committee from 1868 to 1878. From 1875 to 1881, he served as a Democrat in the U.S. House of Representatives, but he lost a bid for reelection in 1880. In 1885-1886, he was solicitor general of the United States. He was a member of the U.S. and Chilean Claims Commission in 1893. In 1898, he was president of the Virginia State Bar Association, and, in 1901-1902, he was president of the state constitutional convention. After 1875, he also practiced law in the District of Columbia. Goode died on July 14, 1909, in Norfolk. Goode, *Recollections of a Lifetime*.

GORDON, James Byron (*General*), son of George and Sarah Lenoir (Gwyn) Gordon and a first cousin of Major General John B. Gordon (*q.v.*), was born on November 22, 1822, in Wilkesboro, Wilkes County, North Carolina. He attended the school of Peter Ney in Iredell County and Emory and Henry College in Virginia before entering the mercantile business in the late 1840s. He later became a farmer. He was an Episcopalian. In 1850, he was elected from Wilkes County to a term in the North Carolina House. At the beginning of the Civil War, Gordon volunteered in the Wilkes Valley Guards, and he served in the 1st North Carolina Cavalry in the Army of Northern Virginia, earning the admiration of General J.E.B. Stuart (*q.v.*). In March 1862, he was promoted to lieutenant colonel and was sent to North Carolina, and in June he went to Virginia, where he served under General Wade Hampton (*q.v.*) during the Seven Days battles and fought at Second Manassas, in Stuart's raid into Pennsylvania, and at Fredericksburg, Chancellorsville, and Brandy Station. He was promoted to brigadier general on September 28, 1863, and he led the 1st Brigade of North Carolina Cavalry at the battles of Auburn, Bethesda Church, and Culpeper Court House. He participated in the Mine Run campaign in Virginia in November and December of 1863, and during the Wilderness campaign he stopped Union General Phillip Sheridan's raid on Richmond, which saved the city. Gordon lost his life on May 18, 1864, at the battle of Spotsylvania, near Richmond. Cowles, *The Life and Services of General James B. Gordon*; *Southern Historical Society Papers*, XXIX.

GORDON, John Brown (*General*), was born on February 6, 1832, in Upson County, Georgia, to the Reverend Zachariah Herndon Gordon and his wife Malinda (Cox). Gordon, whose father's family was from North Carolina, was a first cousin of General James B. Gordon (*q.v.*). He was privately educated at Pleasant Green Academy, attended Franklin College (later the University of Georgia) until 1852, was admitted to the bar the following year, and began a law practice in Atlanta in 1854. Gordon was a Baptist and a Whig who became a Democrat in the late 1850s. He married Fanny Rebecca Harelson on September 18, 1854; they had three sons and three daughters. Gordon also assisted his father in an Alabama coal mining enterprise before the Civil War. He developed a friendship with William Lowndes Yancey (*q.v.*) and became a strong secessionist. At the beginning of the war, Gordon volunteered as a captain in the "Raccoon Roughs," an Alabama company. In December 1861, he became a lieutenant colonel in the 6th Alabama Regiment of Rodes' Brigade. At the battle of Seven Pines in late spring 1862, he took over and led the charge after Rodes (*q.v.*) was wounded. He participated in the battle of Malvern Hill during the Seven Days and was wounded five times in the battle of Sharpsburg. After his recovery, he was promoted to brigadier general on November 1, 1862; his Georgia brigade fought at the battles of Chancellorsville and Gettysburg in 1863. He saw service along the Rapidan in November of that year, but his great fame began with the Wilderness campaign in the spring of 1864. After leading Early's (*q.v.*) Division at the "Bloody Angle" of Spotsylvania Court House, he was promoted to major general on May 14, 1864. In June of that year, he fought at Cold Harbor; he fought in Early's Valley campaign of 1864 at Monocacy in July and at Cedar Creek in

October. He commanded the 2nd Corps of the Army of Northern Virginia before Petersburg, where he held the last of the lines. In March 1865, he planned and led the assault on Fort Stedman near Petersburg, and he was part of the last charge at Appomattox. He surrendered at Appomattox and was soon paroled. After the war, he practiced law in Atlanta. He was a delegate to the National Union convention in 1866 and an unsuccessful Democratic candidate for governor of Georgia in 1868. From 1873 to 1880, he served in the U.S. Senate, winning the seat formerly held by Alexander H. Stephens (*q.v.*). He resigned this post to help build the Georgia Pacific Railroad and to assume a position with the Louisville and Nashville Railroad in 1880. From 1886 to 1890, he was governor of Georgia, and he returned to the U.S. Senate from 1891 to 1897. Gordon published his *Reminiscences of Civil War* (1903) prior to his death on January 9, 1904, in Miami, Florida. Tankersley, *John B. Gordon: A Study in Gallantry*.

GORGAS, Josiah (*General*, *Bureaucrat*), son of Joseph and Sophia (Atkinson) Gorgas, was born in Dauphin County, Pennsylvania, on July 1, 1818. He graduated sixth in a class of fifty-two from the U.S. Military Academy in 1841. Gorgas was a Democrat and an Episcopalian. He married Amelia Gayle, daughter of an ex-governor of Alabama, in December 1853; they had six children, one of whom, William Crawford Gorgas, was later surgeon general of the United States. Upon graduating from West Point, Gorgas was assigned as a second lieutenant to ordnance duty in New York. He was sent abroad in 1845 to study the ordnance of the European armies. During the Mexican War, he distinguished himself in the siege at Vera Cruz. In 1853, he was placed in command of an arsenal near Mobile, Alabama, and was promoted to captain in 1855. A man of conservative temper, he grew to sympathize with the Southern cause and he supported secession. He resigned his commission in April 1861 and volunteered for service in the Confederate Army. He was appointed chief of ordnance, where he directed the Bureau of Foreign Supplies and organized the Mining and Nitre Bureau. He was promoted to brigadier general on November 10, 1864. His responsibilities included supplying the armies with powder, shells, and arms. His efforts to break the blockade were essential to sustaining the war effort. Gorgas's biographer correctly claims that the general was an organizational genius who supplied an army through making the most of a limited manufacturing complex. Gorgas surrendered as the war ended and was soon paroled. After the war, he operated a blast furnace and was superintendent of the Briarfield Iron Works in Alabama. He taught and served as vice-chancellor of the University of the South at Sewanee, Tennessee, from 1868 to 1877. He was president of the University of Alabama in 1877-1878, where he was also a librarian prior to his death on May 15, 1883, in Tuscaloosa, Alabama. Vandiver, *Ploughshares into Swords*.

GOVAN, Daniel Chevilette (*General*), son of Andrew Robison and Mary Pugh (Jones) Govan, was born in Northhampton County, North Carolina, on July 4,

1829. His father served in the U.S. House from South Carolina before moving to Marshall County, Mississippi, in 1832. Govan was educated by private tutors and graduated from the University of South Carolina in 1848. In December 1853, he married Mary F. Otey, a daughter of Episcopal Bishop James H. Otey; they had fourteen children. Govan joined his kinsman, Benjamin McCulloch, in the gold rush to California in 1849, and in 1850 he was the deputy sheriff of Sacramento. He returned to Mississippi in 1852 and became a planter. He moved to Phillips County, Arkansas, in 1860 where he was a planter before the Civil War. When the war began, Govan raised a regiment and volunteered for service in the Confederate Army. At the battle of Shiloh and at the battle of Perryville in the Kentucky campaign, Govan was colonel of the 2nd Arkansas Regiment. He served as a brigade commander at Murfreesboro and at Chickamauga. At the battle of Missionary Ridge, he helped in the victory at Ringgold Gap, winning praise from General Patrick R. Cleburne (q.v.). Promoted to brigadier general on December 29, 1863, he took part in the Atlanta Campaign, where he showed gallant conduct at Pickett's Mill. He was captured in the battle of Jonesboro, Georgia, on September 1, 1864, and was soon exchanged. He served throughout the Tennessee campaign and into the Carolinas in the last months of the war. He surrendered in North Carolina and was paroled in May 1865. After the war, he returned to his plantation in Arkansas and largely refrained from public life. From 1894 to 1896, he served as an Indian agent in the state of Washington. He returned to Mississippi in 1898 and died in Memphis, Tennessee, at the home of one of his children on March 12, 1911. Connolly, *Army of the Heartland*; Warner, *Generals in Gray*.

GRACIE, Archibald, Jr. (*General*), was born to the wealthy merchant, Archibald Gracie, and his wife Elizabeth Davidson (Bethune) on December 1, 1832, in New York City. The younger Gracie spent five years at Heidelburg, Germany, in private schools and graduated fourteenth in a class of forty-six from the U.S. Military Academy in 1854. He was an Episcopalian. He had one son by his marriage to Josephine Mayo on November 19, 1856. Gracie served on a Pacific Coast expedition against the Snake Indians before resigning his military commission in 1856 to become a merchant in Mobile, where he was also agent for Baring Brothers of London in 1857. In 1860, he was a captain of the Washington Light Infantry in Mobile. When the war began, he joined the 3rd Alabama Infantry and participated in the battles of Yorktown and Williamsburg in April and May 1862. After his promotion to colonel, Gracie served in Chattanooga and captured Fort Cliff in Huntsville, Tennessee. He attained the rank of brigadier general on November 4, 1862. Gracie served as military governor of Lexington and was part of the rear guard of Bragg's (q.v.) army at Harrodsburg during the Kentucky campaign. In 1863, he was sent to serve under General James Longstreet (q.v.) at Chickamauga. He won a commendation for bravery at Drewry's Bluff in May 1864 and was recommended for promotion to major general. But before his promotion could be approved, Gracie was killed in the trenches below Petersburg on December 2, 1864. *Confederate Veteran*, V; Owen, *History of Alabama and Dictionary of Alabama Biography*, III.

GRAHAM, Malcolm Daniel (*Congressman*, *Judge*), was born on July 6, 1827, in Autauga County, Alabama, to John and Jeanette (Smith) Graham. He was educated at Transylvania University in Kentucky in the 1840s and lived in Wetumpka and Montgomery, Alabama, before moving to Henderson, Rusk County, Texas, in 1855. He and his wife, the former Amelia Cunningham Ready, had two sons. Graham, a lawyer, served as clerk of the Alabama House of Representatives in 1853 and was a member of the Texas Senate in 1857. From 1859 to 1861, he was attorney general for the state of Texas. He was a Democrat and a secessionist. During the Civil War, he volunteered as a colonel in the Confederate Army but saw little service. He was elected to the first Confederate House. He served on the prestigious Ways and Means Committee, generally supported the administration, and criticized the enrollment officers for their clerical incompetence. Graham also served as presiding judge of Holmes's Corps in the Trans-Mississippi Department during 1865. After the war he returned to Alabama, where he practiced law until his death on October 8, 1878, in Montgomery. Lynch, *The Bench and Bar of Texas*; Owen, *History of Alabama and Dictionary of Alabama Biography*, III.

GRAHAM, William Alexander (*Congressman*), was born on September 5, 1804, in Lincoln County, North Carolina, to General Joseph and Isabella (Davidson) Graham. After attending private academies, he tied for first place in the class of 1824 at the University of North Carolina and was admitted to the North Carolina bar the following year. Graham studied law with Judge Thomas Ruffin (*q.v.*). He became an equity lawyer in Hillsboro, North Carolina. Graham was a Presbyterian. He married Susannah Washington in 1836 and had many children, some of whom had distinguished careers of their own. He served a term in the state House under the borough system from Hillsboro from 1833 to 1835 before being elected in 1836, 1838, and 1840; he also served as speaker during his last two terms. From 1840 to 1843, he served in the U.S. Senate as a member of the Whig party; the Democratic state legislature retired him in 1843. He was governor of North Carolina from 1845 to 1849 and secretary of the navy under Millard Fillmore from 1850 to 1852, when he was the Whig party candidate for vice-president. Two years later, he was elected to a term in the state Senate. In 1860, Graham supported John Bell for president and opposed the calling of the state convention. Although he was strongly opposed to secession, he was a delegate to the convention from Orange County; he not only signed the Ordinance of Secession, but he also ran (unsuccessfully) for president of the convention. He opposed North Carolina's supporting the Confederate Constitution. Retired to private life during most of the war, Graham was elected to the second Confederate Senate in 1863 where he generally opposed the Davis administration. An extreme advocate of states' rights, Graham feared executive tyranny because of the president's excessive use of the veto. He served on the Conference, Finance, Impressment, and Naval Affairs Committees in the Senate. His loyalty and diligence, along with his sound political ability, made him one of the most respected men in the Confederate Senate. In 1864, he urged Governor Zebulon Vance (*q.v.*) to negotiate for a separate peace. He supported the Hampton Roads Conference and in 1865 joined R.M.T. Hunter (*q.v.*) and James L. Orr (*q.v.*) in urging President Davis (*q.v.*) to accept favorable peace terms short of independence. He returned to his law practice in North Carolina when the war ended. He was elected to the U.S. Senate in 1866 but was not allowed to serve. The same year he was a delegate to the Philadelphia union convention. From 1873 to 1875, he was an arbitrator on the issue of the disputed state boundary line. Graham, who was also interested in preserving and collecting the sources of the history of the state, served as president of the North Carolina Historical Society. He died on August 11, 1875, at Saratoga Springs, New York. Ashe, *Cyclopedia of Eminent and Representative Men of the Carolinas*, I; Peele (comp.), *Lives of Distinguished North Carolinians.*

GRAY, Henry (*Congressman*), was born on January 19, 1816, in Laurens District, South Carolina. He graduated from South Carolina College in 1834, was admitted to the bar, and moved to Mississippi in the 1840s where he was a district attorney for Winston County. He served in the state legislature and ran unsuccess-fully for the U.S. House of Representatives before moving to Caddo Parish, Louisiana, in 1851. A secessionist, he lost by one vote a race for the U.S. Senate to Judah P. Benjamin (*q.v.*) in 1859. Gray became a Democrat and was elected to the Louisiana legislature in 1860. He was an intimate friend of Jefferson Davis (*q.v.*), and he enlisted as a private in the early days of the war. In 1862, at Davis's request he organized the 28th Louisiana Regiment, which helped to defend the state against federal troops in 1863. Gray, a colonel, also saw action at the battles of Mansfield and Pleasant Hill during the Red River campaign, and at times he commanded the brigade. He was promoted to brigadier general in 1865 but declined the office. Gray also represented Louisiana in the second Confederate House of Representatives, where he was an ally of General Richard Taylor (*q.v.*) and served on the Judiciary Committee and the special committee to increase the Confederate forces. While in Congress, Gray became an opponent of the Davis administration. After the war, he returned to his law practice in Caddo Parish. He also served in the Louisiana Senate for some years. He died in retirement in Coushatta, Louisiana, on December 11, 1892. Fortier, *A History of Louisiana*, II; New Orleans *Daily Picayune*, December 13, 1892; Taylor, *Destruction and Reconstruction.*

GRAY, Peter W. (*Congressman*), son of William Fairfax Gray, was born in Fredericksburg, Virginia, on December 12, 1819. In the 1830s, his family moved to Houston, Texas, where Gray participated in the war for independence and favored annexation to the United States. He studied law in his father's office and was married. In 1846-1847, he served in the Texas legislature, and in 1848, he was a founder of the Houston Public Library. Gray succeeded his father as district attorney of Houston. He was also a district judge and served in the state Senate in 1854. As a states' rights Democrat and a secessionist, he voted for secession at the state convention and represented Houston in the first Confederate House of Representatives, where he was a staunch supporter of the Confederacy. He served on the House Currency and Judiciary Committees and the Special Committees on homesteads for soldiers disabled in war and on the Sequestration Acts. He did not stand for reelection to the Congress. In 1863, as a volunteer aide on the staff of General John B. Magruder (*q.v.*), he helped to retake Galveston for the Confederacy on New Year's Day. In 1864, he unwillingly accepted President Davis's (*q.v.*) appointment as fiscal agent for the Trans-Mississippi Department. He unsuccessfully tried to raise money to pay off the Confederate debt in the department. This handicapped him in raising money for Kirby Smith's (*q.v.*) army, leaving the western army virtually without funds by February 1865. After the war, Gray returned to his Houston law practice. He was elected first president of the Houston Bar Association in 1870. Four years later, he became an associate justice of the state Supreme Court. Gray died in Houston, Texas, on October 3, 1874. Lynch, *The Bench and Bar of Texas*; Parks, *General Edmund Kirby Smith*.

GREEN, Thomas (*General*), was born on June 8, 1814, in Amelia County, Virginia, to Nathan and Mary (Field) Green. His father, a Tennessee lawyer, was later a judge of the state Supreme Court and president of Lebanon Law College. Green attended Princeton College, Jackson College, and the University of Nashville in Tennessee, before joining the revolutionary army of Texas in 1835. He was a Presbyterian and a bachelor. A major at the battle of San Jacinto, he became a surveyor in LaGrange, Texas, in 1837. A county in Texas now bears his name. In 1839-1840, he was an Indian fighter, and, in 1840, he represented Fayette County in the Texas Congress. Green, who had also studied law with his father, was clerk for the Texas Supreme Court from 1841 to 1861. He served on the Mexican frontier in 1842, and in 1846, he was a captain at the battle of Monterrey during the Mexican War. He volunteered for service in the Confederate Army when the war broke out. Green was named colonel of an Arizona and New Mexico regiment in 1861. He was in all Texas battles of the Civil War, as well as the New Mexico battles of Valverde, Glorieta, and Las Cruces. In January 1863, he participated in the recapture of Galveston, Texas, and on May 20, 1863, he was promoted to brigadier general. He was recommended for promotion to major general but was never confirmed. Green, who was related to General Richard Taylor (*q.v.*), served in Louisiana in the Red River campaign of 1864. He commanded a cavalry division at the battle of Mansfield on April 8 and on April 9 incurred wounds at the battle of Pleasant Hill that were to prove fatal. Green died on April 14, 1864, at Blair's Landing, Louisiana. Evans, *Confederate Military History*, XI; Kerby, *Kirby Smith's Confederacy*.

GREENHOW, Rose O'Neal (*Spy*), was born in 1817 in Port Tobacco, Maryland. Her father died when she was an infant. Little is known about her early life. She was raised a Catholic, and in 1835 she married the famous doctor and author Robert Greenhow. They lived in Richmond and Washington and had four children. In the 1850s, she became one of Washington's most popular hostesses, and her home became a meeting place for many of the country's leading political figures. Mrs. Greenhow was a Southern sympathizer and in a position to overhear many war secrets. (Her true role in the war has been clouded by the romance of the times.) She is said to have discovered Union plans for First Manassas and to have passed them on to the Confederate government, thus helping in that one-sided Southern victory. She was placed under house arrest by the Washington authorities in August 1861 and, at her request, was sent into the Confederate lines in May 1862. In August 1863, she ran the blockade to England and France as an official courier of the Confederate government. She wrote *My Imprisonment and the First Year of Abolition Rule at Washington* (1863). Returning on the *Condor*, she fell overboard off the North Carolina coast and drowned sometime in late 1864. Massey, *Bonnet Brigades*; Ross, *Rebel Rose*.

GREGG, John (*Congressman, General*), was born to Nathan and Sarah (Pearsall) Gregg on September 28, 1828, in Lawrence County, Alabama. He attended the school of Professor Tutwiler at LaGrange, Georgia, and graduated from La Grange College in 1847. Gregg taught school and studied law in Tuscumbia, Alabama, before moving to Fairfield, Freestone County, Texas, in 1851. He was first married to Mollie Winston, and when she died, he married Mary Frances Garth in 1855; both marriages were childless. Gregg, an ardent secessionist, was a circuit court judge in Texas in 1855. He was a member of the Texas secession convention, voted for secession, and was elected to the provisional Confederate Congress at Montgomery. Gregg left Congress in late 1861 and raised an infantry regiment. As lieutenant colonel of the 7th Texas Regiment, he was taken prisoner at Fort Donelson in February 1862. Exchanged after months in prison, he was promoted to brigadier general on August 29, 1862. During the Vicksburg campaign of 1863, he fought Grant at Raymond and Jackson, Mississippi, and he routed the Union General Rosecrans at Chickamauga. He served under John B. Hood (*q.v.*) in all the Virginia campaigns of 1864 and was a hero of the Wilderness. Gregg was killed near Richmond on October 7, 1864. Alexander and Beringer, *Anatomy of the Confederate Congress*; Evans, *Confederate Military History*, XI.

GREGG, Maxcy (*General*), son of Colonel James Gregg and his wife Cornelia (Maxcy), was born on August 1, 1814, in Columbia, South Carolina. He declined his degree from South Carolina College in 1836 and was admitted to the Columbia bar in 1839. Gregg was also an amateur scientist, and he became a lawyer of note. He was an Episcopalian, a Democrat, and a bachelor. During the Mexican War, he was a major in Colonel Milledge Bonham's (*q.v.*) regiment but never fought. He argued against cooperation in favor of immediate secession at the Southern Rights convention of 1852, and at the South Carolina secession convention he helped to frame the Ordinance of Secession. When the war began, Gregg entered the Confederate Army as a colonel of the 1st Regiment of South Carolina Volunteers. Promoted to brigadier general on December 14, 1861, he was a hero of the battle of Cold Harbor and fought in the battle of Malvern Hill in June and July of 1862. Gregg subsequently fought at the battles of Cedar Mountain, Second Manassas, Harper's Ferry, Sharpsburg, and Shepherdstown before he was killed during the battle of Fredericksburg, Virginia, on December 14, 1862. After his death, he became a symbol of courage for the Southern war effort. *Confederate Veteran*, VIII; McCrady, "Gregg's South Carolina Brigade," *Southern Historical Society Papers*, XIII.

GREGG, William (*Businessman*), son of William and Elizabeth (Webb) Gregg, was born on February 2, 1800, in Carmichaels, Monongalia County, Virginia. He was raised as a Quaker by his uncle, Jacob Gregg, but later became an Episcopalian. He was apprenticed to a watchmaker in Lexington, Kentucky, before moving to Columbia, South Carolina, in 1824, where he made a fortune in cotton manufacturing. In 1829, he married Marina Jones, by whom he had three children. He moved to Edgefield, South Carolina, in 1829, where he bought the Vancluse cotton factory. In 1838, he moved to Charleston and became a partner in the jewelry firm of Hayden, Gregg, and Company in Charleston, South Carolina. Influenced by the economic writings of Henry C. Carey, Gregg published *Essays on Domestic Industry* in 1845. The following year he established the Graniteville Manufacturing Company near Aiken, South Carolina. Gregg had become a public figure because of his desires for manufacturing development in the South. He represented Edgefield District in the state House in 1856-1857 and lost a race for the Senate in 1858. In 1860, he wrote articles for *DeBow's Review* urging the South to prepare for war, and he followed his own advice by ordering new machinery for his own mills. Gregg was a delegate to the state secession convention and signed the Ordinance of Secession. During the war, he kept his cotton plant open despite enormous impressments. He urged the Confederacy to strengthen its economic position by relying on private industry and the profit motive to production incentive, while giving priority to purchases for the military, the indigent, and their families. He claimed that the government discouraged industry by not setting up a cooperative policy toward industrial development and finance. He was a vociferous opponent of the blockade-runners, believing the war effort would be better served through support of local industry. After the war, Gregg tried to refit his mills. He died on September 13, 1867, in Kalmia, near Graniteville, South Carolina. Mitchell, *William Gregg*.

GRIMES, Bryan (*General*), was born to Bryan and Nancy (Grist) Grimes on November 2, 1828, at the family plantation "Grimesland" in Pitt County, North Carolina. His father, a supporter of Henry Clay, was a man of great wealth, owning a large estate and many slaves. The younger Grimes attended Bingham School and graduated from the University of North Carolina in 1848. He had one child by his marriage to Elizabeth Hilliard Davis on April 9, 1841, and, after her death, eight children by his marriage to Charlotte Emily Bryan on September 5, 1863. Grimes, like his father, was a Whig and a planter. He had no desire for public office, becoming instead a cultivated gentleman who traveled in Europe during the years before the war. However, as a member of the North Carolina secession convention he was a vehement secessionist. When the war began, he volunteered for service in the Confederate Army. He entered the Confederate Army as a major of the 4th North Carolina Regiment and participated in the Virginia battles of Yorktown, Williamsburg, and Seven Pines in the spring of 1862. In December of that year, he commanded a brigade at the battle of Fredericksburg, and at Chancellorsville in May 1863 he helped to rout Siegel's Corps. Grimes had some success in his attempts to check the peace movement in his state. He declined an opportunity to enter the Confederate Congress in order to remain in the field. At the Wilderness he saved Richard S. Ewell's (*q.v.*) Corps, for which he was promoted to brigadier general on May 19, 1864. He participated in the battle of Winchester in September of that year, and on February 15, 1865, he was promoted to major general in command of Ramseur's Division. Grimes fought at Fort Stedman and in the trenches before Petersburg, and he displayed great heroism during the retreat of Lee's army. He fought at Saylor's Creek on April 6 and commanded one of the last attacks on Appomattox on the very day of the surrender. Grimes, a persistent fighter, opposed the surrender. Nevertheless, he surrendered at Appomattox and was later paroled. After the war, he returned to his plantation, where he enjoyed much success and lived the life of a country gentleman. Grimes, a haughty aristocrat, refused postwar public service and became involved in a legal battle when he attempted to have a group of immigrants deported from the county. He was killed by an assassin hired by those immigrants at Grimesland, North Carolina, on August 14, 1880. Ashe, *Cyclopedia of Eminent and Representative Men of the Carolinas. . .*, I; Peele, (comp.) *Lives of Distinguished North Carolinians*.

H

HALE, Stephen Fowler (*Congressman*), was born to William and Elliner (Manahan) Hale in Crittenden County, Kentucky, on January 31, 1816. His father was a Baptist minister. The younger Hale attended Cumberland University in Kentucky, taught school in Alabama in 1837, read law, and in 1839 attended law school in Lexington, Kentucky. He was a Baptist. In 1839, he moved to Eutaw, Alabama, to set up his law practice. He also owned a small plantation. On June 12, 1844, he married Mary Elinor Kirksey, by whom he had a son. Hale, a Whig, represented Greene County in the Alabama legislature in 1843. During the Mexican War, he was a colonel. He lost a race for the U.S. House in 1853 before returning to the state legislature in 1857-1858 and 1859-1860. In early 1861, Governor Thomas O. Moore (*q.v.*) of Alabama sent him as a commissioner to encourage Kentucky to secede. Hale served in the provisional Congress on the Military Affairs, Judiciary, and Indian Affairs Committees. In the provisional Congress, he offered a plan for the protection of slavery during wartime and he proposed the legislation which banned the payment of debts to Northerners. Rather than stand for election to the first Confederate Congress, he entered the military service. Hale became a lieutenant colonel in the 11th Alabama Infantry and fought at Seven Pines and Gaines' Mill, where he died from wounds near Richmond, Virginia, on July 18, 1862. In 1866, the Alabama legislature named a county after him. Gandrud, *Marriage Records of Greene County, Alabama, 1823-1860*; Owen, *History of Alabama and Dictionary of Alabama Biography*, III.

HAMPTON, Wade (*General*), son of Wade Hampton II and his wife Ann (Fitzsimmons), was born on March 28, 1818, in Charleston, South Carolina. He attended Rice Creek Academy and graduated from South Carolina College in 1836. He studied law not only to start a practice but also to handle his own extensive business affairs. He was a Democrat and an Episcopalian. He was also a famous sportsman. In October 1838, he married Margaret Preston, who died in the summer of 1855. He married Mary Singleton McDuffie, a daughter of Senator George McDuffie of South Carolina, in June 1858. Hampton had three sons and three daughters by his two marriages. Despite his plantation holdings and great

inherited wealth, he doubted the economy of slave labor, and while he acknowledged the right of secession, he disputed it as a matter of policy. Hampton bought
equipment and raised troops for the Confederate Army and entered military service
as a private. At the battle of First Manassas he was slightly wounded while holding
the Warrenton Road against Keyes' Corps and trying to sustain General Barnard
Bee. Soon after his promotion to brigadier general on May 23, 1862, he was
wounded in the foot during the battle of Seven Pines. In July 1862, he became
second in command of J.E.B. Stuart's (*q.v.*) Cavalry Corps of the Army of
Northern Virginia, and he participated in most of Stuart's operations thereafter. He
was wounded three times during the battle of Gettysburg; when he recovered, he
was promoted to major general on August or September 3, 1863. Hampton became
corps commander after Stuart's death in May 1864. In June 1864, he saved
Lynchburg by checking Philip Sheridan at Trevilian Station, capturing three
thousand men in the process. On February 15, 1865, he was promoted to lieutenant
general. He slowed Sherman's advance and covered General Joseph E. Johnston's
(*q.v.*) retreat through South Carolina during the final months of the war. Hampton
refused to surrender and went home to South Carolina. After the war, he tried to
regain his fortune and rescue his ruined lands. A conciliatory person by nature, he
opposed those who advocated continued resistance to the federal government and
worked to end the carpetbag era in South Carolina. He was elected governor in
1876 and again in 1878 and served as a U.S. senator from 1880 to 1891. Hampton
retired from public life when the Populist movement changed the political structure of his state. He died on April 11, 1902, in Columbia, South Carolina.
Wellman, *Giant in Gray*.

HANLY, Thomas Burton (*Congressman*), was born in Nicholsonville, Kentucky, on June 9, 1812. Little is known about his childhood or his family. A
Democrat, he was a farmer and lawyer and settled in Helena, Phillips County,
Arkansas, in 1833. In 1842-1843, he served in the Arkansas House, and in 1846,
he was circuit judge for the First Circuit. He spent the years 1852-1855 in the state
Senate, and he became an associate justice of the state Supreme Court in 1858. As
a delegate to the Arkansas convention in 1861 he voted for secession, but he
wanted the Ordinance of Secession to be submitted to the popular vote. Hanly
represented the Fourth Congressional District of Arkansas in both the first and the
second Confederate House of Representatives. An anti-administration man in the
first House, he became staunchly pro-administration in the second, following an
easy reelection campaign. An active, energetic man, he served on the Claims,
Conference, and Indian Affairs Committees in both Houses. Hanly also served on
the Enrolled Bills, Post Office and Post Roads, Quartermaster's and Commissary,
and Military Transport Committees in the first House, and the Impressments,
Military Affairs, and Pay and Mileage Committees of the second House. He was a
member of the special committee to hold Confederate States' elections in occupied
states in the first House and of the special committee on claims against the

Confederate government in the second. In the first House, Hanly was an enemy of Henry S. Foote (*q. v.*) of Tennessee. As the war came to an end, many Arkansas congressmen left Richmond, but Hanly remained until after the president escaped. He then returned to Arkansas and resumed his law practice. He was an opponent of Reconstruction. Restrictions kept him from public office until the end of the radical regime. He was elected to the state legislature in 1879. Hanly died on June 9, 1880, in Little Rock, Arkansas. Hempstead, *Historical Review of Arkansas*; Thomas, *Arkansas in War and Reconstruction, 1861-1874*.

HARDEE, William Joseph (*General*), was born on October 12, 1815, in Camden County, Georgia, to Major John Hardee, a state senator from Camden County, and his wife Sarah (Ellis). He graduated twenty-sixth in a class of forty-five from the U.S. Military Academy in 1838 and attended cavalry school in Saumur, near Paris, France, during 1840. Hardee was a vestryman in the Episcopal church. He had no political affiliation. He married Elizabeth Dummett on November 14, 1840, and, upon her death, Mary Frances Lewis on January 13, 1863. He had one son and three daughters by his first wife. Hardee began his military career in the U.S. Army as a second lieutenant in the 2nd Dragoons in 1838; he was promoted to first lieutenant in 1839. He served at Fort Jessup, Louisiana. During the Mexican War, he participated in the siege of Vera Cruz, and in 1855, under the direction of then Secretary of War Jefferson Davis (*q. v.*), he published *Hardee's Tactics*, a standard military manual of its time. In 1856, he was named lieutenant colonel of cavalry and commandant of cadets at West Point. He resigned his commission in the U.S. Army in January 1861 and was commissioned a colonel in the Confederate Army. During the Civil War, he preferred field service to high administrative office. He commanded Fort Morgan on Mobile Bay, and on June 17, 1861, he was promoted to brigadier general and was given a territorial command in northeast Arkansas. After his promotion to major general on October 7, 1861, he fought in the front line during the battle of Shiloh and in Bragg's (*q. v.*) army during the Kentucky campaign, where his men bore the brunt of the battle of Perryville. Promoted to lieutenant general on October 10, 1862, he was part of the left wing at the battle of Murfreesboro late in 1862 and held his own at the battle of Missionary Ridge in 1863. Following his participation in the Atlanta campaign, he was given command of the Department of South Carolina, Georgia, and Florida in September 1864. He tried unsuccessfully to stop William T. Sherman in South Carolina and Georgia. During the final months of the war, he fought with General Joseph E. Johnston (*q. v.*) in North Carolina. He surrendered in North Carolina in April 1865 and was later paroled. Hardee, who had acquired a Selma, Alabama, plantation after his second marriage, returned there after the war. He was also in the insurance business and served as president of the Selma and Meridian Railroad prior to his death on November 6, 1873, in Wytheville, Virginia. Hughs, *General William J. Hardee*; Snow, *Southern Generals, Their Lives and Campaigns*.

HARDINGE, Belle Boyd (*Spy*), was a doctor's daughter, born on May 9, 1844, in Martinsburg, Virginia. She attended Mount Washington College in Virginia from 1856 to 1860. She was an Episcopalian. She was married to Samuel Wylde Hardinge in 1865 and, after his death, to John Hammond in 1869. She had a daughter by her first marriage and four children by her second. During the Civil War, she was an informer for General Thomas J. Jackson (*q.v.*), operating out of her uncle's hotel in Washington, D.C. She was a courier, a mail carrier, and a smuggler for the Confederate government. She also took Confederate messages to European allies. In 1865, she published her memoirs, *Belle Boyd in Camp and Prison*. She also was an actress on the English stage, and she acted in many western American theatres. She died on June 11, 1900, in Kilbourne, Wisconsin, where she was speaking to a Grand Army of the Republic post. Boyd, *Belle Boyd in Camp and Prison*; Massey, *Bonnet Brigades*.

HARRIS, Isham Green (*Governor*), son of Isham Green and Lucy (Davidson) Harris of North Carolina, was born in Tullahoma, Franklin County, Tennessee, on February 10, 1818. In 1832, he left home and clerked in a Paris, Tennessee, store. He entered the mercantile business in Tippah County, Mississippi, in the late 1830s before studying law at Winchester Academy and receiving admission to the Mississippi bar in 1841. His 1843 marriage to Martha Travis produced eight children. Harris practiced law in Tippah County from 1841 to 1847. He entered the Mississippi Senate in 1847 and represented Mississippi as a Democrat in the U.S. House of Representatives from 1849 to 1853. In 1853, he moved to Memphis in order to widen his law practice. He also became active in Tennessee politics. As governor of Tennessee from 1857 to 1862, he advocated secession and used his influence to secure his state's secession. His strategy was to convince the people that the state was neither in the Union nor out of it and then to isolate the unionists as traitors to the state's independent position. He hoped to convince others that his prime task was to defend the Mississippi River from all outsiders. Harris organized and commanded the state army and supported the movement to restore Nashville to the Confederacy. During the war, he raised 100,000 troops for the Confederacy. In 1863, Harris lost his bid for reelection. Forced to leave Tennessee in 1863, he served as aide-de-camp to P.G.T. Beauregard (*q.v.*) in 1863, Braxton Bragg (*q.v.*) and Joseph E. Johnston (*q.v.*) in 1864, and John Bell Hood (*q.v.*) until the end of the war. When the war ended he fled to Mexico. In 1876, he returned to his Memphis law practice. He was elected U.S. senator in 1877 and served until 1897. He was a staunch advocate of paper money and was president pro tem of the Senate from 1893 to 1895. He supported the Populist movement in the 1890s. Harris died on July 8, 1897, in Washington, D.C. Caldwell, *Sketches of the Bench and Bar of Tennessee*; Connelly, *Army of the Heartland*.

HARRIS, Nathaniel Harrison (*General*), son of William Mercer and Caroline (Harrison) Harris, was born on August 22, 1834, in Natchez, Mississippi. He attended the University of Louisiana, studied law, and went into law practice in the 1850s with his older brother in Vicksburg, Mississippi. He never married. When the war began, Harris entered the Confederate Army as a captain of the 19th Mississippi Regiment. He displayed gallantry at the Virginia battles of Williamsburg and Seven Pines in the late spring of 1862. While holding the rank of colonel, he commanded a regiment at the battles of Chancellorsville and Gettysburg, as a result of which he was promoted to brigadier general on January 20, 1864. His brigade won fame during the Wilderness campaign of 1864, including the battles of Spotsylvania, Cold Harbor, Petersburg, and Richmond. In March 1865, he commanded the inner line of defenses at Richmond, and at Appomattox he was a division commander. He surrendered with Lee's (*q.v.*) army and was soon paroled. After the war, he returned to his Vicksburg law practice. During the 1870s, he was president of the Mississippi Valley and Ship Island Railroad before going to South Dakota. In 1885, he was appointed registrar of the U.S. Land Office at Aberdeen, South Dakota. Around 1890, he moved to San Francisco and went into business. While on a business trip in Malvern, England, he died on August 23, 1900. Harris, *From the Diary of General Nat H. Harris*.

HARRIS, Thomas Alexander (*Congressman*), was born in 1826 in Warren County, Virginia, and was orphaned at the age of nine. He fought in the Mormon and Iowa War at the age of twelve. He attended the U.S. Military Academy from 1843 to 1845 but did not take a degree. He was twice married, his first wife being Imogene Porter; the name of his second wife is unknown. Sometime during the late 1840s, he moved to Missouri where he practiced law in Hannibal. Harris edited the *Missouri Courier* in Hannibal during the politically divisive 1850s. Although he was a unionist Democrat who supported John Bell for the presidency in 1860, he was at one time a member of the American party and served as its national secretary. During the Mexican War, he participated in the Lopez expedition to Cuba. He was a member of the Missouri legislature, and in 1856, he ran for secretary of state on the anti-Benton ticket. He joined the army when the war began. During the Civil War, he held the ranks of brigadier general in the Missouri State Guard and major in the Confederate Army. After participating in the battle of Lexington in September 1861, he was named to the provisional Confederate Congress, a position which he accepted as a means of improving living conditions among Confederate troops. Elected to the Confederate House in 1862, Harris served until February 1864; he was anti-administration and served on the Military Affairs and Conference Committees. While in the House, he opposed all tax bills and all "unnecessary and irregular warfare." He tried unsuccessfully to leave the Confederacy before the end of the war but was captured in May 1865 while trying to pass through the lines in Florida. He was soon paroled. After the war he was broke. He invested in mining lands in Missouri, went to Texas in 1870, and worked on a New Orleans newspaper before settling in Louisville, Kentucky. He was a member of the Life Insurance Association of America and served as assistant secretary of state for Kentucky in 1880. He died in Peewee Valley, Kentucky, on April 9, 1895. Ryle, *Missouri: Union or Secession*; Yearns, *The Confederate Congress*; Warner and Yearns, *Biographical Register of the Confederate Congress*.

HARRIS, Wiley Pope (*Congressman*), was born in Pike County, Mississippi, on November 9, 1818, to Early and Mary Vivian (Harrison) Harris. His father, who attained wealth in Georgia, lost his property upon moving to Mississippi. After his father's death in 1821, the younger Harris was reared by an uncle, General Wiley Pope Harris. He attended the University of Virginia and studied law at Transylvania University in Kentucky in 1840. Harris began to practice law in Gallatin, Tennessee, in 1840. He married Frances Mayes in 1851, and they had five children. From 1844 to 1850, he was circuit court judge for the Second District and was considered the best judge in Tennessee. He was a delegate to the state constitutional convention in 1851. He was elected as a Democrat to the U.S. House of Representatives in 1853 and again in 1855. Harris moved to Jackson, Mississippi, in 1857 and was a secessionist delegate to the state convention in 1861. He attended the Montgomery convention in the same year, where he served in the provisional Confederate Congress. A member of the Judiciary and Public Lands Committees, he helped to draft the Confederate Constitution. He offered the amendment which made the Confederate government responsible for state debts, and he opposed submitting the Constitution for popular ratification. An early administration supporter, he subsequently blamed Davis (*q.v.*) for the army's failure to mount an offensive after the victory at First Manassas. He declined further service in the Congress. In 1863, he served as the Conscription Bureau's representative in Mississippi, after which he retired to private life. When the war ended he revived his law practice. In 1875, he supported cooperation with the Liberal Republicans in hopes of overthrowing the Adelbert Ames administration in Mississippi. Harris was a delegate to the Tennessee constitutional convention in 1890. He died on December 3, 1891, in Jackson, Tennessee. Davis, *Recollections of Mississippi and Mississippians*; Rowland, *Courts, Judges, and Lawyers of Mississippi, 1798-1935*.

HARRISON, James Thomas (*Congressman*), son of Thomas and ———— (Earle) Harrison, was born in Pendleton, South Carolina, on November 30, 1811. His father, a lawyer, had been an officer during the War of 1812. The younger Harrison graduated with distinction from the University of South Carolina in 1829, studied law under James Louis Petigru, and was admitted to the Charleston bar in 1832. He was a cousin of Wiley Pope Harris (*q.v.*). His marriage to Regina Elewett on February 11, 1840, produced several daughters, one of whom married General Stephen Dill Lee (*q.v.*). Harrison practiced law in Macon, Noxubee County, Georgia, from 1834 until 1836, when he moved to Columbus, Mississippi, his residence for the rest of his life. He was little interested in public life before the war, and he developed an excellent law practice. He was a Baptist. A Democrat (earlier he was a Whig), he was a delegate to the Montgomery Confederate convention of 1861, where he was a member of the Postal Affairs and Printing Committees of the provisional Confederate Congress. He devised rules on governing the convention. He was one of the most distinguished lawyers at the convention, but his talents were never used properly during the war. He was also a chief advisor to Governor Charles Clark of Mississippi, but he saw little further service in the Confederacy. Harrison was a delegate to the state constitutional convention in 1865, the same year he declined the chancellorship of his district. He was elected to the U.S. House of Representatives in 1867 but was refused admittance. Harrison was a geologist in his later years. He died in Columbus, Mississippi, on May 22, 1879. Orr, "Life of Honorable James T. Harrison," *Publications of the Mississippi Historical Society*, VIII.

HARRISON, Thomas (*General*), was born in Jefferson County, Alabama, on May 1, 1823, and was reared in Monroe County, Mississippi. A brother, James E. Harrison, also became a Confederate general. Harrison moved to Texas in 1843 and studied law in Brazoria County before returning to Mississippi. He was a Baptist and a Democrat. He had five children from his 1858 marriage to Sarah Ellis McDonald. He returned to Texas in 1846 and served under Jefferson Davis (*q.v.*) during the capture of Monterrey in the Mexican War. He moved to Houston in 1850 and was elected to the Texas legislature the same year. He lived in Maclin, Texas, from 1851 to 1855, when he moved to Waco, which was to be his home for the rest of his life. When the war began, Harrison entered the Confederate Army as a captain and helped to drive the Union Army from Texas. He served with the "Texas Rangers" at the battle of Shiloh, where he became known as an efficient cavalry officer, and commanded a brigade at the battle of Murfreesboro. Harrison fought in all the great battles of the Army of Tennessee, including Missionary Ridge, Chickamauga, and subsequent campaigns in Georgia and the Carolinas. He was promoted to brigadier general on January 14, 1865, and was wounded slightly in a cavalry skirmish near Johnsonville, North Carolina, two months later. He never resumed his command. After the war, he returned to Waco, where he was a district judge from 1866 until 1877. Harrison later resumed his law practice. He died in Waco on July 14, 1891. Sarrafian, *The Harrison Family of Texas*; Simpson (ed.), *Texas in the War, 1861-1865*.

HARTRIDGE, Julian (*Congressman*), son of a leading merchant, was born in Savannah, Chatham County, Georgia, on September 9, 1829. After attending Chatham Academy and Montpelier Institute in Georgia, he graduated with high distinction from Brown University in 1848 and from Harvard Law School in 1850. On May 11, 1853, he married Mary M. Charlton, by whom he had nine children. Hartridge, a secessionist Democrat and a Baptist, practiced law in Savannah. From 1854 to 1858, he was solicitor general for the Eastern Judicial Circuit of

Georgia. He was elected to and served in the Georgia House in 1858-1859 and was a delegate to the Charleston Democratic convention in 1860. When the war began, he volunteered as a lieutenant in the Chatham Artillery, but he saw little military service. He was also an active, distinguished member of the first and second Confederate House of Representatives, having been elected from Georgia's First Congressional District. He began as a supporter of the Davis administration but turned against it in his second term. During his first term, he served on the Conference and Ways and Means Committees and the special committee to inquire into illegal arrests. In the second Confederate House, he served on the Commerce, Illegal Seizures and Impressments Committees, and on the special committee to increase Confederate forces. In 1863, he advocated the abolition of state commissary impressments. Financially ruined after the war, he recouped some of his losses after resuming his law practice in Savannah. Hartridge served as a Democrat in the U.S. House of Representatives from 1875 to 1879. He died in Washington, D.C., on January 8, 1879. Bell, *Men and Things*; Northen (ed.), *Men of Mark in Georgia*, IV.

HATCHER, Robert Anthony (*Congressman*), son of the merchant Archibald Hatcher, was born on February 24, 1819, in Buckingham County, Virginia. He was educated privately in Lynchburg, Virginia, studied law, and was admitted to the Kentucky bar, where he practiced from 1840 to 1847. He was a Baptist and a Democrat. He was married to a Miss Marr, whose brother was a New Orleans lawyer. In 1847-1848, Hatcher practiced law in New Madrid, Missouri, where he was also circuit attorney of the Tenth Judicial District for six years before the Civil War. He served in the Missouri House in 1850-1851 and attended the state convention as a secessionist in 1861. He was also a merchant in New Madrid in the 1850s. During the early part of the war, he was a major on the staff of General Leonidas Polk (*q.v.*) in the Confederate Army. He was a delegate to the state convention in 1862. Hatcher was elected from the field to serve in the second Confederate House where he was a member of the Enrolled Bills and Ordnance and Ordnance Stores Committees. He defended General John B. Hood (*q.v.*) on the decision to abandon Atlanta. He was generally a Davis administration supporter. When the war ended he returned to New Madrid to practice law. Hatcher served as a Democrat in the U.S. House from 1873 to 1879. In 1877, he moved to Charleston, Missouri, where he practiced law until his death on December 4, 1886. Alexander and Beringer, *The Anatomy of the Confederate Congress*; Downs (ed.), *Encyclopedia of American Biography*, IX.

HAWES, James Morrison (*General*), was born to Richard Hawes (*q.v.*), later Confederate provisional governor of Kentucky, and his wife Hattie Morrison (Nicholas) on January 7, 1824, in Lexington, Kentucky. He graduated twenty-ninth in a class of forty-one from the U.S. Military Academy in 1845. He was an Episcopalian. He married Maria J. Southgate on February 3, 1857. His first military duty was in the Indian Territory. Hawes served in the military occupation of Texas in 1845-1846 and was breveted first lieutenant for his action at Vera Cruz during the Mexican War. From 1848 to 1850, he was an assistant instructor of infantry and cavalry tactics and mathematics at West Point, and from 1850 to 1852, he attended the cavalry school at Saumur, France. He served on the Texas frontier and during the Utah expedition of 1858 as a captain in the 2nd Dragoons. When the war began, he resigned his commission in the U.S. Army and volunteered for service in the Confederate Army. Hawes entered the Confederate Army as a captain and was later named colonel of the 2nd Kentucky Cavalry. He commanded all cavalry under General Albert S. Johnston (*q.v.*) until after the battle of Shiloh, when he asked to be relieved. Appointed brigadier general on March 14, 1862, Hawes then served as a brigade commander under General John C. Breckinridge (*q.v.*). In October 1862, he was sent to Little Rock, and he fought in the battle of Milliken's Bend, Louisiana, on June 7, 1863. In 1864, he fortified Galveston Island. There is no record of his surrender. After the war, Hawes was a hardware merchant in Covington, Kentucky, where he died on November 22, 1889. Evans, *Confederate Military History*, IX; *Kentucky Marriages*.

HAWES, Richard (*Governor*), was born on February 6, 1797, in Caroline County, Virginia, to Richard and Clara (Walker) Hawes. His father, a member of the Virginia legislature, moved to Kentucky in 1810. The younger Hawes attended the school of Professor Samuel Wilson and Transylvania University before being admitted to the Kentucky bar in 1824 and opening his practice in Winchester, Kentucky. He was an Episcopalian. He married Hettie Morrison Nicholas in November 1818. His son, James M. Hawes (*q.v.*), was a Confederate general. In 1832, he served in the Black Hawk War. Hawes, who manufactured hemp in addition to practicing law, had a varied political career—as Clark County representative to the lower house of the Kentucky legislature in 1828, 1829, and 1834, and as Whig congressman from the Ashland District in the U.S. House of Representatives from 1837 to 1841. His brother, Albert Gallatin Hawes, was a Democratic congressman from Kentucky. In 1843, he moved to Paris, Kentucky, where he continued his law practice, and in 1856, he joined the Democratic party. He voted for John Breckinridge (*q.v.*) in 1860 and supported a policy of armed neutrality for Kentucky in 1861. As Confederate provisional governor of Kentucky from 1862 to 1865, he sympathized with the Confederates and had to leave the state in 1864. After the war, he returned to his law practice in Paris, Kentucky, where he was also county judge of Bourbon County from 1866 until his death on May 25, 1877. Clift, *Governors of Kentucky*.

HAYNES, Landon Carter (*Congressman*), was born on December 2, 1816, in Elizabethtown, Tennessee. His family background is unknown. He graduated with honors from Washington College in Tennessee in 1836. He read law in the office of Thomas A. R. Nelson and was admitted to the Jonesboro, Tennessee, bar in 1840. Haynes was married and had two sons. He soon entered politics and became the Democratic leader of east Tennessee. He was a presidential elector in 1844 and 1848. Elected to the state legislature in 1847, Haynes became speaker of the House in 1849 and also served in the state Senate. In his bid for national office, he lost an election to the U.S. House to Thomas A. R. Nelson in 1859. A John C. Breckinridge (*q.v.*) elector, in 1860 he was a strong secessionist. He was elected to the first Confederate Senate because of his reputation as a political leader. In the Senate he was a Davis administration opponent, condemned martial law, and claimed that Tennessee was lost to the Confederacy because of the pro-Eastern military bloc and the incompetence of President Davis (*q.v.*). He believed that suspension of *habeas corpus* would be a subversion of civil authority. Haynes spoke forcefully for the treatment and release of Union prisoners. He was reelected to the second Senate and came to believe that the war effort was futile. Throughout the war he practiced law and defended many of Tennessee's citizens who had been condemned for treason. The war's end found him residing in Statesville, North Carolina, but he soon removed to Memphis where he practiced law and tried to recoup his fortune which had been lost during the war. Haynes never again held public office. He died in Memphis on February 17, 1875. Caldwell, *The Bench and Bar of Tennessee*; *The South in the Building of the Nation*, XI.

HAYS, Harry Thompson (*General*), was born on April 14, 1820, in Wilson County, Tennessee, to Harmon and Elizabeth (Cage) Hays. He was from a fine New Orleans family. After being orphaned as a child, he was reared by an uncle in Wilkinson County, Mississippi. He attended St. Mary's College in Baltimore, Maryland, and began a New Orleans law practice in 1844. Hays, a Catholic and a Whig, married a first cousin, Elizabeth Cage, in 1858. During the Mexican War, he served in the Mississippi Cavalry. Although active in Whig politics during the 1850s, he held no public office but gained a reputation as an excellent lawyer. When the war began, he joined the 7th Louisiana Infantry as a colonel; he served ably at the battle of First Manassas in July 1861. Hays also fought with the Army of Northern Virginia in the Valley campaign of 1862. Following the battle of Port Republic, where he was wounded, he was appointed brigadier general on July 25, 1862, and was assigned to the command of his fellow Louisianian, General Richard Taylor (*q.v.*). Hays was a hero of the battle of Sharpsburg and fought with bravery and valor at Fredericksburg, Chancellorsville, and Gettysburg. In May 1864, he was severely wounded at Spotsylvania Court House after which he saw no further active military service. In the fall of 1864, he was responsible for locating absentees in Mississippi and Louisiana. In May 1865, after the war had ended, he was promoted to major general. He surrendered with Kirby Smith's (*q.v.*) army and was soon paroled. After the war, he practiced law in New Orleans with General Daniel W. Adams (*q.v.*). From 1866 until his removal the following year, he was sheriff of Orleans Parish. Hays returned to his law practice and died on August 21, 1876, in New Orleans. *Biographical and Historical Memoirs of Louisiana*.

HEBERT, Louis (*General*), son of Valery and Clarissa (Bush) Hébert, was born on March 13, 1820, in Iberville Parish, Louisiana. He graduated from Jefferson College in Louisiana in 1840 and was third in a class of forty-one at the U.S. Military Academy in 1845. He was a Catholic and a Democrat. He married Malvine Lambremont in 1848, by whom he had three sons. From 1845 to 1846, he was assistant engineer in the construction of Fort Livingston, Louisiana. In 1846, he resigned his commission in the army to become a sugar planter in Iberville Parish. Elected a major in the state militia he served as a major from 1847 to 1850 and as a colonel from 1858 to 1861. From 1853 to 1855, he served in the state Senate, and from 1855 to 1859, he was chief of engineers for the state. When the war began, Hébert entered the Confederate Army as a colonel of the 3rd Louisiana Regiment and fought in the battle of Wilson's Creek in October 1861 before he was captured during the battle of Elkhorn in March 1862. Shortly thereafter he was exchanged. After his promotion to brigadier general on May 26 of that year, Hébert commanded Little's Division at the battle of Iuka and distinguished himself at the battle of Corinth, both in northern Mississippi in the fall of 1862. He participated in the siege at Vicksburg and in June 1863 was sent to North Carolina, where he had charge of the heavy artillery in the Cape Fear District. At the end of the war, he was chief engineer of the Department of North Carolina. He surrendered in April 1865 and was later paroled. After the war, Hébert returned to planting in Louisiana. He also edited the newspaper *Iberville South* and taught in private schools in Iberville and St. Martin's Parish. Hébert died on January 7, 1901, at Breaux Bridge, Louisiana. Fortier, *A History of Louisiana*, I.

HEBERT, Paul Octave (*General*), son of Paul and Mary Eugenia (Hamilton) Hébert and a first cousin of Louis Hébert (*q.v.*), was born on December 12, 1818, in Iberville Parish, Louisiana. He graduated first in his class at Jefferson College in Louisiana in 1836 and first in a class of forty-two from the U.S. Military Academy in 1840. He was a Catholic and a Democrat. He had five children by his marriage to Cora Wills Vaughan on August 3, 1842, and, after her death, five children by his marriage to Penelope L. Andrews in 1861. He was commissioned second lieutenant in the Engineer Corps. Hébert taught at West Point from 1842 until he resigned in 1845 to become chief engineer for the state of Louisiana, a position which he held for two years. During the Mexican War, he was breveted colonel for his service at Molino del Rey. In 1852, he was a delegate to the state constitutional convention, and from 1853 to 1856, he was governor of Louisiana. Hébert was also a planter in Iberville Parish before the war. When the war began, he entered the 1st Louisiana Artillery as a colonel and was named a brigadier general of state troops in August 1861. Hébert, who held both staff and line positions during the war, was promoted to brigadier general in the Confederate Army on May 26, 1862. He commanded the Department of Texas in the Trans-Mississippi Department and the Subdistrict of North Louisiana. In his former capacity he supervised the defense of Galveston. His only combat was at Milliken's Bend, Louisiana, on June 7, 1863. In May 1865, he surrendered Kirby Smith's (*q. v.*) army to the Union forces; he was later paroled. In 1865, he was again state engineer, and in 1873, he supervised the construction of the Mississippi levees. In the election of 1872, he led the Horace Greeley wing of the Louisiana Democratic Party. Hébert died of cancer on August 29, 1880, in New Orleans. McLure, *Louisiana Leaders*.

HEISKELL, Joseph Brown (*Congressman*), son of Frederick S. and Elizabeth Brown Heiskell, was born on November 5, 1823, in Knox County, Tennessee. He was educated at the University of East Tennessee, studied law, and was admitted to the bar in 1844. He was a Whig, a Presbyterian, and a prohibitionist. He married and had one son. While in the state legislature, he revised the Code of Tennessee in 1857-1858. He also practiced law in Rogersville, Tennessee, before the war. He supported secession and was elected to both Confederate Houses. He served on the Judiciary and War Tax Committees and supported the Davis administration on most important issues. He was involved in bills for the manufacture of small arms and was concerned with outlawing illegal and discriminatory acts of impressment. Heiskell resigned from the second House in 1864 because he felt the government was not doing enough to expedite the exchange of Confederate prisoners. He returned to his law practice and gave no further service to the Confederacy. After the war, he moved to Memphis and practiced law. After Reconstruction, he was elected attorney general of Tennessee and later served as reporter of the state Supreme Court. He died in Memphis on March 7, 1913. Speer (comp.), *Biographical Directory of the Tennessee General Assembly*; Yearns, *The Confederate Congress*.

HELM, Benjamin Hardin (*General*), was born to John Larue and Lucinda Barbour (Hardin) Helm on June 2, 1831, in Elizabethtown, Hardin County, Kentucky. He graduated ninth in a class of forty-two from the U.S. Military Academy in 1851. Helm, a Whig who became a Southern rights Democrat, married Emilie Todd, a half-sister of the wife of Abraham Lincoln, in 1856. In 1852, he resigned from the service to practice law in Elizabethtown and later in Louisville, Kentucky. He served in the Kentucky legislature in 1855-1856 and was state's attorney from 1856 to 1858. In 1861, Lincoln offered him the position as paymaster general in the army. He declined the post. When the Civil War began, Helm organized the 1st Kentucky Cavalry and served as its colonel. He was promoted to brigadier general on March 14, 1862, and was injured at Vicksburg in June of that year. He saw duty in the District of the Gulf and returned as a part-time division commander during the Tullahoma campaign of 1863 in Tennessee. Helm was mortally wounded at the battle of Chickamauga, Georgia, where he died on September 20, 1863. Connelly, *Army of the Heartland*; *Encyclopedia of Kentucky*; McMurtry, *Ben Hardin Helm*.

HEMPHILL, John (*Congressman*), son of the Reformed Presbyterian minister John Hemphill and his wife Jane (Lind), was born on December 18, 1803, in Blackstock, Chester District, South Carolina. He graduated second in the class of 1825 from Jefferson College in Pennsylvania, taught school, studied law in the office of David J. McCord, and was admitted to the South Carolina bar in 1829. Hemphill, a Democrat and a bachelor, practiced law in Sumter, South Carolina, from 1831 to 1838 and edited a nullification newspaper in Sumter in 1832-1833. After fighting in the Florida Seminole War in 1836, he moved to Texas in 1838 where he practiced law at Washington-on-the-Brazos. He was judge of the Fourth Judicial District of Texas from 1840 to 1842. As a delegate to the Texas constitutional convention of 1845, he advocated statehood. Hemphill was chief justice of the state Supreme Court from 1846 to 1858. From 1859 until his expulsion for Confederate sympathies in 1861, he was a states' rights Democrat in the U.S. Senate, where he delivered a speech in January 1861 on the right of a state to withdraw from the Union. On January 6, 1861, he was one of fourteen senators who met to recommend the immediate secession of the Southern states. Extremely active in the provisional Confederate Congress, he was a member of the Commercial and Financial Independence, Finance, and Judiciary Committees, and of the special committee to digest the laws. Hemphill led the Texas provisional delegation at Montgomery and Richmond. He died on January 4, 1862, in Richmond. Lubbock, *Six Decades in Texas*; *The Memoirs of Francis R. Lubbock*; Lynch, *The Bench and Bar of Texas*.

HENRY, Gustavus Adolphus (*Congressman*), was born on October 8, 1804, in Scott County, Kentucky, where his father, General William Henry, was a state senator. He graduated from Transylvania University in 1825 and began a legal career. In 1833, he married Marian McClure. Henry, a Whig, served in the Kentucky legislature in 1831 and 1833. In 1833, he moved to Clarksville, Tennessee, where he lost a bid for election to the U.S. House of Representatives in 1842. He was elected to the Tennessee legislature in 1851-1852. In 1853, he ran unsuccessfully against Andrew Johnson for governor of Tennessee. A unionist, he supported John Bell for the presidency in 1860. Yet, when his state government called, Henry agreed to serve as a commissioner to the Confederate government. As a member of the Confederate Senate from 1861 to 1865, Henry was a loyal supporter of President Davis (*q.v.*). He proposed that the government control the state militias, supported the sequestration bill, and, at the last, proposed that President Davis name Lee (*q.v.*) commander-in-chief of the armies. He turned down a chance to become attorney general of the Confederacy. Henry was a powerful member of the western concentration bloc and a vigorous opponent of

Braxton Bragg (*q. v.*). In Congress, he served on the Conference, Military Affairs, Public Lands, and many special committees. His son, Gustavus Henry, Jr., was a colonel in the Army of Tennessee. After the war, he avoided public affairs and returned to his law practice. He died in Clarksville on September 10, 1880. Speer (comp.), *Biographical Directory of the Tennessee General Assembly*; Yearns, *The Confederate Congress*.

HERBERT, Caleb Claiborne (*Congressman*), was born in Goochland County, Virginia, in 1814. Little is known of his early life or his education. A farmer and a Democrat who lived in Eagle Lake, Colorado County, Texas, he represented the Columbus District in the Texas Senate from 1857 to 1860. He was a secessionist. Herbert represented the Second Congressional District of Texas in the first and second Confederate House of Representatives, where more than half of his votes were cast against administration-sponsored measures. He served on the Committee on Ordnance and Ordnance Stores during his first term and on the Claims and Commerce Committees during his second. In the second Confederate House, Herbert was also a member of the special committee to investigate patient treatment at Stewart Hospital. In May 1863, he was a member of a House committee to investigate Confederate prisons, and he subscribed to the minority view that the punishment of Union prisoners at Castle Thunder in Richmond was cruel and degrading. He quarreled with other members of the Texas congressional delegation over the conscript law, which he so detested that he declared publicly that the state should secede from the Confederacy. After the war, Herbert was denied the seat to which he had been elected in 1865 in the Texas House. He was accidentally killed near Columbus, Texas, on July 15, 1867. Yearns, *The Confederate Congress*.

HETH, Henry (*General*), was born on December 16, 1825, in Chesterfield County, Virginia, to Lieutenant John Heth and his wife Margaret (Pickett), a cousin of the future Confederate General George E. Pickett (*q.v.*). He attended Georgetown College, D.C. and refused an appointment to the U.S. Naval Academy in 1842. In 1847, he graduated last in a class of thirty-eight from the U.S. Military Academy. He was an Episcopalian. He married a first cousin, Harriet Selden, by whom he had three children. Heth was second lieutenant at Matamoros during the Mexican War. In 1855, he also fought the Indians, winning a victory against the Sioux at Bluewater and earning his promotion to captain. From 1858 to 1860, he participated in the Utah expedition, and in 1858, he wrote *A System of Target Practice*. He resigned from the U.S. Army in April 1861 and volunteered for the Confederate Army. At the beginning of the Civil War, Heth organized the Quartermaster's Department at Richmond. As colonel of the 45th Virginia Regiment, he served under General John B. Floyd in West Virginia, where he participated in the battle of Camifax Ferry. Promoted to brigadier general on January 6, 1862, he accompanied General Edmund Kirby Smith (*q.v.*) into

Kentucky. In February 1863, he received command of a division of Ambrose P. Hill's (*q.v.*) Corps of the Army of Northern Virginia. Wounded at the battles of Chancellorsville and Gettysburg, Heth also participated in the battle of Bristoe Station, Virginia, in October 1863. He became a major general on May 24, 1863. A year later, he resisted Grant at the battles of Spotsylvania, Nowell's Turnout, and Bethesda Church. During the siege of Petersburg, he fought along the Weldon Railroad, captured two thousand men at Reams' Station and at Burgess' Mill. He surrendered at Appomattox and was soon paroled. After the war, Heth lived in Richmond where he engaged in mining and insurance business. From 1880 to 1884, he performed river and harbor work as a civil engineer for the U.S. government. He was also a special agent in the Office of Indian Affairs. Heth died on September 27, 1899, in Washington, D.C. Morrison (ed.), *The Memoirs of Henry Heth*.

HILL, Ambrose Powell (*General*), was born on November 9, 1825, in Culpeper County, Virginia, to Major Thomas Hill, a well-to-do merchant, and his wife Fanny (Russell). He attended Simms's Academy in Virginia and graduated fifteenth in a class of thirty-eight from the U.S. Military Academy in 1847. Hill had no political affiliation. He was an Episcopalian until 1840, when illness inspired his conversion to the Baptist church. He married Katherine Goosh Morgan, a sister of General John Morgan (*q.v.*), in May 1859; they had two daughters. During the Mexican War, he was a first lieutenant and later a captain of artillery. A career officer, he fought in the Seminole War in Texas and Florida from 1849 to 1853, and from 1855 to 1860, he was a captain in the office of the superintendent of the U.S. Coast Survey in Washington, D.C. Hill resigned from the federal army in March 1861 and entered the Confederate Army as a colonel of the 13th Virginia Volunteers. After participating in the battle of First Manassas, he was promoted to brigadier general on February 26, 1862. Three months later he was promoted to major general. Hill was hero of the Peninsular campaign in Virginia in 1862, fighting at Williamsburg, in the center of the Army of Northern Virginia during the Seven Days, and at Second Manassas. After fighting at Fredericksburg and Chancellorsville, Hill was promoted to lieutenant general and was given command of the 3rd Corps of the Army of Northern Virginia on May 20, 1863. He led his corps through the battle of Gettysburg and at the debacle of Bristoe Station, Virginia, where he lost many of his men in October 1863. In 1864, he participated in most of the battles of the Wilderness campaign and in the defense of Petersburg, where he repelled the attack on the Weldon Railroad in June. Because of illness from psychological as well as physical causes during much of the later fighting, his military performance was uneven. He was killed near Petersburg while trying to reach his troops on April 2, 1865. Schneck, *Up Came Hill*.

HILL, Benjamin Harvey (*Congressman*), son of John and Sarah (Parham) Hill, was born in Jasper County, Georgia, on September 14, 1823. His father was a man of modest means and limited education. The younger Hill graduated first in his class from the University of Georgia in 1844. He was admitted to the bar in Troup County, Georgia, the following year. Hill became a successful lawyer, planter, and Whig leader in the state. He was a Methodist and a leader of the Sons of Temperance. On November 27, 1845, he married Caroline E. Holt, who was from a famous Georgia family; they had two sons and four daughters. He was elected to the lower House of the state legislature in 1851, where he was a unionist and an opponent of the Know-Nothings, and served until 1853. In 1855, he became an independent unionist and a Know-Nothing himself. He was a presidential elector on the Millard Fillmore slate in 1856 and on the John Bell slate in 1860. He lost a race for governor in 1857 to Joseph E. Brown (*q.v.*). In 1859, he was a unionist in the Georgia Senate. Despite his unionist beliefs, he did not want division at home. As a delegate to the Georgia secession convention, he voted for secession. Hill helped to organize the Confederate government in Montgomery and served in the Confederate Senate throughout the war. In the provisional Congress, he served on the Judiciary Committee, opposed state nullification of Confederate law, and was a major contributor to the debate over the Confederate Constitution. As chairman of the Judiciary of the Confederate Senate, Hill favored the Confederate Supreme Court. He had a violent altercation over the need for conscription with Senator William L. Yancey (*q.v.*). Hill favored overseer exemptions, protested illegal impressments, and was a severe critic of bureaucratic management; proposed the investigation of the Quartermaster and Commissary Departments; and opposed the Hampton Roads Conference. He also offered a plan for a Southern convention in 1864 in order to present a united front for peace bargaining. A Davis defender in Richmond and in Georgia, he served on the Patents, Printing, and Judiciary Committees of the Senate. After the war, Hill lost his money and was arrested. When paroled he returned to his law practice and was active in politics. He denounced the Reconstruction government in an 1867 article entitled "Notes on the Situation." In 1872, he supported Horace Greeley for the presidency. He also helped to reorganize the Georgia Democrartic party. In 1875, he was elected to the U.S. House of Representatives as a Democrat and was reelected the following year. He later served in the U.S. Senate, from 1877 until his death on August 16, 1882, in Atlanta, Georgia. Hill, *Senator Benjamin Harvey Hill of Georgia: His Life, Speeches, and Writings*; Pearce, *Benjamin H. Hill, Secession and Reconstruction*.

HILL, Benjamin Jefferson (*General*), was born on June 13, 1825, in McMinnville, Tennessee. Little is known of his early life. He attended common schools and entered the mercantile business in McMinnville in the 1850s. In 1855, he was elected to the Tennessee Senate and served until the war began. Hill entered the Confederate Army as colonel of the 5th Tennessee Regiment and fought at the battle of Shiloh under General Patrick R. Cleburne (*q.v.*) in the spring of 1862. He was a regimental commander during Braxton Bragg's (*q.v.*) Kentucky campaign and at the battle of Murfreesboro in late 1862. After participating in the 1863 battles of Chickamauga and Chattanooga, he served as provost marshal of the Army of Tennessee throughout the Atlanta campaign, in which he also fought. Promoted to brigadier general on November 30, 1864, he distinguished himself as a cavalry commander during John B. Hood's (*q.v.*) Tennessee campaign. Late in 1864, he participated in the siege of Murfreesboro. In the final months of the war, Hill commanded a brigade under General Nathan B. Forrest (*q.v.*). When the war ended, he surrendered and was soon paroled. After the war, he was a merchant and a lawyer in McMinnville, where he died on January 5, 1880. Speer (comp.), *Biographical Directory of the Tennessee General Assembly*; Warner, *Generals in Gray*.

HILL, Daniel Harvey (*General*), son of Solomon and Nancy (Caheen) Hill, was born on July 21, 1821, in York District, South Carolina. His father, a friend of John C. Calhoun, died four years later. He graduated twenty-eighth in a class of fifty-six from the U.S. Military Academy in 1842. Upon accepting his commission in the army, he held duty in garrisons. On November 2, 1852, he married Isabella Morrison, by whom he had three sons and one daughter. Hill had a lifelong spinal ailment which has been blamed for his gloomy disposition and sarcasm. Although he belonged to no particular political party, he was a rabid secessionist. During the Mexican War, he fought in the battles of Contreras, Churubusco, and Chapultepec, for which he was breveted major. In February 1849, he resigned his military commission to teach mathematics at Washington College in Lexington, Virginia. In 1854, he taught at Davidson College, where he stayed until 1859. Hill, a rigid Presbyterian with an intense desire for reform, also published *A Consideration of the Sermon on the Mount* (1856) and *Crucifixion of Christ* (1860). By 1859, he believed that war would come, and he took a position as commandant at the Military Institute of Charlotte, North Carolina. When the war began, he volunteered for service in the Confederate Army. On July 10, 1861, Hill became the first North Carolinian officer to be promoted to brigadier general. Promoted to major general on March 26, 1862, he fought in the Peninsular campaign, particularly at Seven Pines and during the Seven Days, at the end of which he was challenged to a duel by Robert Toombs (*q.v.*). The duel was avoided, but all cooperation ceased between the two intractable personalities. Hill subsequently participated in the defense of Boonsboro Gap, the battle of Sharpsburg, and the retreat from Fredericksburg, all in late 1862. On July 13, 1863, he was promoted to lieutenant general in command of the 2nd Corps of the Army of Tennessee. He aided Braxton Bragg (*q.v.*) at the battles of Chickamauga and Chattanooga before President Davis (*q.v.*) removed him from the Army of the West because Hill had accused Bragg of incompetence. At Drewry's Bluff in the spring of 1864, Hill was a voluntary aide-de-camp to General P.G. T. Beauregard (*q.v.*) and he later maintained the lines at Petersburg. In 1865, he served as a major general under General Joseph E. Johnston (*q.v.*) in the Carolinas. He surrendered in North Carolina and was soon paroled. After the war, Hill was a newspaper and magazine editor and a writer of religious tracts in North Carolina. From 1877 to 1884, he was president of the University of Arkansas, and from 1885 to 1889, he was president of Middle Georgia Military and Agricultural College. He died on September 24, 1889, in Charlotte, North Carolina. Bridges, *Lee's Maverick General*; Peele (comp.), *Lives of Distinguished North Carolinians*.

HILTON, Robert B. (*Congressman*), was born in Virginia in 1821. Details of his early life are unknown. He worked for a Savannah newspaper in the mid-1840s. A lawyer and a Democrat, he moved to Florida in 1848 and edited the *Tallahassee Floridian* before the Civil War. He was married and had a family. Hilton divided his time between Tallahassee and Savannah, supported the secession of Florida, and enlisted as a private in the Confederate Army. He was also an active member of the first and second Confederate House, representing Florida's Second Congressional District. Besides serving on the Military Affairs Committee of the House during both of his terms, Hilton was a member of the Inauguration, Patents, Post Office and Post Roads, and War Tax Committees during his first term, and of the Conference, Elections, and Territories and Public Lands Committees during his second. In 1865, he also was a member of the special committee set up to persuade state governors to decrease their granting of military exemptions and to levy additional taxes. In May 1863, he sponsored a bill to allow a small number of exemptions for plantation overseers because he believed that slaves needed supervision. He was a major supporter of General Lee's (*q.v.*) promotion to commander-in-chief of the Confederate armies. Hilton lost everything but his personal liberty during the war. After the war, he was a lawyer and newspaper editor in Tallahassee, Florida. He died there on January 10, 1894. Davis, *The Civil War and Reconstruction in Florida*; Groene, *Ante-Bellum Tallahassee*; Warner and Yearns, *Biographical Register of the Confederate Congress*.

HINDMAN, Thomas Carmichael (*General*), was born on January 28, 1828, in Knoxville, Tennessee, to Thomas C. and Sallie (Holt) Hindman. His parents moved to Calhoun County, Alabama, in 1832 and to a plantation in Ripley, Tippah County, Mississippi, in 1841. Young Hindman attended both public and private schools in Mississippi and Lawrenceville Classical Institute in New Jersey before he graduated from Princeton College in 1846. He was a Democrat and a Presbyterian. He married Mary Watkins Briscoe on November 11, 1856; they had two sons and a daughter. Hindman was a second lieutenant in the 2nd Mississippi Regiment during the Mexican War but returned to Mississippi in 1848 to study law. Three years later he was admitted to the Tippah County bar, and in 1854 he entered the state legislature, serving until 1856. While in the state House, Hindman advocated the right of secession and became friendly with Jefferson Davis (*q.v.*). He emigrated to Arkansas, settling in Helena in 1856. He opposed the Know-Nothings and the Johnson faction in Arkansas Democratic politics. From 1859 to

1861, he was a states' rights Democrat in the U.S. House of Representatives. Hindman was a close friend of the future General Patrick R. Cleburne (*q. v.*) and worked for the election of Henry M. Rector (*q. v.*) as governor in 1860, although he deserted him two years later. When the war began, Hindman gave up his seat in Congress and entered the Confederate Army as colonel of the 2nd Arkansas Infantry. He was promoted to brigadier general on September 28, 1861, and to major general on April 18, 1862. He was a division commander at the battle of Shiloh, and in May 1862, he was given command of the Trans-Mississippi Department. Hindman stirred up the people of his state to support the war effort. He restored order and confidence in the Army in the west before he was succeeded by General Theophilus H. Holmes (*q. v.*) in October of the same year. Hindman fought in the battle of Prairie Grove, Arkansas, in December 1862. He was a division commander in the Army of Tennessee at the battles of Chickamauga and Chattanooga, until General Braxton Bragg (*q. v.*) relieved him of his command. However, he fought in the Atlanta campaign until an eye injury forced his permanent retirement from combat. When the war ended, Hindman moved to Mexico and grew coffee there from 1865 to 1868. He then returned to Helena, where he farmed. His opposition to Reconstruction government probably cost him his life at the hands of an assassin on September 28, 1868. *Confederate Veteran*, XXXVIII; Hallum, *Biographical and Pictorial History of Arkansas*.

HODGE, Benjamin Louis (*Congressman, Judge*), was born in Tennessee in 1824. Details of his early life are unknown. He was a Whig farmer, lawyer, and shopkeeper in Shreveport, Caddo Parish, Louisiana, before the Civil War. In November 1860, he signed a petition to arm the state militia, and as a delegate to the Louisiana secession convention he voted for secession. In 1861, he was an unsuccessful candidate for the state Senate. When the war began, he volunteered as a colonel in the Confederate Army and served until 1862, participating in many campaigns. In 1863, he ran fourth in a race for governor of Louisiana. In February 1864, he was named presiding judge of the military court of the Trans-Mississippi Department, but he relinquished the position a month later when he replaced Henry Marshall (*q. v.*) in an uncontested election to the second Confederate House of Representatives. Hodge had no committee assignments, but he cast many votes and, unlike his predecessor, supported the Davis administration. He died in Richmond, Virginia, on August 12, 1864. Bragg, *Louisiana in the Confederacy*.

HODGE, George Baird (*Congressman, General*), was born on April 8, 1828, in Fleming County, Kentucky, the son of William and Sarah (Baird) Hodge. He attended Mayville Seminary in Kentucky and graduated from the U.S. Naval Academy in 1845. He was commissioned as a midshipman and resigned in 1851, holding the rank of lieutenant. He studied law and became a prominent lawyer in Newport, Kentucky. Hodge had a son by his marriage to Katura Tibbetts.

In 1853, he ran unsuccessfully for Congress as a Whig. He later joined the Democratic party, served a term in the state legislature from 1859 to 1861, and was an elector on the John C. Breckinridge (*q.v.*) ticket in 1860. At the beginning of the war, along with Breckinridge and Robert Preston, he was sympathetic to the Confederate cause, and he served as a member of the Executive Council of the provisional government of Kentucky in 1861. He was also in the provisional Confederate Congress, where he was on the special committee. Although he regretted secession, he willingly defended the Confederacy. After enlisting in the Civil War as a private under Simon Buckner (*q.v.*), he was made a captain as a result of his family connections, and he was acting adjutant general of the Breckinridge Division. He showed gallantry in battle at Shiloh where he was made a major. In May 1863, he was promoted to colonel. He served as inspector general at Cumberland Gap and commanded Preston's Cavalry in operations in eastern Tennessee, including Chickamauga. During Wheeler's raid in northern Georgia, he became a cavalry hero. Hodge was promoted to brigadier general on August 4, 1864, and was given command of the district of southwest Mississippi and east Louisiana. He surrendered at Meridian, Mississippi, and was paroled there in May 1865. After the war, he practiced law in Newport, Kentucky, and served as a Democratic elector on the Horace Greeley ticket in 1872. He was elected to the state Senate in 1873 and served until 1877 when he moved to Longwood, Florida. He probably became a farmer in Florida. Hodge died on August 1, 1892, in Longwood, Orange County, Florida. *Encyclopedia of Kentucky;* Evans, *Confederate Military History,* IX.

HOKE, Robert Frederick (*General*), was born to Michael and Frances (Burton) Hoke on May 27, 1837, in Lincolnton, North Carolina. His father died during his childhood, and young Hoke attended Kentucky Military Academy before taking over his family's businesses, which included milling cotton and manufacturing iron. He was an Episcopalian and a Democrat. He married Lyslia A. Van Wyck; they had children. When the war began, he volunteered for service in the Confederate Army. Hoke was a captain at Big Bethel, Virginia, in June 1861. He spent much of 1862 as a lieutenant colonel assisting in the defense of New Bern, North Carolina. He served with the Army of Northern Virginia during the 1862 battles of the Seven Days, Second Manassas, Sharpsburg, and Fredericksburg, and he was promoted to brigadier general on January 17, 1863. He was wounded at the battle of Chancellorsville in April 1863. In January 1864, he was again sent to New Bern to drive the Union Army from eastern North Carolina, and he received a resolution of thanks from the Confederate Congress when he had accomplished this objective. On April 20, 1863, he was promoted to major general and fought at Cold Harbor and the siege of Petersburg before returning to North Carolina for the final months of the war. He surrendered in North Carolina in late April 1865 and was soon paroled. After the war, Hoke returned to his business pursuits. He later developed iron mines in and near Chapel Hill, dealt in real estate, and, in 1877, served as director of the North Carolina Railroad. Hoke sought no postwar public office. He died in Raleigh, North Carolina, on July 3, 1912. Evans, *Confederate Military History*, IV; Freeman, *Lee's Lieutenants*, III.

HOLCOMBE, James Philemon (*Congressman*, *Diplomat*), brother of the eminent physician William Henry Holcombe, was born on September 25, 1820, in Lynchburg, Virginia, to the antislavery physician Dr. William James Holcombe and his wife Ann Eliza (Clayton). He attended Yale College from 1837 to 1839 and studied law at the University of Virginia. He was a Presbyterian. Holcombe had six children by his marriage to Ann Seldon Watts on November 4, 1841. He practiced law at Fincastle, Virginia, prior to moving to Cincinnati, Ohio, in 1844, where he wrote books on law. He was also a member of the Virginia Historical Society. In 1852, he became adjunct professor of constitutional and international law, mercantile law, and equity at the University of Virginia; he was promoted to full professor in 1854. As a states' rights secessionist delegate to the Virginia convention, he helped to bring on secession. Holcombe served in the Confederate House of Representatives from 1862 to 1864 where he was a member of the Judiciary Committee. In 1864, he went to Canada and to Halifax, Nova Scotia, as a commissioner from the Confederate government to attempt to organize Confederate prisoners who had escaped to Canada. He was also a spy, and toward the end of the war he worked with Clement Clay (*q.v.*) and Jacob Thompson (*q.v.*) at the Niagara Conference to attempt to ascertain Lincoln's plans for peace. When the war ended he returned to Virginia. In 1866, he founded Bellevue, a school for boys in Bedford County, Virginia. He later moved to Capon Springs, West Virginia, where he died on August 11, 1883. Kirkland, *The Peacemakers of 1864*; Tyler, *Encyclopedia of Virginia Biography*, III.

HOLDEN, William Woods (*Editor*), was born in Orange County, North Carolina, on November 24, 1818. His parents and his early life are unknown. He was truly a self-made man, who attended a field school and served as a printer's apprentice before studying law and being admitted to the bar in Raleigh in 1841. Holden was a Baptist who later became a Methodist Episcopalian. He married Ann Augusta Young in 1841; his second wife was Louisa Virginia Harrison. Holden, a Whig who became a Democrat in 1843, worked on the Raleigh *Star* and edited the Raleigh *Standard* until late 1864. He was the state printer in the 1840s. In 1848, he supported the movement for free suffrage in North Carolina and used his newspaper to foment radical secessionism. Holden developed an intense desire for public office, and in 1858, he was defeated in races for both the governorship and the U.S. Senate. In 1859, he dropped the paper as a Democratic party organ, supported Stephen Douglas for the presidency, and opposed secession. He served in the state secession convention as a unionist but voted for the "right of revolution." At first Holden was a warm supporter of the war, but while he was printer for the state legislature in 1862, he became hostile toward the Confederacy. In 1864, he formed a secret unionist society in North Carolina called "the Heroes of America" and ran as a peace candidate for governor. When the war ended, President Johnson made him provisional governor of North Carolina in late 1865. As Republican candidate for governor in 1868, he supported Negro suffrage; he was elected to office, but he was impeached in 1870 as a result of corruption during his scandal-ridden administration. He then moved to Washington, D.C., to edit the Republican *Daily Morning Chronicle*. In 1872, he declined the diplomatic post of minister to Peru. From 1873 to 1881, he was postmaster of Raleigh, North Carolina, where he died in retirement on March 1, 1892. "Autobiography of William Woods Holden," *Historical Papers of Trinity College*, III; Raper, "William Woods Holden; A Political Biography."

HOLDER, William Dunbar (*Congressman*), whose grandfather had been a companion of Daniel Boone, was born in Franklin County, Tennessee, on March 6, 1824, to Richard Calloway and ———— (Dunbar) Holder. His mother died when he was only weeks old, and the family moved first to Franklin County, Tennessee, and, in 1839, to Pontotoc, Mississippi. In June 1854, he married a Miss Bowles, by whom he had eight sons and two daughters. He was a U.S. district clerk and a deputy U.S. marshal and became a successful planter, before entering the Mississippi House of Representatives as a Whig in 1853. He served one term. When the war began, he organized the 17th Regiment of Mississippi Infantry, of which he was elected colonel. He fought at First Manassas, Leesburg, and the Seven Days, where he was wounded at Malvern Hill. He later fought at Chancellorsville and received a second, permanently disabling wound at the battle of Gettysburg. He saw no further military service. In 1863, he succeeded Reuben Davis (*q.v.*) as representative from the northeastern district of Mississippi to the Confederate House of Representatives. He served on the Elections, Medical Department, Naval Affairs, and Public Buildings Committees. In early 1865, he was falsely accused of supporting Reconstruction. When the war ended, he returned to Pontotoc to farm. The only public service he seems to have performed was as deputy state auditor of Mississippi in 1886. He died in office in Jackson on April 26, 1900. *Biographical and Historical Memoirs of Mississippi*.

HOLLIDAY, Frederick William Mackey (*Congressman*), son of Dr. Richard John McKim Holliday and his wife Mary Catherine (Taylor), was born on February 22, 1828, in Winchester, Virginia. He attended Winchester Academy and graduated with distinguished honors from Yale in 1847 and from the University of Virginia Law School in 1849. He was a Presbyterian. He had two childless marriages, the first to Hannah Taylor, whom he married in 1868, and, after her death, to Caroline Calvert. Holliday began his law practice in Winchester in 1850 and was commonwealth's attorney for the courts of Winchester and Frederick Counties from 1852 to 1861. When the war began, he volunteered for service as a captain of infantry and fought at Harper's Ferry as part of the Stonewall Brigade. He also saw action at Winchester, McDowell's, and Port Republic, and he was promoted to colonel before losing an arm at the battle of Cedar Run (Slaughter's Mountain) on August 9, 1862. He saw no further military action. Holliday was elected to the second Confederate Congress in 1864 and served for the remainder of the war. He was on the Claims and the Quartermaster's and Commissary Department Committees. He generally supported the Davis administration. After the war, Holliday returned to his law practice in Winchester. He was active in Democratic party politics but was unable to hold public office until after Reconstruction. During his term as Democratic governor of Virginia from 1878 to 1882, he vetoed a plan to repudiate the state debt. He later retired to his farm and died in Winchester on May 20, 1899. Tyler, *Encyclopedia of Virginia Biography*, III.

HOLLINS, George Nichols (*Naval Captain*), whose father was a prominent merchant, was born on September 20, 1799, in Baltimore, Maryland, to John Hollins and his wife Janet (Smith), a sister of General Samuel Smith. He was married twice; both wives were daughters of a Colonel Steritt. Hollins entered the U.S. Navy as a midshipman in 1814 and served on the *Erie*. During the Algerian war of 1815, he served under Stephen Decatur on board the *President*. He also saw duty on the *Guerriere*, the *Columbus*, the *Franklin*, and the *Washington*, and he commanded East India merchant ships. He was promoted to lieutenant in 1828, to commander in 1841, and to captain in 1855, the year he bombarded Graytown, Nicaragua, in retaliation for destruction of American property. When the war began, he resigned from the navy. In March 1861, he went to Montgomery, Alabama, where he worked with Raphael Semmes (*q.v.*) and Josiah Tattnall (*q.v.*). As a commander in the Confederate Navy, he captured the steamer *St. Nicholas* on the Potomac River on June 29, 1861. On July 10, 1861, he was named commander of naval defenses on the James River, and on July 31 of the same year, he was put in charge of the naval station at New Orleans, which he defended against the federal blockade. He later served on the boards of inquiry after New Orleans was taken by Union forces. In December 1861, he was the flag officer in charge of defending the works at Columbus, Kentucky. He later commanded all Confederate naval forces on the Mississippi River and served on the court of inquiry concerning the destruction of the ironclad Virginia. From 1863 on, he held routine duties around Richmond. He surrendered when the war ended, but was soon paroled. After the war, Hollins was a city court officer in Baltimore, where he died on January 18, 1878. Evans, *Confederate Military History*, II; Scharf, *History of the Confederate Navy*.

HOLMES, Theophilus Hunter (*General*), was born on November 13, 1804, in Sampson County, North Carolina, to North Carolina Congressman and Governor Gabriel Holmes and his wife Mary (Hunter). After graduating forty-fourth in a class of forty-six from the U.S. Military Academy in 1829, he began a military career on the Southwest frontier. Holmes, who married Laura Wetmore in 1841, had at least one son. He fought in the Florida Indian Wars from 1839 to 1842, served in the Texas army of occupation, and was breveted major at the battle of Monterrey during the Mexican War. He also participated in expeditions against the Seminoles and the Navajoes, and in March 1855, was promoted to major. In 1861, he lived in New York City and was superintendent of the general recruiting service for the army. He resigned his commission in April 1861 and went to North Carolina to assist in organizing the coastal defenses there. Holmes, an old friend of Jefferson Davis (*q.v.*), was appointed brigadier general in the Confederate Army on June 5, 1861. After participating in the battle of First Manassas, he was promoted to major general on October 7, 1861. He commanded the Department of North Carolina and served as a division commander during the Seven Days' battles before his promotion to lieutenant general on October 10, 1862. In the latter capacity, Holmes commanded the Trans-Mississippi West until relieved by General Edmund Kirby Smith (*q.v.*) in March 1863. Afterwards, he had charge of the District of Arkansas, during which time he participated in the siege of Vicksburg and the attack on Helena in July 1863. In March 1864, he was given command of the Department of Fredericksburg. Holmes was considered inefficient in the field by his superiors, and he was particularly disliked by General Daniel H. Hill (*q.v.*). He returned to North Carolina late in 1864, where he directed reserve operations until the close of the war. He surrendered and was soon paroled. After the war, he retired to a farm in Fayetteville, Cumberland County, North Carolina, where he died on June 21, 1880. Ashe, *Cyclopedia of Eminent and Representative Men of the Carolinas . . .*, I; Freeman, *Lee's Lieutenants*.

HOLT, Hines (*Congressman*), son of George Holt, was born on April 27, 1805, in Baldwin County, Georgia. He graduated from Franklin College (later the University of Georgia) in 1824, studied law, and was admitted to the Columbus, Muscogee County, Georgia, bar. Holt was a Whig. He married and had a large family. He was an eminent lawyer and planter who in 1832, as a delegate to the state convention, had opposed nullification. He held office briefly in the U.S. House of Representatives in 1841 before returning to his law practice. In 1859, he was elected to the state Senate. Holt had once been a Know-Nothing; he was a cooperationist at the time of the state secession convention, for which he was an unsuccessful candidate. During the war, he was too old to serve in the military, but in 1862, he represented the Third District of Georgia in the first Confederate House, where he served on the Conference and Ways and Means Committees as well as the special joint committee to wait on the president. In September 1862, he and Henry S. Foote (*q.v.*) jointly offered the first Congressional peace proposal. Holt was also an ally of the Davis administration. He resigned his seat toward the end of his term and was replaced by Porter Ingram (*q.v.*). Holt returned to Georgia to his law practice and saw no further service in the Confederate government. He did, however, serve in an advisory capacity to Governor Joseph E. Brown (*q.v.*). When the war ended, he practiced law in Columbus, Georgia. He died on November 4, 1868, in Milledgeville, Georgia. Yearns, *The Confederate Congress*.

HOLTZCLAW, James Thadeus (*General*), was born on December 17, 1832, in McDonough, Henry County, Georgia, to Elijah and Elizabeth (Bledsoe) Holtzclaw. He attended Presbyterian High School in Lafayette, Georgia, and East Alabama Institute before refusing an appointment to the U.S. Military Academy in 1853. He read law instead, and in 1855, he was admitted to the bar and began his practice in Montgomery, Alabama. On April 10, 1856, he married Mary Billingslea Cowles, by whom he had a son and a daughter. Holtzclaw attended but never joined the Methodist Episcopal church. He developed a successful law practice in Montgomery but seemed to have had no interest in politics. When the war began, he volunteered for military service in Alabama. In 1861, he helped to capture the Pensacola Navy Yard. He served with the 18th Alabama Regiment as major and lieutenant colonel in 1861 and as colonel in 1862-1863 before being promoted to brigadier general on July 7, 1864. Holtzclaw was wounded at Shiloh in 1862, served in Clayton's Brigade during the battle of Lookout Mountain in 1863, and was part of the rear guard of John B. Hood's (*q.v.*) army on its retreat from Nashville in December 1864. Near the end of the war, he participated in the siege of the Spanish fort at Mobile. Holtzclaw surrendered at Mobile and was paroled at Meridian, Mississippi, in May 1865. He returned to his Montgomery law practice and soon became active in Democratic politics. In 1893, he was appointed to the State Railroad Commission. He died on July 19, 1893, in Montgomery. Owen, *History of Alabama and Dictionary of Alabama Biography*, III.

HOOD, John Bell (*General*), was born on June 29, 1831, in Owingsville, Bath County, Kentucky. His parents, whose ancestors had helped to settle the state, were John W. Hood, a prosperous physician, and his wife Theodocia (French). Young Hood attended a subscription school in Clark County and graduated forty-fourth in a class of fifty-two from the U.S. Military Academy in 1853. Hood, a nonconforming Baptist, became an Episcopalian during the war as a result of his contact with General Leonidas Polk (*q.v.*). He married Anna Maria Hennen on April 30, 1868; they had three sons and eight daughters. A favorite of Robert E. Lee (*q.v.*), he was a career officer in the U.S. Army before the war. He served in California and Texas from 1853 to 1857 and fought in the Indian Wars on the frontier in 1857. In April 1861, Hood resigned his commission and joined the Confederate Army; his first duty was at Yorktown, Virginia. He was a simple man, though tactless and crude, who hated staff duty and was a good fighter but a mediocre strategist. Hood entered the Confederate Army as a captain of cavalry and was promoted to brigadier general on March 6, 1862. In the summer of 1862, he displayed heroism during the Seven Days and at the battle of Second Manassas.

On October 10, 1862, he was promoted to major general. Hood was a hero of the battle of Gettysburg, where he lost an arm; he fought at the battle of Chickamauga just two months later and lost his right leg. He was incapacitated for only a short while. On February 8, 1864, he was promoted to lieutenant general, and on July 18, 1864, he was temporarily promoted to full general. With the failure of the Atlanta counteroffensive which he led, Hood asked to be relieved of his command. He reverted to lieutenant general in rank and subsequently fought under General P.G.T. Beauregard (*q.v.*) at the battles of Franklin and Nashville, Tennessee. He was involved in the most destructive phase of the Confederate war effort in the battles around Nashville. Hood surrendered in Natchez, Mississippi, in late May 1865, and he was soon paroled. After the war, he worked as a factory and commercial merchant in New Orleans. But by the late 1860s, he had made some poor business ventures, and he was soon reduced in circumstances. He wrote a volume of memoirs, *Advance and Retreat* (1878-1879) and opposed the Louisiana lottery. Hood died on August 30, 1879, in New Orleans, a victim of the same yellow fever epidemic which killed his wife and one of his children. Dyer, *The Gallant Hood*.

HOTCHKISS, Jedediah (*Topographer*), son of Stiles and Lydia (Beecher) Hotchkiss, was born in Windsor, Broome County, New York, on November 30, 1828. He was a Presbyterian. He had two daughters by his marriage on December 21, 1853, to Sarah Comfort. In the fall of 1847, Hotchkiss taught school in Augusta County, Virginia, where he founded the Mossy Creek Academy. In 1849, he was a mining geologist in Staunton, Virginia, where he was responsible for the investment of millions of dollars in Virginia iron and coal. In 1858, he moved to Stribling Springs, Virginia, and he later bought a farm at Churchville, where he founded the Loch Willow School for Boys. In June 1861, he dismissed his students and offered his services to the Confederate Army. During the Civil War, Hotchkiss became a topographical engineer, served as chief of engineers on the staff of General "Stonewall" Jackson (*q.v.*), and prepared the maps which were used in Lee's and Jackson's campaigns. He was later made a major and served on the staff of General Richard Ewell (*q.v.*) at Gettysburg. His contributions in mapmaking were of incalculable importance to the war effort. When the war ended, he returned to Staunton, where he ran a school for boys, was a civil and mining engineer, and studied the natural resources of Virginia. He wrote *The Summary of Virginia* in 1875 and edited the magazine *The Virginian* from 1880 to 1886. Hotchkiss devoted most of his life after the war to preserving material on Jackson and the 2nd Corps. He was also a lecturer, and in 1882, he made a geological survey of his state. Hotchkiss died in Staunton on January 17, 1899. *Make Me a Map of the Valley: The Civil War Journal of Stonewall Jackson's Topographer*.

HOTZE, Henry (*Editor, Diplomat*), son of Rudolph and Sophia (Esslinger) Hotze, was born in Zurich, Switzerland, on September 2, 1833. His father was a captain in the French Royal Service. Hotze, who was educated in a Jesuit College, came to the United States, became a citizen, and moved to Mobile, Alabama, in 1855. His wife was the former Ruby Senac of New Orleans. In 1856, he edited Gobineau's *The Moral and Intellectual Diversity of the Races* for publication in the United States. In 1858, he was part of the Mobile delegation to the Southern commercial convention at Montgomery, and he joined the editorial staff of the *Mobile Register*, where he became a friend of the businessman Colin John McRae (*q.v.*). He was secretary at the U.S. legation in Brussels, Belgium, in 1858-1859, and in 1859, he was secretary for the Board of Harbor Commissioners in Mobile. In April 1861, Hotze entered the Confederate Army as a member of the Mobile Cadets. In August of that year, he was sent to purchase supplies in Europe, and in November 1861, he became a Confederate commercial agent in London. Working closely with Edwin De Leon (*q.v.*) in selling the Confederacy to the European governments, he became an advocate of arming and freeing the slaves. From May 1862 to August 1865, he edited the *Index*, an effective London-based propaganda organ for the Confederacy. He disseminated Confederate propaganda in France and wrote editorials for London newspapers. Hotze was also involved in various financial and diplomatic schemes for the Confederacy. He was probably the most talented Confederate in Europe. When the war ended, he remained in Europe and became a journalist. Little is known about the remainder of his life. He died in Zug, Switzerland, on April 19, 1887. Cullop, *Confederate Propaganda in Europe*; Dufour, *Nine Men in Gray*.

HOUSE, John Ford (*Congressman, Judge*), was born in Williamson County, Tennessee, on January 9, 1827, to Edwin Paschall and Margaret S. (Warren) House. His family was poor, and he received his education in the local academy and attended Transylvania University in Kentucky before graduating from the Lebanon Law School in 1850. He began his practice of law in Franklin County, Tennessee. House was a Methodist. He married Julia Franklin Beech on January 7, 1851; their only child died in infancy. A Whig and a unionist, House represented Clarksville in the Tennessee House in 1853 and served for some years. In 1860, he supported John Bell for the presidency. He was elected to the provisional Confederate Congress and served on the Finance Committee, but he declined election to the permanent Congress. He volunteered for service in the Confederate Army and served on the staff of General George E. Maney (*q.v.*) and fought in the battles of Murfreesboro, Chickamauga, Missionary Ridge, Dalton, and New Hope Church. In the spring of 1864, the Richmond war office named him judge advocate for northern Alabama. House returned from the war to find his estate ruined. He recouped part of his losses by reviving his law practice in Clarksville. He became a Democrat, was a delegate to the state constitutional convention in 1870, was elected to the U.S. House of Representatives in 1875, and served there from 1875 to 1883. In 1879, he was chairman of the Ways and Means Committee. He died in retirement in Clarksville, Tennessee, on June 28, 1904. Speer (comp.), *Biographical Dictionary of the Tennessee General Assembly.*

HUBBARD, David (*Bureaucrat*), was born in 1792 in either Tennessee or Old Liberty, Virginia, the son of Revolutionary War soldier Major Thomas Hubbard and his wife Margaret. He attended country schools in Tennessee and was an Episcopalian. He had six children by his marriage to Eliza Campbell. After her death, he married Rebecca Stoddard, a daughter of Benjamin Stoddard. Hubbard served under Andrew Jackson at New Orleans during the War of 1812. He was wounded and became a major in the Quartermaster's Corps. When the war ended he studied law in Tennessee. In 1819, he settled in Huntsville, Alabama, where he worked as a carpenter and practiced law. He moved to Florence, Alabama, in 1823 and became county solicitor, before moving to Moulton, Lawrence County, in 1827 to embark upon a varied career in business and politics. In 1829, he moved to Courtland, Alabama, to buy and sell Chickasaw lands. At various times in his life, Hubbard built and owned cotton factories, tanneries, shoe factories, and flour mills. In the 1840s, he also constructed one of the first railroads in Alabama. A states' rights Democrat who employed slave labor in his factories, Hubbard served on the Ways and Means Committee during his term in the U.S. House of Representatives from 1839 to 1841. He lost a campaign for reelection but served a second term in the House from 1849 to 1851. He was a delegate from Alabama to the Southern commercial convention in 1859 and an elector for John C. Breckinridge (*q.v.*) in 1860. Hubbard had opposed the Compromise of 1850, and, in 1860, warmly supported secession. (Both the *D.A.B.* and the *Biographical Directory of Congress* claim that he served in the Confederate States House. There is no record of his attendance in the Confederate States *House Journal*.) From 1863 until 1865, he was the Confederate commissioner of Indian Affairs, a position which he filled with tact and skill. He was responsible for handling many difficulties with the Indians and managed to hold their loyalty to the Confederacy. After the war, he was financially ruined. He moved to Spring Hill, Tennessee, where he ran a tan yard. Hubbard died at his son's home on January 20, 1874, in Pointe Coupee Parish, Louisiana. Garrett, *Reminiscences of Public Men in Alabama*; Owsley, *King Cotton Diplomacy.*

HUGER, Benjamin (*General*), was born to Francis Kinlock Huger and his wife Harriet Lucas (Pinckney), daughter of General Thomas Pinckney, on November 22, 1805, in Charleston, South Carolina. He graduated eighth in a class of thirty-seven from the U.S. Military Academy in 1825. Huger had five children by his marriage to Elizabeth Celestine Pinckney, a cousin, on February 17, 1831. He was a career officer in the army, serving on topographical duty until 1828; in 1832, he was promoted to captain of ordnance. For twelve years, he commanded the arsenal at Fortress Monroe, and from 1839 to 1846, he was also a member of the

Ordnance Board of the War Department. During the Mexican War, he was chief of ordnance on the staff of General Winfield Scott. As a major of ordnance, he also commanded armories at Harper's Ferry, Charleston, and Pikesville in the prewar years. When Fort Sumter fell, he resigned his commission in the army. Huger entered the Confederate Army as a colonel of artillery but was promoted to brigadier general on June 17, 1861, and to major general on October 7, 1861. In May 1861, he commanded the Department of Southern Virginia and North Carolina. In 1862, he served as a division commander under Generals Joseph E. Johnston (q.v.) and Robert E. Lee (q.v.) at Seven Pines and during the Seven Days. He was not successful in the field, and after the fall of Roanoke Island, for which he was held responsible, Huger was relieved of his command. He was sent west, where he was chief of ordnance and inspector of artillery for the Trans-Mississippi Department from 1863 until the end of the war. He surrendered in late May 1865 and was later paroled. After the war, Huger was a farmer in North Carolina and in Fauquier County, Virginia. He later returned to Charleston, South Carolina, where he died in retirement on December 7, 1877. Davidson, *The Last Foray*; Evans, *Confederate Military History*, V.

HUME, Thomas (*Minister*), was born in Portsmouth, Virginia, on October 21, 1836, to the Baptist clergyman Thomas Hume and his wife Mary Ann (Gregory). He attended Virginia Collegiate Institute, Richmond College, and the University of Virginia. He became a Baptist minister. On October 31, 1878, he married Ann Louise Whitescarver, by whom he had four children. Hume taught French and English at Chesapeake Female College before the Civil War. When the war began, he volunteered for service in the Confederate Army. A staunch Democrat and secessionist, he served as chaplain of the 3rd Virginia Regiment and was official pastor to the Confederate hospitals at Petersburg during the war. After the war, he was principal of Petersburg Classical Institute in the 1860s, president of Roanoke College from 1876 to 1885, and professor of English literature at the University of North Carolina in 1885. It is not known when he died. Silver, *Confederate Morale and Church Propaganda*.

HUMES, William Young Conn (*General*), son of John N. and Jance C. (White) Humes and a cousin of the lawyer and politician Thomas William Humes, was born on May 1, 1830, in Abingdon, Virginia. His father lost his fortune, and young Humes had to borrow money to complete his education. After graduating with honors from Virginia Military Institute in 1851, he taught school to repay his debts. Humes then read law in Knoxville, Tennessee, where he also practiced before moving to Memphis in 1858. He developed a successful law practice. He was an Episcopalian. He had two sons by his marriage to Margaret White in 1854 and, upon her death, four children by his marriage to Sallie Elder in 1864. When the war began, he volunteered for duty in the Confederate Army. Humes served as lieutenant and later as captain of artillery, and he was in charge of the batteries at

Island No. 10 where he was captured in April 1862. He was later exchanged. Promoted to brigadier general on November 16, 1863, he then commanded a cavalry brigade and served as chief of artillery in Joseph Wheeler's (*q.v.*) Corps. He participated in all the engagements of the Atlanta campaign of 1863-1864, and late in 1864, he served under John B. Hood (*q.v.*) during the last days of the Army of Tennessee. He was sent to stop Sherman at Augusta, Georgia, and he defeated Kilpatrick at Aiken, South Carolina, during the final months of the war. Promoted to major general on March 10, 1865, after commanding a division for more than a year, Humes was also present at the battle of Bentonville, North Carolina. He surrendered in North Carolina in April 1865 and was later paroled. After the war, he again practiced law in Memphis before moving to Huntsville, Alabama, where he died on September 12, 1883. Connelly, *Autumn of Glory*; Evans, *Confederate Military History*, III.

HUMPHREYS, Benjamin Grubb (*General*), was born in Bayou Pierre, Claiborne County, Mississippi, on August 28, 1808, to the planter George Wilson Humphreys and his wife Sarah (Smith). He attended schools in Russellville, Kentucky, and Morristown, New Jersey, and clerked in a store before being admitted to the U.S. Military Academy in 1825. He was dismissed from the academy for disciplinary reasons in 1826. Humphreys had two children by his marriage to Mary McLaughlin on March 15, 1832, and, upon her death, twelve children by his marriage to Mildred Maury on December 3, 1839. After serving as an overseer on his father's plantation in 1827, Humphreys read law and became a planter himself. A Whig and a unionist, he represented Claiborne County in the Mississippi House in 1838 and 1839 and in the Senate from 1840 to 1844 before moving to Sunflower County, Mississippi, in 1846. When the war began, he organized the Sunflower Guards. He fought at Seven Pines and during the Seven Days. He earned distinction at the battle of Fredericksburg in December 1862, at Chancellorsville in April 1863, and at Gettysburg in July 1863. Humphreys was promoted to brigadier general on August 14, 1863. He served gallantly and ably under General James Longstreet (*q.v.*) in Georgia and Tennessee, particularly at the battles of Chickamauga and Knoxville. After participating in the Wilderness campaign in May and June 1864, and in Early's (*q.v.*) Valley campaign of July 1864, Humphreys was given command of the Military District of Mississippi in September of that same year. In February 1865, he commanded the District of Southern Mississippi. He surrendered when the war ended. After the war, he was elected governor of Mississippi and served from 1865 until the radical Reconstruction government removed him in 1868. During his term as governor, he urged rejection of the Fourteenth Amendment. Humphreys was also an insurance agent in Jackson and Vicksburg. After 1878, he lived on a plantation in Laflore County, Mississippi, where he died on December 22, 1882. *Biographical and Historical Memoirs of Mississippi*; Freeman, *Lee's Lieutenants*, II; Perman, *Reunion Without Compromise*.

HUNTER, Robert Mercer Taliafaro (*Cabinet Member, Congressman*), son of James and Maria (Garnett) Hunter, was born on April 21, 1809, in Essex County, Virginia. He was privately tutored. He graduated from the University of Virginia in 1829 and from the Winchester Law School in 1830, the same year that he was admitted to the Virginia bar. He and his wife, the former Mary Evelina Dandridge, were married on October 4, 1836; they had eight children. Hunter, who began his career as a states' rights Whig, was elected to the state House in 1833 and served in the state Senate from 1835 to 1837. He represented Essex County as a Democrat in the U.S. House from 1837 to 1843 and from 1845 to 1847, but he was a consistent Democrat only in 1840. From 1839 to 1841, Hunter was the speaker of the House. As U.S. senator from 1847 to 1861, he was a moderate. He favored the annexation of Texas, the Tariff Act of 1857, and the Lecompton Constitution. From 1850 to 1861, he was chairman of the Senate Finance Committee. He declined offers to become secretary of state in the administrations of Franklin Pierce and James Buchanan. In 1860, he was a candidate for the presidency. He favored the secession of Virginia, and he resigned from the U.S. Senate in March 1861. He represented Virginia in the provisional Confederate Congress and in both terms of the Confederate Senate, where he served as president pro tem. In the provisional Congress, he served on the Finance Committee and supported moving the capital to Richmond. Hunter also served as Confederate secretary of state after Robert E. Toombs (*q.v.*) resigned. Hunter sought to align Spain with the Confederacy, wrote principles of self-government into diplomatic correspondence, was a consistent Davis administration supporter, but resigned in February 1862 in order to return to the Confederate Senate. In February 1865, he was a member of the peace commission, along with John A. Campbell (*q.v.*) and Alexander Stephens (*q.v.*). He served on the Conference, Finance, and Foreign Affairs Committees, and finally broke with Davis over the issue of freeing the slaves. In 1865, he advised the government to surrender. When the Confederate government collapsed, he surrendered and was imprisoned for seven months. Upon his release, he returned to his ruined lands in Essex County and began to practice law. He lost a race for the U.S. Senate in 1874. From 1877 to 1880, he was the state treasurer of Virginia, and in 1886, he was collector of customs at the port of Rappahannock. He died on July 18, 1887, in Lloyds, Essex County, Virginia. Ambler (ed.), *Correspondence of Robert M. T. Hunter*; Simms, *Life of Robert M. T. Hunter*.

HUNTON, Eppa (*General*), was born on September 22, 1822, near Warrenton in Fauquier County, Virginia, to Eppa and Elizabeth Marye (Brent) Hunton. Hunton, who lost his father during his childhood, was reared with the help of an uncle, state Senator Charles Hunton. He had a limited education, attending the new Baltimore Academy in Fauquier County, where he studied under the Reverend John Ogilvie, before he taught school himself. Hunton then read law, was admitted to the Virginia bar in 1843, and practiced in Brentsville, Prince William County, Virginia. He was a Democrat. He married Lucy Caroline Weir in June 1848; they had one son. Hunton was a colonel and, in 1847, a general in the county militia. From 1849 to 1861, he was commonwealth's attorney for Prince William County. In 1860, he was a John C. Breckinridge (*q.v.*) elector, and at the state secession convention he favored immediate secession. He resigned from the convention when the war began and entered the military service of the state of Virginia. As colonel of the 8th Virginia Regiment, he fought gallantly at the battle of First Manassas in July 1861 and during the Seven Days in 1862. He was wounded at the battle of Gettysburg and attained the rank of brigadier general on August 9, 1863. He recruited for the Confederate Army at Chaffin's Farm until the spring of 1864, when he fought Grant at Cold Harbor, Drewry's Bluff, Petersburg, and, in 1865, at the battle of Sayler's Creek. He surrendered in April 1865 and was held prisoner for three months. After the war, he practiced law in Warrenton and opposed radical Reconstruction. He was a Democrat in the U.S. House from 1873 to 1881 and was appointed by the Virginia legislature to the U.S. Senate from 1892 to 1895. In 1877, he was the only Southern member of the electoral commission which resolved the disputed Hayes-Tilden election. Hunton, who favored free coinage of silver, supported William Jennings Bryan for president in 1896. After 1881, he practiced law in Washington, D.C. He died in Richmond on October 11, 1908. Freeman, *Lee's Lieutenants*, II-III; Maddex, *The Virginia Conservatives*; Woodward, *Origins of the New South*.

HURST, David Wiley (*Judge*), son of the farmer and merchant seaman Captain Richard Hurst, was born in Amite County, Mississippi, on July 10, 1819. He attended Oakland College in Liberty, Mississippi, was admitted to the bar in 1843, and began his law practice in the office of James M. Smiley in Amite County. He had three sons and one daughter by his marriage on July 13, 1847, to Sarah Tilloston. Hurst, a Whig, served in the Mississippi legislature in 1848. For a time he lived and practiced law in Bay St. Louis, where he was a law partner of John T. Lamkin (*q.v.*), but he returned to Amite County before the Civil War. He was opposed to secession and voted against the Ordinance as a delegate to the constitutional convention. When the war began, he volunteered for service in the Confederate Army. He was a colonel in the 33rd Regiment until severe injury at Corinth, Mississippi, in October 1862 ended his military career. Hurst was named to the Mississippi Supreme Court in 1863, a position which he held for the remainder of the war. His decisions often favored the Confederate cause. After the war, Hurst moved to Vicksburg and then to Summit, Mississippi, where he practiced law until his death on July 10, 1882. *Biographical and Historical Memoirs of Mississippi*; Robinson, *Justice in Grey*.

HUSE, Caleb (*Bureaucrat*), was born in Newburyport, Massachusetts, on February 11, 1831, to Ralph Cross and Caroline (Evans) Huse. He graduated seventh in his class of forty-two from the U.S. Military Academy in 1851 and was assigned to the 1st Regiment of Artillery at Key West, Florida. In 1852, he married Harriet

Pinckney, by whom he had thirteen children. From 1852 to 1859, Huse was an assistant professor of chemistry, mineralogy, and geology at West Point. In 1854, he was promoted to first lieutenant, and in 1860, he was given leave to travel abroad. When he returned, he became commandant of cadets at the University of Alabama. His sympathy with the South led him to support secession, and he resigned from the federal army in February 1861. Huse then volunteered for service in the Confederate Army. In April 1861, he was sent to Europe to purchase supplies for the army. He bought clothing, medicine, and ordnance from Austria and received praise from Josiah Gorgas (*q.v.*) for his purchases. Accused of misappropriations of Confederate funds in 1863, he was cleared and later helped to secure the Erlanger loan. His contributions to the Confederate supply effort were considered crucial by the general staff. He was left penniless after the war, and in 1868, he returned to the United States. In 1876, he ran a school to prepare students for the Military Academy at Sing Sing, New York. Three years later, he moved the school to Highland Falls, New York, where he died on March 11, 1905. Huse, *The Suppliers of the Confederate Army*; Thompson, *Confederate Purchasing Operations Abroad*.

I

INGRAM, Porter (*Congressman*), was born into the poor farming family of Jonathan and Polly (Underwood) Ingram in Marlborough, Vermont, on April 1, 1810. He attended the common school at Marlborough and graduated from Yale College in 1831. He was a Methodist. He married Elizabeth Lewis in 1843, and they had two children. Ingram was a New York school teacher until 1836, when he moved south and settled in Hamilton, Harris County, Georgia. He studied law and later moved to Columbus, Georgia, where he practiced law with Martin Crawford and served as a judge in the city court during the 1850s. Also a successful planter, Ingram did not immediately support secession. During the war, Ingram represented the Sixth District of Georgia in the first Confederate House. He served on the Committee on Medical Departments. He did not stand for reelection. His career during the remainder of the war is unknown. After the war, he returned to law practice in Columbus and retired completely from public life. He died in Columbus, Georgia, on December 3, 1893. Northen (ed.), *Men of Mark in Georgia*, IV.

IVERSON, Alfred, Jr. (*General*), was born on February 4, 1829, in Clinton, Georgia, to Alfred Iverson and his wife Caroline (Holt). His father was a U.S. senator from Georgia at the time of secession. Young Iverson was reared in Columbus, Georgia, and in Washington, D.C. He attended military school in Tuskegee, Alabama, and read law, a subject which he did not like, before entering the army during the Mexican War. He was a Presbyterian and a Democrat. He married Harriet Harris Hutchins of Gwinnett County, Georgia, in 1857 and, upon her death, Adela Branham in 1878; he had children. Iverson was a railroad contractor in the 1840s and a first lieutenant of cavalry in the army before the Civil War. He served posts in Kansas and on the frontier during the Indian Wars of 1858-1859. Iverson resigned from the U.S. Army in 1861. Early in the Civil War, he was captain and later colonel of the 20th North Carolina Regiment. His well-trained regiment showed its skills during the Seven Days. During the battles of Sharpsburg and South Mountain in September 1862, Iverson commanded Garland's Brigade. Promoted to brigadier general on November 1, 1862, he fought at the battle of Fredericksburg in late 1862 and at Chancellorsville and Gettysburg in 1863 before going to Georgia to lead the cavalry in Martin's Division and to organize state troops. In 1864, he fought with Joseph Wheeler's (*q.v.*) Cavalry, and he captured General George Stoneman at Sunshine Church. He surrendered after Appomattox. After the war, he was a businessman in Macon, Georgia, until 1877, when he moved to Orange County, Florida. After farming there, he moved to Osceola County, Florida, where he was in the orange grove business. He died on March 31, 1911, in Atlanta. Freeman, *Lee's Lieutenants*, II; Northen (ed.), *Men of Mark in Georgia*, IV.

J

JACKSON, Claiborne Fox (*Governor*), was born in Fleming County, Kentucky, on April 4, 1807. His parents, Dempsey and Mary (Pickett) Jackson, were Virginians who settled in Kentucky and later emigrated to Howard County, Missouri, where both father and son went into business and soon made enough money to retire. The younger Jackson had a total of five children by his three wives, Jane, Louisa, and Eliza, all of whom were daughters of Dr. John Sappington. Jackson was a states' rights Democrat and belonged to no church. In 1832, he served as a captain in the Black Hawk War. Four years later he entered the state legislature, where he served for twelve years and was elected speaker of the House in 1844 and 1846. Jackson was also cashier of the State Bank of Missouri in Fayette from 1836 to 1840 and has been considered the originator of the banking house system of Missouri. In 1848-1849, he was elected to the state Senate, where he turned against Thomas Hart Benton's domination of state Democratic politics and took extremely proslavery positions. In 1860, he was elected governor of Missouri. A Stephen A. Douglas supporter, Jackson recommended the calling of a state secession convention. But he could not get the state to act, and in September 1861, he was forced to abandon the capital. The state convention then declared the office of governor vacant and a new governor was appointed. He maintained a state government of Confederate supporters in exile. Jackson, who had armed the state militia and had called for 50,000 volunteers as governor, entered the Confederate Army as a brigadier general, but he was compelled to resign for reasons of ill health. He died on December 6, 1862, of cancer in Little Rock, Arkansas. *Appleton's Cyclopedia of American Biography*; Ryle, *Missouri: Union or Secession*.

JACKSON, Henry Rootes (*General, Judge*), was born to Henry and Martha J. (Rootes) Jackson on June 24, 1820, in Athens, Georgia, where his father was a professor at Franklin College (later the University of Georgia). The younger Jackson, a poet, graduated first in his class at Yale in 1839, studied law, and was admitted to the Columbus, Georgia, bar in 1840 before moving to Savannah. He was appointed U.S. district attorney in 1843 and served until 1847. Jackson, a secessionist Democrat, had three sons and one daughter by his 1843 marriage to Cornelia Augusta Davenport. After her death, he married Florence Barclay King in 1866. During the Mexican War, he was named colonel of the 1st Georgia Regiment. From 1849 to 1853, he was a judge of the Superior Court of Georgia, and in 1849, he edited the *Savannah Georgian*. From 1853 to 1859, he served as the U.S. minister to Austria, and in 1860, he was a delegate to the Democratic convention in Charleston. He voted for secession at the Georgia secession convention. Jackson, who became a Confederate judge when the Confederacy was organized in 1861, was also appointed a brigadier general on June 4, 1861. Jackson resigned his judgeship and served in the advance on Cheat Mountain, West Virginia, in September 1861, but his division command was disbanded when Georgia's Governor Joseph E. Brown (*q.v.*) wanted him to defend Savannah. Jackson was promoted to major general in the Georgia state army on December 2, 1861, and became an aide to General W.H.T. Walker (*q.v.*). During the Atlanta campaign, he was used to organize state troops. By September 1864, he was again a brigadier general in the Confederate Army, and he served with General John B. Hood (*q.v.*) from Jonesboro to Franklin to Nashville, where he was captured in late 1864. He was held prisoner until the war ended. After the war, he returned to his law practice in Savannah. From 1885 to 1887, he was U.S. minister to Mexico. From 1875 to 1898, he served as president of the Georgia Historical Society and also as trustee of the Peabody Education Fund. In 1892, he became a director of the Central Railroad and Banking Company of Georgia. He died on March 23, 1898, in Savannah. Myers, *The Children of Pride*; Robinson, *Justice in Grey*.

JACKSON, John King (*General*), was born on February 8, 1828, in Augusta, Georgia. He attended Richmond Academy in Georgia, graduated with honors from South Carolina College in 1846, studied law, and was admitted to the Augusta bar in 1848. Before the war, he practiced law in Augusta, Richmond County, Georgia. He seemed to have had no prewar public career. Jackson married Virginia L. Hardwick in 1849; they had three sons. When the war began, he volunteered for service in the Confederate Army. Early in the war, he was a captain in the Oglethorpe Infantry and colonel of the 5th Georgia Volunteers. He fought at Santa Rosa Island on October 9, 1861, and served as commander of Confederate troops at Pensacola until January 14, 1862, when he was promoted to brigadier general and was sent to help organize the Army of Tennessee. He fought well as a brigade commander at Shiloh and guarded railroad communications during Braxton Bragg's (*q.v.*) invasion of Kentucky in the fall of 1862. Jackson also participated in the battles of Murfreesboro, Chickamauga (where 61 percent of his regiment was killed), Chattanooga, and Missionary Ridge. He accompanied General Joseph E. Johnston (*q.v.*) to Atlanta during the Georgia campaign of 1863-1864. In August 1864, he was given command of the Department of Florida. He served under General William J. Hardee (*q.v.*) in the center of the line during the siege of Savannah, and he had charge of the supply depots in the Carolinas during the final months of the war. He surrendered at the end of the war in North Carolina. After the war he practiced law in Augusta. He obtained relief from the Georgia legislature for personal financial liabilities incurred by Confederate officers during the war years. He died of pneumonia in Milledgeville, Georgia, on February 26, 1866. Northen (ed.), *Men of Mark in Georgia*, V.

JACKSON, Thomas Jonathan ("Stonewall") (*General*), was born on January 21, 1824, in Clarksburg, West Virginia, to Jonathan and Julia Beckwith (Neale) Jackson. He was orphaned while he was young and was reared by an uncle, Cummins Jackson. In 1846, he graduated seventeenth in a class of fifty-nine from the U.S. Military Academy. A Presbyterian and a Democrat, he married Elinor Junkin in 1856 and, after she died, Mary Anna Morrison on July 16, 1857; both marriages were childless. During the Mexican War, he served with General Winfield Scott from Vera Cruz to Mexico City and was breveted for his performance at Churubusco and Chapultepec. He held post assignments after the Mexican War. In 1851, he resigned his military commission in the army to become a professor of military tactics at Virginia Military Institute. A dour, humorless man, Jackson earned a reputation among the students as a relentless instructor. At the outbreak of the Civil War, Jackson volunteered for service and helped to organize troops at Harper's Ferry. Appointed brigadier general under Joseph E. Johnston (*q.v.*) on June 17, 1861, he earned the sobriquet "Stonewall" for his action at the battle of First Manassas. On October 7, 1861, he was promoted to major general in command of the Shenandoah Valley and northwest Virginia. In March 1862, he stopped General N. P. Banks at Winchester and Kernstown, and by the following month he was in command of the sixteen thousand Confederate troops in northern Virginia. In May, he defeated John C. Fremont at Staunton and Banks at Front Royal and Winchester. At the battle of Second Manassas in August 1862, he turned the right flank of General John Pope's army. After capturing the garrison at Harper's Ferry and rescuing Lee (*q.v.*) at Sharpsburg, Jackson was promoted to lieutenant general on October 10, 1862, and was given command of the 2nd Corps of the Army of Northern Virginia. He led the right wing in the battle of Fredericksburg in December 1862. At the battle of Chancellorsville, his daring assault nearly routed General Joseph Hooker's army, but Jackson was subsequently wounded by one of his own sharpshooters. He died of pneumonia at Chancellorsville on May 10, 1863, following the amputation of his left arm. His loss was a near mortal blow to the Confederate war effort. Douglas, *I Rode with Stonewall*; Vandiver, *Mighty Stonewall*.

JACKSON, William Hicks (*General*), was born on October 1, 1835, in Paris, Tennessee, to Dr. Alexander Jackson and his wife Mary W. (Hicks). He attended West Tennessee College in 1852 and graduated thirty-eighth in a class of forty-nine from the U.S. Military Academy in 1856. Jackson, who was a brother of Howell E. Jackson, U.S. senator and Supreme Court justice, married Selene Harding on December 15, 1868; they had a son and two daughters. Before the war, he served as a cavalry officer in the U.S. Army against the Indians in Kansas and New Mexico. Although he opposed the idea of war, he resigned his commission in the army in May 1861 and became a loyal Confederate. He served as a staff officer under General Gideon J. Pillow at Memphis. In November 1861, he was wounded at Belmont, Mississippi, during an attempt to rout General Ulysses S. Grant. At the battle of Shiloh in the spring of 1862, Jackson was a colonel in command of all cavalry from western Tennessee and northern Mississippi. At the battle of Corinth and the raid on Holly Springs, Mississippi, in late 1862, he commanded all cavalry under General Earl Van Dorn (*q.v.*). Promoted to brigadier general on December 29, 1862, Jackson fought in 1863 under General Joseph E. Johnston (*q.v.*). He commanded the cavalry during the relief of Vicksburg and destroyed General William T. Sherman's supplies around Meridian, Mississippi, in early 1864. Later, he was cavalry commander of the left wing of Johnston's Army of Tennessee during the Georgia campaign from Atlanta to Jonesboro, Georgia, and at Spring Hill and Franklin, Tennessee, in November 1864. At Murfreesboro under General Nathan B. Forrest (*q.v.*), he prevented the capture of John B. Hood's (*q.v.*) army and assisted in the retreat from Nashville. Although Jackson was considered for promotion, he never reached the rank of major general because of his feud with the Jefferson Davis family. Jackson never surrendered. From 1865 to

1868, he lived in Jackson, Tennessee, where his father had given him two cotton plantations. When he married, he moved to "Belle Meade," a plantation near Nashville which had been in his wife's family since 1800. He became the largest stock farmer in Tennessee. Jackson also edited the journal *Rural Sun* during the 1880s and at one time served as president of the State Association of Farmers. An Episcopalian and a Whig before the war, he became a Democrat after the war; he was never repatriated. In 1883, he became president of the Safe Deposit, Trust, and Banking Company of Nashville, and in 1894, he became president of the Nashville Gaslight Company. Jackson died on March 30, 1903, at "Belle Meade." Speer (comp.), *Biographical Directory of the Tennessee General Assembly*.

JACKSON, William Lowther (*General*), son of Colonel William Lowther Jackson and his wife Harriet (Wilson) and a second cousin of the future General Thomas J. Jackson (*q.v.*), was born in Clarksburg, Virginia, on February 3, 1825. He read and studied law and was admitted to the Clarksburg bar in 1847. Jackson was a Presbyterian. He married Sarah Creel on August 12, 1854, and they had one son. Before the war, he represented Clarksburg in the Virginia House of Delegates and was also commonwealth's attorney. He was second auditor and superintendent for the state library fund and lieutenant governor of Virginia in the 1850s. A secessionist, he enlisted in the Confederate Army as a private and became colonel of the 31st Virginia Infantry. He served on the staff of his cousin "Stonewall" in 1862, participating in the battles of Port Republic, Cedar Mountain, Second Manassas, Harper's Ferry, and Sharpsburg. In April 1863, as colonel of the 19th Virginia Cavalry, he was assigned to the Department of Western Virginia, and in the summer of 1864, he served in the defense of Lynchburg and in Early's (*q.v.*) Valley campaign. He was promoted to brigadier general on December 19, 1864. He fled to Mexico when the war ended, and in 1866, he went to Louisville, Kentucky, to practice law. From 1872 to 1890, he was continuously elected judge of the circuit court for Jefferson County, Kentucky. He died on March 24, 1890, in Louisville. Evans, *Confederate Military History*, II; Tyler, *Encyclopedia of Virginia Biography*, III.

JEMISON, Robert, Jr. (*Congressman*), son of William and Sarah (Mims) Jemison, was born in Lincoln County, Georgia, on September 17, 1802. He attended the school of Professor N.S.S. Beaman and studied law at the University of Georgia during the 1820s. He was a unionist Whig and a Methodist. He married Priscilla Cherokee Taylor, and they had one son. Jemison moved to Alabama in 1826 and for ten years was a planter. In 1836, he moved to Tuscaloosa, Alabama, where he operated a saw mill, flour mill, toll bridge, and stagecoach line. He served in the lower house of the state legislature from 1840 to 1850 and the upper house from 1851 to 1863. Jemison was a unionist delegate to the Alabama secession convention, and also served as its president. His support of the Confederate Constitution brought many Alabama unionists into the secessionist camp. In the early stages of the war, he assisted in raising Alabama troops for the war effort. In 1863, Jemison was elected to the Confederate Senate to replace the late William L. Yancey (*q.v.*), and he was reelected in 1864. In the Senate he generally opposed the Davis administration and served on the Finance, Claims, Naval Affairs, and Post Roads Committees. After the war, he became a Democrat, ran a railroad, headed a hospital for the insane, and helped to systematize Alabama's postwar finances. Jemison held no further public office because of restrictions. He died in Tuscaloosa on October 17, 1871. Owen, *History of Alabama and Dictionary of Alabama Biography*, III; Smith, *The History and Debates of the Convention of the People of Alabama*.

JENKINS, Albert Gallatin (*Congressman, General*), was born to the shipowner Captain William Jenkins and his wife Janetta (McNutt) on November 10, 1830, in Cabell County, Virginia. He attended Virginia Military Institute, graduated from Jefferson College, Pennsylvania, in 1848 and from Harvard Law School in 1850. Jenkins turned to farming and never practiced law. He was a Presbyterian and a Democrat, and he married Virginia Bowlin in 1858. From 1857 to 1861, he was U.S. congressman from Charleston, Virginia, resigning from the Congress in April 1861. Although he owned slaves, he was a unionist before the war. He volunteered for military service in western Virginia, and served as colonel in the 8th Virginia Regiment. At the beginning of 1862, he was elected to the first Confederate Congress but performed little service there as he preferred military duty. He was appointed a brigadier general in the Confederate Army on August 1, 1862, and served in Ambrose P. Hill's (*q.v.*) Division before being transferred to Stuart's Cavalry. He was captured at Chambersburg, Pennsylvania, in 1863, and upon his exchange he served heroically at Gettysburg and in the Shenandoah Valley. He died on May 21, 1864, of wounds suffered at Cloyd's Mountain, near Dublin, Virginia. Tyler, *Encyclopedia of Virginia Biography*, III.

JENKINS, Charles Jones (*Judge*), was born on January 6, 1805, in Beaufort District, South Carolina. He came to Georgia at the age of eleven with his father, for whom he was named. The younger Jenkins studied under Moses Waddell at the Willington Academy in South Carolina, attended Franklin College (later the University of Georgia) in 1822, and graduated third in his class at Union College in Schenectady, New York, in 1824, where he was also elected to Phi Beta Kappa. He studied law in the office of John M. Berrien in Savannah and was admitted to the Georgia bar in 1826. Jenkins was a Presbyterian. He was first married to a sister of the planter-politicial Augustus Seaborn Jones and, after her death, to a daughter of a Judge Barnes. In 1829, he moved to Augusta, Georgia, where he joined the firm of Augustus B. Longstreet. He was a member of the Troup (anti-Clarke) party. Jenkins, a unionist Whig, was state attorney general in 1831 and solicitor of the Middle Circuit prior to representing Richmond County in the state House of Representatives from 1836 to 1841. Always a Whig candidate in a predominantly Democratic county, he lost a race for reelection in 1842, but was returned to the House from 1843 to 1849. He was speaker of the House in 1840, 1843, and 1845. A supporter of the Compromise of 1850, he reported the resolutions of the "Georgia Platform of 1850" at the state convention that year. In 1851, he refused to run against Berrien for the U.S. Senate and also refused the cabinet post of secretary of the interior. In 1853, he ran unsuccessfully for governor. Jenkins was elected to the state Senate in 1856. During the Civil War, Jenkins could have had the position of attorney general in the Davis cabinet, but instead he spent the war years as an associate justice of the state Supreme Court, a position to which he had been named by Governor Joseph E. Brown (q.v.) in 1860. Although Jenkins was a loyal Confederate, he considered secession a "blunder." His legal decisions during the war were landmark defenses of state sovereignty. After the war, he did not want Georgia to repudiate its war debts. He was elected governor in late 1865 on a platform of opposition to the ratification of the Fourteenth Amendment, but he was deposed by the federal military in 1868. He left Georgia and, for a time, lived in Europe. He returned to Georgia in 1870, but he held no further public office. In 1877, he served as president of the state constitutional convention. He died in Augusta on June 14, 1883. Myers, *The Children of Pride*; Perman, *Reunion Without Compromise*; Robinson, *Justice in Grey*.

JENKINS, Micah (*General*), son of Captain John Jenkins and his wife Elizabeth (Clark), was born on December 1, 1835, on Edisto Island, South Carolina, where his father was a wealthy planter. He graduated first in his class at the South Carolina Military Academy in 1855. In 1856, he married Caroline Jamison, daughter of David F. Jamison, who was later president of the South Carolina secession convention; they had four sons. He was an Episcopalian. Jenkins, a secessionist Democrat, founded King's Mountain Military School in Yorkville, South Carolina, in 1855 and taught there until the beginning of the war. A strong secessionist, when the war began he helped to organize a regiment for the Confederate Army. As colonel of the 5th South Carolina Regiment, he was a favorite of General James Longstreet (q.v.) and was a conspicuous participant at the battle of First Manassas in July 1861. Jenkins, who also fought at the battles of Williamsburg and Seven Pines in the spring of 1862, was promoted to brigadier general on July 22, 1862, following his service during the Seven Days. Severely wounded during the battle of Second Manassas in August of that year, he recovered sufficiently to fight at Fredericksburg in December 1862. In the spring of 1863, he fought in the Suffolk campaign in Virginia. He also served at Gettysburg and commanded Hood's (q.v.) Division at the battle of Chickamauga. In November and December 1863, he participated with Longstreet in the Knoxville campaign. During the second day of the battle of the Wilderness, Jenkins was mortally wounded by one of his own men, in an accident similar to the one which killed General Thomas J. Jackson (*q.v.*) a year earlier at almost exactly the same location. He died on May 6, 1864. Freeman, *Lee's Lieutenants*, I, II.

JOHNSON, Bushrod Rust (*General*), son of Noah and Rachel (Spencer) Johnson, was born on October 7, 1817, in Norwich, Musingum County, Ohio. He attended St. Clairsville Academy, Ohio, and graduated twenty-third in a class of forty-two from the U.S. Military Academy in 1840. He entered the army as a second lieutenant and held various frontier duties. Johnson, nominally a Quaker, was not particularly religious. He married Mary Hatch on April 12, 1852; they had one son. After fighting in the Florida War in 1853-1854 and serving on the Kansas frontier as a first lieutenant in 1844, Johnson fought at Palo Alto, Resaca, and Monterrey during the Mexican War. In 1847, he was forced to resign his commission because he had been discovered smuggling. From 1848 to 1851, he was a professor of philosophy and chemistry at Western Military Institute in Georgetown, Kentucky, where he was superintendent from 1851 to 1855. In 1855, he became superintendent of the Military College of the University of Nashville. A secessionist, he also served as a colonel in the Tennessee Militia during the 1850s. When the war began, he volunteered as a colonel of engineers under Albert Sidney Johnston (*q.v.*) in the provisional Army of Tennessee. Appointed brigadier general in the Confederate Army on January 24, 1862, he was captured at Fort Donelson, escaped, and was later conspicuous at the battle of Shiloh, where he was wounded in the spring of 1862. He fought at the battle of Perryville during the Kentucky campaign of 1862 and at Murfreesboro. As a division commander at the battle of Chickamauga in 1863, he entered the gap in the federal lines and defeated the federal right wing. Johnson also commanded a division under General James Longstreet (*q.v.*) in east Tennessee and participated in the battle of Bean's Station and in the defense of Knoxville in late 1863. On May 21, 1864, he was promoted to major general. He fought at Petersburg and at Drewry's Bluff in 1864 and at Sayler's Creek in 1865. He surrendered with Lee at Appomattox and was paroled. In 1866, he was a professor of engineering, mechanics, and natural philosophy at the University of Nashville, where he was also chancellor from 1870 to 1874. He then retired to a farm near Brighton, Illinois, where he died on September 12, 1880. Cummings, *The Curious Career of Bushrod Rust Johnson*.

JOHNSON, Edward ("Allegheny") (*General*), son of Dr. Edward Johnson, was born on April 16, 1816, in Salisbury, Chesterfield County, Virginia. His family later moved to Kentucky. Johnson was an Episcopalian and a bachelor. He graduated thirty-second in a class of forty-five from the U. S. Military Academy in 1838. He began a career in the army by fighting Indians in Florida from 1838 to 1841, when he was transferred to the Southwest. During the Mexican War, he was breveted captain for his gallantry at Molino del Rey and breveted major for his gallantry at Chapultepec. He later saw frontier duty and was promoted to captain in 1851. In June 1861, he resigned from the U.S. Army and entered service in the Confederate Army. During the early days of the Civil War, he went as a lieutenant colonel of the 12th Georgia Regiment to Virginia. Promoted to brigadier general on December 13, 1861, he fought at McDowells' in "Stonewall" Jackson's (*q.v.*) Valley campaign of May 1862. On February 28, 1863, he was promoted to major general, and he commanded a division of the 2nd Corps under General Richard S. Ewell (*q.v.*) in the attack on Culp's Hill during the battle of Gettysburg in July. He fought in the Wilderness in May 1864 and was captured while defending the "bloody angle" at Spotsylvania Court House. Later he was exchanged, and in September 1864, he joined the Army of Tennessee as a division commander under John B. Hood (*q.v.*). After making a desperate charge during the battle of Franklin in November, he was again captured at Nashville and was not released until after the war ended. After the war, he, was a farmer in Chesterfield County. Johnson died on March 2, 1873, while on a visit to Richmond. Freeman, *Lee's Lieutenants*, III; Tyler, *Encyclopedia of Virginia Biography*, III.

JOHNSON, George W. (*Governor*), son of William Johnson, was born on May 27, 1811, in Georgetown, Kentucky. His grandfather, Colonel Robert Johnson, had been a hero of the Revolutionary War. After studying law at Transylvania University in Kentucky during the early 1830s and practicing law in Georgetown in the 1840s, Johnson turned to farming in Kentucky, where he had extensive cotton holdings. Johnson also owned a cotton plantation in Arkansas, but he resided mainly in Kentucky in the last years of the antebellum period. He married Ann Eliza Viley on August 20, 1833; they had seven children. From 1838 to 1840, he represented Scott County in the Kentucky legislature. Johnson, a Democrat, joined John C. Breckinridge (*q.v.*) in pushing for the secession of Kentucky. He convinced President Davis (*q.v.*) to support the collection of war taxes in Kentucky in order to show that state's support for the South. He also enlisted as a private in the 1st Kentucky Regiment and accompanied Albert Sidney Johnston (*q.v.*) in military councils. At Shiloh, where he was an aide to Breckinridge, he was mortally wounded. He died on a hospital boat on April 9, 1862, having served with the rank of private. After his death, the "Shadow" government virtually disappeared and Kentucky was lost to the Confederacy. Clift, *Governors of Kentucky*; Clift (comp.), *Kentucky Marriages*.

JOHNSON, Herschel Vespasian (*Congressman*), was born to Moses and Nancy (Palmer) Johnson in Burke County, Georgia, on September 18, 1812. He graduated from the University of Georgia in 1834 and was admitted to the Georgia bar the same year. On December 19, 1833, he married Mrs. Ann (Polk) Walker. He had a successful law practice in Augusta and later at Milledgeville. Johnson also ran his plantation "Shady Grove" for several years before he entered Democratic politics in 1840. He was a Presbyterian but in later years was attracted to the Swedenborgian faith. In 1847, he ran unsuccessfully for governor of Georgia. In 1848-1849, Johnson served Georgia in the U.S. Senate, and from 1849 to 1853, he was judge of the superior court for the Ocmulgee Circuit. Johnson moved to Milledgeville in 1850. He joined the Southern Rights party and supported the Compromise of 1850, although he did not approve of it. He also supported the Kansas-Nebraska Act of 1854. From 1853 to 1857, he was governor of Georgia. In 1860, he was the Democratic candidate for vice-president as the running mate of Stephen A. Douglas. Opposed to the secession of his state, Johnson nevertheless was a delegate to the Georgia secession convention and acquiesced on the question, although he never expected the Confederacy to secede. During the war he was a loyal supporter of President Davis (*q.v.*) but took consistently state-rightist positions on various issues, such as conscription. He was elected to the first and second Confederate Senates and served from 1862 to 1865. He was a leader of the peace movement, yet only supported Reconstruction when he believed the Confederacy could no longer protect itself. He served on the Finance, Foreign Affairs, Naval Affairs, and Post Office and Post Roads Committees of the Senate and was highly respected as an able and dedicated legislator. When the war ended, he returned to Milledgeville to his law practice. In 1866, he was elected to the U.S. Senate, but because of the Reconstruction Acts he was unable to serve. He returned to his law practice until 1873, when he was named a judge of the Middle Circuit Court. Johnson died on August 16, 1880, in Jefferson County, Georgia. Flippin, *Herschel V. Johnson of Georgia*; Perman, *Reunion Without Compromise*.

JOHNSON, Robert Ward (*Congressman*), was born in Scott County, Kentucky, on July 22, 1814, to Judge Benjamin and Matilda (Williams) Johnson. He was a nephew of the Kentucky political leader Richard Mentor Johnson. In 1821, his family moved to Arkansas. Johnson received his education at the Choctaw Indian Academy in Kentucky, at St. Joseph's College, Kentucky, in 1833, and at Yale Law School in 1835. In 1836, he married Sara Smith, a daughter of Dr. George W. Smith; they had three children. After her death, in 1862 he married her sister, Laura Smith. Johnson, whose family controlled Arkansas politics from 1836 to 1860, practiced law in Little Rock from 1835 to 1847. From 1840 to 1842, he was prosecuting attorney for the area, as well as the *ex officio* state attorney general. In 1840 and 1842, he ran unsuccessfully for the state legislature. A Democrat, he served in the U.S. House of Representatives from 1847 to 1853 and in the U.S. Senate from 1853 to 1861. He was a unionist supporter of the Compromise of 1850. Throughout the 1850s he edited a powerful party newspaper called the *True Democrat*. In 1860, he refused to run for reelection to the Senate and worked for the secession of Arkansas. Johnson was a delegate to the provisional Confederate Congress in 1862 and a member of the Confederate Senate from 1862 to 1865. A loyal administration man, Johnson's party machine was able to send him to office while his lieutenants were largely denied further political office. He served ably on the Accounts, Indian Affairs, Public Lands, Military Affairs, and Rules Committees. After the war he fled to Texas for a time. When he returned to his large land holdings in Jefferson County, Arkansas, he found his land confiscated and his financial condition ruinous. In the fall of 1868, he moved to Washington, D.C., where he was a law partner of General Albert Pike until 1877, when he returned to Little Rock. He held no further political office. Johnson died in Little Rock on July 26, 1879. Shinn, *Pioneers and Makers of Arkansas*; Thomas, *Arkansas in War and Reconstruction, 1861-1874*.

JOHNSON, Thomas (*Congressman*), was born in Montgomery County, Kentucky, on July 4, 1812. Little is known about his family or his education. He was a farmer and a merchant and lived in Mount Sterling, Montgomery County, Kentucky, in 1860. There is some evidence that he was active in local politics. Elected to the provisional Confederate Congress from the Tenth District of Kentucky, he served on the Committee on Military Affairs. Johnson declined election to the first Confederate Congress. He served in the 2nd Battalion of Kentucky Mounted Rifles from October 1862 until April 1865, when he was taken prisoner. He was married to Elizabeth Dale. Johnson returned to Mount Sterling after the war to his merchant business. He served in the state House in 1876-1877, and in the state Senate from 1878 to 1882. He died in Mount Sterling on April 7, 1906. Boyd (coll.), *Some Marriages in Montgomery County, Kentucky Before 1864*.

JOHNSON, Waldo Porter (*Congressman*), a nephew of Governor Joseph Johnson and the son of William and Olive (Waldo) Johnson, was born on September 16, 1817, in Bridgeport, Harrison County, Virginia, where his father was a farmer and merchant. He graduated from Rector College, Pruntytown, Virginia, in 1839, studied law, and was admitted to the Virginia bar in 1842. Johnson had no religious affiliation. He had five children by his October 27, 1847, marriage to Emily Moore. In 1842, he moved to Osceola, St. Clair County, Missouri, to continue his law practice. During the Mexican War, he served with the 1st Missouri Regiment. Johnson, a Thomas Hart Benton Democrat, was elected to the Missouri House of Representatives in 1847. The following year he was named circuit attorney for St. Clair County, and in 1851 he became judge of the Seventh Judicial Circuit. In 1854, he was an unsuccessful candidate for the U.S. House of Representatives, but he served in the U.S. Senate from 1861 until his expulsion for support of the Confederacy in 1862. Johnson was a member of the peace convention in Washington in 1861, and in a special session of the Senate in July 1861, he offered a resolution for a peace conference. He then joined the Confederate Army as a lieutenant colonel of the 4th Missouri Regiment and was wounded at Pea Ridge, Arkansas, in March 1862. He later helped to evacuate Corinth, and in the fall of 1862, he recruited and organized troops for Governor Sterling Price (*q.v.*)

of Missouri. In the fall of 1863, he was appointed by Governor Thomas C. Reynolds (*q.v.*) to replace R.L.Y. Peyton (*q.v.*) in the Confederate Senate. As a member of the first and second Senates, Johnson served on the Claims, Conference, Engrossment and Enrollment, Foreign Relations, and Indian Affairs Committees. He worked to retain currency standards, opposed too rapid devaluation of the currency, and wanted to restore public confidence in the cabinet through turnover in office. Johnson was an ardent supporter and confidential advisor to President Davis (*q.v.*). After the war, he fled to Hamilton, Ontario, Canada. He returned to Missouri and to his law practice in 1867 and in 1875, was the president of the state constitutional convention. The following year he moved to St. Louis. He returned to Osceola in 1884 and died there on August 14, 1885. Stewart, *The History of the Bench and Bar of Missouri*; Yearns, *The Confederate Congress*.

JOHNSTON, Albert Sidney (*General*), was born to Dr. John Johnston, a physician, and his wife Abigail (Harris) on February 2, 1803, in Washington, Kentucky. Raised in Louisiana, he attended Transylvania University, where he was a close friend of Jefferson Davis (*q.v.*), and graduated eighth in a class of forty-one from the U.S. Military Academy in 1826. He was an Episcopalian and a Democrat. He married Henrietta Preston on January 20, 1829, and, after her death, Eliza Griffin on October 3, 1843. His one son by his first wife, William Preston Johnston (*q.v.*), was aide-de-camp to President Davis during the war. After his graduation from West Point, Johnston entered the army and was sent first to New York and then to St. Louis. He was a regimental adjutant in the Black Hawk War of 1832 before he resigned his commission in Louisville, Kentucky, in 1834. The following year, he enlisted in the Texas army during the war for independence, and after being wounded during a duel, he rose in rank to become commander of the Texas army. From 1838 to 1840, he was secretary of war for the Republic of Texas, and during the Mexican War he fought at Monterrey as a colonel of the Texas volunteers. In the 1840s, he was also a planter in Brazoria County, Texas. Poverty-stricken by 1848, he reentered the U.S. Army as a paymaster in 1849. By 1855, he had risen to colonel of the 2nd Cavalry, and the following year he commanded the Department of Texas. From 1858 to 1860, he fought the Mormons in Utah and had charge of the Department of the Pacific. Johnston, a unionist, felt himself a Texan, and he agreed to resign his commission in the army only if Texas seceded. He resigned in April 1861. On August 30, 1861, he was appointed a full general in the Confederate Army and was placed in command of the Department of the West. Johnston had personality problems as a commander; he could not properly direct the actions of subordinates. His faith in General Leonidas K. Polk (*q.v.*) was shaken by the loss of Forts Henry and Donelson in early 1862. Although his attack on General U. S. Grant at Shiloh resulted in success for the Confederates, Johnston himself was mortally wounded and bled to death on the battlefield on April 6, 1862. Moore, *Destiny's Soldier*; Roland, *Albert Sidney Johnston: Soldier of Three Republics*.

JOHNSTON, George Doherty (*General*), was born on May 30, 1832, in Hillsboro, North Carolina, to George Mulhollen and Eliza Mary (Bond) Doherty Johnston. His family moved to Alabama in 1834. Johnston attended Marion Seminary, graduated from Howard College, Alabama, in 1848, and received a law degree from Cumberland University in Tennessee in 1852. He was a Presbyterian. He married Euphrodia Poellnitz in 1853, and after her death, Maria Barnett, in 1865; his second wife also died and he married Stella Searcy Harris in 1876. He had one son by his first wife and another son by his third. In 1854, Johnston practiced law in Marion, Alabama, where he was also elected mayor in 1856. In 1857-1858, he represented Perry County in the Alabama legislature. When the war began, he enlisted in the Confederate Army as a second lieutenant in the 4th Alabama Regiment. Promoted to lieutenant colonel after the battle of Shiloh in the spring of 1862, he participated in every engagement of the Army of Tennessee from Shiloh to Bentonville, North Carolina. Five days after his promotion to brigadier general on July 26, 1864, he was wounded at the battle of Ezra Church, and he spent the rest of the war on crutches. Even so, he participated in Hood's (*q.v.*) Tennessee campaign and served in the last battles in North Carolina. He surrendered at Durham Station, North Carolina, in April 1865. After the war, he practiced law in Marion until he became commandant of cadets at the University of Alabama from 1871 to 1873. From 1885 to 1890, he was superintendent of the South Carolina Military Academy. He returned to Tuscaloosa, Alabama, and in 1892-1893, he was a member of the U.S. Civil Service Commission. Johnston, who also served in the Alabama Senate in 1900, wrote *Memories of the Old South* (1905). He died on December 8, 1910, in Tuscaloosa. Owen, *History of Alabama and Dictionary of Alabama Biography*, III; Warner, *Generals in Gray*.

JOHNSTON, Joseph Eggleston (*General*), son of Peter Johnston, a speaker of the Virginia House of Delegates, and his wife Mary (Wood) Johnston, was born on February 3, 1807, in Prince Edward County, Virginia. He attended Abingdon Academy and graduated thirteenth in a class of forty-six from the U.S. Military Academy in 1829. He was appointed second lieutenant in the 4th Artillery. Johnston was baptized an Episcopalian during the Civil War by General Leonidas K. Polk (*q.v.*). He married Lydia McLane, daughter of U.S. Senator Louis McLane of Delaware, on July 10, 1845; they had no children. He served in the Black Hawk War in 1832 and on topographical duty with the army in 1834. In 1836, he was promoted to first lieutenant, and he served as an aide-de-camp to Winfield Scott during the Seminole War before resigning his commission in 1837 to become a civil engineer. In 1838, he returned to the army as a first lieutenant of topographical engineers, and he was breveted captain for his gallantry during the Seminole campaign that year. In 1841, he was put in charge of the Topographical Bureau, and the following year he was named adjutant general of Florida. Promoted to captain in 1846, Johnston served during the Mexican War with General Scott at Vera Cruz, Cerro Gordo, Contreras, Churubusco, Molino del Rey,

Chapultepec, and Mexico City. He was breveted major, lieutenant colonel, and colonel and was corps commander for the Department of Texas. In 1858, he was acting inspector general for the Utah expedition. On June 28, 1860, he became quartermaster general for the U.S. Army. In April 1861, he resigned from the army and helped to organize the Virginia Volunteers, of which he was a major general. On May 14, 1861, he was appointed brigadier general in the Confederate Army, and he commanded the garrison at Harper's Ferry before assisting General P.G.T. Beauregard (*q.v.*) at the battle of First Manassas in July. Promoted to full general on August 31, 1861, he ranked fourth in seniority (after Samuel Cooper [*q.v.*], A. S. Johnston [q.v.], and Robert E. Lee [*q.v.*]), which led to a feud between him and President Jefferson Davis (*q.v.*). In May 1862, he was wounded at the battle of Seven Pines, where he attacked but missed the opportunity to destroy McClellan's army. His command then passed to General Lee, and in 1863, Johnston commanded the Department of the West. He unsuccessfully attempted to salvage an already desperate situation at Vicksburg in the first half of that year. After the fall of Vicksburg in July, he replaced Braxton Bragg (*q.v.*) as commander of the Army of Tennessee. In turn, he was replaced by John B. Hood (*q.v.*) in July 1864. Johnston ended the war in the Carolinas, where he unsuccessfully attempted to check William T. Sherman's march north. When the war ended, he surrendered his command to Sherman in North Carolina. He was soon paroled. In 1865, he was employed by the National Express and Transportation Company of Richmond, and the following year he was president of the Alabama and Tennessee River Railroad Company in Savannah, Georgia. Johnston worked for Tilden's election in 1876. He returned to Richmond in 1877 and was a U.S. congressman from Virginia from 1879 to 1881. From 1885 to 1891, he was President Grover Cleveland's railroad commissioner. Johnston was also an insurance agent in Richmond and published *Narrative of Military Operations* (1875). He died in Washington, D.C., on March 21, 1891. Govan and Livingood, *A Different Valor*.

JOHNSTON, Robert (*Congressman*), was born in Rockbridge County, Virginia, on October 14, 1818. He studied law under John W. Brockenbrough (*q.v.*) in Lexington in 1840. He moved to Clarksburg, Virginia (now West Virginia), in 1842 and began a law practice. He served in the House of Delegates from 1855 to 1858. He was married and he had children. In January 1861, he led the meeting of the State Rights party. Although he was a secessionist, he was not elected to the secession convention. However, he was elected to the provisional Confederate Congress without seeking the office and subsequently was elected without opposition to the first Confederate House and, with little opposition, to the second. He was a member of the Committee on Military Appointments and the committee to make the proceedings of the provisional Congress public. In the first and second Confederate Houses, Johnston was also a member of the following committees:

Post Office and Post Roads, the committee to investigate the losses of Forts Donelson and Pillow, Currency, Accounts, Quartermaster's and Commissary Departments, and the committee of State Claims against the Confederate government. When the war ended, he moved to Harrisonburg, Virginia, and practiced law. He was also a judge from 1880 to 1885. Johnston died in Rockingham County on November 6, 1885. Haymond, *History of Harrison County, West Virginia*; Warner and Yearns, *Biographical Register of the Confederate Congress*.

JOHNSTON, Robert Daniel (*General*), was born on March 19, 1837, in Lincoln County, North Carolina, to Dr. William Johnston and his wife Nancy (Forney). He attended a classical school in Rutherfordton, North Carolina, graduated second in the class of 1857 from the University of North Carolina, and studied law at the University of Virginia in 1860-1861. Johnston was a Democrat and an elder in the Presbyterian church. He married a Miss Evans on November 1, 1871. When the war began, he entered the Confederate Army as a captain of the 23rd North Carolina Regiment, and he participated in all battles of the Army of Northern Virginia during the Civil War. He fought at the battle of Williamsburg and was wounded at Seven Pines in May 1862; at the battles of South Mountain and Sharpsburg in September 1862, his actions were heroic. He served as a regimental commander at the battle of Chancellorsville and was promoted to brigadier general on September 1, 1863, after fighting at the battle of Gettysburg. In 1864, he fought in the Wilderness, Spotsylvania, Early's (*q.v.*) Valley campaign, Cedar Creek, and the Petersburg trenches. He surrendered along the Roanoke River and was later paroled at Charlotte, North Carolina. After the war, he practiced law in Charlotte and edited the Charlotte *Observer* for some years. In 1887, he moved to Birmingham, Alabama, where he was president of the national bank from 1885 to 1895. From 1895 to 1908, he was registrar for the U.S. Land Office in Birmingham. Johnston died on February 1, 1919, in retirement in Winchester, Virginia. Owen, *History of Alabama and Dictionary of Alabama Biography*, III.

JOHNSTON, William Preston (*Staff Officer*), son of Albert Sidney (*q.v.*) and Henrietta (Preston) Johnston, was born on January 5, 1831, in Louisville, Kentucky. His mother died when he was four, and he was raised by an uncle, General William Preston. He attended the primary schools of Louisville, the Academy of S. V. Womack, Centre College in Danville, Kentucky, and Western Military Institute in Georgetown, Kentucky, before graduating from Yale College in 1852 and the University of Louisville Law School in 1853. He was an Episcopalian and a Whig who became a Democrat. He married Rosa Elizabeth Duncan on July 6, 1853, and, after her death, Margaret Henshaw Avery in 1888; he had one son and five daughters. Johnston, a strong secessionist, practiced law in Louisville before the war. In 1855, he moved to New York, but he returned to Louisville two years later. When the war began, he entered the Confederate Army as a major of the 2nd

Regiment Kentucky Artillery and was later a lieutenant colonel in the 1st Kentucky Regiment of the Army of Northern Virginia. He became ill and weak from camp fever but recovered and was promoted to colonel and aide-de-camp to Jefferson Davis (*q.v.*) in May 1862. Throughout the war he served as a mediator between Davis and his subordinates. In his capacity as a confidential staff officer he was intimately acquainted with Confederate leaders, whose confidence he earned and maintained. Johnston also participated in the battles of Seven Pines in 1862 and Cold Harbor, Sheridan's Raid, Drewry's Bluff, and Petersburg in 1864. When the war ended, he was captured along with President Davis and was imprisoned. Upon his release he went to Canada. In 1867, he was appointed to the chair of English and history at Washington and Lee University in Lexington, Virginia. He was named president of Louisiana State University in 1880 and served as president of Tulane University from 1883 to 1889. In 1878, he published *The Life of Albert Sidney Johnston*. Johnston died on July 16, 1899, in Lexington, Virginia. Shaw, *William Preston Johnston: A Transitional Figure of the Confederacy*.

JONES, David Rumph (*General*), was born in Orangeburg District, South Carolina, on April 5, 1824, to Donald Bruce and Mary Elvira (Rumph) Jones. He was raised in Dooly County, Georgia, attended the local schools, and in 1846, he graduated forty-first in a class of sixty from the U.S. Military Academy. Jones had two daughters by his marriage to Rebecca Taylor, a niece of President Zachary Taylor. He entered the army as a second lieutenant of infantry. Breveted first lieutenant during the Mexican War, he participated in the siege of Vera Cruz, the battles of Cerro Gordo, Ocaloco, and Churubusco, and the assault and capture of Mexico City. He was stationed in California from 1848 to 1851 and at West Point from 1851 to 1853 as an assistant instructor of infantry. In 1853, he was breveted captain and was made adjutant general for the western division of the U.S. Army. From 1854 to 1858, he was acting judge advocate for the Pacific Department, and from 1858 to 1861, he was assistant adjutant general for the Department of the West. He resigned his commission in February 1861 and volunteered for service in the Confederate Army. After helping to defend Charleston, where he served as chief of staff to General P.G.T. Beauregard (*q.v.*) in the spring of 1861, Jones was appointed brigadier general on June 17, 1861. He fought at the battles of Yorktown, Seven Pines, the Seven Days, Second Manassas, and South Mountain in 1862. At the battle of Sharpsburg that same year, he saved the Confederate right by attacking General Ambrose Burnside. In September 1862, he was promoted to major general, but he was relieved of duty for health reasons. Jones died of heart trouble in Richmond, Virginia, on January 15, 1863. Evans, *Confederate Military History*, V; Northen (ed.), *Men of Mark in Georgia*, IV.

JONES, George Washington (*Congressman*), was born on March 15, 1806, to James and Jane (Slaughter) Jones in King and Queen County, Virginia, where the elder Jones was a sheriff. In March 1816, the family moved to Giles County,

Tennessee, and the younger Jones was apprenticed to the saddler's trade. He was a Democrat and a bachelor. He was elected justice of the peace for Lincoln County, Tennessee, and served from 1832 to 1835. He represented Lincoln County in the Tennessee House from 1835 to 1839 and in the state Senate from 1839 to 1841, during which time he sponsored a bill to abolish imprisonment for debt. From 1840 to 1843, he was the clerk of the Lincoln County court. At one time before the war, he was also president of the Bank of Fayetteville. As a member of the U.S. House of Representatives from 1843 to 1859, he supported the annexation of Texas and the Compromise of 1850 but did not advocate nullification or secession. In 1860, he supported Stephen A. Douglas for president. He was a late convert to secession, and although he was elected a delegate to the peace convention in Washington in 1861, he did not attend. Jones served in the first permanent Confederate House from 1862 to 1864 but refused to stand for reelection. A member of the Rules, Ways and Means, and Currency Committees, Jones generally supported the Davis administration. He performed no further duty in the Confederacy. After the war, he obtained an early pardon from President Johnson and returned to Lincoln County. He was a delegate to the state constitutional convention in 1870 and a member of the Board of Trustees of the Tennessee Hospital for the Insane from 1871 to 1884. Jones held no postwar political office. He died in Fayetteville, Lincoln County, on November 14, 1884. Speer (comp.), *Biographical Directory of the Tennessee General Assembly*.

JONES, Henry Cox (*Businessman*), was born on January 23, 1821, in Franklin County, Alabama, where his father, a planter, had moved from Virginia. His parents were William Stratton and Ann Harris (Cox) Jones. After graduating from La Grange College in 1840, he studied law with Daniel Coleman of Athens, Georgia. Jones was a Democrat and a Methodist. He had ten children by his October 13, 1844, marriage to Martha Louisa Keyes. Jones was admitted to the Alabama bar in 1841 and the same year became a probate court judge. He also developed a profitable law practice. In 1843-1844, he represented Florence, Alabama, in the state House; in 1853, he was elected to the state Senate. In the late 1850s, he entered the cotton goods manufacturing business in Florence. Jones was a Douglas Democrat in 1860 and, as a delegate to the secession convention, refused to vote for or sign the Ordinance of Secession. During the war, he manufactured cottons and woolens under contract from the Confederate government. His factory had one of the most productive operations during the war. After the war he returned to law practice. In 1876, he was an elector on the Tilden slate in Alabama. Jones died in Florence on June 20, 1913. Owen, *History of Alabama and Dictionary of Alabama Biography*, III; Vandiver, *Ploughshares into Swords*.

JONES, John Beauchamp (*Bureaucrat*), was born on March 6, 1810, in Baltimore, Maryland. Little is known of his parents or his early education except that he was raised in Kentucky and Missouri and that he received a common school education. He married Frances T. Curtin in 1840; they had two sons and two daughters. Jones was an Episcopalian and a Democrat. As a young man he entered the newspaper business and worked for many publishers. In 1841, he edited the *Baltimore Saturday Visitor*, where he wrote, printed, and distributed his first novel, *Wild Western Scenes*, a book that became a minor classic of frontier adventure. In 1842, he was appointed editor of the *Madisonian*, the official Whig organ in Washington, D.C. During the Polk administration, he held the consulate at Naples, Italy. Jones wrote many novels during the 1850s. From 1857 to 1860, he published the weekly *Southern Monitor* in Philadelphia and attempted to explain the South to Northerners. In 1859, he wrote an anti-secession novel about the ills of disunion entitled *Wild Southern Scenes*. When the Civil War broke out, he volunteered for duty in the Confederate government in Richmond. He obtained a clerkship in the Confederate War Department as aide to Secretary Leroy Pope Walker (*q.v.*). Jones was in charge of passports, a job from which he could scrutinize the workings of the Confederate bureaucracy. In February 1862, he raised a company for local defense and saw about a month of action at a battery near Richmond. He retired as captain on April 23, 1863, was later conscripted but did not serve, and held various minor posts in the government throughout the remainder of the war. Jones kept a journal of his observations in Richmond, which was published as the *Rebel War Clerk's Diary* in 1866. His gossipy study also penetrated to the personalities and the performance of the Confederate leadership. He is remembered chiefly because of that study. Jones died while the book was in press, on February 4, 1886, in Burlington, New Jersey. *American Mercury*, December 1925.

JONES, Joseph (*Physician*), son of the Reverend Charles Colcock and Mary (Jones) Jones, was born on September 6, 1833, in Liberty County, Georgia. He attended the University of South Carolina and received his A.B. and M.A. from Princeton in 1853 and 1856, respectively. In 1856, Jones also received his M.D. from the University of Pennsylvania. He was married twice, to Caroline S. Davis in 1858 and, after her death, Susan Rayner Polk, daughter of Bishop Leonidas Polk (*q.v.*) in 1870. He had six children. His son, Charles Colcock Jones, was an important historian in Reconstruction Georgia. Jones was a Presbyterian. He was a professor of natural theology at the University of Georgia in 1858 and also served as a professor of chemistry at Savannah Medical College and at the Medical College of Georgia prior to the Civil War. When the war began, he volunteered for military service and became a cavalry officer. He was a full surgeon-major in the Confederate Army. Jones served at Andersonville and became a specialist in the treatment of gangrene. After the war, he settled in New Orleans and practiced medicine, and in 1872, was given a chair in chemistry at the University of Louisiana. He was also appointed president of the Louisiana State Board of Health, and in 1887, he was elected president of the Louisiana State Medical

Society. He wrote *Medical and Surgical Memoirs* (1876-1890, 3 volumes) and was active in founding the Southern Historical Association. He died on February 17, 1896, in New Orleans. Cunningham, *Doctors in Gray*; Myers, *The Children of Pride*.

JONES, Robert McDonald (*Congressman*), was born in the Choctaw territory (southern Mississippi) on October 1, 1808. He was a half-breed Indian and a wealthy farmer who owned more than two hundred slaves. Jones also owned a number of general stores. A leader of the secessionist movement in Red River County, Choctaw Nation, he was reputed to have convinced the Choctaws to support the Confederacy. He was the signer of the joint treaty for the Choctaws and Chickasaws with the Confederate States on July 12, 1861. Jones served as a nonvoting delegate in the first and second Confederate Houses. He was useful in advising the government on policies toward the western Indians. It is believed that he returned to the Choctaw Nation and again took up farming. He died on his estate near Hugo, Oklahoma, on February 22, 1872. Yearns, *The Confederate Congress*; Warner and Yearns, *Biographical Register of the Confederate Congress*.

JONES, Samuel (*General*), was born to Samuel and Ann (Moseley) Jones, on December 17, 1819, in Powhatan County, Virginia. He graduated nineteenth in a class of fifty-two from the U.S. Military Academy in 1841. He was a Presbyterian. He began his military career in the army on the Maine frontier from 1841 to 1843 and on the Florida frontier from 1845 to 1846. From 1846 to 1851, he was assistant professor of mathematics and instructor of infantry and artillery at West Point. Promoted to captain in 1853, he served in New Orleans and Texas until 1858, when he was named assistant judge advocate for the U.S. Army, stationed in Washington, D.C. He resigned his commission in April 1861 and volunteered for service in the Confederate Army. At the battle of First Manassas, he was General P.G.T. Beauregard's (*q.v.*) chief of artillery. Promoted to brigadier general on July 21, 1861, in January 1862 he relieved General Braxton Bragg (*q.v.*) as commander at Pensacola. On March 10, 1863, he was promoted to major general in command of the Department of Alabama and West Florida. In September 1862, he commanded Thomas Hindman's (*q.v.*) Division at Corinth, Mississippi, and was also given the departmental command for east Tennessee. Jones refused to send reinforcements to Braxton Bragg in Kentucky because he believed the request unnecessary; as a consequence, he was transferred to the Department of West Virginia, which he defended from December 1862 until March 1864. He was relieved of his command after losing the confidence of both Virginia lawmakers and General Robert E. Lee (*q.v.*). He then succeeded Beauregard as head of the Department of South Carolina, Georgia, and Florida until January 1865. He surrendered at the war's end and was paroled in Tallahassee in May 1865. From

1866 to 1880, Jones farmed in Mattoax, Virginia. In 1880, he received a clerkship in the U.S. War Department, and in 1885, he went to work in the office of the judge advocate general. He died on July 31, 1887, in Bedford Springs, Virginia. Evans, *Confederate Military History*, III; Jones, *The Siege of Charleston*.

JONES, Thomas McKissick (*Congressman*), was born to Wilson and Rebecca (McKissick) Jones on December 16, 1816, in Person County, North Carolina, but he was brought as a baby to Giles County, Tennessee, where he spent most of the rest of his life. He received his education at Wirtenburg Academy in Pulaski, Tennessee, prior to graduating from the University of Alabama in 1833 and from the University of Virginia in 1835. He read law in 1836 and was admitted to the Pulaski bar where he developed a successful law practice. On December 25, 1838, he married Marietta Perkins, by whom he had nine children. His first wife died, and he married Mrs. Anne G. Wood on May 9, 1883. Jones was a lifelong Democrat and a vestryman in the Episcopal church. He served in the Florida war as captain of a Pulaski regiment. In 1845, he was sent to the Tennessee House of Representatives, and two years later he entered the state Senate. He was a delegate to the Charleston Democratic convention in 1860 and was a member of the provisional Confederate Congress in 1861. A severe critic of the arbitrary abuse of *habeas corpus*, Jones was a Davis administration supporter. He served on the Flag and Seal and Naval Affairs Committees. Jones declined reelection to Congress, entered the army, and was subsequently taken prisoner. Nothing further is known of his wartime career. When the war ended, he returned to his Pulaski law practice. In 1870, he was a delegate to the state constitutional convention. In 1872, he was named judge of the criminal court. He also served as a judge of the state Supreme Court and as mayor of Pulaski. He died there on March 13, 1892. Speer (comp.), *Biographical Directory of the Tennessee General Assembly*.

JONES, William Giles (*Judge*), son of a planter who was a nephew of William Branch Giles and his wife, a Miss Moseley, was born in Powhatan County, Virginia, on November 6, 1808. He attended Hampden-Sidney College and the University of Virginia and was admitted to the Virginia bar in 1830. Jones was a Whig who became a Democrat. He was married to a Miss Branch and, after her death, to a Miss Hobson; he had two sons. In 1834, he moved to Alabama to practice law. He represented Greene County in the Alabama legislature in 1843 and Mobile County in 1849 and 1857-1858, when he was chairman of the Judiciary Committee. In 1858, he was named a judge of the U.S. District Court for the Southern District of Alabama, a position which he retained throughout the Civil War under the Confederacy. His decisions were usually protective of his state, but he remained loyal to the Confederacy. After the war he was arrested and indicted for high treason against the federal government. But he was never tried for that offense; he was soon paroled and sent home. He practiced law in Mobile, where he died in 1883. Owen, *History of Alabama and Dictionary of Alabama Biography*, III; Robinson, *Justice in Grey*.

JORDAN, Thomas (*General*), was born on September 30, 1819, in Luray Valley, Virginia, to Gabriel and Elizabeth Ann (Sibert) Jordan. He graduated forty-first in a class of forty-two from the U.S. Military Academy in 1840. Jordan, a career officer in the U.S. Army before the Civil War, had one son and one daughter by his marriage to a Miss Kearny. He fought in the Seminole War in 1842 and served on frontier duty until 1846, when he was promoted to first lieutenant. During the Mexican War, he fought at Palo Alto and was assistant quartermaster for the army in 1847. From 1848 to 1861, he was stationed on the Pacific Coast. He resigned his commission in May 1861 and volunteered for duty in the Confederate Army. As a captain in the Confederate Army, he was P.G.T. Beauregard's (*q.v.*) chief of staff at the battle of First Manassas, where he directed the disposition of reinforcements. He was then sent west to assist Beauregard in the preparations for the battle at Shiloh, for which he was promoted to brigadier general on April 14, 1862. From July 1862 until the end of the Kentucky campaign, he served as General Braxton Bragg's (*q.v.*) chief of staff. He then was transferred to the same position under Beauregard in Charleston. In May 1864, he received command of the Third Military District of South Carolina. During the war, he was well-known for his superior organizational ability. He surrendered in South Carolina and was later paroled. In 1866, he edited the Memphis *Appeal*. The following year he wrote a book on *The Campaigns of Lt. General Forrest*. In 1869-1870, he was chief of staff for the insurgent army of Cuba. He then returned to edit the *Financial and Mining Record* in New York City, a magazine which he used to support the free coinage of silver. He died on November 27, 1895, in New York City. Evans, *Confederate Military History*, III.

K

KEAN, Robert Garlick Hill (*Bureaucrat*), son of John Vaughan and Caroline (Hill) Kean, was born in Caroline County, Virginia, on October 24, 1828. His father was a schoolteacher and planter of modest means. After attending Episcopal High School in Alexandria, Virginia, Rappahannock Academy, and Concord Academy, Kean attended the University of Virginia, receiving his B.A. in 1852 and his M.A. the following year. He was admitted to the bar in 1853 and began practicing law in Lynchburg, Virginia. Kean was a vestryman in the Episcopal church and a lifelong Democrat. He married Jane Nicholas Randolph, the daughter of Thomas J. Randolph, in 1854. In 1874, his first wife having died, he married Adelaide Prescott. Kean had five children by his marriages. An extreme states' rights advocate, he urged secession and joined the Virginia Home Guard at an early date. When the war began, he entered the Confederate Army as a private in the Southern Army of the Potomac, but after the battle of First Manassas he was made adjutant general to George W. Randolph (*q.v.*), his uncle by marriage. When Randolph became secretary of war, Kean was named chief of the Bureau of War, succeeding Albert Taylor Bledsoe (*q.v.*). He held this office for the remainder of the war, acting as office manager, executive secretary, and research assistant for the various secretaries of war. After the war, he returned to his law practice in Lynchburg. In 1881, he was city attorney in Lynchburg, and in 1890, he was made president of the Virginia Bar Association. He refused to run for political office and wanted to repay all of his war debts. He died in 1898. Younger (ed.), *Inside the Confederate Government: The Diary of Robert Garlick Hill Kean*.

KEEBLE, Edwin Augustus (*Congressman*), was born on February 14, 1807, in Cumberland County, Virginia, to Walter and Amanda (Shrewsbury) Keeble. He attended the University of North Carolina and was admitted to the bar in Murfreesboro, Tennessee, during the late 1820s, where he became an outstanding lawyer. He also owned a small plantation. Keeble had four children by his first marriage. On November 30, 1836, following his first wife's death, he married Mary W. Maney, by whom he had five children. He had a son by his third marriage to Sally Dickinson Bell. Keeble was publisher and editor of the Murfreesboro *Central Monitor* in 1834 and the *Monitor* in 1835. From 1838 to 1855, he was Democratic mayor of Murfreesboro. He also served as speaker of the lower house of Tennessee in the late 1850s and as director of a savings institute prior to the Civil War. He actively supported secession. Keeble was elected to the second Confederate Congress in 1863 without opposition. A Davis administration supporter, he served on the Judiciary Committee. After the war, he returned to the practice of law and was an opponent of the Brownlow administration. He died on August 26, 1868, in Murfreesboro. Sims (ed.), *A History of Rutherford County*; Speer (comp.), *Biographical Directory of the Tennessee General Assembly*.

KEITT, Lawrence Massillon (*Congressman*), was born to George and Mary Magdelene (Wannamaker) Keitt on October 4, 1824, in Orangeburg District, South Carolina. He graduated from South Carolina College in 1843, studied law, and was admitted to the Orangeburg bar in 1845. He and his wife, the former Susanna Sparks, had two daughters. Keitt served in the state House of Representatives from 1848 to 1852, during which time he became a single-state secessionist.

He served as a states' rights Democrat in the U.S. House of Representatives from 1853 until his resignation in 1856 and again from 1856 until 1860. He was also a delegate to the South Carolina secession convention and a member of the provisional Confederate Congress, where he opposed the election of Jefferson Davis (*q. v.*) to the presidency and supported Howell Cobb (*q. v.*) and helped to draft the Constitution and to organize the government. Keitt served on the Foreign Affairs and Indian Affairs Committees of the provisional Congress. He was a leader in the Confederate decision to fire on Fort Sumter. During the war, he also served as brigadier general of the 20th South Carolina Volunteers and commanded the forces on Sullivan's Island. In May 1864, he was sent to Virginia where he was mortally wounded at Cold Harbor. He died on June 2, 1864, near Richmond. Cauthen, *South Carolina Goes to War, 1861-1865*; Lee, *The Confederate Constitutions*; Wakelyn, *The Politics of a Literary Man*.

KELL, John McIntosh (*Naval Commander*), son of John and Margery (Baillie) Kell, was born at Darien, Georgia, on January 26, 1823. In 1841, when he was only seventeen years old, he received an appointment to the U.S. Military Academy. He had six children by his October 1856 marriage to Julia Blanche Munroe. Upon his graduation from the academy, Kell spent seventeen years in active service with the navy. During the Mexican War, he was engaged along the California coast. He was on the expedition sent to Paraguay against Lopez and also on Perry's expedition to Japan. In 1860, he was a junior lieutenant stationed in Pensacola. Early in 1861, Kell resigned his commission and accepted duty in the Confederate Navy. Until June 1864, Kell was an executive officer serving under Admiral Raphael Semmes (*q. v.*). He was first lieutenant and executive officer on the *Sumter*, which captured seventeen merchant vessels for the Confederacy. In August 1862, he was transferred to the *Alabama*, which sunk over sixty merchant men, including the *Hatteras*, before it was sunk by the federal ironclad *Kearsarge* in late 1862. Kell escaped capture and was promoted to full captain in 1863. Late in the war, he commanded the ironclad *Richmond*, which was stationed on the James River. There is no record of his having surrendered. After the war, finding himself broke and the coast country devastated, he moved to Sunnyside, Georgia. He engaged in agricultural pursuits and took no part in his state's political life. From 1886 to 1900, he was adjutant general for Georgia. He also published his *Recollections of a Naval Life* (1900). Kell died in Sunnyside on October 5, 1900. Kell, *Recollections of a Naval Life*.

KELLY, John Herbert (*General*), was born in March 1838 in Carrollton, Pickens County, Alabama, to Isham Harrison and Elizabeth (Herbert) Kelly. Orphaned at the age of seven, he was reared by his grandmother, Harriet Herbert Hawthorne. He was a bachelor. He was educated in the common schools in Pickens County and entered West Point in 1857. He resigned from the academy in late 1860 in order to enter service in the Confederate Army. Kelly had a brilliant military career. He accompanied General William Hardee (*q.v.*) to Missouri, fought as a colonel at the battles of Shiloh and Perryville, and was wounded at the battle of Murfreesboro in late 1862. He was a brigade commander at the battle of Chickamauga and was promoted to brigadier general on November 16, 1863. He commanded a cavalry division throughout the Atlanta campaign. Sent to Tennessee with Wheeler's Cavalry after Atlanta, he was conspicuous in the attempt to halt the federal invasion. Kelly died while leading a charge at the battle of Franklin, Tennessee, on August 20, 1864. *Annals of the Army of Tennessee*; Owen, *History of Alabama and Dictionary of Alabama Biography*, III.

KEMPER, James Lawson (*General*), son of William and Maria Elizabeth (Allison) Kemper, was born on June 11, 1823, in Madison County, Virginia. He attended Virginia Military Institute and received an M.A. from Washington College in Virginia in 1842. He had five children by his marriage to Cremora Conway Cave in 1853. Kemper also studied law and, in 1843, began a practice in Madison County. He volunteered for duty as a captain of Virginia Volunteers during the Mexican War in 1847. From 1848 to 1860, he represented Madison County in the Virginia House of Delegates, where he was chairman of the Military Affairs Committee and also served as speaker during 1858-1860. Although he was not originally a secessionist when the war began, he became a colonel of the 7th Regiment of Virginia Volunteers in May 1861. Kemper fought at the battle of First Manassas. A hero of the battle of Williamsburg, where he led his regiment on May 5, 1862, he was promoted to brigadier general on June 3, 1862 and fought in the battles of Seven Pines and the Seven Days before serving as a division commander at the battle of Second Manassas in August 1862. Later that year, he participated in the battles of South Mountain and Sharpsburg, Maryland, and Fredericksburg, Virginia. He was wounded and captured during the battle of Gettysburg in July 1863, underwent a long recovery, and saw no further field service. Upon his exchange in 1864, he commanded the Conscript Bureau and the Virginia Reserves. He was promoted to major general on September 19, 1864. During the last days of the war, he defended Richmond after the evacuation. He surrendered at the war's end and was paroled at Danville, Virginia. After the war, he returned to Madison County to practice law. A member of the Conservative party of his state, he served as governor of Virginia from 1874 to 1877. In 1877, the Virginia legislature wanted him to seek a seat in the U.S. Senate, but Kemper chose to retire to his farm instead. He died in Gordonsville, Orange County, Virginia, on April 7, 1895. Maddex, *The Virginia Conservatives*; Smith, *Virginia 1492-1892*.

KENAN, Augustus Holmes (*Congressman*), was born to Thomas Holmes and Aurelia (Powell) Kenan in Montpelier, Baldwin County, Georgia, in 1805. Little is known of his education or early training. His first marriage to Henrietta G. Alston ended in divorce. Kenan married Sarah Barnes in the 1830s; they had two sons. He was a Methodist, an ardent Whig, and a close friend of Henry Clay. He settled in Milledgeville, Georgia, where he became a criminal lawyer. For twenty years he was the clerk of the court for Baldwin County. In 1835, he served on the staff of Winfield Scott in the Indian campaign in Florida, where he was also a friend of Joseph E. Johnston (*q.v.*). The same year he helped to remove the Cherokee Indians from Georgia. Before the Civil War, Kenan also served in both houses of the state legislature. At one time he worked for the state arsenal, the state penitentiary, and the state deaf and dumb asylum. Although he was opposed to secession and to slavery, he represented Baldwin County at the Georgia secession convention, where he voted against the Ordinance of Secession thirteen times but finally signed it. As a member of the provisional Congress, he served on the Military Affairs and Engrossment Committees. Although he generally opposed the administration in the provisional Congress, Kenan turned into an administration loyalist upon being elected to the first Confederate House. He served on the Military Affairs and Conference Committees and was an opponent of the Foote faction. He returned often to Georgia to encourage the people to support President Davis (*q.v.*). When his term ended, he refused reelection and retired to his home in Milledgeville. He saw no further service and died at home on June 16, 1865. Cook, *History of Baldwin County, Georgia*; Northen (ed.), *Men of Mark in Georgia*, IV.

KENAN, Oren Rand (*Congressman*), was born into a wealthy cotton- and tobacco-growing family in Kenansville, North Carolina, on March 4, 1804. He attended private schools, read law, and began a practice in 1825. Kenan soon left his law practice to run the family plantation. He served as a Democrat in the North Carolina House from 1834 until 1838, and then dropped out of politics. After the election of Lincoln, he became a secessionist. Elected to the first Confederate House, he supported the Davis administration and vigorously pursued the defense of the North Carolina coast from the Union Navy. A strong localist, Kenan refused to support the tax-in-kind. He did not seek election to the second Congress, and he returned to his plantation. After the war Kenan returned to the practice of law, but he held no further political office. He died near Kenansville on March 3, 1887. Register (comp.), *The Kenan Family and Some Allied Families*.

KENNER, Duncan Farrar (*Congressman, Diplomat*), son of William and Mary (Minor) Kenner, was born on February 11, 1813, in New Orleans, Louisiana, where his father was a prosperous merchant. He attended public schools in New Orleans, graduated from Miami University of Ohio in 1831, and spent the next four years traveling in Europe. Although he studied law under John Slidell (*q.v.*), he never practiced, becoming, in 1835, a sugar planter and horse breeder at his plantation "Ashland" in Ascension Parish. On June 1, 1839, he married Anne Guillelmine Nanine Bringier. Kenner, a Whig, served in the Louisiana legislature from 1836 to 1850 and lost a race for the U.S. Senate in 1849. He was a delegate to the state constitutional conventions of 1844 and 1852, serving as president of the latter. He supported secession. In the provisional Confederate Congress, he served on the Finance and Patents Committees and was responsible for the formation of the Congress under the permanent constitution. Elected to the first Confederate House from the Third District of Louisiana, he was reelected in 1864. He was chairman of the Ways and Means Committee of the Confederate House throughout the war. An administration supporter, he was one of the most important members of the Congress, as much of the administration legislation was steered through his committee. In 1864, he was sent as special commissioner to France and Great Britain, where he promised an end to slavery in return for diplomatic recognition from these nations. After the war, he found his plantation in ruins, but his great business skill enabled him to recoup his losses. He was president of the Louisiana Sugar Planters Association in 1877, and he subsequently became president of the New Orleans Gas Company, the Crescent Cotton Seed Oil Company, and the Louisiana Sugar Company. Kenner also had an active postwar political career. In 1866-1867, he served in the state Senate. He lost a bid for the U.S. Senate in 1879, running as a Democrat. In 1883, President Arthur named him to the U.S. Tariff Commission. He died in New Orleans, Louisiana, on July 3, 1887. Arthur and deKernion, *Old Families of Louisiana*; *Biographical and Historical Memoirs of Louisiana*.

KERSHAW, Joseph Brevard (*General*), son of Colonel John Kershaw and his wife Harrietta (Du Bose), was born on January 5, 1822, in Camden, South Carolina, where his father was at one time mayor. He attended the Cokesbury Conference School in Abbeville, South Carolina, was admitted to the bar in 1843, and began a practice in Camden in 1844, after serving on the governor's staff for a year. Kershaw was a Quaker, a Mason, and a Democrat. He married Lucretia Douglas in 1844; they had four daughters, and their only son later served as rector of St. Michael's Parish in Charleston. During the Mexican War, he was a first lieutenant in the Palmetto Regiment. From 1852 to 1856, he was a member of the state House, and in 1860, he was a delegate to the South Carolina secession convention. When the Civil War began, he entered the Confederate Army as colonel of the 2nd South Carolina Infantry and was stationed at Sullivan's Island near Charleston before going to Virginia to fight with his regiment at the battle of First Manassas. Promoted to brigadier general on February 13, 1862, he fought at Yorktown, the Seven Days, and Fredericksburg in 1862 and at Chancellorsville in the spring of 1863, all with the Army of Northern Virginia. At Gettysburg he overran General Daniel Sickles' position, and he later was a division commander at Chickamauga and a hero of Chattanooga and the Knoxville campaign of 1863. He was promoted to major general on June 2, 1864. Kershaw fought at the Wilderness, Cold Harbor, Spotsylvania, and Petersburg, and in Early's (*q.v.*) Valley campaign in the spring and summer of 1864. In 1865, he opened the attack at Cedar Creek during the final phase of the siege of Richmond. He was captured at Sayler's Creek on April 6, 1865, and paroled in July. He returned to his law practice in Camden. Kershaw was elected to the state Senate in 1865 and was made its president. From 1877 to 1893, he was judge for the Fifth Judicial Circuit, and in 1894, he was named postmaster of Camden. He also wrote for *Battles and Leaders of the Civil War*. Kershaw died in Camden, South Carolina, on April 13, 1894. Brooks, *South Carolina Bench and Bar*; Freeman, *Lee's Lieutenants*, II.

KEYES, Wade, Jr. (*Cabinet Member*), was born in Mooresville, Alabama, in 1821, the son of General George and Nellie (Rutledge) Keyes. He was educated by private tutors and attended La Grange College in Georgia and the University of Virginia before moving to Lexington, Kentucky, in the late 1840s to study law. He had a daughter, Mary, by his marriage to a Miss Whitfield. Keyes was a Methodist and a Democrat. He moved to Tallahassee, Florida, in 1844 where he practiced law and then he moved to Montgomery, Alabama, in 1851. He was the author of two volumes on legal subjects: *An Essay on the Learning of Future Interests in Real Property* (1853) and *An Essay on the Learning of Remainders* (1854). In 1853, Keyes was given the chancellorship for the Southern Division of Alabama. He was a secessionist. When the Civil War began, he volunteered for duty in the Confederate Army but was assigned to staff duty in Richmond. Throughout the Civil War, he served as assistant attorney general for the Confederacy. During Judah P. Benjamin's (*q.v.*) term, Keyes actually conducted the affairs of the office. His opinions were detailed arguments backed by quotations from U.S. court cases. However, Keyes was no politician, and he was never able to obtain a cabinet office which his experience and ability merited. After the war, he had a law practice in Florence, Alabama. Little else is known about his postwar career. He died in Florence. Evans (ed.), *Confederate Military History*, VII; Patrick, *Jefferson Davis and His Cabinet*.

L

LAMAR, Gazaway Bugg (*Banker*), son of Basil and Rececca (Kelly) Lamar, was born in Richmond County, Georgia, on October 2, 1798. He was a relative of Henry Gazaway Lamar, who had represented Macon in the U.S. House of Representatives from 1829 to 1833. He was a Methodist. His October 21, 1821, marriage to Jane Meek Creswell ended tragically in June 1838, when she and their six children drowned in a steamship accident. He had two sons and three daughters by a second marriage to Harriet Cazenove. Lamar's relatives, members of an important Georgia family, were helpful in setting him up in business. His connections with Georgia's political leaders were also helpful in his career. Lamar achieved prominence in the financial circles of Augusta and Savannah. He introduced the first iron steamship, the *John Randolph*, to the United States in 1834, and in the following year he was an incorporator of the Iron Steam-Boat Company of Augusta. He also had an interest in the Mechanics Bank of Augusta. During the late 1830s and early 1840s, he helped his cousin, Mirabeau Lamar, by providing financial assistance to the Republic of Texas. One of his ships, the *Mary Semmes*, was used for transport by the U.S. government during the Mexican War. In 1845, Lamar moved to New York, where he became president of the Bank of Republic. In November 1860, he purchased and shipped ten thousand muskets to Georgia. Lamar supported the secession of Georgia. He was also an intelligence and postal agent for the Confederacy in New York until he moved to Savannah in early 1861 to become president of the Bank of Commerce. In July 1861, he served as president of the Bank Convention of the Confederate States. By 1863, however, he was in financial trouble, and he tried blockade running with Fernando Wood, former mayor of New York City. He considered the war over when Sherman took Atlanta, and he signed the oath of allegiance in an attempt to save his property. At the end of the war, he was arrested on alleged charges of trying to bribe federal officials. President Johnson had him released in late 1865, and he returned to his New York business interests. Lamar died on October 5, 1874, in New York City. *Appleton's Cyclopedia of American Biography, III*; Northen (ed.), *Men of Mark in Georgia*, IV.

LAMAR, Lucius Quintus Cincinnatus (*Diplomat, Judge*), son of Judge L.Q.C. and Sarah Williamson (Bird) Lamar, was born on September 17, 1825, in Putnam County, Georgia, where his father was a lawyer and a judge. He was related to Gazaway Bugg Lamar (*q.v.*). After attending schools in Baldwin and Newton Counties, Georgia, he graduated from Emory College in 1845 and studied law. In 1847, he moved to Columbus, Georgia, where on July 14, he married Virginia Longstreet, a daughter of Augustus B. Longstreet. They had one son and three daughters. She died, and, on January 5, 1887, he married Mrs. Henrietta Dean Holt, the daughter of James Dean of Georgia and the widow of General W. S. Holt. Lamar, a Democrat and a Methodist, practiced law in Oxford, Mississippi, in the late 1840s where he was also an assistant professor of mathematics at the University of Mississippi. In 1851, he became a champion of states' rights. He returned to Georgia, where he served in the state legislature in 1853. In 1855, he again moved to Oxford, where he owned a plantation called "Solitude" and practiced law. Elected to the U.S. House of Representatives from Mississippi in 1858, he was reelected in 1859 and took part in the secession debates of 1859-1860. While a delegate to the Charleston Democratic convention in 1860, he opposed the withdrawal of the Southern wing, fearing Southern disunity. As a member of the anti-Bell party, he opposed precipitant secession, cited the need for a plan of secession, and proposed that the Southern states continue to use the U.S. Constitution as a basis for their laws. In 1860, he was also named to a chair of ethics and metaphysics at the University of Mississippi. The following year, as a member of the Mississippi convention, he helped to frame the Ordinance of Secession. Lamar entered the war as a lieutenant colonel of the 8th Mississippi Regiment in early 1861. He was later promoted to colonel and fought in the battle of Williamsburg, but his military service was cut short by attacks of vertigo. In November 1862, President Davis (*q.v.*) appointed him special commissioner to Russia, France, and England, but the Confederate Senate refused to confirm his appointment. Lamar managed to negotiate some pro-Confederate naval conditions while he was in London. He returned to Georgia near the end of 1863. In March 1864, he defended the suspension of the writ of *habeas corpus* in Georgia, and in December of the same year, he went to Richmond as judge advocate for Ambrose P. Hill's (*q.v.*) Corps. There is no record of his surrender. After the war, Lamar practiced law and held professorships of ethics and metaphysics and of governmental science and law at the University of Mississippi. He was a delegate to the Mississippi constitutional conventions of 1865, 1868, 1875, 1877, and 1881. A compromiser, he served in the U.S. House of Representatives from 1872 to 1877. In 1876, he was elected to the U.S. Senate following an active campaign. He was reelected in 1883 and served until 1885, when he became President Grover Cleveland's secretary of the interior. He opposed the Greenback-Republican fusion. In 1888, he was named to the U.S. Supreme Court. Lamar died in Macon, Georgia, on January 23, 1893. Cate, *Lucius Q. C. Lamar*.

LAMKIN, John Tillman (*Congressman*), was born in Augusta, Georgia, on July 17, 1811, to William and Keziah (Snead) Lamkin. He studied law with James M. Bethune and was admitted to the bar in 1833. In November 1835, he married Thurza Ann Kilgore; they had one son. On Christmas Day 1835, the Lamkins moved to Texas, and they later went to New Orleans, where Lamkin became an accountant. In 1838, he began a law practice in Pike County, Mississippi. From 1841 to 1845, he was district attorney in Holmesville, Pike County. A Whig, he also owned a modest farm. Lamkin seems to have spent the last years before the war in pursuit of his law practice. A Mason and a unionist, he nevertheless acquiesced in support of the Confederacy after his long opposition to secession had failed. In April 1862, he raised the Holmesville Guards of the 33rd Mississippi Regiment, serving as a captain. On October 5, 1863, he was elected to the second Confederate House, defeating the radical secessionist John J. McRae (*q.v.*) for Congress. He served on the Commerce, Patents and Post Office and Post Roads Committees. Lamkin opposed the Davis administration, though he did not join the union faction in Congress. Lamkin had been one of the leading lawyers of his state before the war, but he never recovered financially or emotionally from the war's effects. He died in Holmesville, Mississippi, on May 19, 1870. *Biographical and Historical Memoirs of Mississippi*; Conerly, *Pike County, Mississippi*.

LANDER, William (*Congressman*), son of Samuel and Eliza Ann (Miller) Lander, was born on May 9, 1817, in Tiparo, Ireland. His family moved to the United States in 1818 and settled somewhere in the Northeast. They moved to Lincolnton, North Carolina, in 1826. The younger Lander, whose parents were members of the Church of England, attended Lincolnton Academy and the Cokesburg, South Carolina, Methodist School during the 1820s. He read law under James R. Dodge, was admitted to the bar in 1839, and built up a large practice in Lincolnton. He also owned a small plantation. He had four children by his marriage to Sarah Connor on May 8, 1839. Lander was elected to the North Carolina House in 1852, and from 1852 to 1862, he served as solicitor for the state Circuit Court. A Democrat and a pronounced secessionist, he attended the Democratic national convention in Charleston in 1860. He supported John C. Breckinridge (*q.v.*) for the presidency in 1860. As a delegate to the North Carolina secession convention, he voted for the Ordinance of Secession and continued to serve in the convention until he resigned in 1862 to enter the Confederate House. An active supporter of the Davis administration, Lander served on the Patents, War and Tax, and Quartermaster's Committees. Because of his radical views on pursuing the war effort, he was defeated for reelection by a moderate. Lander played no further role in the Confederate war effort. After the war, he returned to his law practice in Lincolnton, where he died on January 6, 1868. Sherrill, *Annals of Lincoln County, North Carolina*.

LANE, James Henry (*General*), was born on July 28, 1833, at Matthews Court House, Virginia, to Walter Gardner and Mary Ann Henry (Barkwell) Lane. He graduated with honors from Virginia Military Institute in 1854 and received his M.A. from the University of Virginia in 1857. Lane was an Episcopalian and a Democrat. He had four daughters by his marriage to Charlotte Randolph Meade on September 13, 1869. He was an assistant professor of mathematics at Virginia Military Institute from 1857 to 1859 and at Florida State Seminary until 1861, when he became a professor of natural philosophy and instructor of tactics at Charlotte Military Institute in North Carolina. When the Civil War began, he joined the North Carolina Volunteers. As major in the 1st North Carolina Volunteers, he participated in the battle of Big Bethel in June 1861. Lane served throughout the war with the Army of Northern Virginia and was wounded twice in the Peninsular campaign of 1862 before he was promoted to brigadier general on November 1, 1862. Among the major battles in which he participated were Sharpsburg, Fredericksburg, Chancellorsville, the Wilderness, and Petersburg. At the battle of Gettysburg he was part of Pickett's charge, and at Spotsylvania in the spring of 1864 he helped in the defense at the "bloody angle." He surrendered at Appomattox and was later paroled. After the war, he returned penniless to his birthplace in Virginia. He taught in private schools in Virginia for seven years and did further graduate study at the University of Virginia. From 1872 to 1880, he was a professor of natural philosophy and commerce at the Agricultural and Mechanical College of Virginia (later Virginia Polytechnic Institute). From 1880 to 1882, he was a professor of mathematics at the Missouri School of Mines, and from 1882 to 1907, he was a professor of civil engineering at Alabama Polytechnical Institute. Lane died on September 21, 1907, in Auburn, Alabama. Cox, *Address on the Life and Services of General James H. Lane, Army of Northern Virginia*.

LAW, Evander McIvor (*General*), was born on August 7, 1836, in Darlington, South Carolina, to Ezekiel Augustus and Sarah Elizabeth (McIvor) Law. His father was a lawyer and state legislator. The younger Law attended public schools, Old St. John's Academy, and South Carolina Military Academy in Charleston, where he graduated in 1856. He was a Democrat and a Presbyterian. He married Jane Elizabeth Lotta on March 9, 1863; they had three sons and one daughter. Before the war, he practiced law in Darlington. He was an assistant professor of belles lettres at the Citadel in 1857 and a professor of history and belles lettres at Kings Mountain Military Academy in Yorkville, South Carolina, from 1858 to 1860. In 1860, he moved to Tuskegee, Alabama, to found a military high school. When the Civil War began, he volunteered for service in the Confederate Army. He helped to recruit Alabama troops for the Confederate Army and was elected lieutenant colonel of the 4th Alabama Regiment. Law served under General Barnard Bee during the battle of First Manassas and won praise from General Thomas J. Jackson (*q.v.*) for his performance as a brigade leader during the Seven Days in the summer of 1862. After fighting at Second Manassas and Sharpsburg, he was promoted to brigadier general on October 3, 1862. At the battle of Gettysburg the following July, he assumed command of Hill's Division on the second day of the battle and led the assault on Round Top, where he lost two thousand men. He performed heroically at the battle of Chickamauga and was wounded at Cold Harbor in June 1864. During the last months of the war, he commanded a cavalry force under General Joseph E. Johnston (*q.v.*) in the Carolinas. He was promoted to major general on March 20, 1865. He surrendered in North Carolina. After the war, he returned to South Carolina to become a planter and to enter the railroad business. In the late 1860s, he moved to Tuskegee, Alabama. In 1872, he organized the Alabama Grange, and in 1881, he was named associate principal of Kings Mountain Institute in Alabama. When it closed in 1881 he moved to Florida. He established the Southern Florida Military Institute at Bartow, Florida, in 1894, and in 1908, he retired from the institute. In 1905, he edited the Bartow *Courier-Herald* from which he retired in 1915. Law died in Bartow in 1920. Freeman, *Lee's Lieutenants*, II, III; *Southern Bivouac*, II; *Southern Historical Society Papers*, VIII.

LAWTON, Alexander Robert (*General, Bureaucrat*), was born to Alexander James and Martha (Mosse) Lawton on November 4, 1818, in St. Peter's Parish, Beaufort District, South Carolina. He graduated thirteenth in a class of thirty-one from the U.S. Military Academy in 1839 and was assigned to the artillery. He resigned in 1841, studied law at Harvard in 1842, and began his practice in Savannah, Georgia, the following year. On November 5, 1845, he married Sarah Hillhouse Alexander, by whom he had two daughters. From 1849 to 1854, Lawton was president of the Augusta and Savannah Railroad. An immediate secessionist, in 1855 he was elected to the state legislature, where he was considered its strongest member. In 1860, he was elected to the Georgia Senate. When Georgia seceded, he resigned from the Senate and assisted in organizing a state regiment. As colonel of the 1st Volunteer Georgia Regiment, he seized Fort Pulaski, the first overt act of the war in Georgia. On April 13, 1861, he was commissioned a brigadier general and put in charge of Georgia's coastal defenses. In 1862, he was sent to Richmond, and he participated in the Valley campaign and the Seven Days. At the battle of Second Manassas, he commanded Ewell's (*q. v.*) division. Lawton was wounded at the battle of Sharpsburg in 1862 and was disabled until May 1863. Because he was an excellent military organizer, President Davis (*q. v.*) named him quartermaster general on February 17, 1864, a position which he did not want but which he filled for the duration of the war. There is no record of his surrender. After the war, he practiced law in Savannah. From 1870 to 1875, he served in the state legislature. In 1876, he was the chairman of the state electoral college, and the following year he was vice-president of the Georgia constitutional convention. In 1880, he ran unsuccessfully for the U.S. Senate as a Democrat. President Cleveland nominated him minister to Russia in 1885, but since his disabilities had not been removed, he could not serve. Two years later, after their removal, he became minister to Austria, a post which he held until 1889. Lawton died in retirement in Clifton Springs, New York, on July 2, 1896. Northen (ed.), *Men of Mark in Georgia*, IV; Vandiver, *Ploughshares into Swords*.

LEACH, James Madison (*Congressman*), was born to William and Nancy (Brown) Leach on January 17, 1815, in Randolph County, North Carolina. He attended Caldwell Institute and graduated from the U.S. Military Academy in 1838. He resigned his commission shortly after graduation. He studied law, was admitted to the bar in 1842, and began his practice in Lexington, North Carolina. On June 24, 1846, he married Eliza Montgomery. From 1848 to 1858, Leach served in the state House as a member of the Whig, and later the American, party. While in the U.S. House of Representatives from 1859 to 1861, he opposed secession. However, when the war began, he resigned from Congress and volunteered for service in the Confederate Army. During the war, he held the ranks of captain and lieutenant colonel in the army and served as a unionist in the second Confederate House in 1864-1865. He claimed to have been a member of the peace party which advocated Reconstruction. He served on the Illegal Seizures and the

Quartermaster's and Commissary Departments Committees. After the war, he became a Democrat and served in the state Senate in 1865, 1866, and 1879. He also practiced law in Lexington. He served as a conservative in the U.S. House of Representatives from 1871 to 1875. Leach died in Lexington, North Carolina, on June 1, 1891. Barnes, *A History of the Congress of the United States, 1875-1877*; Hamilton, *Reconstruction in North Carolina*.

LEACH, James Thomas (*Congressman*), was born in 1805 in Johnston County, North Carolina. He married Elizabeth W. Sanders on July 19, 1833, and they had at least one son. He studied medicine at Jefferson Medical College in Philadelphia. He was a doctor and a farmer who served in the North Carolina legislature from 1858 to 1860 as a Whig. He opposed secession. While a state senator from Johnston County, Leachburg, North Carolina, during the early stages of the war, he became a strong supporter of Jonathan Worth (*q.v.*). In his campaign for the second Confederate House, Leach denied the right of secession. He was a unionist in the Confederate Congress, and he opposed the Davis administration on almost every issue. In September 1863, he published a broadside, "Fellow-Citizens of the Third Congressional District," which earned him a place in the leadership of the peace movement of the second Congress. He opposed allowing reporters in the legislative sessions, opposed arming slaves, and wrote a resolution calling for peace without independence. After the war he returned to his plantation in Johnston County. In 1867, he was an ally of William W. Holden (*q.v.*) and a member of the pro-Reconstruction radicals of North Carolina. He died in Johnston County on March 28, 1883. Hamilton, *Reconstruction in North Carolina*; Zuber, *Jonathan Worth: A Biography of a Southern Unionist*.

LEE, Fitzhugh (*General*), son of Commodore Sydney Smith Lee and his wife Anna Maria (Mason), who was a sister of James M. Mason (*q.v.*), was born on November 19, 1835, in Fairfax County, Virginia. He was a nephew of General Robert E. Lee (*q.v.*), and his father was an officer in the Confederate Navy. Lee graduated forty-fifth in a class of forty-nine from the U.S. Military Academy in 1856. He was an Episcopalian. He had five children by his April 19, 1871, marriage to Elen Bernard Foule. Lee was wounded in May 1859 during the Indian campaigns in Texas, where he served as a second lieutenant under Edmund Kirby Smith (*q.v.*), and as adjutant to Earl Van Dorn (*q.v.*). In May 1860, he became a cavalry instructor at West Point. On May 3, 1861, he resigned from the U.S. Army and volunteered his services to Virginia. At the battle of First Manassas, he was adjutant general to General R. S. Ewell (*q.v.*) and in August 1861, he was lieutenant colonel of the 1st Virginia Cavalry. Promoted to brigadier general on July 24, 1862, he fought with the Army of Northern Virginia at Sharpsburg and Gettysburg. On August 3, 1863, he was promoted to major general, and late that same year he was given command of a cavalry division in the Army of Northern Virginia. He helped to halt Grant's advance at Spotsylvania Court House in May

1864, but later that year he was severely wounded at the battle of Winchester. After his recovery, in the spring of 1865, he commanded all cavalry in the Army of Northern Virginia, and he was one of three corps commanders on the Council of War prior to the surrender at Appomattox. He surrendered at Farmville, Virginia, on April 11, 1865, and was soon paroled. After the war, he was a farmer in Stafford County, Virginia, until he was called out of retirement to serve as Democratic governor of Virginia from 1885 to 1889. In 1890, he was an internal revenue collector in Virginia. Lee ran unsuccessfully for the U.S. Senate in 1893. He served as U.S. consul general to Havana from 1896 to 1898. At the outbreak of the Spanish-American War, he was commissioned a major general in the army but never actually fought. He died on April 28, 1905, in Washington, D.C. Tyler, *Encyclopedia of Virginia Biography*, III; *Who's Who in America*, 1905.

LEE, George Washington Custis (*General*), was born to Robert Edward (*q.v.*) and Mary Anne Randolph (Custis) Lee on September 16, 1832, at Fortress Monroe, Virginia. He graduated first in a class of forty-six from the U.S. Military Academy in 1854 and served in the Engineering Bureau of the army from 1855 to 1861. He was an Episcopalian and a bachelor. He resigned his commission on May 2, 1861, and volunteered for duty in the Confederate Army. As a major of engineers, he helped to fortify Richmond in July 1861, and the following month he was promoted to colonel and named aide-de-camp to President Davis (*q.v.*). Lee was promoted to brigadier general on June 25, 1863, and to major general on October 20, 1864. He saw active field service only during the final months of the war, when he organized the clerks and mechanics of Richmond for the emergency defense of that city. He was a trusted member of Davis's staff. Lee was captured with General R. S. Ewell (*q.v.*) at Sayler's Creek, Virginia, in April 1865. He was soon paroled and returned to Virginia. From 1865 to 1871, he was a professor of civil and military engineering and applied mechanics at Virginia Military Institute, and from 1871 to 1896, he was president of Washington and Lee University. He died in retirement at Burke's Station, Virginia, on February 18, 1913. Freeman, *Robert E. Lee*, III.

LEE, Robert Edward (*General-in-Chief of the Armies*), was born on January 19, 1807, in Westmoreland County, Virginia. He was the son of Henry Lee, the famous "Light Horse Harry" of the American Revolution, and his wife Anne Hill (Carter). Henry Lee was governor of Virginia—and he was also a compulsive gambler who lost all his money in land speculation before dying in 1818. Hence, Robert was raised in genteel poverty. He attended school in Alexandria and graduated from West Point in 1829, second in a class of forty-six. His first assignment was as second lieutenant of engineers at Fort Pulaski, Georgia. He was an Episcopalian and a Whig. He married Mary Ann Randolph Custis, who came from a wealthy and established Virginia family, and they had seven children. He held a series of engineering assignments: Fort Monroe, 1831-1834; assistant in the chief engineer's office in Washington, 1834-1837; superintendent of engineers at St. Louis Harbor 1837-1841; and engineer at Fort Hamilton, New York, 1841-1846. He was promoted to first lieutenant in 1836 and to captain in 1838. In 1847, he served in the Mexican War at Buena Vista, Vera Cruz, Cerro Gordo, Churubusco, and Chapultepec (where he was wounded). He was breveted a colonel in 1848. From 1848 to 1852, he served as head of construction at Fort Carroll in Baltimore Harbor, and from 1852 to 1855, he was superintendent at West Point. In 1855, Lee was made lieutenant colonel of the 2nd Cavalry, but his wife's illness kept him in Virginia for most of the late 1850s. In 1859, he was called upon to put down John Brown's raid. The Army high command, fearing secession sentiment in the Virginian, sent him to command the Department of Texas in 1860, and in March 1861, he was named colonel of the 1st Cavalry. Lee was a unionist who owned no slaves, but his first loyalty was to Virginia. Thus, when Virginia seceded, he resigned his commission in the U.S. Army. In April 1861, he was placed in charge of all Confederate forces, and he soon became military advisor to President Jefferson Davis (*q.v.*) with the rank of general. He was sent to examine the defenses of the South Atlantic seaboard but returned to Richmond in March 1862. When Joseph E. Johnston (*q.v.*) was wounded at Seven Pines, Lee became commander of the Army of Northern Virginia. He stopped McClellan in the Seven Days' battles in June and July 1862. He defeated Pope at Second Manassas on August 29-30, 1862, but was decisioned at Sharpsburg in September. He was decisive at Fredericksburg in December 1862 and stopped Hooker at Chancellorsville in May 1863. Believing that another thrust north would win the war for the Confederacy, he persuaded President Davis to allow the Pennsylvania campaign, which ended in disaster for the Confederacy at Gettysburg on July 1-3, 1863. A genius at field fortification, he magnificently held the Union armies from Richmond in the Wilderness campaign from May to June 1864. When Grant decided to take Richmond from the South, Lee defended Petersburg from July 1864 until April 1865. Grant finally broke through his lines on April 2, 1865, and Lee was forced to surrender the Army of Northern Virginia at Appomattox on April 9, 1865. He had previously been named general-in-chief of the Confederate Armies and had resisted a congressional move to make him dictator of the Confederacy. Always close to Davis, Lee had the unique ability to advise the president and to subordinate his efforts to the general war effort. Because of his concern with the defense of Richmond, Lee has recently become a controversial figure in military history. It is doubtful that the image of the ''lost cause'' will ever be disentangled from the compassion and supposed military genius of Lee. After the war, he was paroled to Richmond, and he devoted the rest of his life to rebuilding Washington College (later Washington and Lee University in honor of Lee) in Lexington, Virginia, as its president. He was indicted for treason but was never brought to trial. He died in Lexington on October 12, 1870. Freeman, *Robert E. Lee: A Biography*, I-IV.

LEE, Stephen Dill (*General*), was born to Thomas and Caroline (Allison) Lee on September 22, 1833, in Charleston, South Carolina. He graduated seventeenth in a class of forty-six from the U.S. Military Academy in 1854. He had one child by his marriage to Regina Harrison on February 9, 1865. Lee served as adjutant of Florida and quartermaster of his regiment during the Seminole War of 1857. He also saw frontier service in Kansas and the Dakotas from 1858 to 1861. He resigned his commission in the U.S. Army in February 1861 and volunteered for duty in the Confederate Army. As aide-de-camp to General P.G.T. Beauregard (*q.v.*), Lee was sent to demand the surrender of Fort Sumter in the early days of the war. After fighting at Seven Pines, the Seven Days, and Second Manassas and serving with distinction as artillery commander at Sharpsburg, he was promoted to brigadier general on November 6, 1862. He repulsed Sherman at Chickasaw Bayou, and in May 1863, he was the hero of the battle of Champion Hills. Captured during the siege of Vicksburg, he was soon exchanged. On August 3, 1863, he was promoted to major general, and on June 23, 1864, he was promoted to lieutenant general in command of the Department of Mississippi and Alabama. He succeeded Hood (*q.v.*) as commander of the Army of Tennessee and covered the Confederate retreat from Nashville, where he was severely wounded in late 1864. However, he continued to command the Army of Tennessee in the North Carolina campaigns until the war ended. He surrendered in North Carolina on April 16, 1865, and was paroled that May. After the war, he moved to Columbus, Mississippi, and became a planter. A Democrat, he served in the state Senate in 1878 and was a delegate to the constitutional convention of 1890. From 1880 to 1899, he was president of Mississippi Agricultural and Mechanical College, and in 1899, he headed the Vicksburg National Park Association. Author of *The South Since the War* (1899), he was also head of the United Confederate Veterans. He died on May 28, 1908, in Vicksburg. *Confederate Veteran*, VI.

LEE, William Henry Fitzhugh ("Rooney") (*General*), second son of Robert Edward (*q.v.*) and Mary Anne Randolph (Custis) Lee, was born on May 31, 1837, at the Custis home "Arlington." He attended Harvard University for one year before entering the U.S. Army in 1857. He served in Utah but resigned his commission in 1859 to take charge of the family estates in Kent County, Virginia. He was a Democrat and an Episcopalian. He married Charlotte Wickham in 1859 and, after her death, Mary Tabb Bolling in 1867. When the Civil War began, Lee organized a cavalry company. He entered the Confederate Army in May 1861 as colonel of the 9th Virginia Cavalry and served under General J.E.B. Stuart (*q.v.*) in all cavalry campaigns of the Army of Northern Virginia. He was promoted to brigadier general on September 15, 1862. He fought at the battles of Fredericksburg and Chancellorsville before being wounded and captured at the battle of Brandy Station in June 1863. He was exchanged in March 1864 and on April 23, 1864, became the youngest major general in the Confederacy. At the time of the surrender at Appomattox, he was second in command of all cavalry. He was paroled soon after the surrender. After the war, he returned to the management of his family's farmlands in Virginia and served as president of the Virginia Agricultural Society during the 1870s. From 1875 to 1879, he served in the state Senate, and from 1887 to 1891, he was a Democrat in the U.S. House of Representatives. He died in Loudoun County, Virginia, on October 15, 1891. Freeman, *Lee's Lieutenants*, II-III; *Robert E. Lee*, II-IV.

LESTER, George Nelson (*Congressman*), was born in Abbeville District, South Carolina, on March 13, 1824, the son of Richard Henry and Mary (Sims) Lester. When he was four years old, he moved with his parents to Gwinnet County, Georgia, where he spent his youth hard at work on his father's farm. Largely self-educated, he read law under N. L. Hutchins of Lawrenceville, Georgia, and began his law practice in 1843. His marriage to Margaret L. Irwin on November 1, 1843, produced seven children. Lester became a successful lawyer in Cumming, Forsyth County, and then moved to Cobb County, Georgia, where he was elected to the state legislature in the 1850s and served as chairman of the Judiciary Committee. In 1855, he became a reporter for the state Supreme Court. He was a Democrat and a secessionist. When the Civil War began, he volunteered for service in the Confederate Army and organized the 41st Georgia Regiment. Lester fought in the Kentucky campaign in the fall of 1862, losing his right arm in the battle of Perryville. Later, he joined the state reserves and in 1864 represented the Sixth District of Georgia in the second Confederate House. He served on the Quartermaster's and Commissary Departments Committee, but he was often absent from Richmond. After the war, he practiced law in Marietta, Georgia. During Reconstruction, he was commissioner of the Home Department for the Georgia Bureau of Immigration. He was judge of the Blue Ridge Circuit and helped Judge Irwin to revise the state legal code during the 1880s. In 1888, he served as president of the Georgia electoral college. In 1890, he became attorney general of Georgia. Lester died in Marietta on March 30, 1892. Northen (ed.), *Men of Mark in Georgia*, III.

LETCHER, John (*Governor*), son of William Houston and Elizabeth (Davidson) Letcher, was born on March 29, 1812, in Lexington, Rockbridge County, Virginia. He attended Randolph-Macon College, graduated from Washington College in Lexington in 1833, and was admitted to the Virginia bar in 1839. He was a Democrat and a Presbyterian. He had nine children by his marriage to Mary S. Holt. Letcher, who developed an excellent legal practice in Lexington, also edited the *Valley Star*, a strongly Democratic newspaper in a Whig county, from 1840 to 1850. In 1847, he signed the Ruffner paper advocating the abolition of slavery in West Virginia, but as a member of the U.S. House of Representatives from 1851 to 1859, he defended the South and became a proslavery spokesman. He served on the House Ways and Means Committee. While a delegate to the state constitutional convention in 1850-1851, he favored a white basis of electoral representation. However, in 1859 the Whigs of his state labeled him an abolitionist in a heated gubernatorial campaign in which he carried only two congressional districts in the east. Elected governor of Virginia in 1860, he supported Stephen A. Douglas for president the same year. He helped to organize the peace convention in Washington in 1861, yet he gave strong support to the Confederacy. His calling of the General Assembly led to that body's taking Virginia out of the Union. Letcher tried to keep western Virginia within the Confederacy and helped to organize the provisional army of the state. In June 1864, Union troops burned his home in Lexington. An able administrator, Letcher generally ran only a caretaker government because the Confederate government controlled Virginia. After the war, he practiced law in Lexington, served as a Democrat in the state House from 1875 to 1877, and was a member of the Board of Visitors at Virginia Military Institute from 1866 to 1880. Letcher died on January 26, 1884, in Lexington. Boney, *John Letcher of Virginia*.

LEWIS, David Peter (*Congressman, Judge*), was born to Peter C. and Mary Smith (Buster) Lewis in 1820 in Charlotte County, Virginia. His parents later moved to Madison County, Alabama. The younger Lewis attended college and, from 1842 until 1861, practiced law in Huntsville. Aside from the fact that he was a Democrat, never married, and owned a plantation, little is known about his early life. Although he voted against secession as a delegate to the convention, he signed the Alabama Secession Ordinance. As a member of the provisional Congress, he served on the Patents and Indian Affairs Committees; he resigned before the end of his term and retired to private life. In 1863, Governor John Shorter (*q.v.*) named him judge of the Circuit Court of Alabama. A committed unionist, Lewis fled to Nashville before the war ended, but he did not cooperate with the Union forces. After the war, he returned to Alabama and his law practice. He was elected Republican governor of Alabama in 1873-1874, achieving a reputation as an excessive spender. At the end of Reconstruction, he was vilified by former Confederates and was forced to retire to private life. He died on July 3, 1884, in Huntsville, Alabama. Owen, *History of Alabama and Dictionary of Alabama Biography*, III; Woolfolk, ''Five Men Called Scalawags,'' *Alabama Review*, XVII.

LEWIS, David W. (*Congressman*), was born on October 24, 1815, in Hancock County, Georgia, to Thomas and Nancie (Hardwick) Lewis. He attended schools in Sparta, Georgia, and the University of North Carolina before graduating from Franklin College (later the University of Georgia) in 1837. He had six children by his marriage to Martha E. Meriwether. Lewis served as private secretary to Governor George R. Gilmer before he began a law practice in Sparta in 1843. Lewis was a Whig until 1854 and owned a sizable plantation. From 1845 to 1855, he represented Hancock County in the Georgia state legislature. He also helped to establish the Georgia State Agricultural Society. He supported the secession of his state. As the representative from Georgia's Fifth District to the first Confederate House, he achieved a reputation as a wise, cautious public servant who supported the Davis administration. He served on the Rules, Territories and Public Lands, and Printing Committees. He refused service in the second Congress and returned to his plantation. When the war ended, he again practiced law for a time. From 1873 to 1885, he was president of the Northern Georgia Agricultural College. Lewis died in Hancock County on December 28, 1885. Northen (ed.), *Men of Mark in Georgia*.

LEWIS, John W. (*Congressman, Manufacturer*), was born on February 1, 1801, in Spartanburg District, South Carolina, to Joel and ——— (Merham) Lewis. His father died while he was young. Lewis attended Cedar Springs Academy and studied medicine with Dr. Richard Harris of Greenville, South Carolina. He married Maria Earle in 1834. In 1830-1831, he served in the South Carolina legislature. He also began another career as a Baptist preacher. In 1840, he moved to Canton, Georgia, where he became a pastor and built iron furnaces. He was elected as a Democrat to the Georgia Senate in 1845. In Georgia, Lewis became a wealthy farmer as well as a physician and a preacher. He was an early benefactor of Governor Joseph E. Brown (*q.v.*), who at one time had taught school in Lewis's home. In 1846, he loaned Brown money to go to Yale; in return, when Brown became governor, he made Lewis his superintendent of state roads in 1857, and Lewis made sweeping changes in personnel and train schedules. A secessionist, he was defeated for election to the first Confederate House. He was Brown's appointee to the Confederate Senate in 1861-1862, where, with his keen business sense, he was considered one of the most practical members. An opponent of the administration, he was a member of the congressional bloc which supported Beauregard (*q.v.*) for commander of the armies in the west. He served on the Finance, Post Office and Post Roads, and special committees. After he resigned from the Senate in 1862, he manufactured salt for the Confederacy at Saltville, Georgia. Lewis died in Canton, Georgia, in June 1865. Hill, *Joseph E. Brown and the Confederacy*; *History of the Baptist Denomination in Georgia*.

LEWIS, Joseph Horace (*General*), was born to John and Eliza Martz (Reed) Lewis on October 29, 1824, in Glasgow, Barren County, Kentucky. He was from a well-to-do family. Lewis graduated from Centre College in Danville, Kentucky, in 1843 and read law under Judge C. C. Tompkins before being admitted to the Glasgow bar in 1845. He had two children by his marriage to Sarah H. Rogers on November 29, 1845. Following the death of his first wife, he married Cassandra (Flournoy) Johnson, daughter of Thompson B. Flourney, on March 29, 1883. Lewis served three terms as a Whig in the Kentucky House between 1845 and 1853 before he joined the Democrats after the rise of the Know-Nothing party. He was an ardent Southerner who supported John C. Breckinridge (*q.v.*) for president in 1860. He ran unsuccessfully as a Democrat for the U.S. House in 1857 and again in 1861, losing to a unionist. When the war began, he volunteered to recruit troops for the Confederate Army. In September 1861, he became colonel of the 6th Kentucky Regiment, with whom he fought at the battles of Shiloh, Corinth, Stone River, Murfreesboro, Jackson, and Chickamauga. Promoted to brigadier general on September 30, 1863, he led the Orphan Brigade, which fought during the Atlanta campaign at Missionary Ridge, Ringgold Gap, Mill Creek Gap, Resaca, New Hope Church, Pine Mountain, Kenesaw Mountain, and Peachtree Creek. After the fall of Atlanta, the brigade joined General Joseph Wheeler's (*q.v.*) Cavalry Corps, with whom they fought through the battle of Bentonville, North Carolina. He surrendered at Washington Court House, North Carolina, at the conclusion of the war and was soon paroled. Lewis returned to his Glasgow law practice, and in 1868, he was elected to the Kentucky legislature. From 1870 to 1873, he served as a Democrat in the U.S. House. A circuit judge in 1880, he was later named to the state Court of Appeals, where he was chief justice from 1882 to 1904. He retired to his farm in Glasgow, where he died on July 6, 1904. Levin (ed.), *The Lawyers and Lawmakers of Kentucky*.

LOGAN, George W. (*Congressman*), was born to John and Martha (Harton) Logan on February 22, 1815, in Chimney Rock, North Carolina, where his father kept a tavern. He studied law, was admitted to the North Carolina bar, and began a practice in Rutherfordton, North Carolina. He also dealt in real estate and farmed. He was a Baptist and a Whig. He had five children by his marriage to Amelia Dovey Wilson, and after her death he married Mary Elizabeth Cabiness. In 1838-1839, he was clerk and master in equity in the local court. From 1841 to 1849, he was clerk of the county court, and in 1855-1856, he was county solicitor. In 1858, he was editor of the *Rutherford Engineer*. Although he was a staunch unionist, Logan supported the Confederate cause. He had no role in the early years of the Civil War. In 1863, he was elected to the second Confederate House as a peace candidate by the Red String Organization, a band of war deserters from the Rutherfordton area whose platform was hostility to President Davis (*q.v.*). They were a small farmer class who lacked full social recognition and were thought to base their political views on envy and hatred of higher social classes. In Congress, Logan worked on proposals for peace, based on state action. He served on the Printing and Ordnance and Ordnance Stores Committees. He and his allies returned to the unionist cause before the end of the war, preparing for power once the war had ended. When the war ended, Logan became a lieutenant of William W. Holden (*q.v.*), joined the Republican party, and was a delegate to the state convention in 1865. In 1866, he served in the state legislature, and he was a Superior Court judge from 1868 until his defeat in 1874. He knew only a little about law, however, and was an incompetent judge; even the Republicans deserted him. In 1870, he was a member of the Rutherfordton City Council. He was part of a faction which controlled the *Star*, a newspaper hostile to the Ku Klux Klan. In 1883, he was involved in a railroad company. He died on October 18, 1899, in Rutherfordton. Griffin, *History of Old Tryon and Rutherford Counties*.

LOMAX, Lunsford Lindsay (*General*), was born on November 4, 1835, in Newport, Rhode Island, to Major Mann Page and Elizabeth Virginia (Lindsay) Lomax of Virginia. He attended schools in Richmond and Norfolk and graduated twenty-first in a class of forty-nine from the U.S. Military Academy in 1856. He had children by his marriage to Elizabeth Winter Payne on February 20, 1873. Lomax served as a first lieutenant on frontier duty in Kansas and Nebraska until April 1861, when he resigned his U.S. Army commission to enter the Confederate Army as assistant adjutant general to General Joseph E. Johnston (*q.v.*). He was later inspector general to General Ben McCulloch in Texas and to the Army of Tennessee under General Earl Van Dorn (*q.v.*). Lomax fought in many battles in the west, including Pea Ridge, Farmington, Corinth, Vicksburg, Baton Rouge, and Spring Hill. As colonel of the 11th Virginia Cavalry, he fought at Brandy Station, West Virginia, in June 1863 and at Gettysburg in July. He was promoted to brigadier general on July 23, 1863, and to major general on August 10, 1864. During the spring and early summer of 1864, he served under Fitzhugh Lee (*q.v.*) at the Virginia battles of Culpeper, Wilderness, Cold Harbor, and Yellow Tavern. Lomax also distinguished himself in Early's (*q.v.*) Valley campaign, and after the battles of Winchester, Reams' Station, and Woodstock, he was named commander of Early's Cavalry wing on October 31. In March 1865, he took command of the Ninth Valley District, which at that time included northern Virginia. He surrendered his division in May 1865 at Greensboro, North Carolina, and was soon paroled. From 1865 to 1885, Lomax farmed near Warrenton, Virginia. From 1885 to 1899, he was president of Blacksburg College (later merged into Virginia Polytechnic Institute), and between 1899 and 1905, he helped to compile the *Official Records of the Union and Confederate Armies*. In 1905, he was named commandant of Gettysburg National Military Park. He died on May 28, 1913, in Washington, D.C. Ellsworth, *West Point in the Confederacy*; McDonald (ed.), *Make Me a Map of the Valley*.

LONG, Armistead Lindsay (*General*), was born on September 3, 1825 (or September 13, 1827) in Campbell County, Virginia, to Colonel Armistead and Callista (Cralle) Long. He graduated seventeenth in a class of forty-four from the U.S. Military Academy in 1850. Long, whose father-in-law, Edwin V. Sumner, was a U.S. Army general, had two children by his marriage to Mary Heron Sumner. He had garrison duty at Fort Moultrie, South Carolina, from 1850 to 1852 and frontier duty from 1852 to 1860. He resigned from the army on June 10, 1861, and volunteered for duty in the Confederate Army, as inspector general and chief of artillery for General William W. Loring (*q.v.*) in West Virginia. In the fall of 1861, he was promoted to colonel and was appointed military secretary to General

Robert E. Lee (*q.v.*), who had much confidence in his abilities. Long also commanded the artillery of the 2nd Corps of the Army of Northern Virginia. He became famous for his disposition of artillery at the battles of Fredericksburg, Chancellorsville, and Gettysburg. He attained the rank of brigadier general on September 21, 1863, after which he fought at Bristoe Station in October and the Mine Run campaign in November and December 1863 in Virginia. In the summer of 1864, he organized the artillery which accompanied Jubal Early (*q.v.*) on his Valley campaign. Long was also present at Waynesboro, Virginia, in March 1865 and accompanied General John B. Gordon's (*q.v.*) Corps on its withdrawal from Richmond. He surrendered at Appomattox and was later paroled there. From 1865 until he went blind in 1870, he was chief engineer for the James River and Kanawha Canal Company in Virginia. He published *Memoir of Lee* (1886). He died on April 29, 1891, in Charlottesville, Virginia. Evans, *Confederate Military History*, III; Freeman, *Lee's Lieutenants*, II, III.

LONGSTREET, James (*General*), son of the planter James Longstreet and his wife Mary Ann (Dent), was born on January 8, 1821, in Edgefield District, South Carolina. His mother was related by marriage to General U. S. Grant. Longstreet was reared by his uncle, Judge Augustus B. Longstreet, in Alabama and Georgia and graduated fifty-fourth in a class of sixty-two from the U.S. Military Academy in 1842. Although his upbringing was Episcopalian, he became a Roman Catholic after the war. Longstreet married Maria Louise Garland on March 8, 1848, and, after her death, Helen Dortch on September 8, 1897; both marriages were childless. A career officer in the U.S. Army before the war, he held early duties in Missouri and Louisiana. During the Mexican War, he fought under General Zachary Taylor at Palo Alto, Resaca, and Monterrey and under General Winfield Scott during the siege of Vera Cruz and the battles of Cerro Gordo and Chapultepec, where he was wounded. He was breveted captain and major for his war service. From 1849 to 1851, he was chief of the Commissary Department in Texas. Promoted to captain in 1852 and to major in 1858, he served in New Mexico and was in the Paymaster Department in Washington, D.C., in 1861. He resigned his commission on June 1, 1861, and volunteered for service in the Confederate Army. On June 17, 1861, he became a brigadier general, and he served in the battle of First Manassas under Beauregard (*q.v.*) before being promoted to major general on October 7, 1861. Although he made some mistakes at Seven Pines, he had a distinguished record in the Peninsular campaign of 1862. In addition, he inflicted great losses on the Union army by his occupation of Mayre's Heights during the battle of Fredericksburg in December, following his promotion to lieutenant general on October 9, 1862. Upon his last promotion, he commanded the 1st Corps of the Army of Northern Virginia. Longstreet was unequaled as a field tactician but had little talent for independent command. He arrived too late to participate in the battle of Chancellorsville, and as commander of the right wing at the battle of Gettysburg, he was accused of losing the battle by his delay in attacking on the second day. In September 1863, he was sent to support General Braxton Bragg (*q. v.*) in the west, and although he was responsible for the victory at Chickamauga in September, he was unsuccessful at Knoxville in November and December. On May 5, 1864, he was wounded during the battle of the Wilderness, and he saw no more action until late fall of that year. However, he commanded his corps during the final months of the war and was present with Lee (*q. v.*) and surrendered at Appomattox. He was soon paroled. After the war, he was president of an insurance company in New Orleans; in 1869, he was a surveyor for the port of New Orleans and also had a cotton factory there; and in 1878, he was a supervisor of internal revenue. Longstreet, who had probably been a Democrat before the war, joined the Republican party in the postwar years, and through his connections with ex-President Grant was appointed U.S. minister to Turkey in 1880. The following year he moved to Gainesville, Georgia, and became U.S. marshal for the district of Georgia. In 1897, he was U.S. railroad commissioner for the Pacific Railroad. Longstreet published his memoirs, *From Manassas to Appomattox*, in 1896. He died on January 2, 1904, in Gainesville. Eckenrode and Conrad, *James Longstreet*; Sanger and Hay, *James Longstreet*, I-II.

LORING, William Wing (*General*), son of Reuben and Hannah (Kenan) Loring, was born on December 4, 1818, in Wilmington, North Carolina. During his youth, his father moved to St. Augustine, Florida, where he became a planter and built a sugar mill. Young Loring attended school in Alexandria, Virginia, and Georgetown College, D.C. He was an Episcopalian and a lifelong bachelor. Loring, who had his first contact with Indian fighting in the Everglades at the age of fourteen, rose to senior captain and major during the Seminole War in 1836-1838. He studied law under Senator David Yulee and was admitted to the St. Augustine, Florida, bar in 1842. From 1842 to 1845, he was a member of the Florida House. He ran unsuccessfully for the state Senate in 1845. During the Mexican War, he served under General Winfield Scott and was breveted lieutenant colonel and colonel. He lost his left arm in the fighting around Mexico City. Loring accepted an appointment as lieutenant colonel in the U.S. Army in March 1848. He was colonel in command of the Department of Oregon during the army's attempt to control the lawlessness of "gold fever," from 1849 to 1851. From 1851 to 1856, he was an Indian fighter on the frontier. He studied military science in Europe before returning to command the Department of New Mexico in 1860. An opponent of secession, he nevertheless worked to persuade other officers to join the Confederate Army. He resigned from the U.S. Army on May 13, 1861. Loring, who had been a colonel in the federal army at the time of his resignation, became a brigadier general in the Confederate Army on May 20, 1861, and he took charge of Confederate forces in West Virginia. In September of the same year, he participated in the Cheat Mountain campaign, which provoked a major clash over command duties with General Thomas J. Jackson (*q. v.*). On February 17, 1862, he was promoted to major general and was given command of the Army of

Southwestern Virginia. In December 1862, he was transferred to command of the 1st Corps of the Army of Mississippi. In May 1863, his forces were cut off from the rest of the Confederate troops during the battle of Baker's Creek, which prevented their capture at Vicksburg. Loring also served under General Leonidas Polk (*q.v.*) in northern Mississippi and commanded Polk's Corps in the Army of Tennessee after Polk's death. He participated in the Atlanta campaign under Generals Joseph E. Johnston (*q.v.*) and John B. Hood (*q.v.*). His last service was in the Carolinas and in April 1865, he surrendered. He was soon paroled. After the war, Loring was a New York banker. In 1869, he traveled to Egypt, where he became inspector general in the service of the Khedive. In 1870, he commanded Alexandria and the Egyptian coastal defenses. Following his command of the army in 1875-1876 during the Abyssinian War, he was made pasha. In 1879, he returned to Florida and later went to New York. He ran unsuccessfully as a Democrat for the U.S. Senate from Florida in 1881, losing to Charles W. Jones. Loring died on December 30, 1886, in New York City following a heart attack. Loring, *A Confederate Soldier in Egypt*; Wessels, *Born to Be a Soldier: The Military Career of William Wing Loring*.

LOVELL, Mansfield (*General*), was born to Dr. Joseph Lovell, U.S. Army surgeon general, and his wife Margaret (Mansfield), on October 20, 1822, in New York City. He graduated ninth in a class of fifty-six from the U.S. Military Academy in 1842. In 1849, he married Emily M. Plympton. His early military duty was in the 4th Artillery. Lovell served in the U.S. Army under General Zachary Taylor. Wounded at Monterrey in 1846, he was also breveted captain during the Mexican War for his performance at Chapultepec. After his resignation from the army in 1854, he was employed by Cooper and Hewitt's Iron Works in Trenton, New Jersey, until 1858, when he became deputy street commissioner for New York City. He resigned to enter the Confederate Army when the Civil War began. On October 7, 1861, he became a major general in command of Department Number One of the Confederate Army, with headquarters in New Orleans. In April 1862, he evacuated the city after burning all his papers. Although a board of inquiry in November 1863 declared that Lovell had not been to blame for the loss of the city, he was removed from his command. He held no further significant command after the battle of Corinth in October 1862. Lovell, who commanded the 1st Corps, was praised for his leadership during and after this battle. In 1864, he was a volunteer staff officer to General Joseph E. Johnston (*q.v.*), and Johnston attempted to secure his assistance during the Atlanta campaign. There is no record of his surrender or parole. After the war, Lovell was an engineer in New York City, where he removed the obstructions in the East River. For a time in the early 1880s, he was a rice planter on the Savannah River. He died on June 1, 1884, in New York City. Fortier, *A History of Louisiana*, II; Wright, *General Officers of the Confederate Army*.

LOWREY, Mark Perrin (*General*), was born on December 29, 1828, in McNairy County, Tennessee, to Adam and Marguerite (Doss) Lowrey. Reared in poverty by his mother, he worked as a brickmason for a time. He had no formal education. During the Mexican War, he enlisted in the 2nd Mississippi Volunteers but saw no active service. Lowrey married Sarah R. Holmes in 1849. From 1853 until 1861, he was a Baptist minister and held various pastorates around Kossuth, Mississippi. When the Civil War broke out, he volunteered for duty in the Confederate Army and served in northern Mississippi and Tennessee as colonel of the 4th Mississippi Volunteers. In 1862, he became colonel of the 32nd Mississippi Regiment. After serving with distinction during the battles of Chickamauga and Missionary Ridge, he was promoted to brigadier general on October 4, 1863. General Patrick R. Cleburne (*q. v.*) called him the bravest man in the Confederate Army. Lowrey was a division commander during the Hundred Days from Dalton to Atlanta and the battles of Franklin and Nashville in 1864 and in the Carolinas in 1865. He also preached to the troops during the war. He resigned from the army in March 1865 and returned to Mississippi. After the war, he reorganized the Mississippi churches. From 1868 to 1877, he was president of the Mississippi Baptist convention. In 1873, he founded Blue Mountain Female College in Mississippi. He died on February 27, 1885, in transit near Middleton, Tennessee. Evans, *Confederate Military History*, VII.

LUBBOCK, Francis Richard (*Governor*), son of Dr. Henry T. W. and Susan Ann (Saltus) Lubbock, was born on October 16, 1815, in Beaufort, South Carolina. His father died in 1829, and he had to give up a private school education to become a clerk in Charleston. In 1834, Lubbock moved to New Orleans, and on February 5 of the following year, he married Adele Baron, a French Creole woman. After her death, he married Mrs. Sarah E. (Black) Porter in December 1883, and upon her death he married Lou Scott on August 12, 1903. Lubbock moved to Texas in 1836 where he operated a store and a ranch at Velasco, near Houston. In 1837, he became assistant clerk of the Texas House of Representatives, and the following year he was promoted to chief clerk in the comptroller's office. From 1841 to 1857, he was clerk of the District Court for Harris County, Texas. Lubbock, a Democrat and a secessionist, was elected lieutenant governor of Texas in 1857 but lost a bid for reelection in 1859. He was a Texas delegate to the Charleston Democratic convention in 1860. The following year he was elected governor of Texas and served until 1863. During his term in office, he raised money for the Confederate war effort and established a military board, a state foundry, and a percussion cap factory. He also worked to keep Texas loyal to the Confederacy. At the end of his term as governor, he volunteered for military duty. He was a lieutenant colonel in the Confederate Army and served on President Davis's (*q. v.*) staff in 1864. He fled Richmond at war's end with the president, was captured and imprisoned in Fort Delaware, and later paroled. At the end of the war, he had lost his ranch. He moved to Galveston in the late 1860s where he was a tax collector, and he operated a commission house in Houston and Galveston. From 1878 to 1891, he was state treasurer in Austin, where he lived at the time of his death on June 22, 1905. Lubbock, *Six Decades in Texas: The Memoirs of Francis R. Lubbock*.

LYNCH, Patrick Nieson (*Bishop*), was born on March 10, 1817, in Ireland. His parents emigrated two years later to the United States, where they settled in Cheraw, South Carolina. Lynch attended the seminary of St. John the Baptist and received his D.D. from the College of the Propaganda at Rome in 1840. He was ordained a Catholic priest in 1840 and was sent to Charleston, South Carolina, as the pastor of St. Mary's Church. He later became principal of Collegiate Institute and vicar-general of the diocese in 1850. On March 14, 1858, he became the third bishop of Charleston. He became a staunch secessionist and an active defender of slavery. During the war, he urged his parishoners to flock to the Confederate cause. He administered the sacrament at Fort Sumter and worked with the Sisters of Mercy at Charleston Hospital. His cathedral was destroyed by fire in December 1861. In April 1864, he left the South as a Confederate emissary to France and to the Pope. He traveled to Rome, where he remained for the rest of the war, but he never presented himself as an official agent of the Confederate government abroad. His mission was to persuade the Pope to condemn the Union's use of Irish immigrants in the army and to stop the Union from buying the services of Europeans for duty in the war. He even attempted to intervene on behalf of the Confederacy with Napoleon III. After the war, he returned to Charleston to rebuild his burned church. He spent the rest of his life trying to restore relations between the North and the South. Lynch died in Charleston on February 26, 1882. Blied, *Catholics in the Civil War*; Owsley, *King Cotton Diplomacy*.

LYON, Francis Strother (*Congressman*), was born on February 25, 1800, in Danbury, Stokes County, North Carolina, to James and Behetheland (Gaines) Lyon. His father was a tobacco farmer. He attended common schools in North Carolina before moving to St. Stephens, Alabama, in 1817. A bank clerk, he studied law and was admitted to the Demopolis, Alabama, bar in 1821. Lyon was an Episcopalian. On March 4, 1824, he married Sarah Serena Glover and they had seven children. He was a popular lawyer, and from 1822 to 1830, he served as secretary of the state Senate. Elected to the state Senate in 1833, he became president of that body the following year. He served as a Whig in the U.S. House of Representatives from 1835 to 1839, after which he returned to his law practice and to agriculture. From 1847 to 1853, he was involved in the settlement of state bank claims. He became a secessionist and joined the Yancey (*q.v.*) wing of the state Democratic party. In 1860, he was part of the Alabama delegation which withdrew from the Charleston Democratic convention. He was elected to the Alabama House in 1861 and to the provisional Confederate Congress, where he declined to serve because of pressing matters in the Alabama legislature. He was elected to both permanent Confederate Houses. An administration supporter, he served on the Ways and Means, Currency, War Tax, and many special committees. During the war, he subscribed to the cotton loan, and when the war ended, he found that his fortune was gone. He returned to his law practice in Demopolis and became active in Democratic party politics. He was a delegate to the state constitutional convention in 1875 and was elected to the state Senate the following year. Lyon died in Demopolis in retirement on December 31, 1882. Owen, *History of Alabama and Dictionary of Alabama Biography*, IV.

LYONS, James (*Congressman*, *Judge*), son of Dr. James Lyons, was born in Hanovertown, Virginia, on October 12, 1801. He graduated from the College of William and Mary in 1817 and began his law practice in Richmond in 1818. Lyons, who in 1824 arranged the Marquis de Lafayette's visit to Virginia, was married to Henningham Watkins and, after her death, to Imogen Bradfute Penn. He had eight children. A states' rights Whig, he made an address in 1840 opposing the bank of the United States and the high protective tariff. He served in the House and later the Senate of the Virginia legislature during the 1850s and was considered an ardent secessionist. When the Civil War began, he held various local political offices and supported the Confederate war effort. In February 1862, he replaced John Tyler (*q.v.*) who had died, in the first Confederate House of Representatives, where he served until he was defeated for election by William C. Wickham (*q.v.*) in February 1864. In the House he was a supporter of the Davis administration, and he served on the Buildings and Commerce Committees, as well as on several special committees. In 1864, he favored a tax-in-kind on all agricultural products. He lost his election campaign despite the support of the Richmond *Enquirer*, which had applauded his secessionism. Later in 1864, he was appointed a trial judge in charge of handling political prisoners. When the war ended, he returned to his Richmond law practice. Lyons was closer to President Davis (*q.v.*) after the war than during it; he assisted in the ex-president's legal defense. He practiced law in Richmond and died there on December 15, 1882. Tyler, *Encyclopedia of Virginia Biography*, IV.

M

MCCALLUM, James (*Congressman*), was born to Daniel and Sarah (Smith) McCallum in Robeson County, North Carolina, on October 2, 1806. His family moved to Tennessee in the late 1810s. He received little schooling but read law in Pulaski, Tennessee, and was admitted to the Tennessee bar around 1828. McCallum was a Mason and an elder in the Presbyterian church. He married Elizabeth Brown on February 14, 1829, and they had nine children, two of whom died in infancy. From 1842 to 1861, he was clerk and master of the Chancery Court at Pulaski. He also at one time served in the Tennessee legislature. There is no record of his service to the Confederacy in the early stages of the war. During the war, he served in the second Confederate House in 1864-1865, although he had not supported secession. He served on the Accounts, Medical Department, and Post Office and Post Roads Committees and was an administration supporter. McCallum, who had been a Whig before the war, joined the Democratic party after the war. In 1870, he was made a director of the Pulaski Savings Bank. He held no postwar public office. He died in Pulaski on September 16, 1889. Speer (comp.), *Biographical Directory of the Tennessee General Assembly*.

MCCAUSLAND, John (*General*), was born to the Irish immigrants John and Harriet (Kyle) McCausland on September 13, 1836, in St. Louis, Missouri. His father became a merchant in Lynchburg, Virginia. After receiving his preparatory education at Point Pleasant, Mason County, Virginia, McCausland graduated first in the class of 1857 from Virginia Military Institute and studied at the University of Virginia the following year. He was married and had three sons and one daughter. McCausland was assistant professor of mathematics at Virginia Military Institute from 1858 until 1861. When the war began, he left his position and volunteered for the Confederate Army. He organized the Rockbridge Artillery during the first months of the Civil War. Lee (*q.v.*) sent him to Kanawha Valley to organize a regiment, and he was later transferred to serve under General Albert S. Johnston (*q.v.*) at Bowling Green, Kentucky. He showed courage at Fort Donelson, for which he was promoted to colonel, and he participated in the battle of Shiloh in 1862. In 1862-1863, he fought in Virginia, where he was a hero of Port Republic and effective at Lynchburg. Following his command of Confederate troops at the battle of Cloyd's Mountain, he was promoted to brigadier general on May 18, 1864. McCausland executed a brilliant flanking attack at the battle of Monocacy, Maryland, in July 1864, and he accompanied Early (*q.v.*) during his Washington raid and his Valley campaign. On July 30, he gave the orders for the burning of Chambersburg, Pennsylvania. In 1865, he fought before Petersburg, and he participated in the battle of Five Forks on April 1. He refused to surrender and for a while he was a fugitive. After the war, he spent two years in Europe and Mexico before returning to his six-thousand-acre farm in Mason County, West Virginia, where he spent the rest of his life quietly. He died on January 22, 1927, at his farm near Henderson, West Virginia. Early, *Autobiographical Sketch and Narrative of the War Between the States*; Shawkey, *West Virginia*, V.

MCCAW, James Brown (*Physician*), son of Dr. William Reid and Ann Ludwell (Brown) McCaw, was born on July 21, 1823, in Richmond, Virginia, where his father had been an eminent physician. He attended Richmond Academy and studied medicine at the University of the City of New York in 1843, where he was a pupil of Valentine Mott. He returned to Richmond in late 1843 and soon became an important physician. McCaw had nine children by his 1845 marriage to Delia Patterson. A founder of the Medical Society of Virginia in the late 1840s, he edited the *Virginia Medical and Surgical Journal* from 1853 to 1855 and the *Virginia Medical Journal* from 1856 to 1859. In 1858, he was made a professor at the Medical College of Virginia. When the Civil War began, he volunteered for service in the Confederate Cavalry Corps. In 1862, he was made surgeon in charge and commandant at the Chimborazo Hospital in Richmond, the largest hospital in the Confederacy and then one of the largest in the world. Seventy-six thousand soldiers were treated there. In 1864, he became editor of the *Confederate States Medical Journal*, a position which he held until the end of the war. At the end of the hostilities, he returned to his medical practice in Richmond. From 1868 to 1883, he was a professor of chemistry and medicine and dean from 1871 to 1883 of the faculty at the Medical College of Virginia. He died on August 13, 1906, in Richmond. Cunningham, *Doctors in Gray*; Tyler, *Encyclopedia of Biography*, IV.

MCCOWN, John Porter (*General*), was born on August 19, 1815, in Seviersville, Tennessee. He graduated tenth in a class of forty-two from the U.S. Military Academy in 1840 and entered the Artillery Corps. He was a Mason, but no other details are known of his personal life. After assisting in the removal of Indians to the west in 1840, he served on the frontier during the Canada border disturbances of 1840-1841. In 1845-1846, he was part of the military occupation of Texas, and during the Mexican War, he was breveted captain for his gallantry at Cerro Gordo. Following frontier duty on the Rio Grande, he was promoted to captain in the 4th U.S. Artillery in January 1851. McCown also fought the Seminoles of Florida in 1856-1857, participated in the Utah expedition of 1858, and served at garrisons in Nebraska and the Dakotas from 1858 to 1861. He resigned his commission on May 17, 1861, and entered the Confederate Army as a lieutenant colonel of artillery. Promoted to brigadier general on October 12, 1861, he contributed to the victory at Belmont, Missouri, on November 7 of that year. On March 10, 1862, he was promoted to major general, around the same time that he was blamed by General Braxton Bragg (*q.v.*) for the loss of New Madrid, Missouri. After fighting at Fort Pillow in April through June 1862, McCown was given temporary command of the Army of the West. During Bragg's Kentucky campaign, he commanded the 3rd Division, and following the Confederate defeat at the battle of Murfreesboro, Bragg preferred charges against him for incompetence. McCown was found guilty by court martial, and in 1863, he was sent to Mississippi where he spent the remainder of the war in obscurity. McCown, who was himself hot-tempered, never forgave Bragg, whose animosity toward him was personal as well as professional. During the last days of the war, he successfully defended a crossing of the Catawba River near Morgantown, North Carolina. He surrendered in North Carolina and was soon paroled. After the war, he taught school in Knoxville before moving to Little Rock, Arkansas, in 1870, where he owned a farm. He died in Little Rock on January 22, 1879. Arkansas *Democrat*, January 22, 1879; Eliot, *West Point in the Confederacy*.

MCDOWELL, Thomas David (*Congressman*), son of Dr. Alexander McDowell, was born in Elizabethtown, Bladen County, North Carolina, on January 4, 1823. McDowell attended Donaldson Academy and graduated from the University of North Carolina in 1843. After studying law and being admitted to the North Carolina bar, he began his law practice in Elizabethtown in 1844. He was a Whig in the North Carolina House from 1846 to 1850 and a Democrat in the state Senate from 1854 to 1858. He was active in the Presbyterian church and maintained a plantation in North Carolina. An advocate of states' rights and an immediate secessionist, he was elected to the provisional Confederate Congress and to the first Confederate House of Representatives, where he was a member of the Joint Committees on Commerce and the Inauguration. He supported the Davis administration in the provisional Congress but opposed it in the first Confederate House. While he was elected unanimously to office, he became unpopular among his fellow congressmen because of his extreme states' rights views. He was defeated for the second Congress because he was out of step with the moderate movement in the state. After the war, McDowell rapidly sank into oblivion, and he returned to his law practice and retired from public life. There is little record of his postwar career. He died on May 1, 1898, in Elizabethtown. *Bladen County, North Carolina, Abstracts of Wills*; *University of North Carolina Magazine*, June 1898; Wheeler, *Reminiscences and Memoirs of North Carolina*.

MACFARLAND, William H. (*Congressman*), was born on February 9, 1799, in Lunenburg County, Virginia. He attended the College of William and Mary and became a lawyer in Richmond during the 1820s. MacFarland was a vestryman in the Episcopal church and a unionist Whig. In 1836, he was president of the Richmond and Petersburg Railroad. He delivered a funeral oration for James Madison while lieutenant governor of Virginia in 1837. From 1837 to 1865, he was president of the Farmer's Bank of Richmond. He also owned coal mines and was a financier. MacFarland supported public education, and in 1846, he was a member of the Richmond Educational Association. In 1850, he helped to organize the Richmond Historical Society. In 1860, he was elected to the Virginia secession convention as a unionist. He was an anti-administration member of the provisional Confederate Congress, where he served on the Commercial Affairs and Inauguration Committees and the special committee for comfort of wounded soldiers. He ran unsuccessfully for the first Confederate House against former President John Tyler (*q. v.*), who accused MacFarland of threatening his debtors with foreclosures if they failed to support him. MacFarland gave no further public service to the Confederacy. In 1864, he helped to provide artificial limbs for soldiers. Throughout the war, he provided needed business advice to the Confederate government. After the war, he helped to achieve a civil rather than a military government for Richmond in the early days of Reconstruction. He signed Jefferson Davis's (*q. v.*) parole bond. In 1867, along with R.M.T. Hunter (*q. v.*) and Thomas Jefferson Randolph, MacFarland joined the Conservative party. He died in Greenbrier County, West Virginia, on January 10, 1872. Christian, *Richmond, Her Past and Present*; Scott, *Houses of Old Richmond*.

MCGEEHEE, Edward (*Businessman*), was born in Oglethorpe, Georgia, on November 18, 1786. He came to Mississippi on a flatboat and settled in Wilkinson County around 1810, where he was a noted planter. In 1811, he married Margaret L. Crosby. Prior to the Civil War, he built the West Feliciana Railroad, founded the Woodville Bank, owned one of the first cotton factories in the state, and contributed large sums of money to churches and colleges. Little is known of his full business career, except that he became the wealthiest man in Mississippi. He spent a few terms in the Mississippi legislature but otherwise shunned public office. He declined an offer to become Zachary Taylor's secretary of the treasury. McGeehee favored the colonization of slaves. One of the richest and most knowledgeable businessmen along the Gulf Coast when the Civil War began, he turned his fortune and his abilities to work for the Confederacy. He gave food crops to the western army. After the war, he retired to his plantation in Bowling Green, Mississippi, and died there on October 1, 1880. *History of Oglethorpe County, Georgia*.

MCGOWAN, Samuel (*General*), was born on October 9, 1819, in Laurens County, South Carolina, where his parents, William and Jeannie (McWilliams) McGowan, had emigrated from Ireland. He attended the school of Thomas Lewis Lesly, graduated from South Carolina College in 1841, and was admitted to the

Abbeville, South Carolina, bar the following year, after schooling himself in the law. He rose to eminence in the South Carolina legal profession. He was an Episcopalian and a Democrat. He had seven children by his marriage to Susan Caroline Wardlaw, the eldest daughter of Judge David R. Wardlaw. During the Mexican War, he was a captain in the Quartermaster's Department. McGowan also served in the South Carolina House for twelve years and was elected a major general in the state militia in the late 1850s. When South Carolina seceded, he joined the state brigade. After assisting P.G.T. Beauregard (*q.v.*) in the capture of Fort Sumter and serving as aide-de-camp to Milledge L. Bonham (*q.v.*) during the battle of First Manassas, McGowan went to Virginia as colonel of the 14th South Carolina Regiment in 1862. Wounded at the first battle of Cold Harbor and again at Second Manassas in the summer of 1862, he recovered sufficiently to succeed General Maxcy Gregg (*q.v.*) as brigade commander during the battle of Fredericksburg. Promoted to brigadier general on April 23, 1863, he displayed extraordinary bravery when wounded a third time during the battle of Chancellorsville. In 1863, he fought at the Wilderness and at the "Bloody Angle" of Spotsylvania. He surrendered at Appomattox and was soon paroled. After the war, McGowan returned to his law practice in Abbeville, practicing from 1869 to 1879. He became a member of the state constitutional convention in 1865 and was elected to the U.S. House the same year but was not permitted to take his seat. A leader in the anti-Republican struggles of the state, he was elected to the South Carolina legislature in 1878 and served as an associate justice of the state Supreme Court from 1879 until he was defeated for reelection in 1893. He died on August 9, 1897, at Abbeville. Brooks, *South Carolina Bench and Bar*; *Confederate Veteran*, V; *Encyclopedia of Eminent South Carolinians*.

MCGUIRE, Hunter Holmes (*Physician*, *Bureaucrat*), was born on October 11, 1835, in Winchester, Virginia, to Dr. Hugh Holmes and Ann Eliza (Moss) McGuire. He studied medicine at Winchester Medical College in 1855 and at the University of Pennsylvania and Jefferson Medical College in 1856. He was an Episcopalian. He married Mary Stuart in 1866, and they had nine children, two of whom became doctors. He practiced medicine in Winchester for only about a year, and in 1857, became a professor of anatomy at the Winchester Medical College. In 1858, he returned to Philadelphia for further study, but after John Brown's raid at Harper's Ferry in 1859, McGuire, a secessionist, agreed to pay the fees of all Southern students who were studying in the North to return to Richmond. He then went to New Orleans to teach in the Medical Department of the University of Louisiana. After Virginia seceded, he returned home and volunteered in the Confederate Army as a private. He was at Harper's Ferry prior to his appointment as a surgeon in May 1861. He served under "Stonewall" Jackson (*q.v.*) as medical director of the Army of the Shenandoah, was promoted to brigadier general in 1862, and was surgeon to Jackson and later to the 2nd Army Corps under the command of General Richard S. Ewell (*q.v.*). He became medical director of the Army of Northern Virginia and of the Army of the Valley of Virginia in 1864, organized the Reserve Corps Hospital, and perfected the Ambulance Corps. He was captured in March 1865 and paroled when the war ended. From 1865 to 1878, he held the chair of surgery at the Medical College of Virginia. One of the founders of the Medical Society of Virginia in the 1870s, he was also president of the American Medical Association in 1892. In 1875, he was the president of the Association of Medical Officers of the Army of the Confederate States. From 1893 until his death in Richmond on September 19, 1900, McGuire was president of the College of Physicians in Richmond. Cunningham, *Doctors in Gray*; Freeman, *Lee's Lieutenants*; *Southern Historical Society Papers*, XXVIII.

MACHEN, Willis Benson (*Congressman*), was born on April 10, 1810, in Caldwell County, Kentucky, to Henry and Nancy (Tarrant) Machen. He attended Cumberland College in Kentucky, married Margaret A. Chittenden, and was a farmer in Eddyville, Lyon County, Kentucky. He also was a merchant and manufacturer there in the 1850s and served as a delegate to the state constitutional convention in 1849-1850. In 1854-1855, he was a member of the upper house of the Kentucky legislature, and in 1856 and 1860, he was elected to the lower house. A secessionist and a Democrat, he was a leader in the Kentucky separationist movement. He also served in both permanent Confederate Houses, where he was a supporter of the administration. After the war, he returned to his farm. He served as state railroad commissioner in 1880, and he owned and operated iron furnaces in Lyon County during the 1880s. Machen died in Eddyville on September 29, 1893. *Biographical Directory of the American Congress*.

MACKALL, William Whann (*General*), was born on or about January 18, 1817, in Cecil County, Maryland. He graduated eighth in a class of fifty from the U.S. Military Academy in 1837. Mackall attended the Episcopal church but was without religious affiliation. He married Aminta Sorrel, daughter of a Savannah merchant, on May 7, 1843; they had five children. A career officer in the U.S. Army before the Civil War, he was severely wounded in 1838 during the Seminole War. He served on the border during the Canadian disturbances of 1840 and on the Maine frontier in 1841-1842. During the Mexican War, he was breveted captain for his performance at Monterrey and major for his services at Contreras and Churubusco. During the 1850s, he was also adjutant general for the Western and Eastern Divisions, and in 1856, he was named adjutant general for the Department of the Pacific. He was opposed to slavery and accepted secession with reluctance. He resigned his commission on July 3, 1861, and joined the Confederate Army. In the early days of the war, he was adjutant general to General A. S. Johnston (*q. v.*). Promoted to brigadier general on March 6, 1862, he was captured during the Confederate loss at Island Number 10 the following month. He was later exchanged. Mackall was given command of the District of the Gulf in December 1862. From April to September 1863, he served as Braxton Bragg's (*q. v.*) chief of staff, and from January 1864 until the end of the war, he was chief of staff to General J. E. Johnston (*q. v.*). He refused to surrender under John B. Hood (*q. v.*) and was relieved of command. Mackall saw no further military service. After the war, he farmed his plantation "Langley" in Fairfax County, Virginia. He died near McLean, Virginia, on August 12, 1891. Evans, *Confederate Military History*, II; Mackall, *A Son's Recollections of His Father*.

MCLAWS, Lafayette (*General*), son of James and Elizabeth (Huguenin) McLaws, was born on January 15, 1821, in Augusta, Georgia. He attended the University of Virginia from 1837 to 1838 and was forty-eighth in a class of fifty-six at the U.S. Military Academy in 1842. His wife was Emily Allison Taylor, a niece of President Zachary Taylor. Commissioned into the infantry in 1842, McLaws served on the frontier and had an undistinguished career during the Mexican War. He was promoted to captain of infantry in 1851 and participated in the Utah expedition of 1858. The following year he escorted the Mormons to California. When the Civil War began, he resigned his commission and volunteered for duty in the Confederate Army. After entering the 10th Georgia Regiment, he was promoted to brigadier general on September 25, 1861. He distinguished himself at the battles of Yorktown and Williamsburg in April and May of 1862. On May 23, 1862, he was promoted to major general and was given command of a division of the 1st Corps of the Army of Northern Virginia. He assisted in the capture of Harper's Ferry and aided General Thomas J. Jackson (*q. v.*) at Sharpsburg, where his heroism won praise from Longstreet (*q. v.*). At the battle of Fredericksburg, he was heroic in the defense of Mayre's Heights, and at Chancellorsville he defeated Major General John Sedgwick. At Gettysburg, he drove back General Daniel Sickles on the second day of the battle. Later the same year, he accompanied General James Longstreet (*q. v.*) west, where he fought at the battles of Chickamauga and Knoxville. Following Knoxville, McLaws turned against Longstreet, was relieved for lack of cooperation, court-martialed, but was subsequently exonerated by President Davis (*q. v.*). In 1864, he commanded the District of Georgia against Sherman's advance. He ended the war while serving with General Joseph E. Johnston (*q. v.*) in the Carolinas. He surrendered at Greensboro, North Carolina, and was subsequently paroled. After the war, he was in the insurance business in Augusta before moving to Savannah in 1874, where he was a tax collector in 1875 and collector for the port in 1876. He was also postmaster of Savannah in 1876. McLaws died there in retirement on July 24, 1897. Freeman, *Lee's Lieutenants*, I-II; Young, *The Battle of Gettysburg*.

MCLEAN, James Robert (*Congressman*), was born in Enfield, North Carolina, on September 21, 1823. He was orphaned at an early age. Raised by relatives, he attended the local schools, studied law under John A. Gilmer (*q. v.*) and was admitted to the North Carolina bar in 1844. McLean also farmed in Guilford County, North Carolina. A Presbyterian and a Democrat, he married and had a large family. He moved his law practice to Rockford, North Carolina, in 1845, and in 1850-1851, he served in the state legislature. In 1852 he moved back to Greensboro in Guilford County, and he lived there when the war broke out. McLean was an active secessionist. In the first Confederate House he represented the Sixth Congressional District of North Carolina. He served on the Foreign Affairs and Claims Committees, and on the special committee for the relief of individuals who had lost their lands to the Northern invaders. Although he did not seek reelection, he had ably served the Davis administration and he had urged the citizens of North Carolina to pursue a vigorous defensive war. For three months in the fall of 1864, he was a major in a regiment of the North Carolina senior reserves. He also fought in the last Confederate battle in North Carolina at Bentonville. When the war ended, he returned to his law practice in hopes of recovering his wartime losses. He died in Greensboro on April 15, 1870. Arnett, *Greensboro*; Connor, *North Carolina Biography*, VI.

MCMULLEN, Fayette (*Congressman*), was born on May 18, 1805, in Bedford County, Virginia. He received an academic education but worked as a farmer, stagecoach driver, and teamster. McMullen, a unionist Democrat, was married twice, his second marriage being to Mary Wood in July 1858. He represented Washington District in the Virginia Senate from 1838 to 1849 and was the Democratic congressman from Rye Cove, Virginia, in the U.S. House from December 1849 to March 1857. In 1857, President Buchanan appointed him governor of the Washington Territory. He served until 1858 and then returned to his farm in Smyth County, Virginia. He opposed secession but supported the Confederacy. Defeated for election to the first Confederate House of Representatives, he was elected as a peace candidate to the second House, where he served on the Post Office and Post Roads, Public Buildings, and Territories and Public Lands Committees, and on the select committee on alleged depredations of the Confederate soldiers in southwest Virginia and east Tennessee. He was an anti-administration man. In December 1864, he tried to get Congress to take anti-inflationary measures; he advocated price controls, with a fair standard of value for all goods. When the war ended, he returned to his farm in Smyth County. He held no public office, although he ran for Congress many times. McMullen ran as a Greenbacker for governor in 1878. He died in a railroad accident on November 8, 1880. *Appleton's Cyclopedia of American Biography*.

MCQUEEN, John (*Congressman*), son of James McQueen, was born on February 9, 1804, in Queensdale, Robeson County, North Carolina. He attended the University of North Carolina and was admitted to the Bennetsville, South Carolina, bar in 1828. He developed a successful law practice, but after 1850, he considered himself a planter rather than a lawyer. McQueen was an Episcopalian and a Democrat; he was married and had a family. He served in the South Carolina Militia from 1833 to 1837 and was a member of the U.S. House of Representatives

from 1849 until he resigned in 1860. The most radical of South Carolina secessionists, he was a commissioner to Texas in 1861 and was mentioned as a gubernatorial
candidate in 1862. As a member of the first Confederate House of Representatives
from South Carolina's First Congressional District, he supported the Davis
administration and served on the Accounts, Foreign Affairs and Inauguration
Committees. He voted to suspend the writ of *habeas corpus*, and he defended
Secretary Judah P. Benjamin (*q.v.*) on the loss of Forts Henry and Donelson. In
1864, he was defeated for the second Confederate House by James Witherspoon
(*q.v.*), a Davis critic. He returned to private life. McQueen's plantation was ruined
during the war years and he lost much of his fortune. Nevertheless, he attempted to
farm his lands. He died at Society Hill, South Carolina, on August 30, 1867.
Cauthen, *South Carolina Goes to War, 1861-1865*.

MCRAE, Colin John (*Diplomat, Businessman*), brother of John Jones McRae
(*q.v.*) and son of John and Elizabeth Mary McRae, was born in Sneedsboro, North
Carolina, on October 22, 1812. His family moved to Mississippi five years later.
The young McRae was tutored privately and attended Frederick's School and
Catholic College in Biloxi, Mississippi. His schooling ended when his father died
in 1835. In 1838, he was a member of the Mississippi legislature. He was a
Democrat and a Presbyterian and never married. McRae moved to Mobile,
Alabama, in 1840, where he speculated in land and operated a cotton commission
house. During the 1850s, he and his brother John were promoters and stockholders
of the Mobile and Ohio and the Mobile and New Orleans Railroads. In 1857, they
were engaged in buying and selling land and slaves, and in 1859, they speculated
in mineral lands in central Alabama. An extreme secessionist, McRae was elected
to represent Mobile County in the provisional Confederate Congress, where he
served on the Finance and Engrossment Committees. He was also a major
financial agent of the Confederate government. In the fall of 1862, he traveled
throughout the South, buying cotton for the Confederacy, and shipping it to
England through the blockade. In January 1863, he helped to negotiate and
manage the Erlanger loan, for which he was the European agent. He was the chief
Confederate financial agent in Europe. In addition, he returned home for a time in
late 1863 and established an important arsenal and ordnance plant at Selma,
Alabama. He also became an agent of the Confederate Ordnance Bureau. In 1863,
he participated in the attempt to recruit Polish citizens to fight for the Confederacy.
After the war, he tried to prevent the holders of the Erlanger bonds from suing to
recover their losses. He returned to Mississippi and again engaged in business
pursuits. He helped to pay for the Jefferson Davis (*q.v.*) trial defense. In the fall of
1867, he was went to South America to establish a colony of American exiles. He
bought a plantation and store at Puerto Cortes, where he dealt in cattle, mahogany,
and mercantile goods. He died at Belize, British Honduras, in February 1877.
Davis, *Colin J. McRae: Confederate Financial Agent*.

MCRAE, John Jones (*Congressman*), was born to John and Elizabeth Mary McRae on January 10, 1815, in Sneedsboro, North Carolina, where his father was a merchant. The family moved to Mississippi in 1817, and McRae attended Frederick's School before being sent by his brother Colin (*q.v.*) to Miami University in Ohio, where he graduated in 1834. He studied law and in 1835 was admitted to the Mississippi bar. He developed a decent legal practice in Wayne County, Mississippi. In 1835, he married Mrs. McGuire, a widow. He was a Democrat and a Presbyterian. During the 1840s, McRae edited the newspaper *Eastern Clarion* at Paulding, Mississippi, and was a promoter for the Mobile and Ohio Railroad in the 1850s. McRae was a states' rights delegate in the state legislature in 1848 and 1850, serving as speaker of the house in the latter term. The state legislature appointed him acting U.S. senator in 1851-1852, and he was elected and served as governor of Mississippi from 1854 to 1858. In 1858, he was elected to the U.S. House of Representatives as a states' rights Democrat; he was reelected in 1860 and resigned in 1861. Elected from the Seventh Congressional District to the Confederate House, he served on the Ways and Means and Special Committees, and he supported the Davis administration. When the Piney Woods area of Mississippi became increasingly unsettled because of military losses, McRae was blamed for not pushing the war effort more vigorously, as a result of which he was defeated for reelection by John Lamkin (*q.v.*). McRae assisted his brother in business for the Confederate government for the remainder of the war. When the war ended, he returned to his law practice in Mississippi. His fortune lost and in poor health, he traveled to South America to live with his brother. He died at Belize, British Honduras, on May 31, 1868. *Biographical and Historical Memoirs of Mississippi*.

MCTYEIRE, Holland Nimmons (*Minister*), son of John and Elizabeth Amanda (Nimmons) McTyeire, was born in Barnwell District, South Carolina, on July 28, 1824. He attended Cokesbury and Collinswood Schools and graduated from Randolph-Macon College in Virginia in 1844. McTyeire had six children by his November 8, 1847, marriage to Amelia Townsend. In 1845, he was ordained a Methodist minister in Virginia and was made pastor of the church at Williamsburg. The following year, he was made pastor in Mobile, Alabama. He moved to New Orleans in 1849 and served a number of churches there. In 1851, he founded the *Christian Advocate* in New Orleans and edited it until 1858. From 1858 until 1862, he edited the official periodical of the Methodist church, South, the *Advocate*, in Nashville, Tennessee. He was a minister in Montgomery, Alabama, from 1863 to 1866. A staunch secessionist, McTyeire served as a propagandist for the war effort. As a preacher to the troops, he was an inspiration for renewed effort to win the war. When the war ended, he became a bishop of the church, serving in that capacity in Montgomery for twenty years. A prolific author, he wrote six books, including a *History of Methodism* (1887). He also participated in the founding of Vanderbilt University in the 1870s and was its president for thirteen years. He died in retirement on February 15, 1889, in Nashville. Owen, *History of Alabama and Dictionary of Alabama Biography*, IV; Silver, *Confederate Morale and Church Propaganda*.

MACWILLIE, Malcolm H. (*Congressman*), was a lawyer in La Mesilla, Dona Ana County, Arizona Territory. There is no record of his family or his upbringing. When Colonel John R. Baylor (*q.v.*) organized the military government of the territory in the 1850s, MacWillie became his attorney general. He was appointed to both permanent Houses of the Confederate Congress as a nonvoting delegate, and was a Davis administration supporter. In 1863, MacWillie attempted to obtain territorial status for New Mexico, but the Confederate government refused. In the second Congress, he worked with Elias Boudinot (*q.v.*) to gain relief for Indian property taken by Confederate military authorities. Little is known about his life after the war. Farish, *History of Arizona*; Robinson, *Justice in Grey*.

MAFFITT, John Newland (*Naval Commander*), son of the Methodist minister John Newland Maffitt and his wife Ann Carnick, was born at sea on February 22, 1819. He attended school in Fayetteville, North Carolina, and became a midshipman in the U.S. Navy at the age of thirteen. He was a member of the Methodist-Episcopal church, and he had two children by his November 17, 1840, marriage to Mary Florence Murell. She died in 1852, and on August 3, 1852, he married Mrs. Caroline Laurens Read, by whom he had two sons. After her death, he had three children by his marriage to Emma Martin on November 23, 1870. Maffitt served on the frigate *Constitution* in 1835. He held continuous duty until 1842 when he served on the U.S. Coastal Survey. He worked sixteen years on charting the Atlantic Coast, and in 1858, he was made assistant superintendent of the Coast Survey. He was promoted to lieutenant on June 25, 1843, the same year he commanded the brig *Dolphin*, which stopped slave ships and captured the *Echo*. The following year, he commanded the *Crusader*, which performed similar tasks. Maffitt resigned his command on April 28, 1861, and entered the service of the Confederate Navy. In the early days of the war, he was commissioned a lieutenant; he participated in the battle of Hilton Head, South Carolina, and mapped roads and obstructed the Coosaw River for Robert E. Lee (*q.v.*) in November 1861. In January 1862, he was promoted to captain. His ship, the *Cecile*, ran the blockade, bringing in arms, ammunition, and military stores, until Maximilian became emperor of Mexico. Maffitt commanded the *Florida* in early 1863, which he equipped and sent to Mobile. In 1863, he seized many vessels from New York to the Equator. Under his command the *Florie* and the *Lucile* destroyed $10 million in property from September 1863 until June 1864. In the fall of 1864, Maffitt commanded the ironclad *Albemarle* and was stigmatized by the federal navy as a pirate. He never surrendered. When the Confederate cause seemed hopeless, in March 1865 he became a captain in the British navy. He returned to the United States two years later and settled on a farm, where he wrote his reminiscences, *The*

Nautilus (1878). He also wrote a sketch of Raphael Semmes (*q.v.*) for the *South Atlantic Magazine* in 1877. Maffitt died in Wilmington, North Carolina, on May 15, 1886. Maffitt, *The Life and Services of John Newland Maffitt.*

MAGRATH, Andrew Gordon (*Judge, Governor*), son of John and Marie (Gordon) McGrath, was born on February 8, 1813, in Charleston, South Carolina. He attended Bishop England's School in Charleston, graduated first in his class at South Carolina College in 1831, studied law under James L. Pettigru, and graduated from Harvard Law School in 1835. McGrath was an Episcopalian and had five children by his March 8, 1843, marriage to Emma Mitchell; he and his second wife, Mary E. McCord, had no children. He developed an excellent law practice in Charleston. He represented St. Philip's and St. Michael's parishes in the South Carolina House of Representatives in 1838-1840, 1862-1864, and 1866-1867. In 1848, he was a Zachary Taylor Democrat. As a delegate to the Southern rights convention in 1852, he believed secession inexpedient. He was also a district judge in South Carolina from 1856 until his resignation in 1860. He was a member of the secession convention and of the South Carolina Executive Council in 1860 and served as Governor Francis Pickens's (*q.v.*) secretary of state. When the Civil War began, he was appointed district judge for South Carolina. During the war, he tried some famous cases on prize law and declared unconstitutional the Confederate tax on securities. He became unpopular with President Davis (*q.v.*) because of his court decisions. In 1864, he was elected governor of the state and his term was marked by his extreme states' rights view. In 1865, he offered a plan to other Confederate governors to continue the war, even after Richmond fell, by making a pact to send state militias to the aid of other beleaguered states. At the end of the war, he was arrested and imprisoned. After his release in November 1865, he lived quietly and practiced law in Charleston. He died there on April 9, 1893. Brooks, *South Carolina Bench and Bar*; Cauthen, *South Carolina Goes to War.*

MAGRUDER, John Bankhead (*General*), son of Thomas and Elizabeth (Bankhead) Magruder, was born on August 15, 1810, in Winchester, Virginia. He graduated fifteenth in a class of forty-two from the U.S. Military Academy in 1830, and he married Henrietta Von Rapff in 1831, by whom he had at least three children. After graduation from West Point, he began a career in the army, where he became a first lieutenant of artillery in 1836 and served in forts in Texas and Florida. During the Mexican War, he was breveted major for his performance at Cerro Gordo and lieutenant colonel after being wounded at Chapultepec. Off the field, however, Magruder earned a reputation as a dandy and party giver during the 1850s. He commanded Fort Adams in Rhode Island from 1855 until 1859. He resigned his commission on March 16, 1861, and entered the service of the Confederacy. Magruder entered the Confederate Army as a colonel and was promoted to brigadier general on June 17, 1861, following his victory at Big

Bethel, Virginia. On October 7, 1861, he was promoted to major general. In the spring and early summer of 1862, he delayed McClellan during the Peninsular campaign and the Seven Days, but because he failed to command efficiently or to take advantage of his superior force, he was transferred to command the District of Texas in October of that year. Magruder fortified the state, dispersed the blockade from Galveston harbor, and supervised the retaking of Galveston by the Confederates in January 1863. He saw little further action. When the Civil War ended, he refused to ask for parole. He went to Mexico in 1865 and became a major general in Maximilian's army. He later returned to Texas, where he lectured about his Mexican War experiences. Magruder died in poverty in Houston, Texas, on February 19, 1871. Freeman, *Lee's Lieutenants*, I; Kerby, *Kirby Smith's Confederacy: The Trans-Mississippi South, 1863-1865*.

MAHONE, William (*General*), was born on December 1, 1826, in Monroe, Southampton County, Virginia, to Colonel Fielding J. Mahone and his wife Martha (Drew). He attended Littletown Academy and graduated from Virginia Military Institute in 1847. Mahone was a Democrat and an ardent secessionist and attended the Episcopal church. By his marriage to Otelia Butler on February 8, 1855, he had thirteen children, only three of whom reached maturity. He taught at Rappahannock Military Academy from 1847 to 1851 and was chief engineer from 1851 to 1861 for the Norfolk and Petersburg Railroad, of which he was also president in 1861. He lived in Petersburg, Virginia. When Virginia seceded, he was appointed quartermaster general for the state army. He became colonel of the 6th Virginia Infantry at the beginning of the war, and he helped to capture the Norfolk Navy Yard and supervised the construction of the defenses at Drewry's Bluff. He was promoted to brigadier general on November 16, 1861. After fighting at Seven Pines and the Seven Days, he was wounded during the battle of Second Manassas but recovered sufficiently to participate in such major battles as Fredericksburg, Chancellorsville, Gettysburg, the Wilderness, and Spotsylvania, all with the Army of Northern Virginia. On July 30, 1864, he was promoted to major general, following his heroic action at the battle of the Crater where he captured Warren's Corps. Lee (*q.v.*) considered him an excellent general. There is no record of his having surrendered. After the war, he returned to the railroad and joined the Readjuster party in Virginia. He was president of the Norfolk and Tennessee Railroad Company from 1867 until 1877, prior to losing a bid for the governorship of Virginia in 1878. In 1880, he was elected to the U.S. Senate, but he lost a subsequent bid for reelection six years later. Mahone dominated Republican party politics in his state after the war; he was also friendly to the Populists in the last years of his life. He died on October 8, 1895, in Washington, D.C. Blake, *William Mahone of Virginia*.

MALLET, John William (*Scientist*), was born to Robert and Cordelia (Watson) Mallet on October 10, 1835, in Dublin, Ireland. He received his Ph.D. from the

University of Gottingen, Germany, in 1852 and graduated from Trinity College, Dublin, with an A.B. in 1853. In 1854, he came to the United States and was a professor of chemistry at Amherst College. He was an Episcopalian, and he never relinquished his British citizenship. He had three children by his marriages to Mary Elizabeth Ormond in 1857 and to Mrs. Josephine (Pages) Burthe in 1888. Mallet was a chemist in the geological survey of Alabama in 1855-1856, and he was a professor of chemistry at the University of Alabama in Tuscaloosa from 1855 to 1860. When the Civil War began, he enlisted in the Confederate Army as a private and was soon promoted to colonel of artillery serving on Rodes' (*q.v.*) staff. In 1862, he was placed in charge of the ordnance labs in Richmond, whose machinery he had helped to design. Despite insufficient equipment, he made advances in artillery which were of utmost importance to the war effort. When the war ended, he moved to New Orleans and was professor of chemistry at the University of Louisiana from 1865 to 1868. From 1868 to 1908, he taught at the University of Virginia, with the exception of the years 1883-1884, which he spent at the University of Texas. Mallet was a fellow of the Royal Society of London. He died on November 6, 1912, in retirement in Charlottesville, Virginia. Tyler, *Encyclopedia of Virginia Biography*, V; *Who's Who in America*, 1912-1913.

MALLORY, Stephen Russell (*Cabinet Member*), son of Charles and Ellen (Russell) Mallory, was born in 1812 or 1813 in Trinidad, West Indies. His family moved to Key West, Florida, in 1820, and two years later his father died. Mallory was an Episcopalian. He attended school in Mobile, Alabama, and, in 1826, the Moravian School for Boys in Nazareth, Pennsylvania. From 1833 to 1840, he served as customs inspector at Key West prior to studying law and being admitted to the bar in Key West in 1840. In 1838, he married Angela Moreno; they had two daughters and three sons, one of whom shared not only his father's name but his career in the U.S. House and Senate. Mallory was a county judge in Monroe County, Florida, from 1840 to 1845, when he became the collector at the port of Key West. He soon developed an outstanding legal reputation and became active in Democratic party politics. The Florida legislature elected him to the U.S. Senate in 1851 where he served for ten years and was on the Naval Affairs Committee. Mallory was a convert to the cause of secession in 1860. When Florida seceded from the Union, he resigned from the Senate and moved to his home in Pensacola. On March 4, 1861, President Davis (*q.v.*) named him secretary of the Navy, a position which he held throughout the war. His job was heavily administrative and organizational, but his department was always a poor relation to the War Department. The two departments never fully cooperated. He encountered problems with the scarcity of skilled labor and manufacturing, and he was forced to contract with private firms. But unlike the secretary of war who was constantly hampered by President Davis's interference, Mallory was truly commander of the navy, for Davis knew little about naval warfare. Together with naval agent James D. Bulloch (*q.v.*) Mallory was sent to England as an envoy in 1862, developed a new war cruiser which drove federal shipping from the seas, and experimented with planned economic warfare—although he would never use navy ships to run the blockade. It was his idea that the Confederate Navy should use its limited resources for specializing in the use of ironclads. As the war ended, he left Richmond with President Davis and was taken prisoner in La Grange, Georgia, on May 20, 1865. After his release from prison in March 1866, he practiced law in Pensacola, where he lived at the time of his death on November 9, 1873. Durkin, *Stephen R. Mallory: Confederate Navy Chief*.

MANEY, George Earl (*General*), son of Thomas and Rebecca (Southall) Maney, was born on August 24, 1826, in Franklin, Tennessee. He attended Nashville Seminary and graduated from the University of Nashville in 1845. His marriage to Bettie Crutcher on June 23, 1853, produced two sons and three daughters. During the Mexican War, Maney served as a lieutenant in the Tennessee Infantry, but he left military service in 1848. Two years later, he was admitted to the Tennessee bar and he practiced in Nashville before the war. When the Civil War began, he volunteered for service in the Confederate Army. After entering as colonel of the 1st Tennessee Infantry, he fought in the Cheat Mountain campaign of September 1861 in northwestern Virginia. In February 1862, he asked to be sent to Tennessee. As commander of the 2nd Brigade of the Army of Mississippi, he distinguished himself at the battle of Shiloh, for which he was promoted to brigadier general on April 16, 1862. He participated in the battles of Perryville, Murfreesboro, Chickamauga, and Missionary Ridge before being wounded at Chattanooga in late 1863. He was captured during the battle of Atlanta in August 1864, and although he was subsequently released and ended the war years in the Carolinas, he saw no further action. He surrendered in Greensboro, North Carolina, and was subsequently paroled on May 1, 1865. He returned to his Nashville law practice and became president of the Tennessee and Pacific Railroad in 1868. He joined the Republican party, served in the Tennessee legislature, and entered and then withdrew from the gubernatorial race of 1876. President Arthur appointed Maney U.S. minister of Colombia in 1881 and to Bolivia in 1882; President Harrison appointed him U.S. minister to Uruguay and Paraguay in 1889-1900. He remained in Paraguay until 1894 and then retired to Washington, D.C. He died in Washington on February 9, 1901. Connelly, *Autumn of Glory*; Washington *Evening Star*, February 11, 1901.

MANIGAULT, Arthur Middleton (*General*), was born on October 26, 1824, in Charleston, South Carolina, to the wealthy rice planter Joseph Manigault and his wife Charlotte (Drayton). He left the College of Charleston in 1841 to study the export trade and to enter business. Manigault was an Episcopalian and a Democrat, and he had five children by his marriage to Mary Procter Huger on April 18, 1850. During the Mexican War, he was a first lieutenant in the Palmetto Regiment. From 1847 to 1856, he was a commission merchant in Charleston. In 1856, he moved to Georgetown County, where he had inherited a rice plantation, "White Oak." At the time of the firing on Fort Sumter, Manigault was inspector general on the staff of P.G.T. Beauregard (*q.v.*). When the Civil War began, he was colonel of the 10th South Carolina Regiment, and he helped to construct the batteries for the defense of Winyah Bay and Corinth. After serving as a brigade commander under General Braxton Bragg (*q.v.*) during the battle of Shiloh, he served with the Army of Tennessee at Stone's River, Chickamauga, and the Atlanta campaign. He was promoted to brigadier general on April 26, 1863. Manigault sustained two wounds during the war—at Resaca, Georgia, in May 1863 and at Franklin, Tennessee, in November 1864. He saw no further active duty. When the war ended, he returned to rice planting in Georgetown. Manigault served as adjutant and inspector general of South Carolina from 1880 to 1886. He died in Georgetown on August 17, 1886. Davidson, *The Last Foray*.

MANLY, Basil (Minister), son of the planter Basil Manly and his wife Elizabeth (Maultsby), was born in Pittsborough, North Carolina, on January 29, 1798. He attended Bingham School and graduated first in his class of 1821 at South Carolina College. On December 23, 1824, he married Sarah Murray Rudulph, by whom he had five children. Manly, who had begun to preach in 1818, was ordained in the Baptist ministry in 1822 and settled in Edgefield, South Carolina. In the 1820s, he was a pastor in Charleston, South Carolina, where he assisted in the founding of Furman Institute in 1823. He preached at the First Baptist Church in Charleston from 1826 to 1837. From 1837 to 1855, he was president of the University of Alabama. He owned a plantation in Tuscaloosa, where he also helped to found the Alabama Historical Society. In 1859, he helped to establish a hospital for the insane in Tuscaloosa. At the Alabama Baptist convention in 1860, Manly, a vehement secessionist, condemned the federal government. He ran unsuccessfully for the state legislature as a secession candidate and was the chaplain at the inauguration of Jefferson Davis (*q.v.*) in Montgomery. When the war began, he was preaching in Montgomery. His sermons in the field were an inspiration to the Confederate troops. In 1864, he suffered a stroke, and when he recovered he returned to South Carolina. Manly died on December 21, 1868, in Greenville, South Carolina. Wilson, "Basil Manly, Apologist for Slavocracy," *Alabama Review*, XV.

MANN, Ambrose Dudley (*Diplomat*), was born at Hanover Courthouse, Virginia, on April 26, 1801. He moved to Kentucky early in life and left the U.S. Military Academy in 1831 to study law in Greeney's County, Kentucky. He was a Whig who became a Democrat, and he married Hebe Grayson Carter. He practiced law in Greeney's County and became active in Whig politics. Mann was appointed U.S. consul to Bremen, Germany, in 1842, U.S. commissioner to Hungary in 1849, and U.S. minister to Switzerland in 1850. From 1854 to 1856, he was assistant secretary of state. Late in the 1850s, he began to write about Southern economic independence, and he championed a Southern merchant marine. For a time he settled in Richmond, Virginia, from where he volunteered for service in the Confederate government. During the war, the Confederate government sent him on a special mission to England in 1861. The mission proved unsuccessful, but Mann did influence the English and Belgian press. From 1862 until the end of the war, he lived in Belgium, where he attempted to win King Leopold's support of the Confederate cause. In 1863-1864, he went to the Vatican to attempt to persuade the Pope to stop the recruitment of Irish and Germans to fight in the Union Army. After the war, he lived in Paris and was a journalist. He died there on November 20, 1889. Cullop, *Confederate Propaganda in Europe*; Moore (ed.), *The Letters of A. Dudley Mann to Jefferson Davis, 1869-1889*.

MARMADUKE, John Sappington (*General*), was born to Meredith Miles and Lavinia (Sappington) Marmaduke on March 14, 1833, in Arrow Rock, Missouri. His father was a Democratic governor of Missouri in 1844. Young Marmaduke attended country schools, Masonic College in Lexington, Missouri, Yale, and Harvard. He graduated thirtieth in a class of thirty-eight from the U.S. Military Academy in 1857. He was a Democrat and a bachelor and had no religious affiliation. Before the war, Marmaduke served on the frontier as a career officer in the U.S. Army. He participated in the Utah expedition and was promoted to second lieutenant in the 7th Infantry during the Mormon War of 1858-1860. Marmaduke resigned from the federal army in 1861 and volunteered for duty in the Confederate Army. He began his service under General William Hardee (*q.v.*) as lieutenant colonel and later colonel of the 1st Arkansas Battalion. After winning praise for his role during the battle of Shiloh, where he was also wounded, he was promoted to brigadier general on November 15, 1862, following the siege of Corinth. In December of that year, he was conspicuous at the battle of Prairie Grove, Arkansas. Marmaduke was assigned to a cavalry division in the Trans-Mississippi Department under General Thomas Hindman (*q.v.*), and during 1853 he twice accompanied General Sterling Price (*q.v.*) on a series of raids into Missouri. He participated in the battles of Fayetteville and Helena in late 1863. During his participation in the defense of Little Rock in September 1863, he fought a duel with and killed General L. M. Walker, for which he was arrested. He was soon released, however. Marmaduke attacked Pine Bluff, Arkansas, the following month, and during the Red River campaign in the spring of 1864 he was brilliant at the battle of Poison Spring. Marmaduke was taken prisoner at the battle of Mine Creek, during Price's Missouri raid in October 1864. He was not released until after the war, although he was promoted to major general on March 17, 1865. Upon his release in the summer of 1865, he traveled in Europe before entering the commission and insurance business in St. Louis in 1866. From 1871 to 1874, he edited the *St. Louis Journal of Agriculture*, and in 1874, he served as secretary of the State Agricultural Board. From 1880 to 1885, he was a member of the State Railroad Commission. Marmaduke served one term as Democratic governor of

Missouri, from 1885 to 1887. He died on December 28, 1887. Kerby, *Kirby Smith's Confederacy: The Trans-Mississippi South, 1863-1865*; Wright, *General Officers of the Confederate Army*.

MARSHALL, Henry (*Congressman*), was born to the wealthy merchant and planter Adam Marshall and his wife in Darlington District, South Carolina, on December 28, 1805. He was a cousin of the Confederate general Maxcy Gregg (*q.v.*). He was a Presbyterian and attended Union College in New York during the late 1820s. Sometime thereafter, he moved to Louisiana where he served in the state Senate before the Civil War. Marshall also farmed in Mansfield, Louisiana, for some years before the war. He was a secessionist member of the Louisiana secession convention and a member of the provisional Confederate Congress, and he served on the Territories, Public Lands and Claims Committees, and on the Select Committee of Three to receive the tax. Marshall was elected to the first Confederate House, where his committee assignments included Claims, Quartermaster's and Commissary Departments, Military Transport, Conference, Inauguration, Patents, and Territories and Public Lands. He was anti-administration during both of his terms. Marshall refused to run for the second Congress and was replaced by Benjamin L. Hodge (*q.v.*). He believed that the Davis government had not shown enough interest in saving southern Louisiana from the Union invasion. Little else is known of his wartime career. He died in De Soto Parish, Louisiana, on July 13, 1864. Bragg, *Louisiana in the Confederacy*; *Memories of Northwest Louisiana*.

MARSHALL, Humphrey (*General, Congressman*), son of John James and Ann Reed (Birney) Marshall, was born on January 13, 1812, in Frankfort, Kentucky. He graduated forty-second in a class of forty-five at the U.S. Military Academy in 1832 and became a member of the Mounted Rangers. In January 1833, he married Frances Elizabeth MacAlister; they had nine children. He resigned his army commission in 1833 and studied law. Marshall was admitted to the Frankfort bar in 1833 and moved to Louisville, Kentucky, the following year where he developed a good law practice and also became a planter. He fought in the 1833 Black Hawk War, and upon return from the war he entered political life. In 1836, he served on the Louisville City Council. He became active in the state militia in the late 1830s and in 1846 was lieutenant colonel in the militia. During the Mexican War, he was the ranking colonel of cavalry and participated in the charge of Buena Vista. He served in the U.S. House of Representatives as a Whig from 1849 to 1852 and as a member of the American party from 1855 to 1859, when he defeated General William Preston (*q.v.*) for election in 1855. From 1852 to 1854, he served as President Fillmore's minister to China. In 1859, he became a secessionist, although he later tried to save the Union and favored an armed neutrality. In 1860, he supported John C. Breckinridge (*q.v.*) for president. He attempted to keep Kentucky neutral in 1860, but when Lincoln called for the invasion of Kentucky he joined the Confederate Army. He was commissioned a brigadier general on October 30, 1861, and was placed in charge of an independent department, the Army of Southwest Virginia. He fought at the battle of Middle Creek in January 1862 and participated in Bragg's (*q.v.*) invasion of Kentucky. In June 1863, he resigned his commission to practice law in Richmond. He was elected to the second Confederate House from Kentucky where he served on the Military Affairs Committee and was an administration opponent. Marshall was a leader of the Kentucky bloc, opposed to General Bragg, and agitated for another invasion of Kentucky. After the war, he returned to his law practice in Louisville, where he died on March 28, 1872. Connelly and Jones, *The Politics of Command*; Levin (ed.), *The Lawyers and Lawmakers of Kentucky*.

MARTIN, Augustus Mary (*Bishop*), was born on February 2, 1803, in Breton, St. Malo, France. After serving at Beauvois, France, as subdeacon in 1824 and deacon in 1825, he was ordained in the Catholic priesthood in 1828. Martin came to the United States in 1841 and served as acting chaplain of the Ursuline Convent at New Orleans the following year. From 1843 to 1853, he held pastorates in Louisiana, and on July 29, 1853, he was named Bishop of Natchitoches. During the Civil War, he sided with the Confederacy. In August 1861, he gave a sermon on the morality of the Confederate war effort, which was said to have converted many Gulf Coast Catholics to the Southern cause. Throughout the war, he preached for Confederate victories, and he tried to sustain morale after New Orleans had fallen. He was a consistent defender of states' rights and believed in support of the government under which he lived. After the war, he continued as bishop of Natchitoches until his death in New Orleans on September 29, 1879. Blied, *Catholics in the Civil War*; Rice, *American Catholic Opinion and the Slavery Controversy*.

MARTIN, James Green (*General*), was born on February 14, 1819, in Elizabeth City, North Carolina, to William and Sophia Scott (Dauge) Martin. His father was a planter, physician, shipbuilder, and North Carolina assemblyman. Young Martin attended St. Mary's Academy in Raleigh and graduated fourteenth in a class of forty-two from the U.S. Military Academy in 1840. He was an Episcopalian and had four children by his marriage to Marian Murray Reed on July 12, 1844; his second marriage was to Hetty King on February 8, 1858. For six years following his graduation from West Point, Martin served on the Maine frontier. During the Mexican War, he lost his right arm at Churubusco and was promoted to captain in 1847. He later served again on the frontier, and he was quartermaster under General Albert S. Johnston (*q.v.*) during the Utah expedition. After North Carolina seceded, he resigned from the army in June 1861 and entered the service of the Confederate Army. At the beginning of the Civil War, he was adjutant general of North Carolina, in charge of organizing and equipping state troops. In September 1861, he was named commander of North Carolina forces. Martin raised twelve thousand more troops than the state quota for the Confederate Army. In May 1862, he was appointed brigadier general and was given command of all Confederate troops in North Carolina. After driving federal forces from Newport in the fall of 1863, he became a hero in the defense of Petersburg, Virginia, in 1864, fighting at Howlett's House and Turkey Ridge. During the last part of the war, his health failed, and he was given command of the District of Western North Carolina. He surrendered in North Carolina on May 10, 1865, and was soon paroled. After the war, he moved to Asheville, North Carolina, where he studied law; he practiced law from 1866 until his death on October 4, 1878. Barrett, *The Civil War in North Carolina*; Wright, *General Officers of the Confederate Army*.

MARTIN, John Marshall (*Congressman*), was born in Edgefield District, South Carolina, on March 18, 1832. He graduated from the Citadel in 1852. He moved to Ocala, Florida, from Edgefield in 1856. Before the war, he was a planter. He was active in local Democratic party politics, and he supported the secession of Florida. During the Civil War, he organized the Marion Light Infantry in Florida, of which he was captain in 1861. He also was elected to the first Confederate House of Representatives from the First District of Florida. Martin served on the Naval Affairs Committee and the special committee for the relief of sick soldiers. At the end of his term in the House, he refused reelection and returned to the field. In the spring of 1864, Martin was colonel of the 9th Florida Regiment. He saw service in the Army of Tennessee during the Nashville campaign in late 1864. When the war ended, he returned to his Ocala plantation. He was also part of a company which wanted to construct an electric railroad. He died at Ocala on August 10, 1921. Ott and Chazel, *Ocali County*; Rerick, *Memoirs of Florida*, II.

MARTIN, William Thompson (*General*), son of John Henderson and Emily Moore (Kerr) Martin, was born on March 25, 1823, in Glasgow, Kentucky. He graduated from Centre College in Danville, Kentucky, in 1840, and, following his family's move to Vicksburg, Mississippi, was admitted to the Natchez bar in 1842. He was a unionist Whig and an opponent of secession. On January 5, 1854, he married Margaret Dunlop Conner, by whom he had four sons and five daughters. Martin forsook private practice to become district attorney of Natchez from 1844 until 1860. When Mississippi seceded, he organized the Adams County Cavalry, and when the war began, he volunteered with his company for service in the Confederate Army. He was a major of the 2nd Mississippi Cavalry and, along with J.E.B. Stuart (*q.v.*), he was a cavalry leader during the Peninsular campaign and at the Seven Days' battles in Virginia in 1862. At the battle of Sharpsburg in September, he was a personal aide to General Robert E. Lee (*q.v.*). Promoted to brigadier general on December 2, 1862, he was transferred to the Army of the West. Martin distinguished himself in Tennessee, where he participated in the Tullahoma campaign of the summer of 1863 and the battle of Spring Hill in

November 1864. At the battle of Chickamauga and during the Atlanta campaign, he commanded a division of General Joseph Wheeler's (*q.v.*) Cavalry Corps. On November 10, 1863, he was promoted to major general. From late 1864 until the end of the war, he commanded the District of Northwest Mississippi. There is no record of his surrender. After the war, he returned to Natchez and practiced law. He was also active in Democratic politics: he was a delegate to the state constitutional conventions of 1865 and 1890, and from 1882 to 1894, he served in the Mississippi Senate. In 1905, he was postmaster of Natchez. Also involved in a railroad company, he was president of the Natchez, Jackson, and Columbus Railroad in 1884. Martin died on March 16, 1910, in Natchez. Evans, *Confederate Military History*, VII; *Who's Who in America*, 1906-1910.

MASON, James Murray (*Congressman, Diplomat*), was born on November 3, 1798, in Fairfax County, Virginia, to General John and Anna Maria (Murray) Mason. He attended Georgetown Academy and graduated from the University of Pennsylvania in 1818 and from the College of William and Mary Law School in 1820. Mason was an Episcopalian and had eight children by his marriage on July 25, 1822, to Elizabeth Margaretta Chew. He began his law practice in the Richmond office of Benjamin Watkins Leigh in 1822 and moved to Winchester, Virginia, where he soon became a successful lawyer. He represented Winchester in the Virginia House of Delegates in 1826-1827 and 1829-1831. From 1837 to 1839, he served as a Jackson Democrat in the U.S. House of Representatives. As U.S. senator from 1847 to 1861, he chaired the Foreign Relations Committee and drafted the Fugitive Slave Law of 1850. A secessionist, Mason was a Virginia delegate to the provisional Confederate Congress. In November 1861, President Davis (*q.v.*) appointed him commissioner of the Confederacy to Great Britain and France, where he acted as central agent for the Confederate purchasing agents, helped the propagandists raise money, and sold bonds. U.S. officials seized Mason and his diplomatic colleague John Slidell (*q.v.*) from the British steamer *Trent* while en route to Europe. They were held prisoner in Boston until January 1862. Great Britain felt insulted over the seizure, and early diplomatic relations with the North began on a cool note. Mason's purchasing of battleships led to the "Alabama Claims" and diplomatic problems with Europe. Though he made successful loans, his tour was a failure because he was unable to secure European recognition for the Confederacy. When the war ended he fled to Canada. In 1868, he settled near Alexandria, Virginia, where he lived at the time of his death on April 28, 1871. Mason, *The Public Life and Diplomatic Correspondence of James M. Mason*.

MAURY, Dabney Herndon (*General*), nephew of M. F. Maury (*q.v.*), was born on May 21, 1822, in Fredericksburg, Virginia, to Captain John Minor Maury and his wife Eliza (Maury). He left his study of law at the University of Virginia in 1842 to pursue a military career, and in 1846, he graduated thirty-seventh in a class of fifty-nine from the U.S. Military Academy. In 1852, he married Nannie R. Mason; they had one son and two daughters. Wounded at Cerro Gordo during the Mexican War, Maury was breveted first lieutenant before serving as an assistant professor in infantry tactics at West Point from 1850 to 1852. From 1852 to 1858, he served as a lieutenant on frontier duty in Texas, and from 1858 to 1860, he was superintendent of the cavalry school at Carlisle, Pennsylvania. In 1859, he published *Skirmish Drill for Mounted Troops*, and the following year he was breveted captain and named adjutant general of New Mexico. When the Civil War began, he resigned from the federal army. He served as adjutant general in the Confederate Army and, early in 1862, was appointed chief of staff to General Earl Van Dorn (*q.v.*), with whom he fought in the battles of Elkhorn Tavern and Pea Ridge. He was promoted to brigadier general on March 12, 1862, and to major general on November 12, 1862, after serving as a division commander at the battle of Corinth. He saw action at Yazoo Pass and Steele's Bayou during the Vicksburg campaign, and he commanded the Department of East Tennessee, with headquarters at Knoxville, until May 1863, when he was made commander for the District of the Gulf, a position which he retained throughout the remainder of the war. He was captured when Mobile fell, but he was later paroled. After the war, he was penniless and he had no previous business experience to help him find a job. Maury returned to his family home in Fredericksburg where he taught school, wrote a school history of Virginia, and helped to organize the Southern Historical Society in 1869. He also served as a member of the executive committee of the National Guard and was U.S. minister to Colombia from 1885 to 1889. He wrote his *Recollections of a Virginian* prior to his death on January 11, 1900, at his son's home in Peoria, Illinois. *Confederate Veteran*, III; Evans, *Confederate Military History*, III.

MAURY, Matthew Fontaine (*Naval Commander, Scientist, Diplomat*), was born in Spotsylvania County, Virginia, on January 14, 1806, to Richard and Diana (Minor) Maury. When Matthew was five, his father emigrated to Tennessee, and he attended Hayseth Academy there before becoming a midshipman at the age of nineteen. He was an Episcopalian and married Ann Herndon, a cousin, in 1834. Maury commanded his first vessel in 1831; he wrote a text on navigation in 1834; and he was promoted to lieutenant in 1837. In 1843, he was in charge of the depot of charts and instruments in Washington, D.C. He wrote *Physical Geography of the Sea and Its Meteorology* in 1855 and was named president of the National Meteorological Institute in 1856. Although almost all his duty was on shore, President Buchanan promoted him to commander in 1858. On April 20, 1861, he resigned his commission and went to Richmond. He was named commander in the Confederate Navy and chief of harbor and river defenses. He mined the James River and invented the electric torpedo. In 1862, he was sent to England where he purchased and outfitted cruisers and experimented in torpedo defenses. He remained there for the duration of the war. After the war, he moved to Mexico where he was a member of Prince Maximilian's cabinet. He also moved to England from 1866 to 1868 to instruct military students in the uses of torpedoes. In 1868, he returned to Virginia, where he was professor of meteorology at Washington and Lee University. Maury died on February 1, 1873, in Lexington, Virginia. Alderman (ed.), *Library of Southern Literature*, VIII; Williams, *Matthew Fontaine Maury*.

MAXEY, Samuel Bell (*General*), was born on March 30, 1825, in Tompkinsville, Kentucky, to Rice and ——— (Bell) Maxey. He attended common schools and graduated fifty-eighth in a class of fifty-nine from the U.S. Military Academy in 1846. Maxey had children by his marriage to Matilda Cassa Denton on July 19, 1853. He fought at Vera Cruz and Cerro Gordo and was breveted first lieutenant during the Mexican War before resigning his commission to go to Kentucky in 1849. He studied law in Paris, Texas, and was admitted to the bar in Kentucky in 1850, beginning his law practice in Albany, Kentucky. From 1852 to 1856, he was clerk of county and circuit courts and master of chancery for Clinton County. In 1857, he moved to Paris, Texas, and joined the Democratic party. He was district attorney for Lamar County in 1858-1859, and in 1861, he declined a seat in the Texas Senate in order to join the Confederate Army. When the Civil War began, Maxey raised the 9th Regiment of Texas Infantry, of which he was colonel. He was promoted to brigadier general on March 7, 1862. In 1863, he fought at Port Hudson, Mississippi, with General Joseph E. Johnston (*q.v.*) and at Chattanooga. On December 11, 1863, he was given command of the Indian Territory. Maxey reorganized and trained the Indian troops into an efficient fighting force during the Red River campaign of 1864. General Kirby Smith (*q.v.*) subsequently recommended Maxey for promotion to major general, but the position was never granted. There is no record of his surrender. After the war, Maxey returned to his law practice in Paris. He declined judicial appointment to the Eighth District of Texas in 1873. He was also active in postwar Democratic party politics. From 1875 until he lost a bid for reelection in 1887, Maxey served as a Democrat in the U.S. Senate where he often supported farms for western Indians. He died on August 16, 1895, in retirement in Eureka Springs, Arkansas. *Biographical Directory of Congress*; Kerby, *Kirby Smith's Confederacy: The Trans-Mississippi South, 1863-1865*; Ramsdell, *Reconstruction in Texas*.

MAXWELL, Augustus Emmett (*Congressman*), was born on September 21, 1820, in Elberton, Georgia, to Simeon and Elizabeth (Fortson) Maxwell. The family moved to Greene County, Alabama, in 1822. The younger Maxwell graduated from the University of Virginia in 1841, studied law in Alabama, and was admitted to the Alabama bar in 1843. Maxwell was a Democrat and a vestryman in the Episcopal church. He had three children by his 1843 marriage to Sarah Roane Brockenbrough and, after her death, five children by his 1853 marriage to Julia H. Anderson. Maxwell practiced law in Eutaw, Alabama, from

1843 to 1845, when he moved to Tallahassee, Florida. With help from his Brockenbrough in-laws, he entered public life and was attorney general of Florida in 1846-1847, a member of the state House in 1847, secretary of state in 1848, state senator in 1849-1850, and U.S. congressman from 1853 to 1857. He left Congress in 1857 and practiced law in Pensacola, Florida. From 1857 to 1861, he was a U.S. naval agent at Pensacola. He supported secession. Maxwell was elected to the Confederate Senate and served from 1862 to 1865. An administration supporter, he feared excessive speculation on war goods. He was involved in the peace movement of 1864. He served on the Commerce, Patents, Engrossment and Enrollments, Foreign Affairs, Indian Affairs, and Naval Affairs Committees. In 1865-1866, he was a judge of the Florida Supreme Court, but resigned in late 1866 to become president of the Pensacola and Montgomery Railroad and the law partner of Stephen Mallory (*q.v.*). From 1877 to 1885, he was appointed a state circuit court judge. In 1885, he was a delegate to the state constitutional convention, and from 1887 to 1891, he was chief justice of the Florida Supreme Court. He then retired from public life but resumed his law practice in Pensacola. He died on May 5, 1903, in Chipley, Florida. Rerick, *Memoirs of Florida*; Yearns, *The Confederate Congress*.

MEMMINGER, Christopher Gustavus (*Cabinet Member*), was born on January 7 or 9, 1803, in Nayhingen, Wurttenberg, Germany, to Christopher Godfrey and Eberhardina (Kohler) Memminger and was brought to Charleston, South Carolina, as an infant. His father had died in Germany. His mother died when he was four, and he was placed in a Charleston orphan house. He was an Episcopalian. He graduated second in the class of 1819 at South Carolina College and was admitted to the bar in 1824, the same year he became an American citizen. His 1832 marriage to Mary Wilkinson produced eight children. She died and Memminger married her sister, Sarah A. Wilkinson, in 1878. He became a successful lawyer in Charleston. An opponent of nullification, he served in the lower house of the state legislature during 1836-1852 and 1854-1860. For twenty years he was chairman of the Ways and Means Committee of the state House. In 1855, he served on the Committee of Free Schools in Charleston. He was a unionist delegate to the Southern rights convention in 1852, South Carolina's emissary to persuade Virginia to secede in 1860, and a delegate to the South Carolina secession convention. He supported secession and was elected to the provisional Confederate Congress, where he served on the Commercial Affairs Committee and chaired the committee which drafted the provisional constitution. President Davis (*q.v.*) appointed him secretary of the treasury in 1861, and he served until June 15, 1864, when he resigned because he saw no way to remedy the Confederacy's financial condition. His businesslike manner offended many politicians, but his relationship with the president was excellent. He was aware of the necessity to raise finances, but his attempts to control the inflation caused by loans, dwindling supplies, and worthless bonds were unsuccessful. With little cooperation from Congress, Memminger's taxation schemes also failed. Attempts to float bond issues abroad failed largely because of Confederate military reverses. After his resignation, he retired to North Carolina and gave no further service to the Confederacy. He received a pardon in 1867 and returned to his law practice in Charleston. In 1868, he founded a company which manufactured sulphuric acid. He died in Charleston on March 7, 1888. Capers, *The Life and Times of C. G. Memminger*.

MENEES, Thomas (*Congressman*), son of Benjamin Williams and Elizabeth (Harrison) Menees, was born on June 26, 1823, in Mansker's Creek, Davidson County, Tennessee. He attended and taught in country schools in Robertson County, Tennessee, and studied medicine at Transylvania University, where he received his M.D. in 1846. He was a Democrat, a Mason, and a steward in the Methodist Episcopal church. Menees had four children by his marriage to Elizabeth Hooper on April 21, 1853. She died and he married Mrs. Mary Jane Walker, on August 14, 1863, by whom he had a daughter. Menees practiced medicine in Springfield, Tennessee, from 1846 to 1855, and he then went into business. In 1857, he served in the state Senate, but he lost a bid for the U.S. House of Representatives two years later because of the power of the Whigs in his area. After returning to private life, he made railroad investments. He was a secessionist and supported John C. Breckinridge (*q. v.*) for president in 1860. He was elected to the first Confederate House from Tennessee's Eighth Congressional District soon after the war began and was reelected in 1864. An administration supporter, he served on the Medical Departments, Territories and Public Lands, and Printing Committees. After the war, he practiced medicine in Nashville. In 1873, he was a professor of medicine at the University of Nashville, and the following year he was made dean of the medical faculty at Vanderbilt University. He died in Nashville on September 6, 1905. Wooldridge, *History of Nashville*.

MERRICK, Edwin Thomas (*Judge*), son of Thomas and Anna (Brewer) Merrick, was born on July 9, 1809, in Wilbraham, Massachusetts. He attended Wesleyan Academy at Wilbraham from 1830 to 1832, studied law, and moved to New Lisbon, Ohio, where he was admitted to the Ohio bar in 1833. He developed a practice in Carrollton, Ohio. His marriage to Caroline E. Thomas on December 3, 1840, produced two sons. He was a Methodist. Merrick moved to Clinton, Louisiana, in 1838 and was admitted to the bar there in 1839. His practice flourished and he became involved in local politics. In 1845, he was the judge of the Seventh District Court at New Orleans, and the following year he was the successful Whig nominee to the state Supreme Court. In 1855, he was named chief justice of the state Supreme Court. Although Merrick opposed secession, he believed in the right of secession, and he remained chief justice of the state Supreme Court on behalf of the Confederacy throughout the war. He was reelected in 1863 but was removed by the occupying federal forces and, in 1865, retired to his plantation at Pointe Coupee. After the war, his plantation in West Feliciana Parish was seized, and he went to New Orleans to practice law. In 1871, he wrote a treatise, *Laws of Louisiana and Their Sources*. He died on January 2, 1897, in retirement in New Orleans. Fortier, *A History of Louisiana*, II.

MILES, William Porcher (*Congressman*), was born at Walterboro, Colleton District, South Carolina, on July 4, 1822, to James Saunders and Sarah Bond (Worley) Miles. He attended Willington Academy, graduated first in his class at the College of Charleston in 1842, studied law, and was admitted to the Charleston bar in 1843. In 1863, he married Betty Bevine, the daughter of a Virginia and Louisiana planter. Miles soon gave up the law, and from 1843 to 1855, he was an assistant professor of mathematics at the College of Charleston. During a term as mayor of Charleston from 1855 to 1857, he perfected the city's system of drains. He was elected and served as Democratic member of the U.S. House of Representatives from 1857 to 1860 and helped to stem the tide of the Know-Nothing movement in South Carolina. Miles resigned from Congress in December 1860 and was elected to the state secession convention. He was chairman of the Foreign Relations Committee of the South Carolina secession convention and was elected a member of the Military Affairs and Printing Committees of the provisional Confederate Congress in Montgomery. Miles favored limits on the president's term in office, advocated the inclusion of nonslaveholding states in the Confederacy, and offered amendments to the Confederate Constitution. He represented Charleston in the Confederate House from 1862 to 1865 and was chairman of the important Military Affairs Committee. Miles was P.G.T. Beauregard's (*q.v.*) major spokesman in Richmond, supported the anti-Bragg faction, proposed a Confederate Supreme Court, favored conscription, and desired a streamlined, reorganized army. A brilliant legislator and excellent administrator, he supported President Davis (*q.v.*) until 1864, when he accused the president of no longer wishing to defend Charleston. Miles also served on the Conference and on many special committees. He held some military duty and was a colonel on Beauregard's staff at First Manassas. From 1865 to 1880, he lived as a country gentleman at Oakridge, Nelson County, Virginia (he had married into wealth). From 1880 to 1882, he was president of the University of South Carolina. In 1882, he became manager of a sugar plantation in Ascension Parish, Louisiana. One of the largest plantations in the South, it produced 20 million pounds of sugar annually. Miles also founded a sugar experiment station. He played no role in postwar politics. He died on May 11, 1899, in Burnside, Louisiana. Ashe, *Cyclopedia of Eminent and Representative Men of the Carolinas of the Nineteenth Century*, I; Wakelyn, *The Politics of a Literary Man*.

MILLER, Samuel Augustine (*Congressman*), was born in Shenandoah County, Virginia, on October 16, 1819. He attended Gettysburg College from 1835 to 1839. He read law, was admitted to the Virginia bar in 1841, and became a specialist in land titles. Miller had five children by his marriage to a Miss Quarrier. In 1842, he moved to Kanawha County, Virginia, where he became president of the Kanawha Salt Company. He also practiced law in Charleston, (West) Virginia and supported the Union. But when the Civil War began, he joined the Confederate Army as a private and rose to the rank of major. From the fall of 1862 to the end of the war, he also represented southwest Virginia in the first and second Confederate House of Representatives. During his first term, he served on the Territories and Public Lands Committees and on the special committee on the manufacturing of arms. In the second Confederate House, he served on the Elections, Indian Affairs, and Army Pay Committees and on the special committee to study violations of impressment laws. Miller considered himself a unionist in the Confederate House. After the war he fled briefly to Canada. He was charged with treason in late 1865, but later, after the charges were dismissed, returned to the practice of law in Charleston, West Virginia. He lost almost all of his property during the war. He served in the legislature in 1874. Miller died in Parkersburg on November 19, 1890. Atkinson (ed.), *Bench and Bar of West Virginia*.

MILTON, John (*Governor*), was born to Homer Virgil and Elizabeth (Robinson) Milton in Louisville, Georgia, on April 20, 1807. He attended the academy in Louisville, studied law, and practiced in Mobile, Alabama, and New Orleans before moving to Jackson County, Florida, to farm in 1846. Milton had four children by his marriage to Susan Amanda Cobb on December 9, 1826, and, after her death, eleven children by his marriage to Caroline Howze in 1840. He was a secessionist and a prohibitionist. In 1833, he ran for Congress on the nullifier ticket in Georgia. From 1835 to 1837, he was a captain of volunteers in the Seminole War in Florida. He entered politics in Florida, and in 1849, he was a Democratic state senator from Jackson County. Milton served as governor of Florida from 1860 to 1864, during which time he cooperated with the Confederate government far more than did any other Confederate governor. He besieged the U.S. arsenal at Apalachicola and Forts Marion and Augustine in the early days of the war, raised troops, and supplied food and clothing for the army. He would have preferred the military to the civilian life, and he opposed all peace propaganda. When his term ended, he retired to private life in Jackson County. Milton died of a stroke, apparently caused by worry and overwork, in Marianna, Florida, on April 1, 1865. *Makers of America, Florida Edition*, I.

MITCHEL, Charles Burton (*Congressman*), was born in Gallatin, Tennessee, on September 19, 1815. Nothing is known of his early family life. He was educated in the common schools, attended the University of Nashville, and graduated from the Jefferson Medical School in Philadelphia, Pennsylvania, in 1836. He then removed to Washington, Arkansas, where he practiced medicine for twenty-five years. He was a Presbyterian and was active in Democratic politics. He was elected to the state legislature in 1848 and was the state receiver of public moneys from 1853 to 1856 but lost a race for the U.S. House of Representatives in 1860. Mitchel was elected to the U.S. Senate in March 1861 but resigned the following July. He was married to Sallie Ann ———— and they had one son. Mitchel belonged to the union wing of the Arkansas Democratic party, largely because he was an opponent of the Robert W. Johnson (*q.v.*) family machine. He was elected to the first Confederate Senate after the war began, and he was reelected in 1864. In the Senate, he was an administration supporter who urged more care in planning the defense of the Mississippi River. He opposed the military command of General Thomas Hindman (*q.v.*) and called for General Kirby Smith (*q.v.*) to be named as commander of the Trans-Mississippi District. Mitchel died in office while home in Little Rock on September 20, 1864. *Arkansas Gazette*, September 21, 1864; *Biographical Directory of the American Congress*.

MONROE, Thomas Bell (*Congressman*), was born on October 7, 1791, in Albemarle County, Virginia. His parents moved to Barren County, Kentucky, when he was young, and he pursued a public school education. Early active in Kentucky politics, Monroe was elected to a term in the state legislature in 1816. He studied law two years later, and became a lawyer in Frankfort, Kentucky, in 1819. His marriage to Eliza Palmer Adair produced a son and namesake who was a major in the Confederate Army. Monroe was also an educator; at one time he taught as a lecturer in the Law Department of Transylvania University. In 1823, he became secretary of state for Kentucky. From 1825 to 1828, he was reporter of the decisions of the Court of Appeals, and he also published *Monroe's Kentucky Reports*. In 1830, he was elected U.S. district attorney for Kentucky, and from 1834 to 1861, he was a judge of the U.S. District Court for Kentucky. A secessionist, he was a lifetime Democrat. He represented Franklin County in the provisional Confederate Congress, where he served on the Foreign Affairs, Judiciary, and Military Affairs Committees. Monroe refused to stand for election to the permanent Congress and, instead, practiced law during the war. He retired from public life, simply because he was too old to perform any active service. Monroe died on December 24, 1865, in Frankfort, Kentucky. Collins, *Historical Sketches of Kentucky*.

MONTAGUE, Robert Latane (*Congressman*), son of Lewis Brooke and Catherine Street (Jesse) Montague, was born on May 23, 1819, in Ellaslee, Middlesex County, Virginia. He attended Fleetwood Academy in Virginia, studied law in Fredericksburg, and graduated from the College of William and Mary in 1842. He began an active legal practice in Saluda, Virginia, and also became involved in local politics. He had a small farm. He was a Democrat and a Baptist, and he married Cordelia Gay Eubank on December 14, 1852. Montague was a member of the state legislature from 1850 to 1852, commonwealth attorney of Middlesex County in 1857, and lieutenant governor under John Letcher (*q.v.*)

in 1860. In 1861, he served as president of the Virginia secession convention and was a leader in the state secession movement. During the war, he was a member of the state Executive Council, and he helped to organize Virginia troops for service in the Confederate Army. Montague was also a conspicuous member of the second Confederate House from 1863 to 1865. A staunch Davis supporter, he served on the Ordnance and Ordnance Stores Committee and on special investigatory committees. When the war ended, he returned to his law practice in Saluda. When his disabilities were finally removed in 1872, he represented Middlesex County in the House of Delegates. He was judge of the Eighth Judicial District of Virginia from 1875 until his death on March 2, 1880, in Middlesex County. McGregor, *Disruption of Virginia*.

MOORE, Andrew Barry (*Governor*), was born to Captain Charles and Jane (Barry) Moore on March 7, 1807, in Spartanburg, South Carolina. His father was a planter. After moving to Alabama as a youth, the younger Moore received a local primary school education and was admitted to the bar of Marion, Alabama, in 1833. Moore was a Presbyterian and had three children by his marriage to Mary Gorree in 1837. He was elected to the state legislature from Marion in 1839 and 1842 and served as speaker of that body from 1843 to 1845. In 1848, he was a presidential elector on the Whig ticket, but he joined the Democratic party in 1857. In 1851, he became a judge on the state circuit court, leaving the bench to run unopposed for governor in 1857. He was reelected in 1859. Moore, an ardent advocate of states' rights, became a leader for secession in Alabama. By ordering the seizure of Pensacola in 1861, he helped the Confederate government to collect munitions and supplies. He also organized troops for the defense of Alabama. After his term as governor was over in late 1861, he was made special aide-de-camp to Governor John Shorter (*q. v.*) and held the position for the rest of the war. He practiced law from the end of the war until his death on April 5, 1873, in Marion. Fleming, *Civil War and Reconstruction in Alabama*; Owen, *History of Alabama and Dictionary of Alabama Biography*, IV.

MOORE, James William (*Congressman*), was born in Montgomery County, Kentucky, on February 12, 1818. He never married. He was a lawyer and a circuit court judge in Mount Sterling, Montgomery County, Kentucky, prior to the Civil War. He served as judge of his district from 1851 until 1858. He was a secessionist Democrat and was among the first in his state to denounce the election of Lincoln. In 1861, he was a delegate to the Kentucky convention. Moore was a member of the Judiciary Committee in the first Confederate House of Representatives and served on the Joint Judiciary Committee in the second. Although he took frequent leaves of absence from the House, he was an influential member of the Judiciary Committee and supported the Davis administration. In 1862, he urged price limits on woolen goods and salt. He was destitute in 1861, and the war did not improve his financial status. He intended to settle in Richmond, Virginia, after the war, but he returned to his home in Mount Sterling, practiced law, and died there on September 17, 1877. Yearns, *The Confederate Congress*.

MOORE, John Creed (*General*), was born on February 23, 1824, in Hawkins County, Tennessee. He attended Emory and Henry College in Virginia and graduated seventeenth in a class of forty-three from the U.S. Military Academy in 1849. Breveted second lieutenant in the 4th Artillery for his participation in the Seminole War in 1849-1850, Moore served in Santa Fe, New Mexico, in 1852-1853 and at Fort Union, Nebraska, in 1853-1854. In 1855, he took a leave of absence and resigned his U.S. Army commission in late 1855 to teach school in Tennessee. In 1860, he taught at Shelby College in Kentucky. He moved to Galveston, Texas, before the beginning of the Civil War. When the war began, he joined the Confederate Army as colonel of the 2nd Texas Infantry. He displayed gallantry at the battle of Shiloh, and on May 26, 1862, he was promoted to brigadier general. He also participated in the attack on Corinth, Mississippi. He was captured during the Vicksburg campaign and was exchanged shortly there-after. Later, he served under General Braxton Bragg (*q.v.*) at the battles of Missionary Ridge and Chattanooga in the fall of 1863. In December 1863, he was assigned to command the Eastern and Western Districts of the Department of the Gulf, with headquarters in Mobile. For unexplained reasons he resigned his commission in February 1864. He returned to Galveston and took no further part in the war effort. After the war, he taught school at Mexia and Dallas, Texas, and wrote many articles about the war. Moore died in retirement on December 31, 1919, in Osage, Texas. Johnson, *Texans Who Wore the Gray*.

MOORE, Samuel Preston (*Surgeon General*), son of Stephen West and Eleanor Screven (Gilbert) Moore, was born in Charleston, South Carolina, in 1813. He attended school in Charleston and received his M.D. from the Medical College of the State of South Carolina in 1834. In 1845, he married Mary Augusta Brown. Moore joined the U.S. Army and was given a western assignment as an assistant surgeon in the army in 1835. He served with distinction in the Mexican War. In 1849, he was an army surgeon with the rank of major. When the Civil War began, he resigned his commission, After practicing medicine in Little Rock, Arkansas, Moore was named surgeon general of the Confederacy in June 1861. In 1863, he went to Richmond, where he became first president of the Association of Army and Navy Surgeons of the Confederate States. He also found medicine from indigenous plants of the South, and in 1864, he started the *Confederate States Medical Journal*. Moore created the Reserve Surgical Corps, was a director of relief associations, established pharmaceutical laboratories, and proposed plans for staff coordination as the Confederacy became materially weakened and unable to supply adequate medical facilities. After the war, he remained in Richmond, where he resumed his medical practice. Moore served on the Richmond school board from 1877 to 1883. He died in Richmond on May 31, 1889. Burrage and Kelly, *American Medical Biographies*; Pilcher, *The Surgeon-Generals of the United States Army*.

MOORE, Thomas Overton (*Governor*), was born in Sampson County, North Carolina, on April 5 or 10, 1804, to John and Jean (Overton) Moore. He was educated in Sampson County and, in 1829, moved to Rapides Parish, Louisiana, where he managed his uncle's sugar plantation and later became a successful planter in his own right. His marriage to Bethiah Jane Leonard on November 30, 1830, produced five children. Moore, a Democrat, entered local politics and was elected to the lower house of the Louisiana legislature in 1848 and to the upper house in 1856. He was an ardent secessionist. In 1860, he was elected governor of the state, and he not only called the secession convention, but in 1861, he called for five thousand Louisiana troops for the Confederacy in addition to the three thousand already requested by President Davis (*q.v.*). He cooperated with the Confederate government. Moore later sponsored a stay law which suspended forced sales of agricultural goods to the Confederate Army. Although his administration ended in June 1862 after the fall of New Orleans, he moved the capital to Shreveport and acted as governor of the northern part of the state for the remainder of the war. In 1864, his plantation, home, and sugar mill were destroyed. After the war he fled to Havana. When given a pardon, he returned to his plantation in 1866 and attempted to recoup his losses. Moore had no further public career. He died in Rapides Parish (near Alexandria) on June 25, 1876. *Biographical and Historical Memoirs of Louisiana*; Bragg, *Louisiana in the Confederacy*.

MOREHEAD, John Motley (*Congressman*), son of John and Obedience (Motley) Morehead, was born on July 4, 1796, in Pennsylvania County, Virginia. The family moved to Rockingham County, North Carolina, in 1798. The younger Morehead attended the school of Dr. David Caldwell and graduated from the University of North Carolina in 1817. He was a Presbyterian and had eight children by his marriage to Ann Eliza Lindsey on September 6, 1821. Morehead, who was a tutor in 1817-1818, studied law and was admitted to the Wentworth, North Carolina, bar in 1819. He represented Rockingham County in the state legislature in 1821. He subsequently moved to Greensboro, where he represented Guilford County in the legislature in 1826-1827. Morehead, who identified with the western group in North Carolina's politics, was a Jackson Democrat until 1835, when he became a Whig. He was a delegate to the state constitutional convention in 1835 and president of the national Whig party convention in 1848. Besides being a successful lawyer, he was a businessman who established and controlled large cotton factories in North Carolina and served during the 1840s as first president of the North Carolina Railroad. Morehead gave state aid to the railroads and favored internal improvements during his term as governor of North Carolina from 1841 to 1845. In addition to his business enterprises, he founded and owned the Edgeworth Seminary for young ladies during the 1850s. Morehead was a state senator in 1860 and a delegate to the Washington Peace Conference in 1861. When the Civil War began, he favored an active role for North Carolina. As a member of the provisional Congress, he served on the Committee on Commercial and Financial Independence. When his term ended, Morehead worked for the extension of the Confederate States railroads throughout North Carolina so as to facilitate that state's contributions to the war effort. When the war ended, he continued in the railroad business. He died on August 28, 1866, at Rockbridge, Alum Springs, Virginia. Konkle, *John Motley Morehead and the Development of North Carolina, 1796-1866*.

MORGAN, John Hunt (*General*), son of Calvin and Henrietta (Hunt) Morgan, was born on June 1, 1825, in Huntsville, Alabama. He was reared in Lexington, Kentucky, and attended Transylvania University in the mid-1840s. He was an Episcopalian. He married Rebecca Gratz Bruce on November 21, 1848, and, after her death, Martha Ready in 1863; he had no children. After fighting at Buena Vista during the Mexican War, Morgan returned to Lexington in 1847 to become a merchant and a manufacturer of hemp. In 1857, he founded the Lexington Rifles. He supported the secession of Kentucky. At the beginning of the war, he joined General Simon B. Buckner (*q.v.*) at Bowling Green, Kentucky. In April 1862, he became a colonel in the 2nd Kentucky Cavalry, and on December 11, 1862, he was promoted to brigadier general. Morgan was most famous for his raids into Tennessee, Kentucky, Indiana, and Ohio, which made him dreaded in the North. On his most famous raid into Ohio in 1863, he was captured but later escaped, and in April 1864, he was given command of the Department of Southwestern Virginia. Morgan was killed in a surprise attack on September 4, 1864, in Greenville, Tennessee. Swiggett, *The Rebel Raider: A Life of John Hunt Morgan*.

MORGAN, John Tyler (*General*), son of the merchant and planter George Morgan and his wife Frances (Irby), was born on June 20, 1824, in Athens, Tennessee. The family moved to Calhoun County, Alabama, in 1833. He attended the pioneer school of Charles P. Samuel and studied law under William P. Chilton (*q.v.*) before being admitted to the Tuskegee, Alabama, bar in 1845. He was a devout Methodist and a secessionist Democrat. Morgan married Comelia Willis on February 11, 1846; they had two sons and two daughters. Morgan practiced law in Tuskegee before moving to Selma in 1855. Active in political life, he held no prewar office. He was a presidential elector on the John C. Breckinridge (*q.v.*) ticket, and at the state convention he was aligned with William Lowndes Yancey (*q.v.*). When the Civil War began, he enlisted in the Confederate Army. He recruited a mounted Alabama regiment for the Confederate Army and served under General N. B. Forrest (*q.v.*) in mid-Tennessee during 1861-1862. He declined a promotion to brigadier general on June 6, 1863, but accepted a later promotion to the same rank on November 17, 1863. Morgan participated in the Knoxville campaign and also distinguished himself in his harassment of Sherman during the Atlanta campaign. He fought in North Carolina as well. In the last days of the war, he recruited Mississippi Negroes for enlistment in the Confederate Army. There is no record of his surrender. When the war ended, he returned to his Tuskegee law practice. During Reconstruction, he advocated local self-government and white supremacy. In 1876, he was a Democratic elector for Samuel Tilden, and the same year he was elected to the U.S. Senate from Alabama. He served for over thirty years. During his fifth term, he became a Populist. Morgan, who was also chairman of the Foreign Affairs Committee of the Senate, was perhaps best known for his persistent efforts on behalf of the construction of the Panama Canal. He served in the Senate until his death on June 11, 1907, in Washington, D.C. Morgan, *A History of the Family of Morgan*; *Who's Who in America*, 1906-1907; Woodward, *Origins of the New South*.

MORGAN, Simpson Harris (*Congressman*), was born in Rutherford County, Tennessee, in 1821. There is no information on his early life. Morgan married into the family of Augustus H. Garland (*q.v.*). He moved to Clarksville, Red River County, Texas, in 1844, where he became a lawyer and a farmer. He became a railroad promoter and served as president of the Texas and Pacific Railroad. Elected from the Sixth Texas Congressional District to the second Confederate House, he served on the Impressment and Judiciary Committees. He was an administration supporter. Morgan died in Monticello, Arkansas, on December 15, 1864. Alexander and Beringer, *Anatomy of the Confederate Congress*; *Journal of the Confederate Congress*, VII.

MORRIS, William S. (*Bureaucrat*), was a businessman and a medical doctor in Georgia before the Civil War. Early in his career he became an important stockholder in the American Telegraph Company. When the Civil War began, he volunteered for service in the Confederate government. Postmaster General John Reagan (*q.v.*) chose him as chief of the military telegraph. He was efficient in maintaining an effective telegraph system throughout the South during the war years. Morris used the American Telegraph Company stations in the South as independent units for rapid communication. There is evidence that he returned to private business at the war's end, but it is unknown where. Thompson, *Wiring a Continent*.

MORTON, Jackson C. (*Congressman*), was born in Fredericksburg, Spotsylvania County, Virginia, on August 10, 1794. His parents died while he was a boy, and he was reared by an uncle, William Mogen. He attended Washington College in Virginia in 1814 and graduated from the College of William and Mary in 1815.

Morton, who was in the lumber and manufacturing business in Pensacola, Florida, in 1820, later became a wealthy planter in Mortonia, Florida. He entered political life as a Whig, served in the Florida territorial legislature in the 1836-1838 term, and helped to frame the state constitution in 1838. From 1841 to 1845, he was a naval agent in Pensacola, and from 1848 to 1855, he served Florida in the U.S. Senate. In 1850, he was a radical secessionist, but by 1860 he was a cooperationist who wanted Florida to secede only after Alabama had seceded. He retired from active politics in 1855 and returned to his lumber business. When the Civil War began, he volunteered for duty in the Confederate Army; he saw no service and, instead, served in politics. During the war, Morton was a delegate to the provisional Confederate Congress, where he served on the committee to draw up the permanent Confederate Constitution and on the Commercial Affairs Committee. He also served on the Commercial Affairs, Flag and Seal, Inauguration, and Indian Affairs Committees after he was elected to the first and second Confederate House of Representatives. Morton opposed the Davis administration for its lack of protection of the Florida coast. When the war ended, he returned to his business in Florida, and took no further part in public life. Morton died on November 20, 1874, in Santa Rosa County, Florida. Davis, *The Civil War and Reconstruction in Florida*; Lee, *The Confederate Constitutions*.

MUNNERLYN, Charles James (*Congressman*), was born to Charles Lewis and Hannah (Shackleford) Munnerlyn on February 14, 1822, in Georgetown, South Carolina. His family first moved to Florida, and then, in 1837, to Decatur, Georgia. He attended Emory College in Georgia and studied law under A. B. Longstreet during the 1840s. He never practiced law, becoming instead a large planter in Decatur County. He was a Methodist. He married Eugenia Shackleford on February 20, 1845, and they had nine children. He never joined a political party and seems to have largely stayed out of politics until the war began. Munnerlyn was a strong secessionist and served as a delegate to the Georgia secession convention. When the Civil War began, Munnerlyn enlisted as a private in the 1st Georgia Volunteers and saw service in Pensacola and West Virginia during 1861 and 1862. He was elected from the Second Congressional District of Georgia to the first Confederate House. He favored the conscript law, served on the Claims, Naval Affairs, and special committees, and generally supported the administration. After he was defeated for reelection, he entered the army. President Davis (*q.v.*) promoted him to major and ordered him to organize the regular reserves in Florida and to deliver supplies in Virginia. He also furnished 100,000 head of cattle for the army and helped Confederate officers to leave the country. When the war ended, he returned to his plantation in Georgia, only to find his lands destroyed. He entered business in hopes of recouping his losses. Munnerlyn helped to build the Atlanta and Gulf Railroad during the late 1870s. He served as ordinary of Decatur County in 1884. He died in Decatur County on May 17, 1898. Avery, *History of Georgia*; Northen (ed.), *Men of Mark in Georgia*, V.

MURRAH, Pendleton (*Governor*), was born in South Carolina around 1820. Early in life he moved to Alabama and then to Marshall, Henderson County, Texas, where he studied law and served in the state legislature in 1857. He was a Democrat and an intense foe of the Know-Nothings. Murrah practiced law and was a political opponent of Sam Houston. He supported secession. When the Civil War began, he volunteered for service in the Confederate Army. During the early part of the war, Murrah was a colonel in a Texas brigade and saw service on the frontier. In 1863, he was elected governor of Texas by a large majority. His administration was marked by conflict with Confederate authorities and disagreement with local Confederate military commanders, such as his argument with General John B. Magruder (*q. v.*) over the Conscription Act. In the closing days of the war, he made an independent effort to make favorable peace terms for Texans. Shortly after the war, he called for a state constitutional convention in hopes of reorganizing the government. But he was branded a traitor by the federal authorities and was forced to flee to Mexico before it convened. Murrah died in July 1865 in Monterrey, Mexico. Lubbock, *Six Decades in Texas: The Memoirs of Francis R. Lubbock*; Ramsdell, *Reconstruction in Texas*; Wright (comp.), *Texas in the War*.

MURRAY, John Porry (*Congressman*), was born in Jackson County, Tennessee, on July 14, 1830. Little is known of his family or his early life. He was a member of the Methodist Episcopal church, and he became an important lawyer and a Democratic leader in Gainesboro, Tennessee. Murray had two sons and three daughters by his marriage to Evelyn Eaton. He secured the nomination of Andrew Johnson for governor and was a circuit court judge before the war. There is evidence that he supported the secession of Tennessee. When the Civil War began, he volunteered for service in the Confederate Army. From September 1861 to August 1863, he was colonel of the 28th Regiment of Tennessee Volunteers. In 1863, he was elected by the Fourth Congressional District to serve in the second Confederate House of Representatives, where he served on the Impressments, Indian Affairs, and Ordnance and Ordnance Stores Committees. An anti-Davis man, he opposed an alliance with France and was unpopular with the Southern press. He was a staunch defender of the western bloc, and he attempted to get increased military protection for the Cumberland area because of its production of war supplies. After the war, he was the first Confederate official to call on Andrew Johnson; he was granted a pardon. He then returned to his Gainesboro law practice and stayed out of politics. Murray died in Jackson County, on December 21, 1895. Alexander and Beringer, *Anatomy of the Confederate Congress*.

MYERS, Abraham Charles (*Bureaucrat*), son of the Charleston lawyer Abraham Myers, was born in May 1811 in Georgetown, South Carolina. He graduated thirty-second in a class of forty-three from the U.S. Military Academy in 1833, accepted a commission as a second lieutenant, and was stationed at Baton Rouge, Louisiana, the same year. Myers was Jewish. In the 1850s, he married Marion Twiggs, daughter of General David E. Twiggs; they had children. A professional soldier, he served in the Indian wars in Florida in 1836-1838 and 1841-1842. He was made a captain in the Quartermaster Department in 1839, and during the Mexican War, he was breveted a major at Palo Alto and a colonel at Churubusco. In 1848, he was named chief quartermaster of the army in Mexico. He continued to hold various military duties in the Southern states for the next thirteen years. He resigned his commission on January 28, 1861. He volunteered for service in the Confederate Army, and on March 15, 1861, President Davis (*q.v.*) named him quartermaster general of the Confederacy. Myers served until August 10, 1863. In this capacity he procured supplies and established government shops. He opposed impressment but was forced to practice it. Unfortunately, he was never able to provide adequately for the armies, nor could he overcome problems with his subordinates. After he was superseded in his position, he left for Georgia, impoverished and hating President Davis. He held no further office in the Confederacy. When the war ended, he traveled in Europe until 1877 and later came to Lake Roland, Maryland. He moved to Washington, D.C., and died there on June 20, 1888. Goff, *Confederate Supply*; Vandiver, *Ploughshares into Swords*.

N

NEWSOM, Ella King (*Nurse*), was born in Brandon, Rankin County, Mississippi, probably in the 1830s. She was the daughter of T.S.N. King, a Baptist minister, who removed with his family to Arkansas when Ella was a small child. She married a rich Arkansan, Dr. Frank Newsom, who soon died and left her a wealthy widow. She belonged to the Baptist church. When the Civil War began, she volunteered for duty as a nurse and taught nurses in the Memphis city hospital. She was also a nurse in the front lines at Bowling Green, Kentucky, managed the Southern Mother's Home in Memphis in 1863, organized a hospital in Nashville, and saw service at Chattanooga, Atlanta, Corinth, and Abingdon, Virginia. She earned the sobriquet "The Florence Nightingale of the Southern Army." After the war, she married an ex-Confederate colonel named Trader and had several children who died in infancy. She was widowed again in 1875 and became an employee of the Pension Office in Washington, D.C. Mrs. Newsom wrote a book on her wartime experiences called *Reminiscences of War Time* (1905). She lived until at least 1913, but died soon after in Washington, D.C. Richard, *The Florence Nightingale of the Southern Army*; Simkins and Patton, *Women in the Confederacy*.

NICHOLLS, Francis Redding (*General*), son of Thomas Clark and Louisa Hanna (Drake) Nicholls, was born on August 20, 1834, in Donaldsonville, Louisiana. He attended Jefferson Academy in New Orleans and graduated twelfth in a class of thirty-four from the U.S. Military Academy in 1855. He was a Democrat and a Catholic, and he married Caroline Zilpha Guion on April 26, 1860. Nicholls fought the Seminoles in Florida before resigning his commission in 1856 to study law at the University of Louisiana. He was admitted to the Louisiana bar in 1858 and began his practice in Napoleonville, Louisiana. He was a unionist before the war, but when the Civil War began he entered the army as a lieutenant colonel in the 8th Louisiana Regiment. He fought at the battle of First Manassas, and in the spring of 1862, he participated in Thomas J. Jackson's (*q.v.*) Valley campaign, where in May he lost his left arm at the battle of Winchester. He was promoted to brigadier general on October 14, 1862, and commanded the post at Lynchburg, Virginia. While leading the 2nd Louisiana Brigade at the battle of Chancellorsville in May of the following year, he lost his left foot, a wound which ended his field command. Nicholls turned down a subsequent promotion to major general. In 1864, he went to the Trans-Mississippi Department to head the Volunteer and Conscript Bureau until the end of the war. There is no evidence that he ever surrendered. After the war, he practiced law in Napoleonville until 1876, when he became governor of Louisiana following a much-disputed election. When his term ended, he returned to the practice of law. He was elected governor again in 1888, and he was chief justice of the state Supreme Court from 1892 to 1911. Nicholls helped end the Louisiana lottery prior to his 1911 retirement to his plantation near Thibodeaux, Louisiana. He died there on January 4, 1912. Evans, *Confederate Military History*, X; Fortier, *A History of Louisiana*, II.

NISBET, Eugenius Aristides (*Congressman*), was born on December 7, 1803, in Greene County, Georgia, to the physician James C. Nisbet and his wife Penelope (Cooper). He attended Powellton Academy and the University of South Carolina, graduated first in his class from the University of Georgia in 1821, and studied law in Litchfield, Connecticut, in 1822. He was admitted to the bar by special permission because he was under age and began his practice in Madison, Georgia, on the Ocmulgee Circuit in 1824. He became a successful lawyer. On April 12, 1825, Nisbet married Amanda Battle, by whom he had twelve children. One of his daughters married Confederate General Martin L. Smith (*q.v.*). Nisbet was a Presbyterian. He was active in Whig politics and ran for political office. He served in the state House from 1827 to 1830 and in the Senate from 1830 to 1837, when he moved to Macon. He was a states' rights Whig and a follower of the Troup faction and later became a leader of the Know-Nothing party in Georgia. He lost a close race for the U.S. House of Representatives in 1836 but ran again in 1838 and won, serving from 1839 to 1841. From 1845 to 1853, he was one of the first three associate judges of the state Supreme Court. He became a Democrat in 1855, supporting James Buchanan and later Stephen Douglas for the presidency. In 1850, he was the president of a state educational convention. He also continued the practice of law in Macon. Nisbet became a secessionist in the late 1850s. As a member of the of the secession convention, he was chairman of the committee which drew up the Ordinance of Secession. He was elected to the provisional Confederate Congress and served on the committee to draft the provisional Constitution and the Foreign Affairs and Territories Committees. He supported a single term of eight years for the president. When Nisbet resigned from Congress on December 10, 1861, the Confederacy lost one of its most able politicians. He ran unsuccessfully for governor against Joseph Brown (*q.v.*) in 1861. Nisbet practiced law in Macon throughout the war, and he volunteered for judicial duty. After the war, he wrote and lectured, and in 1868 he received an honorary Doctor of Laws degree from the University of Georgia. He died on March 18, 1871, in Macon, Georgia. Lee, *Confederate Constitutions*; Lewis (ed.), *Great American Lawyers*, IV.

NORTHROP, Lucius Bellinger (*Bureaucrat*), was born on September 8, 1811 in Charleston, South Carolina, to the notable and well-to-do family of Amos Bird and Claudia Margaret (Bellinger) Northrop. After graduating twenty-second in his class of thirty-three from the U.S. Military Academy in 1831, he was breveted second lieutenant and was sent west on Indian service, where he became a friend of Jefferson Davis (*q.v.*). He was promoted to first lieutenant in 1834 but retired from combat in 1839, after being wounded in the Seminole War. He was a Democrat and, originally Episcopal, became a Roman Catholic when he married Maria Euphenia Joanna De Bernalieu in 1841. In 1842-1843, he served in the Subsistence Department in Washington. He also studied medicine at Jefferson Medical College in Philadelphia during the 1840s. In 1848, he was dropped from the army for practicing medicine on private patients, but when Jefferson Davis (*q.v.*) was named secretary of war that same year, he reinstated Northrop and promoted him to the rank of captain. From 1853 to 1861, Northrop also practiced medicine in Charleston. After South Carolina seceded from the Union, Northrop resigned his army commission and volunteered for service in the Confederate Army. During the Civil War, he held the rank of colonel and was appointed commissary general by President Davis; it was his duty to provide food for the military. He was bitterly criticized for being too close to Davis, for failing to coordinate the transportation system, and for his arbitrary use of impressment. He made additional enemies when he required commissary agents to be responsible to him. As a result, the Confederate House voted for his removal, a position which was also supported by General Robert E. Lee (*q. v.*). He left office voluntarily early in 1865 and held no further duty in the Confederacy. In his defense, it could be argued that Northrop was the victim of a limited transportation system and crop growing area in the early days of the war and of the blockade in the later days. After the war ended, he was arrested in Richmond but was later released. Northrop then farmed near Charlottesville, Virginia, from 1867 until 1890. He died on February 9, 1894, in the soldiers' home at Pikesville, Maryland. Felt, "Lucius B. Northrop and the Confederate Subsistence Department," *Virginia Magazine of History and Biography*, LXIX; Hay, "Lucius B. Northrop: Commissary General of the Confederacy," *Civil War History*, IX.

NORTON, Nimrod Lindsay (*Congressman*), son of Hiram and ———— (Spencer) Norton, was born on April 18, 1830, in Carlisle, Nicholas County, Kentucky. He attended Fredonia Academy in New York and the Military Institute of Kentucky before moving to Fulton, Mississippi, in the 1850s to farm. He had a daughter and a son by his 1853 marriage to Mary C. Hall. Norton was a Mason and an opponent of secession. When the war began, he volunteered for service in the Confederate Army. During the war, he organized a company under Sterling Price (*q. v.*), whom he served as a staff officer. He also was elected to the second Confederate House. He served on the Claims, Territories, and Public Lands Committees, but was frequently absent from Richmond. After the war, he moved to Texas, where he farmed on the Lavaca River. He provided the granite which was used in building the Texas capitol. He lived in Austin from 1870 until his death on September 28, 1903. Brown, *Indian Wars and Pioneers of Texas*.

O

OCHILTREE, William Beck (*Congressman*), was born on October 10, 1811, in Fayetteville, Cumberland County, North Carolina, to David and Lucy (Beck) Ochiltree. In his youth, his family moved to Florida and later to Alabama, where he studied law and was admitted to the bar in 1832. Ochiltree was an Episcopalian. In 1834, he married Novaline (Kennard) Peck, and in 1839, he and his wife moved to Texas, where they helped to settle Nacodoches. Ochiltree later became an important lawyer in Nacodoches. In 1842, he was named judge of the Fifth Judicial District of Texas. He was secretary of the treasury of the Republic of

Texas in 1844 and attorney general in 1845, the year he also served as a delegate to the state constitutional convention. In 1846, he was elected a district judge, and in 1855-1856, he was elected to the state House. Ochiltree was a Whig leader and chairman of the Judiciary Committee in the state House. He moved to Marshall, Texas, in 1859 and signed the Texas Secession Ordinance in 1861. He was a delegate to the provisional Confederate Congress. He also raised the 18th Texas Infantry, which he served as colonel. While in Congress, he served on the Inauguration, Military Affairs, Pay and Mileage, Postal Affairs, and Territories Committees and was considered an administration supporter. He refused election to the first House but fought with his regiment in the western campaigns. Ochiltree resigned his commission in 1863 and returned to his law practice. He held no further position in the Confederacy. He died in Marshall, Texas, on December 27, 1867. *Appleton's Cyclopedia of American Biography*, IV; Lynch, *The Bench and Bar of Texas*.

OLDHAM, Williamson Simpson (*Congressman*), son of Elias and Mary (Bratton) Oldham, was born on June 19, 1813, in Franklin County, Tennessee, where his father was a poor farmer. At the age of eighteen, the younger Oldham opened a school in the Tennessee mountain country. He read law and was admitted to the bar in Tennessee in 1836. That same year he moved to Fayetteville, Arkansas, where he developed a successful law practice. On December 12, 1837, he married the wealthy Mary Vance McKissick, daughter of Colonel James McKissick; the couple had five children prior to her death. On December 26, 1850, Oldham married Mrs. Anne S. Kirk, and, after her death, he married Agnes Harper on November 19, 1857. He was elected to represent Washington County in the Arkansas legislature in 1838 and served as speaker of that body in 1842. From 1844 to 1848, he was an associate justice of the state Supreme Court, leaving this post to oppose a fellow Democrat. R. W. Johnson (*q.v.*), in a race for the U.S. Senate. He was unsuccessful in his bid and moved to Austin, Texas, the following year to practice law. In 1852, he was president of the Austin Railroad Association. From 1854 to 1857, he edited the *Texas State Gazette* and helped to prepare the Digest of Laws of Texas. After 1855, Oldham was a political enemy of Sam Houston. In 1860, he moved to Brenham, Texas, and supported John C. Breckinridge (*q.v.*) for the presidency. In 1861, he was a strong secessionist and an active member of the secession convention. He was sent as a commissioner to Arkansas to try to win that state over to the Confederacy, and he served in the provisional Confederate Congress at Montgomery. He was outspoken in committing the Confederate Constitution to state sovereignty. As a member of the Confederate Senate throughout the war, he was faithful to the Davis administration and through his close association with the Texas legislature proved a powerful force in keeping Texas loyal to the Confederacy. Oldham was a champion of states' rights during the war; he opposed conscription, the restricted planting of cotton, and the suspension of the writ of *habeas corpus*. He served on the Indian Affairs, Naval

Affairs, Commerce, Finance, Judiciary, and Joint committees and was one of the most diligent congressmen in Richmond. After the war, he went to Mexico and Canada, where he became a photographer and wrote *The Last Days of the Confederacy* (1866). He returned to Texas in 1867 and remained an unreconstructed rebel, refusing to take the loyalty oath. Oldham died of typhoid fever in Houston on May 8, 1868. King, "The Political Career of William Simpson Oldham," *Southwestern Historical Quarterly*, XXXIII.

O'NEAL, Edward Ashbury (*General*), was born to Edward and Rebecca (Wheat) O'Neal on September 20, 1818, in Madison County, Alabama. He graduated with highest honors from LaGrange College in 1836, read law, and was admitted to the Alabama bar in 1840. He developed a successful law practice in Florence, Alabama, in 1840. He was a Democrat, a Methodist, and a strong secessionist. O'Neal had six children by his marriage of April 12, 1833, to Olivia Moore. One son was later a major in the Confederate Army and another son ran for governor of Alabama. Active in local politics, O'Neal was elected to the state legislature in 1841 and ran an unsuccessful race for the U.S. House of Representatives in 1848. He became a secessionist leader in northern Alabama. When the Civil War began, he volunteered for service in the Confederate Army. After serving as colonel of an Alabama Brigade at the battles of Yorktown, Seven Pines, and the Seven Days in Virginia in 1862, he was wounded at the battle of South Mountain in September 1862. While commanding Rodes' (*q.v.*) Brigade at the battle of Chancellorsville in May 1862, he was wounded a second time. He was promoted to brigadier general on June 6, 1863, and served as a division commander at Gettysburg. In 1864, he recruited for the army in northern Alabama and commanded Cantey's Brigade during the Atlanta campaign, where he fought at Marietta and Peach Tree Creek. There is no record of his surrender. After the war, he lived in Florence, Alabama, resumed his law practice, and became a leader in the Democratic party. From 1882 to 1886, he was governor of Alabama. He died on November 7, 1890, in Florence. Owen, *History of Alabama and Dictionary of Alabama Biography*, IV; Wright, *General Officers of the Confederate Army*.

ORR, James Lawrence (*Congressman*), son of Christopher and Martha (McCann) Orr and brother of Jehu A. Orr (*q.v.*) was born in Craytonville, Pendleton District, South Carolina, on May 12, 1822. He graduated from the University of Virginia in 1842 and was admitted to the bar in Anderson, South Carolina, the following year. In the fall of 1844, he married Mary Jane Marshall, by whom he had five children. Orr was a Presbyterian and a Democrat. From 1844 to 1846, he edited the Anderson *Gazette*. In 1846, he gave up the newspaper, resumed the practice of law, and became active in politics. He was elected to the state House and served from 1844 to 1848. From 1849 to 1859, he served as a Democrat in the U.S. House of Representatives, where he was speaker from 1857 to 1859. He was a delegate to the Southern Rights convention in 1851 and to the Democratic national convention in 1860. A staunch Douglas Democrat, he had long favored the cooperative effort of the Southern states. He was also a delegate to the South Carolina secession convention and was sent to Washington to negotiate the surrender of the forts in Charleston harbor. Throughout the war he served in the Confederate Senate. A member of the Beauregard (*q.v.*) bloc, Orr was a critic of Bragg (*q.v.*) and, along with Wigfall (*q.v.*), deserted the administration in 1862. He quarrelled with Davis (*q.v.*) in 1864, when Orr wanted to negotiate for peace. Even so, he served ably on the Foreign Affairs, Rules, Finance, Printing, Commerce, and many special and joint committees. He also worked to aid South Carolina soldiers in Richmond. When the war ended, he returned to his law practice in Anderson. Orr supported President Johnson's program of Reconstruction and so, in 1865, was sent as a special commissioner to the president to negotiate for a provisional government in South Carolina. He was a delegate to the state constitutional convention in 1865 and was elected governor of South Carolina in 1866. In 1868, he lost the confidence of the Democrats of his state by becoming a Republican, and for the next two years he served as the elected judge of the Eighth Circuit Court. In 1872, he supported Grant's policy of declaring the Ku Klux Klan an outlaw organization and became Grant's minister to Russia. He died of pneumonia in St. Petersburg, Russia, on May 5, 1873. Cauthen, *South Carolina Goes to War, 1861-1865*; Perman, *Reunion Without Compromise*.

ORR, Jehu Amaziah (*Congressman*), son of Christopher and Martha (McCann) Orr and brother of James L. Orr (*q.v.*), was born on April 10, 1828, in Craytonville, South Carolina. His family moved to Mississippi in 1843, and he attended Erskine College in South Carolina and Princeton College during the mid-1840s. He was a Democrat and an elder in the Presbyterian church. He married Elizabeth Ramsay Gates in 1852 and, after her death, Cornelia Ewing Van de Graaf in 1857. In 1849, Orr began to practice law in Houston, Mississippi, and in 1850, was named secretary of the state Senate. He became active in politics, and in 1852, he was elected to the lower house of the state legislature. Two years later he was named U.S. attorney for the North District of Mississippi. Orr, an opponent of secession, supported Stephen Douglas in the election of 1860, but as a delegate to the Mississippi convention the following year, he voted for secession. He served in the provisional and second Confederate Congress, where he favored the Hampton Roads Conference and blamed Davis (*q.v.*) for the failure of peace negotiations. He served on the Claims, Patents, Engrossment, and Foreign Affairs Committees. During 1862-1863, as a colonel in the Confederate Army he fought in Mississippi campaigns. After the war, he returned to his Houston law practice and advised partial enfranchisement of the Negro. From 1870 to 1876, he was judge of the Sixth Judicial Circuit of Mississippi. In the late 1870s, he moved to Columbus,

Mississippi, and became a successful lawyer; he held no further public office. He died on March 9, 1921, in Columbus, Mississippi. *Biographical and Historical Memoirs of Mississippi.*

OULD, Robert (*Bureaucrat, Judge*), was born in Georgetown, D.C., on January 31, 1820. He attended Jefferson College in Pennsylvania and graduated from Columbia College, D.C., in 1837 and from the College of William and Mary in 1842. He was a Democrat and a Catholic. He practiced law in the District of Columbia from 1842 to 1861. He was a member of a committee to codify the District's laws and was district attorney for D.C. before the war. Loyal to the South, he volunteered for government duties in the Confederacy after the Civil War began. From January to March 1862, he was assistant secretary of war, appointed by President Davis (*q.v.*). In July 1862, he became agent for the exchange of Confederate prisoners, where he paid careful attention to details and later had charge of the Confederate Secret Service. He was also judge advocate of the Confederate courts-martial during 1864-1865. After the war, he was indicted for treason on the charge of misappropriation of funds belonging to federal prisoners in the Confederacy. He spent only eight weeks in prison and was cleared of all accusations, after which he practiced law in Richmond, Virginia. He died there in 1882. Robinson, *Justice in Grey.*

OURY, Granville Henderson (*Congressman*), was born on March 12, 1825, in Abingdon, Washington County, Virginia. He moved to Bowling Green, Missouri, with his family in 1836 and was admitted to the Missouri bar in 1848. A Democratic lawyer and a farmer, he moved to San Antonio, Texas, before joining the mining rush to California in 1849. In 1856, he went to Tucson, Arizona, to practice law. He was a district court judge for Arizona and New Mexico before the Civil War. Oury, a secessionist, was elected to represent the Arizona Territory as a nonvoting delegate to the provisional Confederate Congress. His appointment was primarily a symbolic gesture to show the Confederate government's concern for territories. Oury resigned from the Congress in 1861 to serve as a captain in Herbert's Battalion of the Arizona Cavalry in the Confederate Army. He also served as a colonel under General Henry Sibley in various western campaigns during 1862. In Arizona he fought the unionist policies of John Robert Baylor (*q.v.*) and Malcolm MacWillie (*q.v.*). After the war, he returned to his Tucson law practice. In 1866, he was elected speaker of the territorial House, and two years later he became attorney general of the territory. From 1881 to 1885, he served as a Democrat in the U.S. House of Representatives. Oury died on January 11, 1891. *Biographical Directory of the American Congress.*

OWENS, James Bryan (*Congressman*), was born in Barnwell District, South Carolina, in 1816. He graduated from Furman College, Greenville, South Carolina, and in 1853, moved to Marion County, Florida, where he and his three brothers all owned cotton plantations. He married in the 1850s. Active in politics, Owens served in the Florida legislature before the war. As a delegate to the Charleston Democratic convention in 1860, he favored John C. Breckinridge (*q.v.*) and tried to prevent a rift in the party before the war. He represented Marion County at the Florida secession convention, where he voted for secession. Elected to the provisional Confederate Congress, he was on the committee to draft a permanent Confederate Constitution, and he opposed the Davis administration. When his term in Congress ended, he took no part in the war, and he returned to his plantation in Marion County. Owens was also an itinerant Baptist minister during the war years. In 1867, he attempted to work with resettling and helping Negroes under Reconstruction. He entered the orange-growing business. He died in Ocala on August 1, 1889. Ott and Chazel, *Ocali Country*; Tebeau, *A History of Florida*.

P

PAGE, Richard Lucian (*General*), son of William Byrd and Ann (Lee) Page, was born on December 20, 1807, in Clarke County, Virginia, where his father was a planter. The younger Page was a first cousin of Robert E. Lee (*q.v.*). He became a naval midshipman in 1824 on both the *Constitution* and the *Constellation*. Page had three children by his 1841 marriage to the former Alexina Taylor of Norfolk. He was made a lieutenant in 1834 and, in 1845, became executive officer on the *Independence*, on which he served during the Mexican War. From 1852 to 1854, he commanded the *Perry*, and in 1855, he was promoted to commander. He served as assistant inspector of ordnance from 1855 to 1856, when he was placed in command of the sloop of war *Germantown*. After Virginia seceded, he resigned from the U.S. Navy. At the beginning of the war, he was an aide to Governor John Letcher (*q.v.*) of Virginia, and he superintended the fortification of the James and the Nansemond Rivers. On June 10, 1861, he was commissioned a commander in the Confederate Navy, and he served as an ordnance officer at Norfolk and later as captain in command of naval forces on the Savannah. He fought in the naval battle off Port Royal in 1862. On March 1, 1864, he was promoted to brigadier general. He commanded the outer works at Mobile Bay and was engaged in the heroic defense of Fort Morgan, Alabama, in August 1864. He surrendered after the fall of Mobile in August 1864 and was held a prisoner until September 1865. After his release, he lived in Norfolk, where he was superintendent of public schools from 1875 to 1883. Page died on August 9, 1901, in retirement at Blue Ridge Summit, Pennsylvania. Tyler, *Encyclopedia of Virginia Biography*, IV; Warner, *Generals in Gray*.

PALMER, Benjamin Morgan (*Chaplain*), was born on January 25, 1818, in Charleston, South Carolina, to the Reverend Edward Palmer and his wife Sarah (Bunce). He attended Amherst College from 1832 to 1834 and graduated first in the class of 1838 at the University of Georgia. He also attended the Columbia Theological Seminary in South Carolina from 1839 to 1841, and in 1842, he was licensed to preach in the Presbyterian church. On October 7, 1841, he married Mary Augusta Howe, by whom he had six children, only two of whom lived to maturity. Palmer was pastor of the First Presbyterian Church in Savannah from 1841 to 1843 and of a Presbyterian church in Columbia, South Carolina, from 1843 to 1855. While in Columbia, he also founded and edited the *Southern Presbyterian Review*. From 1853 to 1856, he was a professor of church history and government at the seminary in Columbia, and from 1856 to 1902, he was a pastor of the First Presbyterian Church in New Orleans, Louisiana. He was a staunch secessionist with a wide and respected reputation. In 1860, he was perhaps the most influential person in New Orleans in urging his state to join the Confederate cause. He was a Confederate commissioner to ten general assemblies in 1861 and served as chaplain of the Army of Tennessee throughout the war. His zealous sermons urged the troops to renewed efforts. Palmer also founded the Confederate Presbyterian Church. After the war, he supported relief for the persecuted Jews of Russia in 1882. He published a life of *James Henly Thornwell* in 1876. Palmer also became a member of the Anti-Lottery League in 1891. He died in a streetcar accident in New Orleans on May 25, 1902. *Library of Southern Literature*, IX; Silver, *Confederate Morale and Church Propaganda*.

PARSONS, Mosby Munroe (*General*), was born on May 21 or August 5, 1822, in Charlottesville, Virginia. His family moved to Cole County, Missouri, in 1835 and settled in Jefferson City. Parsons attended St. Charles College, Missouri, studied law, and began his practice in Jefferson City in 1846. He married Mary Wells on September 18, 1850. During the Mexican War, he participated in the invasion of California and was promoted to captain. Active in Missouri Democratic politics, he was elected attorney general of Missouri in 1853 and served until 1857. He represented Cole County in the Missouri House in 1857 and was elected to the state Senate in 1859. A secessionist, he allied with Governor Claiborne Jackson (*q.v.*) in attempting to persuade his state to secede. When the Civil War began, he organized the Missouri State Militia. He fought under General Sterling Price (*q.v.*) at the battles of Carthage, Wilson's Creek, and Lexington, Missouri, and was a hero of the battle of Elkhorn, Arkansas, in March 1862. After his promotion to brigadier general on November 5, 1862, he served in the Arkansas campaign of 1862-1863 and in Taylor's Red River campaign in Louisiana in 1864. His able performance at the battle of Pleasant Hill in April 1864 won Parsons recommendation for promotion to major general; although he was never confirmed, he was assigned to the duties of this rank from April 30, 1864, until the end of the war. He accompanied Price on his last great raid through Missouri in late 1864, fighting at Mark's Mill and Jenkins' Ferry. He refused to surrender at war's end. Parsons went to Mexico and joined the Mexican imperialist forces which were fighting Maximilian. He was killed, probably near China, Mexico, on August 17, 1865. Conrad (ed.), *Encyclopedia of the History of Missouri*, V; Sona and Sona, *Marriage Records of Cole County, Missouri*.

PAYNE, William Henry Fitzhugh (*General*), was born on January 27, 1830, in Clifton, Fauquier County, Virginia, to Arthur Alexander and Mary Conway Mason (Fitzhugh) Payne. His father was a breeder of fine horses. Young Payne attended the University of Missouri and Virginia Military Institute, from which he graduated in 1849. He was a Democrat. He married Mary Elizabeth Winston Payne, daughter of W. Winter Payne on September 29, 1852; they had ten children. Payne studied law at the University of Virginia and became a lawyer in 1850. He was commonwealth's attorney for Fauquier County from 1852 to 1861. When Virginia seceded, he entered the Confederate Army as a captain of the Black Horse Cavalry. He was wounded and taken prisoner at the battle of Williamsburg during the Peninsular campaign of 1862 but recovered and was soon exchanged. He participated in J.E.B. Stuart's (*q.v.*) raid into Pennsylvania the following fall. In June 1863, he was again wounded and taken prisoner while he held Warrenton, Virginia, against attack. He was again exchanged. After serving in Early's (*q.v.*) Valley campaign during the summer of 1864, he served at Cedar Creek in October. Payne was promoted to brigadier general on November 1, 1864. He was wounded a third time at the battle of Five Forks during the siege of Richmond on April 1, 1865. Payne was captured in Warrenton and spent fourteen months in federal prisons. Upon his release in May 1866, he practiced law in Warrenton. He served in the Virginia House in 1879. In the 1880s, Payne moved to Washington, D.C., where he became counsel for the Southern Railroad. He died in Washington, D.C., on March 29, 1904. *Confederate Veteran*, XII; *Southern Historical Society Papers*, XXXVI.

PEARSON, Richmond Mumford (*Judge*), was born on June 28, 1805, in Rowan County, North Carolina, the son of Richmond and Elizabeth (Mumford) Pearson. One of his paternal uncles had served in the U.S. House of Representatives. He attended schools in Washington, D.C., and Salisbury, North Carolina, before graduating from the University of North Carolina in 1823. He was admitted to the Salisbury bar in 1826 and began his practice there. On June 12, 1831, he married Margaret McClung Williams; she died and in 1859, he married Mary (McDowell) Bynum. A son and namesake later served in the U.S. Congress.

Pearson, a Whig, was a member of the state House from 1829 to 1835. In 1836, he served as a superior court judge, and in 1848, he became an associate justice of the state Supreme Court. He was named chief justice in 1858. During this time, he also taught law in Surrey County. Pearson opposed secession and had no love for the Confederacy, although he remained chief justice of the state Supreme Court throughout the war. Even so, Pearson's decisions were mostly in favor of the Confederacy. He grew unpopular because of his opposition to conscription, and he became a rallying point for unionist sentiment in North Carolina. In 1865, he was defeated as a candidate for delegate to the state convention but was reelected chief justice. He joined the Republican party in 1868 and supported William W. Holden (*q.v.*). Pearson died in office on January 5, 1878. Ashe, *Cyclopedia of Eminent and Representative Men of the Carolinas*, I; Robinson, *Justice in Gray*.

PEGRAM, John (*General*), son of James West and Virginia (Johnson) Pegram, was born on January 24, 1832, in Petersburg, Virginia. He graduated tenth in a class of forty-six from the U.S. Military Academy in 1854. He was an Episcopalian. He married Hetty Cary in January 1865, only three weeks before his death. Before the Civil War, Pegram served with the army in California, Kansas, the Dakotas, and New Mexico. He was promoted to first lieutenant in 1857. He resigned from the U.S. Army on May 10, 1861. After entering the Confederate Army as a lieutenant colonel, he participated in the battle of Rich Mountain, West Virginia, on July 11, 1861. Promoted to brigadier general on November 7, 1862, he led Georgia and Louisiana cavalry regiments at the battles of Stone's River, Murfreesboro, and Chickamauga. Although he was never promoted to major general, he was given division commands under Nathan B. Forrest (*q.v.*) in Tennessee and under Jubal Early (*q.v.*) and J. B. Gordon (*q.v.*) in Virginia. He was wounded at the Wilderness in the spring of 1864, and upon his recovery he fought at Cold Harbor under Early before he succeeded General R. E. Rodes (*q.v.*) as division commander at the battle of Winchester. Pegram commanded Rodes' Division at Fisher's Hill and Cedar Creek, as well as a division in Gordon's Corps during the sieges of Petersburg and Richmond, between December 1864 and February 1865. He was killed at Hatcher's Run near Petersburg on February 6, 1865. Freeman, *Lee's Lieutenants*, III; Wright, *Generals of the Confederacy*.

PEMBERTON, John Clifford (*General*), son of John Pemberton, a naval officer, and his wife Rebecca (Clifford), was born on August 10, 1814, in Philadelphia, Pennsylvania. Educated privately during his early years, he graduated twenty-seventh in a class of fifty from the U.S. Military Academy in 1837. He was a Quaker and probably a Democrat. Pemberton had five children by his marriage to Martha Thompson of Virginia on January 18, 1846. As a second lieutenant in the 4th Artillery Regiment, he fought the Seminoles in Florida in 1837. Pemberton held duty on the Canadian border from 1840 to 1842. He was an artillery officer during the Mexican War, where he was also breveted captain and major. In 1858, he fought the Mormons in Utah. He resigned his commission on April 24, 1861, and went to Richmond, where he organized the Virginia Cavalry and Militia. On June 17, 1861, he entered the Confederate Army as a brigadier general. He was promoted to major general on January 15, 1862, and was assigned to command the Department of South Carolina, Georgia, and Florida. Promoted to lieutenant general on October 13, 1862, he received command of the Department of Mississippi, Tennessee, and East Louisiana. After being hampered by conflicting orders, Pemberton was soundly beaten at Vicksburg by General U. S. Grant, to whom he surrendered the city on July 4, 1863. Upon his exchange Pemberton resigned his command on May 18, 1864. During the last part of the war, he was a lieutenant colonel of artillery around Richmond. There is no record of his surrender. After the war, he farmed near Warrenton, Virginia, until 1875 when he moved to Philadelphia. He died on July 18, 1881, in Penllyn, Pennsylvania. Pemberton, *Pemberton, Defender of Vicksburg*.

PENDER, William Dorsey (*General*), was born to the wealthy planter James Pender and his wife Sarah (Routh) on February 6, 1834, in Edgecombe County, North Carolina. He clerked in his brother's store before attending the U.S. Military Academy where he graduated nineteenth in a class of forty-six in 1854. He was an Episcopalian. He had three sons by his marriage to Mary Frances Shepperd on March 3, 1859. Pender served with the U.S. Army Dragoons in New Mexico, California, Washington, and Oregon before the war. He fought in numerous battles with the Indians and served as adjutant of the 1st Dragoons in San Francisco. While distressed by the idea of civil war, his loyalty to his home state ultimately prevailed and he resigned his commission on March 21, 1861. He entered the Confederate Army as a captain of artillery in the provisional army. After recruiting troops in Baltimore, he became a colonel of the 3rd North Carolina Volunteers, which participated at the battle of First Manassas in July 1861. After serving as a brigade commander during the battle of Seven Pines, he was promoted to brigadier general on June 3, 1862, and fought during the Seven Days before being wounded at Second Manassas, where he fought in Jackson's Corps. Pender also participated in the 1862 battles of Winchester, Harper's Ferry, and Sharpsburg and was heroic at the battle of Fredericksburg. At the battle of Chancellorsville in May 1863, he was a division commander under General A. P. Hill (*q.v.*). On May 27, 1863, he was promoted to major general. He was a hero of the first day of the battle of Gettysburg, but on the second day he was wounded in the leg. Pender died of infection following the amputation of the leg on July 18, 1863, in Staunton, Virginia. Peele (comp.), *Lives of Distinguished North Carolinians*.

PENDLETON, William Nelson (*General*), was born on December 26, 1809, in Richmond, Virginia, to Edmund and Lucy (Nelson) Pendleton. He grew up on a plantation in Richmond, where he attended John Nelson's School before graduating fifth in a class of forty-two from the U.S. Military Academy in 1830. He was an Episcopalian and a Democrat. He had one son and three daughters by his marriage to Anzolette Elizabeth (Page) on July 15, 1831. His only son, Colonel Alexander Swift Pendleton, died in the battle of Winchester in September 1864. Pendleton served at Fort Moultrie and taught at West Point before resigning his commission in the U.S. Army in 1833 over the issue of nullification in South Carolina. He taught mathematics at Bristol College, Pennsylvania, in 1833 and at Newark College, Delaware, in 1837. In 1837, he was ordained an Episcopal clergyman in Pennsylvania. Pendleton taught at Episcopal Boys' High School in Wilmington, Delaware, in 1840 before removing to Baltimore in 1843. In 1847, he was rector of All Saints' Church, Frederick, Maryland, and six years later he became rector of a church in Lexington, Virginia. Pendleton was sympathetic to the Confederate cause and entered the Confederate Army as a captain and commander of the Rockbridge Artillery. Promoted to colonel, he served as chief of artillery to General J. E. Johnston (*q.v.*) at the battle of First Manassas. Following his promotion to brigadier general on March 26, 1862, he was chief of artillery for the Army of Northern Virginia and held the position for the rest of the war. He did not distinguish himself at the Seven Days' battles in the summer of 1862, but he performed excellently during the battle of Gettysburg a year later. During the siege of Petersburg, he made gallant stands at the battles of Rice's Station and Farmville, and he helped to arrange the details for the surrender of Lee's army. He continued as a minister to the troops during the war. Pendleton was paroled and he returned to Lexington. He was rector of Grace Church in Lexington, Virginia, until his death on January 15, 1883. Lee, *Memoirs of William Nelson Pendleton, D.D.*

PERKINS, John, Jr. (*Congressman*), son of John and Mary Bynum (Rivers) Perkins, was born in Natchez, Mississippi, on July 1, 1819. He was educated by private tutors and graduated from Yale College in 1840 and from Harvard Law School in 1842. In 1843, he began a law practice in New Orleans, Louisiana, which he relinquished four years later to become a cotton planter in Louisiana. Perkins, whose father was a Presbyterian, was himself a Catholic and a Democrat. He was also a close friend of J.D.B. DeBow (*q.v.*). His first marriage, to Mary Potts in 1850, ended when his wife deserted him. Perkins subsequently married Evelyn May. He had no children. He traveled in Europe in 1848-1849 and lived in Paris, where he was engaged in research for the Louisiana Historical Society, which he helped to organize. Active in local politics in 1851, he was judge of the Circuit Court for Madison Parish, and from 1853 to 1855, he served as a Democrat in the U.S. House of Representatives. He took over his father's plantation in 1857, but, although his father had been rich in land, Perkins made no money as a planter. As chairman of the state secession convention in 1861, he wrote the Secession Ordinance. In the provisional Confederate Congress, he served on the Printing and Foreign Affairs Committees and assisted in drafting the Constitution. Perkins also represented Madison Parish in the permanent Confederate House from 1862 to 1865 and was praised by the Louisiana legislature for his relief work on behalf of Confederate soldiers in Richmond. He favored the tax-in-kind, generally supported the administration, and served on the Foreign Affairs, Rules, Ways and Means, and Commerce Committees. He incurred heavy debts during the war, and when the war ended, he did not return to his plantation. He traveled extensively in Mexico and tried to establish a coffee plantation in Cordoba, Spain. He remained in Europe until 1878. Perkins died on November 28, 1885, in Baltimore, Maryland. Calhoun, "The John Perkins Family of Northeast Louisiana," *Louisiana Historical Quarterly*, XIX.

PERRY, Edward Aylesworth (*General*), son of Asa Perry, a farmer, and his wife Philura (Aylesworth), was born on March 15, 1831, in Richmond, Berkshire County, Massachusetts. He attended Richmond Academy and left Yale College in 1851 to teach at Greenville Academy in Alabama. He also studied law and was admitted to the Alabama bar in 1857. He was a Mason and a Presbyterian and was without political affiliation before the war. On February 1, 1859, he married Wathen Taylor; they had five children. In 1857, he moved to Pensacola, Florida, to practice law. When the Civil War began, he ceased his practice and volunteered for service in the Confederate Army. Early in the war, he raised a company which later became part of the 2nd Florida Regiment. As colonel, he accompanied the regiment to Virginia and fought under General James Longstreet (*q.v.*) at the battles of Seven Pines and the Seven Days in the summer of 1862. Longstreet praised Perry's valor and efficiency, and he was promoted to brigadier general on August 28, 1862. He fought at Fredericksburg and, in May 1863, at the battle of Chancellorsville, where he contracted typhoid fever. At the battle of Gettysburg, his brigade sustained heavy losses. Perry, who had been wounded at the battle of Frayser's Farm during the Seven Days, was wounded a second time and was permanently disabled at the Wilderness in May 1864. He spent the rest of the war with reserve forces in Alabama. There is no record of his surrender. After the war, he had a lucrative law practice in Pensacola and made numerous real estate investments. He remained active in Democratic politics throughout Reconstruction. From 1884 to 1888, he was Democratic governor of Florida. During his term of office, he helped to write a new state constitution. Perry died suddenly of a stroke during a visit to Kerrville, Texas, on October 15, 1889. *Florida Law Journal*, July 1949; Rerick, *Memoirs of Florida*, I.

PETTIGREW, James Johnston (*General*), was born to Ebenezer and Ann B. (Shepherd) Pettigrew on July 4, 1828, in Tyrrell County, North Carolina. His father was a Whig congressman, but Pettigrew himself was a Democrat. He was an Episcopalian and he never married. After graduating from the University of North Carolina in 1846, he was appointed by President Polk to a professorship at the

Naval Observatory in Washington, D.C. In 1848, he studied law under James L. Pettigru of Charleston, South Carolina, and he also spent two years of study in Berlin before returning to Charleston to practice law in 1852. Active in local politics, in 1856 he was elected to the South Carolina legislature, where he opposed reopening the slave trade. He was defeated for reelection in 1858. The following year he went abroad to fight for the Italian army in the unification struggle. He returned to Charleston in 1859 to assist in improving the militia. When the Civil War began, he commanded at Castle Pinckney and was a colonel of the militia. He refused the position of adjutant general of the state, preferring to fight as a colonel of the 12th North Carolina Regiment. Promoted to brigadier general on February 26, 1862, he fought at Williamsburg and Yorktown and was wounded and captured at Seven Pines. Two months later, he was exchanged, and he commanded the defenses at Petersburg and eastern North Carolina before leading his brigade at the battle of Gettysburg. Pettigrew led this division after his commander, General Henry Heth (*q.v.*), was wounded. He performed brilliantly in his attack on the federal center during the third day of the battle. However, he was mortally wounded during the retreat to the Potomac, and he died on July 17, 1862, near Winchester, Virginia. Clark (ed.), *Histories of the Several Regiments and Battalions from North Carolina in the Great War, 1861-1865*, IV.

PETTUS, Edmund Winston (*General*), son of John and Alice Taylor (Winston) Pettus and brother of John J. Pettus (*q.v.*), was born on July 6, 1821, in Limestone County, Alabama. He attended common schools, Clinton College in Tennessee, studied law under William Cooper of Tuscumbia, Alabama, and was admitted to the Alabama bar in 1842. Pettus practiced law in Gainsville, Sumter County, Alabama. He married Mary L. Chapman on June 27, 1844; they had three children. He was solicitor for the Seventh Alabama Judicial Circuit in 1844 before serving as a lieutenant during the Mexican War. He was judge of the Seventh Circuit from 1855 to 1858, when he moved to Cahaba in Dallas County, Alabama. He was a commissioner to Mississippi from Alabama at the time of secession. When the Civil War began, he volunteered for service in the Confederate Army and distinguished himself in the western command. After his service during the siege of Vicksburg, he was promoted to brigadier general on September 18, 1863. He subsequently fought with the Army of Tennessee at the battles of Missionary Ridge, where he commanded the right under General William Hardee (*q.v.*), and Chattanooga, and during the Atlanta campaign at Kenesaw Mountain, Atlanta, and Jonesboro in 1864. He was also sent to defend Columbia, South Carolina. In March 1865, he was seriously wounded in North Carolina. He surrendered in North Carolina and was soon paroled. Pettus returned to Selma, Alabama, to practice law and became a prominent Democratic politician. He was elected as a Democrat to the U.S. Senate in 1896 and served until his death on July 27, 1907, in Hot Springs, North Carolina. Hardy, *Selma: Her Institutions and Her Men*.

PETTUS, John Jones (*Governor*), was born on October 9, 1813, in Wilson County, Tennessee, to John and Alice Taylor (Winston) Pettus. He was a brother of General Edmund Pettus (*q.v.*). After attending schools in Limestone County, Alabama, and studying law in Sumter County, Alabama, he moved to Kemper County, Mississippi, in the 1840s where he became a planter and an active secessionist. Pettus was a Democrat and a Presbyterian and was married. He served in the lower house of the Mississippi legislature from 1846 to 1848 and in the upper house from 1848 to 1858. In January 1854, he was acting governor of the state, and the same year he served as president of the state Senate. From 1859 to 1863, he was governor of Mississippi. A slow, unimaginative person, Pettus was not a successful governor, but he defended the state against union forces and kept Vicksburg from falling for a year. During his term, the markets were closed by the blockade and the military enrollment was exhausted. Pettus wanted the legislature to restrict the shipment of cotton north, and he encouraged the agricultural production of provisions and grain. He issued cotton and Treasury notes and favored conscription. Pettus was unwilling to run for a second term as governor, and in 1864, he became a colonel in the state militia and served for the remainder of the war. After the war, he moved to Arkansas, where he lived a life of seclusion. He died on January 25, 1867. Bettersworth, *Mississippi in the Confederacy*; Woods, ''A Sketch of the Mississippi Secession Convention of 1861,'' *Publications of the Mississippi Historical Society*, VI.

PEYTON, Robert Ludwell Yates (*Congressman*), son of Townshend Dade Peyton, was born in Loudoun County, Virginia, on February 8, 1822. His family had lived in Virginia since 1622. His father liberated the family's slaves following the Nat Turner insurrection, and the family moved to Ohio, where the younger Peyton graduated from Miami University in Oxford, Ohio. He took a law degree from the University of Virginia in 1840 and became a planter and a lawyer. Peyton, who never married, was at one time engaged to a daughter of Governor Sterling Price (*q.v.*) of Missouri. In 1847-1848, he came to Harrisonville, Cass County, Missouri, where he practiced law and became active in local politics. Peyton ran unsuccessfully for circuit attorney of the Sixth Circuit and for the state legislature in 1855. In 1858, he was elected to the state Senate and began a law partnership with R. O. Boggess of Kansas City. He was a states' rights Democrat and a secessionist of the John C. Calhoun school. When the Civil War began, he was a colonel of the Missouri State Guards. Peyton served in the provisional Confederate Congress and was elected to the first Confederate Senate by the Missouri legislature at Neosha. In the Senate he served on the Claims, Commerce, Engrossment and Enrollment, and Indian Affairs Committees, and on the special committee to investigate the management of the Navy Department. In his military capacity, Peyton served in the 3rd Cavalry Regiment under General Sterling Price and fought in sixty engagements before contracting malaria around Vicksburg.

He died in Bladon Springs, Alabama, on September 3, 1863. *History of Cass and Bates County, Missouri*; Peyton, *History of Augusta County, Virginia*; Slaughter, *History of Bristol Parish*.

PHELAN, James (*Congressman, Judge*), son of John and Priscilla Oakes (Ford) Morris Phelan, was born in Huntsville, Alabama, on October 11, 1821. On September 22, 1846, he married Eliza Jones Moore. A son and namesake later served in the U.S. House of Representatives from Tennessee. Phelan was apprenticed at the age of fourteen on the Huntsville *Democrat*, where he remained employed until 1842. In 1842, he edited *Flag of the Union*, the Democratic organ of Tuscaloosa. The following year he was named state printer. He studied law and was admitted to the Huntsville bar in 1846, where he practiced until he moved to Aberdeen, Mississippi, in 1849. Until 1861, he was a famous lawyer in Aberdeen. In 1860, he was elected as a secessionist to the Mississippi Senate. A personal friend and advisor to Jefferson Davis (*q.v.*), Phelan served in the first Confederate Senate, where in January 1863, he introduced a bill authorizing the impressment of all cotton in the South. That action probably cost him his seat in the Senate; his friendship with Davis and the support of Bragg (*q.v.*) were also upsetting to his constituents. He served on the Indian Affairs, Judiciary, Printing, and Conference Committees. He later served as a presiding military court judge for the remainder of the war. After the war he was impoverished. He returned to his law practice in Alabama and later moved to Memphis, Tennessee, in 1867. Phelan died in Memphis on May 17, 1873. Lynch, *The Bench and Bar of Mississippi*.

PICKENS, Francis Wilkinson (*Governor*), was born on April 7, 1805, in Colleton District, South Carolina, to Governor Andrew Pickens and his wife Susannah Smith (Wilkinson). He attended Franklin College (later the University of Georgia) and South Carolina College in 1827 prior to being admitted to the bar in 1829. Pickens never practiced law, however. Having inherited wealth, he was a planter in Edgefield District, South Carolina, on his plantation "Sydney." Pickens was married three times: to Eliza Simkins in 1828, who died; to Marion Antoinette Dearing in 1843, who also died; and to Lucy Petway Holcombe, by whom he had one child in 1858. He served in the state House from 1832 to 1834 and was a nullifier Democrat in the U.S. House from 1834 to 1843. From 1844 to 1846, he served in the state Senate. He was a delegate to the Nashville convention in 1850. Although a secessionist, he joined the cooperationist camp after 1852, and later, after joining James L. Orr (*q.v.*) and the national Democrats, he hesitated on secession before running with the strong tide of public opinion in South Carolina. President Buchanan named him U.S. minister to Russia and he served from 1858 to 1860. He returned to South Carolina and was elected governor in 1860. As governor during the early days of the war, Pickens could not adequately defend South Carolina, and in December 1861, the legislature elected an executive council to control the affairs of state. When his term ended in 1862, Pickens retired to his estate. He held no further office in the Confederacy. After the war, he was deeply in debt. He urged a state constitutional convention in 1865 to accomplish presidential Reconstruction. Pickens died in Edgefield, South Carolina, on January 25, 1869. Cauthen, *South Carolina Goes to War, 1861-1865*; Perman, *Reunion Without Compromise*; Potter, *Lincoln and His Party in the Secession Crisis*.

PICKETT, George Edward (*General*), was born on January 28, 1825, in Richmond, Virginia, to Robert Pickett, a Henrico County planter, and his wife Mary (Johnston). He attended Richmond Academy and studied law with his uncle in Quincey, Illinois, in 1842. Appointed to West Point, he graduated last in a class of fifty-nine in 1846. First married to Sally Minge in January 1851, after her death, he married La Salle Corbell on September 5, 1863, by whom he had two children. During the Mexican War, he participated in the siege of Vera Cruz and fought at Cerro Gordo, Contreras, Churubusco, Molino del Rey, Chapultepec, and Mexico City. He was breveted first lieutenant and captain. After serving on the Texas frontier from 1849 to 1855, he was promoted to captain of the 9th Infantry. Pickett spent the year 1856 at Fortress Monroe in Virginia before being assigned to duty in the Washington Territory from 1857 to 1861. He resigned his commission when the Civil War began and volunteered for service in the Confederate Army. A colonel of Virginia troops, he was promoted to brigadier general on February 13, 1862. His brigade served gallantly under James Longstreet (*q.v.*) during the battle of Williamsburg and the Seven Days, where Pickett was wounded at Gaines' Mills. Following his promotion to major general on October 11, 1862, his division held the center for Lee (*q.v.*) at the battle of Fredericksburg the following December. But his greatest fame came on the third day of the battle of Gettysburg, where he led his small division against the virtually impregnable federal center at Cemetery Ridge. The casualties were enormous and included all but one field and general officer in his division. The following September, Pickett was sent to recruit in southern Virginia and North Carolina. In January 1864, he fought at New Bern, and in the spring of 1864, he saved Petersburg from capture. Defeated at the battle of Five Forks on April 1, 1865, he was relieved and discredited by Robert E. Lee following the battle of Sayler's Creek on April 6. He surrendered at Appomattox and was soon paroled. After the war Pickett was a poor man; he became a life insurance salesman in Richmond. He died in Norfolk, Virginia, on July 30, 1875. Pickett, *The Heart of a Soldier As Revealed in the Intimate Letters of General George E. Pickett*; Stewart, *Pickett's Charge*.

PICKETT, John T. (*Diplomat*), son of James Chamberlayne and Ellen (Desha) Pickett, was born in Maysville, Macon County, Kentucky, probably in the 1820s. His grandfather, Joseph Desha, was a governor of Kentucky and his father was a diplomat and a Democrat. He was educated in Scott County, Kentucky, and attended the U.S. Military Academy during the 1840s. He later studied law at Lexington Law School in Kentucky. An expansionist, he was part of the Lopez expedition to Cuba in 1850. He commanded at the battle of Cardenas and also served at one time as a general in the Hungarian army. Pickett served as U.S. consul at Turk's Island and as U.S. envoy to Vera Cruz from 1853 to 1861. When the Civil War began, he resigned his position and went to Richmond. In 1861, he was secretary of the Confederate peace mission to Washington. During the war, he was a Confederate commissioner in Mexico in 1861-1862 and special envoy extraordinary to Mexico in 1865. He was also at one time General John C. Breckinridge's (*q.v.*) chief of staff. He urged that Negroes be freed to be put into the military service of the Confederacy. He returned from Mexico when the war ended and settled in Washington, D.C. In 1870, he sold the diplomatic correspondence of the Confederate States, known as the "Pickett Papers," to the U.S. government for $75,000. Prior to his death in the 1890s, he lived and practiced law in Washington, D.C. Collins, *Historical Sketches of Kentucky*, II; Owsley, *King Cotton Diplomacy*.

PIERCE, George Foster (*Minister*), was born to the Methodist preacher Lovick Pierce and his wife Ann (Foster) on February 3, 1811, in Greene County, Georgia. He graduated from Franklin College (later the University of Georgia) with honors in 1829 and received his M.A. degree there in 1832. In 1829, he studied law with his uncle, Thomas Foster, but never practiced. Pierce had seven children by his marriage to Ann Maria Waldron on February 4, 1834. In 1831, he was ordained in the Methodist ministry and preached widely from Savannah to Charleston; five years later he was named an elder of the Augusta District. He was president of the Georgia Female College at Macon from 1838 until his resignation in 1840, when he edited the *Southern Lady's Book*. Pierce engaged in pastoral work in Georgia from 1842 to 1848. In 1845, he helped to organize the Methodist Episcopal Church South, a proslavery, pro-Southern branch of the church. From 1848 to 1854, he served as president of Emory College at Oxford, Georgia. In 1854, he was named a bishop of Georgia, a position which he retained throughout the Civil War. He published his *Incidents of Western Travel* in 1857. As Bishop, Pierce supported Georgia's secession. During the war, he raised food supplies for the Confederacy and he also preached to the troops. After the war, he resisted all attempts to reunite the Methodist church. Pierce died on September 3, 1884, in Sparta, Georgia. Fitzgerald, *Bishop George F. Pierce*.

de POLIGNAC, Prince Camille Armand Jules Marie (*General*), son of the Prince de Polignac, president of the Council of Ministers to Charles X of France, was born on February 16, 1832, at Millemont, France. Educated at the College of Stanislaus in Paris during the early 1850s, he served in the French Army during the

Crimean War. He resigned his commission in 1859 to study plant life in Central America and was living there at the outbreak of the Civil War. He was first married to Marie Adolphine Langenberger; he had one son and one daughter by his second marriage to Elizabeth Marguerite Knight. After offering his services to the Confederate Army when the Civil War began, he was made lieutenant colonel and chief of staff to General P.G.T. Beauregard (*q.v.*). He was promoted to brigadier general on January 10, 1863, and to major general on June 13, 1864. During the second half of the war, he served in the Army of Tennessee. In the Red River campaign in Louisiana in the spring of 1864, he distinguished himself while commanding his own and Mouton's Brigade in the battles of Mansfield and Pleasant Hill. In March 1865, the Confederate government sent him to France to seek the aid and intervention of Napoleon III. After the war, he remained in France and retired to his estate, where he wrote articles on the Civil War. In the Franco-Prussian War of 1870-1871, he led the 1st Division and was awarded the French Legion of Honor. He later gained a reputation as a mathematician and civil engineer. He conducted surveying expeditions in Algeria prior to his death on November 15, 1913, in Paris, France. *Confederate Veteran*, XXIII; Fortier, *A History of Louisiana*, II; Hatton, "Prince Camille de Polignac and the American Civil War, 1863-1865," *Louisiana Studies*, III.

POLK, Leonidas (*General*), was born on April 10, 1806, in Raleigh, North Carolina, to William and Sarah (Hawkins) Polk. He graduated eighth in a class of thirty-eight from the U.S. Military Academy in 1827. He resigned his commission to enter the ministry and was ordained an Episcopal priest in 1830. Polk was a Democrat who probably became a Whig. He had two sons and five daughters by his marriage to Frances Devereux of Raleigh in May 1830. After serving a parish in Richmond, Virginia, Polk settled in Tennessee during the 1830s. In 1838, he became missionary bishop of the Southwest, and three years later, he was named the first Protestant Episcopal bishop of Louisiana. He was a close friend of Jefferson Davis (*q.v.*) since their West Point days. Polk helped to establish the University of the South before the Civil War. When the war began, he offered his services to the Confederate Army. On June 25, 1861, he was appointed a major general in the Confederate Army, and President Davis gave him command of Department Number 2, which included much of the west. He supervised the building of fortifications in New Madrid, Missouri, Fort Pillow, Island Number 10, Memphis, Tennessee, and Columbus, Kentucky. On November 7, 1861, he commanded Confederate troops at the battle of Belmont, Missouri. After General Albert S. Johnston (*q.v.*) assumed command of the Army of Tennessee, Polk commanded the 1st Corps at the battles of Shiloh, Perryville, Corinth, and Murfreesboro. On October 10, 1862, he was promoted to lieutenant general. At the battle of Chickamauga in September 1863, he commanded the right wing. Polk also commanded the Department of Alabama early in 1864 before he joined

General Joseph E. Johnston (*q.v.*) at Resaca during the Atlanta campaign. He was killed on reconnaissance at Pine Mountain, near Marietta, Georgia, on June 14, 1864. Parks, *General Leonidas Polk*; Polk, *Leonidas Polk*, I-II.

POLK, Lucius Eugene (*General*), a nephew of Leonidas Polk (*q.v.*) and son of Dr. William Julius Polk and his wife Mary Rebecca (Long), was born on July 10, 1833, in Salisbury, North Carolina. Two years later his father moved to Columbia, Tennessee, where he became a large planter. The younger Polk, an Episcopalian and a Democrat, graduated from the University of Virginia in 1852. He was married to a cousin, Sallie Moore Polk, on August 19, 1863, and they had five children, one of whom was later U.S. Congressman Rufus King Polk of Pennsylvania. In 1853, Polk settled near Helena, Arkansas, and soon became a prosperous planter. He had no political ambition before the Civil War. When the war began, he enlisted as a private in the Confederate Army in the West and served under General William Hardee (*q.v.*). He was promoted to colonel after he was wounded during the battle of Shiloh in April 1862. Severely wounded at the battle of Richmond, Kentucky, on August 30, he was wounded yet again at the battle of Perryville in October, after covering the retreat from Corinth only days before. He was promoted to brigadier general on December 13, 1862, and won praise for his performance at the battle of Murfreesboro. He was heroic during the battle of Chickamauga and fought at Missionary Ridge before a final wound during the battle of Kenesaw Mountain in June 1864 disabled him for further service. He returned to his father's home in Tennessee. After the war, he lived quietly on his plantation in Columbia, Maury County, Tennessee. In 1887, he served as a Democrat in the state Senate. Polk died on December 1, 1892, in Columbia, Tennessee. Connelly, *Autumn of Glory*; Polk, *Polk Family and Kinsmen*.

POLLARD, Edward Alfred (*Editor*), was born to Richard and Pauline Cabell (Rivers) Pollard on February 27, 1831, in Nelson County (later Albemarle County), Virginia. He attended Hampden-Sidney College in 1846, the University of Virginia from 1847 to 1849, and graduated from the College of William and Mary Law School in 1850. He was an Episcopalian and a Democrat. Pollard married early in life, and his wife died in 1850. After the Civil War, he married Marie Antoinette Nathalie Granier-Dowell. During 1850-1855, he was a journalist in California and traveled widely in Mexico, Nicaragua, China, and Japan. During the Buchanan administration, he was clerk of the Judiciary Committee of Congress. In 1859, he published *Black Diamond*, a book of secessionist essays, and in 1861, he became co-editor of the Richmond *Examiner*. During the war, he supported the struggle for Southern independence, and despite his hatred of Jefferson Davis (*q.v.*), his performance was unaffected and he was one of the ablest Confederate leaders. Nevertheless, he remained better known for his anti-Davis polemics than for his ability as a journalist or historian. He published his

Southern History of the War, an attempt to blame Confederate losses on the president, between 1862 and 1866. In 1864, he ran the blockade to Europe, where he intended to be a journalist representative for the South, but he was captured. He was not exchanged until January 1865. After the war, Pollard returned to Richmond. In 1866, he published *The Lost Cause*. He continued to write extensively about the war for the rest of his life. He published two magazines, *Southern Opinion* in 1867 and *The Political Pamphlet* in 1868. He left the *Examiner* in 1867 and moved the following year to New York where he became a free-lance journalist. Pollard died in Lynchburg, Virginia, on December 12, 1872. Andrews, *The South Reports the Civil War*; Reynolds, *Editors Make War*.

POPE, Joseph Daniel (*Bureaucrat*), son of Joseph James and Sarah (Jenkins) Pope, was born on March 6, 1820, in Beaufort District, South Carolina. He attended Waterloo Academy, graduated from the University of Georgia in 1841, studied law under James L. Pettigru, and was admitted to the South Carolina bar in 1845. He was an Episcopalian. Pope married Catherine A. Scott on December 11, 1845. Besides practicing law at Beaufort, he served in the lower house of the South Carolina legislature from 1854 to 1860 and in the upper house from 1863 to 1865. He was also a delegate to the state secession convention. When the Civil War began, he was made head of the Confederate Revenue Department. Secretary of the Treasury Memminger (*q.v.*) placed him in charge of printing and issuing Confederate money and of printing all Confederate Treasury notes. During his tenure, he recommended the creation of a centralized government printing agency in Columbia, South Carolina. He retained this position throughout the war. Pope lost his property during the war and practiced law in Columbia, South Carolina, after 1865. In 1884, he was named professor of law at the University of South Carolina, and in 1906, he became the first dean of the law school there. He died in Columbia, South Carolina, on March 21, 1908. Brooks, *South Carolina Bench and Bar*; Todd, *Confederate Finance*.

PORCHER, Francis Peyre (*Physician*), was born on December 14, 1825, in St. Johns, Berkeley County, South Carolina, the son of Dr. William Porcher and his wife Isabella Sarah (Peyre). He attended Mount Zion Academy, graduated from South Carolina College in 1844, and was first in the class of 1847 at the Medical College of South Carolina in Charleston, where he later taught. He also studied in France from 1847 to 1849. Porcher had five children by his marriage to Virginia Leigh, a daughter of Benjamin W. Leigh. After her death, he had four children by his marriage to Margaret Ward. Porcher practiced medicine and taught at the Medical College until the war began. He was an authority on botany, and, in the 1850s, he helped to establish the Charleston Preparatory Medical School. When the Civil War began, he volunteered for medical service in the Confederate government. In 1863, he wrote *Resources of the Southern Fields and Forests*, which was published by order of the surgeon general of the Confederacy. This work was perhaps the most useful guide to field treatment and the extraction of plant medicine used in the Confederacy. He was surgeon to the Holcombe Legion throughout most of the war and was also on the staff of the Naval Hospital at Fort Nelson (Norfolk) and the South Carolina Hospital at Petersburg, Virginia. When the war ended, he returned to Charleston to teach at the Medical College. From 1873 to 1876, Porcher edited the *Charleston Medical Journal and Review*. He attained an international reputation in medicine and botany. He died on November 19, 1895. *Confederate Veteran*, XXXIII; Kelly and Burrage, *American Medical Biographies*.

POWER, John Logan (*Bureaucrat, Editor*), was born in Tipperary County, Ireland, on March 1, 1834. His father died in 1840, and his mother remarried in the United States, where he was reared in poverty. Little is known of his early life or even where he lived. He was a Presbyterian. He married Jane Wilkinson in December 1857 and had a large family. Power moved to New Orleans in 1854 and to Jackson, Mississippi, in 1855. He was a printer in the office of *Flag of Our Union* and the Presbyterian paper *True Witness*, both in New Orleans, and he was co-owner and manager of Ethelbert Barksdale's (*q.v.*) *Mississippian* in Jackson, from 1855 to 1860. In January 1860, he published the *Jackson Daily News*, and the following year he was the official reporter of the state secession convention, for which he published the proceedings. After the Civil War began, he continued to edit his newspaper, and he actively supported the war effort. In 1864, he was named Mississippi superintendent of Army records and clerk of the state House. The following year he was secretary of the state constitutional convention. His services to the state during the war were largely in recording events of the war and providing printed information upon which other leaders could take action. After the war, he started the *Mississippi Standard* in Jackson, which later became the *Clarion*. In 1875, he was state printer, and in 1895 and 1899, he was elected secretary of state in Mississippi. He died in Jackson, Mississippi, on September 24, 1901. Bettersworth, *Mississippi in the Confederacy*; *Biographical and Historical Memoirs of Mississippi*.

PRATT, Daniel (*Businessman*), was born on July 20, 1799, in Temple, New Hampshire, to Edward and Asenath (Flint) Pratt. In 1831, he married Esther Ticknor, by whom he had three children. Pratt moved to Savannah, Georgia, in 1820, when he became a carpenter. The following year, he moved to Milledgeville, Georgia, where he labored at this trade for ten years. In 1831, Pratt moved to Clinton, Georgia, to take over the cotton gin factory owned by Samuel Griswold. Two years later, he moved to Elmore County, Alabama, and in 1838, he settled in Autauga County, Alabama, near Montgomery. There, in an area later known as "Prattville," he built a cotton, grist, and lumber mill. By 1859, his property was assessed at $519,000. In 1860, Pratt was elected to the Alabama House. Although he was ardently Southern in his sympathies, he opposed secession. During the war, however, he organized and equipped the "Prattville Dragoons" and served as a director of the Northern and Southern Railroad. His business interests were used to assist in feeding and clothing the Confederate armies. In 1872, he was a director of the Red Mountain Iron and Coal Company. Pratt died on May 13, 1873. Armes, *The Story of Coal and Iron in Alabama*; Tarrant, *Honorable Daniel Pratt: A Biography*.

PRESTON, John Smith (*General*), was born on April 20, 1809, near Abingdon, Virginia, to Francis Smith and Sarah (Buchanan) Preston. He attended Hampden-Sidney College from 1823 to 1825 and the University of Virginia from 1825 to 1827, before studying law at Harvard. He was a Presbyterian and a Democrat. He had children by his marriage to Caroline Martha Hampton, daughter of the future Confederate General Wade Hampton (*q.v.*), on April 28, 1830. Preston practiced law in Abingdon before moving to Columbia, South Carolina, in 1840. He then acquired a large and profitable sugar plantation in Louisiana, "The Homus," moved there in 1841, and made a fortune. He returned to South Carolina in 1848. From 1848 to 1856, he was a member of the South Carolina state Senate. From 1856 to 1860, he lived in Europe. He returned in 1860 and was chairman of the South Carolina delegation to the Democratic convention in Charleston. The following February, he was a commissioner to Virginia to urge that state's secession. When the Civil War began, Preston volunteered for service in the Confederate Army. At Fort Sumter and First Manassas, he was an aide to General P.G.T. Beauregard (*q.v.*). In August 1861, he was named assistant adjutant general in command of the 2nd Brigade of Kentucky troops. Preston assumed command of the Confederate prison camp at Columbia, South Carolina, in January 1862 and held this position until Secretary of War James A. Seddon (*q.v.*) named him superintendent of the Bureau of Conscription in Richmond on July 30, 1863. Preston managed this bureau ably until the end of the war. He was promoted to brigadier general on June 10, 1864. When the war ended, he returned to South Carolina. He remained "unreconstructed," and he argued against reconciliation with the North. He lived in England for a time before returning to South Carolina in 1868. Preston lived in semi-retirement and traveled to make speeches in defense of the right of secession. He died in Columbia on May 1, 1881. Connelly and Jones, *The Politics of Command*; Tyler, *Encyclopedia of Virginia Biography*, III.

PRESTON, Walter (*Congressman*), son of the farmer and large landowner John W. Preston, was born in July 1819 in Abingdon, Virginia. He attended the University of Virginia and Yale College around 1840, studied law, and was admitted to the Virginia bar. Preston, a Whig, practiced law and was a planter in Abingdon. For a time he lived in Arkansas. He also served in the Arkansas legislature and was a candidate for attorney general of Virginia before the war. Until April 6, 1861, he considered himself an opponent of secession, but he later served in the provisional Confederate Congress and defeated Fayette McMullen (*q.v.*) by a large majority for a seat in the first Confederate House of Representatives. He was a supporter of the Davis administration in the provisional Congress but not in the first House, where he was a member of the Conference, Foreign Affairs, Quartermaster's and Commissary Departments Committees, and the special committee on the election of Confederate congressmen in the states held by the enemy. After his term in the House ended, he returned to private life. He practiced law in Abingdon and held no further office in the Confederacy. While he suffered financially from the war, he remained moderately well-to-do. Preston died in Abingdon in November 1867. Summers, *History of Southwest Virginia*.

PRESTON, William (*General, Diplomat*), a nephew of the Virginia Congressman Francis Smith Preston and a cousin of the South Carolina Senator William Campbell Preston, was born on October 16, 1816, to William and Caroline (Hancock) Preston in Louisville, Kentucky. He attended Augusta College, St. Joseph's College in Kentucky and Yale College in 1836 before graduating from Harvard Law School in 1838. He began a law practice in Louisville the following year. In 1840, he married Margaret Wickliffe, by whom he had one son and five daughters. Preston was a Catholic and a Whig who later joined the Democratic party. During the Mexican War, he was a lieutenant colonel in the 4th Kentucky Volunteers. He was a delegate to the state constitutional convention in 1849, and the following year he was elected to the Kentucky House. Preston's career as a Whig included a term in the state Senate from 1851 to 1853 and a term in the U.S. House of Representatives from 1852 to 1855. He lost a bid for reelection in 1854 and became a Democrat around the same time. From 1858 to 1861, he was President Buchanan's envoy extraordinary and minister plenipotentiary to Spain. He resigned his post when the Civil War began and he returned to Louisville. More nationalist than secessionist, Preston volunteered for the Confederate Army and served as a colonel on the staff of Albert Sidney Johnston (*q.v.*) at Shiloh. He was promoted to brigadier general on April 14, 1862, and he saw action at Vicksburg, Baton Rouge, Murfreesboro, and other points in mid-Tennessee. In April 1863, he relieved Humphrey Marshall (*q.v.*) in southwest Virginia. He served as a division commander at the battle of Chickamauga, and in 1864, he served under General Edmund Kirby Smith (*q.v.*) in the Trans-Mississippi Department. In 1864, he was also envoy extraordinary and minister plenipotentiary from the Confederate government to Maximilian, emperor of Mexico. In 1865, he was promoted to major general. He was a member of the Kentucky bloc and a vigorous opponent of Braxton Bragg (*q.v.*). Preston never surrendered. After the war, he traveled to Mexico, the West Indies, England, and Canada. He returned to Kentucky in 1866 and was elected to the state House of Representatives the following year, serving there until 1869, when he moved to Lexington, Kentucky, to practice law. In 1880, he was a delegate to the Democratic national convention. Preston died on September 21, 1887, in Lexington. Connelly and Jones, *The Politics of Command*; Duke, *Reminiscences of William Basil Duke*.

PRESTON, William Ballard (*Congressman*), was born in Smithfield, Montgomery County, Virginia, on November 25, 1805, to Governor James Patton Preston and his wife Ann (Taylor). He graduated from the College of William and Mary in 1823, studied law at the University of Virginia, and was admitted to the Virginia bar in 1826. He became an outstanding lawyer. He was a Presbyterian. He married Lucinda Staples Redd on November 21, 1839 and they had three sons. Preston served in the lower house of the Virginia legislature in 1830-1832 and 1844-1845 and in the upper house from 1840 to 1844. He also served a term as a Whig in the U.S. House from 1847 to 1849. In 1849-1850, he was President Zachary Taylor's secretary of the navy. Preston resumed his law practice, and in 1858, he traveled to France to propose a steamship line between the two countries. An opponent of secession, Preston was a delegate to the state constitutional convention in 1861, and he was elected to the provisional Confederate Congress. During his term, he tried to prevent war, although he presented his state's Ordinance of Secession to that body. A powerful member of the western bloc, along with other members of the Preston family, he actively supported the career of P.G.T. Beauregard (*q.v.*). He also served on the powerful Military Affairs Committee. Preston died in office in Smithfield on November 16, 1862. Connelly and Jones, *The Politics of Command*; Sobel, *Biographical Directory of the United States Cabinet*; Tyler, *Encyclopedia of Virginia Biography*, III.

PRICE, Sterling (*General*), son of Pugh Williamson and Elizabeth (Williamson) Price, was born on September 14 or 20, 1809, in Farmville, Prince Edward County, Virginia. He attended Hampden-Sidney College in Virginia in 1826-1827 and studied law under Creed Taylor near Farmville. He was a Presbyterian and a Democrat. He married Martha Head on May 14, 1833. Price settled on a farm in Keytesville, Chariton County, Missouri, in 1831. He was elected as a Democrat from Chariton County to the state House in 1836, 1840, and 1842; in 1844, he was also chosen speaker of that body. Elected to the U.S. House in 1844, he resigned two years later to fight in the Mexican War. He was named brigadier general of volunteers and also participated in the march on Chihuahua and served as military governor of New Mexico. During his term as governor of Missouri from 1853 to 1857, he was an anti-Benton Democrat. He was a member of the State Banking Commission from 1857 to 1861. Price was an ardent unionist; nevertheless, he became president of the Missouri secession convention in 1860. When the war began, he joined the secessionists and helped to organize the Missouri State Guard, of which he was made major general in June 1861. He defeated federal forces at Wilson's Creek and Lexington, Missouri, in 1861 before going to Arkansas. He was promoted to brigadier general on March 6, 1862. He was wounded in the battle of Elkhorn but recovered sufficiently to participate in the battles of Shiloh, Iuka, and Corinth later the same year. He also fought at Helena, Alabama, in 1863. Late in 1864, he attempted to retake Missouri for the Confederacy but was turned back at Westport, and at the end of the war he was in Texas with what remained of his command. Political discrimination against him in Richmond kept him from promotions in rank which he might otherwise have received. Price refused to surrender when the war ended. He traveled to Mexico on an unsuccessful colonization scheme. In 1866, he returned to Missouri, disillusioned and impoverished. He died on September 29, 1867, in St. Louis. Shalhope, *Sterling Price*.

PRYOR, Roger Atkinson (*Congressman*, *General*), son of the Presbyterian minister Theodorick Bland Pryor and his wife Lucy Eppes (Atkinson), was born in Petersburg, Dinwiddie County, Virginia, on July 19, 1828. He attended the Classical Academy of Petersburg, graduated first in his class at Hampden-Sidney College in 1845, and received his law degree from the University of Virginia Law School in 1848. The following year, he was admitted to the Virginia bar but soon abandoned his practice because of ill health. On November 8, 1848, he married Sara A. Rice, the future author of *Reminiscences of Peace and War* (1904). They had seven children. Pryor was a Democrat and a radical secessionist. He joined the staff of the Washington, D.C., *Union* in 1852 and of the Richmond *Enquirer* in 1853. He became well-known for his opposition to the Know-Nothing party. From 1854 to 1857, he served as special U.S. minister to Greece. Upon his return, he joined the staff of the ultra-secessionist newspaper, *The South*, in Washington, D.C., and also worked on the Washington *States*. From 1859 to 1861, he was a Democrat in the U.S. House of Representatives. He was a delegate to the Charleston Democratic convention in 1860 and supported Breckinridge (*q. v.*) for president. After urging the attack on Fort Sumter, he resigned from the U.S. Congress on March 3, 1861, and was elected to the provisional and the first permanent Confederate House of Representatives. He served on the Military Affairs and special committees but resigned from Congress in April 1862. He also had a distinguished military career, serving as colonel at the battles of Yorktown and Williamsburg and as brigadier general at Seven Pines, Gaines' Mill, Frayser's Farm, Second Manassas, Harper's Ferry, and Sharpsburg. He was promoted to brigadier general on April 16, 1862, but resigned as general on August 26, 1863, because he had been reassigned and left without a command. He became a special courier without rank during 1864 and was captured at Petersburg in November 1864. Pryor was confined at Fort Lafayette until the end of the war. After the war, he moved to New York and urged Southern acquiescence toward the Reconstruction government while on the staff of the New York *Daily*

News. He practiced law in New York City from 1866 to 1890, during which time he also served as a Democratic judge of the state Court of Common Pleas from 1890 to 1894 and on the state Supreme Court from 1894 to 1899. He died in New York City on March 14, 1919. Tyler, *Encyclopedia of Virginia Biography*, III.

PUGH, James Lawrence (*Congressman*), was born on December 12, 1820, in Burke County, Georgia, to Robert and Anne Silvia (Tilman) Pugh. His family moved to Pike County, Alabama, in 1824, and his father died six years later. Pugh attended school in Louisville, Alabama, and at Rocky Mountain Academy; in 1834, he went to night school in Irwinton, Alabama. In 1836, he fought in the Indian War on the Alabama frontier. He studied law in the office of John Gill Shorter (*q.v.*) and was admitted to the Alabama bar in 1841. In 1847, he married Sarah Sarena Hunter, by whom he had six children, three of whom died in infancy. Born a Presbyterian, he became an Episcopalian when he married. He farmed and practiced law in Eufaula, Alabama, as a member of the firm of Pugh and Cochran. He was also active in local politics. Pugh, who was originally a Whig, joined the Democratic party after he lost a race for the U.S. House in 1849. He served a term in the House as a Democrat from 1859 to 1861. When the Civil War began, he enlisted as a private in the Eufaula Rifles of the 1st Alabama Regiment and served one year. Pugh was elected to the Confederate House of Representatives and served from 1861 to 1865. He supported the Davis administration throughout the war and was a member of the pro-Bragg bloc. He served on the Military, Public Buildings, and Currency Committees. After the war, he returned to his law practice in Eufaula. He was a delegate to the state constitutional convention in 1875 and a Democratic elector for Samuel Tilden in 1876. Two years later, he ran unsuccessfully for the U.S. Senate; he was finally elected to that body in 1880 and served until 1897. He was also chairman of the Judiciary Committee of the Senate. He declined a nomination to the U.S. Supreme Court in 1888. When his term ended, Pugh settled in Washington, D.C., and practiced law. Pugh died in Washington, D.C., on March 9, 1907. Connelly and Jones, *The Politics of Command*; Owens, *History of Alabama and Dictionary of Alabama Biography*, IV.

PURYEAR, Richard Clauselle (*Congressman*), son of John and Sally (Clausel) Puryear, was born in Mecklenburg County, Virginia, on February 9, 1801. He attended the common schools, married, and, in the 1830s, became a planter near Huntsville, North Carolina. He was a Baptist. At one time, Puryear was magistrate of Surry County, North Carolina. In 1838, 1844, 1846, and 1852, he was elected to the state House, and he also served at one time in the state Senate. He was a Whig in the U.S. House of Representatives from 1853 to 1857 but lost a campaign for reelection in 1856. In 1859, he was elected to the House on the American party ticket. At the time of the North Carolina state secession convention, Puryear was a unionist, but he was later a delegate to the provisional Confederate Congress at Richmond. He was a member of the Committee on Naval Affairs. When his term ended, he returned to his farm in North Carolina. Nothing further is known of his wartime career, save that he supported William W. Holden's (*q.v.*) peace movement. After the war, he planted and in 1866, was a delegate to a peace congress in Philadelphia. He was an ally of Governor Jonathan Worth (*q.v.*) and sought to make an alliance between the Republican party and its southern Democratic supporters. He died on July 30, 1867, in Yadkin County, North Carolina. *Biographical Directory of the American Congress*; Hamilton, *Reconstruction in North Carolina*.

Q

QUINTARD, Charles Todd (*Chaplain*, *Physician*), was born in Stamford, Connecticut, on December 22, 1824, to well-to-do parents, Isaac and Clarissa (Hoyt) Shaw Quintard. He attended Trinity School in New York and received his M.A. from Columbia College in 1846 before studying medicine with Dr. James R. Wood. In 1847, he received his M.D. from New York University Medical College. The following year, he settled in Athens, Georgia, to practice medicine. His marriage to Katharine Hand produced three children. In 1851, Quintard became professor of physiology and pathological anatomy at Memphis Medical College in Tennessee, where he was also editor of the *Memphis Medical Register*. An Episcopalian, he came under the influence of Tennessee Bishop James H. Otey; in 1855, he became a deacon, and the following year he was ordained and became rector of Cavalry Church in Memphis. He was also rector of a church in Nashville prior to the war. He sympathized with the Southern cause. During the Civil War, Quintard was both medical officer and chaplin of the 1st Tennessee Regiment, and he saw action at the battles of Cheat Mountain, Perryville, Murfreesboro, Chickamauga, and Franklin. When the war ended, he moved to Nashville and was elected the second bishop of Tennessee in late 1865. An adherent of the Oxford Movement in 1867, he was instrumental in the second founding of the University of the South in Sewanee, Tennessee. In 1872, he resigned his position there as vice-chancellor, favoring Josiah Gorgas (*q.v.*) as his successor. He continued in his pastoral duties for the remainder of his life. He died on February 15, 1898, in Darien, Georgia. Guerry, *Men Who Made Sewanee*; Noll, *Doctor Quintard*.

QUINTERO, Juan (*Diplomat*), was born in Havana, Cuba. He lived in Mexico, where he was a farmer, before becoming a U.S. citizen in 1853. He was a Catholic and a lawyer. There is some evidence that he lived in New Orleans for a time before the Civil War began. When the war began, he entered the service of the Confederate government. During the Civil War, Quintero managed delicate and involved diplomatic missions for the Confederacy with skill and success. In May 1861, President Davis (*q.v.*) sent him to the Vidaurri government in Mexico to try to obtain an agreement on the border security and an alliance with the Confederacy. He was also sent to Monterrey as resident diplomat, but President Davis kept him from making an alliance with Mexico. Quintero broke the blockade to bring cotton from Texas to Mexico. In 1863, he protected the friendship with Vidaurri and kept President Juarez neutral on Confederate rights. His relations with the Mexican government were most helpful to the Confederacy. He apparently also succeeded in keeping Mexican border bandits from attacking Confederate supply trains. After the war, Quintero had charge of a land office in Austin, Texas. There is no record of his death. Kerby, *The Confederate Invasion of New Mexico and Arizona*; Lonn, *Foreigners in the Confederacy*; Owsley, *King Cotton Diplomacy*.

R

RAINS, Gabriel James (*General*), son of Gabriel M. and Hester (Ambrose) Rains and brother of George W. Rains (*q.v.*), was born on June 4, 1804, in Craven County, North Carolina. The younger Rains received a common school education in North Carolina and graduated thirteenth in a class of thirty-eight from the U.S. Military Academy in 1827. His marriage to Mary Jane McClellan produced six children. Upon accepting his appointment in the U.S. Army, Rains served in the West as a lieutenant in the 7th U.S. Infantry. He was promoted to captain in 1837 and was wounded during the Seminole War in Florida in 1838, for which he was breveted major. After serving on posts in Louisiana and Florida, he recruited troops for the Mexican War. Rains also fought the Indians during the Seminole

War of 1849-1850. He was promoted to major in 1851 and was transferred to California the following year. In 1860, he was promoted to lieutenant colonel. Rains resigned his commission in the summer of 1861 and volunteered for duty in the Confederate Army. After entering as a colonel, he was promoted to brigadier general on September 23, 1861. As he had experimented with explosives during his federal army career, the Confederates assigned him to the mining defenses of Yorktown and Williamsburg, Virginia. Rains also organized a plan of torpedo protection for the Southern harbors and invented the explosive subterra shell in 1862. During the Virginia Peninsular campaign of 1862, he fought heroically at the battles of Seven Pines and during the Seven Days. In May 1863, he ran the Bureau of Conscription in Richmond and was given a series of secret missions. On June 17, 1864, he was named chief of the Torpedo Bureau, under the jurisdiction of the War Department. There is no record of his surrender. After the war, he lived in Atlanta before moving to Charleston, South Carolina, in 1876, where from 1877 to 1880 he was a clerk in the Quartermaster Department of the U.S. Army. He died in Aiken, South Carolina, on August 6, 1881. Charleston *News and Courier*, August 1881; Freeman, *Lee's Lieutenants*, I.

RAINS, George Washington (*Bureaucrat*), son of Gabriel M. and Hester (Ambrose) Rains and brother of the future Confederate General Gabriel James Rains (*q.v.*), was born in Craven County, North Carolina, in 1817. His parents moved to Alabama while he was young, and after attending New Bern Academy in North Carolina, he graduated third in a class of fifty-six from the U.S. Military Academy in 1842 and began a military career in the Corps of Engineers. He married Frances Josephine Ramsdell on April 23, 1856. Rains was assistant engineer at Fort Warren in Boston in 1842-1843 and was garrisoned at Fort Monroe in 1843-1844. From 1844 to 1846, he was assistant professor of chemistry, mineralogy, and geology at West Point. In 1846, he was promoted to first lieutenant and was stationed at the Quartermaster Depot at Port Isabel, Texas. During the Mexican War, he was breveted captain and later major, seeing action at Vera Cruz, Cerro Gordo, Contreras, Churubusco, and Molino del Rey. In 1847-1848, he was an aide-de-camp to Generals Winfield Scott and Gideon Pillow. In 1848-1849, he was stationed at the garrison at New Orleans; the following year he fought in the Seminole War in Florida. He was promoted to captain in 1856 but resigned the same year to become part-owner and president of the Washington Iron Works and Highland Iron Works in Newburgh, New York, positions which he held until 1861. During this time, he patented steam engines and boilers. When the Civil War began, he joined the Confederate Army. Rains enlisted as a lieutenant colonel in the Confederate Artillery and was responsible for equipping powder mills at Augusta, Georgia. These mills produced 2,750,000 pounds of gunpowder for the Confederacy during the war years. He was placed in charge of all munitions production in Augusta in April 1862. Rains also initiated the wholesale collection of nitre and authored *Notes on Making Saltpetre from the Earth of the Caves* (1863). After the war, he remained in Augusta. He was professor of chemistry and pharmacy at the University of Georgia from 1867 to 1884, serving as dean of the faculty in 1884. For the next ten years, he held the position of professor emeritus, a title which he abandoned when he went into business in New York in 1894. In 1882, Rains published *History of the Confederate States Powder Works*. He died in Newburgh on March 21, 1898. Appleton's *Cyclopedia of American Biography*; Vandiver, *Ploughshares into Swords*.

RALLS, John Perkins (*Congressman*), was born to the Virginia family of Hector and Sallie (Stowe) Ralls on January 1, 1822, in Greene County, Georgia. He attended the academy in Greensboro, Georgia, and graduated from the medical college at Augusta, Georgia, in 1845. Ralls was a Democrat, a prohibitionist, and a member of the Methodist Episcopal church. He married Agnes Mary Hamilton on August 1, 1847; the couple had six children. Ralls trained in hospitals in Paris, France, in 1846-1847 before becoming county and city physician in Gadsden, Alabama. He had an active and successful practice. A delegate to the Alabama secession convention, he also was elected to the Confederate Congress and served in 1862-1863. Ralls served in Congress as a Davis administration loyalist and was defeated for reelection in 1864. A committed Reconstructionist, Ralls was a member of the Indian Affairs, Medical Department, and Special Committees. A man of talent, he retired to his medical practice and held no other office in the Confederacy. Ralls was a delegate to the state constitutional convention in 1875 and served in the Alabama legislature in 1878. He died in Gadsden on November 23, 1904. Fleming, *Civil War and Reconstruction in Alabama*; Owen, *History of Alabama and Dictionary of Alabama Biography*, IV.

RAMSAY, James Graham (*Congressman*), was born in Iredell County, North Carolina, on March 1, 1823. He graduated from Davidson College in 1838, studied medicine at Jefferson Medical College in Philadelphia, and graduated in 1848. He was a friend of Francis Burton Craige (*q.v.*). He was a farmer and a doctor in Mt. Vernon, Rowan County, North Carolina, before the war. Ramsay, who was married and had at least one daughter, was a member of the Presbyterian church and a unionist Whig. From 1856 to 1862, he served in the state Senate. He claimed that his unionism kept him from being elected to the first Confederate House of Representatives. However, through the efforts of William W. Holden's (*q.v.*) newspaper and the peace party of his district, he was elected to the second Confederate House, where he served on the Medical Department and Naval Affairs Committees. In the House, Ramsay favored raising the pay of Confederate officials. In March 1865, he was reported as absent without leave from Richmond. Later that year, he returned to Charlotte to practice medicine with J.M.K. Henderson. He was a candidate for the state constitutional convention in June 1865 but was disqualified from taking the oath because he had not been pardoned. He became a Republican and served in the state Senate in 1883. He died in Salisbury on January 10, 1903. Brawley, *The Rowan Story*; Rumple, *A History of Rowan County*.

RAMSEUR, Stephen Dodson (*General*), was born on May 31, 1837, in Lincolnton, North Carolina, to Jacob A. and Lucy M. Ramseur. He came from a well-to-do family. He attended schools in Lincolnton and Milton and Davidson College from 1853 to 1855 before graduating fourteenth in a class of forty-one from the U.S. Military Academy in 1860. He was a Presbyterian. He married Ellen E. Richmond on October 22, 1863. Ramseur was commissioned a second lieutenant in the U.S. Army and served at Fortress Monroe before resigning on April 5, 1861, to enter the Confederate Army. As an artillery officer, he was sent to Mississippi, to Raleigh, North Carolina, and then to Yorktown. Elected colonel of artillery under General John B. Magruder (*q.v.*), he fought at Williamsburg before being wounded at the battle of Malvern Hill during the Seven Days in 1862. On November 1, 1862, he was promoted to brigadier general and was given a brigade in Rodes' (*q.v.*) Division. He was again wounded in the battle of Chancellorsville in May 1863 and, upon his recovery, was conspicuous in the fighting during the first day of the battle of Gettysburg. For his heroism during the battle of Spotsylvania in May 1864, he was promoted to major general on June 1, 1864, and was given Jubal Early's (*q.v.*) Division, with whom he fought in the relief of Lynchburg and at Monocacy and Winchester during Early's Valley campaign. He was killed during the battle of Cedar Creek on October 20, 1864. Evans, *Confederate Military History*, IV; Peele (comp.), *Lives of Distinguished North Carolinians*.

RANDOLPH, George Wythe (*Cabinet Member*), a grandson of Thomas Jefferson, was born to Governor Thomas Mann Randolph and his wife Martha (Jefferson) at Monticello (near Charlottesville, Virginia) on March 10, 1818. From 1831 to 1836, he was a midshipman in the U.S. Navy. He attended Harvard College and, in 1837-1839, the University of Virginia. He practiced law in Richmond and developed an excellent practice. Randolph was an Episcopalian and a Democrat and married Mary E. (Adams) Pope in 1852. A secessionist, he voted for secession at the 1861 Virginia state convention. When the Civil War began, he resigned from the convention and joined the Confederate Army. During the war, he served as a major in command of artillery under General John B. Magruder (*q.v.*) at Big Bethel in June 1861, and on February 12, 1862, he became a brigadier general. On March 17 or 22, 1862, he was named secretary of war in the Davis cabinet, a position which he held until November 15 or 17 of the same year. During his brief stint as head of the War Department, Randolph antagonized President Davis (*q.v.*), the Congress, and various Confederate generals. He thought strategically, and his concern for the western line of defense forced Davis to focus his attention on that part of the Confederacy. He also favored a stringent conscription law and a scheme of decentralization for the army. Randolph quit his post when his scheme for the west was rejected, although it received praise from Josiah Gorgas (*q.v.*). During his term as secretary of war, Randolph contracted tuberculosis, resigned, and moved to the south of France for reasons of health. After the war, he returned to Virginia. Randolph died of pulmonary pneumonia on April 3, 1867, at "Edge Hill" near Charlottesville. Jones, "Some Aspects of George W. Randolph's Service as Confederate Secretary of War," *Journal of Southern History*, XXVI; Patrick, *Jefferson Davis and His Cabinet*; Tyler, *Encyclopedia of Virginia Biography*, III.

RANSOM, Matt Whitaker (*General*), was born on October 8, 1826, in Warren County, North Carolina, to Robert and Priscilla West Coffield (Whitaker) Ransom. A brother, Robert (*q.v.*), also became a general in the Confederate Army. He attended Warrenton Academy, graduated from the University of North Carolina in 1847, and practiced law in Warrenton until 1853, when he became a planter in Northampton County. He had eight children by his marriage to Martha Anne Exum on January 19, 1853. A zealous Whig, Ransom's dislike of nativism prompted him to join the Democratic party in 1855. From 1858 to 1860, he served in the state House. The unionist Ransom was a peace commissioner to the provisional Confederate Congress in Montgomery. However, in April 1861, he resigned himself to secession and enlisted as a private in the 1st North Carolina Regiment. In 1862, he fought at Seven Pines, was wounded at Malvern Hill during the Seven Days, and returned to fight at the battles of Sharpsburg and Fredericksburg before being sent to North Carolina with his brigade in January 1863. He fought in the battles of Weldon and Plymouth and defeated the enemy at Suffolk but was forced to withdraw from New Bern to protect Richmond. On June 13, 1863, he was promoted to brigadier general, and he served as a brigade commander at Gettysburg. During the siege of Petersburg, he held the Crater line. Late in 1864, he served as a division commander, fighting at Hare's Hill and in April 1865, at Five Forks, He surrendered at Appomattox and was soon paroled. He returned to planting and practiced law in Weldon, North Carolina. From 1872 until he was defeated for reelection in 1895, he was a Democrat in the U.S. Senate. In 1895, President Cleveland appointed him U.S. minister to Mexico. He remained in Mexico for two years. Ransom died near Garysburg, Northampton County, in retirement on October 8, 1904. *Biographical Directory of the American Congress*; *Charlotte Daily Observer*, October 9, 1904; *Who's Who in America*, 1903-1905.

RANSOM, Robert, Jr. (*General*), was born to Robert and Priscilla West Coffield (Whitaker) Ransom on February 12, 1828, in Warren County, North Carolina. He graduated eighteenth in a class of forty-four from the U.S. Military Academy in 1850. By his marriage to Minnie Hurtt in 1856 he had eight children;

in 1884, after his first wife's death, he married Katherine DeWitt Lumpkin. Ransom, who spent 1850-1851 at the cavalry school in Carlisle, Pennsylvania, was a splendid horseman in the Dragoons, and he served as a scout in Kansas and New Mexico before returning to West Point as a cavalry instructor in 1854. The following year he was promoted to first lieutenant. After participating in the Sioux expedition, he was promoted to captain in 1861. He resigned his commission when the Civil War began. Like his brother Matt (*q.v.*), Robert Ransom entered the Confederate Army. He served as a captain and later colonel of cavalry, with a command in Vienna, Virginia, in the early days of the war. Promoted to brigadier general on March 6, 1862, he later organized Johnston's and Beauregard's Cavalry in the west and southwest. He fought in the Seven Days' battles and at Harper's Ferry, distinguished himself at Sharpsburg, and commanded a division at Fredericksburg. On May 26, 1863, he was promoted to major general and went to North Carolina to defend the Weldon Railroad. In April 1864, he was sent to Richmond. He fought at the Bermuda Hundred and Drewry's Bluff and commanded the cavalry during General J. A. Early's (*q.v.*) raid on Washington in July 1864. In November of the same year, illness forced him to accept a command in Charleston, South Carolina, where he remained for the rest of the war. There is no record of his surrender. A farmer in Warren County, North Carolina, until 1878, Ransom was also an express agent and city marshal at Wilmington, North Carolina, and a civil engineer in charge of river and harbor improvements in New Bern, North Carolina, prior to his death in New Bern on January 14, 1892. Evans, *Confederate Military History*, IV.

READ, Henry E. (*Congressman*), was born in Larue County, Kentucky, on December 25, 1824. There is no record of his childhood or education. He farmed in Larue County at an early age. During the Mexican War, he performed gallant service; he was wounded at Chapultepec. From 1853 to 1855, he was a member of the Kentucky House, and from 1857 to 1865, he served in the Kentucky Senate. Read was a lawyer and a politician. He supported secession and was elected from Kentucky's Third Congressional District to the first and second Confederate House of Representatives. During his first term, he served on the Commerce and Patents Committees but was absent much of the time because he also fought in a number of battles as a colonel of cavalry. In the second Confederate House, he was a member of the Patents, Impressments, Medical Department, and Quartermaster's and Commissary Departments Committees. He was probably a member of the western concentration bloc. Destitute after the war, he became a merchant in Larue County. Read took his own life on November 9, 1869, in Louisville, Kentucky. Alexander and Beringer, *Anatomy of the Confederate Congress*; Collins, *Historical Sketches of Kentucky*.

READE, Edwin Godwin (*Congressman*), was born on November 13, 1812 , at Mount Turziah, Person County, North Carolina, to Robert R. and Judith A.

(Gooch) Reade. His father died while he was still young, and Reade worked as a farmer before he studied law and was admitted to the North Carolina bar in 1835. He began his practice at Roxboro, North Carolina, and eventually became a famous lawyer. He also owned a small farm. Reade's first marriage, to Emily A. L. Moore, was childless; after her death, he married Mrs. Macy Parmele in 1871. He was a Whig whose sentiments were anti-Catholic and anti-foreign. He served a term in 1855-1857 in the U.S. House of Representatives as a member of the American party. He declined to run for reelection. In 1861, Lincoln wanted to name him to his cabinet, but Reade refused. Reade, who was a unionist, also declined the opportunity to attend the North Carolina secession convention. In 1863, Governor Zebulon Vance (q.v.) appointed him to the Confederate Senate, but Reade served for only two months. In his short term, he was a vigorous foe of the administration and joined forces with William W. Holden (q.v.). Because of his early support of Reconstruction, the Vance forces campaigned to defeat him for reelection and succeeded. While in the Senate, Reade served on the Committee on Finance. He returned to his law practice and gave no further service to the Confederacy. He was president of his state's reconstruction convention in 1865, and he was a supporter of President Andrew Johnson. In 1868, he joined the Republican party and became an exponent of Negro suffrage. From 1868 to 1879, he was an associate justice of the Supreme Court of North Carolina. He was also a banker in Raleigh, North Carolina, prior to his death there on October 18, 1894. Ashe, *Cyclopedia of Eminent and Representative Men of the Carolinas*; Hamilton, *Reconstruction in North Carolina*; Yearns, *The Confederate Congress*.

REAGAN, John Henninger (*Cabinet Member*), was born to Timothy R. and Elizabeth (Lusk) Reagan on October 8, 1818, in Sevier County, Tennessee. He was a self-made man who attended such Tennessee schools as Nancy Academy, Boyds Creek Academy, and Maryville Seminary before serving as an Indian fighter and surveyor of public lands in Texas from 1839 to 1843. He was a Methodist. On April 19, 1844, Reagan married Martha Music, a widow with six children. His second marriage, to Edwina Moss Nelms on December 23, 1852, produced six more children, four of whom reached maturity. After his second wife's death in 1863, Reagan married Molly Ford Taylor on May 31, 1866, and had three more children. From 1844 to 1851, Reagan had a small farm in Kaufman County, Texas. In 1844, he began to study law; within two years he was serving as a probate judge, and in 1847, he was elected to a term in the state legislature. From 1852 to 1857, he was a district judge in Palestine, Texas. Reagan, a secessionist, also served two terms as a Democrat in the U.S. House of Representatives from 1857 to 1861 and was a delegate to the Texas secession convention. He resigned from Congress when the Civil War began. As a deputy to the provisional Confederate Congress in Montgomery, he helped to frame the Confederate Constitution. Throughout the war, he was postmaster general in the Davis cabinet, where he remained loyal to the Davis administration and strove to make the Post Office

Department self-sufficient. An expert on clerical details, he was able to hire an excellent administrative staff. But he never had the necessary machinery with which to deliver the mail properly. He did try to operate the department with its own revenue. He also served as secretary of the treasury for the last few months of the war and advised the president on terms of surrender. Reagan was imprisoned when the war ended and was not released until December 1865. He returned to his law practice in Texas. He was a delegate to the Texas constitutional convention in 1875, a congressman from 1875 to 1887, a U.S. senator from 1887 to 1891, and chairman of the Texas Railroad Commission from 1897 to 1901. He died in Palestine, Texas, on March 6, 1905. Proctor, *Not Without Honor*; Reagan, *Memoirs*.

RECTOR, Henry Massey (*Governor*), son of the Virginian Elias Rector and his wife Fannie Bardella (Thurston), was born in Louisville, Kentucky, on May 1, 1816. He was a nephew of Wharton Rector and was also related to Robert W. Johnson (*q.v.*), who later served in the Confederate Congress. Rector lost his father when he was six. He attended school in Louisville and worked for his stepfather's salt works prior to moving to Hot Springs, Arkansas, in 1835, where he had inherited land from his father. His marriage to Jane Elizabeth Field in October 1838 produced four sons and two daughters, and, after her death, his marriage to Ernestine Flora Linde in February 1860 produced one daughter. Rector also served as a state bank teller in 1839-1840, U.S. marshal in 1842-1843, and Democratic state senator in 1848. In 1854, he practiced criminal law in Little Rock. Five years later, when he was named to the state Supreme Court, he intended to shelve politics, but the following year found him leading the revolt against the domination of the Robert Johnson faction in the state. Elected governor in 1860, Rector called the state convention to urge secession and he seized the arsenal at Little Rock. However, he later refused to permit Arkansas troops to leave the state, and he threatened to secede from the Confederacy. On November 4, 1862, he resigned the governorship in the face of political pressure against his resistance to the Confederate government. Rector held no other office in the Confederacy. After the war, he was a planter in Pulaski County, Arkansas. He was elected as a delegate to the state constitutional conventions of 1868 and 1874, but he held no political office. He died on August 12, 1899, in retirement in Hot Springs, Arkansas. *Arkansas Gazette*, August 13, 1899; Hallum, *Biographical and Pictorial History of Arkansas*.

REYNOLDS, Thomas C. (*Governor*), was born in Charleston, South Carolina, on October 11, 1821. His family moved to Virginia, where he graduated from the University of Virginia in 1842 and was admitted to the bar in 1844, after traveling in Europe and studying at Heidelberg. Reynolds spoke French, Spanish, and German fluently. In 1846, he was appointed secretary of the U.S. legation at Madrid. He moved to St. Louis in 1850. In 1851, Reynolds, who was a secessionist and an anti-Benton Democrat, clashed and duelled with the Benton Democrat

B. Gratz Brown over Reynolds's support of Know-Nothingism; Reynolds was unhurt, but Brown was wounded in the knee. From 1853 to 1857, he was U.S. district attorney for Missouri. A leading spirit of the secessionist movement in Missouri and an ally of Claiborne Jackson (*q. v.*), Reynolds was elected lieutenant governor in 1860, and he quickly called for the organization of state troops to serve the Confederacy. In January 1861, he printed a private circular in favor of secession. After Governor Jackson's death, the Confederate troops in Missouri made Reynolds governor for the remainder of the war. He gave Confederate generals almost absolute power over Missouri troops and the right to whatever provisions were necessary to pursue the war. Since Missouri was largely under federal control, he was unable to perform many of the political duties of the governorship. Reynolds was also a volunteer aide to General Joseph Shelby (*q. v.*) during Sterling Price's (*q. v.*) Missouri Raid of 1864. After the war, Reynolds fled to Mexico and became a counselor to Maximilian. In 1868, he returned to Missouri, where he was elected to the legislature in 1874. Two years later, he was a member of a U.S. commission to visit South and Central America. He took his own life on March 30, 1887, in St. Louis, Missouri. Bay, *Reminiscences of the Bench and Bar of Missouri*; Conrad (ed.), *Encyclopedia of the History of Missouri*, VI; Ryle, *Missouri: Union or Secession*.

RHETT, Robert Barnwell (*Congressman, Editor*), was born on December 24, 1800, in Beaufort, South Carolina, to James and Marianna (Gough) Smith. His formal education ended at the age of seventeen. In 1824, he was admitted to the bar and began a law practice in Beaufort. He married Elizabeth Washington Burnet in 1827 and, after her death, Catherine Dent in 1853. Rhett developed a good law practice and also owned a plantation, but his major interest was politics. He served in the South Carolina legislature from 1826 to 1832, where he was a vigorous nullifier. He was also attorney general of South Carolina in 1832, and he was elected as a Democrat to the U.S. House of Representatives in 1837 and served until 1849. In the early 1840s, he organized a radical secessionist movement in Barnwell County called the Bluffton Movement. He was a delegate to the Nashville convention in 1850 and the Southern Rights convention in 1852. Rhett also served in the U.S. Senate from 1850 to 1852. He owned and edited the *Charleston Mercury* and used his paper to take an extreme position in favor of secession. At the South Carolina secession convention in 1860, he drafted the Secession Ordinance and called for the Montgomery convention. As a member of the provisional Confederate Congress, he chaired the committee for drafting the permanent Confederate Constitution, opposed the closing of the African slave trade, and supported a six-year presidential term. He was considered a possibility for president, but his extreme secessionism destroyed his chances. His contributions to the permanent Constitution were major, and he also served on the Foreign Affairs and Financial Independence Committees. He was defeated in his bid for a seat in the first Confederate House because of his known criticism of the Davis administration. As editor of the Charleston *Mercury* throughout the war, he became a vigorous opponent of the Davis administration. When the war ended, he temporarily retired to private life. He was a delegate to the Democratic national convention in 1868. Rhett moved to St. James Parish, Louisiana, where he died on September 14, 1876. Cauthen, *South Carolina Goes to War; 1861-1865*; White, *Robert Barnwell Rhett*.

RIPLEY, Roswell Sabine (*General*), was born on March 14, 1823, in Worthington, Ohio, to Christopher and Julia (Caulkins) Ripley. He graduated seventh in a class of thirty-nine from the U.S. Military Academy in 1843, and on December 22, 1853, he married Alicia Middleton of Charleston, South Carolina. After accepting his commission in the army, Ripley served on garrison duty until 1846, when he became an assistant professor of mathematics at West Point. During the Mexican War, he fought at Monterrey and Vera Cruz, was breveted captain after Cerro Gordo, and major after Chapultepec. He published a history based on his war experiences, *The War with Mexico*, in 1849. In 1853, he resigned his army commission to become a Charleston, South Carolina, businessman. He also served as an officer in the state militia. When the Civil War began, he volunteered for service in the Confederate Army. As a lieutenant colonel of state troops, he occupied Fort Moultrie and later Fort Sumter after its fall in April 1861. He was appointed brigadier general in the Confederate Army on August 15, 1861, and remained in Charleston to command the Department of South Carolina, Georgia, and Florida until he was sent to join the Army of Northern Virginia the following year. Ripley commanded a brigade in General Daniel H. Hill's (*q.v.*) Division during the Seven Days and the battle of South Mountain before being wounded during the battle of Sharpsburg in September 1862. He was then reassigned to command the 1st Artillery District in Charleston until 1865, when he was ordered to join General Joseph E. Johnston (*q.v.*) in North Carolina. He surrendered in North Carolina and was later paroled. After the war, he traveled to Paris and to England, where he launched an unsuccessful manufacturing venture. He returned to Charleston in 1868 and did business there and in New York City, where he died on March 29, 1887. Evans, *Confederate Military History*, V; Freeman, *Lee's Lieutenants*, II, III.

RIVES, Alfred Landon (*Chief of the Engineering Bureau*), son of William Cabell (*q.v.*) and Judith (Walker) Rives, was born in Paris, France, on March 25, 1830. His father was an important political leader in Virginia and a power in the Confederate Congress. After attending Concord Academy, he graduated sixth in his class at Virginia Military Institute in 1848, studied engineering at the University of Virginia, and graduated in 1854 from the Ecole des Ponts et Chausees, the engineering school of France. He married Sadie MacMurdo, by whom he had three children. In the late 1850s, Rives served in the Engineering Corps of the

Virginia Midland Railroad and in the U.S. Corps of Engineers under Montgomery Meigs. As secretary of the interior during the Pierce administration, he supervised the construction of the Cabin John Bridge. When the Civil War began, he left Washington, D.C., and joined the Confederate Army. He was a captain and later a colonel of engineers during the Civil War, serving also as acting chief of the Engineering Bureau of the Confederacy. His speed at bridge construction and his genius for fortifications were instrumental in the success of the Army of Northern Virginia. After the war, he was an engineer and architect in Richmond, Virginia. He was division engineer of the Chesapeake and Ohio Railroad in 1868, chief engineer of the Mobile and Birmingham Railroad in 1870, and vice-president of the Richmond and Danville Railroad in 1883. Involved in the construction of the Panama Canal, he was superintendent of the Panama Railroad in 1887. Rives died on February 27, 1903, at Castle Hill, near Richmond, Virginia. Nichols, *Confederate Engineers*; Tyler, *Encyclopedia of Virginia Biography*, III.

RIVES, William Cabell (*Congressman*), was born to Robert and Margaret Jordan (Cabell) Rives on May 4, 1792, in Amherst County, Virginia. He attended Hampden-Sidney College, graduated from the College of William and Mary in 1809, and was admitted to the Charlottesville bar in 1814. On March 24, 1819, he married Judith Page Walker. Alfred Landon Rives (*q.v.*) was his son. He developed an excellent law practice and became active in politics. A delegate to the Virginia constitutional convention of 1816, he also served in the House of Delegates from 1817 to 1820 and in 1822. After moving to Albemarle County, Virginia, in 1822, he was elected as a Democrat to the U.S. House of Representatives in 1823 and served until 1829. From 1829 to 1832, and again from 1849 to 1853, he was U.S. minister to France. He also served terms in the U.S. Senate as a Democrat from 1832 to 1834 and 1836 to 1839 and as a Whig from 1841 to 1845. Rives turned Whig in 1841 in support of President Tyler (*q.v.*) on the bank issue. He was also a successful planter and an historian of some note. His three-volume biography of *James Madison* (finished after the war) was a standard work for years. In 1861, he was a member of the peace commission to Washington and a Virginia delegate to the provisional Confederate Congress, where he was noted for his caution. He also served in the Confederate House in 1864. Although he favored reunion, he did not support the Reconstruction forces in the Confederate Congress because he feared they might hinder the war effort. Rives proposed to consolidate the army under Lee's (*q.v.*) command, and he generally supported the Davis administration. He served ably on the Foreign Affairs Committee. After the war, he completed his biography of Madison. Rives died in Charlottesville on April 25, 1868. Ambler, *Sectionalism in Virginia, 1776-1861*; Tyler, *Encyclopedia of Virginia Biography*, III.

ROBERTS, Oran Milo (*Judge*), was born in Laurens District, South Carolina, on July 9, 1815, to Obe and Margaret Ewing Roberts. His father died in 1825, and the family moved to Alabama. Roberts graduated from the University of Alabama in 1836 and was admitted to the Alabama bar the following year. He practiced law with William P. Chilton (*q. v.*). His marriage to Frances W. Edwards in December 1837 produced six children. After her death in December 1887, he married Catherine E. Border. Roberts, a Democrat, became active in Alabama politics; he served in the Alabama legislature from 1838 until 1840 before moving to San Augustine, Texas, in 1841. In 1844, he was a district attorney, and two years later, he became judge of the Fifth Texas Judicial District, eventually resigning to return to his law practice. In 1857, he was elected an associate justice of the Texas Supreme Court, and in 1864, he was elected chief justice of that body, succeeding Judge Royal Wheeler. A secessionist and an advocate of states' rights, Roberts was also president of the Texas secession convention. As Confederate judge during the Civil War, he was active on behalf of the government. In 1862, he had a military career of some importance in the Trans-Mississippi West as colonel of the 11th Regiment of Texas Infantry. He left the army to become chief justice of the Texas Supreme Court. After the war, he practiced law in Tyler, Texas. In 1866, he was chairman of the Judiciary Committee of the state convention and was elected to the U.S. Senate but was denied his seat because of federal restrictions on Confederate leaders. From 1868 to 1870, he was a professor of law at the high school in Gilmer, Texas. In 1874, he was again elected chief justice of the Texas Supreme Court. From 1878 to 1882, he was governor of the state. Roberts was also an educational reformer, and he served as professor of law at the University of Texas from 1883 until his death on May 19, 1898, in Austin, Texas. Robinson, *Justice in Gray*; Lynch, *The Bench and Bar of Texas*.

ROBERTSON, Jerome Bonaparte (*General*), was born on March 14, 1815, in Woodford County, Kentucky, to Cornelius and Clarissa (Hill) Robertson. Orphaned at the age of twelve and penniless, he worked as a hatter in Union County, Kentucky, before studying medicine for three months at Transylvania University in 1835. By his marriage to Mary Elizabeth Cummins on May 4, 1838, he had three children, one of whom was also a general in the Confederate Army. After her death, he married Mrs. Harriet (Hendley) Hook in 1879. Robertson moved to Texas in 1835 and served as a captain in the Texas army during the war for independence. In 1837, he settled in Washington County, Texas, to practice medicine. From 1838 to 1844, he was an Indian fighter, and in 1845, he moved to Independence, also in Washington County, where he developed a medical practice of some note. He also used his military reputation to gain political attention. Robertson was elected to the state House in 1848 and to the Senate in 1850. He was a secessionist delegate to the state convention of 1861. When the Civil War began, he volunteered for service in the army. He served as a captain in the 5th Texas Infantry and rose to colonel by June 1862. Robertson participated in the battles of the Seven Days, was wounded during the battle of Second Manassas in August 1862, but recovered sufficiently to fight at South Mountain in September before being promoted to brigadier general on November 1, 1862. The following July, he led Hood's (*q.v.*) Texas Brigade, with whom he fought in some forty battles during the remainder of the war, including the battle of Gettysburg where he was again wounded. His clash with General James Longstreet (*q.v.*), under whom he served at Chickamauga and during the Knoxville campaign, provoked a court martial trial, and Robertson was temporarily removed from command. Robertson spent the rest of the war in Texas and Arkansas, in the Trans-Mississippi Department in command of the Reserve Corps. There is no record of his surrender. After the war, he practiced medicine in Texas until 1868. In 1874, he was superintendent of the State Bureau of Immigration, and from 1879 to 1891, he was a promoter of west Texas railroads. In 1879, Robertson moved to Waco, Texas, where he died on January 7, 1891. Connelly, *Autumn of Glory*; Monaghan, *Civil War on the Western Border, 1845-1865*.

ROBINSON, Cornelius (*Congressman*), was born to Todd and Martha (Terry) Robinson on September 25, 1805, in Wadesboro, Anson County, North Carolina. He attended the University of North Carolina and was admitted to the bar in 1824, although he never practiced law. Robinson, whose grandfather had been a Tory, was himself a Democrat and a Methodist who operated a planting and commission business in Mobile, Alabama, throughout the antebellum period. His marriage to Martha Owen De Jarnette on January 3, 1828, produced five children. He served in the Indian Wars in 1836 and as a brigadier general during the Mexican War. He was a member of the Alabama secession convention and a staunch supporter of secession. During the Civil War, he was a member of the staff of Braxton Bragg (*q.v.*) and served in the provisional Confederate Congress in 1861-1862. He was a member of the Post Office Committee. He did not stand for election to the permanent Congress but did have various minor military duties throughout the remainder of the war. After the war, he was a planter in Lowndes County, Alabama, where he died at Church Hill on July 29, 1867. Denman, *The Secession Movement in Alabama*; Owen, *History of Alabama and Dictionary of Alabama Biography*, IV.

RODDEY, Philip Dale (*General*), was born on April 2, 1826, in Moulton, Lawrence County, Alabama, to Mrs. Sarah Roddey. Little is known of his family background. He was poor, received little education, and worked as a tailor before serving as county sheriff from 1846 to 1849. Roddey had two sons and one daughter by his marriage to Margaret A. McGaughey. In 1849, he entered the steamboat business in Chickasaw, Colbert County, Alabama. When the Civil War began, Roddey formed a cavalry troop and volunteered for the Confederate Army. Roddey showed gallantry at Shiloh, where he headed off an invading army in northern Alabama in the spring of 1862. In December 1862, he became colonel of the 4th Alabama Cavalry, which he had organized, and his regiment fought in middle Tennessee and northern Alabama with Generals Nathan B. Forrest (*q.v.*)

and Joseph Wheeler (*q. v.*). Prior to his promotion to brigadier general on August 3, 1863, he commanded the District of Northern Alabama. After his promotion, he led a cavalry division during the Atlanta campaign of 1863-1864 and kept Hood's (*q. v.*) Alabama communications open. In 1865, he was defeated with Forrest at Selma, Alabama, during a final desperate attempt to halt the federal invasion. He surrendered and was paroled in May 1865. After the war, he was a commission merchant in New York. He died during a business trip to London, England, on July 20, 1897. Owen, *History of Alabama and Dictionary of Alabama Biography*, IV; Riley, *Makers and Romance of Alabama History*.

RODES, Robert Emmett (*General*), was born to General David Rodes and his wife Martha (Yancey) on March 29, 1829, in Liberty, Bedford County, Virginia. He attended schools in Lynchburg and graduated with distinction from Virginia Military Institute in 1848, where he also taught civil engineering from 1849 to 1851. Married to Virginia Hortense Woodruff on September 10, 1857, he had two sons. He was assistant engineer for the Southside Railroad in Richmond from 1851 to 1854. He also worked on railroad construction in Marshall, Tennessee, in 1855. In the following year, he helped to build the Alabama Great Southern Railroad. Rodes was an engineer in North Carolina in 1856 and in Missouri in 1857. From 1857 to 1861, he was chief engineer for the lower portion of the Northwestern and Southwestern Railroad from Jefferson, Missouri, to Meridian, Mississippi. At the outbreak of the Civil War, he was a professor of applied mechanics at Virginia Military Institute. When the Civil War began, he volunteered for duty in the Confederate Army. Rodes entered the army as a colonel of the 5th Alabama Infantry and was promoted to brigadier general on October 21, 1861. After fighting at the battle of Seven Pines in May 1862, he was wounded at Fair Oaks. Before he had recovered sufficiently, Rodes again led his brigade at the battle of Gaines' Mill during the Seven Days and was ill for several months afterward. He was wounded a second time at the battle of Sharpsburg but fought again at Fredericksburg in December 1862. The following May he led Daniel H. Hill's (*q. v.*) Division in a flank march during the battle of Chancellorsville. For his performance on this occasion, Rodes was promoted to major general on May 7, 1863, and he led the division thereafter at the battles of Gettysburg, the Wilderness, Spotsylvania, and during Early's (*q. v.*) Valley campaign of 1864. He was killed at Winchester, Virginia, on September 19, 1864. Tyler, *Encyclopedia of Virginia Biography*, III; Walker, *Biographical Sketches of the Graduates and Eleves of the Virginia Military Institute*.

ROGERS, Samuel St. George (*Congressman*), was born on June 30, 1832, in Pulaski, Tennessee. He studied law in Columbus, Georgia. He was a large landholder and a lawyer who began his law practice in Ocala, Marion County, Florida, in 1851. During the 1850s, he became colonel of the Ocala Militia, and he defended the town against the Seminole Indians. He was a strong secessionist.

When the Civil War began, he volunteered for duty in the Confederate Army. During the war, he was a major and later a lieutenant colonel in the Marion Light Artillery. He also commanded the 2nd Florida Infantry in 1862, and in 1863, he served in P.G.T. Beauregard's (*q.v.*) Corps as a member of the military court of the Department of South Carolina, Georgia, and Florida. Rogers succeeded John M. Martin (*q.v.*) in the second Confederate House of Representatives. He was elected because of his dedicated service to the Confederate cause. In the second House, he served on the Enrolled Bills, Impressments, Indian Affairs, and Naval Affairs Committees, and on special committees concerning conscription, increasing the military force, and lessening the number of exemptions. He supported the Davis administration on a majority of issues. He returned to his plantation when the war ended and held no postwar political office. Rogers died in Terre Haute, Indiana, on September 11, 1880. Alexander and Beringer, *Anatomy of the Confederate Congress*; Ott, *Ocali Country*; Warner and Yearns, *Biographical Register of the Confederate Congress*.

ROSS, Lawrence Sullivan (*General*), was born on September 27, 1838, at Benton's Post, Iowa, to Captain Shapley P. and Catherine (Fulkerson) Ross. He graduated from Alabama's Florence Wesleyan University with distinction in 1859. Ross was a Methodist and a Democrat. He had six children by his marriage to Elizabeth Tinsley in 1859. He was an Indian fighter with Earl Van Dorn (*q.v.*) at the battle of Wichita, Kansas, in 1858, and in 1860, he was captain of a group of sixty rangers who protected the frontier from Commanche attacks. When the Civil War began, Ross enlisted in the Confederate Army as a private, was later a colonel of the 6th Texas Regiment, and participated in a total of 135 battles during the war. He helped to make allies for the Confederacy among some of the Indian tribes, fought under Ben McCulloch as a raider in the Texas Cavalry at the battle of Elkhorn, Arkansas, in March 1862, and led a regiment in the heroic defense of Hatchie Bridge at the battle of Corinth, Mississippi, the following October. During the Holly Springs raid in December 1862, he delayed Grant's advance upon Richmond, and he was promoted to brigadier general on the field of battle of Yazoo City, although his promotion was not confirmed until December 21, 1863. Ross subsequently served under Generals Joseph E. Johnston (*q.v.*) and John B. Hood (*q.v.*) during the Atlanta campaign. He was said to be the eyes of Hood, whose army he saved from annihilation, because of his ability to scout the whereabouts of the enemy. There is no record of his surrender. He returned to the Brazos River area of Texas when the war ended. He was penniless, but he later made a small fortune in planting. In 1873, he was sheriff of McLennan County, Texas, and two years later, he was a delegate to the state constitutional convention. Ross also served in the Texas Senate from 1881 to 1885 and was governor from 1887 to 1891. He was president of Texas Agricultural and Mechanical College from 1891 until his death on January 3, 1898, at College Station, Texas. Daniell (comp.), *Personnel of the Texas State Government*.

ROSSER, Thomas Lafayette (*General*), son of John and Martha Melvina (Johnson) Rosser, was born on October 15, 1836, in Campbell County, Virginia. His father moved the family to Texas in 1849, and young Rosser resigned from the U.S. Military Academy two weeks before he would have graduated in 1861. He had two daughters and a son by his marriage to Elizabeth Barbara Winston on May 28, 1863. When the Civil War began, he volunteered for service in the Confederate Army. In the first days of the war, Rosser instructed the Washington Artillery of New Orleans and saw action at Blackburn's Ford and the battle of First Manassas, where he shot down McClellan's observation balloon. A captain at the battle of Yorktown in May 1862, he was promoted to lieutenant colonel of artillery after being wounded at the battle of Mechanicsville. Rosser commanded the 5th Virginia Cavalry with great distinction during J.E.B. Stuart's (*q.v.*) expedition to Catlett's Station, at the battles of South Mountain and Sharpsburg in September 1862, and at Kelly's Ford, where he was wounded in December 1862. After fighting at the battles of Chancellorsville and Gettysburg, he was promoted to brigadier general and was given command of the Laurel Brigade on September 28, 1863. Rosser subsequently fought at the Wilderness, where he was wounded at Trevilian Station, and participated in the "cattle raid" near Petersburg. In October 1864, he assumed command of Jubal Early's (*q.v.*) Cavalry, which he managed to save at the battle of Cedar Creek on October 19. Promoted to major general on November 1, 1864, he fought at New Creek in Beverly, West Virginia, at Five Forks on April 1, and at the skirmish at High Bridge on April 6-7, 1865. He was captured at Hanover Court House, Virginia, in May 1865 and was later paroled. When the war ended, he returned to Texas. Rosser was chief engineer for the North Pacific Railroad from 1871 to 1881 and chief engineer for the Canadian Pacific Railroad from 1881 to 1883. He lived in various places in the Far West. He also studied law, and in 1885, he became a gentleman farmer near Charlottesville, Virginia. During the Spanish-American War, President McKinley made him a brigadier general in the U.S. Army, but he never actually fought. In 1905, he was named postmaster at Charlottesville, where he died on March 29, 1910. *Confederate Veteran*, 1910; Freeman, *Lee's Lieutenants*, III; Tyler, *Encyclopedia of Virginia Biography*, III.

ROYSTON, Grandison Delaney (*Congressman*), son of Joshua and Elizabeth S. (Watson) Royston, was born on December 9, 1809, in Carter County, Tennessee. He attended the Presbyterian Academy in Washington County, Tennessee, studied law, and was admitted to the Tennessee bar in 1831. He was a Presbyterian and a lifelong Democrat. Royston married Clarissa Bates in May 1835, and they had two sons and a daughter. In 1832, Royston moved to Fayetteville, Washington County, Arkansas, and taught school briefly before moving to Washington, Hempstead County, Arkansas, where he attained a statewide reputation as a lawyer. From 1833 to 1835, he served as prosecuting attorney for the Third Circuit. In 1836, he was elected by Hempstead County to help frame and adopt the statehood constitution. He was elected to the legislature the same year, and in 1837, he was speaker of the state House. President Jackson, who had named Royston U.S. district attorney for Arkansas in 1836, reneged on his appointment, but in 1841, President Tyler (*q.v.*) named him to the same post. As state Senator in 1858, Royston became known as the "father" of the state levee system. He also owned a successful plantation. Although he did not believe in secession, he followed his state out of the Union and served in the Confederate House in 1861. He favored placing General Kirby Smith (*q.v.*) in charge of the Trans-Mississippi District. Declining reelection, he was succeeded in Congress by Rufus Garland (*q.v.*). While in Congress, he was an administration supporter. He served on the Medical Department, Post Office and Post Roads, and Quartermaster's Committees. Royston saw no further service in the Confederacy after he left office early in 1864 and he returned to his law practice. He was a delegate to the state constitutional convention in 1874. Royston died in Washington, Arkansas, on August 14, 1889. Hallum, *Biographical and Pictorial History of Arkansas*; Hempstead, *Historical Review of Arkansas*.

RUFFIN, Thomas (*Statesman*), was born on November 17, 1787, in King and Queen County, Virginia, to Sterling and Alice Roana Ruffin. He attended the Classical Academy in Warrenton, North Carolina, graduated with honors from Princeton College in 1805, studied law, and was admitted to the North Carolina bar in 1808, having moved there the previous year. On December 7, 1809, he married Annie M. Kirkland, by whom he had fourteen children. Ruffin was a Democrat and a devout Episcopalian. He represented Hillsboro in the North Carolina House in 1813, 1815, and 1816. Named judge of the superior court in 1825, he also was affiliated with the Bank of North Carolina in 1828 prior to becoming chief justice of the state Supreme Court in 1832. Twenty years later, he resigned from the bench to become a progressive and successful farmer; in 1854, he was president of the Agricultural Society of North Carolina. In 1860, he supported John C. Breckinridge (*q.v.*) for the presidency. As a delegate to the Washington Peace conference, he tried to prevent disunion, but he later voted for his state's Secession Ordinance. He helped to prepare North Carolina for war by obtaining military supplies. He was too old for active service, but his support of President Davis (*q.v.*) and the war effort served to control unionism in North Carolina. After the war, he opposed congressional Reconstruction and dissented from the violence of the Ku Klux Klan. He died on January 15, 1870, in Hillsboro, North Carolina. Peele (comp.), *Lives of Distinguished North Carolinians*.

RUFFIN, Thomas (*Congressman*), was born on September 9, 1820, in Louisburg, Franklin County, North Carolina. Little is known of his family life. He was probably related to Thomas Ruffin (*q.v.*). He studied law at the University of North Carolina and practiced in Goldsboro throughout the antebellum period. Ruffin was a circuit attorney in Missouri from 1844 to 1848. Upon returning to

North Carolina, he entered politics and served as a Democrat in the U.S. House from 1853 to 1861. He was a secessionist and his constituents elected him to the provisional Confederate Congress in Richmond in 1861. Ruffin also served in the Confederate Army as a colonel in the 1st North Carolina Cavalry. He was wounded at Bristoe Station, Virginia, and was taken prisoner. He died from his wounds on October 13, 1863, at Alexandria, Virginia. *Biographical Directory of the American Congress*; Freeman, *Lee's Lieutenants*, II.

RUSSELL, Charles Wells (*Congressman*), was born on July 19, 1818, in Sisterville, Tyler County, Virginia, to the Irish immigrants Joshua and Catherine (Wells) Russell. He attended Linsly Institute, Wheeling, Virginia, later West Virginia, and Jefferson College in Pennsylvania from 1837 to 1839, and taught school in Richmond, Virginia, before beginning a law practice in Wheeling. He was a Democrat and a secessionist. Rusell had three sons by his marriage to Margaret Moore. In 1851, he wrote a book about the monopolistic practices of the Wheeling and Welmont Bridge Company, a work which enhanced his political career. During the Civil War, he represented Wheeling in the provisional and both permanent Confederate Houses. He served ably on the Judiciary, Naval Affairs, and Conference Committees. He supported the Davis administration, concentrated on saving West Virginia for the Confederacy, and, in 1863, advocated the strengthening of the conscript law and restricting overseer exemptions. After West Virginia was lost to the Confederacy, he believed that a force of ten thousand troops could bring it back. Russell also believed that the Confederacy had lost its chance to get additional border state support when it refused Maryland a seat in the Congress. After the war, he traveled in Canada. In 1866, he moved to Baltimore, Maryland, where he practiced law and wrote two novels, *Roebuck*, and *The Fall of Damascus*. He died on November 22, 1867. Russell, *Roebuck*.

RUST, Albert (*Congressman, General*), was born in 1818 in Fauquier County, Virginia. He attended Common schools in Virginia and emigrated to Arkansas in 1837, where he studied law and was admitted to the bar in El Dorado, Union County. Rust was a Democrat and a Methodist; he married and had a family. He was also a prominent Arkansas farmer and slaveowner. From 1842 to 1848 and from 1852 to 1854, he served in the state House. He was a member of the U.S. House from 1855 to 1857 and ran unsuccessfully for reelection in 1856 before being returned to that body from 1859 to 1861. In 1860, his name was mentioned as a candidate for the U.S. Senate seat of Robert W. Johnson (*q.v.*). Although he was a unionist who supported Stephen A. Douglas for president in 1860, he eventually supported secession. He resigned from Congress in March 1861 and volunteered for service in the Confederate Army. Early in the war, he raised the 3rd Regiment of Arkansas Infantry, which participated in the Cheat Mountain campaign in western Virginia during the fall of 1861 and served in Virginia under General "Stonewall" Jackson (*q.v.*) in 1862. Promoted from colonel to general in the provisional Confederate Army in March 1862, he did not attain the permanent rank of brigadier general until two years later. Meanwhile, he had fought at Corinth in October 1862 and had served under Sterling Price (*q. v.*) in April 1863, under Hindman (*q. v.*) in Arkansas, and under Pemberton (*q. v.*) and Taylor (*q. v.*) in Louisiana early in 1864. Rust also was elected to the provisional Confederate Congress in 1861, where he was a member of the Postal Affairs Committee. In the fall of 1864, having lost his command because of some question of his loyalty to the Confederate cause, Rust gave up active military service and moved to Austin, Texas, until August 1865. During the last part of the war, he expressed unionist sentiments and was a bold critic of the Confederate government. After the war, he returned to Arkansas, where he served in the U.S. House of Representatives during the early years of Reconstruction. In 1869, he was a Republican candidate for the U.S. Senate, but he withdrew his name before the election. He died in El Dorado, Arkansas, on April 3, 1870. *Arkansas Gazette*, April 7, 1870; *Biographical Directory of the American Congress*; Thomas, *Arkansas in War and Reconstruction*.

S

ST. JOHN, Isaac Munroe (*Bureaucrat*), son of Isaac Richards and Abigail Richardson (Munroe) St. John, was born on November 18, 1827, in Augusta, Georgia, where his father was in the newspaper business. He graduated from Yale College in 1845, practiced law briefly in New York City, and became editor of the *Baltimore Patriot* in 1847. St. John had six children by his marriage to Ella J. Carrington on February 28, 1865. From 1848 to 1855, he was a civil engineer on the staff of the Baltimore and Ohio Railroad. In 1855, he returned to Georgia, where he was in charge of construction of the Blue Ridge Railroad until 1860. When the Civil War began, St. John resigned from the railroad and volunteered for service in the Confederate Army. He served under John B. Magruder (*q. v.*) in the Virginia Peninsula in 1861 as a private in the Engineering Corps. In February 1862, he was promoted to captain of engineers, and in April of that year he was sent to Richmond to head the Nitre and Mining Bureau, where he supervised the making of gunpowder for the Confederacy. On February 16, 1865, he was promoted to brigadier general and was named commissary general of the Confederate Army. As commissary general during the final months of the war, he devised a system of collecting supplies directly from the people and making them immediately available for use. He surrendered in Richmond at the war's end and was soon paroled. From 1866 to 1869, St. John was chief engineer of the Louisville, Cincinnati, and Lexington Railroad in Louisville, Kentucky. In 1870-1871, he was city engineer for Louisville, and in 1873, he served as chief engineer of the Elizabeth, Lexington, and Big Sandy Railroad. St. John died in White Sulphur Springs, West Virginia, on April 7, 1880. Goff, *Confederate Supply*; Vandiver, *Ploughshares into Swords*; Wright, *General Officers of the Confederate Army*.

SALE, John Burress (*Staff Officer*), was born to the eminent clergyman Alexander Sale and his wife Sarah (Burress) on June 7, 1818, in Amherst County, Virginia. His father later moved to Lawrence County, Alabama, where Sale graduated from LaGrange College and was also admitted to the bar in 1837. He was married four times: to Susan Turner, Nannie T. Mills, Lou Leigh, and Annie Cornelius. His first three wives died in childbirth. Sale practiced law in Moulton, Alabama, in 1839 and was named a probate judge the following year. He later moved to Aberdeen, Mississippi, where he practiced law from 1845 to 1861. In 1861, he lived in Memphis, Tennessee. During the Civil War, he helped to organize the Tennessee Volunteers and served as lieutenant colonel of the 27th Mississippi Regiment. He was also Braxton Bragg's (*q.v.*) chief of staff and judge advocate general for the Army of Tennessee. He was head of the Bragg bloc and lobbied for the general in Richmond. He also served as Bragg's emissary to Joseph Johnston (*q.v.*) in the crucial western campaigns of 1864. Sale helped Bragg draw up plans for the offensive of 1864. After the war, he returned to Memphis, where he resumed a successful law practice. He died in Memphis, Tennessee, on January 24, 1876. Connelly and Jones, *The Politics of Command*; Evans, *Confederate Military History*, I.

SANDERSON, John Pease (*Congressman*), was born in Sunderland, Vermont, on November 28, 1816. He graduated from Amherst in 1839. He was a secessionist Democrat, a lawyer, and a slaveholding planter in Jacksonville, Florida, before the Civil War. He became involved in the development of the Southern Railway system. His wife was from a well-to-do Florida planting family. He served in the Florida House in 1843, the Senate in 1848, and was solicitor of the Eastern Circuit from 1849 to 1854. During the war, Sanderson served for fifteen days in the provisional Confederate Congress, where he was a member of the Claims, Military Affairs, and Public Lands Committees. He finished the unexpired term of George T. Ward (*q.v.*), who resigned the office in February 1862. In 1864, Sanderson was conscripted but was found unfit for service. However, he served as a clerk in the Quartermaster Corps for six months. Later, he was also an appraiser of confiscated property for the Conscript Bureau. At the end of the war, "Ortega," his plantation on the St. John's River in Duval County, along with all of his stock, crops, and equipment, was confiscated by federal troops. His land was eventually returned to him, but he spent some time recouping his losses. He practiced law in Jacksonville. Sanderson died in New York City on June 28, 1871. Davis, *Civil War and Reconstruction in Florida*; Warner and Yearns, *Biographical Register of the Confederate Congress*.

SCOTT, Robert Eden (*Congressman*), son of John and Elizabeth (Pickett) Scott, was born on April 22, 1808, in Virginia. He graduated from the University of Virginia in 1827 and was admitted to the bar at Warrenton, Virginia, in 1829. On March 10, 1831, he married Elizabeth Taylor. After her death, Scott married Ann Morson and, after her death, Heningham Watkins Lyons. He served as commonwealth's attorney for Warrenton, and he represented his district in the state legislature during the 1850s. He was elected to the constitutional convention of 1850. He was a Whig and he also operated a small plantation in Warrenton. In 1861, after being offered, and declining, the position of secretary of the navy in the Lincoln cabinet, Scott attended the Virginia secession convention as a unionist. He voted for secession, however, and also offered Virginia's final compromise to the nonslaveholding states. He served in the provisional Confederate Congress and was on the Special Committee. He was a candidate for reelection when he was killed in an accident on May 3, 1862. Alexander and Beringer, *Anatomy of the Confederate Congress*; McGregor, *Disruption of Virginia*.

SEDDON, James Alexander (*Congressman, Cabinet Member*), was born in Falmouth, Virginia, on July 13, 1815, to the merchant-banker Thomas Seddon and his wife Susan (Alexander). He graduated from the University of Virginia in 1835 and was admitted to the Virginia bar in 1838. Seddon was an ardent follower of John C. Calhoun. He practiced law in Richmond, where he became a well-known lawyer. He married Sarah Bruce, daughter of a wealthy planter, in 1845. In 1845-1847 and 1849-1851, he served as a Democrat in the U.S. House of Representatives, after which he retired to his plantation in Goochland County, Virginia. As a delegate to the peace convention at Washington in 1861, he favored secession. He was also a Virginia delegate to the provisional Confederate Congress at Richmond. From November 21, 1862, to February 16, 1865, Seddon was secretary of war in the Davis cabinet. He saw the war in large terms and devised much of the Confederates' offensive strategy of concentration and total war. He was successful at decentralizing authority within the army, and he created the Department of the West. However, he proved to be a poor administrator, unable to work with the Commissary Department or to coordinate his ideas and policies with those of the president. Early in 1865, he resigned because of illness and retired to his plantation. After the war, he considered his life a failure. He was imprisoned but was later released. He went into business in Richmond and, for a while, supported the Conservate party of Virginia. Seddon died on his plantation in Goochland County on August 19, 1880. Boutwell, *Reminiscences*, II; Curry,

"James A. Seddon, A Southern Prototype," *Virginia Magazine of History and Biography*, LXVII; Maddex, *The Virginia Conservatives*; Patrick, *Jefferson Davis and His Cabinet*.

SEMMES, Raphael (*Admiral*), was born to Richard Thompson and Catherine Taliaferro (Middleton) Semmes on September 27, 1809, in Charles County, Maryland. He attended the U.S. Military Academy until 1826, later studied law, and was admitted to the Maryland bar in 1834. In 1837, he was commissioned a lieutenant in the U.S. Navy. He was a Catholic, and he had six children by his marriage to Annie Elizabeth Spencer on May 5, 1837. Semmes, who moved his residence to Mobile, Alabama, in 1849, served on the *Porpoise*, the *Cumberland*, and the *Ruritan* during the Mexican War, and he participated in the blockading of Vera Cruz. After the war, he inspected lighthouses along the Gulf Coast. He was promoted to commander in 1855. In 1861, he was in charge of the Lighthouse Bureau, a position which he relinquished to purchase materials for the Confederate Navy. Semmes resigned from the federal navy on February 15, 1861, and went to Montgomery, where the Confederate government authorized him to purchase munitions. He was named a commander in the Confederate Navy. He captured merchantmen and fitted out the *Sumter*. He was subsequently promoted to captain and placed in command of the *Alabama*. When that ship sank on June 19, 1864, Semmes was captured by the English, who would not release him to U.S. authorities. Upon his release in February 1865, he became a rear admiral and commanded the Confederate fleet on the James River. He surrendered at Greensboro, North Carolina, and was paroled in May 1865. Semmes returned to Mobile after the war. In 1866, he was a professor at Louisiana Military Institute, and from 1867 until 1877, he practiced law and edited the Memphis *Daily Bulletin*. He died on August 30, 1877, in Mobile. Meriwether, *Raphael Semmes*; Roberts, *Semmes of the Alabama*.

SEMMES, Thomas Jenkins (*Congressman*), son of the merchant Raphael Semmes and his wife Matilda (Jenkins) and first cousin of Raphael Semmes (*q.v.*), was born on December 16, 1824, in Georgetown, D.C. He attended primary school in Georgetown, graduated with high honors from Georgetown College in 1842, and from Harvard Law School in 1845. He was a Democrat and a Catholic. On January 8, 1850, he married Mary Eulalia Knox, by whom he had three sons and two daughters. He began his law practice in the District of Columbia. In December 1850, he moved to New Orleans, where he practiced law with a former Harvard classmate, Matthew C. Edwards. In 1855, he attacked the Know-Nothing party and became active in politics. The following year, he was elected to the Louisiana state legislature, and in 1857-1858, he was attorney for the Eastern District of Louisiana. From 1859 to 1861, he was state attorney general, and at the convention of 1861 he helped to draft the Louisiana Secession Ordinance. When the Civil War began, he was named judge of the Confederate District Court for Louisiana. Semmes served in the Confederate Senate from 1862 to 1865 and was on the Finance, Judiciary, and Flag and Seal Committees. He was loyal to the Davis administration on most issues. Semmes helped to prepare the tax-in-kind bill and wrote the Judiciary Committee report against martial law. He favored special military exemptions for overseers and was one of the leaders in the movement in behalf of P.G.T. Beauregard's (*q.v.*) command of the western armies. Semmes was a leader in the western concentration bloc. When the war ended, he made a quick trip to Washington, obtained a pardon, and returned to New Orleans to practice law. Semmes took no part in postwar politics. He was a delegate to the Louisiana constitutional conventions of 1879 and 1898, held the chair of civil law at the University of Louisiana from 1873 to 1879, and was president of the American Bar Association in 1886. He died in New Orleans on June 23, 1899. *Biographical and Historical Memoirs of Louisiana*, II; *Southern Historical Society Papers*, XXV.

SEXTON, Franklin Barlow (*Congressman*), was born on April 29, 1828, in New Harmony, Posey County, Indiana. Three years later, his family moved to San Augustine County, Texas, where Sexton graduated from Wesleyan College in 1846, served as an apprentice in a printing office, studied law, and was admitted to the Texas bar in 1848. He developed an excellent law practice in San Augustine, Texas. He was a Mason and a member of the Methodist church; he was married and had a daughter. Sexton, a Democrat who served in the Texas legislature during the 1850s, was also a farmer and a slaveholder. He was a secessionist and became a state senator in 1861. He served in the Confederate Army during the early days of the war. In 1862, he was elected from the Fourth Congressional District of Texas to the first Confederate House of Representatives; he was reelected in 1863. Sexton, a pro-administration man, served on the Commerce, War Tax, Quartermaster's and Commissary Departments, and Military Transportation Committees during his first term and on the Joint, Post Office and Post Roads, and Ways and Means Committees during his second term. He preferred increased taxation to curb inflation. He was reputed to have been one of the hardest working and most efficient men in Congress. After the war, he practiced law in San Augustine before moving to Marshall, Texas, in 1872. In 1876, he supported Samuel Tilden for the presidency. Sexton served on the Texas Supreme Court prior to his death in El Paso, Texas, on May 15, 1900. Estill (ed.), "Diary of a Confederate Congressman, 1862-1863," *Southwestern Historical Quarterly*, XXXIX; Wright (comp.), *Texas in the War*.

SHELBY, Joseph Orville (*General*), was born to Orville and Anna M. (Boswell) Shelby on December 12, 1830, in Lexington, Kentucky. He was related to Governor Isaac Shelby of Kentucky, and his family included prominent planters and rope manufacturers in Kentucky and Tennessee. He attended Kentucky schools and Transylvania University before moving to Waverly, Lafayette County, Missouri, at the age of nineteen. In 1858, he married a remote cousin,

Elizabeth N. Shelby, by whom he had seven children. A wealthy man, Shelby inherited his father's rope factory and plantation. By 1861, he was one of the wealthiest landowners of Missouri and owned plantations in Lafayette and Bates Counties. During the Kansas border troubles of the 1850s, he was sympathetic to slavery and actively sided with the South. At the beginning of the war, he organized a company of cavalry for the Confederacy and he went on to engage in every campaign of the Civil War west of the Mississippi River, including the battles of Elkhorn and Prairie Grove, Arkansas; Newtonia and Cane Hill, Missouri; and Corinth, Mississippi. In December 1862 he captured the steamer *Sunshine* at Booneville, Mississippi, and in 1863, while leading a division at the battle of Helena, Arkansas, he was wounded. After his promotion to brigadier general on December 15, 1863, he won fame as a raider with General Sterling Price (*q.v.*) through Arkansas and Missouri in 1864. When the war ended, rather than surrender, he set out for Mexico with six hundred men, including fellow Confederate generals Sterling Price, H. B. Lyon, and John McCausland (*q.v.*), on a military expedition which later became an unsuccessful colonization scheme. In 1867, he returned to Bates County, where he again became a planter. Shelby was U.S. marshal for the Western District of his state in 1893; he died in Adrion, Missouri, on February 13, 1897. O'Flaherty, *General J. Shelby, Undefeated Rebel.*

SHELLEY, Charles Miller (*General*), was born on December 28, 1833, in Sullivan County, Tennessee, to the contracter and builder William Percy Shelley and his wife Margaret (Etter). His father was a brigadier general in the state militia. In 1836, the family moved to Selma, Alabama, and Shelley, who had little formal education, later followed his father's profession. Shelley became a successful businessman in Talladega, Alabama, and refrained entirely from prewar politics. He was a Methodist. He married Kathleen McConnell on June 15, 1865, and, after her death, Ann Olivia McConnell. He had two sons and one daughter. When the Civil War began, he became a lieutenant of artillery in the Confederate Army. After fighting in the battle of First Manassas, Shelley fought in Bragg's (*q.v.*) Kentucky campaign of 1862, having recruited the 30th Alabama Regiment of which he was colonel. After participating at the battle of Port Gibson, Mississippi, in May 1863, he was captured at Vicksburg in July. Following his release, Shelley fought with the Army of Tennessee in every battle from Chattanooga to Greensboro, including Missionary Ridge, the Atlanta campaign, and the battles of Franklin and Nashville, Tennessee. He was promoted to brigadier general on September 17, 1864. Shelley's Brigade was devastated at Franklin and he saw no further service. There is no record of his surrender. After the war, he returned to his business in Alabama. After serving as sheriff of Dallas County from 1874 to 1876, he was a Democratic congressman from Alabama from 1877 to 1885. From 1885 to 1889, he had a presidential appointment as fourth auditor of the U.S.

Treasury. He was also associated with the law firm of Shelley, Butler, and Martin in Alabama. He moved to Birmingham, Alabama, in the 1890s where he promoted industrial pursuits until his death on January 19 or 20, 1907. *Biographical Directory of the American Congress*; Evans, *Confederate Military History*, VII; Owen, *History of Alabama and Dictionary of Alabama Biography*, IV.

SHEWMAKE, John Troup (*Congressman*), was born in Burke County, Georgia, on January 22, 1826. He studied at Princeton for one year, clerked in an Augusta law office, and was admitted to the bar in 1848. Before the war, he was a lawyer in Augusta, Georgia. During the war, he served in the Georgia State Senate and was elected to the second Confederate House in 1863. Although he was supposed to have been a staunch administration supporter, Shewmake voted more than half of the time against the Davis administration's war measures. He served on the Accounts and Naval Affairs Committees. His major work was in the area of impressment where he wanted to relieve livestock operatives from the obligation to furnish meat to the government. Shewmake probably became an ally of Governor Brown (*q.v.*). When the war ended, he returned to his Augusta law practice. He served two terms in the Georgia Senate from 1879 to 1883. Shewmake died in Augusta on December 1, 1898. Wiley (ed.), *Letters of Warren Aiken*; Yearns, *The Confederate Congress*.

SHORTER, John Gill (*Governor, Congressman*), was born on April 23, 1818, to General Reuben Clarke and Bary Butler (Gill) Shorter in Monticello, Georgia, where his father was a planter, physician, and legislator. After graduating from Franklin College (later the University of Georgia) in 1837, Shorter moved to Alabama, where he was admitted to the Eufaula bar in 1838. He was a Baptist and a Democrat. He had one daughter by his January 12, 1843, marriage to Mary Jane Butler. After four years in law practice, Shorter became involved in Alabama politics. In 1842, he was solicitor for his district. He represented Barbour County in the state Senate in 1845 and in the state House in 1851. From 1852 to 1861, he was a circuit court judge. In 1861, Governor Moore (*q.v.*) appointed him a commissioner to Georgia to urge the secession of that state. In the provisional Confederate Congress, Shorter served as chairman of the Committee on Engrossment and the committee to organize the executive branch of the government. He also wrote that part of the permanent Confederate Constitution which provided for the admission of new states. He was a strong supporter of the Davis administration. In 1861, he was elected governor over Thomas H. Watts (*q.v.*). As governor of Alabama, Shorter constructed the defenses for Mobile, supported conscription, and collected taxes according to schedule. However, he was blamed for Alabama's wartime reverses, and in 1863, Watts defeated him for the governorship by a margin of three to one. He held no other office in the Confederate government. After the war, Shorter practiced law and shunned public life. He died in Eufaula, Alabama, on May 29, 1872. Fleming, *Civil War and Reconstruction in Alabama*; Owen, *History of Alabama and Dictionary of Alabama Biography*, IV.

SHOUP, Francis Asbury (*General*), was born on March 22, 1834, in Laurel, Indiana, to the merchant George Grove Shoup and his wife Jane (Conwell). He attended Asbury University (later DePauw University) in Indiana and graduated fifteenth in a class of thirty-four from the U.S. Military Academy in 1855. He had three children by his 1870 marriage to Ester Habersham Elliott, daughter of Episcopal Bishop Stephen Elliott (*q.v.*). Shoup had garrison duty at Key West and Fort Moultrie and was promoted to second lieutenant in the U.S. Army in 1855. He fought the Seminoles in Florida in 1856-1858. In 1860, he resigned from the service to study law, and he was admitted to the St. Augustine bar the following year. When the Civil War began, he volunteered for service in the Confederate Army. Shoup, who served at a battery at Fernandina, Florida, in 1861, became a major of artillery in a Kentucky regiment in October 1861 and served as General William Hardee's (*q.v.*) chief of artillery at the battle of Shiloh in March 1862. He was inspector of artillery under P.G.T. Beauregard (*q.v.*) and was General Thomas C. Hindman's (*q.v.*) chief of artillery in Arkansas, where he fought at Prairie Grove in December 1862. On September 12, 1862, he was promoted to brigadier general, and the following April he went to Mobile as chief of artillery to General Simon B. Buckner (*q.v.*). After serving as a brigade commander during the siege of Vicksburg, Shoup was General Joseph E. Johnston's (*q.v.*) chief of artillery during the Atlanta campaign in 1864, and he saved the guns during the retreat of the Army of Tennessee. He constructed the works of the Chattahoochee River and became General John B. Hood's (*q.v.*) chief of staff in Tennessee late in 1864. Shoup also requested that the Confederate Congress approve the enlistment of Negro troops in the Confederate Army. There is no record of his surrender. In 1865, Shoup taught mathematics at the University of Mississippi. Three years later, he was ordained an Episcopal priest, and he was later rector of churches at Waterford, New York, Nashville, and New Orleans. From 1869 to 1883, he taught metaphysics at the University of the South in Sewanee, Tennessee. He also taught engineering, physics, and mathematics there in 1883. Shoup died in retirement on September 4, 1896, in Columbia, Tennessee. Durden, *The Gray and the Black: Confederate Debate on Emancipation*; Noll, *Doctor Quintard*; Noll, *History of the Church in the Diocese of Tennessee*.

SIMMS, William Elliott (*Congressman*), son of William Marmaduke and Julia (Shropshire) Simms, was born on January 2, 1822, in Cynthiana, Harrison County, Kentucky. He attended public schools and was a member of the Law Department of Transylvania University in 1846, the year he was also admitted to the bar in Paris, Kentucky. Simms had three children by his September 27, 1866, marriage to Lucy Ann Blythe. He was a captain in the Mexican War and represented Bourbon County in the state House during 1849-1851. He was a secessionist and in 1857, he edited the *Kentucky State Flag*, a secessionist newspaper. He also practiced law in Paris, Kentucky, for some years before the war and became active in politics. From 1859 to 1861, he served as a Democrat in the U.S. House of Representatives. In 1861, he was one of three commissioners sent by the state of Kentucky to treat with the Confederate government. When the Civil War began, he enlisted in the Confederate Army as a colonel of the 1st Battalion Kentucky Cavalry. He was also elected a Confederate senator from Kentucky, serving throughout the war years, and was captain of the Confederate Congress militia. He supported the Davis administration throughout the war, favored an invasion of Kentucky, and served on the Accounts, Indian Affairs, Naval Affairs, Foreign Relations, Public Buildings, and many special committees. He was one of the most diligent and able politicians in the Confederate Senate. Simms fled to Canada after the war. Because of his political disabilities, his political career was ended by the war. He returned to Paris, Kentucky, in 1866 and became a wealthy farmer in the postwar years. He died on June 25, 1898, in Paris. Collins, *Historical Sketches of Kentucky*, II.

SIMPSON, William Dunlap (*Congressman*), was born on October 27, 1823, in Laurens County, South Carolina, to John W. and Elizabeth (Saterwhite) Simpson. His father had been a doctor in Belfast, Ireland. The younger Simpson attended Laurens Academy in South Carolina and graduated with distinction from South Carolina College in 1843. He also attended Harvard Law School prior to his admittance to the South Carolina bar in 1846. Simpson was a Democrat and an elder in the Presbyterian church. He had eight children by his marriage to Jane E. Young in March 1847. He developed an excellent law practice in Laurens District and also participated in local politics. He served in both houses of the South Carolina legislature during the 1850s. In the early days of the Civil War, he was an aide to General Milledge Bonham (*q.v.*) during the siege of Fort Sumter. He participated in the battle of First Manassas as a major and later served as a lieutenant colonel of the 14th South Carolina Regiment. Wounded at Germantown, he also saw action in the Seven Days and at Sharpsburg. He replaced Bonham in the Confederate Congress when Bonham became governor in 1863. He supported the Davis administration in the first House but turned against it in the second. He was a watchdog over the treatment of Northern prisoners and served on the Claims, Elections, Impressments, and Quartermaster's and Commissary Departments Committees. Ruined financially after the war, he returned to his law practice at Laurens Court House. He was elected to the U.S. House of Representatives in 1866 but was denied his seat by the federal authorities. In 1876 and 1878, he was elected lieutenant governor of South Carolina, and in 1879, he became governor of the state. The following year he was named chief justice of the state

Supreme Court. Simpson died in Columbia, South Carolina, on December 26, 1890. Charleston *News and Courier*, December 27, 1890; Faunt and Reynolds, *Biographical Directory of the Senate of the State of South Carolina*.

SIMS, Frederick William (*Bureaucrat*), son of Frederick and Katherine Willis (Wellborn) Sims, was born in Clinton, Jones County, Georgia, in 1828. He later moved to Macon, Georgia, where his father was mayor in 1842. He was married to Catherine M. Sullivan on September 12, 1850, and after her death, to Sarah Louisa Munroe on December 10, 1862, by whom he had six children. In the 1850s, Sims was the chief accountant for the Central Railroad of Georgia. In 1856, he published the Savannah *Republican* along with a partner, James Roddey Sneed. Two years later he became sole proprietor of the paper. When the Civil War began, he volunteered for duty in the Confederate Army. In late 1862, he was captured while a captain in Company B, 1st Georgia Regiment, and was later released. On June 2, 1863, he was named assistant adjutant general, serving as inspector, agent, and supervisor of railroad transportation for Confederate troops. He was promoted to lieutenant colonel in January 1864. His contributions to the war effort in the last years of the war were invaluable; it was said that he kept the Army of Northern Virginia in troops. After the war, he headed the firm of F. W. Sims and Company, cotton factors and commission merchants in Savannah. In September 1874, he became business manager of the *Savannah Daily Advertiser*. Sims took his own life on May 25, 1875, in San Francisco. Black, *The Railroads of the Confederacy*; Goff, *Confederate Supply*; Myers, *The Children of Pride*.

SINGLETON, Ortho Robards (*Congressman*), was born on October 14, 1814, in Nicholasville, Jessamine County, Kentucky. His early life is unknown. He attended St. Joseph's College in Bardstown, Kentucky, and studied in the Law Department at the University of Lexington before being admitted to the Kentucky bar in 1838. Singleton was a Catholic; he was married and had one daughter. Sometime in the early 1840s, he moved to Mississippi, where he practiced law and owned a small plantation in Canton, Madison County. He served in the Mississippi House in 1846-1847 and in the Senate from 1848 to 1854. He was a Democrat in the U.S. House of Representatives from 1853 to 1855 but lost a bid for reelection in 1854. He was returned to the House from 1857 until his withdrawal in 1861. A secessionist, he served in both sessions of the permanent Confederate House of Representatives, where he supported the Davis administration. During his first term, he was a member of the Joint, Inauguration, and Indian Affairs Committees, as well as the special committee on claims of families of deceased soldiers. In his second term, he was a member of the Conference and Indian Affairs Committees and the special committee on the Confederate States Treasury. He was also an aide-de-camp to General Robert E. Lee (*q.v.*) in 1864. Before the war ended, Singleton had become disillusioned with the Confederate cause. After the war, he returned to his law practice in Mississippi. Once the federal restrictions on his public service were lifted, he again served as a Democrat in the U.S. House of Representatives from 1875 to 1887. He moved to Forest, Mississippi, in 1883. Singleton died in Washington, D.C., on January 11, 1889. *Biographical Directory of the American Congress*.

SLAUGHTER, James Edwin (*General*), was born to Letitia (Madison) Slaughter in June 1827 at his family's estate at Cedar Mountain, Virginia. The name of his father is not known. He was a Presbyterian and a descendant of President James Madison. He attended Virginia Military Institute in 1845-1846, withdrawing to enter the U.S. Army during the Mexican War, where he served in the 1st Artillery. In 1852, he was promoted to first lieutenant. He left the army in May 1861 and volunteered for the Confederate Army. Slaughter entered as a captain of artillery and was Braxton Bragg's (*q.v.*) inspector general at Pensacola in the Department of Alabama and West Florida. For his role in the bombardment of Pensacola, he was promoted to brigadier general on March 8, 1862. During the battle of Shiloh, he was assistant inspector general on the staff of General Albert S. Johnston (*q.v.*). In May, he rejoined Bragg's staff as inspector general for the Army of Mississippi, and he fought in the Kentucky campaign of 1862 before receiving a line command in Mobile, Alabama. In April 1863, he became chief of artillery and staff to General John B. Magruder (*q.v.*) in Galveston, Texas, and he had charge of the East Subdistrict of Texas for the remainder of the war. On May 12, 1865, Slaughter led Confederate forces at the battle of Brownsville, Texas, the last battle of the war. He did not surrender and, instead, left for Mexico where he lived for several years. He returned to Mobile by 1870, where he was a civil engineer and postmaster. He moved to New Orleans in the 1880s. Slaughter died during a visit to Mexico City on January 1, 1901. Warner, *Generals in Gray*; Washington *Evening Star*, January 4, 1901.

SLIDELL, John (*Diplomat*), was born in 1793 in New York City to John and Margery (Mackenzie) Slidell. His father was a merchant, insurance agent, and banker. The younger Slidell graduated from Columbia College in 1810, studied law, and was admitted to the New York bar. He was engaged in the mercantile business in New York until he was ruined by the embargo during the War of 1812. A duel forced his removal to New Orleans in 1819, where he developed an outstanding commercial law practice. He married a Creole, Mathilde Deslonde, in 1835; they had a son and two daughters. Slidell, a Democrat, served in the Louisiana House before losing a race for the U.S. House in 1828. He was U.S. district attorney in New Orleans in 1829-1833 and lost bids for the U.S. Senate in 1834, 1836, and 1848. He served as a states' rights Democrat in the U.S. House of Representatives from 1843 to 1845 and in the Senate from 1853 until his resignation in 1861. In 1845, Slidell was U.S. minister to Mexico, and in 1853, he sold bonds for the New Orleans and Nashville Railroad in London. He supported the Lecompton Constitution for Kansas and was an enemy of Stephen Douglas. He broke with President Buchanan in 1861 and was converted to secession by Lincoln's election. When the Civil War began, President Davis (*q. v.*) appointed him Confederate ambassador to France. He was captured by federal authorities during the *Trent* affair in November 1861 with his colleague James M. Mason (*q. v.*); both were imprisoned, released in January 1862, and allowed to go on to England. The event had the effect of hindering early diplomatic relations between England and the federal government. As Confederate minister to France, he failed to gain French recognition of the Confederacy, but he negotiated the Erlanger loan. (One of his daughters married Erlanger's son.) He was unsuccessful in his attempt to build ships for the Confederacy in France, and he became deeply involved in Napoleon's Mexican venture. After the war, he remained in Paris until the fall of the Second Empire in 1870. He neither sought nor was offered pardon. He died at Cowes, Isle of Wight, England, on July 26 or 29, 1871. Owsley, *King Cotton Diplomacy*; Sears, *John Slidell*.

SMITH, Charles Henry (*Humorist*), son of the merchant Asahel Reid Smith and his wife Caroline Ann (Maguire), was born in Lawrenceville, Gwinnett County, Georgia, on June 15, 1826. He left the University of Georgia in 1848 to manage his father's store. In 1849, he married Mary Octavia Hutchins, by whom he had thirteen children. A Democrat and a lawyer, he rode the circuit in 1851 in the vicinity of Rome, Georgia. Smith also practiced law in Rome until the end of the antebellum period. During the war, he was a major on the staff of Generals Francis Bartow (*q. v.*) and George T. Anderson (*q. v.*). In 1864, he became judge advocate of Marion, Georgia. He also wrote wartime letters which appeared in the Rome *Confederacy* and other Southern newspapers under the pen name "Bill Arp." These letters are historically valuable for the insight they give into Southern sentiments and attitudes. His humorous anecdotes and tales became famous among the troops, and his stories circulated throughout the Confederacy. After the war, he practiced law and contributed weekly letters to the Atlanta *Constitution* for a period of twenty-five years. He served in the Georgia legislature in 1865-1866 and was mayor of Rome in 1868-1869. In 1866, he published *Bill Arp, So Called*. Smith moved to Carterville, Bartow County, Georgia, in 1877 and died there on August 24, 1903. Brantley, *Georgia Journalism of the Civil War Period*; Ginther, "Alias Bill Arp," *Georgia Review*, IV.

SMITH, Edmund Kirby (*General*), was born on May 16, 1824, in St. Augustine, Florida, to Colonel Joseph Lee Smith and his wife Frances (Kirby). His father, a federal judge, was also a lawyer and a Republican from Connecticut. Kirby Smith attended Hallowell School in Virginia and graduated twenty-fifth in a class of forty-one from the U.S. Military Academy in 1845. He accepted a commission in the infantry. He was a Democrat and a vestryman in the Episcopal church. By his marriage to Cassie Selden of Virginia on September 24, 1861, he had five sons and six daughters. He was breveted three times during the Mexican

War and was an assistant professor of mathematics at West Point from 1849 to 1852. He was promoted to captain in 1855 and fought the Commanche Indians in Texas before the outbreak of the Civil War. Although Kirby Smith opposed secession, he resigned his army commission when Florida seceded and volunteered for duty in the Confederate Army. As General Joseph E. Johnston's (*q.v.*) chief of staff, he helped to organize the Army of Shenandoah in 1861. He was commissioned a brigadier general on June 17, 1861, and in July he was wounded during the battle of First Manassas, where he led the 4th Brigade. Promoted to major general on October 11, 1861, Kirby Smith was given a division in Beauregard's (*q.v.*) command, and in March 1862, he assumed command of the Department of East Tennessee. He accompanied Braxton Bragg (*q.v.*) during his Kentucky campaign, winning a victory at Richmond, Kentucky, on August 30, 1862. His performance in Kentucky earned him a promotion to lieutenant general on October 9, 1862. Kirby Smith became disgusted with Bragg over his unwillingness to engage the enemy. In February 1863, he was transferred to command the Trans-Mississippi Department, a position he kept for the rest of the war. The spring after his promotion to full general on February 19, 1864 (which was never confirmed), his army was victorious in the Red River campaign in Louisiana. When he surrendered his troops to Union General E.R.S. Canby on May 26, 1865, Kirby Smith was almost the only Confederate general remaining in the field. He was soon paroled. He then fled to Mexico and Cuba but later returned to Florida to serve from 1866 to 1868 as president of the Atlantic and Pacific Telegraph Company. From 1870 to 1875, he was president of the University of Nashville, and from 1875 until his death on March 28, 1893, he was a professor of mathematics at the University of the South in Sewanee, Tennessee. He died at Sewanee on March 28, 1893. Parks, *General Edmund Kirby Smith*.

SMITH, Gustavus Woodson (*General*), was born to Byrd and Sarah Hatcher (Woodson) Smith on January 1, 1822, in Georgetown, Scott County, Kentucky. He graduated eighth in a class of fifty-six from the U.S. Military Academy in 1842. Smith was a member of the Democratic party. His marriage to Lucretia Bassett on October 3, 1844, was childless. Smith was commissioned a second lieutenant in the U.S. Army Corps of Engineers in 1845. During the Mexican War, he served with the Corps of Engineers and was breveted three times. He saw action at Vera Cruz, Cerro Gordo, Contreras, Churubusco, and Chapultepec. From 1849 until his resignation in 1854 to join Quitman's Cuban filibustering expedition, he was an assistant professor of engineering at West Point. He moved to New Orleans and went with Quitman to Cuba before moving to New York City in 1856. Smith was chief engineer for the Trenton Iron Works from 1856 to 1858. From 1858 to 1861, he was street commissioner for New York City. When the Civil War began, he volunteered for service in the Confederate Army. On September 19, 1861, he was commissioned a major general. He commanded a wing of the Army of Northern Virginia during the Peninsular campaign of the spring of 1862 until forced by paralysis to retire from the field. During the battle of Seven Pines, he headed the army after General Joseph E. Johnston (*q.v.*) had been wounded. On November 17-20, 1862, he was secretary of war *ad interim* in the Davis cabinet. Smith, who feuded with President Davis (*q.v.*), was then transferred to Charleston, South Carolina, where he served under Beauregard (*q.v.*). He resigned from the army on February 17, 1863, angered that promotions had been granted to men with lesser seniority than he. Smith then served as superintendent of the Etowah Mining and Manufacturing Company in Georgia, and he was a major general in the Georgia Militia from June 1864 until the end of the war. He participated in numerous battles in Georgia and let his troops effectively and efficiently. He surrendered in Macon, Georgia, in April 1865 and was soon paroled. From 1866 to 1870, he was superintendent of an iron works in Chattanooga, Tennessee, and from 1870 to 1875, he was insurance commissioner of Kentucky. In 1876, he moved to New York City, where he died on June 4, 1896. Smith also published a number of books including *The Battle of Seven Pines* (1891) and *Confederate War Papers* (1884). Freeman, *Lee's Lieutenants*, III; Myers, *The Children of Pride*; Patrick, *Davis and His Cabinet*.

SMITH, James Argyle (*General*), was born on July 1, 1831, in Maury County, Tennessee. His family life is unknown. He graduated forty-fifth in a class of fifty-two from the U.S. Military Academy in 1853 and served in the West as a career officer in the U.S. Army until 1861. He participated in the Sioux Expedition of 1855 and the Utah expedition of 1858. In December 1859, he was promoted to first lieutenant. He resigned his commission on May 9, 1861, in order to join the Confederate Army. In 1862, he held the rank of major and was assistant adjutant general for General Leonidas Polk (*q.v.*), with whom he fought heroically during the battle of Shiloh in the spring. After being promoted to colonel, he fought at Perryville during the Kentucky campaign, and at Murfreesboro and Chickamauga. He was promoted to brigadier general on September 30, 1863, following the battle of Missionary Ridge. He was painfully wounded during the Atlanta campaign but recovered and later assumed command of Cleburne's (*q.v.*) Division after the latter's death at the battle of Franklin, Tennessee. He spent the final months of the war in the Carolinas. He surrendered in North Carolina and was paroled at Greensboro in May 1865. From 1865 to 1877, he was a farmer and public school teacher in Jackson, Mississippi, and from 1877 to 1886, he was state superintendent of education in Mississippi. Smith died on December 6, 1901, in Jackson. *Association of Graduates, United States Military Academy*; Evans, *Confederate Military History*, VII.

SMITH, James Milton (*Congressman*), son of a farmer, was born on October 24, 1823, in Twiggs County, Georgia. He did woodwork and worked as· a blacksmith, attended school at Culloden in Monroe County, studied law, and was admitted to the Georgia bar in 1846. Smith, who became an able Columbus,

Georgia, lawyer, was married to Hester Ann Brown on June 8, 1848, and, after her death, to Mrs. Florida Abercrombie Wellborn on September 1, 1881; he had no children. In 1855, he ran unsuccessfully for the U.S. House as a states' rights Democrat. He was a unionist but finally supported secession. In July 1861, he enlisted as a major in the Upson Volunteers of the 13th Georgia Infantry. He was promoted to lieutenant colonel in February 1862 and later left the military for reasons of health. In 1863, he represented the Seventh Congressional District of Georgia in the second Confederate House. Smith was an active member of the Military Affairs Committee and served on the joint committee to exempt state officers from service in the Confederate Army. An extreme defender of states' rights, he supported the Davis administration on all issues except those he felt affected Georgia's efforts to protect itself. After the war, Smith practiced law in Columbus with Peter W. Alexander (*q.v.*) and was associated with Alexander H. Stephens (*q.v.*) and Lucius Gartrell (*q.v.*). He was elected speaker of the House in the Georgia legislature of 1870. He became the first Democratic governor of Georgia after the carpetbagger regime had been ousted from state politics; he served from 1870 to 1876. Chairman of the State Railroad Commission from 1879 to 1885, Smith was also a Baptist pastor from 1881 to 1882. From 1887 to 1890, he was judge of the superior court of the Muscogee District. He died in Columbus, Georgia, on November 20, 1890. Telfair, *A History of Columbus, Georgia*.

SMITH, Martin Luther (*General*), son of Luther Smith, was born on September 9, 1819, in Tomkins County, New York. He graduated sixteenth in a class of fifty-six from the U.S. Military Academy in 1842. On July 27, 1846, he married Sarah E. Nisbet, daughter of Eugenius Nisbet (*q.v.*) of Athens, Georgia, who was a major figure in Georgia politics. Smith, a career officer in the U.S. Army before the Civil War, served with the topographical engineers during the Mexican War. Following his promotion to first lieutenant in 1853, he made surveys for improvements on the Savannah River in Georgia. In 1856, he was promoted to captain, and he spent the next five years making surveys in Texas and serving as chief engineer for the Fernandina and Cedar Keys Railroad in Florida. He resigned from the army on April 1, 1861, and was commissioned a major in the Confederate States Corps of Engineers at the beginning of the war. Smith was promoted to brigadier general on April 11, 1862, and to major general on November 4, 1862. He was chief of engineers for the Army of Northern Virginia before being sent west in 1862, where he planned and constructed the river defenses for New Orleans and Vicksburg. In June 1862, he was put in charge of the Third District of southern Mississippi and east Louisiana. While he was chief in command at Vicksburg, he resisted the naval attack of General William T. Sherman in December 1862. He later commanded a division and was captured during the siege of Vicksburg. Following his exchange, he was chief engineer for the Army of Northern Virginia from April through July 1864, for the Army of Tennessee from July to October 1864, and for the defense of Mobile until the end of the war. He surrendered at Mobile and was paroled in May 1865. After the war, he was an engineer in Athens, Georgia. He died in Savannah on July 29, 1866. *Confederate Veteran*, VI; Nichols, *Confederate Engineers*.

SMITH, Robert Hardy (*Congressman*), was born on October 21, 1814, in Camden County, North Carolina, to Robert Hardy and Elizabeth (Gregory) Smith. He attended the U.S. Military Academy during the early 1830s but did not graduate. He taught in Dallas County in 1834 and was admitted to the North Carolina bar in 1835. Smith was married three times: to Evalina Inge on January 12, 1839; after her death, to his sister-in-law Emily Inge on November 25, 1845; and after her death, to Helen Herndon on April 9, 1850. He had three children. After moving to Livingston, Alabama, in 1836, he developed a law practice and entered politics. He represented Sumter County in the Alabama legislature in 1849. He became the leader of the Whigs in the Alabama House but lost his bid for the state Senate in 1851. A political compromiser, he opposed the radicalism of the Nashville convention of 1850. In 1853, he moved to Mobile, Alabama, to practice law. In 1860, he was a unionist member of the anti-Yancey (*q.v.*) faction in the state and supported John Bell for the presidency. Yet, when Alabama seceded, he went to North Carolina to persuade that state to secede. Smith was elected to the Confederate Congress in 1861. He served on the Naval Affairs and Accounts Committees of the provisional Confederate Congress and helped to frame the Confederate Constitution. He introduced the item veto, supported the speedy addition of constitutional amendments, and probably served on the secret committee of three which perfected the style of the Constitution. During the war, he served as colonel of the 36th Alabama Infantry, resigning in April 1862 because of sickness. Smith performed no further service in the Confederate cause. After the war, he returned to the practice of law in Mobile, where he died on March 13, 1878. Lee, *The Confederate Constitutions*; Owen, *History of Alabama and Dictionary of Alabama Biography*, IV.

SMITH, William (*General, Congressman, Governor*), son of Colonel Caleb Smith and his first cousin Mary Waugh (Smith), was born on September 6, 1797, in Marengo, King George County, Virginia. He attended private schools in Virginia, Plainfield Academy in Connecticut, and, in 1814, Nelson's Classical School in Hanover County, Virginia, before studying law and being admitted to the Virginia bar in 1819. He had eleven children by his marriage to Elizabeth H. Bell in 1821. Smith, who began a law practice in Culpeper County, Virginia, in 1818, ran a line of mail and passenger coaches in 1827. From 1836 to 1841, he served in the state Senate. He also served one term as a Democrat in the U.S. House of Representatives from 1841 to 1843 but lost a bid for reelection. In 1842, he moved to Fauquier County, Virginia, to practice law, and from 1846 to 1849, he was the governor of Virginia. In 1849, he moved to San Francisco, where he was president of California's first Democratic state convention in 1850. He declined a seat in the U.S. Senate in 1851. He returned to Virginia in 1852 and again served in the U.S. House from 1853 to 1861. When the war began, he volunteered for service in the Confederate Army. During the Civil War, he served in the 49th Virginia Infantry, first as colonel, as brigadier general in 1863, and later that same year, as major general. He saw action at the battles of First Manassas, Yorktown, Gettysburg, Fredericksburg, and the Peninsular campaign, and he was severely wounded in the battle of Sharpsburg. He was a self-made fighter who earned the respect of his troops and had utter contempt for the West Point graduates who shared command with him. In 1862, he served for a time in the Confederate House, representing the Ninth Virginia Confederate District. A secessionist, he supported the Davis administration and served on the Claims, Naval Affairs, and Special Committees. Smith was elected governor of Virginia in 1864 and served until May 1865. As governor during the last year of the war, he helped the Confederate commissary obtain food and supplies and moved the seat of state government to Lynchburg in April 1865. After the war he was a farmer in Warrenton, Fauquier County, and served a term in the lower house of the state legislature from 1877 to 1879. Smith died on May 18, 1887, in Warrenton. Fahrlner, "William 'Extra Billy' Smith, Governor of Virginia, 1864-1865," *Virginia Magazine of History and Biography*, LXXIV; Smith, *Virginia, 1492-1892*.

SMITH, William Ephraim (*Congressman*), was born in Augusta, Richmond County, Georgia, on March 14, 1829, to Samuel and Susan (Horton) Smith. He studied law, was admitted to the Georgia bar in 1848, and began a practice in Albany, Georgia. He was also a planter. Smith married Caroline Williams on August 7, 1860, and, after her death, her sister, Mary Williams, in 1872. He was ordinary of Doughterty County in 1853 and solicitor general of the Southwest Circuit from 1858 to 1868. He was a Whig and a unionist until the war started. During the Civil War, he enlisted as a first lieutenant in the 1st Georgia Volunteer Infantry. Promoted to captain in 1862, he lost a leg in the battle of King's School House in June of that year. He saw no further military duty in the war. From 1863 until the end of the war, he represented the Second District of Georgia in the Confederate House. He served on the Ordnance and Ordnance Stores and the Territories and Public Lands Committees. Smith was generally a Davis administration opponent. When the war ended, he returned to his Albany law practice. He served as a Democrat to the U.S. House of Representatives from 1875 to 1881 and in the state Senate from 1886 to 1888. He again practiced law until his death on March 11, 1890, in Albany, Dougherty County, Georgia. Northen (ed.), *Men of Mark in Georgia*, V.

SMITH, William Nathan Harrell (*Congressman*), was born on September 24, 1812, in Murfreesboro, Hartford County, North Carolina, to Dr. William L. Smith and his wife Ann (Harrell), who died the following year. He attended academies at Murfreesboro, Kingston, Rhode Island, and Colchester, Connecticut, prior to graduating from Yale College in 1834. He also studied law at Yale in 1836 and began his practice in North Carolina in 1839. He was a member of the Presbyterian church. In January 1839, he married Mary Olivia Wise, by whom he had three children. He developed a successful law practice and entered politics. Smith, a Whig, represented Hartford County in the North Carolina House in 1840 and in the North Carolina Senate in 1848. In 1848, he was solicitor for the state Judicial District. He ran unsuccessfully for the U.S. House in 1857 but went on to serve in the state Senate in 1858 and the U.S. House from 1859 to 1861, where he fell one vote short of being elected speaker. Although he was a political ally of the Know-Nothings, he disapproved of their actions. Smith, who had been a unionist, served in the provisional and both permanent Confederate Houses. He served on the Claims, Rules, Elections, Medical Department, and Conference Committees. Always conservative, he opposed the Davis administration but voted against the suspension of the writ of *habeas corpus*. He advocated the elimination of military exemptions for those who furnished substitutes to fight in their places, and he opposed the peace movement. When the war ended, he returned to his Murfreesboro law practice and was elected to the North Carolina House in 1865. He did not join the Republican party, but he collaborated with the carpetbag forces in North Carolina. He opposed the Reconstruction Act of 1868. Two years later, he moved briefly to Norfolk, Virginia, but he practiced law in Raleigh around 1871 and was involved in the defense of William W. Holden (*q.v.*). He was a member of the Democratic state committee, and from 1878 to 1889, he was chief justice of the North Carolina Supreme Court. Smith died in Raleigh on November 14, 1889. Ashe, *Cyclopedia of Eminent and Representative Men of the Carolinas*, I; Hamilton, *Reconstruction in North Carolina*.

SMITH, William Russell (*Congressman*), son of Ezekiel and Elizabeth (Hampton) Smith, was born on March 27, 1815, in Russellville, Kentucky, where his father was a planter. He was orphaned early in life. Smith attended the University of Alabama until 1834, later studied law, and was admitted to the bar in Greensboro, Alabama, in 1835. He was a Catholic and was married three times. Smith had a son by his 1843 marriage to Jane Binion; three children by his marriage to Mary Jane Murray on January 3, 1847; and two sons by his marriage to Wilhelmine M. Easley on June 14, 1854. In 1837 Smith fought in the Creek War. He edited a magazine in Mobile and the Whig paper *Moniter* in 1838. In 1839, he was mayor of Tuscaloosa. In 1841-1842, he served as a Whig in the state legislature, but he left the Whig party the following year to write for the Democratic newspaper *The Southern*. He was a circuit court judge in 1850 and a member of the U.S. House from Tuscaloosa from 1851 to 1857, losing a bid for reelection in 1856. He was also a delegate to the Alabama secession convention, where he was initially a leader of the unionist group. Yet, he became a cautious secessionist and gave his full allegiance to his state. He also compiled the proceedings of the convention. In 1861, he raised the 6th Alabama Regiment and was made colonel of the 26th Regiment. He also served in the Confederate House throughout the war. Generally in opposition to the Davis administration, he served on the Printing, Flag and Seal, Foreign Affairs, and special committees. When the war ended, he practiced law in Tuscaloosa. Smith ran unsuccessfully for governor in 1865 and for Congress in 1878. In 1870-1871, he was president of the University of Alabama. Smith moved to Washington, D.C., in 1879 and practiced law until he died there on February 26, 1896. Fleming, *Civil War and Reconstruction in Alabama*; Smith, *William Russell Smith of Alabama*.

SNEAD, Thomas Lowndes (*Congressman*), was born to Jesse and Jane L. (Johnson) Snead on January 10, 1828, in Henrico County, Virginia. He graduated from Richmond College in 1846 and from the University of Virginia in 1848 and was admitted to the Virginia bar in 1850. Snead had a son and a daughter by his November 24, 1852, marriage to Harriet Vairin Reel. He moved in 1850 to St. Louis, Missouri, where he practiced law, and he was editor and owner of the St. Louis *Bulletin* in 1860-1861. He was a Democrat and a secessionist. When the Civil War began, he was made aide-de-camp to Missouri Governor Claiborne Jackson (*q.v.*) and became adjutant general of the Missouri State Guard in 1861. He saw action at the battles of Bonneville, Carthage, Wilson's Creek, and Lexington. In October 1861, he was a commissioner from Missouri to negotiate a military convention with the Confederate States. He was named chief of staff for the Army of the West in late 1861, and in 1862, he became assistant adjutant general in the Confederate Army, serving with Sterling Price (*q.v.*) in Arkansas, Missouri, and Mississippi. In May 1864, he was elected by Missouri soldiers to the second Confederate House, where he served on the Committee on Foreign Affairs and the special committee to increase the military force. He was a Davis administration supporter. After the war, he moved to New York City, where he was managing editor of the *Daily News* in 1865-1866. He was admitted to the New York bar in 1866. He wrote *The Fight for Missouri* in 1886. Snead practiced law in New York City until his death on October 17, 1890. *Library of Southern Literature*, XI.

SORREL, Gilbert Moxley (*General*), son of Francis and Matilda A. (Moxley) Sorrel, was born on February 23, 1838, in Savannah, Georgia, where his father was a successful businessman and commission merchant. His sister was married to the future General William W. Mackall (*q.v.*). Sorrel was a Presbyterian. He was a clerk in the Banking Department of the Central Railroad of Georgia and a member of a Savannah Militia Company in 1860. When the Civil War began, he volunteered for service in the Confederate Army. He served as captain and voluntary aide-de-camp to General James Longstreet (*q.v.*) at the battle of First Manassas, and in September 1861, he was named adjutant general of Longstreet's Brigade. Thereafter he was present during every engagement of the 1st Corps of the Army of Northern Virginia until the wounding of Longstreet at the Wilderness, including Seven Pines, the Seven Days, Sharpsburg, Gettysburg, Chickamauga, and the Knoxville campaign. On October 24, 1864, following a chest wound which he suffered at Petersburg, Sorrel was promoted to brigadier general and was named assistant adjutant general for the Army of Northern Virginia and chief of staff for the 1st Corps. Afterwards he returned to the field, where he was wounded at Hatcher's Run, Virginia, in February 1865. There is no record of his surrender. After the war, he was a merchant, businessman, and steamship company official in Savannah. Sorrel also completed his memoirs, *Recollections of a Confederate Staff Officer*, published posthumously in 1905. He died on August 10, 1901, in Roanoke, Virginia. Northen (ed.), *Men of Mark in Georgia*, V; Sorrel, *Recollections of a Confederate Staff Officer*.

SOULE, Pierre (*Diplomat*), was born on August 31, 1801, in Castillon, France, to Judge Joseph Soulé and his wife, Jeanne (Lacroix). He attended the Jesuit College in Toulouse and the academy in Bordeaux. A Catholic who had been destined for the priesthood, he was a shepherd in the Pyrenees and taught school in Paris before becoming a lawyer in 1822. In 1828, he married Armantine Mercier, by whom he had one son. In 1825, Soulé was sent to prison for publishing revolutionary articles, but he escaped to England. The following year, he traveled to Haiti and later the United States, where he lived in Baltimore, New Orleans, Tennessee, and Kentucky. He worked as a gardener, learned English, studied law, and was admitted to the New Orleans bar in the 1830s. He became a successful lawyer and an active politician. In 1845, he served a term as a Democrat in the state Senate, and from 1847 until his resignation in 1853, he was a states' rights Democrat in the U.S. Senate. While U.S. minister to Spain from 1853 to 1855, he was the author of the Ostend Manifesto in 1854. In 1855 he retired to private law practice. He supported Stephen A. Douglas at the Charleston convention in 1860. Although he opposed secession, Soulé followed Louisiana out of the Union and later served as a brigadier general of special services on the staff of General P.G.T. Beauregard (*q.v.*) during the defense of Charleston. Since President Davis (*q.v.*) was hostile to him, his military title was an honorary one. Soulé also ran the blockade to Havana in 1864 and attempted to recruit a foreign legion to fight for the Confederacy. Because he was a member of the Beauregard bloc and its lobbyist in Richmond, the administration distrusted him. After the war he moved to Havana and was part of a scheme to settle Confederate veterans in Sonora. He returned to New Orleans, where he died on March 26, 1870. Ettinger, *The Mission of Pierre Soulé to Spain, 1853-1855*; Moore, "Pierre Soulé: Southern Expansionist and Promoter," *Journal of Southern History*, XXI; Winters, *The Civil War in Louisiana*.

SPARROW, Edward (*Congressman*), was born on December 29, 1810, in Dublin, Ireland. When he was a youth, his family brought him to Ohio. He attended Kenyon College in Ohio, studied law, was admitted to the Ohio bar, and came to Louisiana in 1831. He was considered an important antebellum Louisiana lawyer; he also was the owner of "Arlington" plantation. He was a Catholic and had several children by his marriage to Minerva Parker. Sparrow was clerk of court for Concordia Parish in 1833 and sheriff from 1834 to 1840. During the Mexican War, he was a brigadier general in the state militia. He moved to Carroll Parish, Louisiana, in 1852. A Whig and a political ally of Alexander DeClouet (*q.v.*), he was a member of the Baton Rouge convention in 1860 and voted for secession at the Louisiana convention in 1861. In the provisional Confederate Congress, he served on the Military Affairs, Indian Affairs, and Flag and Seal Committees, as well as the committee to draft a permanent Confederate Constitution. In the first and second Confederate Senates, he was chairman of the important Military Affairs Committee. Sparrow was an ally of Thomas Semmes (*q.v.*) and Augustus H. Garland (*q.v.*) in the Senate. In 1862, he was alienated from the Davis administration, and, along with Robert M. T. Hunter (*q.v.*) of Virginia, moved into the General Joseph E. Johnston camp (*q.v.*). A foe of Braxton Bragg (*q.v.*), he was a close friend of P.G.T. Beauregard (*q.v.*), for whose reinstatement to active command he worked in 1862. In 1864, he supported the suspension of the writ of *habeas corpus* and opposed the exemption of Confederate businesses from heavy taxation. In 1865, he dissented from the majority view in the Senate by proposing to let commissioners determine market and impressment prices. Toward the end of the war, he favored the surrender of the Trans-Mississippi Department at a time when such a sentiment was considered treasonable in his home district of northern and western Louisiana. After the war, he returned to private practice and never again held political office. Sparrow died in Lake Providence, Louisiana, on July 4, 1882. Calhoun, "A History of Concordia Parish, Louisiana," *Louisiana Historical Quarterly*, XV; Connelly and Jones, *The Politics of Command*; Lee, *The Confederate Constitutions*.

STAPLES, Waller Redd (*Congressman*), was born in Stuart, Patrick County, Virginia, on February 24, 1806, to Colonel Abram Penn and Mary (Penn) Staples. He attended the University of North Carolina and graduated with honors from the College of William and Mary in 1846. He studied law in the Montgomery County, Virginia, office of William B. Preston (*q.v.*) and began his own practice there in 1848. Staples was a Whig and never married. In 1853-1854, he served a term in the state legislature. As a member of the Virginia secession convention in 1861, he opposed immediate secession. He was later sent as a delegate to the provisional Confederate Congress at Montgomery. During the war, he served on the staff of Colonel Robert Trippe (*q.v.*) and was a member of the Confederate House of Representatives from 1862 to 1865. An opponent of arbitrary conscription laws, he turned against the Davis administration in 1864. He served on the Military

Affairs, Elections, Patents, and numerous special committees. When the war ended, he returned to his law practice. In 1870, he was elected judge of the Virginia Supreme Court of Appeals, a position which he lost to the Readjusters in 1882. From 1884 to 1887, he helped to construct the state legal code, and he served as counsel for the Richmond and Danville Railroad Company. He became a Democrat after the war and lived in Richmond from 1882 until his death on August 20, 1897. Johnston (comp.), *Memorials of Old Virginia Clerks*; Tyler, *Encyclopedia of Virginia Biography*, III.

STEPHENS, Alexander Hamilton (*Vice-President*), was born in Crawfordsville, Wilkes County, Georgia, on February 11, 1812. He was the son of Andrew Baskins Stephens, a poor merchant's clerk, and his wife Margaret (Grier). His father died in 1826. With the help of a benefactor, Stephens was able to attend Franklin College (later the University of Georgia), from which he graduated first in the class of 1832. He had odd jobs, taught school, studied law, and was admitted to the Crawfordsville bar in 1834. He early became a successful lawyer and turned his attentions to public service. He was a Presbyterian, a lifelong bachelor, and a Whig. He served in the Georgia legislature from 1836 to 1840, and again in 1842. He served in the U.S. House of Representatives from 1843 to 1859, where his intelligence and biting oratory soon carried him to leadership in the Whig party. He was a staunch unionist who was personally responsible for the Georgia unionist movement in 1850. In 1859, he decided that his party no longer had any power in the South, but he remained active in politics as a supporter of Stephen A. Douglas in 1860. After the presidential election, he called for a convention of all the Southern states in the hopes of at least forging a united Southern effort if he could not forestall disunion. He was a union delegate to the Georgia secession convention, but signed the Ordinance of Secession. As a delegate to the Montgomery convention to create the Confederacy, he was a leader in constructing a conservative constitution. The provisional Confederate Congress elected him vice-president of the Confederacy in February 1861. He was also the commissioner to Virginia to persuade that state to join the Confederacy. A staunch states' rights enthusiast, actions of the Davis government soon drove him into political opposition. He returned to Georgia, became a champion of Governor Joseph E. Brown (*q.v.*), and sabotaged much of the Confederate government's relations with that state. In 1862, Stephens became the leader of the Senate opposition to the Davis administration. Along with R.M.T. Hunter (*q.v.*) and John A. Campbell (*q.v.*), he was a delegate to the abortive Hampton Roads Peace Mission in late 1864. When the war ended, he was arrested and held prisoner in Boston for six months. When released he settled in Atlanta, Georgia. In 1866, he was elected to the U.S. Senate but was never able to present his credentials; as with many other leaders, the federal government refused him public office during Reconstruction. He became a vehement foe of Reconstruction. In 1871, he bought the Atlanta *Southern Sun* and, in his editorials, opposed the Democratic fusion with the

Liberal Republicans in 1872. From 1873 to 1882, he again served in the U.S. House, and in 1882-1883, he was governor of Georgia. He also published the best selling history, *A Constitutional View of the Late War Between the States* (1868-1870). He died on March 4, 1883, in Atlanta, Georgia. Von Abele, *Alexander H. Stephens*.

STEPHENS, Linton (*State Legislator*), was born to Andrew Baskins and Matilda S. (Linsay) Stephens, on July 1, 1823, in Wilkes County, Georgia. He was orphaned at the age of three. He attended the academy at Culloden, Georgia, and graduated first in the class of 1843 at Franklin College (later the University of Georgia). He was raised by his half-brother, Alexander Stephens (*q.v.*), and was that powerful man's spokesman in Georgia. He studied law under Judge N. Beverley Tucker at the University of Virginia and attended Harvard Law School before being admitted to the Crawfordsville, Georgia, bar in 1846. In January 1852, he married Emmeline (Thomas) Bell, a daughter of Judge James Thomas, by whom he had three daughters. He had three more children by his June 1867 marriage to Mary W. Salter, after his first wife's death. Stephens served in the Georgia House from 1849 until 1852, when he moved to Hancock County, Georgia. He represented Hancock County in the state House from 1853 to 1855 but was unsuccessful in his campaigns for the U.S. House in 1855 and 1857. In 1859, he became an associate justice of the Georgia Supreme Court, and while he held this position he established the legal rights of slaves. He opposed secession at the Georgia convention in 1861, but when the Civil War began, he volunteered for service in the Confederate Army. During the war, he raised the 15th Regiment of Georgia Volunteers, and he served as lieutenant colonel in Virginia until his health forced him to leave military service in 1862. As a member of the Georgia House from 1862 to 1865, he worked for peace. In 1863, he helped his state to raise a battalion for its own defense. Along with his brother, he joined Governor Brown (*q.v.*) in the Georgia peace movement, which included a united Confederate effort at conciliation with the North. After the war, he practiced law in Georgia and opposed the liberal Republicans in 1872. He died in Hancock, Georgia, on July 14, 1872. Bryan, *Confederate Georgia*; Waddell, *Biographical Sketch of Linton Stephens*.

STEUART, George Hume (*General*), son of George Hume Steuart, was born on August 24, 1828, in Baltimore, Maryland. His father, who was descended from an old Maryland family, had been a general during the War of 1812. Steuart graduated thirty-seventh in a class of thirty-eight from the U.S. Military Academy in 1848 and served on the Texas frontier with the U.S. Army from 1848 until 1855. He was promoted to first lieutenant and captain of cavalry in 1855. Steuart had garrison duty in Kansas, Nebraska, and Colorado before participating in the Cheyenne expedition of 1856, the Utah expedition of 1858, and the expedition against the Commanches in 1860. He resigned from the army on April 22, 1861, and volunteered for service in the Confederate Army, entering as a captain of cavalry. He fought as colonel of the 1st Maryland Infantry under General Arnold Elzey (*q.v.*) at the battle of First Manassas. Promoted to brigadier general on March 6, 1862, he served with General Thomas J. Jackson (*q.v.*) in the Valley campaign of 1862 and was wounded at Cross Keys on June 8. Disabled for some time, he later distinguished himself in the assault on Culp's Hill during the battle of Gettysburg and helped to hold the "bloody angle" at Spotsylvania, where he was taken prisoner in May 1864. Steuart was later exchanged and fought under Pickett (*q.v.*) during the Petersburg campaign and at the battle of Five Forks in April 1865. He surrendered at Appomattox and was later paroled. After the war, he farmed in Anne Arundel County, Maryland. He died in retirement on November 22, 1903, in South River, Maryland. Evans, *Confederate Military History*, II.

STEVENS, Walter Husted (*General*), son of Samuel Stevens, was born on August 24, 1827, in Penn Yan, New York. Following his graduation in 1848 from the U.S. Military Academy, where he was fourth in a class of thirty-eight, he married a sister of the future Confederate States General Louis Hébert (*q.v.*) of Louisiana, and he became Southern in his outlook. He was commissioned in the Army Corps of Engineers. During the 1840s and 1850s, he was engaged in fortification repair in New Orleans, where he was superintending engineer for the U.S. Army in 1854-1856. In 1853, he surveyed the Texas rivers and harbors, and from 1853 to 1857, he was a lighthouse inspector along the Texas coast. In 1860, he built the New Orleans custom house. He resigned from the army on March 2, 1861, and volunteered for the Confederate Army. Stevens served on General P.G.T. Beauregard's (*q.v.*) staff during the battle of First Manassas as a captain of engineers, where he also laid out the battle works. As chief engineer for the Army of Virginia, he laid out the fortifications for General Joseph E. Johnston's (*q.v.*) army at the battle of Seven Pines and the rest of the Peninsular campaign of 1862. Promoted to colonel, he supervised the strengthening of the defenses of Richmond in 1863-1864. On August 28, 1864, he was promoted to brigadier general and was named chief engineer for the Army of Northern Virginia. He was responsible for the construction of the Petersburg defenses. Stevens surrendered at Appomattox and was paroled there. After the war, he went to Mexico, where he was a superintendent and constructing engineer for a railroad which was being built between Mexico City and Vera Cruz. He died on November 12, 1867, at Vera Cruz. *Confederate Veteran*, XXX; Nichols, *Confederate Engineers*; Tyler, *Encyclopedia of Virginia Biography*, III.

STEVENSON, Carter Littlepage (*General*), son of Carter Littlepage and Jane (Herndon) Stevenson, was born on September 21, 1817, in Fredericksburg, Virginia. After graduating forty-second in a class of forty-five from the U.S. Military Academy in 1838, he served as a first lieutenant during the Florida War in 1840. He was married to Martha P. Griswold and had children. During the

Mexican War, Stevenson fought with distinction at Palo Alto and Resaca de la Palma and was promoted to captain in 1847. He served on the Texas frontier, fought in the Seminole War in 1856-1857, and participated in the Utah expedition in 1858-1861. He resigned his commission on June 6, 1861, to enter the service of the Confederacy. Stevenson was promoted to brigadier general on March 6, 1862, and was sent to east Tennessee, where he forced the withdrawal of federal forces from Cumberland Gap and participated in Braxton Bragg's (*q.v.*) Kentucky campaign. On October 10, 1862, he was promoted to major general and was given a division under Bragg's command. After fighting in the battle of Murfreesboro, he was sent to reinforce Pemberton (*q.v.*) at Vicksburg, where he fought at Champion's Hill and commanded the Confederate right. At the battle of Missionary Ridge in September 1863, he commanded a division under General William Hardee (*q.v.*). Stevenson later served under General J. B. Hood (*q.v.*) in the Army of Tennessee, where he was temporary commander of Hood's Corps in the Atlanta campaign and distinguished himself at Resaca and Kenesaw Mountain. He held the center as a division commander at Nashville late in 1864 and ended the war in the Carolinas. Stevenson surrendered in North Carolina and was paroled in Greensboro in May 1865. After the war, he was a civil and mining engineer in Virginia. Stevenson died on August 15, 1888, in Carolina County, Virginia. Connelly, *Autumn of Glory*; Tyler, *Encyclopedia of Virginia Biography*, III.

STEWART, Alexander Peter (*General*), was born on October 2, 1821, in Rogersville, Tennessee, to William and Elizabeth Spylser (Decherd) Stewart. He attended Carrick Academy in Winchester, Tennessee, and graduated twelfth in a class of fifty-six from the U.S. Military Academy in 1842. He was a Presbyterian, a Mason, and a unionist Whig. Like his prosperous father, Stewart disapproved of slavery, although he admitted the constitutional right of secession. He had four sons by his marriage to Harriet Byron Chase on August 27, 1845. Stewart accepted a commission and served in the U.S. Army in Beaufort, South Carolina, before returning to West Point as an assistant professor of mathematics in 1843. Two years later, he resigned from the army to accept a chair in mathematics and natural philosophy at Cumberland University in Lebanon, Tennessee. He held this position until the beginning of the Civil War, except for 1849 and 1855, when he taught at the University of Nashville. He was also a city surveyor in Nashville. When the Civil War began, he volunteered for duty in the Confederate Army. Stewart became a brigadier general on November 8, 1861, and commanded a brigade under General Leonidas Polk (*q.v.*) at Shiloh the following March. After fighting at Perryville and Murfreesboro in 1862, he was promoted to major general on June 5, 1863. He participated in the battles of Chickamauga, Chattanooga, and Atlanta, and on June 23, 1864, he was promoted to lieutenant general and was given command of Polk's Corps in the Army of Tennessee. He spent the final months of the war with General Joseph E. Johnston (*q.v.*) in North Carolina, where he was wounded. He surrendered in North Carolina and was paroled in May 1865. Poor at the end of the war, Stewart taught at Cumberland University in Tennessee and worked as a surveyor from 1865 to 1870, when he moved to St. Louis. From 1870 until 1874, he was associated with the Mutual Life Insurance Company of St. Louis. He returned to St. Louis in 1886, having been chancellor of the University of Mississippi for twelve years. He died on August 30, 1908, during a visit to Biloxi, Mississippi. Wingfield, *General A. P. Stewart, His Life and Letters*.

STRICKLAND, Hardy (*Congressman*), was born in Jackson County, Georgia, on November 24, 1818. He attended local schools. He became a successful farmer in Cumming, Georgia. From 1847 until 1858 he served in the Georgia legislature. He was a secessionist Democrat, who supported John C. Breckinridge (*q.v.*) for the presidency in 1860, and voted for secession as a delegate to the Georgia convention. Strickland, who lived in Cumming, Forsyth County, represented the Ninth Congressional District of Georgia in the first permanent Confederate House, where he served on the Accounts and Patents Committees. He was a Davis administration opponent. He refused reelection and returned to his farm. There is no record of further service to the Confederacy. He lost nearly all of his personal property in the war but worked to recover it after the war ended. Strickland held no public office in the postwar years. He died in Forsyth County on January 24, 1884. Alexander and Beringer, *The Anatomy of the Confederate Congress*; Temple, *The First Hundred Years. . . . .*

STUART, James Ewell Brown (*General*), was born to Archibald and Elizabeth Letcher (Pannill) Stuart on February 6, 1833, in Patrick County, Virginia. His father was a prosperous country lawyer and Democratic congressman. Stuart, the seventh son, was educated in Wytheville, Virginia, and attended Emory and Henry College from 1848 to 1850. He graduated thirteenth in a class of forty-six from the U.S. Military Academy in 1854. Although his mother was Episcopalian, he became a Methodist after a revival experience, but he returned to the Episcopal church in 1859. He was a temperance advocate, deeply religious, and romantic. He was probably a Democrat. On November 14, 1855, he married Flora Cooke, daughter of U.S. Brigadier General Philip St. George Cooke; they had one son and one daughter. After accepting his commission in 1854, Stuart served in Texas and New Mexico on the western frontier with the Mounted Rifles. He was wounded at Solomon's Fork, Kansas, in 1857 and was voluntary aide-de-camp to Robert E. Lee (*q.v.*) at Harper's Ferry in 1859. He was promoted to captain in 1861, and when the Civil War began, he resigned from the U.S. Army to enter the 1st Virginia Cavalry. After serving under General Joseph E. Johnston (*q.v.*) at the battle of First Manassas, he was promoted to brigadier general on September 24, 1861. Stuart soon acquired a reputation for his boldness and skill as a cavalry officer. Before the Seven Days during the Virginia Peninsular campaign of 1862, he responded to Lee's request for information about McClellan's position by riding completely around McClellan's army. After his promotion to major general on July 25, 1862, he commanded all cavalry in the Army of Northern Virginia until his death. His battle credits included brilliant performances at Second Manassas, Sharpsburg, and Fredericksburg in 1862. After General Thomas J. Jackson (*q.v.*) was killed during the battle of Chancellorsville in May 1863, Stuart assumed command of the 2nd Army Corps. His cavalry division fought brilliantly at the battle of Brandy Station, Virginia, in June 1863 but, owing to ambiguous instructions from Lee, was late in arriving on the field at the battle of Gettysburg. Stuart was mortally wounded at the Yellow Tavern during the battle of Cold Harbor in the Wilderness campaign in the spring of 1864. He died on May 12, 1864, in Richmond, Virginia. Davis, *Jeb Stuart: The Last Cavalier*.

SWAIN, David Lowry (*Educator*), son of George and Caroline (Lowry) Swain, was born on January 4, 1801, in Asheville, North Carolina. His father, a hatter and farmer, also served in the state legislature at one time. Having attended Newton Academy, the younger Swain finished his junior year at the University of North Carolina in 1821 before studying law and being admitted to the North Carolina bar the following year. On January 12, 1823, he married Eleanor H. White, who bore him seven children. Swain was a Presbyterian and a unionist Whig. He served terms in the North Carolina House of Commons from 1825 to 1830, when he became a judge of the Superior Court. He was an early follower of Henry Clay. He was elected governor in 1833 and served until 1836. In 1835, he named himself president of the University of North Carolina, a position which he held for most of the rest of his life. Swain, who also taught constitutional and international law and political economics, was not only an able university financier, but he aided such noted historians as Caruthers, Wiley, Wheeler, and Hawks. As a unionist Whig, he opposed secession, but he accepted a commission to represent North Carolina to the Confederate government in Montgomery in early 1861. He managed to keep the university alive both during and after the Civil War. Despite the reduced circumstances of the University, Swain believed that its continuance provided incentives to look to the future of the South. He helped to control Governor Zebulon Vance's (*q.v.*) excesses of states' rights; in turn, Vance wanted Swain to serve in the Confederate Senate. In April 1865, Vance named him a special commissioner to General Sherman to arrange the terms of surrender and to save the university campus from destruction. After the war, Swain consulted with President Johnson on Reconstruction in North Carolina. He died in Chapel Hill, North Carolina, on August 27, 1868. Peele (comp.), *Lives of Distinguished North Carolinians*.

SWAN, William Graham (*Congressman*), was born in Alabama in 1821. Little is known of his early career except that he studied law and moved to Tennessee during the 1840s. He was a lawyer and a secessionist Whig and was married to

Margaret P. Swan. During the 1850s, he was an influential citizen of Knoxville, Tennessee, where in 1854 he was granted the exclusive right to light the city with gas. With his friend, John H. Crozier, Swan controlled and edited the Knoxville *Register* throughout the 1850s. He was a political opponent of William G. Brownlow, also a Whig; when Brownlow's paper became the official Whig organ in the city, the *Register* became a Democratic paper. Swan was also a judge and state attorney general before the war. He was mayor of Knoxville in 1855-1856. When the Civil War began, he enlisted in the Confederate Army as a private but later campaigned successfully for the first and second Confederate House of Representatives as the poor man's friend, using his own paper for publicity. Swan, who supported the Davis administration during both of his terms, was a member of the Inauguration, Military Affairs, and Conference Committees during his first term. He retained his seat on the Military Affairs Committee in his second term, when he also served on the Printing Committee and on the special committee to remove the seat of Confederate government from Richmond. Swan, who himself owned no slaves, vehemently opposed arming the slaves in 1864. He was a bitter enemy of Henry S. Foote (*q.v.*), also a congressman from Tennessee, because of Foote's opposition to President Davis (*q.v.*). After the war, Swan returned to his law practice and business interests in Knoxville. But he moved to Memphis shortly thereafter and died there on April 10, 1869. Green, *Law and Lawyers*; Patton, *Unionism and Reconstruction in Tennessee*; Temple, *Notable Men of Tennessee from 1833 to 1875.*

T

TALIAFERRO, William Booth (*General*), was born to Warner T. and Frances (Booth) Taliaferro on December 28, 1822, in Belleville, Gloucester County, Virginia. He was related to Confederate Secretary of War James A. Seddon (*q.v.*). He graduated from the College of William and Mary in 1841 and attended Harvard Law School. He was an Episcopalian and a Democrat. He had one son by his marriage to Sally N. Lyons on February 17, 1853. When the Mexican War began, Taliaferro became a captain in the 11th United States Infantry and was later promoted to major. Having developed a successful law practice in Belleville, he entered local politics. He was a member of the Virginia House from 1850 to 1853 and an elector for President James Buchanan in 1856. During John Brown's raid on Harper's Ferry in 1859, he commanded the Virginia Militia. When the Civil War began, he volunteered for duty in the Confederate Army. In the early days of the war, he was in the Peninsula as a major general of militia. He served as a colonel of the 23rd Virginia Infantry under General Robert S. Garnett in western Virginia before his promotion to brigadier general on March 6, 1862. Taliaferro then participated in Jackson's (*q.v.*) Valley campaign, was seriously wounded on August 29 at Second Manassas, but recovered to fight at Fredericksburg in December before he was ordered to Beauregard's (*q.v.*) command. In March 1863, he was given command of the District of Savannah, East Florida, and South Carolina. He defended Fort Wagner near Charleston in July 1863. In December 1864, he again held a division command, and in the final months of the war, he guarded the route for the escape of General William Hardee's (*q.v.*) troops. He surrendered around Bentonville, North Carolina, and was paroled in May 1865. He returned to his Belleville law practice and became active in opposition to Reconstruction. Taliaferro was elected to the Virginia House in 1874 and served until 1879. He was a judge of the Gloucester County Court from 1891 to 1897. Taliaferro also was a member of the Board of Visitors of Virginia Military Institute and of the College of William and Mary. He died on February 27, 1898, on his estate, "Dunham Massie," in Gloucester County. Evans, *Confederate Military History*, II; Tyler, *Encyclopedia of Virginia Biography*, III.

TAPPAN, James Camp (*General*), was born on September 9, 1825, in Franklin, Williamson County, Tennessee, to Benjamin and Margaret (Camp) Tappan. He attended Phillips Exeter Academy, New Hampshire, graduated from Yale College in 1845, and read law in Vicksburg, Mississippi, before beginning a practice in Helena, Arkansas, in 1848. He married Mary E. Anderson in June 1854. He developed a successful law practice and became active in local politics. A Democrat, he served in the Arkansas legislature in 1851-1852 and was a receiver for the U.S. Land Office at Helena from 1852 to 1860. When the Civil War began, he joined the Confederate war effort. He entered the Confederate Army as a colonel of the 13th Arkansas Regiment and was a hero of the battle of Belmont, Missouri, on November 7, 1861. After participating in the charge on the "Hornet's Nest" at the battle of Shiloh the following March, Tappan fought in the battles of Richmond and Perryville, Kentucky, during Bragg's (*q.v.*) campaign in October 1862. He was promoted to brigadier general on November 5, 1862. Tappan served under General Sterling Price (*q.v.*) on the Little Rock expedition in Arkansas in 1863, on the Camden expedition, and in the battle of Jenkins' Ferry in the spring of 1864. Later, he also fought at the battles of Mansfield and Pleasant Hill, Louisiana, during the Red River expedition, also in the spring of 1864. He was on Price's last raid into Missouri. There is no record of his surrender. After the war, he returned to his law practice in Helena. Tappan remained out of politics until after Reconstruction. He was speaker of the Arkansas House from 1896 to 1899 and declined a nomination for governor. He died in Helena on March 19, 1906. *Bench and Bar of Arkansas*; *Confederate Veteran*, XXIX.

TATTNALL, Josiah (*Naval Commander*), was born on November 9, 1795, at Bonaventure, near Savannah, Georgia, to Governor Josiah and Harriet (Fenwick) Tattnall. He was orphaned at the age of nine. He attended English schools from 1805 to 1811 and was commissioned a midshipman in the U.S. Navy in 1812. On September 6, 1821, he married Harriette Fenwick Johnson. Tattnall fought at the battle of Bladensburg during the War of 1812, participated in the Barbary War, and was promoted to lieutenant in 1818. From 1818 to 1821, he served on the *Macedonian* in the Pacific squadron. He served on the *Jackal* in 1823-1824 and on the *Erie* in the West Indies in 1828-1829. In 1831-1832, he helped to protect American commerce in the Gulf of Mexico. Promoted to commander in 1838, he was commandant of the Boston Navy Yard from 1838 to 1843. During the Mexican War, he commanded the Mosquito Division which bombarded Vera Cruz. He became a captain in 1850 and served on the *Saranac* during the Cuban insurrection. In 1854-1855, he cruised the Pacific Ocean, and he also commanded a squadron stationed in the East Indies and lived in San Francisco prior to the Civil War. He resigned from the U.S. Navy on February 20, 1861, and entered the service of the Confederate Navy, even though he opposed secession. He was commissioned a senior flag officer and named a captain in March 1861. He commanded the Confederate attack on Port Royal in November of that year. In March 1862, he commanded the *Virginia* (formerly the *Merrimac*), which he destroyed to prevent her capture after the unsuccessful battle with the *Monitor*, an action for which he was censured by a court of inquiry. Tattnall returned to Georgia and commanded the Georgia naval defenses in 1863. In January 1865, he destroyed the entire Union fleet in the Savannah River. He was captured in North Carolina and paroled in May 1865. Tattnall moved to Halifax, Nova Scotia, in 1866 but returned to Savannah in 1870 to become inspector of the port. He died there on November 9, 1871. *Appleton's Cyclopedia of American Biography*; Scharf, *History of the Confederate Navy*.

TAYLOR, Richard (*General*), was born on January 27, 1826, near Louisville, Kentucky, to President Zachary Taylor and Margaret Mackall (Smith). He was sent to study in Edinburgh and in France in the early 1840s. He entered Harvard in 1843 and graduated from Yale College in 1845. He then traveled widely before settling down in 1848 to manage his father's cotton plantation in St. Charles Parish, Louisiana. Taylor married Louise Marie Bringier in February 1851; they had five children. He became active in local politics and, in 1856, deserted the Whig for the Democratic party. Elected to the Louisiana Senate in 1856, he served until 1861. Taylor attended the Charleston Democratic convention and opposed the deep South's disruption of the party. Elected to the Louisiana secession convention, he voted for secession and urged preparations for war early in 1861. When the Civil War began, he joined the 9th Louisiana Infantry and was elected its colonel. He was appointed brigadier general on October 21, 1861, and participated with Thomas J. Jackson (*q. v.*) in the celebrated Valley campaign of 1862. He was promoted to major general in July 1862 and was given command of the District of West Louisiana. He was victorious at the battles of Sabine Pass and Mansfield during the Red River campaign in the spring of 1864. Promoted to lieutenant general on May 16, 1864, he was assigned to the Department of East Louisiana, Mississippi, and Alabama. But Taylor asked to be relieved of his command after he clashed with General Kirby Smith (*q. v.*) over the latter's refusal to follow up the advantages gained during the Red River campaign. After performing badly at Henderson's Hill, Taylor was assigned to the Department of Mississippi, which he surrendered in May 1865. Shortly thereafter he was paroled. After the war he was penniless. He pled the cause of the South during Reconstruction, for a time lived in New Orleans, traveled to Europe in 1873, and returned two years later to live in Virginia. Taylor's memoirs, *Destruction and Reconstruction* (1879), are probably the best written memoirs of any Civil War general. He died on April 17, 1879, in New York City. Johnson, *Red River Campaign*; Taylor, *Destruction and Reconstruction*.

TERRY, William (*General*), was born on August 14, 1824, in Amherst County, Virginia. His early life is unknown. After graduating from the University of Virginia in 1848, he taught school and studied law. In 1851, he was admitted to the bar in Wytheville, Virginia, where he also became a merchant and editor of the Wytheville *Telegraph* before the Civil War. He was a Mason and a Democrat. He was married to Emma Wigginton, by whom he had four sons and three daughters. Terry was a lieutenant in the state militia during John Brown's raid on Harper's Ferry in 1859, and, when the Civil War began, he entered the Confederate Army as a lieutenant of the 1st Virginia Infantry. Promoted to major after the battle of First Manassas, he fought in the Seven Days' battles before being wounded at the battle of Second Manassas in August 1862. He was promoted to colonel in September 1863 and to brigadier general on May 19, 1864. He was again wounded during the defense of Petersburg in 1864 but returned to fight with the Army of Northern Virginia until he was severely wounded during the sortie at Fort Stedman in March 1865. He surrendered and was paroled in the spring of 1865. After the war, he returned to his law practice at Wytheville. He was inactive in politics during the early years of Reconstruction, but served in the U.S. House of Representatives from 1871 to 1873 and from 1875 to 1877. In 1880, he was a delegate to the Democratic national convention. Terry drowned in an accident near his home on September 5, 1888, in Wytheville. Goode, *Recollections of a Lifetime*; Warner, *Generals in Gray*.

THOMAS, Edward Lloyd (*General*), son of Edward Lloyd Thomas, was born on March 23, 1825, in Clarke County, Georgia. His father was from a prominent Maryland family. After graduating from Emory College in Georgia with distinction in 1846, he enlisted in the Mexican War as a private in 1847 and was promoted to lieutenant for his performance at Vera Cruz. Thomas was a Methodist and a secessionist. He married Jennie Gray of Talbot County, Maryland. In 1848, he refused a commission in the U.S. Army to become a planter and country gentleman in Newton County, Georgia. At the beginning of the Civil War, he raised the 35th Georgia Infantry, of which he was colonel. Thomas took over the command when General James J. Pettigrew (*q.v.*) was wounded at the battle of Seven Pines and served under Daniel H. Hill (*q.v.*) during the Seven Days, where he was wounded at Mechanicsville after opening the battle. He was promoted to brigadier general on November 1, 1862, and fought with Lee (*q.v.*) in every battle of the Army of Northern Virginia until the end of the war, including Fredericksburg, Chancellorsville, Gettysburg, the Wilderness, and Petersburg. He surrendered at Appomattox and was soon paroled. After the war, he retired to his Georgia plantation until 1885, when President Cleveland named him to the Land and Indian Bureaus. He was also an Indian agent for the Sac and Fox Agency. Thomas died on March 10, 1898, at South McAlester, Indian Territory, in what is now part of Oklahoma. *Confederate Veteran*, VI; Northen (ed.), *Men of Mark in Georgia*, VI.

THOMAS, James Houston (*Congressman*), was born on September 22, 1808, in Iredell County, North Carolina. Nothing is known of his early life. He moved to Columbia, Maury County, Tennessee, in the 1820s. He graduated from Jackson College in Tennessee in 1830, studied law, and was admitted to practice in Tennessee in 1831. A successful lawyer and large farmer in Columbia, he became a Democratic politician and served as attorney general of Tennessee from 1836 to 1842. He was elected to the U.S. House in 1847 and served until 1851; reelected in 1859, he served until the outbreak of the war. He was a secessionist. In the provisional Congress, Thomas served on the Foreign Affairs Committee. He was a staunch advocate of the Confederate invasion of Kentucky and believed that the state would provide many troops for the Confederate cause. He returned to private law practice in February 1862, but the federal invasion forced him to flee Tennessee for Alabama. When he returned to Tennessee in 1864, the state's unionist officials arrested him for treason. He was held prisoner until the end of the war. After the war, he returned to the practice of law and settled in Fayetteville, Tennessee. He died there on August 4, 1876. Alexander and Beringer, *Anatomy of the Confederate Congress*; Amnesty Petition, National Archives, Record Group #94.

THOMAS, John J. (*Congressman*), was born in Albemarle County, Virginia, August 8, 1813. There is no record of his early life, although there is evidence that he moved to Kentucky sometime in the 1820s. He was a planter in Christian County, Kentucky, throughout the antebellum period. On August 11, 1837, Thomas married Lucy M. Quarles, and they had children. He was a Baptist. From 1845 until 1850 he held a clerkship in the post office department in Washington, D.C. Thomas became active in politics and served in the Kentucky House of Representatives from 1851 to 1853. In the provisional Congress, he served on the Commissary Committee. He supported the Davis administration. He did not stand for election to the first Congress, but he served as an aide to General John Stuart Williams (*q.v.*) until the end of the war. From 1865 until 1873 he was a tobacco broker in Clarksville, Tennessee. Thomas was a tobacco inspector in New York City from 1873 until 1878, when he moved to Paducah, Kentucky. His date of death is unknown, though he lived with a daughter in Camden, Arkansas, in 1895. Alexander and Beringer, *Anatomy of the Confederate Congress*.

THOMASON, Hugh French (*Congressman*), son of Colonel Daniel Thomason and his wife Mary Jane (Denton), was born in Smith County, Tennessee, on February 22, 1826. His father died in 1839, and he moved to Washington County, Arkansas, where he taught school in 1845. He studied law in 1846, and in 1847, he was admitted to the Arkansas bar. Thomason lived in Fayetteville from 1847 until 1861, when he moved to Van Buren in Crawford County, Arkansas. In 1851, he was prosecuting attorney for the Fayetteville Circuit. Originally a Democrat, Thomason joined the Know-Nothings after the passage of the Kansas-Nebraska Act. In 1856, he ran unsuccessfully as an American party candidate for the U.S. House of Representatives. He supported John Bell for the presidency in 1860. He played a prominent role at the Arkansas secession convention in 1861, advocating a convention of all Southern states. During the second session of the state convention, he acquiesced on the secession issue. He was a delegate to the provisional Confederate Congress at Montgomery but was defeated by Felix Batson (*q.v.*) for election to the permanent Congress in 1861 because he had not been an original secessionist. In Congress, he served on the Territorial Committee. After 1861, he took no further part in the war. However, as a state legislator in 1866 he offered a general amnesty bill for all ex-Confederates. He was an Arkansas commissioner to Washington, D.C., during Reconstruction, and he joined the Democratic party in the late 1860s. In 1874, he was a delegate to the state constitutional convention and ran unsuccessfully for Congress. From 1880 to 1886, he was a state senator. There is evidence that he died in Crawford County, Arkansas, sometime after 1900. Shinn, *Pioneers and Makers of Arkansas*; Thomas, *Arkansas in War and Reconstruction*.

THOMPSON, Jacob (*Diplomat*), was born on May 15, 1810, in Caswell County, North Carolina, to Nicholas and Lucretia (Van Hook) Thompson. His father, a tanner, had married into wealth. The younger Thompson attended Bingham Academy in Orange County, North Carolina, and graduated from the

University of North Carolina in 1831. After tutoring at the university, he studied law in Greensboro and was admitted to the bar in 1835. He was an Episcopalian. Thompson moved to Natchez in 1836 and then to Pontotoc, Mississippi, in 1837. He married a wealthy Mississippian, Catherine Ann Jones, in 1838; they had one son. Thompson, who wanted to serve in the state legislature, lost a race for attorney general but became a Democratic leader in northern Mississippi before moving to Oxford, Mississippi, in late 1837. From 1839 to 1851, he served in the U.S. House of Representatives, where he was chairman of the Indian Affairs Committee and supported the Mexican War. He lost a bid for reelection in 1850. In return for his support, President Franklin Pierce offered him the consulship at Havana in 1853 but he declined it. In 1855, he lost a campaign for the U.S. Senate to Jefferson Davis (*q.v.*). From 1857 to 1861, he was secretary of the interior in the Buchanan cabinet. He centralized and personally controlled the management of the department, but his reputation suffered because of fraud in the Indian trust fund. A secessionist, he resigned his cabinet post in January 1861 to organize Confederate troops in Mississippi. When the Civil War began, he entered the Confederate Army as a lieutenant colonel and served as a voluntary aide to General P.G.T. Beauregard (*q.v.*). General John L. Pemberton (*q.v.*) appointed him inspector general of the Confederate Army in 1862. Thompson was captured but released after the battle of Vicksburg. He left the army early in 1863 to become active in the Mississippi legislature, and in 1864-1865, he conducted a secret mission to Canada for President Davis. He sought to cooperate with secret organizations in the western states which conspired against the U.S. government. As part of the Knights of the Golden Circle, Thompson worked with Clement Vallandingham to release and arm 25,000 Confederate prisoners in the North; the scheme did not succeed. Fearing he would be accused as a traitor to the federal government after the war, he did not return to his home. From 1865 to 1867, he traveled in Canada and in Europe. He returned in 1868 to Oxford, Mississippi, and to Memphis, Tennessee, in 1870, where he acquired extensive property holdings. He died on March 24, 1885. Bivins, "Life and Character of Jacob Thompson"; Owsley, *King Cotton Diplomacy*.

THOMPSON, John Reuben (*Diplomat, Editor*), son of John Thompson, a Northern merchant, and his wife Sarah (Dyckman), was born on October 23, 1823, in Richmond, Virginia. He attended the East Haven School in Connecticut and the University of Virginia, studied law in the office of James A. Seddon (*q.v.*) in 1844, and graduated from the University of Virginia Law School in 1845. He was an Episcopalian, a Whig, and a lifelong bachelor. In 1847, his father bought him the *Southern Literary Messenger*, which he owned until 1860. Thompson also practiced law in Richmond in 1853-1854, after which he sailed for Europe and gave the magazine over to his printers. He returned to Richmond in 1856 and continued to edit his magazine. He edited the magazine *Southern Field and Fireside* in Augusta, Georgia, in 1861. He was a secessionist. During the Civil

War, his health prevented military service, but he served as aide to Governor John Letcher (*q.v.*) of Virginia in 1862. In 1863, he went abroad in the diplomatic service of the confederacy. Living in London, he joined the editorial staff of the *Index*, a persuasive and influential Confederate propaganda organ. He also served for a time as editor of the *Southern Illustrated News* and contributed to *The Standard* in Richmond. After the war, he continued to live in London until he became literary editor for the New York *Post* in 1866. In early 1873, he went to Colorado for his health, but he died on April 30, 1873, in New York City. Cullop, *Confederate Propaganda in Europe*.

THORNWELL, James Henley (*Minister*), was born on December 9, 1812, in Marlborough District, South Carolina, to James and Martha (Terrell) Thornwell. His father died while he was young, and his mother raised him in poverty. After attending an old field school and Cheraw Academy, he graduated first in the class of 1831 from South Carolina College. Although his mother was a Baptist, he was converted to Presbyterianism. Thornwell had two sons by his marriage to Nancy White Witherspoon on December 3, 1835. After serving as principal of Cheraw Academy, he became a candidate for the Presbyterian ministry at Andover, Massachusetts, and studied at Harvard before obtaining his first pastorate in Lancaster, South Carolina, in 1835. In 1837, he was a professor of logic and belles lettres at South Carolina College, and after serving a pastorate in Columbia, South Carolina, he returned to the college faculty in 1841. He was involved in the Old-New School controversy within the church, and he supported state aid to education. In 1851, he was minister of a church in Charleston, but he left the same year to become president of South Carolina College. In 1855, he resigned to become a professor at the Presbyterian seminary in Columbia. In 1856, he became an editor of the *Southern Quarterly Review*. By 1860, he had become a strong secessionist. As editor of the *Presbyterian Review* during the Civil War, he defended secession, and he not only directed the separation of the Southern Presbyterians from the Northern, but he called for the organization of a Confederate Presbyterian church. During the winter of 1861-1862, he wrote propaganda to rally popular interest in the war; his tract "Our Danger and Our Duty" was widely circulated in the army. He died on August 1, 1862, in Charlotte, North Carolina. Palmer, *The Life and Letters of James Henley Thornwell*; Silver, *Confederate Morale and Church Propaganda*.

TIBBS, William Henry (*Congressman*), was born at Appomattox, Virginia, on June 10, 1816. He moved to Smith County, Tennessee, when he was a child. A merchant and a farmer before the war, he lived in Columbus, Georgia, in the 1830s and assisted in the removal of Indians from northern Georgia before moving to Tennessee. He was a merchant in Cleveland, Tennessee, in 1860. A Whig and a secessionist, he was a political ally of Isham Harris (*q.v.*) in Tennessee and was considered the leading secessionist in the Third Congressional District, which he represented in the first Confederate House of Representatives. He served on the Joint, Enrolled Bills, and Indian Affairs Committees of the House. Tibbs had trafficked in slaves before the war, and while he served in the Confederate House, he continued to buy slaves for speculative purposes. He also spied and informed on Union sympathizers in Richmond. After introducing and securing the passage of the Conscription Act, Tibbs refused to seek reelection. He entered the Confederate Army as a colonel and saw service in the western campaigns throughout the remainder of the war. After the war, he enjoyed some business success in Dalton, Georgia, and died there on October 18, 1906. *Confederate Veteran*, XV; Hurlburt, *History of the Rebellion in Bradley County*.

TIFT, Nelson (*Businessman*), son of Amos and Hanna Tift, was born in 1810 in Groton, Connecticut. At the age of nineteen, he came to Charleston, South Carolina, where he spent nine years in the mercantile business before founding the city of Albany, Georgia, in 1835. He and his wife, the former Annie Maria Mercer, had seven children. Before the war, he was an extremely successful factory owner in Albany. In 1844, he edited the weekly paper, *The Patriot*, which later became the *Albany Herald*. During the 1850s, Tift was also a justice of the peace. He supported secession and volunteered his business interests to the Confederate cause. The Albany beef and pork packing establishment, cracker and barrel factories, and grist mill, all of which Tift had built, furnished supplies for the hard-pressed Confederate Army. In 1863, he constructed the Confederate ram *Mississippi* at New Orleans under the direction of Stephen Mallory (*q.v.*). Tift believed that it alone could defend New Orleans. He later burned the ship to keep it from falling into Captain David Farragut's hands. He then went to Savannah, where he converted a merchant vessel into the gunboat *Atlanta* in 1864. When the war ended, he returned to his Albany business interests. He was elected to the Fortieth Congress after the war but never served because the federal authorities contested the election. Tift was also a railroad builder in the postwar years and, in 1877, was a delegate to the Georgia constitutional convention. He died in Albany, Georgia, on November 21, 1891. Northen (ed.), *Men of Mark in Georgia*, III.

TOMPKINS, Sally Louisa (*Nurse*), was born on November 9, 1833, in Matthews County, Virginia. She was a daughter of the wealthy Richmond philanthropist Colonel Christopher Tompkins and Maria Booth (Patterson) Tompkins. She was an Episcopalian and she never married. She attended various Richmond private schools for girls. In the late antebellum period, she handled the family philanthropic ventures. During the Civil War, she served as a nurse in the combat field. She also established the Robertson Hospital in Richmond in 1861 and became its director; the hospital treated over 1,500 soldiers. President Davis (*q.v.*) commissioned her captain of cavalry, making her the only woman in the war known to have received a commission in the regular army. After the war, she did charity work and service for the Episcopal church. She died in Richmond on July 25, 1916. *Confederate Veteran*, XVI; Simpkins and Patton, *Women in the Confederacy*.

TOOMBS, Robert Augustus (*Congressman, General, Cabinet Member*), son of the cotton planter Robert and Catherine (Huling) Toombs, was born on July 2, 1810, in Washington, Wilkes County, Georgia. He attended local private schools, Franklin College (later the University of Georgia), and graduated from Union College, Schenectady, New York, in 1828. He studied law at the University of Virginia in 1829, and he was admitted to the Georgia bar in 1830. Toombs married Julia DuBose on October 18, 1830; they had three children. He became a successful lawyer and planter in his native county of Wilkes, Georgia. In 1836 he commanded a company of Georgia volunteers in the Creek War. Toombs entered politics, and in 1837 he was elected to the Georgia legislature; he served from 1837 to 1840 and from 1842 to 1844. In 1844, he was elected as a Whig to the U.S. House, in which capacity he served from 1845 to 1853. He became a staunch defender of Southern interests, soon left the Whig party for a faction of the Constitutional Union party, and negotiated the Georgia support for the compromise of 1850. He was elected to the U.S. Senate in 1852 and reelected in 1858. In 1856 he became a Democrat, and he supported John C. Breckinridge (*q.v.*) for president in 1860. In the secession crisis Toombs supported the Crittenden Compromise of 1860-1861, but, as a member of the committee of thirteen senators for compromise, he realized that the Republican members would support no compromise on any matter concerning the extension of slavery. He advocated secession of Georgia, resigned from the Senate on February 4, 1861, and, as a member of the Georgia secession convention, wrote the address justifying the Ordinance of Secession. Chosen as a delegate to the Montgomery Convention, he actively sought the presidency of the Confederacy. Toombs lost the election to Jefferson Davis (*q.v.*) and accepted the post of secretary of state in the provisional Confederate government. He also helped to shape the permanent Confederate Constitution and was responsible for much of the conservative acts found in the Constitution. Toombs found little to challenge him in office, soon grew contemptuous of the president's handling of the war effort, and resigned from office early in July 1861. He joined the Georgia state militia and was given command of a brigade in Virginia. Daniel Harvey Hill (*q.v.*), his commanding officer, admonished him for faulty use of tactics after Malvern Hill, and Toombs challenged Hill to a duel. Fortunately, the need for service in the front line left no time for Hill to take up the challenge. Toombs performed well at Antietam, even though wounded in the left hand. He demanded promotion and, when refused, resigned from the army. He returned to Georgia, lost an election for the Confederate Senate in 1863, and in 1864, became inspector-general of the Georgia militia. At home when the war ended, Toombs, learned that a warrant existed for his arrest for treason to the federal Union; in May 1865, he ran to Cuba and then to London. He returned home in 1867 and was cleared of any charge, but he never applied for a pardon. He rebuilt his Washington law practice, and became important in public affairs, though he never again held public office. As a Democrat, he was a foe of the Georgia carpetbagger government, and he supported the election of Rutherford B. Hayes in 1877, in hopes of ridding the South of further federal intervention. In 1879, he was instrumental in persuading the state legislature to create a committee to regulate railroad rates. Toombs died on December 15, 1885, in Washington, Georgia. Phillips, *Robert Toombs*; Thompson, *Robert Toombs of Georgia*.

TRENHOLM, George Alfred (*Cabinet Member*), was born in Charleston, South Carolina, on February 25, 1807, to the shipper William Trenholm and his wife Irena (de Greffin). His father died young, and he left school in the early 1820s to join the firm of John Fraser and Company, shippers of sea-island cotton. He was made a partner in the firm, which became known as Fraser, Trenholm, and Company, and in 1853 he was its principal owner, with foreign connections and unlimited credit abroad. One of the richest men in the South, he owned interests in steamships, hotels, cotton presses, wharves, plantations and slaves, banks, and railroads. Trenholm had thirteen children by his April 3, 1828, marriage to Anna Helen Homes. He served in the South Carolina legislature from 1852 to 1856, and he was a Democrat who supported secession. During the war, he put his financial wisdom and business at the disposal of the Confederacy. He financed a flotilla of boats, including the ironclad gunboat *Chicora*, and he ran the blockade to Nassau. Through the Liverpool branch of his firm, he acted as a financial agent for the Confederate government, and he helped to shape Confederate fiscal policy. From July 18, 1864, until the end of the war, he served as secretary of the treasury in the Davis cabinet. Trenholm refused to repudiate the policies of his predecessor as secretary, Christopher G. Memminger (*q.v.*). He opposed inflation and speculation and, after it was too late to affect the finances of the war, recommended interest-bearing Confederate bonds. His tax reforms were too little, and he tried unsuccessfully for a foreign loan. He was arrested after the war and upon his release he returned to his business interests in Charleston. Although he was bankrupt in 1867, he reorganized his cotton brokerage business and remade his fortune. In 1874, he was elected as a Democrat to the South Carolina House of Representatives. Trenholm died on December 10, 1876, in Charleston, South Carolina. Patrick, *Jefferson Davis and His Cabinet*.

TRIMBLE, Isaac Ridgeway (*General*), was born on May 15, 1802, in Culpeper County, Virginia, to John Trimble and his wife. The family moved to Fort Sterling, Kentucky, in 1805. In 1822, he graduated seventeenth in a class of twenty from the U.S. Military Academy and was commissioned in the artillery. He had two sons by his first marriage to Maria Cattell Presstman and, after her death, was married to his sister-in-law Ann Ferguson Presstman. During the 1820s, Trimble surveyed the military roads of Ohio. He left the U.S. Army in 1832 to become a civil engineer for various railroads, including the Baltimore and Susquehanna, the Philadelphia, Wilmington, and Baltimore, and the Baltimore and Providence. In 1860, he engaged in railroad building in the West Indies, and from 1859 to 1861, he was general superintendent of the Baltimore and Potomac Railroad, with headquarters in Baltimore. When the Civil War began, he volunteered for duty in the Confederate Army. Trimble, who has been called Maryland's most distinguished soldier in the Confederate Army, burned the bridges around Baltimore in April 1861 to impede the passage of federal troops toward Washington. He served as a colonel of engineers of Virginia forces and worked on the Norfolk defenses before he was promoted to brigadier general on August 9, 1861. Directed by General Joseph E. Johnston (*q.v.*) to construct batteries along the Potomac River, Trimble led a brigade in Ewell's (*q.v.*) Division during Jackson's (*q.v.*) Valley campaign and during the Seven Days. He helped to defeat General John Pope on August 9, 1862, at the battle of Cedar Mountain, and on August 27, he led two regiments which captured all supplies and ammunition at Manassas Junction. He was wounded seriously a few days later during the battle of Second Manassas, and upon his recovery Trimble took command of Jackson's Division when the latter became a corps commander in October. He led this division at the battle of Chancellorsville in May 1863. Promoted to major general on April 23, 1863, in June he commanded the left wing of the Army of Northern Virginia in the Shenandoah Valley. At the battle of Gettysburg, he commanded Pender's Division and lost his leg after being wounded in Pickett's charge. Trimble was also captured at Gettysburg and was not exchanged until February 1865. He never rejoined the army. After the war, he moved to Baltimore, where he was a consulting engineer until his death there on January 2, 1888. Freeman, *Lee's Lieutenants*, II; Tyler, *Encyclopedia of Virginia Biography*, III.

TRIPLETT, George W. (*Congressman*), son of Hedgman Triplett, was born in Franklin County, Kentucky, on February 8, 1809. Little is known of his early life or education. He married Pamela Head in 1827 and, in 1833, moved to Daviess County, Kentucky, where he became a public surveyor, merchant, and later a farmer. A Whig, he served in the state Senate during the 1850s. When the Civil War began, he volunteered for service in the Confederate Army. As a major, he served on the staff of Generals Helm (*q.v.*), Hanson, and Van Dorn (*q.v.*), all in Kentucky. In 1862, he was chief quartermaster of John C. Breckinridge's (*q.v.*) Corps. When Breckinridge joined the Davis cabinet, Triplett succeeded him in the second Confederate House of Representatives, where he served on the Claims Committee. He was generally a Davis administration supporter. After the war, he was a judge in Daviess County. He died in Owensboro, Kentucky, on June 25, 1894. Alexander and Beringer, *Anatomy of the Confederate Congress*.

TRIPPE, Robert Pleasant (*Congressman*), was born on December 21, 1819, in Monticello, Jasper County, Georgia, to Robert and Elizabeth (Bass) Trippe. He attended Randolph-Macon College and graduated first in the class of 1839 at Franklin College (later the University of Georgia). In 1840, he was admitted to the Georgia bar. A member of the Methodist Episcopal church, he had six children by his 1842 marriage to Anne O'Neal. Trippe practiced law in Forsyth, Georgia, became interested in politics, and served in the Georgia House from 1849 to 1852. He ran unsuccessfully for the U.S. House in 1852 but was later elected and served two terms as a Whig (1855-1859). He was a supporter of the Know-Nothing faction in Georgia. In 1859-1860, he served in the state Senate, preferring that to national political office. At first a unionist and a John Bell supporter in 1860, he supported secession in the Georgia convention. He was a member of the first Confederate House of Representatives. He served on the Commerce, Elections, Quartermaster's, and Special Committees and was generally an administration supporter. He also served in the Confederate Army from 1862 to 1865. After the war, he practiced law in Forsyth and Atlanta, Georgia. He was a founder of Monroe College in Forsyth, and from 1873 to 1875, he was an associate judge of the state Supreme Court. In 1880, he was elected to the state legislature and he served for a number of years. Trippe died in Atlanta, Georgia, on July 22, 1900. Northen (ed.), *Men of Mark in Georgia*, VI.

TUCKER, John Randolph (*Naval Commander*), was born to John and Susan (Douglas) Tucker on January 31, 1812, in Alexandria, Virginia. He was a nephew of Thomas Jefferson. Commissioned a midshipman in the U.S. Navy in June 1826, he was promoted to lieutenant in 1837. On June 7, 1838, he married Virginia Webb, by whom he had three children. Tucker held the rank of commander and was executive officer on the *Stromboli* during the Mexican War. He was promoted to commodore in 1855 and served in both the Home and Mediterranean Squadrons prior to the Civil War. In 1860, he was an ordnance officer at Norfolk Navy Yard. He resigned his commission on April 18, 1861, and volunteered for service in the Confederate Navy. During the war, Tucker commanded Virginia vessels on the James River. In March 1862, he commanded the *Yorktown*, which ran the batteries at Newport News. He also commanded the *Patrick Henry*, which fought in engagements at Hampton Roads and participated in the attack on Drewry's Bluff in late 1862. He was promoted to captain and on May 13, 1863, he commanded the flagship *Chicora* in Charleston Harbor. In April 1865, he participated in the battle of Sayler's Creek. Tucker surrendered at Sayler's Creek, was imprisoned, and was released on July 24, 1865. After the war, he was agent for the Southern Express Company in Raleigh, North Carolina. As a rear admiral in the Peruvian navy, he fought in the war with Spain in 1866. Tucker was also president of the Peruvian Hydrographic Commission and surveyed the upper Amazon River. He died in Petersburg, Virginia, on June 12, 1883. Rochelle, *Life of John Randolph Tucker*.

TURNER, Joseph Addison (*Editor, Businessman*), son of the writer and politician William Turner and his wife Lucy (Butler), was born on September 23, 1826, in Putnam County, Georgia. He attended Phoenix Academy and Emory College, Georgia, but had to leave school in 1846 for financial reasons. After teaching at Phoenix Academy in 1846, he moved the following year to Eatonton, Georgia, where he studied law with Junius Wingfield and was admitted to the bar. He was a Methodist and a Union Democrat. Turner married the wealthy Lou Dennis on November 28, 1850; they had three sons and three daughters. In 1848, he moved to Monticello in Jasper County, Georgia, and wrote for the *Southern Literary Messenger*. The following year he started *Turner's Monthly*, but it soon failed and he returned to Eatonton to farm and to practice law. He spent much time working for and editing insignificant magazines. In 1855, he supported Herschel V. Johnson (*q.v.*) for governor and opposed the Know-Nothings. In 1856, he ran unsuccessfully for solicitor general of the Ocmulgee Circuit, and in 1857, he lost a bid for the state Senate. In 1858, he became anti-Democratic, and in 1859, he was elected to the Georgia Senate. Turner was neither a secessionist nor a submissionist. He edited *The Countryman* in 1862, a newspaper which, with its humor, was well received by the troops. Through his paper, he stressed unity and cooperation in the South, denounced Governor Joseph Brown (*q.v.*), and supported President Davis (*q.v.*). Turner wrote for other newspapers and, in addition, he organized a hat factory and contracted for hat deliveries to the army during the war years. He was denounced by Governor Joseph Brown as a speculator in war profits. After the war, he was ruined financially, and his paper was suppressed by the federal military authorities. He ran unsuccessfully for judge in Putnam County in 1866. He died in Eatonton, Georgia, on February 29, 1868. Andrews, *The South Reports the Civil War*; Huff, ''Joseph Addison Turner's Role in Georgia Politics, 1851-1860,'' *Georgia Historical Quarterly*, L; Huff, ''Joseph Addison Turner: Southern Editor During the Civil War,'' *Journal of Southern History*, XXIX; Turner, *Autobiography of ''The Countryman.''*

TURNER, Josiah, Jr. (*Congressman*), was born to Josiah and Eliza (Evans) Turner on December 27, 1821, in Hillsboro, North Carolina. He attended Caldwell Institute and the University of North Carolina, and in 1845, he was admitted to the North Carolina bar. In 1856, he married Sophia Devereux, by whom he had four sons and one daughter. Turner, who had a substantial law practice in Hillsboro, also served as a Whig in the North Carolina House from 1852 to 1856 and in the Senate from 1855 to 1862. He voted against the calling of the state secession convention, but as soon as his state left the Union, he was commissioned a captain of cavalry. After he was disabled in the battle of New Bern, he was elected in 1863 as a peace candidate to the second Confederate House, where he was hostile to the Davis administration. He vehemently opposed the government's use of slave labor and maintained that Davis (*q.v.*) had become an abolitionist. Yet, he only owned four slaves. He opposed the tax-in-kind, believed Davis incompetent to run the war, and, although in favor of peace, would not accept North Carolina's plan for reconstruction in 1864. He served on the Foreign Affairs and Indian Affairs Committees. When the war ended, he returned to his law practice in Hillsboro. He was elected to the U.S. House but was denied his seat by federal authorities. From 1866 to 1868, he was president of the North Carolina Railroad. As editor of the Raleigh *Sentinel* that same year, he worked for the defeat of the carpetbag government in the state. Although Turner was considered erratic and violent, he was probably the person who was singly most responsible for the overthrow of Reconstruction in North Carolina. In 1876, he gave up his newspaper, and two years later, he lost a race in which he campaigned as an Independent for the U.S. House. He was elected to the state House but was expelled in 1879 because he was accused of having supported the Reconstruction governments. He spent the years of his life after 1884 as a partisan Republican. Turner died on October 26, 1901. Ashe, *Cyclopedia of Eminent and Representative Men of the Carolinas*, III; Hamilton, *Reconstruction in North Carolina*; Yearns, *The Confederate Congress*.

TYLER, John (*Congressman*), son of Judge John Tyler and his wife Mary (Armistead), was born on March 29, 1790, in Charles City County, Virginia. He graduated from the College of William and Mary in 1807, studied law, and was admitted to the Virginia bar in 1809. Tyler was an Episcopalian. He had seven children by his marriage to Letitia Christian on March 29, 1813, and, after her death, seven children by his marriage to Julia Gardner on June 26, 1844. He served in the lower house of the Virginia legislature from 1811 to 1816 and from 1823 to 1825 was a Democrat-Republican in the U.S. House. From 1825 to 1827, he was governor of Virginia. From 1827 to 1836 he was a member of the U.S. Senate, of which he was president *pro tempore* in 1835. In 1829 and 1830, he was a delegate to the Virginia constitutional convention, and in 1838, he was president of the Virginia African Colonization Society. He was elected vice-president of the United States in 1840, succeeding to the presidency upon William Henry Harrison's death and serving until 1845. He then retired to his Virginia plantation. In 1859, Tyler was named chancellor of the College of William and Mary. In 1861, he was president of the Washington peace convention, where he attempted to conciliate both sides on the secession issue. As a delegate to the provisional Confederate House in 1861, he supported secession, and he urged Southern troops to assume the offensive and to occupy Washington. His presence lent stability to the early Richmond Congress. Tyler died in Richmond, Virginia, on January 18, 1862. Chitwood, *John Tyler: Champion of the Old South*.

V

VANCE, Zebulon Baird (*Governor*), was born to David and Margaret (Baird) Vance on May 13, 1830, in Buncombe County, North Carolina. He attended Washington College in eastern Tennessee but left school when his father died in 1844. In 1851, he obtained a loan from David Swain (*q. v.*) to attend the University of North Carolina Law School, and the following year he opened a law office in Asheville, North Carolina. He was a Presbyterian. Vance had four sons by his marriage to Harriet N. Espy on August 3, 1853. A second marriage, to Florence Steele Martin in 1880, was childless. He early became interested in politics. After serving as county solicitor in 1853, Vance was elected as a Whig to the state legislature in 1854. In 1858, he was elected as a Democrat to the U.S. House of Representatives. Vance, a unionist, supported John Bell for the presidency in 1860. He refused to be a candidate for the Confederate Congress in 1861. When the Civil War began, he joined the state army as a colonel. He fought at New Bern, North Carolina, in March 1862 and participated in the Seven Days' battles before Richmond. He was elected governor of North Carolina in September 1862, and was reelected in 1864, retaining the governorship until the end of the war. As governor, he worked hard to maintain the loyalty and fighting spirit of North Carolinians. He refused to follow a course of separate state rights, and he never allowed the suspension of *habeas corpus* during the war. Imprisoned at the end of the war, he was allowed to return to his law practice in July 1865. As a delegate to the Conservative convention, he opposed Negro suffrage. He was elected to the U.S. Senate in 1870 but could not take his seat because of federal disabilities; in 1872, he lost a second bid for a Senate seat. As Democratic governor of North Carolina from 1876 to 1878, he tried to help the Negro. As U.S. senator from 1879 to 1894, he warned against the encroachments of money power in the nation. Vance died in office on April 14, 1894, in Washington, D.C. Dowd, *Life of Zebulon B. Vance*; Tucker, *Zeb Vance, Champion of Personal Freedom*.

VAN DORN, Earl (*General*), son of Peter A. and Sophie Donelson (Caffery) Van Dorn, was born on September 20, 1820, in Port Gibson, Mississippi. His mother was the niece of Rachel Donelson, the wife of Andrew Jackson. He graduated fifty-second in a class of fifty-six from the U.S. Military Academy in 1842 and was commissioned in the infantry. Van Dorn was a Presbyterian. He had one son by his marriage to Caroline Godbold. During the Mexican War, he was breveted captain in 1847 for his gallantry at Cerro Gordo and major for his performance at Contreras and Churubusco. He fought the Seminole Indians in Florida, was wounded during an expedition against the Commanches, and was promoted to captain in 1855 and to major of the 2nd U.S. Cavalry in 1860. Van Dorn resigned from the army in January 1861 and volunteered for service in the Confederate Army. A brigadier general of Mississippi troops at the outbreak of the Civil War, Van Dorn was sent to command the Department of Texas in April 1861. He was promoted to brigadier general in the Confederate Army on June 5 of that year. He commanded Forts Jackson and St. Philip in New Orleans before rising to major general on September 19, 1861, with command of the 1st Division of the Army of the Potomac. In January 1862, he assumed command of the Army of the West in the Trans-Mississippi Department. After he was defeated at the battle of Elkhorn, Arkansas, in March 1862, Van Dorn was transferred to the Army of Mississippi, which he led to disastrous defeat at the battle of Corinth, Mississippi, in October 1862. After this battle, he was court-martialed for neglect of duty, but the charges were disproved. Late in December, Van Dorn partially redeemed himself by a brave and daring defeat of Grant's army at the battle of Holly Springs, Mississippi, which forced a Union retreat from the vicinity of Vicksburg. General Joseph E. Johnston (*q.v.*) then put him in charge of the cavalry in the Army of Mississippi. In March 1863, he routed a federal brigade at Spring Hill, Tennessee. On May 7, 1863, Van Dorn was killed in Spring Hill by a physician who charged that Van Dorn had "violated the sanctity of his home." Hartje, *Van Dorn*.

VENABLE, Abraham Watkins (*Congressman*), was born to Samuel Woodson and Carrington Venable on October 17, 1799, in Springfield, Prince Edward County, Virginia. He graduated from Hampden-Sidney College in 1816 and abandoned his medical studies to enter Princeton College, from which he graduated in 1819. In 1821, he was admitted to the Virginia bar, and three years later, he made his home in Kinderton, North Carolina. He was a Presbyterian and had a son by his marriage. In 1829, Venable moved to Oxford, Granville County, North Carolina, where he developed an outstanding law practice and an interest in politics. He served as a Democrat in the U.S. House of Representatives from 1847 to 1853, losing a bid for reelection in 1852. In 1860, he supported John C. Breckinridge (*q.v.*) for the presidency. He was a delegate to the provisional Confederate House of Representatives. He was generally an administration supporter, though he refused to support government encroachment upon the rights of states. In 1864, he retired from public life and returned to his law practice. Venable died in Oxford, North Carolina, on February 24, 1876. Moore, *History of North Carolina*; Venable, *The Venables of Virginia*.

VEROT, Jean Pierre Augustin Marcellin (*Clergyman*), son of Jean-Pierre Augustin Marcellin Verot and his wife Magdeleine (Marcet), was born in LePuy, France, on May 23, 1805. He was ordained a Catholic priest in 1828, as a member of the Society of St. Sulpice. He attended the college of Annoney and the ecclesiastical seminary of Issy in the 1820s. In 1830, he was sent to Baltimore, Maryland, where he served as a professor of mathematics at St. Mary's College until 1852. In 1853, he taught at St. Charles College in Baltimore and did parochial work. He was named first vicar apostolic of Florida in 1858. During the Civil War, as third bishop of Savannah, he openly defended slavery and greatly influenced Southern Catholics to support the Confederacy through his "A Tract for the Times: Slavery and Abolition" (1861). Unlike most American bishops, who sought to avoid the sectional controversy, he favored the formation of the Confederacy, to which he was later politically committed. He encouraged the Catholics of Savannah to contribute financially to the Confederacy, and he worked hard to persuade people to accept the suffering of war. He also continued to work with the Catholic church in Florida. Verot promoted and paid for the *Pacificator*, a paper which was designed to rally Southern Catholic support for the Confederacy. After the war, he was a delegate to the First Vatican Council and was named first bishop of St. Augustine, Florida, in the 1870s. He died in St. Augustine on June 10, 1876. Gannon, *Rebel Bishop: The Life and Era of Augustin Verot*.

VEST, George Graham (*Congressman*), son of John Jay and Harriet (Graham) Vest, was born in Frankfort, Franklin County, Kentucky, on December 6, 1830. He graduated from Centre College, Kentucky, in 1848 and studied law at Transylvania University in Lexington, Kentucky, in 1853, where he was valedictorian of his class. Vest was a Democrat and an old-school Presbyterian. He had two children by his marriage to Sallie E. Sneed in 1854. In 1853, he came to Missouri, where he was admitted to the bar and began a practice in Georgetown, Pettis County. He moved to Booneville, Cooper County, Missouri, in 1856. Vest was considered the best lawyer in central Missouri before the war. He supported Stephen A. Douglas for president in 1860. In 1860-1861, he served in the lower house of the Missouri legislature, where he was chairman of the Committee on Federal Relations. Although elected to the legislature as a unionist, he became a staunch secessionist after Lincoln's call for troops. He was the author of the Ordinance of Secession at the Neosho convention in the fall of 1861. Vest volunteered for service in the Confederate Army, but he was used exclusively as a military lawyer. In 1862, he served as a judge advocate in Sterling Price's (*q.v.*) forces. He also was an anti-administration member of the Inauguration and Judiciary Committees of the provisional Confederate Congress and a pro-administration member of the first and second Confederate House of Representatives. During his first term, Vest served on the Elections Committee and on the special committee to investigate the outrages of the enemy against the civilian population in North Carolina. In January 1863, Vest favored drafting Marylanders living in Richmond. Vest served on the Conference and Judiciary Committees of the second Confederate Senate, to which he was appointed by Governor Thomas Reynolds (*q.v.*) in January 1865. In the last debates of the Congress, he urged the evacuation of Richmond and the end to needless bloodshed. Vest practiced law in Sedalia, Missouri, in 1865 before moving to Booneville and, in 1877, to Kansas City. From 1879 to 1903, he was a Democrat in the U.S. Senate. He favored the Wilson tariff and opposed the acquisition of Puerto Rico. Vest wrote *Missouri: Its History and Resources*. He died on August 9, 1904, in Sweet Springs, Saline County, Missouri. *The Bench and Bar of Missouri Cities*; French, *Senator George G. Vest*; Stewart, *The History of the Bench and Bar of Missouri*.

VILLERE, Charles J. (*Congressman*), son of the large slaveholder Jules Villeré and his wife Marie, was born in St. Bernard Parish, Louisiana, in 1830. He was educated at St. Mary's College, Baltimore , studied law in New Orleans, and was admitted to the bar in 1849. He was a Catholic and he had one daughter by his marriage. One of his sisters was the first wife of P.G.T. Beauregard (*q.v.*). Before the war, he was a lawyer, planter, and secessionist Democrat in Pointe à la Hache, Plaquemines Parish. He served from 1854 to 1858 in the state legislature. When the Civil War began, he volunteered for service in the Confederate Army and was appointed an aide to General Beauregard. He also served in the first and second Confederate House of Representatives, where he was a member of the Claims, Military Affairs, and Commerce Committees during his first term and of the Impressments and Military Affairs Committees during his second. Villeré was an active, important member of the Confederate House, where he was hostile to the Davis administration and was part of the anti-Bragg bloc. He was Beauregard's spokesman in the House. After the war he was a Louisiana sugar planter. He died in Jefferson Parish on January 7, 1899. Basso, *Beauregard*; Connelly, *Autumn of Glory*; Warner and Yearns, *Biographical Register of the Confederate Congress*.

W

WADLEY, William Morrill (*Bureaucrat*), was born in Brentwood, New Hampshire, in 1812. Little is known of his family or education. Wadley was a self-made man of immense intelligence. He started out as a blacksmith, and he settled in Savannah, Georgia, in about 1834, beginning work on the Central Railroad the following year. A railroad troubleshooter, he soon secured contracts for new roads and earned a reputation as an excellent manager. By 1861, he was one of the leading railroad men in the South and one of Georgia's great commercial developers. Wadley had a son by his marriage to Rebecca Barnard Everingham in the late 1830s. He supported secession. When the Civil War began, he was a railroad quartermaster living in Jefferson County, Georgia. In 1862 he was named military superintendent of all Confederate railroads. Before he became superintendent, he advocated public control of all railroads; in retaliation, Congress refused to approve his appointment. President Davis (*q.v.*) then appointed him to the Iron Commission, a position he held throughout the remainder of the war. After the war, broken in health and finances, he moved to New Orleans. Prior to his death in Saratoga Springs, New York, on August 10, 1882, he was president of the Vicksburg, Shreveport, and Texas Railroad and the Central Railroad of Georgia. Black, *The Railroads of the Confederacy*; Catherwood (ed.), *Life of William M. Wadley*; Northen (ed.), *Men of Mark in Georgia*, VI; Vandiver, *Ploughshares into Swords*.

WALKER, James Alexander (*General*), son of Alexander and Hannah (Hinton) Walker, was born on August 27, 1832, in Mount Meridian, Augusta County, Virginia. Walker was dismissed from Virginia Military Institute during his senior year (1852) at the instigation of a faculty member, Thomas J. Jackson (*q.v.*). (The charges were never aired.) He later studied law at the University of Virginia in 1854-1855, was admitted to the Virginia bar, and began his practice in Newbern, Pulaski County. In November 1858, he married Sarah Ann Poage, by whom he had four sons and two daughters. Walker was an engineer on the Covington and Ohio Railroad in 1856 and commonwealth's attorney for Pulaski County, Virginia, in 1860. When the Civil War began, he volunteered for duty in the Confederate Army. He entered as a captain in the Pulaski Guards of the Stonewall Brigade, headed by his former antagonist. After serving at Harper's Ferry, he was promoted to colonel of the 13th Virginia Infantry upon the recommendation of Ambrose P. Hill (*q.v.*) in February 1862. He participated in Jackson's Valley campaign and the battles of Sharpsburg and Fredericksburg in 1862. On May 15, 1863, at Jackson's request, Walker was promoted to brigadier general and was placed in command of the Stonewall Brigade. He later fought at Gettysburg, Mine Run, Winchester and the Wilderness, where he was wounded at Spotsylvania on May 12, 1864. The following July, he protected Lee's (*q.v.*) communications and supplies in his defense of the Richmond Railroad. He fought at Hare's Hill in February 1865 and led Early's (*q.v.*) Division at Appomattox. He surrendered at Appomattox and was soon paroled. After the war, he farmed and practiced law in Pulaski County. He served a term in the state House from 1871 to 1872 and was lieutenant governor of Virginia in 1877. A Democrat until 1893, Walker became a Republican because of his opposition to government free trade policies. During his two Republican terms in Congress from 1895 to 1899, Walker helped to develop the mineral resources of his state. After he lost a bid for reelection in 1898, he returned to his law practice in Wytheville, Virginia, where he died on October 21, 1901. Couper, *One Hundred Years at Virginia Military Institute*; Evans, *Confederate Military History*, III; Tyler, *Encyclopedia of Virginia Biography*, III.

WALKER, John George (*General*), son of Missouri state treasurer John Walker, was born on July 22, 1822, in Jefferson City, Missouri. He attended Jesuit College in St. Louis during the early 1840s and was commissioned a lieutenant in the U.S. Army in 1846. He was a Catholic and he married Mellissa Smith on July 6, 1856. Walker was breveted captain in 1847 during his Mexican War service. He remained in the regular army after the war, serving in the west and southwest before resigning his commission as captain in July 1861. He entered the Confederate Army as a major of cavalry and was promoted to lieutenant colonel and colonel before rising to brigadier general on January 9, 1862. He served under General Theophilus H. Holmes (*q.v.*) at the battle of Second Manassas and supported Jackson (*q.v.*) at Harper's Ferry, after which he was gallant as a division commander during the battle of Sharpsburg. Following his promotion to major general on November 8, 1862, Walker was transferred to a division command of Texas infantry in the Trans-Mississippi Department. He participated in the Red River campaign in the spring of 1864, and in June of that year, he relieved General Richard Taylor (*q.v.*) as commander of the District of West Louisiana. At the end of the war, he held a division command in the District of Texas, New Mexico, and Arizona. Walker refused to surrender, and after the war, he escaped to Mexico and England. He returned to Winchester, Virginia, in the late 1860s, where he was in the mining and railroad business before going to Columbia as U.S. consul-general at Bogota. Walker was also a commissioner to South America for the Pan-American convention. He died on July 20, 1893, in Washington, D.C. *Appleton's Cyclopedia of American Biography*; Wright, *General Officers of the Confederate Army*.

WALKER, Leroy Pope (*Cabinet Member, General*), was born into the patrician family of John Williams and Matilda (Pope) Walker on February 7, 1817, in Huntsville, Alabama. He attended the University of Alabama and the University of Virginia and was admitted to the Alabama bar in 1837. Walker had two sons by his marriage to a Miss Hopkins in 1843 and, after her death, three children by his marriage to Eliza Dickson Pickett in July 1850. He became an outstanding legislator, a brilliant lawyer, and a champion of Southern rights. He represented Lawrence County in the Alabama legislature in 1843-1844 and Lauderdale County from 1847 to 1851 and in 1853. In 1849, he was chosen speaker of the House. In 1850, he became judge of the Fourth Judicial Circuit, and in 1855, he moved to Huntsville to practice law. A staunch lifelong Democrat, Walker was a delegate to both the Charleston and the Richmond Democratic conventions in 1860 and chaired the delegation at Charleston. In 1861, he served as a commissioner to urge the secession of Tennessee. From February 16 to September 16, 1861, Walker was secretary of war in the Davis cabinet. His appointment was a political one which resulted in confusion and lack of organization and coordination in the Confederate Army. Yet, he did manage to focus on the need for arms and set up Confederate purchasing operations abroad. He equipped the early fighting units, but he had almost no influence on military strategy. Congress eventually turned against Walker and forced his resignation. After his term as secretary of war, he served in the Department of Alabama and West Florida as brigadier general until 1862, when he became judge of a military court for the remainder of the war. When the war ended, he practiced law in Huntsville. In 1875, he presided over the Alabama constitutional convention. He died in Huntsville on August 23, 1884. Harris, *Leroy Pope Walker*.

WALKER, Reuben Lindsay (*General*), son of Meriwether Lewis and Maria (Lindsay) Walker, was born on May 29, 1827, in Logan, Albemarle County, Virginia. After graduating from Virginia Military Institute in 1845, he practiced civil engineering and farmed in New Kent County, Virginia. He first married Maria Eskridge in 1848; following her death, he married Sally Elam in 1857. Walker had a total of eight children by his two wives. When the Civil War began, he volunteered for duty in the Confederate Army. He was elected a captain of Purcell Battery, but in March 1862, he was promoted to major and chief of artillery in Ambrose P. Hill's (*q.v.*) Division. As colonel and chief of artillery of the 3rd Army Corps, he commanded sixty-three guns at the battle of Gettysburg. In February 1865, he was promoted to brigadier general of artillery. Walker participated in a total of sixty-three battles during the war and was acclaimed as an artillery expert. There is no record of his surrender. After the war, he returned to his Virginia farm. In 1872, he moved to Selma, Alabama, where he was superintendent of the Marine and Selma Railroad until 1874. Back in Virginia in 1876-1877, he worked for the Richmond and Danville Railroad. From 1884 to 1888, he lived in Austin, Texas. Walker returned to Virginia, where he died in New Kent County on June 7, 1890. Evans, *Confederate Military History*, III.

WALKER, Richard Wilde (*Congressman*), son of John Williams and Matilda (Pope) Walker, was born on February 16, 1823, in Huntsville, Alabama. He attended Spring Hill College in Mobile and the University of Virginia before graduating with honors from Princeton College in 1841. Walker was a Presbyterian and a Whig. He had three sons and a daughter by his marriage to Mary Simpson. In 1844, he was admitted to the Huntsville bar. In 1845, he moved to Florence, Alabama, where he was district solicitor from 1848 to 1851. Walker, who was also a slaveholding planter, was elected in 1851 to represent Lauderdale County in the state House. Four years later, he was elected speaker of the House.

In 1853, he was the Whig nominee for governor, but he made no contest for the office. Appointed to the state Supreme Court in 1859, he was elected to the position the following year. He was a close political ally of Alexander Stephens (*q.v.*), and he held the opposite political views of his brother, Leroy Pope Walker (*q.v.*), whom he nevertheless supported for the post of secretary of war in 1861. In the provisional Confederate Congress, he headed the Alabama delegation and served on the Commercial and Financial Independence, Foreign Affairs, and provisional and permanent Constitution Committees. Walker was responsible for the provision in the permanent Confederate Constitution which combined the Confederate district and circuit courts. Although he supported the Davis administration in the provisional Congress, he later turned against it. In 1863, the Alabama legislature chose him to replace Clement C. Clay (*q.v.*), a Davis supporter, in the second Confederate Senate. In the Senate, he served on the Joint, Commerce, Engrossment and Enrollment, Judiciary, Post Office and Post Roads, and Public Buildings Committees. When the war ended, he returned to his Huntsville law practice. Federal disabilities kept him from participating in political life. Walker died on June 16, 1874, in Huntsville. Lee, *Confederate Constitutions*; Owen, *History of Alabama and Dictionary of Alabama Biography*, IV.

WALKER, William Henry Talbot (*General*), was born to Freeman and Mary Washington (Creswell) Walker on November 16, 1816, in Augusta, Georgia. His father, who died when William was eleven, was a U.S. senator from Georgia and a mayor of Augusta. Walker attended Richmond Academy in Augusta and graduated forty-sixth in a class of fifty from the U.S. Military Academy in 1837. He was a Democrat who was not a strong secessionist. He had two sons and two daughters by his marriage to Mary Townsend. In 1837-1838, he fought the Indians in Florida, where he was breveted first lieutenant for his performance at the battle of Okeechobee. He resigned from the army after being seriously wounded in 1838 but was reappointed in 1840. Promoted to captain in 1845, he was twice breveted for bravery during the Mexican War, where he was again seriously wounded at Molino del Rey. From 1854 to 1856, he was an instructor of infantry tactics and commandant of cadets at West Point. He resigned his major's commission in the U.S. Army in December 1860. Commissioned a brigadier general in the Confederate Army on May 25, 1861, he saw service in Pensacola and northern Virginia before resigning his commission in October 1861 to join the anti-Davis forces under Georgia Governor Joseph Brown (*q.v.*). He served as major general of the 1st Division of Georgia Volunteers with a command in Savannah before being reappointed to brigadier general in February 1863. Walker served ably at Vicksburg under General Joseph E. Johnston (*q.v.*), at whose request he was promoted to major general on May 23, 1863. His later service was with the Army of Tennessee, and he was killed while supporting General John B. Hood (*q.v.*) at Atlanta. Walker died in Atlanta on July 22, 1864. *Atlanta Constitution*, July 27, 1930; *Confederate Veteran*, VII; Taylor, *Destruction and Reconstruction*.

WALTHALL, Edward Cary (*General*), was born on April 4, 1831, in Richmond, Virginia, to Barrett White and Sally (Wilkinson) Walthall. His father later went bankrupt and moved the family to Holly Springs, Mississippi, in 1841, where young Walthall attended St. Thomas Hall Academy, read law, and was admitted to the Mississippi bar in 1852. He was an Episcopalian and a Democrat. Walthall's marriages to Sophie Bridger in 1856 and, after her death, to Mary Lecky Jones in 1859 were both childless. After practicing law in Coffeeville, Mississippi, from 1852 until 1856, he was district attorney for the Tenth Judicial District of Mississippi from 1856 to 1860. When the Civil War began, he volunteered for duty in the Confederate Army. He entered the Confederate Army as a first lieutenant of the 15th Mississippi Infantry and soon rose to the rank of lieutenant colonel. In 1861-1862, he served under General Felix Zillicoffer in Kentucky, distinguishing himself despite the Confederate defeat at Mill Springs in January 1862. He helped to drive federal troops from Cumberland Gap and served under P.G.T. Beauregard (*q.v.*) at Corinth and under General James R. Chalmers (*q.v.*) at Munfordville. With the organization of the Army of Mississippi, he was promoted to brigadier general on December 13, 1862. At Chickamauga in the late summer of 1863, he held the main road against Union General George H. Thomas, and in mid-November during the Chattanooga campaign, he attempted to hold Lookout Mountain and was painfully wounded in the foot and captured at Missionary Ridge. Walthall was later exchanged. He was promoted to major general on June 6, 1864, and after the burning of Atlanta he commanded Cantey's Division of Polk's Army of Mississippi. He repulsed Sherman at Kenesaw Mountain, lost two horses at the battle of Franklin, and defended the rear of the Army of Tennessee while commanding eight brigades on the retreat from Nashville in late 1864. Walthall, along with Generals Nathan B. Forrest (*q.v.*) and John B. Gordon (*q.v.*), has been considered one of the three most famous and ablest volunteer leaders of the South. He fought in North Carolina in 1865, was captured at the war's end, and was paroled in May 1865. After the war, he practiced law in Coffeeville, where he was a friend of L.Q.C. Lamar (*q.v.*) and strove for good government through active participation in Democratic politics. In 1871, he moved to Grenada, Mississippi, where he practiced law until 1885. During this time, he was general attorney for the Mississippi Central Railroad Company. In 1885, he was appointed to the U.S. Senate. He was elected to that position the following year and he served continuously except for one year. He died on April 21, 1898, in Washington, D.C. *Confederate Veteran*, VI; Evans, *Confederate Military History*, VII.

WARD, George T. (*Congressman*), was born in Fayette County, Kentucky, in 1810. Little is known of his early life, save that he attended Transylvania University in 1824. He was an Episcopalian and a Whig party leader, and he was a slaveholding planter in Tallahassee, Leon County, Florida, before the war. During the 1840s, Ward was a director of the Union Bank of Tallahassee. In 1841, he lost some of his family in a yellow fever epidemic. Ward lost a race for the governorship of Florida in 1852 to the moderate James E. Broome. By 1860, he was a constitutional unionist, and at the Florida secession convention he and Jackson Morton (*q.v.*) unsuccessfully attempted to defer action on secession. In May 1861, the governor of Florida appointed him to the vacancy in the provisional Confederate Congress left by the resignation of James P. Anderson (*q.v.*). Ward was an active member of Congress, serving on the Claims, Military Affairs, Public Lands, and Commercial and Financial Independence Committees. He resigned from Congress in February 1862 to serve in the Confederate Army, where his career was undistinguished. He served under General John B. Magruder (*q.v.*) and as a colonel at Yorktown under General Ambrose P. Hill (*q.v.*). Ward was killed during the Peninsular campaign while commanding the 2nd Florida Regiment at Fort Magruder, near Williamsburg, Virginia, on May 5, 1862. Alexander and Beringer, *Anatomy of the Confederate Congress*; Freeman, *Lee's Lieutenants*, I.

WARE, Horace (*Businessman*), was born to Jonathan and Roxana (Howe) Ware on April 11, 1812, in Lynn, Massachusetts. He attended schools in North Carolina and Massachusetts before settling in Bibb County, Alabama, in the 1820s, where he learned the iron business from his father. Ware had seven children by his marriage to Martha A. Woodruff. Following her death, he married Mary Harris in 1863. After building a water power forge in Bibb County, Ware discovered an iron ore bed in Shelby County in 1840 and developed the cold blast furnace for manufacturing pig iron. He manufactured cooking utensils and stoves and pioneered in the rolling mill business in Alabama. In 1859, he erected a mill for the manufacture of iron bars, and he used slave labor in his factory prior to the war. During the Civil War, he was a major partner in the Shelby Iron Works and managed iron properties in Talladega County, Alabama. The iron works delivered 12,000 tons a year to the government. Despite labor shortages and rising costs, Ware's efforts marked the high point of self-sustained Confederate war production. His property was destroyed by federal troops, but he continued in the factory business after the war was over. In 1872, he formed the Alabama Iron Company. He sold his interest in this business in 1881 to buy the Kelly furnace in Texas, a venture which he sold in 1883. Ware died in Birmingham, Alabama, in July 1890. Armes, *The Story of Coal and Iron in Alabama*; Owen, *History of Alabama and Dictionary of Alabama Biography*, IV.

WARREN, Edward (*Surgeon*), son of Dr. William Christian Warren and his wife, the former Miss Alexander, was born in Tyrrell County, North Carolina, in 1828. After finishing boarding school in Fairfax County, Virginia, he attended the University of Virginia and received his M.D. from Jefferson Medical College, Pennsylvania, in 1851. He was an Episcopalian and a Whig who originally opposed secession. He married Elizabeth Cotton Johnstone in 1857. Warren advocated the establishment of a state medical examining board during his years of practice in his home town of Edenton, North Carolina. In 1854-1855, he practiced medicine in Paris, France, and in 1856, he won the Fiske Fund prize for ''The Influence of Pregnancy on the Development of Tuberculosis.'' Warren was a professor of medicine at the University of Maryland in 1860-1861, and in 1861, he edited the *Baltimore Journal of Medicine*. When the Civil War began, he volunteered his services to the Confederate Army. Early in the war, he cited the need for more medical officers in the Confederate Army. He himself served as North Carolina surgeon general and medical inspector for the Confederacy. As a member of the Confederate States Medical Examining Board, he voted against the relaxation or absence of standards for the practice of medicine in the South. In 1863, he wrote *An Epitome of Practical Surgery for Field and Hospital*, which was used by every Confederate medical officer. After the war, he reorganized the Washington University Medical School in Baltimore and directed the school from 1867 to 1872. In 1872, he helped to found the Baltimore College of Physicians and Surgeons, and the following year he was chief surgeon in the service of Ismail Pasha in the Middle East. Warren died in Paris, France, on September 16, 1893. Cunningham, *Doctors in Gray*; Warren, *A Doctor's Experiences in Three Continents*.

WATIE, Stand (*General*), was born to David and Susannah Oowatie (or Uweti) on December 12, 1806, in Rome, Georgia. He attended the mission school at Brainard, Georgia, and completed his formal education at Cornwall, Connecticut. A Cherokee Indian, he was baptized in the Moravian church. He married Sarah E. Bell in 1843; they had three sons and two daughters, none of whom lived to maturity. In the early 1830s he assisted his uncle, Elias Boudinot, Sr., in editing the Cherokee *Phoenix*. When the Cherokees gave up their Georgia lands in 1835, Stand Watie moved to Oklahoma. At this time, the Cherokee Nation split into two factions, and he became the leader of the minority (later pro-Southern) faction. Watie became a successful planter in Oklahoma. However, following the Confederate victory at the battle of Wilson's Creek, Missouri, in 1861, he convinced John Ross, a leader of the other Cherokee faction, to support the Confederacy. He was in large part responsible for the Cherokee treaty with the Confederacy. Watie volunteered for military service late in 1861. He was first a colonel under General Ben McCulloch, whom he protected from ''Jayhawkers'' in October 1861. He commanded the first Cherokee regiment in the Confederate Army. He fought other Indians at the battle of Chusto-Talasah in December 1861 and participated in the battle of Elkhorn in March 1862. He was a gallant, daring officer whose loyalty enabled the Confederates to retain allies in the Indian Territory. Following his capture of the steamboat *Williams* in June 1864, he was promoted to brigadier general in September. Watie surrendered in late June 1865 and was soon paroled. After the war, he returned to planting in the Indian Territory. He died at Honey

Creek Indian Territory, in what is now Delaware County, Oklahoma, on September 9, 1871. Anderson, *Life of General Stand Watie*.

WATKINS, William Wirt (*Congressman*), was born in Jefferson County, Tennessee, on April 1, 1826. Little is known of his early life, save that he was raised in Boone County, Arkansas. He practiced law in Carrollton, Arkansas, during the 1850s, and he served in the Arkansas Senate from 1856 to 1860. In February 1861, he was a unionist delegate to the Arkansas secession convention. He favored cooperation with the border slave states and, after the firing on Fort Sumter, voted for secession. Elected to the provisional Congress from Carroll County, he served on the Commerce and Inauguration Committees. He then returned to private life and resumed his law practice in Carrollton. In 1866, he was elected to the Arkansas Senate, and he served in the state Senate from 1878 until 1882. He died in Harrison, Arkansas, on January 15, 1898. Thomas, *Arkansas in War and Reconstruction*; Warner and Yearns, *Biographical Register of the Confederate Congress*.

WATSON, John William Clark (*Congressman*), was born in Albemarle County, Virginia, on February 27, 1808, to John and Elizabeth (Finch) Watson. He graduated from the University of Virginia Law School in 1830. On September 8, 1831, he married Catherine Davis, by whom he had eight children, two of whom were killed in the Civil War. Watson was an elder in the Presbyterian church, a Whig, and an uncompromising prohibitionist. He practiced law in Abingdon, Virginia, from 1831 until 1845, when he moved to Holly Springs, Mississippi, to practice law with J. W. Clapp. As a delegate to the Mississippi state conventions of 1851 and 1860, he opposed secession. In the 1850s, he established a newspaper in Holly Springs to promote unionism, and he ran unsuccessfully for the state convention in 1861. Later, Watson acquiesced on the secession issue, and he was elected to the Confederate Senate from 1863 to 1865. His election seems to have been a reaction against the state's Democrats for precipitating secession. An opponent of the Davis administration, his experience and abilities rapidly made him a leader in the Confederate Senate. He served on the Claims, Engrossment and Enrollment, Impressments, Judiciary, and Printing Committees. He rejected the government peace plan for Reconstruction and met with moderates to submit plans for peace based on Southern independence. After the war, Watson declined to assist in the trial defense of ex-President Davis (*q.v.*). He was a member of the Reconstruction constitutional convention. He was active in the overthrow of the Adebert Ames regime and he also led northern Mississippians against the changes in the state constitution in 1868. He supported the Mississippi revisionists in 1875. From 1876 to 1882, he sat on the circuit bench. Watson again practiced law in Holly Springs from 1882 until his death on September 24, 1890. Bettersworth, *Mississippi in the Confederacy*; *Biographical and Historical Memoirs of Missis-*

sippi, Garner, *Reconstruction in Mississippi*; Lynch, *The Bench and Bar of Mississippi*.

WATTERSON, Henry (*Editor*), son of Harvey Magee Watterson and Talitha Black, was born in Washington, D.C., on February 16, 1840. He attended the Protestant Episcopal Academy of Philadelphia during the early 1850s and was privately tutored at home. In 1856, the family moved back to Maury County, Tennessee, where the younger Watterson worked on the family plantation. In 1858, he became a reporter for the *New York Times*, and in 1859, he worked on the *Daily States* in Washington, D.C. Like his father, he was a Democrat and a unionist, and he became a secessionist in 1861. When the Civil War began, he volunteered for the Confederate Army, where he joined the staff of General Leonidas Polk (*q.v.*). He also worked on a pro-Southern newspaper in Nashville during 1862 but was forced to abandon the paper when Nashville fell to the enemy. He became editor of the Chattanooga *Rebel* in early 1863 and wrote editorials attempting to bolster the soldiers' morale by supporting development of a Southern nation. Forced to wander with his press because of attacks on Chattanooga, he became assistant editor of the *Atlanta Southern Confederacy* in 1863. In 1864, he returned to the military as chief of scouts for General Joseph Johnston (*q.v.*), and he aided General Polk at Resaca. Watterson was later transferred to the staff of General John B. Hood (*q.v.*), but he left the army after the fall of Atlanta to become editor of the Montgomery *Mail* in Alabama. On his last wartime duty, a trip to Liverpool, England, to raise money, he was captured. Upon his release in May 1865, he moved to Cincinnati and worked on a newspaper. Two years later, he became editor of the *Louisville Journal* (later the *Courier-Journal*), a Kentucky newspaper which he edited for fifty years. He was one of the great spokesmen for the idea of a "New" South. Watterson married Rebecca Ewing of Nashville on December 20, 1865. As a Democratic member of the U.S. House in 1876-1877, he was an intimate advisor of Samuel Tilden, and he was a major political figure in the administration of Woodrow Wilson. He died in Jacksonville, Florida, on December 22, 1921. Andrews, *The South Reports the War*; Maccosson, *"Marse Henry"*; Wall, *Henry Watterson, Reconstructed Rebel*.

WATTS, Thomas Hill (*Cabinet Member, Governor*), was born to the prominent planter John Hughes Watts and his wife Prudence (Hill) on January 3, 1819, near Greenville in Butler County, Alabama. He attended Mount Airy Academy, graduated with honors from the University of Virginia in 1839, and was admitted to the bar in 1841. He was a Baptist and a secessionist Whig. He had six children by his January 10, 1841, marriage to Eliza Brown Allen. He became a successful lawyer in Greenville and soon entered politics. Watts represented Butler County in the Alabama legislature in 1842, 1844, and 1845. In 1846, he moved his law practice to Montgomery, Alabama. In 1847, 1849, and 1853, he represented

Montgomery County in the Alabama Senate. After serving as an elector for Zachary Taylor in 1848, he became a Know-Nothing and ran unsuccessfully for Congress in 1856. In 1860, he supported John Bell for the presidency and advocated remaining in the Union, but after Lincoln's election he became a secessionist, and by November 1860, he was a supporter of William Lowndes Yancey (*q.v.*). As a delegate to the Alabama secession convention, he served as chairman of the Judiciary Committee and voted for secession. After losing a race to John Shorter (*q.v.*) for governor of the state, he served as colonel of the 17th Alabama Infantry at Pensacola and Corinth. From March 17, 1862, to October 1, 1863, Watts was attorney general in the Davis cabinet. His task was to supervise court proceedings and to audit accounts. He also wrote over one hundred legal opinions for other cabinet members and congressmen. He opposed military interference with the civil jurisdiction of the courts. He lobbied to no avail for the Congress to provide for a supreme court. He resigned as attorney general to become governor of Alabama, feeling closer to his state than to the Confederate government. He was elected and served as governor from December 1863 until the end of the war. As governor, Watts defended states' rights and opposed the encroachment of Richmond on his powers. At the end of the war, he was imprisoned in the North. He had been wealthy before the war, but federal troops had destroyed all of his property and freed his two hundred slaves. Upon his release, he returned to his Montgomery law practice. In 1868, he joined the Democratic party, of which he became a staunch member. In 1880-1881, he represented Montgomery in the Alabama legislature, and in 1889-1890, he served as president of the Alabama bar. Watts also worked for the Baptist church prior to his death in Montgomery on September 16, 1892. Culver, "Thomas Hill Watts: A Statesman of the Old Regime," *Alabama Historical Society, Transactions*, IV; Denman, *The Secession Movement in Alabama*.

WAUL, Thomas Neville (*Congressman, General*), was born in Statesburg, Sumter District, South Carolina, on January 5, 1813. He attended the University of South Carolina but had to leave school in 1831 when his father died. He was a Democrat and a Baptist. He married Mary Simmons in 1835; they had no children. In 1832, Waul headed west, where he taught school in Florence, Alabama, and studied law with Sargeant Prentiss in Vicksburg, Mississippi. Admitted to the Mississippi bar in 1835, he became district attorney for the Vicksburg area the same year. Waul also was elected a circuit judge in Vicksburg and practiced law in Grenada, Mississippi, and in Louisiana. Having made his fortune as a lawyer and cotton planter, he moved to Gonzales County, Texas, in 1850. Sometime during the 1850s, he moved to New Orleans, but by 1860, he had returned to Texas, where he was elected to serve in the provisional Confederate Congress at Montgomery. Waul participated little in congressional affairs but he served on the Commerce and Indian Affairs Committees. He rejected candidacy to the first Confederate House of Representatives in order to join the army. "Waul's Legion" fought at Corinth and participated in Pemberton's retreat and the defense of Yazoo, Mississippi, in 1863, which temporarily saved Vicksburg for the Confederacy. He was captured at Vicksburg in 1863, and upon his exchange, he was promoted to brigadier general in 1864. During the Red River campaign in March 1864, he fought at Mansfield and Pleasant Hill to defend Texas from General N. P. Banks. He was sent to Arkansas, where he fought in the battle of Jenkins' Ferry, in April 1864. There is no record of his surrender. After the war, he was a delegate to the first Texas Reconstruction convention in 1865. Having lost his fortune during the war years, he moved to Galveston to practice law. There, he recouped his losses. He later retired to a farm in Hunt County, Texas, where he died near Greenville on July 28, 1903. *Confederate Veteran*, III; Evans, *Confederate Military History*, XI; Lynch, *Bench and Bar of Texas*.

WELSH, Israel (*Congressman*), was born on January 20, 1822, in St. Stephens, Alabama. He moved to Wahalak, Mississippi, in 1834. Much of his early life is unknown. He eventually practiced law at Macon, Mississippi. He also farmed during the 1850s. Welsh served in the Mississippi state legislature in 1858. He was a delegate to the constitutional convention of 1861 from Noxubee County. After voting for secession, he volunteered for the Confederate Army and served as a private in the 11th Mississippi Regiment. After election to the first Confederate Congress from the Third Mississippi District, he served on the Post Office and Quartermaster's Committees and was an active member of Congress and a general supporter of the Davis administration. In the second Congress, he was on the Pay and Mileage, Post Office and Post Roads, and War Tax Committees. He actively opposed the use of substitutes, supported the democratic election of officers, and was against the impressment of slaves. After the war, Welsh returned to Noxubee County and practiced law. He died there on May 18, 1869. Rowland, *History of Mississippi*, II; Yearns, *The Confederate Congress*.

WHARTON, John Austin (*General*), was born to William Harris and Sarah Ann (Groce) Wharton on July 3, 1828, in Nashville, Tennessee. The family moved to Texas, where his father and uncle fought in the war for independence. (Wharton County is named for them.) Young Wharton lost his father as a child, and he grew up on a large plantation in Brazoria County, Texas. He was educated in Poughkeepsie, New York, and at the University of South Carolina from 1850 to 1852. He read law under William Preston (*q.v.*) of South Carolina before being admitted to the Brazoria County bar in 1854. He was a Presbyterian and a Democrat. He married Penelope Johnson, daughter of Governor David Johnson of South Carolina; they had one daughter. Wharton was sheriff and district attorney of Brazoria County in 1859. He was a secessionist delegate to the Texas secession convention. When the Civil War began, he volunteered for service in the Confederate Army. As captain and later colonel of the 8th Texas Cavalry, he commanded the Texas Rangers following the death of General B. F. Terry. He won distinction at the battle of Shiloh. He was promoted to brigadier general on November 18, 1862, and he distinguished himself at Bardstown and Perryville during the Kentucky campaign. He saw action at the battles of Murfreesboro and Chickamauga before his promotion to major general on November 10, 1863. As a cavalry commander during the Red River campaign in the spring of 1864, he pursued Union general N. P. Banks, but afterward, poor health forced him to retire from field duty. While on leave, he was shot and killed in a Houston, Texas, hotel on April 6, 1865, during a quarrel with Colonel George Baylor. Henderson, *Texas in the Confederacy*; *Confederate Veteran*, V; Rogers, *A History of Brazoria County, Texas*.

WHEELER, Joseph (*General*), was born to Joseph and Julia Knox (Hull) Wheeler on September 10, 1836, in Augusta, Georgia. His father went bankrupt and moved the family to Connecticut before returning to Georgia in 1845. Wheeler attended public schools, the Episcopal Academy at Cheshire, Connecticut, and graduated nineteenth in a class of twenty-two from the U.S. Military Academy in 1859. He was a Democrat and an Episcopalian. He had two sons and five daughters by his marriage to Daniella (Jones) Sherrod on February 8, 1866. Wheeler served with the U.S. Army at Fort Craig, New Mexico, before resigning his commission in the army on April 22, 1861. He was commissioned a first lieutenant in the Confederate Army in Augusta, Georgia, and he served with the artillery at Pensacola and as colonel of the 19th Alabama Infantry at the battles of Shiloh and Perryville prior to his promotion to brigadier general on October 30, 1862. The preceding July, he had reorganized the cavalry of the Army of Mississippi at the request of General Braxton Bragg (*q.v.*). Wheeler, who fought in 127 Civil War battles, including Murfreesboro, Tullahoma, Chickamauga, Dalton, Resaca, Adamsville, Cassville, Kenesaw Mountain, Decatur, Atlanta, and Bentonville, was promoted to major general and cavalry commander of the Army of Mississippi on January 19, 1863, and to lieutenant general on February 4, 1864. By May 1864, he was the senior cavalry general in the Confederate Army. He was wounded three times during the war and had sixteen horses shot from under him. Wheeler was captured in Georgia in May 1865 and paroled the following June. From 1865 to 1869, he was a commission merchant in New Orleans. In 1869, he moved to Wheeler Station, Lawrence County, Alabama, where he was a planter and studied law. He served as a Democrat in the U.S. House from Alabama from 1880 to 1882 and from 1884 to 1899. As a major general of volunteers in the U.S. Army during the Spanish-American War, he commanded a cavalry division in Cuba, and in 1899, he was sent to help pacify the Philippines. He retired from the army in 1900 and was thereafter a historian. Wheeler, who published *Cavalry Tactics* (1863) during the Civil War, was often unsuccessful as an independent commander, but when protecting and covering a main army he excelled any other Confederate cavalryman. He died on January 25, 1906, in Brooklyn, New York. Dyer, *"Fightin' Joe" Wheeler*.

WHITE, Daniel Price (*Congressman*), was born on November 26, 1814, in Greensburg, Green County, Kentucky, to William P. and Judith (Taylor) White. He attended Kentucky's Centre College and Transylvania University during the 1830s and began a medical practice in Greensburg in 1837. He soon became a well-known and successful doctor. White had three sons and a daughter by his marriage to Nancy F. Clark. After twelve years as a doctor, he abandoned medicine for agricultural and business pursuits. White became active in local politics, and in 1847, he entered the state legislature. Reelected to many terms as a Democrat, by 1857, he had been named speaker of the House. Although he was a secessionist, White supported Stephen A. Douglas for president in 1860. He was elected to the provisional Confederate Congress and served until 1862. He supported an invasion of Kentucky but did little else in Congress. White returned to Kentucky when his term ended and again took up medicine. He practiced there and for a time in Tennessee throughout the remainder of the war. When the war ended, White moved to Louisville, Kentucky, where he became a partner in the tobacco firm of Grover, Clark, and Company from 1867 to 1875. He died there on April 12, 1890. *Encyclopedia of Kentucky*; Howe and Scott, *Green County Historical Fort Book*.

WHITFIELD, Robert Henry (*Congressman*), was born in Nansemond County, Virginia, on September 14, 1814. He received a law degree from the University of Virginia in 1839. He was a lawyer and farmer from Smithfield, Isle of Wight County, Virginia; he was married to Rebecca Ann Peebles, and they had five children. In 1861, he was a unionist delegate to the Virginia secession convention, but he finally voted for the Ordinance of Secession after Lincoln called for troops. There is no record of his early war service. Elected to the second Confederate House of Representatives from Virginia's Second Congressional District, he served on the Naval Affairs and Patents Committees. Whitfield took many leaves of absence before resigning his office on March 7, 1865. He lost most of his financial assets after the war and was in poor health in 1866. He died in Smithfield on October 5, 1868. Alexander and Beringer, *The Anatomy of the Confederate Congress*; Warner and Yearns, *Biographical Register of the Confederate Congress*.

WHITING, William Henry Chase (*General*), son of Levi and Mary A. Whiting, was born on March 22, 1824, in Biloxi, Mississippi. He graduated from Boston High School in Massachusetts, was first in his class at Georgetown College, D.C., in 1840, and graduated first in a class of forty-one at the U.S. Military Academy in 1845, with the highest grade average of any cadet up to that time. He was a Catholic. He had one son by his marriage to Kate D. Walker. From 1845 to 1856, he supervised river and harbor fortifications with the Army Corps of Engineers in California, Florida, Georgia, and North Carolina. He was promoted to first lieutenant in 1853 and to captain in 1858. From 1856 to 1861, he worked on improvements of the Savannah River. Whiting resigned his commission on February 20, 1860, to enter the service of the Confederate Army. He entered as a major of engineers in the defense of Charleston and was General Joseph E. Johnston's (*q.v.*) chief of engineers at the battles of First Manassas and Seven Pines. He was promoted to brigadier general on August 28, 1861. He assisted Thomas J. Jackson (*q.v.*) in the Valley campaign of 1862, where he commanded Hamilton P. Bee's (*q.v.*) Brigade and provided successful strategy for the campaign against McClellan. After the Seven Days, Whiting was transferred to North Carolina, where he made Fort Fisher at the mouth of the Cape Fear River the strongest in the Confederacy. He was promoted to major general on February 28, 1863, but his military career came to a standstill when, following an exceptionally bad showing at Port Walthall Junction during the fighting around Petersburg in the summer of 1864, he was accused of being drunken. He was transferred to a command in North Carolina. During his defense of Fort Fisher in January 1865, he was mortally wounded and captured during hand-to-hand combat. He died on Governor's Island, New York, on March 10, 1865. Freeman, *Lee's Lieutenants*, I; Nichols, *Confederate Engineers*.

WICKHAM, Williams Carter (*Congressman, General*), son of William Fanning Wickham, an Episcopal clergyman, and his wife Ann (Carter), was born on September 21, 1820, in Richmond, Virginia. He studied law at the University of Virginia in the early 1840s and was admitted to the Virginia bar in 1842. He married Lucy Penn Taylor on January 11, 1848; they had two sons. Wickham developed a good law practice and also farmed his father's estate in Hanover County. He became interested in politics and was elected in 1849 to the Virginia House of Burgesses, where he became an influential Whig leader. In the late 1850s, he left the Virginia legislature to become presiding judge of the county court of Hanover. In 1859, he was elected to the state Senate. As a member of the Virginia secession convention, he opposed secession and voted against the Ordinance of Secession. But when the Civil War began, he formed a cavalry company which fought at First Manassas. While a colonel of cavalry in May 1862, he was wounded in the Williamsburg Peninsula campaign. Upon his recovery, he fought under General J.E.B. Stuart (*q.v.*) at the battles of Second Manassas, Sharpsburg, Fredericksburg, Boonsboro, Chancellorsville, and Gettysburg. On September 1, 1863, he was promoted to brigadier general of cavalry, and he went on to participate in the battles of Brandy Station, Spotsylvania Court House, Cold Harbor, and Yellow Tavern. After he was elected to the second Confederate Congress from Virginia's Third Congressional District, he resigned from the army in 1864. While in Congress, he worked for the success of the Hampton Roads Peace Conference. He served well on conferences and special committees and, as a member of the Military Affairs Committee, was especially sensitive to securing military promotions for deserving leaders. He generally opposed the Davis administration. At the end of the war, he wanted to restore friendly relations between the sections, to reorganize labor in the South, and to persuade the South to accept its defeat. Wickham moved to Richmond in May 1865 in order to develop a law practice. He became estranged from his old associates in April 1865, and he joined the Republican party. He was president of the Virginia Central Railroad in 1865 and of the Chesapeake and Ohio Railroad in 1868, the year he worked for the election of U.S. Grant. In 1880, he refused Rutherford B. Hayes' offer to become secretary of the navy. An opponent of the Readjusters, Wickham served in the Virginia Senate from 1883 to 1888, retaining his political independence throughout. He died in Richmond on June 23, 1888. Freeman, *Lee's Lieutenants*, III; Maddex, *The Virginia Conservatives*; Woodward, *Origins of the New South*.

WIGFALL, Louis Trezevant (*Congressman*), was born to the planter Levi Durand Wigfall and his wife Eliza (Thompson) on April 21, 1816, in Edgefield District, South Carolina. He attended the University of Virginia in 1834-1835 and graduated from South Carolina College in 1837. In 1835, he fought in the Seminole War as a volunteer lieutenant. After studying law at the University of Virginia, he was admitted to the Edgefield, South Carolina, bar in 1839. Wigfall was an Episcopalian and a Democrat. He had five children by his marriage to Charlotte Maria Cross. Wigfall fought political duels with Thomas Bird and Preston Brooks, as a result of which he moved to Marshall, Texas, in 1848. The following year, he was elected to the Texas House, and in 1850, he advocated secession in Texas, as he had when he was a "Bluffton Boy" in his native South Carolina. From 1857 to 1860, he served as a Southern Rights Democrat in the Texas Senate, and from 1859 to 1861, he served as a Democrat in the U.S. Senate, where he delivered his famous Southern Address in December 1860. Wigfall was a bitter enemy of Sam Houston. He resigned from the Senate in March 1861 and volunteered for service in the Confederate Army. He had previously urged the Confederate government to take Fort Sumter; upon his resignation he went to Charleston for the bombardment of Fort Sumter. On October 21, 1861, he was commissioned a brigadier general commanding the "Texas Brigade" of the Confederate Army. He resigned his commission in early 1862 to enter the provisional Congress. As a Confederate senator from Texas from 1862 to 1865, he believed in strong military measures, supported conscription, upheld impressment, and voted to suspend the writ of *habeas corpus*. Although he was legalistic in outlook, he opposed the formation of the Confederate States Supreme Court. He became a bitter opponent of President Davis (*q.v.*) and supported the military cause of General Joseph E. Johnston (*q.v.*). He was a member of the Abingdon-Columbia bloc and a supporter of General P.G.T. Beauregard (*q.v.*) for commander of the Army in the West. Scholars maintain that he supported the western bloc because of his fierce hostility to the blunders of the Davis administration. In the Senate, he served on the Foreign Affairs, Military Affairs, Territories, and Joint Committees. He was one of the most powerful politicians in Congress. From 1865 to 1872, Wigfall lived in London. In 1873, he moved to Baltimore and, in 1874, to Galveston, Texas, where he died on February 18, 1874. Connelly and Jones, *The Politics of Command*; King, *Louis T. Wigfall*.

WILCOX, Cadmus Marcellus (*General*), was born on May 29, 1824, in Wayne County, North Carolina, to Reuben and Sarah (Garland) Wilcox. His family moved to Tipton County, Tennessee, when he was two, and he attended Cumberland College and the University of Nashville in Tennessee from 1840 to 1842. He graduated fifty-fourth in a class of fifty-nine from the U.S. Military Academy in 1846. He was a Democrat and a lifelong bachelor. Wilcox went to Monterrey as an aide to Major General John A. Quitman during the Mexican War. Later promoted to first lieutenant for his gallantry at Chapultepec and Mexico City, he was promoted to first lieutenant in 1851. From 1852 to 1857, he was assistant instructor of military tactics at West Point. He took a year's furlough to Europe for health reasons and published *Rifles and Rifle Practice* (1859) before returning to active duty as a captain in New Mexico in 1860. Although he was a unionist, he resigned from the U.S. Army on June 9, 1861, and entered the Confederate Army as colonel of the 9th Alabama Regiment. He was promoted to brigadier general on October 21, 1861. Wilcox rendered important service at the battle of Williamsburg, led three brigades at Gaines' Mill, and was a hero at Frayser's Farm during the Seven Days. He also fought at Seven Pines, Chancellorsville, and Gettysburg before his promotion to major general on August 13, 1863. Thereafter, he participated in all major engagements of the Army of Northern Virginia to Appomattox. His retention of Fort Gregg at the end of the war enabled Lee (*q.v.*) to hold the interior line below Petersburg. He surrendered at Appomattox and was soon paroled. After the war, he declined a command in the Egyptian army. He lived in Washington, D.C., where he held various government posts, including chief of the railroad division of the U.S. Land Office in 1886. Wilcox died on December 2, 1890, in Washington, D.C. Evans, *Confederate Military History*, VII; Freeman, *Lee's Lieutenants*, II.

WILCOX, John Alexander (*Congressman*), was born on April 18, 1819, in Greene County, North Carolina. Little is known of his family. He attended common schools and moved to Tennessee and later, in the 1840s, to Aberdeen, Mississippi. Wilcox was secretary of the Mississippi Senate in 1846 and a lieutenant colonel in the Mexican War. He was elected on the Union Whig ticket from Mississippi to the U.S. House of Representatives in 1851, but he lost a campaign for reelection the following year. In 1853, he moved to San Antonio, Bexar County, Texas, where he practiced law for some years. He voted for secession at the state convention, where he also helped to prepare the Ordinance of Secession and was a member of the Committee on the (Secession) Address. In the first Confederate House of Representatives, he served the First Texas Congressional District and was a member of the Military Affairs, Inauguration, Enrolled

Bills, and Territories and Public Lands Committees. He was generally a Davis administration supporter. Wilcox also served as a colonel on the staff of General John B. Magruder (*q.v.*) and participated in the retaking of Galveston on New Year's Day 1863. When he died of apoplexy on February 7, 1864, in Richmond, Virginia, he was so poor that the Confederate Congress had to pay for his funeral. Johnson, *Texans Who Wore the Grey*.

WILKES, John (*Businessman*), was born to Charles and Jane Jeffrey (Renwick) Wilkes on March 31, 1827, in New York City. He was sent to sea as a boy. He graduated first in the class of 1847 from the U.S. Naval Academy. In April 1854, he married Jane Renwick Smedburg, by whom he had nine children. During the Mexican War, Wilkes served on the cruiser *Mississippi*, which participated in attacks on the Brazos and at Vera Cruz. After traveling to China and Manila, he returned to the United States in 1852. He resigned his commission in early 1853. In December 1853, he moved to Charlotte, North Carolina, where he bought mining and milling property. Five years later, he owned the Mecklenburg Flour Mills. Wilkes, who in 1860 was a member of the Home Guards and part of a local vigilance committee, gave one of his mills to supply the army in Virginia. He also built the Atlantic Coast Line Railroad from Greensboro, North Carolina, to Danville, Virginia, and he began a railroad from Raleigh to Lockville. In 1859, he bought the Mecklenburg Iron Works, which he gave to the Confederacy two years later. Wilkes was also a large supplier of the Confederate Navy. His entire fortune, expertise, and business interests in foodstuffs and clothing were given over to the war effort. Although he never held office in the Confederacy, from the beginning of the war he served as a financial advisor to the state government officials of North Carolina. After the war, he received a federal pardon and tried to rebuild his fortune. He obtained a charter for the First National Bank of Charlotte, of which he was president from 1865 to 1869. In 1869, he was ruined financially by a venture into manufacturing, the Rock Island Woolen Mills, and he returned to the Iron Works. An alderman and a vestryman of St. Peter's Parish in Charlotte, he represented the diocese of North Carolina in the general convention of the Episcopal church in 1886 and for some time thereafter. He probably died in Charlotte sometime around 1900. Ashe, *Cyclopedia of Eminent and Representative Men of the Carolinas*.

WILKES, Peter Singleton (*Congressman*), was born in Maury County, Tennessee, in 1827. He lived in Springfield, Greene County, Missouri, before the Civil War. There is some evidence that he practiced law. In 1860, he was a John C. Breckinridge (*q.v.*) Democrat and a secessionist. When the Civil War began, he volunteered as a private in the 1st Missouri Infantry. No record exists of his military career. He was elected to the second Confederate House from Missouri's Sixth Congressional District, and he served on the Indian Affairs and Post Office Committees. He was also a member of the select committee on the claims of the states in February 1865. Wilkes generally supported the Davis administration. He never returned to Missouri. Wilkes moved to Stockton, California, and became a successful lawyer. He died there on January 2, 1900. Kirkpatrick, "Missouri's Delegation in the Confederate Congress," *Civil War History*, V; Warner and Yearns, *Biographical Register of the Confederate Congress*.

WILKINSON, John (*Businessman, Naval Captain*), son of Jesse Wilkinson, was born on November 6, 1821, in Norfolk, Virginia, where his father was a commodore in the U.S. Navy. He was commissioned a midshipman in 1837 and attended the Philadephia Naval School. He was a bachelor. Wilkinson served on the *Oregon* and the *Portsmouth* and, in 1846, on the *Saratoga* in the Gulf of Mexico. He was promoted to master in June 1850 and to lieutenant later the same year. In 1858-1859, he served in the Paraguay expedition on the *Southern Star*. He resigned his commission on April 6, 1861, to serve in the Confederacy. Wilkinson began his Confederate naval career as a lieutenant on duty at Fort Powhatan. In the spring of 1862, he was taken prisoner at New Orleans while executive officer on the ram *Louisiana*. He was later exchanged. On August 12 of the same year, he went to England, where he bought war munitions and machinery for the Confederacy. He also purchased the steamer *Giraffe*, which he renamed the *Robert E. Lee* and used to run the blockade. Wilkinson made repeated voyages between Wilmington, North Carolina, and Bermuda, exchanging cotton for arms and ammunition. In October 1863, he attempted unsuccessfully to release Confederate prisoners from Johnson's Island, and he later engaged in Canadian intrigue to free more Confederate prisoners. As captain in command of the ironclad *Albemarle* and later the *Chickamauga* in 1864, he destroyed merchant vessels, and in 1865, he commanded the blockade runner *Chamelon*. There is no record of his surrender. After the war, he was a businessman in Nova Scotia before returning to the family homestead in Amelia County, Virginia, in 1874. In 1877, he published *Narrative of a Blockade Runner*. Wilkinson died on December 29, 1891, in Annapolis, Maryland. Tyler, *Encyclopedia of Virginia Biography*, III; Vandiver (ed.), *Confederate Blockade Running Through Bermuda*.

WILLIAMS, James (*Editor, Diplomat*), was born to Ethelred and Mary (Copeland) Williams on July 1, 1796, in Grainger County, Tennessee. Little is known of his early life. He married Lucy Graham, by whom he had three children. In 1841, Williams was editor of the Knoxville *Post* in Knoxville, Tennessee. Two years later, he was elected to a term as a Whig in the Tennessee legislature. As captain of the steamboat *Chattanooga*, he engaged in river trade in 1850. In 1851, he moved to Chattanooga, where he owned the Tennessee River Mining Manufacturing and Navigation Company. In 1852, he helped to organize the Knoxville and Charleston Railroad Company, and in 1856, he moved to Nashville, Tennessee, where he published *Letters of an Old Whig*. After becoming a Democrat in 1856, he served as U.S. minister to Turkey from 1857 to 1861. He returned to Tennessee in 1861 in order to oppose secession. Yet, when the Civil War began, he volunteered for service in the Confederate government. President Davis (*q. v.*) sent him to London in 1861 where he sold Confederate bonds and wrote pro-Southern articles in the *Times* and the *Index*. In 1861, he published *Letters on Slavery from the Old World*, and in 1862, he published *The South Vindicated* in London. In 1863, as a result of diplomatic negotiations with the French government, he recommended that President Davis send a minister to Mexico. But, for all his good relations with Maximilian and Napoleon, he could never gain French recognition of the Confederacy. In 1864, he also went to Germany on behalf of the Confederate government. Williams also wrote *The Rise and Fall of the Model Republic* (1863). When the war ended, he remained in Germany. He died in Gratz, Austria, on April 10, 1869. Cullop, *Confederate Propaganda in Europe*; Hale and Merritt, *A History of Tennessee*, III; Owsley, *King Cotton Diplomacy*.

WILLIAMS, John Stuart (*General*), was born on July 10, 1818, in Mount Sterling, Montgomery County, Kentucky, to General Samuel L. Williams and his wife Frances (Clarke). He attended the common schools of Kentucky and received his B.A. and his M.A. degrees from Miami University in Oxford, Ohio, in 1838 and 1844, respectively. He studied law and, in 1840, was admitted to the bar in Paris, Kentucky, where he practiced for five years. He was a Methodist and a Whig. Williams married Ann Harrison in 1842. During the Mexican War, he served as colonel of the 4th Regiment Kentucky Volunteers and was cited for his bravery at Cerro Gordo. Later, he raised livestock, became interested in politics, and served in the Kentucky House in 1851 and 1853. He opposed secession. When the Civil War began, Williams enlisted as colonel of the 5th Kentucky Volunteers, and in April 1862, he was promoted to brigadier general under Humphrey Marshall (*q.v.*). In 1863, he commanded the Department of East Tennessee which stopped the advance of General Ambrose Burnside. In November 1863, he was relieved of command because of illness. He later assisted in defeating a union attack on the salt works at Abingdon, Virginia. In 1864, he served in Joseph Wheeler's (*q.v.*) Cavalry Corps. Williams surrendered at Appomattox and was soon paroled. After the war, he farmed in Winchester, Kentucky, and worked as a railroad promoter. In 1873 and 1875, having joined the Democratic party, he was elected to the state legislature, but he lost a bid for the governorship in 1875. From 1879 to 1885, he served as a Democrat in the U.S. Senate, but was defeated for reelection. Williams died in retirement on July 17, 1898, in Mount Sterling, Kentucky. *Appleton's Cyclopedia of American Biography*; Boyd (comp.), *Some Marriages in Montgomery County, Kentucky Before 1864*; Evans, *Confederate Military History*.

WILLIAMS, Thomas Henry (*Physician*), son of Isaac F. and Rebecca R. (Stuart) Williams, was born in Dorchester County, Maryland, in 1822. He studied medicine under Alexander Hamilton Bagby and graduated from the University of

Maryland in 1849. He joined the U.S. Army and was stationed in the West as an assistant surgeon for some years. When the Civil War began, he resigned from the army and joined the Confederate war cause. He was medical director and inspector of hospitals in Virginia in 1861. Besides serving as assistant to the surgeon general of the Confederate Army, Williams organized the Confederate Medical Corps and set up most of the large hospitals in the Confederacy. While medical director of the Army of Northern Virginia in 1863, he worked to overcome the disastrous civilian treatment of wounded federal soldiers. He sought better communications between the commanders in the field and the Medical Corps on troop movements and when the enemy was to be engaged so as to better prepare for the treatment of casualties. He claimed that the inability to coordinate staff and line decisions cost many lives. After the war, he practiced medicine in Richmond, Virginia, before moving to Cambridge, Maryland, in the 1880s, where he was active in organizing the Cambridge Hospital. He died in Cambridge on September 22, 1904. Cunningham, *Doctors in Gray*; Kelly and Burrage (eds.), *American Medical Biographies*.

WILSON, William Sidney (*Congressman*), was born into the prominent family of Ephraim Wilson on November 7, 1816, in Snow Hill, Maryland. Little is known of his early career. He was a Democrat and a lifelong bachelor. He became a lawyer in Port Gibson, Claiborne County, Mississippi, sometime during the 1840s and served in the state legislature from 1858 to 1861. He was a secessionist. As a delegate to the provisional Confederate Congress at Montgomery, he served on the Engrossment and Patents Committees before resigning on April 29, 1861, to enter the Confederate Army. Wilson was a lieutenant colonel in the 2nd Regiment of Mississippi Infantry. He saw much action in the Gulf Coast operations and in Virginia. A Mississippi town was named in his honor. He was mortally wounded at the battle of Sharpsburg and died on November 3, 1862. Handy, *A Genealogical Compilation of the Wilson Family*; Lee, *Confederate Constitutions*.

WINDER, John Henry (*General*), was born to General William H. Winder, who had fought in the War of 1812, and his wife Gertrude (Polk) on February 21, 1800, in Somerset County, Maryland. After graduating eleventh in a class of thirty from the U.S. Military Academy in 1820, he served at Fort McHenry and on the Florida frontier before resigning his army commission in 1823. He was married to Elizabeth Shepherd in 1823, and after her death, to Mrs. Catherine A. Cox. Winder returned to the army in 1827 as a second lieutenant of artillery. Promoted to first lieutenant in 1833, he served in the Seminole War and rose to captain in 1842. During the Mexican War, he was breveted twice for gallantry. He was an instructor at West Point during Jefferson Davis's (*q.v.*) student days, and he retained Davis's respect despite severe criticism of Winder's later policies. In November 1860, he was promoted to major of artillery in the U.S. Army, but he resigned to enter the Confederate Army. On June 21, 1861, he was commissioned brigadier general in command of Libby and Belle Isle military prisons in Richmond. By 1864, he commanded all prisons in Alabama and Georgia as well, and in November of that year, he was named commissary general of all prisons east of the Mississippi River. As provost marshal general of Richmond, Winder was also responsible for maintaining order in the city, for the arrest and return of deserters, and, for a time, for fixing commodity prices in the city. He was much criticized for alleged cruelty to prisoners and for the poor conditions of most Confederate prisons. Winder died from anxiety and fatigue on February 7, 1865, in Florence, South Carolina. Charleston *Daily Courier*, February 9, 1865; Scharf, *The Chronicles of Baltimore*.

WISE, Henry Alexander (*General*), was born on December 3, 1806, in Drummondtown, Accomec County, Virginia, to Major John Wise and his wife Sarah Corbin (Cropper). He was a descendant of John Wise, who had come to Virginia in 1650. His father, a lawyer and planter, had been a Federalist speaker of the Virginia Senate. Wise, orphaned at the age of six, was later adopted by his father's relatives. He attended Margared Academy in Virginia, graduated first in his class from Washington College (Pennsylvania) in 1825, and studied law with Henry St. George Tucker. He was a Presbyterian and a temperance Democrat, except for the years 1840-1844 when he supported the Whigs. Wise had a total of seven children by his marriages to Ann Eliza Jennings on October 8, 1828, to Sarah Sargeant in November 1840, and to Mary Elizabeth Lyons in November 1853. (His first two wives died.) A son, O. Jennings Wise, was killed during the Civil War; son, John Sargeant Wise, was later a U.S. congressman from Virginia. Wise lived and practiced law in Nashville, Tennessee, during the late 1820s before returning to Accomec County in 1830. He developed a successful law practice and became active in state politics. He was elected to the U.S. House in 1833 and served until 1837. In 1842, the Senate refused to confirm his appointment as U.S. minister to France, but from 1844 to 1847, he was James Knox Polk's minister to Brazil. He was a delegate to the Virginia constitutional convention of 1850 and governor of the state from January 1856 to 1860. When the Civil War began, he volunteered to serve in the Confederate Army and was commissioned a brigadier general on June 5, 1861. At first, he was a commander in the Kanawha Valley under General Robert E. Lee (*q.v.*). He spent most of the war years in command of coastal defenses in Virginia and South Carolina; at Roanoke Island, under P.G.T. Beauregard (*q.v.*) in Charleston; and in early 1864 in Florida. In May 1864, he fought at Drewry's Bluff, after which he participated in the siege of Petersburg and the defense of Richmond. His promotion to major general on April 6, 1865, was never formally approved. Wise surrendered at Appomattox and was soon paroled. After the war, he practiced law in Richmond and wrote *Seven Decades of the Union* (1872). He died in Richmond on September 14, 1876. Wise, *The Life of Henry A. Wise of Virginia*.

WITHERS, Jones Mitchell (*General*), was born on January 12, 1814, in Huntsville, Alabama, to John Wright and Mary Herbert (Jones) Withers. His father had been a Virginia planter. He attended Greene Academy in Alabama and graduated forty-fourth in a class of fifty-six from the U.S. Military Academy in 1835 but shortly thereafter resigned his commission in the army to study law. Withers was a Presbyterian and a Democrat. He had ten children by his marriage to Rebecca Eloise Forney on January 12, 1837. He was admitted to the Alabama bar in 1838. He was private secretary to Governor Clement C. Clay (*q.v.*) of Alabama, secretary of the state Senate, and director of a state bank prior to 1841, when he became a lawyer and commission merchant in Mobile. He was a lieutenant colonel, and later colonel, during the Mexican War but again declined to remain in the army. In 1855, he was elected to the U.S. House on the American party ticket, and from 1858 to 1861, he was mayor of Mobile. When the Civil War began, he resigned as mayor and volunteered for the Confederate Army. On July 10, 1861, he was commissioned a brigadier general. He had charge of the defense of Mobile in 1861, was a division commander at the battle of Shiloh, and was promoted to major general on August 16, 1862. Withers participated in Braxton Bragg's (*q.v.*) Kentucky campaign and was commended for his service during the battle of Murfreesboro. In 1864, he was assigned to the District of Montgomery, where he was in charge of the reserve forces of Alabama until the end of the war. Withers surrendered at Mobile and was later pardoned. He returned to Mobile to continue his law practice. Withers was again elected mayor of Mobile in 1867 and was city treasurer in 1878-1879. He was also a cotton broker and editor of the Mobile *Tribune* prior to his death in Mobile on March 13, 1890. Owen, *History of Alabama and Dictionary of Alabama Biography*, IV.

WITHERS, Thomas Jefferson (*Congressman, Judge*), was born to Randolph and Sarah (Bailey) Withers near Rock Hill, York County, South Carolina, in 1804. He attended Ebenezer Academy and graduated second in the class of 1828 at South Carolina College. He moved to Camden, South Carolina, and was admitted to the bar in 1829. In 1831, he married Elizabeth Tunstall Boykin, sister of Mary Boykin Chesnut, and the following year he became solicitor of the circuit. He was a Democrat and also owned a plantation during the antebellum period. From 1846 to 1860, he served as a common law judge and he was also a member of the Court of Appeals. He was editor of the *Columbia Telescope* for a time in the 1850s. Withers, who had been opposed to single state secession, was a delegate to the South Carolina secession convention and was one of the leaders of the provisional Confederate Congress at Montgomery, which he helped to organize. Elected to the first Confederate Senate, he refused to serve, returning instead to his judgeship in Camden. Withers, who did not think of himself as a politician, wanted delegates to the Montgomery convention to be ineligible for other than diplomatic offices in the Confederacy. Though his brother-in-law, James Chesnut (*q.v.*), had coerced him into supporting Jefferson Davis (*q.v.*) for president, his inability to get along with

Davis no doubt influenced his decision to return to South Carolina. Yet, as a judge, he was only moderately states' rights and largely an administration defender. The war destroyed much of his estate, and Withers died a poor man on November 7, 1865, in Camden, South Carolina. Brooks, *South Carolina Bench and Bar*; Kirkland and Kennedy, *Historic Camden*.

WITHERSPOON, James Hervey (*Congressman*), was born in Lancaster Court-house, South Carolina, on March 23, 1810, to Colonel James Harvey and Jane (Donnom) Witherspoon. The younger Witherspoon graduated from South Carolina College in 1831. He was a Presbyterian and a slaveholding planter from Lancaster District, South Carolina. He was married, and his daughter, Nancy White, married Reverend James Henley Thornwell (*q.v.*). Witherspoon, a Democrat, was probably a secessionist. When the Civil War began, he volun-teered for duty in the Confederate Army. As a colonel in the Confederate Army, he was an ally of Wade Hampton (*q.v.*) and served with Hampton in many engage-ments. Witherspoon defeated John McQueen (*q.v.*) for election to the second Confederate House of Representatives. McQueen lost because he was too pro-Davis to suit his district. Witherspoon served on the Foreign Affairs, Ordnance and Ordnance Stores, and Post Office and Post Roads Committees. He was a Davis administration loyalist. After the war, he returned to his plantation in Lancaster. He died there on October 3, 1865. Cauthen, *South Carolina Goes to War*; Wardlaw (comp.), *Genealogy of the Witherspoon Family*.

WOFFORD, William Tatum (*General*), was born to William Hollingsworth and Nancy M. (Tatum) Wofford on June 28, 1824, in Habersham County, Georgia. He attended local schools and Gwinnett County Manual Labor School in Georgia before graduating from Franklin College (later the University of Georgia) in 1844. He studied law, was admitted to the Georgia bar in 1845, and began his law practice in 1846 in Cassville, Georgia. He was a Methodist and a unionist Democrat. He had three daughters by his marriage to Julia A. Dwight in 1859; after she died, he married Margaret Landon. Wofford fought at Vera Cruz in 1847 as a captain of volunteers during the Mexican War. He was a prosperous planter in Cassville as well as lawyer before the Civil War. In addition, he was clerk of the lower house of the Georgia legislature from 1849 to 1853, and he edited the Cassville *Standard* in 1852. He was a delegate to the Southern commercial conventions in 1857 and 1858 and voted against secession as a delegate to the Georgia secession convention in 1861. However, when his state seceded, Wofford entered the Confederate Army as a colonel in the 18th Georgia Infantry. After participating in the battles of Second Manassas, South Mountain, and Sharpsburg in 1862, he became a brigade commander following the death of General Thomas R. R. Cobb (*q.v.*) at the battle of Fredericksburg. He was promoted to brigadier general on April 23, 1863. He was a brigade commander at the battle of Chancel-lorsville and fought on the second day of the battle of Gettysburg under General

James Longstreet (*q.v.*), whom he accompanied to east Tennessee later in 1863. After participating in the assault at Knoxville, he returned to Virginia with the 1st Corps of the Army of Northern Virginia and fought at Spotsylvania, Petersburg, and the Wilderness, where he was wounded. In January 1865, he was assigned to command the Department of Northern Georgia at the request of Georgia Governor Joseph Brown (*q.v.*). Wofford surrendered at Resaca, Georgia, on May 2, 1865. He was paroled and returned to Cassville. He was elected to the U.S. House in 1865 but was denied a seat by the federal authorities. Thereafter, he was a planter and railroad organizer around Cassville. He served on the boards of several educational institutions and was a delegate to the state constitutional convention of 1877. Wofford died on May 22, 1884, in Cartersville, Georgia. Bryan, *Confederate Georgia*; Myers, *The Children of Pride*; Northen (ed.), *Men of Mark in Georgia*, III.

WOOD, John Taylor (*Naval Commander*), son of U.S. Surgeon General Robert Crooks Wood and Anne Marshall (Taylor), daughter of President Zachary Taylor, was born at Fort Snelling in the Northwest Territory (later Minnesota) on August 13, 1830. He was commissioned a midshipman in the U.S. Navy in 1847. On November 26, 1856, he married Lola Mackubin, by whom he had eleven children. Wood served on the frigates *Ohio* and the *Brandywine* in the Mexican War and was promoted to lieutenant in 1855. In 1861, he was an assistant professor of seamanship and gunnery at the U.S. Naval Academy but resigned his commission on April 21, 1861, and went to Louisiana. In October of that year, he was commissioned a lieutenant in the Confederate Navy. He was stationed at batteries at Evansport and Aquia Creek during the blockade of the Potomac. After the pivot gun was developed, Wood commanded the *Virginia* and received the surrender of the *Congress* in early 1862. He also commanded the sharpshooters which repulsed the federal fleet at Drewry's Bluff before being called to Davis's (*q.v.*) staff as a colonel of cavalry and naval aide-de-camp in 1863. Wood disliked his staff position, preferring active combat. He participated in boat expeditions on the Chesapeake Bay, and he captured the transport schooners *Elmore* and *Allegheny* on the Potomac River in early 1864. In August 1864, he was promoted to captain and was placed in command of the cruiser *Tallahassee*, which captured thirty other vessels during the war. In early 1865, he declined an offer to command the James River squadron. At the end of the war, Wood fled to Cuba and then to Halifax, Nova Scotia, where he dealt in shipping and marine insurance and where he lived at the time of his death on July 19, 1904. Evans, *Confederate Military History*, I.

WORTH, Jonathan (*State Legislator*), was born to Dr. David Worth and his wife Eunice (Gardner) on November 18, 1802, in Guilford County, North Carolina. He attended Caldwell Institute and the Academy at Greensboro before beginning a law practice in Asheville, North Carolina, in 1823. On October 20,

1824, he married Martitia Daniel, by whom he had eight children. Worth, whose family was Quaker, was himself of no religious denomination. He developed a law practice in Asheville and became active in local politics. In 1830, he was elected to the state legislature, where he took an anti-nullification stand the following year, and served until 1835. In 1840, he was elected to the state Senate on the William Henry Harrison ticket and served on a committee on public schools. He ran unsuccessfully as a Whig for the U.S. House in 1841 and 1845. A self-made businessman who also owned several plantations, he became an influential Whig in North Carolina politics. During his 1858 term in the state Senate, he investigated state railroad affairs. Devoted to the Union, he opposed secession in the state Senate and opposed the calling of a state convention. While he declined to be a candidate for public office in the national Confederate government, he also urged that the state prepare for war. Although he did not join the peace movement, he did oppose the Davis administration. In 1862, he was again elected to the state Senate, and as public treasurer of the legislature, he supervised the entire financial operations of the state during the war. He redeemed bonds and reduced the state debt. Worth was a dominant political figure in the defense of states' rights, and he was an ally of Governor Vance (*q.v.*). In 1865, he was in charge of the North Carolina archives. After the war, Governor William W. Holden (*q.v.*) appointed him provisional treasurer of the state, and Worth himself wanted to run for governor in an effort to restore unity. In 1866, he was reelected to the Senate and favored the ratification of a new state constitution. Worth died on September 5, 1869, in Raleigh, North Carolina. Hamilton (ed.), *Correspondence of Jonathan Worth*; Zuber, *Jonathan Worth*.

WRIGHT, Ambrose Ransom (*General*), was born on April 26, 1826, in Louisville, Jefferson County, Georgia, to the wealthy planter Ambrose Wright and his wife Sarah (Hammond). He read law under Herschel V. Johnson (*q.v.*) (who later became his brother-in-law) before being rejected by his family for marrying without their consent. Wright's 1843 marriage to Mary Hubbell Savage ended with her death in 1854; he later married Carrie Hazlehurst. He had one son. Admitted to the Dooly County, Georgia, bar in 1848, he returned in 1850 to Jefferson County, having inherited part of his father's estate. He was an active Democrat who later joined the American party. In 1859, he moved to Augusta, Georgia, and the following year he was a presidential elector on the John Bell ticket. After the presidential election, he became a secessionist, and he was a member of a committee which attempted to encourage the secession of Maryland. Wright enlisted as a private in the Confederate Army after the Civil War began and was elected colonel of the 3rd Georgia Regiment. In the fall of 1861, he was victorious in an engagement at Chiamicomico Island, North Carolina. Following his performance at the battle of Seven Pines, he was promoted to brigadier general on June 3, 1862. He then fought with the Army of Northern Virginia in every major engagement from Malvern Hill to Petersburg. At the battle of Sharpsburg in

September 1862, he was badly wounded but returned to action at Chancellorsville. He guarded Manassas Gap during the retreat following the battle of Gettysburg. Wright, who also had the strong support of Jefferson Davis (*q.v.*), was elected president of the Georgia Senate in the fall of 1863; he influenced that body by his military performance, though he never took his seat. On November 26, 1864, he was promoted to major general and transferred to a division command under General William Hardee (*q.v.*) at Savannah, Georgia. He saved the city of Augusta from sacking in late 1864 and later followed General J. E. Johnston's (*q.v.*) army to North Carolina. Wright surrendered in North Carolina at the war's end and was paroled in May 1865. Impoverished after the war, he reopened his law practice in Augusta, where he also edited the *Chronicle and Sentinel* for some years. He tried unsuccessfully for the Democratic nomination to the U.S. Senate in 1871 and died on December 21, 1872, in Augusta, Georgia. Bryan, *Confederate Georgia*; Northen (ed.), *Men of Mark in Georgia*, IV.

WRIGHT, Augustus Romaldus (*Congressman*), was born to William and Mary (McCall) Wright on June 16, 1813, in Wrightsboro, Columbia County, Georgia, where his father was a wealthy planter. After attending the public schools in Appling, Georgia, and Franklin College (later the University of Georgia), the younger Wright studied law in Litchfield, Connecticut, and was admitted to the Crawfordsville, Georgia, bar in 1835. He was a Baptist. He had six children by his marriage to Elizabeth Richardson and, after her death, eleven children by his 1847 marriage to Adaline Allman. Wright developed a successful law practice in Crawfordsville and he also owned a plantation. From 1842 to 1849, Wright served as judge of the Superior Court of the Cherokee Circuit. In 1852, he switched his party affiliation from Whig to Democrat. Three years later he moved to Rome, Georgia, to practice law. He became interested in politics, and in 1857, he was elected to the U.S. House, where he served until 1859. Wright was a delegate to the Georgia convention of 1857 and the Southern commercial convention of 1858. A unionist, he supported Stephen A. Douglas for president in 1860 and opposed secession while a delegate to the Georgia secession convention of 1861. Still, he declined President Lincoln's offer of the Union provisional governorship of Georgia. He was elected to the provisional Confederate Congress and he served on the Naval Affairs and the Public Lands Committees. Wright was also elected to the first and second Confederate Houses from Georgia's Tenth Congressional District. He served on the Naval Affairs, Public Lands, Medical Department, Printing, and Pay and Mileage Committees. He was mentioned as a candidate for governor in 1863, but Wright's antagonism toward Governor Joseph E. Brown (*q.v.*) precluded any support from the state's leaders. While in Congress he generally opposed the Davis administration. He also organized Wright's Legion in 1863 and saw active service as colonel of the 38th Georgia Infantry. In 1864, he spent two weeks in Washington, D.C., on a peace mission for the Confederacy. After the war, he was disfranchised. He was a delegate to the Georgia constitutional convention of 1877 and practiced law in Rome, Georgia, where he lived at the time of his death, on March 31, 1891. Myers, *Children of Pride*; Northen (ed.), *Men of Mark in Georgia*.

WRIGHT, John Vines (*Congressman, Judge*), son of Major Benjamin Wright and his wife Martha Ann Harwell (Hicks) and brother of Confederate General Marcus Joseph Wright (*q.v.*), was born on June 28, 1828, in Purdy, McNairy County, Tennessee. He attended universities in Kentucky and Tennessee, studied both medicine and law, and was admitted to the Purdy bar in 1851. He was an Episcopalian and a Democrat. On November 23, 1858, he married Georgia Hays, who at that time owned 100 slaves and much valuable land; they had eight children. He developed a decent law practice but was more interested in politics. Wright defeated a Whig to serve in the U.S. House of Representatives from 1855 to 1861. When the Civil War began, he resigned from Congress to enter the Confederate Army. In 1861, he was commissioned a colonel of the 13th Tennessee Infantry and participated in the battle of Belmont. During the war years, Wright also served as judge of the Circuit Court of Tennessee, chancellor and judge of the state Supreme Court, and representative from Tennessee's Tenth Congressional District in the first and second Confederate Houses. He served on the Committee on Naval Affairs and generally opposed the Davis administration. Perhaps because of his judicial work, Wright spent little time in Richmond. He lost much of his fortune during the war. After the war, he moved to Alabama and, in 1870, to Columbia, Tennessee. A member of the anti-repudiation wing of the Democratic party, he ran unsuccessfully for governor of Tennessee in 1880 on a state credit ticket. Three years later, he moved to Nashville. In 1886, he was chairman of the Northwest Indian Commission and lived in Washington, D.C. From 1887 to 1908, he was a member of the legal division of the General Land Office. Wright died in Washington, D.C., on June 11, 1908. Alexander and Beringer, *Anatomy of the Confederate Congress*; Speer (comp.), *Biographical Directory of the Tennessee General Assembly*.

WRIGHT, Marcus Joseph (*General*), son of Major Benjamin Wright and his wife Martha Ann Harwell (Hicks) and brother of John Vines Wright (*q.v.*), was born on June 1, 1831, in McNairy County, Tennessee. He attended the academy of McNairy County at Purdy, studied law, and moved to Memphis in the 1850s, where he was a clerk in the common law and chancery court before the war. He was a Whig and an Episcopalian. He was married to Martha Spencer Elcan and, after her death, to Pauline Womack; he had three sons and three daughters. When the Civil War began, Wright entered the service of the Confederacy as a lieutenant colonel of the 154th Tennessee Militia. He fought at the battle of Belmont, Missouri, in November 1861 and was wounded at the battle of Shiloh. In February 1862, he was military governor of Kentucky, and he later distinguished himself at the battle of Perryville, where he served under General Benjamin F. Cheatham (*q.v.*). He was promoted to brigadier general on December 20, 1862, and was given command of Daniel S. Donelson's (*q.v.*) Brigade, which he led in the battles of Chickamauga, Chattanooga, and Missionary Ridge in 1863. During the defense of Atlanta in 1864, he commanded the district post. After the fall of Atlanta, he commanded the district post at Macon, Georgia, and in 1865, the entire District of North Mississippi and West Tennessee. He surrendered at Grenada, Mississippi, and he was later paroled. After the war, he was sheriff of Shelby County and practiced law in Memphis. He also edited the Columbia, Tennessee, *Journal* for some years and was an agent for the Confederate Archives in Washington, D.C. He helped to compile the *Official Records of the Union and Confederate Armies*, and he wrote profusely on the history of the war. He died on December 27, 1922, in Washington, D.C. Speer (comp.), *Biographical Directory of the Tennessee General Assembly*; *Who's Who in America*, 1922-1923.

WRIGHT, William Bacon (*Congressman*), was born in Columbus, Georgia, on July 4, 1830, and came to Paris, Lamar County, Texas, in 1855 to practice law. Little is known of his early life, save that he at one time lived in Alabama. In 1857, he helped to found a Presbyterian male academy in Paris, of which he was the first president, and he became a famous lawyer in northeast Texas. He was a Democrat. Unlike most residents of Lamar County, Wright was a secessionist, and in December 1860, he was elected chairman of a committee to draw up a plan for the secession of the state. As representative from the Sixth Texas District in the first Confederate House, he served on the Patents, Claims, Enrolled Bills, and Indian Affairs Committees. He was generally an administration supporter. After his congressional service, he was a major in the Quartermaster Corps, serving under General E. Kirby Smith (*q.v.*). He served in the western theatre until the war's end. After the war, he returned to practice law in Paris and was active in politics in Texas. In 1875, he was a member of the Judiciary Committee of the Texas constitutional convention. In 1885 he moved to San Antonio and died there on August 10, 1895. Johnson, *Texans Who Wore the Gray*; Warner and Yearns, *Biographical Register of the Confederate Congress*.

Y

YANCEY, William Lowndes (*Congressman*, *Diplomat*), was born on August 10, 1814, in Ogeechee, Warren County, Georgia, to Benjamin Cudworth and Caroline (Bird) Yancey. His father was a lawyer and a midshipman in the U.S. Navy. The elder Yancey died when his son was young; the mother remarried. The younger Yancey attended Mount Zion Academy in Hancock County, Georgia, academies in New York State, and Williams College from 1830 to 1833. He studied law and, in 1834, was admitted to the bar in Greenville, South Carolina, where he also planted and edited the Greenville *Mountaineer* from 1834 until 1836. He was a Presbyterian and a Democrat. He married Sarah Caroline Earle, daughter of a wealthy Greenville planter, on August 13, 1835; they had ten children. As a result of a duel over politics, in 1836 Yancey moved to Cahaba, Alabama, where he planted and edited the *Cahaba Democrat* and the *Cahaba Gazette* before being admitted to the bar in Wetumpka, Alabama. He was elected to the Alabama state House in 1841 and to the state Senate two years later. In 1844-1845, he served in the U.S. House. Yancey, who moved to Montgomery in 1846, led the Alabama delegation at the Charleston Democratic convention in 1860. At the Alabama constitutional convention of 1861, he introduced the ordinance to dissolve the Union. He attended the Georgia secession convention and urged that state to secede. President Davis (*q.v.*) appointed him chairman of a committee sent to England and France to obtain diplomatic recognition of the Confederate government abroad; the mission failed in 1862. Yancey was also elected to the first Confederate Senate, where he opposed centralization in government. He was a consistent opponent of the Davis administration. He served on the Foreign Affairs, Public Lands, Rules, Territories, and Naval Affairs Committees. Yancey became a rallying point for those radical secessionists who believed that the Davis administration was a hindrance to an effective war effort. He died in office on July 28, 1863, in Montgomery, Alabama. DuBose, *The Life and Times of William Lowndes Yancey*; Venable, "The Public Career of William Lowndes Yancey," *Alabama Review*, XVI.

YANDELL, David Wendel (*Physician*), was born to Lunsford Pitts and Susan Juliet (Wendel) Yandell on September 4, 1826, in Murfreesboro, Tennessee. He was reared in Lexington and Louisville, Kentucky, attended Centre College in Danville, Kentucky, and received his medical degree from the University of Louisville in 1846. He also had two years of medical training in London, Dublin, and Paris during the late 1840s. Yandell had three daughters and a son by his 1851 marriage to Frances Jane Crutcher. He practiced and taught medicine in Louisville from 1848 until 1851, when he retired to a farm near Nashville for reasons of health. In 1853, he returned to Louisville, where he founded the Stokes Dispensary and taught classes in clinical medicine. When the Civil War began, he volunteered his talents to the Confederate Army. During the Civil War, he served under General Simon B. Buckner (*q.v.*), and on the staffs of Generals Albert Sidney Johnston (*q.v.*) and Joseph E. Johnston (*q.v.*). He was medical director for the Department of the West throughout the war and saw action at the battles of Shiloh, Murfreesboro, and Chickamauga, among other battles. He was Joseph Johnston's political confidant, opposed Braxton Bragg's (*q.v.*) military operations in the west, and argued against the administration's inadequate supplying of the Army of Tennessee. After the war, he returned to Louisville, where he rejoined the faculty of the University of Louisville in 1867 and became a professor of clinical surgery two years later. In 1870, he published *American Practitioner*, and, in 1887, he was surgeon general for the Kentucky Militia. Yandell died in Louisville on May 2, 1898. Connelly, *Autumn of Glory*; Cunningham, *Doctors in Gray*; Kelly and Burrage, *American Medical Biographies*.

YOUNG, Pierce Manning Butler (*General*), son of Dr. Robert Maxwell and Elizabeth Caroline (Jones) Young, was born on November 15, 1836, at Spartanburg, South Carolina. His father moved to Bartow County, Georgia, in 1839. Young graduated from Georgia Military Institute in 1856 and entered the U.S. Military Academy, but he had not graduated when the Civil War began. Young was a Presbyterian, a Mason, a Democrat, and a lifelong bachelor. He resigned from the academy when the Civil War began and volunteered for the Confederate Army, entering as a second lieutenant of the 1st Georgia Regiment. He rose in rank to lieutenant colonel by November 1861. In 1862, he performed gallantly under General J.E.B. Stuart (*q.v.*) in the Army of Northern Virginia during the Maryland campaign, particularly during the charge at South Mountain. After his brilliant fighting at the battle of Brandy Station the following June, he was promoted to brigadier general on September 28, 1863. Young led Hampton's Brigade in the Bristoe and Mine Run campaigns during the last quarter of 1863. In 1864, he was temporarily placed in charge of Hampton's Division, which he led in the defense of Augusta in November and in the defense of Savannah in December. On December 30, 1864, he was promoted to major general. Young, who was disliked by General Joseph Wheeler (*q.v.*), spent the last few months of the war serving under General Wade Hampton (*q.v.*) in the Carolinas. He surrendered in North Carolina and was paroled in May 1865. After the war, he was a planter in Cartersville, Georgia, and had an active political career. He was elected to but not seated in the U.S. House in 1868; he subsequently served two terms from 1870 to 1875 and lost a bid for a third. He was a delegate to the Democratic national conventions of 1872, 1876, and 1880. In 1878, he was a commissioner to the Paris Expedition. Young was President Cleveland's U.S. consul-general to St. Petersburg, Russia, from 1885 to 1887 and U.S. minister to Guatemala and Honduras from 1893 to 1896. While on his way home from Honduras, he died on July 6, 1896, in New York City. *Confederate Veteran*, V; Northen (ed.), *Men of Mark in Georgia*, VI.

YOUNG, William Hugh (*General*), son of Hugh F. Young, a general in the Texas Reserves during the Civil War, was born on January 1, 1838, in Booneville, Missouri. His father took him to Grayson County, Texas, as an infant. He attended Washington College in Tennessee and McKenzie College in Texas and studied military tactics at the University of Virginia from 1859 to 1861. At the beginning of the Civil War, he raised a company in Texas, of which he was elected captain. His company fought with the Army of Tennessee at the battle of Shiloh, after which he was promoted to colonel. He was cited for gallantry at the battles of Perryville and Murfreesboro. After being wounded at Murfreesboro, he fought at the battles of Vicksburg, Chickamauga, and Kenesaw Mountain and compiled a brilliant war record. He was promoted to brigadier general on August 15, 1864, and took command of General Matthew D. Ector's (*q.v.*) Brigade for the remainder of the Atlanta Campaign. He then accompanied General John B. Hood (*q.v.*) to Tennessee, where his left foot was shot off at Allatoona and he was captured in October 1864. He was paroled on July 24, 1865. After the war, he was a lawyer, real estate agent, and freight line operator in San Antonio, Texas, where he also was affiliated with the Nueces River Irrigation Company and edited the San Antonio *Express*. He died in San Antonio on November 28, 1901. *Confederate Veteran*, X; Johnson, *Texans Who Wore the Gray*.

Chronology of Events

Chronology

1828-1832. Nullification Movement in South Carolina
April 6-August 2, 1832. Black Hawk War
November 1835. Republic of Texas
November 1835-August 1843. Second Seminole War
February 1845. Annexation of Texas
1846. Bluffton Movement (S.C.)
May 13, 1846-February 2, 1848. Mexican War
June 10, 1850. Nashville Convention
June 29-September 20, 1850. Compromise of 1850
1855-1857. William Walker's filibustering expedition to Latin America
1857-1858. Mormon Expedition
October 19-December 21, 1857. Lecompton Constitution
October 16-18, 1859. John Brown's Raid
April 1860. Charleston Democratic Convention
November 1860. Election of Abraham Lincoln
December 20, 1860. South Carolina secedes
January 9, 1861. Mississippi secedes
January 10, 1861. Florida secedes
January 11, 1861. Alabama secedes
January 19, 1861. Georgia secedes
January 26, 1861. Louisiana secedes
February 1, 1861. Texas secedes
February 4, 1861. Montgomery Convention begins
February 4, 1861. Washington Peace Conference
February 9, 1861. Jefferson Davis elected provisional president of the Confederate States of America.
April 12, 1861. Fort Sumter
April 15, 1861. Lincoln calls for federal troops
April 17, 1861. Virginia secedes
May 6, 1861. Arkansas secedes
May 7, 1861. Tennessee legislature secedes
May 20, 1861. North Carolina secedes

June 10, 1861. Bethel (first engagement of the Civil War)
July 21, 1861. First Manassas
August 10, 1861. Wilson's Creek
February 12-16, 1862. Fort Donelson
March 6-7, 1862. Shiloh
March 6-8, 1862. Elkhorn Tavern
April 5-May 4, 1862. Siege of Yorktown
April 14-June 5, 1862. Fort Pillow
April 25, 1862. Federal capture of New Orleans
May 1862. Front Royal
June 26, 1862. Meadow Ridge
June 27, 1862. Cold Harbor
June 30, 1862. Frayser's Farm
July 1, 1862. Malvern Hill
August 9, 1862. Cedar Mountain
August 29-30, 1862. Second Manassas
September 14, 1862. South Mountain
September 17, 1862. Sharpsburg
October 3-4, 1862. Corinth
October 7-8, 1862. Perryville
December 13, 1862. Fredericksburg
December 29, 1862. Chickasaw Bluffs
December 31, 1862-January 3, 1863. Murfreesboro
January 1, 1863. Helena
January 1, 1863. Emancipation Proclamation
May 1, 1863. Port Gibson
May 2-4, 1863. Chancellorsville
June 9, 1863. Brandy Station
July 1-3, 1863. Gettysburg
July 4, 1863. Vicksburg surrenders
September 19-20, 1863. Chickamauga
September 22, 1863. Missionary Ridge
November 23-25, 1863. Chattanooga
November 24, 1863. Lookout Mountain
March 23-May 3, 1864. Camden expedition
April 8, 1864. Mansfield
May 5-7, 1864. Wilderness
May 8-21, 1864. Spotsylvania Court House
May 9-13, 1864. Dalton
May 11, 1864. Yellow Tavern
May 12-16, 1864. Drewry's Bluff
May 14-15, 1864. Resaca
May 25-June 5, 1864. New Hope Church

June 3, 1864. Cold Harbor

June 10, 1864. Kenesaw Mountain

June 15, 1864-April 2, 1865. Siege of Petersburg

June 20, 1864. Abingdon

July 9, 1864. Monocacy

July 30, 1864. The Crater

August 31-September 1, 1864. Jonesboro

September 1, 1864. Atlanta evacuated

September 19, 1864. Winchester

November 30, 1864. Franklin

December 15-16, 1864. Nashville

February 3, 1865. Hampton Roads Peace Conference

March 19-21, 1865. Bentonville

April 3, 1865. Richmond evacuated

April 9, 1865. Appomattox Courthouse

April 11, 1865. Mobile evacuated

April 14, 1865. Lincoln assassinated

April 26, 1865. Greensboro

May 12, 1865. Brownsville

May 26, 1865. Kirby Smith surrenders at New Orleans

December 18, 1865. Thirteenth Amendment

February 19, 1866. Freedmen's Bureau Bill

April 9, 1866. Civil Rights Act

June 16, 1866. Fourteenth Amendment

March 2, 1867. First Reconstruction Act

March 30, 1870. Fifteenth Amendment

May 22, 1872. Amnesty Act (disabilities removed from all but 500 ex-Confederates)

November 7-December 6, 1876. Disputed presidential election of 1876

April 10-24, 1877. End of Reconstruction (all federal troops removed from ex-Confederate
    states)

Appendixes

Geographical Mobility Before and After the Civil War

Place and date of birth, residence in 1860, and place and date of death are included. This appendix is divided into two large categories: birth in the South; and birth in the North, the territories, and abroad.

THE SOUTH

Alabama

Name	Birth	1860 Residence	Death
Callahan, Samuel B.	Eufaula 1834	Okmulgee, Okla. Territory	Muskogee, Okla. 2/17/11
Chambers, Henry C.	Limestone County 7/26/23	Robson Landing, Miss.	Carson, Miss. 5/1/71
Clay, Clement C.	Huntsville 12/13/16	Madison County	Madison County 1/3/82
Cruikshank, Marcus H.	Autauga County 12/12/26	Talladega	Talladega 10/10/81
Graham, Malcolm D.	Autauga County 7/6/27	Henderson, Tex.	Montgomery 10/8/78
Gregg, John	Lawrence County 9/28/28	Fairfield, Tex.	Richmond, Va. 10/7/64
Harrison, Thomas	Jefferson County 5/1/23	Waco, Tex.	Waco, Tex. 7/14/91
Jones, Henry C.	Franklin County 1/23/21	Florence	Florence 6/20/13
Kelly, John H.	Carrollton 3/38	West Point, N.Y.	Franklin, Tenn. 8/20/64

Name	Birth	1860 Residence	Death
Keyes, Wade, Jr.	Mooresville 1821	Montgomery	Florence —
Morgan, John H.	Huntsville 6/1/27	Lexington, Ky.	Greenville, Tenn. 9/4/64
O'Neal, Edward A.	Madison County 9/20/18	Alabama	Florence 11/7/90
Pettus, Edmund W.	Limestone County 7/6/21	Cahaba	Hot Springs, N.C. 7/27/07
Phelan, James	Huntsville 10/11/21	Aberdeen, Miss.	Memphis, Tenn. 5/17/73
Roddey, Philip D.	Moulton 4/2/26	Chickasaw	London, England 7/20/97
Swan, William G.	— 1821	Knoxville, Tenn.	Memphis, Tenn. 4/10/69
Walker, Leroy P.	Huntsville 2/7/17	Huntsville	Huntsville 8/23/84
Walker, Richard W.	Huntsville 2/16/23	Florence	Huntsville 6/16/74
Watts, Thomas H.	Greenville 1/3/19	Montgomery	Montgomery 9/16/92
Welsh, Israel	St. Stephens 1/20/22	Macon, Miss.	Noxubec County, Miss. 5/18/69
Withers, Jones M.	Huntsville 1/12/14	Mobile	Mobile 3/13/90

Florida

Name	Birth	1860 Residence	Death
Brooke, John M.	Tampa 12/18/26	—	Virginia 1904
Smith, Edmund K.	St. Augustine 5/16/24	—	Sewanee, Tenn. 3/28/93

Georgia

Name	Birth	1860 Residence	Death
Akin, Warren	Elbert County 10/9/11	Cassville	Cartersville 12/17/77
Alexander, Edward P.	Washington 5/26/35	—	Savannah 4/28/10
Alexander, Peter W.	Elberton 3/21/24	Thomaston	Marietta 9/23/86

Name	Birth	1860 Residence	Death
Anderson, George T.	Covington 2/3/24	Georgia	Anniston, Ala. 4/4/01
Anderson, Robert H.	Savannah 10/1/35	Washington Territory	Savannah 2/8/88
Bartow, Francis S.	Savannah 9/6/16	Savannah	Manassas, Va. 7/21/61
Bass, Nathan	Putnam County 10/1/08	Floyd County	Rome 9/2/90
Battle, Cullen A.	Powelton 6/1/29	Tuskegee, Ala.	Greensboro, N.C. 4/8/05
Bell, Hiram P.	Jackson County 1/19/27	Georgia	Atlanta 8/16/09
Benning, Henry L.	Columbus 4/2/14	Columbus	Columbus 7/8/75
Blandford, Mark H.	Warren County 7/13/26	Buena Vista	Columbus 1/31/02
Boggs, William R.	Augusta 3/18/29	Port Isobel, Tex.	Winston-Salem, N.C. 9/11/11
Boudinot, Elias C.	Rome 8/1/35	Arkansas	Indian Territory 9/27/90
Bowen, John S.	Savannah 10/30/30	St. Louis, Mo.	Raymond, Miss. 7/13/63
Bryan, Goode	Hancock County 8/31/11	Richmond County	Augusta 8/16/65
Bulloch, James D.	Savannah 6/25/23	—	Liverpool, England 1/7/01
Campbell, John A.	Washington 6/24/11	Mobile, Ala.	Baltimore, Md. 3/12/89
Carter, John C.	Waynesboro 12/19/37	Memphis, Tenn.	Franklin, Tenn. 12/10/64
Clanton, James H.	Columbia County 1/8/27	Montgomery, Ala.	Knoxville, Tenn. 9/26/71
Clark, William W.	Augusta 9/23/19	Covington	Baltimore, Md. 8/6/83
Clayton, Henry D.	Pulaski County 3/7/27	Clayton, Ala.	Tuscaloosa, Ala. 10/3/89
Clayton, Philip	Athens 3/19/15	Washington, D.C.	Callao, Peru 3/22/77
Clopton, David	Putnam County 9/29/20	Tuskegee, Ala.	Montgomery, Ala. 2/5/92
Clusky, Michael W.	Savannah 5/?/32	Memphis, Tenn.	Louisville, Ky. 1/13/73

Name	Birth	1860 Residence	Death
Cobb, Howell	Jefferson County 9/17/15	Washington, D.C.	New York, N.Y. 10/9/68
Cobb, Thomas R. R.	Jefferson County 4/10/23	Athens	Fredericksburg, Va. 12/13/62
Colquitt, Alfred H.	Monroe 4/20/24	Baker County	Washington, D.C. 3/26/94
Crawford, Martin J.	Jasper County 3/17/20	Columbus	Columbus 7/23/83
Cumming, Alfred	Augusta 1/30/29	Frontier	Rome 12/5/10
Curry, Jabez L. M.	Lincoln County 6/5/25	Talladega, Ala.	Asheville, N.C. 2/12/03
Davis, Nicholas, Jr.	Athens 1/14/75	Huntsville, Ala.	Huntsville, Ala. 11/3/74
Doles, George P.	Milledgeville 5/14/30	Milledgeville	Cold Harbor, Va. 6/2/64
Echols, Joseph H.	Washington 12/25/16	Oglethorpe	Lexington 9/23/85
Ector, Matthew D.	Putnam County 2/28/22	Henderson, Tex.	Tyler, Tex. 10/29/79
Evans, Augusta J.	Columbus 5/8/35	Mobile, Ala.	Mobile, Ala. 5/9/09
Evans, Clement A.	Stewart County 2/25/33	Lumpkin	Atlanta 7/2/11
Forman, Thomas M.	— 1809	Glynn County	— —
Forsyth, John	Augusta 10/31/12	Mobile, Ala.	Mobile, Ala. 5/2/74
Gartrell, Lucius J.	Wilkes County 1/7/21	Atlanta	Atlanta 4/7/91
Gilmer, Francis M.	Ogelthorpe County 6/8/10	Montgomery, Ala.	Montgomery, Ala. 1/9/92
Gordon, John B.	Upson County 2/6/32	Alabama	Miami, Fla. 1/9/04
Hardee, William J.	Camden County 10/12/15	West Point, N.Y.	Wytheville, Va. 11/6/73
Hartridge, Julian	Savannah 9/9/29	Savannah	Washington, D.C. 1/8/79
Hill, Benjamin H.	Jasper County 9/14/23	La Grange	Atlanta 8/16/82
Holt, Hines	Baldwin County 4/27/05	Columbus	Milledgeville 11/4/68

Name	*Birth*	*1860 Residence*	*Death*
Holtzclaw, James T.	McDonough 12/17/32	Montgomery, Ala.	Montgomery, Ala. 7/19/93
Iverson, Alfred, Jr.	Clinton 2/4/29	Frontier	Atlanta 3/31/11
Jackson, Henry R.	Athens 6/24/20	Savannah	Savannah 3/23/98
Jackson, John K.	Augusta 2/8/28	Augusta	Milledgeville 2/26/66
Jemison, Robert, Jr.	Lincoln County 9/17/02	Tuscaloosa, Ala.	Tuscaloosa, Ala. 10/17/71
Johnson, Herschel V.	Burke County 9/18/21	Milledgeville	Jefferson County 8/16/80
Jones, Joseph	Liberty County 9/6/33	Savannah	New Orleans, La. 2/17/96
Kell, John M.	Darien 1/26/23	Pensacola, Fla.	Sunnyside 10/5/00
Kenan, Augustus H.	Montpelier 1805	Milledgeville	— 12/16/65
Lamar, Gazaway B.	Richmond County 10/2/98	New York, N.Y.	New York, N.Y. 10/5/74
Lamar, Lucius Q. C.	Putnam County 9/17/25	Oxford, Miss.	Macon 1/23/93
Lamkin, John T.	Augusta 7/17/11	Holmesville, Miss.	Holmesville, Miss. 5/19/70
Lewis, David W.	Hancock County 10/24/15	Sparta	Hancock County 12/28/85
McGeehee, Edward	Oglethorpe 11/18/86	Wilkinson County, Miss.	Bowling Green, Miss. 10/1/80
McLaws, Lafayette	Augusta 1/15/21	Frontier	Savannah 7/24/97
Maxwell, Augustus E.	Elberton 9/21/20	Pensacola, Fla.	Chipley, Fla. 5/5/03
Milton, John	Louisville 4/20/07	Jackson Cnty, Fla.	Marianna, Fla. 4/1/65
Nisbet, Eugenius A.	Greene County 12/7/03	Macon	Macon 3/18/71
Pierce, George F.	Greene County 2/3/11	Georgia	Sparta 9/3/84

Name	Birth	1860 Residence	Death
Pugh, James L.	Burke County 12/12/20	Eufaula, Ala.	Washington, D.C. 3/9/07
Ralls, John P.	Greene County 1/1/22	Gadsden, Ala.	Gadsden, Ala. 11/23/04
St. John, Isaac M.	Augusta 11/18/27	Augusta	White Sulphur Springs, W.Va. 4/7/80
Shewmake, John T.	Burke County 1/22/26	Augusta	Augusta 12/1/98
Shorter, John G.	Monticello 4/23/18	Eufaula, Ala.	Eufaula, Ala. 5/29/72
Sims, Frederick, W.	Clinton 1828	Savannah	San Francisco, Ca. 5/25/75
Smith, Charles H.	Lawrenceville 6/15/26	Rome	Carterville 8/24/03
Smith, James M.	Twiggs County 10/24/23	Columbus	Columbus 11/20/90
Smith, William E.	Augusta 3/14/29	Albany	Albany 3/11/90
Sorrel, Gilbert M.	Savannah 2/23/38	Savannah	Roanoke, Va. 8/10/01
Stephens, Alexander H.	Crawfordsville 2/11/12	Crawfordsville	Atlanta 3/4/83
Stephens, Linton	Wilkes County 7/1/23	Crawfordsville	Hancock 7/14/72
Strickland, Hardy	Jackson County 11/24/18	Cumming	Forsyth County 1/24/84
Tattnall, Josiah	Savannah 11/9/95	San Francisco, Calif.	Savannah 11/9/71
Thomas, Edward L.	Clarke County 3/23/25	Clarke County	Indian Territory 3/10/98
Toombs, Robert A.	Washington 7/2/10	Washington	Washington 12/15/85
Trippe, Robert P.	Monticello 12/21/19	Forsyth	Atlanta 7/22/00
Turner, Joseph A.	Putnam County 8/23/26	Eatonton	Eatonton 2/29/68
Walker, William H. T.	Augusta 11/16/16	—	Atlanta 7/22/64
Watie, Stand	Rome 12/12/06	Oklahoma, Indian Territory	Oklahoma, Indian Territory 9/9/71

Name	Birth	1860 Residence	Death
Wheeler, Joseph	Augusta 9/10/36	—	Brooklyn, N.Y. 1/25/06
Wofford, William T.	Habersham County 6/28/24	Cassville	Cartersville 5/22/84
Wright, Ambrose R.	Louisville 4/26/26	Augusta	Augusta 12/21/72
Wright, Augustus R.	Wrightsboro 6/16/13	Rome	Rome 3/31/91
Wright, William B.	Columbus 7/4/30	Paris, Tex.	San Antonio, Tex. 8/10/95
Yancey, William L.	Ogeechee 8/10/14	Montgomery, Ala.	Montgomery, Ala. 7/28/63

Kentucky

Name	Birth	1860 Residence	Death
Adams, Daniel W.	Frankfort 5/1/21	New Orleans, La.	New Orleans, La. 6/14/72
Adams, William W.	Frankfort 3/22/19	Vicksburg, Miss.	Jackson, Miss. 5/1/88
Baylor, John R.	Paris 7/20/22	Waterford, Tex.	Montell, Tex. 2/6/04
Bledsoe, Albert T.	Frankfort 11/9/09	Virginia	Alexandria, Va. 12/8/77
Bradley, Benjamin F.	Scott County 10/5/25	Georgetown	Georgetown 1/22/97
Breckinridge, John C.	Lexington 1/21/21	Washington, D.C.	Lexington 5/17/75
Bruce, Eli M.	Flemingsburg 2/22/28	Nicholas County	New York, N.Y. 12/15/66
Bruce, Horatio W.	Vanceburg 2/22/30	Louisville	Louisville 1/22/03
Buckner, Simon B.	Hart County 4/21/23	Hart County	Hart County 1/8/14
Burnett, Theodore L.	Spencer County 11/14/29	Taylorsville	Louisville 10/30/17
Chilton, William P.	Adair County 8/10/10	Macon Co., Ala.	Montgomery, Ala. 1/21/71
Chrisman, James S.	Monticello 9/14/18	Monticello	Monticello 7/29/81
Churchill, Thomas J.	Jefferson County 3/10/24	Little Rock, Ark.	Little Rock, Ark. 3/14/05

Name	Birth	1860 Residence	Death
Clark, John B.	Madison County 4/17/02	Fayette, Mo.	Fayette, Mo. 10/29/85
Crittenden, George B.	Russellville 3/20/12	Frontier	Danville 11/27/80
Crockett, John W.	Jessamine County 5/17/18	Henderson	Madisonville 6/20/74
Davis, Jefferson	Christian County 6/3/08	Biloxi, Miss.	New Orleans, La. 12/6/89
Duke, Basil C.	Orangeburg 3/31/15	Mayslick	Memphis, Tenn. —
Duke, Basil W.	Scott County 5/28/38	St. Louis, Mo.	New York, N.Y. 9/16/16
Ewing, George	Logan County 11/29/08.	Russellville	Adairsville 5/20/88
Fagan, James F.	Louisville 3/1/28	Little Rock, Ark.	Little Rock, Ark. 9/1/93
Field, Charles W.	Woodford County 4/6/28	West Point, N.Y.	Washington, D.C. 4/2/92
Freeman, Thomas W.	Anderson County 1824	Bolivar, Mo.	St. Louis, Mo. 10/24/65
Gholson, Samuel J.	Madison County 5/19/08	Athens, Miss.	Aberdeen, Miss. 10/16/83
Gibson, Randall L.	Versailles 9/10/32	Lafourche Parish, La.	Hot Springs, Ark. 12/15/92
Hale, Stephen F.	Crittenden County 1/31/16	Eutaw, Ala.	Richmond, Va. 7/18/62
Hanly, Thomas B.	Nicholsonville 6/9/12	Helena, Ark.	Helena, Ark. 6/9/80
Hawes, James M.	Lexington 1/7/24	Frontier	Covington 1/22/89
Helm, Benjamin H.	Elizabethtown 6/2/31	Louisville	Chickamauga, Ga. 9/20/63
Henry, Gustavus A.	Scott County 10/8/04	Clarksville, Tenn.	Clarksville, Tenn. 9/10/80
Hodge, George B.	Fleming County 4/8/28	Newport	Longwood, Fla. 8/1/92
Hood, John B.	Owingsville 6/29/31	Frontier	New Orleans, La. 8/30/79
Jackson, Claiborne F.	Fleming County 4/4/07	Fayette, Mo.	Little Rock, Ark. 12/6/62

Name	Birth	1860 Residence	Death
Johnson, George W.	Georgetown 5/27/11	Scott County	Shiloh, Tenn. 4/9/62
Johnson, Robert W.	Scott County 7/22/14	Jefferson County, Ark.	Little Rock, Ark. 7/26/79
Johnson, Thomas	Montgomery Co. 7/4/12	Mount Sterling	Mount Sterling 4/7/06
Johnston, Albert S.	Washington 2/2/03	Frontier	Pittsburgh Landing, Tenn. 4/6/62
Johnston, William P.	Louisville 1/5/31	Louisville	Lexington, Va. 7/16/99
Lewis, Joseph H.	Glasgow 10/29/24	Glasgow	Glasgow 7/6/04
Machen, Willis B.	Coldwell County 4/10/10.	Eddyville	Eddyville 9/29/93
Marshall, Humphrey	Frankfort 1/13/12	Louisville	Louisville 3/28/72
Martin, William T.	Glasgow 3/25/23	Natchez, Miss.	Natchez, Miss. 3/16/10
Maxey, Samuel B.	Tompkinsville 3/30/25	Lamar County, Texas	Eureka Spgs., Ark. 8/16/95
Moore, James W.	Montgomery Co. 2/12/18	Mount Sterling	Mount Sterling 9/17/77
Norton, Nimrod L.	Carlisle 4/18/30	Missouri	Austin, Tex. —
Pickett, John T.	Maysville —	Vera Cruz, Mex.	Washington, D.C. —
Preston, William	Louisville 10/16/16	Spain	Lexington 9/21/87
Read, Henry E.	Larue County 12/25/24	Kentucky	Louisville 11/9/69
Rector, Henry M.	Louisville 5/1/16	Little Rock, Ark.	Hot Springs, Ark. 8/12/99
Robertson, Jerome B.	Woodford County 3/14/15	Independence	Waco, Tex. 1/7/19
Shelby, Joseph O.	Lexington 12/12/30	Waverly, Mo.	Adrion, Mo. 2/13/97
Simms, William E.	Cynthiana 1/2/22	Paris	Paris 6/25/98
Singleton, Ortho R.	Nicholasville 10/14/14	Canton, Miss.	Washington, D.C. 1/11/89

Name	Birth	1860 Residence	Death
Smith, Gustavus W.	Georgetown 1/1/22	New York, N.Y.	New York, N.Y. 6/4/96
Smith, William R.	Russellville 3/27/15	Mobile, Ala.	Washington, D.C. 2/26/96
Taylor, Richard	Louisville 1/27/36	St. Charles Parish, La.	New York, N.Y. 4/17/79
Triplett, George W.	Franklin County 2/8/09	Daviess County	Owensboro 6/25/94
Vest, George G.	Frankfort 12/6/30	Booneville, Mo.	Sweet Springs, Mo. 8/9/04
Ward, George T.	Fayette County 1810	Tallahassee, Fla.	Fort Magruder, Va. 5/5/62
White, Daniel P.	Greensburg 11/16/14	Greensburg	Louisville 4/12/90
Williams, John S.	Mount Sterling 7/10/18	Paris	Mount Sterling 7/17/98

Louisiana

Name	Birth	1860 Residence	Death
Beauregard, Pierre G. T.	St. Bernard Parish 5/28/18	Gulf Coast	New Orleans 2/20/93
DeClouet, Alexander	St. Martin's Parish 6/9/12	Louisiana	Lafayette Parish 6/26/90
Dupré, Lucius Jacques	St. Landry Parish 4/18/22	New Orleans	Opelousas 3/5/69
Hébert, Louis	Iberville Parish 3/13/20	Louisiana	Breaux Parish 1/7/01
Hébert, Paul O.	Iberville Parish 12/2/18	Iberville Parish	New Orleans 8/29/80
Kenner, Duncan F.	New Orleans 2/11/13	Ascension Parish	New Orleans 7/3/87
Nicholls, Francis R.	Donaldsonville 8/20/34	Napoleonville	Thibodeaux 1/4/12
Villeré, Charles J.	St. Bernard Parish 1830	Pointe à la Hache	Jefferson Parish 1/7/99

Maryland

Name	Birth	1860 Residence	Death
Archer, James J.	Stafford 12/19/17	California	Richmond, Va. 10/24/64

Name	Birth	1860 Residence	Death
Breckinridge, Robert J.	Baltimore 9/14/34	Lexington, Ky.	Danville, Ky. —
Buchanan, Franklin	Baltimore 9/11/00	Washington, D.C.	Talbot County 5/11/74
Carroll, David W.	Baltimore 3/11/16	Pine Bluff, Ark.	Little Rock, Ark. 6/24/05
Elzey, Arnold	Somerset County 12/18/16	Augusta, Ga.	Baltimore 2/21/70
Greenhow, Rose O.	Port Tobacco 1817	Washington, D.C.	North Carolina 1864
Hollins, George N.	Baltimore 9/20/99	—	Baltimore 1/18/78
Jones, John B.	Baltimore 3/6/10	Philadelphia, Pa.	Burlington, N.J. 2/4/66
Mackall, William W.	Cecil County 1/18/17	Frontier	Fairfax Co., Va. 8/12/91
Semmes, Raphael	Charles County 9/27/09	—	Mobile, Ala. 8/30/77
Steuart, George H.	Baltimore 8/24/28	—	South River 11/22/03
Williams, Thomas H.	Dorchester County 3/?/22	—	Cambridge 9/22/04
Wilson, William S.	Snow Hill 11/7/16	Port Gibson, Miss.	Sharpsburg, Va. 11/3/62
Winder, John H.	Somerset County 2/21/00	—	Florence, S.C. 2/7/65

Mississippi

Name	Birth	1860 Residence	Death
Barry, William T. S.	Columbus 12/10/21	Lowndes County	Columbus 1/29/68
Cooper, Douglas H.	Amite County 11/1/15	Wilkinson County	Byron County, Okla. 4/29/79
Darden, Stephen H.	Fayette 11/19/16	Gonzales County, Tex.	Wharton, Tex. 5/16/02
Davis, Joseph R.	Wilkinson County 1/12/25	Canton	Biloxi 9/15/96
Davis, Varina H.	Natchez 5/7/26	Biloxi	New York, N.Y. 10/16/06

Name	Birth	1860 Residence	Death
Harris, Nathaniel H.	Natchez 8/22/34	Vicksburg	Malvern, England 8/23/00
Harris, Wiley P.	Pike County 11/9/18	Jackson	Jackson, Tenn. 12/3/91
Humphreys, Benjamin G.	Bayou Pierre 8/28/08	Sunflower County	Leflore County 12/22/82
Hurst, David W.	Amite County 7/10/19	Amite County	Summit 7/10/82
Jones, Robert M.	Choctaw, Indian Territory 10/1/08	Red River County	Hugo, Okla. 2/22/72
Newsom, Ella K.	Brandon —	Arkansas	Washington, D.C. —
Perkins, John, Jr.	Port Gibson 9/20/20	—	Spring Hill, Tenn. 5/7/63
Van Dorn, Earl	Port Gibson 3/22/24	Savannah, Ga.	Governors Is., N.Y. 3/10/65

Missouri

Name	Birth	1860 Residence	Death
Cockrell, Francis M.	Warrensburg 10/1/34	Warrensburg, Miss.	Washington, D.C. 12/13/15
Cooke, John R.	Jefferson Barracks 6/9/33	Frontier	Richmond, Va. 4/10/91
McCausland, John	St. Louis 9/13/36	Lynchburg, Va.	Henderson, W. Va. 1/22/27
Marmaduke, John S.	Arrow Rock 3/14/33	Frontier	St. Louis 12/28/87
Walker, John G.	Jefferson City 7/22/22	—	Washington, D.C. 7/20/93
Young, William H.	Booneville 1/1/38	Grayson County, Tex.	San Antonio, Tex. 11/28/01

North Carolina

Name	Birth	1860 Residence	Death
Armistead, Lewis A.	New Bern 2/18/16	Frontier	Gettysburg, Pa. 7/4/63
Arrington, Archibald H.	Nashville 11/13/09	Nashville	Nashville 7/20/72
Ashcraft, Thomas	Sampson County 8/6/86	Talladega, Ala.	Clay County, Ala. 12/18/66

Name	Birth	1860 Residence	Death
Ashe, Thomas S.	Hawfields 7/19/12	Wadesboro	Wadesboro 2/4/87
Ashe, William S.	Rocky Point 8/12/13	Wilmington	Wilmington 9/14/62
Avery, William W.	Burke County 5/25/16	North Carolina	Morgantown, Tenn. 7/3/64
Baker, James M.	Robeson County 7/20/22	Lake City, Fla.	Jacksonville, Fla. 6/20/92
Baker, Laurence S.	Gates County 5/15/30	—	Suffolk, Va. 4/10/07
Barringer, Rufus	Poplar Grove 12/2/21	Concord	Charlotte 2/3/95
Bragg, Braxton	Warren County 3/22/17	Lafourche Parish, La.	Galveston, Tex. 9/27/76
Bragg, Thomas	Warrenton 11/9/10	Northampton County	Raleigh 1/21/72
Bridgers, Robert R.	Edgecombe Co. 11/28/19	North Carolina	Columbia, S.C. 12/10/88
Clark, Henry T.	Tarboro 1808	Tarboro	Tarboro 4/14/74
Clingman, Thomas L.	Huntersville 6/27/12	Asheville	Morgantown 11/3/97
Cox, William R.	Scotland Neck 3/11/32	Edgecomb County	Richmond, Va. 12/26/19
Craige, Francis B.	Rowan County 3/13/11	Salisbury	Concord 12/30/75
Daniel, Junius	Halifax 6/27/28	Shreveport, La.	Spotsylvania, Va. 5/13/64
Dargan, Edmund S.	Wadesboro 4/15/05	Mobile, Ala.	Mobile, Ala. 11/22/79
Davidson, Allen T.	Haywood County 5/9/19	Cherokee County	Asheville 1/24/05
Davis, George	New Hanover Co. 3/1/20	Wilmington	Wilmington 2/23/96
Dortch, William T.	Nash County 8/23/24	Goldsboro	Goldsboro 11/21/89
Ellis, John W.	Rowan County 7/?/20	Salisbury	Red Sulphur Springs, Va. 7/7/61
Forney, John H.	Batley Forge 8/12/29	West Point, N.Y.	Jacksonville, Ala. 9/13/02

Name	Birth	1860 Residence	Death
Forrest, Nathan B.	Chapel Hill 7/13/21	Memphis, Tenn.	Memphis, Tenn. 10/24/77
Fuller, Thomas C.	Fayetteville 2/27/32	Fayetteville	Raleigh 10/20/01
Gaither, Burgess S.	Iredell County 3/16/07	North Carolina	Morgantown 2/23/92
Gentry, Meredith P.	Rockingham Co. 9/15/09	College Grove, Tenn.	Nashville, Tenn. 11/2/66
Gilmer, Jeremy F. F.	Guilford County 2/23/18	San Francisco, Ca.	Savannah, Ga. 12/1/83
Gilmer, John A.	Guilford County 11/4/05	Greensboro	Greensboro 5/14/68
Gordon, James B.	Wilkesboro 11/22/22	Wilkesboro	Spotsylvania, Va. 5/18/64
Govan, Daniel C.	Northampton Co. 7/4/29	Phillips County, Ark.	Memphis, Tenn. 3/12/11
Graham, William A.	Lincoln County 9/5/04	North Carolina	Saratoga Springs, N.Y. 8/11/75
Grimes, Bryan	Pitt County 11/2/28	Pitt County	Grimesland 8/14/80
Hoke, Robert F.	Lincolnton 5/27/37	—	Raleigh 7/3/12
Holden, William W.	Orange County 11/24/18	Raleigh	Raleigh 3/92
Holmes, Theophilus H.	Sampson County 11/13/04	Washington, D.C.	Fayetteville 6/21/80
Johnston, George D.	Hillsboro 5/30/32	Marion, Ala.	Tuscaloosa, Ala. 12/8/10
Johnston, Robert D.	Lincoln County 3/19/37	Charlottesville, Va.	Winchester, Va. 2/1/19
Jones, Thomas M.	Person County 12/16/16	Pulaski, Tenn.	Pulaski, Tenn. 3/13/92
Kenan, Owen R.	Kenansville 3/4/04	Kenansville	Kenansville 3/3/87
Leach, James M.	Randolph County 1/17/15	Lexington	Lexington 6/1/91
Leach, James T.	Johnston County 1805	Leachburg	Johnston County 3/28/83
Logan, George W.	Chimney Rock 2/22/15	Rutherfordton	Rutherfordton 10/18/99

Name	Birth	1860 Residence	Death
Loring, William W.	Wilmington 12/4/18	New Mexico	New York, N.Y. 12/30/86
Lyon, Francis S.	Danbury 2/25/00	Demopolia, Ala.	Demopolia, Ala. 12/31/82
McCallum, James	Robeson County 10/2/06	Pulaski, Tenn.	Pulaski, Tenn. 9/16/89
McDowell, Thomas D.	Elizabethtown 1/4/23	North Carolina	— 5/1/98
McLean, James R.	Enfield 9/21/23	Greensboro	Greensboro 4/15/70
McQueen, John	Queensdale 2/9/04	South Carolina	Society Hill, S.C. 8/30/67
McRae, Colin J.	Sneedsboro 10/22/12	Mobile, Ala.	Belize, British Honduras 2/77
McRae, John J.	Sneedsboro 1/10/15	Paulding, Miss.	Belize, British Honduras 5/31/68
Manly, Basil	Pittsborough 1/29/98	Tuscaloosa, Ala.	Greenville, S.C. 12/21/68
Martin, James G.	Elizabeth City 2/14/19	Frontier	Asheville 10/4/78
Moore, Thomas O.	Sampson County 4/10/04	Rapides Parish, La.	Alexandria, La. 6/25/76
Ochiltree, William B.	Fayetteville 10/18/11	Marshall, Tex.	Marshall, Tex. 12/27/67
Pearson, Richmond M.	Rowan County 6/28/05	Salisbury	— 1/5/78
Pender, William D.	Edgecombe County 2/6/34	Frontier	Staunton, Va. 7/18/63
Pettigrew, James J.	Tyrrell County 7/4/28	Charleston, S.C.	Winchester, Va. 7/17/63
Polk, Leonidas	Raleigh 4/10/06	Sewanee, Tenn.	Marietta, Ga. 6/14/64
Polk, Lucius E.	Salisbury 7/10/33	Helena, Ark.	Columbia, Tenn. 12/1/92
Rains, Gabriel J.	Craven County 6/4/03	California	Aiken, S.C. 8/6/81
Rains, George W.	Craven County 1817	Newburgh, N.Y.	Newburgh, N.Y. 3/21/98

Name	Birth	1860 Residence	Death
Ramsay, James G.	Iredell County 3/1/23	Mount Vernon	Salisbury 1/10/03
Ramseur, Stephen D.	Lincolnton 5/31/37	Fortress Monroe, Va.	Cedar Creek, Va. 10/20/64
Ransom, Matt W.	Warren County 10/8/26	Northampton County	Garysburg 10/8/04
Ransom, Robert, Jr.	Warren County 2/12/28	Frontier	New Bern 1/14/92
Reade, Edwin G.	Mount Turziah 11/13/12	Roxboro	Raleigh 10/18/94
Robinson, Cornelius	Wadesboro 9/25/05	Mobile, Ala.	Church Hill, Ala. 7/29/67
Ruffin, Thomas	Louisburg 9/9/20	Goldsboro	Alexandria, Va. 10/13/63
Smith, Robert H.	Camden County 10/21/14	Mobile, Ala.	Mobile, Ala. 3/13/78
Smith, William N. H.	Murfreesboro 9/24/12	Murfreesboro	Raleigh 11/14/89
Swain, David L.	Asheville 1/4/01	Chapel Hill	Chapel Hill 8/27/68
Thomas, James H.	Iredell County 8/22/08	Columbia, Tenn.	Fayetteville, Tenn. 8/4/76
Thompson, Jacob	Caswell County 5/15/10	Oxford, Miss.	Memphis, Tenn. 3/24/85
Turner, Josiah, Jr.	Hillsboro 12/27/21	Hillsboro	Raleigh 10/26/01
Vance, Zebulon B.	Buncombe County 5/13/30	Asheville	Washington, D.C. 4/14/94
Warren, Edward	Tyrrell County 1828	Baltimore, Md.	Paris, France 9/16/93
Wilcox, Cadmus M.	Wayne County 5/29/24	New Mexico	Washington, D.C. 12/2/90
Wilcox, John A.	Greene County 4/18/19	San Antonio, Tex.	Richmond, Va. 2/7/64
Worth, Jonathan	Guilford County 11/18/02	Ashboro	Raleigh 9/5/69

South Carolina

Anderson, Richard H.	Hill Crest 10/7/21	Fort Kearney, Neb.	Beaufort 6/26/79

Name	Birth	1860 Residence	Death
Ayer, Lewis M., Jr.	Barnwell District 11/12/21	Barnwell District	Anderson 3/8/95
Baker, Alpheus	Abbeville 3/23/28	Eufaula, Ala.	Louisville, Ky. 10/22/91
Barnwell, Robert W.	Beaufort 8/1/01	South Carolina	Columbia 11/5/82
Bee, Hamilton P.	Charleston 7/22/22	Texas	San Antonio, Tex. 10/2/97
Bonham, Milledge L.	Edgefield District 12/25/13	South Carolina	White Sulphur Springs, N.C. 8/27/90
Boyce, William W.	Charleston 10/24/18	Winnsboro	Fairfax Co., Va. 2/3/90
Bratton, John	Winnsboro 3/7/31	Winnsboro	Winnsboro 1/12/98
Brown, Albert G.	Chester District 5/31/13	Washington, D.C.	Terry, Miss. 6/12/80
Brown, Joseph E.	Pickins District 4/15/21	Atlanta, Ga.	Atlanta, Ga. 11/30/94
Butler, Matthew C.	Greenville 3/8/36	South Carolina	Columbia 4/14/09
Campbell, Josiah A. P.	Abbeville District 3/2/30	Kosciusko, Miss.	Canton, Miss. 1/10/17
Cantey, James	Camden 12/30/18	Russell County, Ala.	Fort Mitchell, Ala. 6/30/74
Capers, Ellison	Charleston 10/14/37	Charleston	Columbia 4/22/08
Chesnut, James, Jr.	Camden 1/18/15	Camden	Camden 2/1/85
Chisholm, John J.	Charleston 4/16/30	Charleston	Petersburg, Va. 11/2/03
Conner, James	Charleston 9/1/29	Charleston	Richmond, Va. 6/26/83
Dawkins, James B.	Union District 12/14/20	Gainesville, Fla.	Gainesville, Fla. 2/12/83
Deas, Zachariah C.	Camden 10/25/19	Mobile, Ala.	New York, N.Y. 3/6/82
DeBow, James D. B.	Charleston 7/10/20	New Orleans, La.	Elizabeth, N.J. 2/27/67
De Leon, David C.	Camden 1813	Frontier	Albuquerque, N.M. 9/3/72

Name	Birth	1860 Residence	Death
De Leon, Edwin	Columbia 5/4/18	Washington, D.C.	New York, N.Y. 12/1/91
Elliott, Stephen	Beaufort 8/31/06	Savannah, Ga.	Savannah, Ga. 12/21/66
Farrow, James	Laurens 4/3/27	Spartanburg	Laurens 7/2/92
Ferguson, Samuel W.	Charleston 11/3/34	California	Jackson, Miss. 2/3/17
Furman, James C.	Charleston 12/5/09	Greenville	Greenville 3/3/91
Gist, States R.	Union District 9/3/31	Union District	Franklin, Tenn. 11/30/64
Gray, Henry	Laurens District 1/19/16	Caddo Parish, La.	Coushatta, La. 12/11/92
Gregg, Maxcy	Columbia 8/1/14	Columbia	Fredericksburg, Va. 12/14/62
Hampton, Wade	Charleston 3/28/18	South Carolina	Columbia 4/11/02
Harrison, James T.	Pendleton 11/30/11	Columbus, Miss.	Columbus, Miss. 5/22/79
Hemphill, John	Blackstock 12/18/03	Washington-on-the Brazos, Tex.	Richmond, Va. 1/4/62
Hill, Daniel H.	York District 7/21/21	Charlotte, N.C.	Charlotte, N.C. 9/24/89
Huger, Benjamin	Charleston 11/22/05	Charleston	Charleston 12/7/77
Jenkins, Charles J.	Beaufort District 1/6/05	Augusta, Ga.	Augusta, Ga. 6/14/83
Jenkins, Micah	Edisto Isle 12/1/35	Yorkville	Chancellorsville, Va. 5/6/64
Jones, David R.	Orangeburg Dist. 4/5/24	Frontier	Richmond, Va. 1/15/63
Keitt, Lawrence M.	Orangeburg Dist. 10/4/24	Orangeburg	Richmond, Va. 6/2/64
Kershaw, Joseph B.	Camden 1/5/22	Camden	Camden 4/13/94
Law, Evander M.	Darlington 8/7/36	Tuskegee, Ala.	Bartow, Fla. 1920
Lawton, Alexander R.	Beaufort District 11/4/18	Savannah, Ga.	Clifton Springs, N.Y. 7/2/96

Name	Birth	1860 Residence	Death
Lee, Stephen D.	Charleston 9/22/33	Frontier	Vicksburg, Miss. 5/28/08
Lester, George N.	Abbeville Dist. 3/13/24	Cobb County, Ga.	Marietta, Ga. 3/30/93
Lewis, John W.	Spartanburg Dist. 2/1/01	Canton, Ga.	Canton, Ga. 6/65
Longstreet, James	Edgefield Dist. 2/8/21	New Mexico	Gainesville, Ga. 1/2/04
Lubbock, Francis R.	Beaufort 10/16/15	Harris County, Tex.	Austin, Tex. 6/22/05
McGowan, Samuel	Laurens County 10/9/19	Abbeville	Abbeville 8/9/97
McTyeire, Holland N.	Barnwell Dist. 7/28/24	Nashville, Tenn.	Nashville, Tenn. 2/15/87
Magrath, Andrew G.	Charleston 2/8/13	Charleston	Charleston 4/9/93
Manigault, Arthur M.	Charleston 10/26/24	Georgetown	Georgetown 8/17/86
Marshall, Henry	Darlington Dist. 12/28/05	Louisiana	DeSoto Parish, La. 7/13/64
Martin, John M.	Edgefield District 3/18/32	Ocala, Fla.	Ocala, Fla. 8/10/21
Miles, William P.	Walterboro 7/4/22	Charleston	Burnside, La. 5/11/99
Moore, Andrew B.	Spartanburg 3/7/07	Montgomery, Ala.	Marion, Ala. 4/5/73
Moore, Samuel P.	Charleston 1813	Little Rock, Ark.	Richmond, Va. 5/31/89
Munnerlyn, Charles J.	Georgetown 2/14/22	Decatur Co., Ga.	Decatur Co., Ga. 5/17/98
Murrah, Pendleton	— —	Marshall, Tex.	Monterey, Mexico 7/65
Myers, Abraham C.	Georgetown 5/11	—	Washington, D.C. 6/20/88
Northrop, Lucius B.	Charleston 9/8/11	Charleston	Pikesville, Md. 2/9/94
Orr, James L.	Craytonville 5/12/22	Anderson	St. Petersburg, Russia 5/5/73
Orr, Jehu A.	Craytonville 4/10/28	Houston, Miss.	Columbia, Miss. 3/9/21

Name	Birth	1860 Residence	Death
Owens, James B.	Barnwell District 1816	Marion County, Fla.	Ocala, Fla. 8/1/89
Palmer, Benjamin M.	Charleston 1/25/18	New Orleans, La.	New Orleans, La. 5/25/02
Pickens, Francis W.	Colleton District 4/7/05	Columbia	Edgefield 1/25/69
Pope, Joseph D.	Beaufort Dist. 3/6/20	Beaufort	Columbia 3/21/08
Porcher, Francis P.	St. John's 12/14/25	Charleston	— 11/19/95
Reynolds, Thomas C.	Charleston 10/11/21	St. Louis, Mo.	St. Louis, Mo. 3/30/87
Rhett, Robert B.	Beaufort 12/24/00	Charleston	St. James Parish, Louisiana 9/14/76
Roberts, Oran M.	Laurens District 7/9/15	San Augustine, Tex.	Austin, Tex. 5/19/98
Simpson, William D.	Laurens District 10/27/23	Laurens District	Columbia 12/27/90
Thornwell, James H.	Marlboro Dist. 12/9/12	Columbia	Charlotte, N.C. 8/1/62
Trenholm, George A.	Charleston 2/25/07	Charleston	Charleston 12/10/76
Waul, Thomas N.	Sumter District 1/5/15	Gonzales County, Tex.	Greenville, Tex. 7/28/03
Wigfall, Louis T.	Edgefield Dist. 4/21/16	Marshall, Tex.	Galveston, Tex. 2/18/74
Withers, Thomas J.	Rock Hill 1804	Camden	Camden 11/7/65
Witherspoon, James H.	Lancaster Dist. 3/23/10	Lancaster Dist.	Lancaster District 10/3/65
Young, Pierce M. B.	Spartanburg 11/15/36	—	New York, N.Y. 7/6/96

Tennessee

Name	Birth	1860 Residence	Death
Adams, John	Nashville 7/1/25	Frontier	Franklin 11/30/64
Anderson, James P.	Winchester 2/16/22	Monticello, Fla.	Memphis 9/20/72

Name	Birth	1860 Residence	Death
Atkins, John D. C.	Manly's Chapel 6/4/25	Paris	Paris 6/2/08
Barksdale, Ethelbert	Smyrna 1/4/24	Jackson, Miss.	Jackson, Miss. 2/17/93
Barksdale, William E.	Smyrna 8/21/21	Lowndes County, Miss.	Gettysburg, Pa. 7/2/63
Bate, William B.	Bledsoe's Lick 10/7/26	Nashville	Washington, D.C. 3/9/05
Batson, Felix I.	Dickson County 9/6/19	Clarksville, Ark.	Clarksville, Ark. 3/11/71
Bradford, Alexander B.	Jefferson County 6/2/99	Holly Springs, Miss.	Bolivar, Miss. 7/10/73
Brown, John C.	Giles County 1/6/27	Pulaski	Red Boiling Springs 8/17/89
Campbell, Alexander W.	Nashville 6/4/28	Jackson	Jackson 6/13/93
Caruthers, Robert L.	Smith County 7/31/00	Lebanon	Lebanon 10/2/82
Cheatham, Benjamin F.	Nashville 10/20/20	Nashville	Nashville 9/4/86
Colyar, Arthur St. C.	Washington Co. 6/23/18	Franklin	Nashville 12/13/07
Currin, David M.	Murfreesboro 11/11/17	Memphis	Richmond 3/25/64
Davis, Reuben	Winchester 1/18/13	Aberdeen, Miss.	Huntsville, Ala. 10/14/90
DeWitt, William H.	Smith County 10/24/27	Carthage	Chattanooga 4/11/96
Dibrell, George G.	Sparta 4/12/22	Sparta	Sparta 5/9/88
Donelson, Daniel S.	Sumner County 6/23/01	Sumner County	Byhalia, Miss. 4/17/63
Featherston, Winfield S.	Rutherford Co. 8/8/20	Holly Springs, Miss.	Holly Springs, Miss. 5/28/91
Finley, Jesse J.	Lebanon 11/18/12	Marianna, Fla.	Lake City, Fla. 11/6/04
Foster, Thomas J.	Nashville 7/11/09	Lawrence County, Ala.	Kentucky 2/24/87
Gardenhire, Erasmus L.	Overton County 11/12/15	Sparta	Carthage 4/4/99

Name	Birth	1860 Residence	Death
Garland, Augustus H.	Tipton County 6/11/32	Little Rock, Ark.	Washington, D.C. 1/26/99
Garland, Rufus K.	Tipton County 5/22/30	Hempstead Co., Ark.	Prescott, Ark. 12/12/86
Harris, Isham G.	Tullahoma 2/10/18	Nashville	Washington, D.C. 7/8/97
Haynes, Landon C.	Elizabethtown 12/2/16	Tennessee	Memphis 2/17/75
Hays, Harry T.	Wilson County 4/14/20	New Orleans, La.	New Orleans, La. 8/21/76
Heiskell, Joseph B.	Knox County 11/5/23	Knoxville	Memphis 3/7/13
Hill, Benjamin J.	McMinnville 6/13/25	McMinnville	McMinnville 1/5/80
Hindman, Thomas C.	Knoxville 1/28/28	Helena, Ark.	Helena, Ark. 9/28/68
Hodge, Benjamin L.	— 1824	Shreveport, La.	Richmond 8/12/64
Holder, William D.	Franklin County 3/6/24	Pontotoc, Miss.	Jackson, Miss. 4/26/00
House, John F.	Williamson Co. 1/9/27	Franklin County	Clarksville 6/28/04
Hubbard, David	* 1792	Courtland, Ala.	Pointe Coupeé Parish, La. 1/20/74
Jackson, William H.	Paris 10/1/35	Frontier	Nashville 3/30/03
Lowrey, Mark P.	McNairy County 12/29/28	Kossuth, Miss.	Middleton 2/27/85
McCown, John P.	Seviersville 8/19/15	Frontier	Little Rock, Ark. 6/22/79
Maney, George E.	Franklin 8/24/26	Nashville	Washington, D.C. 2/9/01
Menees, Thomas	Mansker's Creek 6/26/23	Tennessee	Nashville 9/6/05
Mitchel, Charles B.	Gallatin 9/19/15	Washington, Ark.	Little Rock, Ark. 9/20/64
Moore, John C.	Hawkins County 2/23/24	Kentucky	Osage, Tex. 12/31/10

* Born in Tennessee or Virginia

Name	Birth	1860 Residence	Death
Morgan, John T.	Athens 6/20/24	Selma, Ala.	Washington, D.C. 6/11/07
Morgan, Simpson H.	Rutherford Co. 1821	Clarksville, Tex.	Monticello, Ark. 12/15/64
Murray, John P.	Jackson County 7/14/30	Gainesboro	Jackson County 12/21/95
Oldham, Williamson S.	Franklin County 6/19/13	Brenham, Tex.	Houston, Tex. 5/8/68
Pettus, John J.	Wilson County 10/9/13	Kemper County, Miss.	Arkansas 1/25/67
Reagan, John H.	Sevier County 10/8/18	Palestine, Tex.	Palestine, Tex. 3/6/05
Rogers, Samuel St. G.	Pulaski 6/30/32	Ocala, Fla.	Terre Haute, Ind. 9/11/80
Royston, Grandison D.	Carter County 12/9/09	Washington, Ark.	Washington, Ark. 8/14/89
Shelley, Charles M.	Sullivan Co. 12/28/33	Selma, Ala.	Birmingham, Ala. 1/20/07
Smith, James A.	Maury County 7/1/31	—	Jackson, Miss. 12/6/01
Stewart, Alexander P.	Rogersville 10/2/21	Lebanon	Biloxi, Miss. 8/30/03
Tappan, James C.	Franklin 8/9/25	Helena, Ark.	Helena, Ark. 3/19/02
Thomason Hugh F.	Smith County 1826	Van Buren, Ark.	—
Watkins, William W.	Jefferson Co. 4/1/26	Carrollton, Ark.	Harrison, Ark. 1/15/98
Wharton, John A.	Nashville 7/3/28	Brazoria County, Tex.	Houston, Tex. 4/6/65
Wilkes, Peter S.	Maury County 1827	Springfield, Mo.	Stockton, Calif. 1/2/00
Williams, James	Grainger County 7/1/96	Ankara, Turkey	Gratz, Austria 4/10/69
Wright, John V.	Purdy 6/28/28	Purdy, Ky.	Washington, D.C. 6/11/08

Virginia

Name	Birth	1860 Residence	Death
Allen, Henry W.	Prince Edward Co. 4/29/20	Baton Rouge, La.	Mexico City 4/22/67

Name	Birth	1860 Residence	Death
Anderson, Clifford	Nottoway County 3/23/33	Macon, Ga.	Georgia 1899
Anderson, Joseph R.	Frincastle 2/6/13	Richmond	Is. of Shoals, N.H. 9/7/92
Ashby, Turner	Fauquier County 10/23/28	Shenandoah Valley	Harrisonburg, Pa. 6/6/62
Bagby, George W.	Buckingham Co. 8/13/28	Richmond	Richmond 11/29/83
Baldwin, John B.	Augusta County 1/11/20	Staunton	Staunton 9/30/73
Barron, Samuel	Hampton 11/28/09	—	Essex County 2/26/88
Beale, Richard L. T.	Hickory Hill 5/22/19	Hague	Hague 4/21/93
Bell, Casper W.	Prince Edward Co. 2/2/19	Brunswick, Mo.	Brunswick, Mo. 10/27/98
Bocock, Thomas S.	Buckingham Co. 5/18/15	Appomattox Co.	Appomattox Co. 8/5/91
Boteler, Alexander R.	Shepherdstown 5/16/15	Shepherdstown	Shepherdston, W.V. 5/8/92
Branch, Anthony M.	Buckingham Co. 7/16/23	Huntsville, Tex.	Huntsville, Tex. 10/3/67
Brockenbrough, John W.	Hanover County 12/23/06	Lexington	Lexington 2/20/77
Brooke, Walker	Winchester 12/25/13	Lexington, Miss.	Vicksburg, Miss. 2/19/69
Burnett, Henry C.	Essex County 11/25/25	Cadiz, Ky.	Cadiz, Ky. 9/28/66
Burton, James H.	— —	Virginia	— —
Cabell, William L.	Danville 1/1/27	Frontier	Dallas, Tex. 2/22/11
Caperton, Allen T.	Monroe County 11/21/10	Monroe County	Washington, D.C. 7/26/76
Chalmers, James R.	Halifax County 1/11/31	Holly Springs, Miss.	Memphis, Tenn. 4/9/98
Chambliss, John R., Sr.	Sussex County 3/4/09	Hicksford	Hicksford 4/3/75
Chilton, Robert H.	Loudon County 2/25/14	Washington, D.C.	Columbus, Ga. 2/18/79
Clapp, Jeremiah W.	Washington Co. 9/24/14	Holly Springs, Miss.	Memphis, Tenn. 9/5/98

Name	Birth	1860 Residence	Death
Clayton, Alexander M.	Campbell County 1/15/01	Lamar, Miss.	Lamar, Miss. 9/30/89
Collier, Charles F.	Petersburg 9/27/17	Petersburg	Petersburg 6/29/99
Conrad, Charles M.	Frederick Co. 12/24/04	New Orleans, La.	New Orleans, La. 2/11/78
Cooke, John E.	Winchester 11/3/30	Richmond	Clark County 9/20/86
Cooke, William M.	Portsmouth 12/11/23	St. Louis, Mo.	Petersburg 4/14/63
Corse, Montgomery D.	Alexandria 3/14/16	Alexandria	Alexandria 2/11/95
Crenshaw, William G.	Richmond —	Richmond	—
Crump, William W.	Henrico County 11/25/19	Richmond	Richmond 2/27/97
Dabney, Robert L.	Louisa County 3/5/20	Richmond	Victoria, Tex. 1/3/98
Daniel, John M.	Stafford County 10/24/25	Richmond	Richmond 3/30/65
Davis, William G. M.	Portsmouth 5/9/12	Tallahassee, Fla.	Alexandria 3/11/98
De Jarnette, Daniel C.	Bowling Green —	Virginia	White Sulphur Springs, W. Va. 8/20/81
Dickinson, James S.	Spotsylvania 1/18/18	Grove Hill, Ala.	Grove Hill, Ala. 7/23/82
Early, Jubal A.	Franklin County 11/3/16	Franklin County	Lynchburg 3/2/94
Echols, John	Lynchburg 3/20/23	Staunton, W. Va.	Staunton, W. Va. 5/24/96
Elliott, John M.	Scott County 5/20/20	Floyd Co., Ky.	Frankfort, Ky. 3/26/79
Ewell, Richard S.	Georgetown, D.C. 2/8/17	Williamsburg	Nashville, Tenn. 1/25/72
Fearn, Thomas	Danville 11/15/89	Huntsville, Ala.	Huntsville, Ala. 1/16/63
Foote, Henry S.	Fauquier County 9/20/00	Vicksburg, Miss.	Nashville, Tenn. 5/19/80
Fry, Birkett D.	Kanawha County 6/24/22	Tallassee, Ala.	Richmond 1/21/91

Name	Birth	1860 Residence	Death
Funsten, David	Clarke County 10/14/19	Alexandria	Alexandria 4/6/66
Garland, Landon C.	Nelson County 3/21/10	Tuscaloosa, Ala.	Nashville, Tenn. 2/13/95
Garnett, Muscoe R. H.	Essex County 7/25/21	Essex County	Essex County 2/14/64
Gholson, Thomas S.	Gholsonville 12/9/09	Richmond	Savannah, Ga. 12/13/68
Goode, John, Jr.	Bedford County 5/27/29	Bedford County	Norfolk 7/14/09
Gray, Peter W.	Fredericksburg 12/12/19	Houston, Tex.	Houston, Tex. 10/3/74
Green, Thomas	Amelia County 6/8/14	Austin, Tex.	Blair's Land., La. 4/14/64
Gregg, William	Carmichaels 2/2/00	Edgefield District, S.C.	Kalmia, S.C. 9/13/67
Hardinge, Belle B.	Martinsburg 5/9/44	Washington, D.C.	Kilbourne, Wisc. 6/11/00
Harris, Thomas A.	Warren County 1826	Missouri	PeeWee Valley, Ky. 4/9/95
Hatcher, Robert A.	Buckingham Co. 2/24/19	New Madrid, Mo.	Charleston, Mo. 12/4/86
Hawes, Richard	Caroline County 2/6/97	Paris, Ky.	Paris, Ky. 5/25/77
Herbert, Caleb C.	Goochland County 1814	Eagle Lake, Tex.	Columbus, Tex. 7/15/67
Heth, Henry	Chesterfield Co. 12/16/25	Frontier	Washington, D.C. 9/27/99
Hill, Ambrose P.	Culpeper County 11/9/25	Washington, D.C.	Petersburg 4/2/65
Hilton, Robert B.	— 1821	Tallahassee, Fla.	Tallahassee, Fla. 1/10/94
Holcombe, James P.	Lynchburg 9/25/20	Charlottesville	Capon Springs, W. Va. 8/22/83
Holliday, Frederick W.M.	Winchester 2/22/28	Winchester	Winchester 5/20/99
Hume, Thomas	Portsmouth 10/21/36	—	—
Humes, William Y. C.	Abingdon 5/1/30	Memphis, Tenn.	Huntsville, Ala. 9/12/83

Name	Birth	1860 Residence	Death
Hunter, Robert M. T.	Essex County 4/21/09	Washington, D.C.	Lloyds 7/18/87
Hunton, Eppa	Warrenton 9/22/22	Brentsville	Richmond 10/11/08
Jackson, Thomas J.	Clarksburg 1/21/24	Lexington	Chancellorsville 5/10/63
Jackson, William L.	Clarksburg 2/3/25	Richmond	Louisville, Ky. 3/24/90
Jenkins, Albert G.	Cabel County 11/10/30	Charleston	Dublin 5/21/64
Johnson, Edward	Chesterfield Co. 4/16/16	Georgia	Richmond 3/2/73
Johnson, Waldo P.	Bridgeport 9/16/17	Osceola, Mo.	Osceola, Mo. 8/14/85
Johnston, Joseph E.	Prince Edward Co. 2/3/07	Washington, D.C.	Washington, D.C. 3/21/91
Johnston, Robert	Rockbridge Co. 10/14/18	Clarksburg	Rockingham Co. 11/6/85
Jones, George W.	King & Queen Co. 3/15/06	Fayetteville, Tenn.	Fayetteville, Tenn. 11/14/84
Jones, Samuel	Powhaton County 12/17/19	Washington, D.C.	Bedford Springs 7/31/87
Jones, William G.	Powhaton County 11/6/08	Mobile, Ala.	Mobile, Ala. 1883
Jordan, Thomas	Luray Valley 9/30/19	California	New York, N.Y. 11/27/95
Kean, Robert G. H.	Caroline County 10/24/28	Lynchburg	Lynchburg 1898
Keeble, Edwin A.	Cumberland Co. 2/14/07	Murfreesboro, Tenn.	Murfreesboro, Tenn. 8/26/68
Kemper, James L.	Madison County 6/11/23	Madison County	Gordonsville 4/7/95
Lane, James H.	Matthews Ct Hse. 7/28/33	Florida	Auburn, Ala. 9/21/07
Lee, Fitzhugh	Fairfax County 11/19/35	West Point, N.Y.	Washington, D.C. 4/28/05
Lee, George W. C.	Fortress Monroe 9/16/32	—	Burke's Station 2/18/13
Lee, Robert E.	Westmoreland Co. 1/19/07	Texas	Lexington 10/12/70

Name	Birth	1860 Residence	Death
Lee, William H. F.	Arlington 5/31/37	Kent County	Loudoun County 10/15/91
Letcher, John	Lexington 3/29/12	Richmond	Lexington 1/26/84
Lewis, David P.	Charlotte County 1820	Huntsville, Ala.	Huntsville, Ala. 7/3/84
Long, Armistead L.	Campbell County 9/13/27	—	Charlottesville 4/29/91
Lyons, James	Hanovertown 11/12/01	Richmond	Richmond 12/18/82
McCaw, James B.	Richmond 7/12/23	Richmond	Richmond 8/13/06
MacFarland, William H.	Lunenburg Co. 2/9/99	Richmond	Greenbrier Co., WV 1/10/72
McGuire, Hunter H.	Winchester 10/11/35	New Orleans, La.	Richmond 9/19/00
McMullen, Fayette	Bedford County 5/18/05	Virginia	Richmond 11/8/80
Magruder, John B.	Winchester 8/15/10	—	Houston, Tex. 2/19/71
Mahone, William	Monroe 12/1/26	Virginia	Washington, D.C. 10/8/95
Mann, Ambrose D.	Hanover Ct. House 4/26/01	—	Paris, France 11/20/89
Mason, James M.	Fairfax County 11/3/98	Washington, D.C.	Alexandria 4/28/71
Maury, Dabney H.	Fredericksburg 5/21/22	Carlisle, Pa.	Peoria, Ill. 1/11/00
Maury, Matthew F.	Spotsylvania Co. 1/14/06	—	Lexington 2/1/73
Miller, Samuel A.	Shenandoah Co. 10/16/19	Kanawha County	Parkersburg, W. Va. 11/19/90
Monroe, Thomas B.	Albemarle Co. 10/7/91	Franklin County, Ky.	— 12/24/65
Montague, Robert L.	Ellaslee 5/23/19	Middlesex County	Middlesex County 3/2/80
Morehead, John M.	Pennsylvania Co. 7/4/96	Greensboro, N.C.	Rockbridge 8/28/86
Morton, Jackson C.	Fredericksburg 8/10/94	Pensacola, Fla.	Santa Rosa Co., Fla. 11/20/74

Name	Birth	1860 Residence	Death
Ould, Robert	Georgetown, D.C. 1/31/20	Washington, D.C.	Richmond 1882
Oury, Granville H.	Abingdon 3/12/25	Tucson, Az.	—
Page, Richard L.	Clarke County 12/20/07	Virginia	Blue Ridge Summit, Pa. 8/9/01
Parsons, Mosby M.	Charlottesville 5/21/22	Jefferson City, Mo.	China, Mexico 8/17/65
Payne, William H. F.	Clifton 1/27/30	Fauquier County	—
Pegram, John	Petersburg 1/24/32	Frontier	Near Petersburg 2/6/65
Pendleton, William N.	Richmond 12/26/09	Lexington	Lexington 1/15/83
Peyton, Robert L. Y.	Loudon County 2/8/22	Kansas City, Mo.	Bladon Springs, Alabama 9/3/63
Pickett, George E.	Richmond 1/28/25	Washington Terr.	Norfolk 7/30/75
Pollard, Edward A.	Nelson County 2/27/31	Richmond	Lynchburg 12/12/72
Preston, John S.	Abingdon 4/20/09	Columbia, S.C.	Columbia, S.C. 5/1/81
Preston, Walter	Abingdon 7/?/19	Abingdon	Abingdon 11/?/67
Preston, William B.	Smithfield 11/25/05	Smithfield	Smithfield 11/16/62
Price, Sterling	Farmville 9/14/09	Keytesville, Mo.	St. Louis, Mo. 9/29/67
Pryor, Roger A.	Petersburg 7/19/28	Washington, D.C.	New York, N.Y. 3/14/19
Puryear, Richard C.	Mecklenburg Co. 2/9/01	Surry County, N.C.	Yadkin Co., N.C. 7/30/67
Randolph, George W.	Monticello 3/10/18	Charlottesville	Near Charlottesville 4/3/67
Rives, William C.	Amherst County 5/4/92	Albemarle County	Charlottesville 4/25/68
Rodes, Robert E.	Liberty 3/29/29	Missouri	Winchester 9/19/64

Name	Birth	1860 Residence	Death
Rosser, Thomas L.	Campbell County 10/15/36	Texas	Charlottesville 3/29/10
Ruffin, Thomas	King & Queen Co. 11/17/87	Hillsboro, N.C.	Hillsboro, N.C. 1/15/70
Russell, Charles W.	Sisterville 7/19/18	Wheeling	Baltimore, Md. 11/22/67
Rust, Albert	Fauquier County 1818	El Dorado, Ark.	El Dorado, Ark. 4/3/70
Sale, John B.	Amherst County 6/7/18	Memphis, Tenn.	Memphis, Tenn. 1/24/76
Scott, Robert E.	— 4/22/08	Warrenton	— 5/3/62
Seddon, James A.	Falmouth 7/13/15	Goochland Co.	Goochland Co. 8/19/80
Semmes, Thomas J.	Georgetown, D.C. 12/16/24	New Orleans, La.	New Orleans, La. 6/23/99
Slaughter, James E.	Cedar Mountain 6/27	—	Mexico City 1/1/01
Smith, William	Marengo 9/6/97	Warrenton	Warrenton 5/18/87
Snead, Thomas L.	Henrico County 1/10/28	St. Louis, Mo.	New York, N.Y. 10/17/90
Staples, Waller R.	Stuart 2/24/06	Montgomery County	Richmond 8/20/97
Stevenson, Carter L.	Fredericksburg 9/21/17	—	Caroline Co. 8/15/88
Stuart, James E. B.	Patrick County 2/6/33	—	Richmond 5/12/64
Taliaferro, William B.	Belleville 12/28/22	Gloucester County	Gloucester Co. 2/27/98
Terry, William	Amherst County 8/14/24	Wytheville	Wytheville 8/5/88
Thomas, John J.	Albemarle Co. 8/8/13	Christian County, Ky.	— —
Thompson, John R.	Richmond 10/23/23	Augusta, Ga.	New York, N.Y. 4/30/73
Tibbs, William H.	Appomattox 6/10/16	Cleveland, Tenn.	Dalton, Ga. 10/18/06
Tompkins, Sally L.	Matthews Co. 11/9/33	Richmond	Richmond 7/25/16

Name	Birth	1860 Residence	Death
Trimble, Isaac R.	Culpeper Co. 5/15/02	Baltimore, Md.	Baltimore, Md. 1/2/88
Tucker, John Randolph	Alexandria 1/31/12	Norfolk	Petersburg 6/12/83
Tyler, John	Charles Cty. Co. 3/29/90	Williamsburg	Richmond 1/18/62
Venable, Abraham W.	Springfield 10/17/99	Oxford, N.C.	Oxford, N.C. 2/24/76
Walker, James A.	Mount Meridian 8/27/32	Pulaski County	Wytheville 10/21/01
Walker, Reuben L.	Logan 5/29/27	New Kent Co.	New Kent Co. 6/7/90
Walthall, Edward C.	Richmond 4/4/31	Coffeeville, Miss.	Washington, D.C. 4/21/98
Watson, John W. C.	Albemarle Co. 2/27/08	Holly Springs, Miss.	Holly Springs, Miss. 9/24/90
Watterson, Henry	Washington, D.C. 2/16/40	Washington, D.C.	Jacksonville, Fla. 12/22/21
Whitfield, Robert H.	— 1815	Smithfield	— —
Wickham, Williams C.	Richmond 9/21/20	Hanover County	Richmond 7/23/88
Wilkinson, John	Norfolk 11/6/21	—	Annapolis, Md. 12/29/91
Wise, Henry A.	Drummondtown 12/3/06	Accomec County	Richmond 9/14/76

THE NORTH

Name	Birth	1860 Residence	Death
Allen, William W.	New York City 1835	Alabama	Sheffield, Ala. 11/24/94
Cheves, Langdon	Philadelphia 6/17/14	Savannah, Ga.	Charleston, S.C. 7/10/63
Clark, Charles	Lebanon, Ohio 5/24/11	Bolivar County Miss.	Bolivar Co., Miss. 12/17/77
Clark, Willis G.	New York 10/27/27	Mobile, Ala.	Roanoke, Va. 9/10/98
Conrow, Aaron H.	Cincinnati, Ohio 6/9/24	Richmond, Mo.	Camarzo, Mexico 8/14/65

Name	Birth	1860 Residence	Death
Cooper, Samuel	Hackensack, N.J. 6/12/98	—	Alexandria, Va. 12/14/76
De Fontaine, Felix G.	Boston, Mass. 1834	Charleston, S.C.	Columbia, S.C. 12/11/96
Flanagin, Harris	Roadstown, N.J. 11/31/17	Arkadelphia, Ark.	Arkadelphia, Ark. 10/23/74
French, Samuel G.	Gloucester County, N.J. 11/22/18	Greenville, Miss.	Florala, Ala. 4/20/10
Gardner, Franklin	New York, N.Y. 1/29/33	Frontier	Vermilionville, La. 4/29/73
Gorgas, Josiah	Dauphin Co., Pa. —	Mobile, Ala.	Tuscaloosa, Ala. 5/15/83
Gracie, Archibald, Jr.	New York, N.Y. 12/1/32	Mobile, Ala.	Petersburg, Va. 12/2/64
Hotchkiss, Jebediah	Windsor, N.Y. 11/30/28	Churchville, Va.	Staunton, Va. 1/17/99
Huse, Caleb	Newburyport, Mass. 2/11/31	Tuscaloosa, Ala.	Highland Falls, N.Y. 3/11/05
Ingram, Porter	Marlborough, Vt. 4/1/10	Columbus, Ga.	Columbus, Ga. 12/3/93
Johnson, Bushrod R.	Norwich, Ohio 10/7/17	Nashville, Tenn.	Brighton, Ill. 9/12/80
Lomax, Lunsford L.	Newport, R.I. 11/4/35	Frontier	Washington, D.C. 5/28/13
Lovell, Mansfield	New York, N.Y. 10/20/22	New York, N.Y.	New York, N.Y. 6/1/84
Merrick, Edwin T.	Wilbraham, Mass. 7/9/09	New Orleans, La.	New Orleans, La. 1/2/97
Pemberton, John L.	Philadelphia, Pa. 8/10/74	Virginia	Penllyn, Pa. 7/18/81
Perry, Edward A.	Richmond, Mass. 3/15/31	Pensacola, Fla.	Kerrville, Tex. 10/15/89
Pratt, Daniel	Temple, N.H. 7/10/99	Autauga County, Ala.	— 5/13/73
Quintard, Charles T.	Stamford, Conn. 12/22/24	Nashville, Tenn.	Darien, Ga. 2/15/98
Ripley, Roswell S.	Worthington, Ohio 3/14/23	Charleston, S.C.	New York, N.Y. 3/29/87

Name	Birth	1860 Residence	Death
Sanderson, John P.	Sunderland, Vt. 11/28/16	Jacksonville, Fla.	New York, N.Y. 6/28/71
Sexton, Franklin B.	New Harmony, Ind. 4/29/28	San Augustine, Tex.	El Paso, Tex. 5/15/00
Shoup, Francis A.	Laurel, Ind. 3/22/34	St. Augustine, Fla.	Columbia, Tenn. 9/4/96
Slidell, John	New York, N.Y. 1793	New Orleans, La.	Cowes, Isle of Wight, England 7/26/72
Smith, Martin L.	Tompkins County, N.Y. 9/9/19	—	Savannah, Ga. 7/29/66
Stevens, Walter H.	Pen Yan, N.Y. 8/24/27	New Orleans, La.	Vera Cruz, Mex. 11/12/67
Tift, Nelson	Groton, Conn. 1810	Albany, Ga.	Albany, Ga. 11/21/91
Wadley, William M.	Brentwood, N.H. 1812	Savannah, Ga.	Sara. Spgs., N.Y. 8/10/82
Ware, Horace	Lynn, Mass. 4/11/12	Shelby County, Ala.	Birmingham, Ala. 7/90
Wilkes, John	New York, N.Y. 3/31/27	Charlotte, N.C.	—

TERRITORIES

Name	Birth	1860 Residence	Death
Alcorn, James L.	Golconda, Ill. 11/4/16	Delta, Miss.	Eagles Nest, Miss. 12/20/94
Armstrong, Frank C.	Choctaw Agency 11/22/35	Frontier	Bar Harbor, Mich. 9/8/09
Maffitt, John N.	At sea 2/22/19	—	Wilmington, N.C. 5/15/86
Ross, Lawrence S.	Benton's Post, Io. 9/27/38	Texas	College Station, Tex. 1/3/98
Wood, John T.	Fort Snelling, N.W. Terr. 8/13/30	Annapolis, Md.	Halifax, Nova Scotia 7/19/04

Name	Birth	1860 Residence	Death

FOREIGN BORN

Name	Birth	1860 Residence	Death
Benjamin, Judah P.	St. Croix, West Indies 8/6/11	New Orleans, La.	Paris, France 5/8/84
Browne, William M.	Dublin, Ireland 7/7/27	Athens, Ga.	Athens, Ga. 4/28/83
Cleburne, Patrick R.	County Cork, Ireland 3/17/28	Helena, Ark.	Franklin, Tenn. 11/30/64
Colston, Raleigh E.	Paris, France 10/31/25	Lynchburg, Va.	Richmond, Va. 7/29/96
Cooper, Charles P.	Cuba 8/13/27	Athens, Ga.	Jacksonville, Fla. 1/9/95
Devine, Thomas J.	Halifax, Nova Scotia 2/28/20	San Antonio, Tex.	San Antonio, Tex. 3/16/90
Ford, Samuel H.	London, England 2/19/19	Louisville, Ky.	St. Louis, Mo. 7/5/05
Hotze, Henry	Zurich, Switzerland 9/2/33	Mobile, Ala.	Zug, Switzerland 4/19/87
Lander, William	Tiparo, Ireland 5/9/17	Lincolnton, N.C.	Lincolnton, N.C. 1/6/68
Lynch, Patrick N.	Ireland 3/10/17	Charleston, S.C.	Charleston, S.C. 2/26/82
Mallet, John W.	Dublin, Ireland 10/10/32	Tuscaloosa, Ala.	Charlottesville, Va. 11/6/12
Mallory, Stephen R.	Trinidad, West Indies 1812-1813	Washington, D.C.	Pensacola, Fla. 11/9/73
Martin, Augustus M.	Breton, France 2/2/03	Natchitoches, La.	Louisiana 9/29/75
Memminger, Christopher G.	Nayhingen, Germany 1/7/03	Charleston, S.C.	Charleston, S.C. 3/7/88
de Polignac, Camile A.J.M.	Millemont, France 2/16/32	Central America	Paris, France 11/15/13
Power, John L.	Tipperary County, Ireland 3/1/34	Jackson, Miss.	Jackson, Miss. 9/24/01

Name	Birth	1860 Residence	Death
Quintero, Juan	Havana, Cuba —	—	—
Rives, Alfred L.	Paris, France 3/25/30	Virginia	Richmond, Va. 2/27/03
Soulé, Pierre	Castillon, France 8/28/02	New Orleans, La.	New Orleans, La. 3/26/70
Sparrow, Edward	Dublin, Ireland 12/29/10	Carroll Parish La.	Lake Providence, Louisiana 7/4/82
Verot, Jean Pierre Augustin M.	LePuy, France 5/23/05	Savannah, Ga.	St. Augustine, Fla. 6/10/76

appendix II / *Principal Occupations*
Prewar, Wartime, Postwar

When postwar occupation is not indicated, the leader either died during the war or disappeared into obscurity. An asterisk (*) means that the leader died during the war or died too soon after the war to start a career.

Name	Prewar	Wartime	Postwar
Adams, Daniel W.	Lawyer	Military	Lawyer-Businessman
Adams, John	Military	Military	*
Adams, William W.	Planter	Military	Businessman
Akin, Warren	Lawyer	Congressman	Lawyer
Alcorn, James L.	Lawyer-Planter	Military	Lawyer
Alexander, Edward P.	Military	Military	Businessman
Alexander, Peter W.	Lawyer-Editor	Journalist	Lawyer
Allen, Henry W.	Lawyer-Planter	Governor	Journalist
Allen, William W.	Planter	Military	Planter
Anderson, Clifford	Lawyer	Congressman	Lawyer

Name	Prewar	Wartime	Postwar
Anderson, George T.	Military-Planter	Military	Businessman
Anderson, James P.	Lawyer-Planter	Military-Congressman	Businessman
Anderson, Joseph R.	Businessman	Military	Businessman
Anderson, Richard H.	Military	Military	Farmer-Laborer
Anderson, Robert H.	Military	Military	Businessman-Local Government Official
Archer, James J.	Military	Military	*
Armistead, Lewis A.	Military	Military	*
Armstrong, Frank C.	Military	Military	Laborer-Government Official
Arrington, Archibald H.	Lawyer-Planter	Congressman	Lawyer
Ashby, Turner	Planter-Businessman	Military	*
Ashcraft, Thomas	Farmer-Inventor	Manufacturer	*
Ashe, Thomas S.	Lawyer	Congressman-Senator	State Politician
Ashe, William S.	Planter-Lawyer	Military	*
Atkins, John D. C.	Planter-Lawyer	Congressman	Planter
Avery, William W.	Lawyer	Congressman	*
Ayer, Lewis M., Jr.	Lawyer-Planter	Congressman	Minister-Educator
Bagby, George W.	Physician-Journalist	Journalist	Writer
Baker, Alpheus	Lawyer	Military	Lawyer
Baker, James M.	Lawyer-Planter	Senator	Lawyer

Name	Prewar	Wartime	Postwar
Baker, Laurence S.	Military	Military	Businessman
Baldwin, John B.	Lawyer	Congressman	Lawyer-State Politician
Barksdale, Ethelbert	Journalist	Congressman	Farmer-Editor
Barksdale, William E.	Lawyer-Editor	Military	*
Barnwell, Robert W.	Lawyer-Politician	Senator	Educator
Barringer, Rufus	Lawyer	Military	Lawyer-Farmer
Barron, Samuel	Military	Military	Farmer
Barry, William T. S.	Lawyer-Planter	Congressman	Lawyer
Bartow, Francis S.	Lawyer	Congressman	*
Bass, Nathan	—	Congressman	Farmer
Bate, William B.	Lawyer	Military	Lawyer-State Politician
Batson, Felix I.	Lawyer	Congressman	Lawyer
Battle, Cullen A.	Lawyer	Military	Newspaperman
Baylor, John R.	Lawyer	Congressman	Lawyer
Beale, Richard L. T.	Lawyer	Military	Farmer-Lawyer
Beauregard, Pierre G. T.	Military	Military	Businessman
Bee, Hamilton P.	Politician	Military	Businessman
Bell, Casper W.	Lawyer-Newspaperman	Congressman	Lawyer
Bell, Hiram P.	Lawyer	Congressman	Lawyer
Benjamin, Judah P.	Lawyer-Planter	Cabinet	Lawyer

Name	Prewar	Wartime	Postwar
Benning, Henry L.	Lawyer	Military	Lawyer
Blandford, Mark H.	Lawyer-Businessman	Congressman	Lawyer
Bledsoe, Albert T.	Educator	Sub-Cabinet	Writer-Editor
Bocock, Thomas S.	Lawyer	Congressman	Lawyer
Boggs, William R.	Military	Military	Architect-Engineer
Bonham, Milledge L.	Lawyer-Politician	Military-Governor-Congressman	Lawyer-Businessman
Boteler, Alexander R.	Planter-Businessman	Congressman	Lawyer-Government Official
Boudinot, Elias C.	Lawyer-Editor	Congressman	Farmer
Bowen, John S.	Military-Architect	Military	*
Boyce, William W.	Lawyer-Planter	Congressman	Lawyer
Bradford, Alexander B.	Lawyer-Businessman	Congressman	Lawyer
Bradley, Benjamin F.	Farmer-Lawyer	Congressman	Farmer-Lawyer
Bragg, Braxton	Military	Military	Engineer
Bragg, Thomas	Lawyer	Cabinet	Lawyer
Branch, Anthony M.	Lawyer	Congressman	Lawyer
Bratton, John	Planter-Physician	Military	Planter-State Politician
Breckinridge, John C.	Lawyer	Military-Cabinet	Lawyer-Businessman
Breckinridge, Robert J.	Lawyer	Congressman	Lawyer
Bridgers, Robert R.	Lawyer-Planter	Congressman	Businessman
Brockenbrough, John W.	Lawyer	Congressman	Lawyer-Educator

Name	Prewar	Wartime	Postwar
Brooke, John M.	Military	Military	Military-Educator
Brooke, Walker	Lawyer	Congressman	Lawyer
Brown, Albert G.	Lawyer-Planter	Senator	Farmer
Brown, John C.	Lawyer	Military	Lawyer-Businessman
Brown, Joseph E.	Lawyer-Politician	Governor	Lawyer-Politician
Browne, William M.	Journalist	Military	Educator
Bruce, Eli M.	Merchant	Congressman	Businessman
Bruce, Horatio W.	Lawyer	Congressman	Lawyer-Educator
Bryan, Goode	Military-Planter	Military	Planter
Buchanan, Franklin,	Military	Military	College President
Buckner, Simon B.	Military	Military	Editor-Politician
Bulloch, James D.	Military	Military	Merchant-Writer
Burnett, Henry C.	Lawyer	Senator	Lawyer
Burnett, Theodore L.	Lawyer	Congressman	Lawyer
Burton, James H.	—	Armorer	—
Butler, Matthew C.	Lawyer	Military	Lawyer-Businessman
Cabell, William L.	Military	Military	Lawyer-Businessman
Callahan, Samuel B.	Rancher	Congressman	Rancher
Campbell, Alexander W.	Lawyer	Military	Lawyer-Banker
Campbell, John A.	Lawyer	Sub-Cabinet	Lawyer

Name	Prewar	Wartime	Postwar
Campbell, Josiah A. P.	Lawyer	Congressman	Lawyer
Cantey, James	Lawyer-Planter	Military	Planter
Capers, Ellison	Educator	Military	Minister-Educator
Caperton, Allen T.	Lawyer-Financier	Senator	Businessman-State Politician
Carroll, David W.	Lawyer	Congressman	Lawyer
Carter, John C.	Lawyer	Military	*
Caruthers, Robert L.	Lawyer-Educator	Governor-Congressman	Educator
Chalmers, James R.	Lawyer	Military	Lawyer
Chambers, Henry C.	Planter	Congressman	Farmer
Chambliss, John R., Sr.	Lawyer-Planter	Congressman	Lawyer
Cheatham, Benjamin F.	Farmer	Military	Local Government Official
Chesnut, James, Jr.	Lawyer	Congressman-Military	Lawyer
Cheves, Langdon	Lawyer-Planter	Engineer	*
Chilton, Robert H.	Military	Military	Manufacturer
Chilton, William P.	Lawyer	Congressman	Lawyer
Chisholm, John J.	Physician-Educator	Physician	Physician-Educator
Chrisman, James S.	Lawyer	Congressman	Lawyer
Churchill, Thomas J.	Planter-Lawyer	Military	State Politician
Clanton, James H.	Lawyer	Military	Lawyer
Clapp, Jeremiah W.	Planter-Lawyer	Congressman	State Politician

Name	Prewar	Wartime	Postwar
Clark, Charles	Planter-Lawyer	Governor-Military	Lawyer
Clark, Henry T.	Planter-Lawyer	Governor	Farmer-Lawyer
Clark, John B.	Lawyer	Congressman-Senator	Lawyer
Clark, William W.	Lawyer-Planter	Congressman	Lawyer-Businessman
Clark, Willis G.	Journalist	Newspaper Editor	Businessman
Clay, Clement C.	Lawyer-Planter	Senator-Diplomat	Lawyer-Planter
Clayton, Alexander M.	Planter-Lawyer	Congressman-Judge	Businessman
Clayton, Henry D.	Lawyer	Military	Lawyer-Farmer
Clayton, Philip	Lawyer-Planter	Sub-Cabinet	Diplomat
Cleburne, Patrick R.	Lawyer	Military	*
Clingman, Thomas L.	Lawyer	Military	Mining Promoter-Politician
Clopton, David	Lawyer	Congressman	Lawyer-Businessman
Clusky, Michael W.	Politician-Editor	Congressman	Newspaper Editor
Cobb, Howell	Lawyer-Politician-Planter	Congressman-Military	Lawyer-Planter
Cobb, Thomas R. R.	Lawyer	Military-Congressman	*
Cockrell, Francis M.	Lawyer	Military	Lawyer-Politician
Collier, Charles F.	Lawyer-Farmer	Congressman	Lawyer-Politician
Colquitt, Alfred H.	Lawyer-Farmer	Military	Lawyer-Farmer
Colston, Raleigh E.	Educator	Military	Military-Educator
Colyar, Arthur S. C.	Lawyer	Congressman	Lawyer-Journalist-Businessman

Name	Prewar	Wartime	Postwar
Conner, James	Lawyer	Military	Lawyer
Conrad, Charles M.	Lawyer	Congressman	Lawyer
Conrow, Aaron H.	Lawyer	Congressman	Adventurer
Cooke, John E.	Lawyer-Writer	Writer-Military	Writer-Planter
Cooke, John R.	Military-Engineer	Military	Merchant
Cooke, William M.	Lawyer	Congressman	*
Cooper, Charles P.	Lawyer	Cabinet Advisor	Lawyer
Cooper, Douglas H.	Planter-Lawyer	Military	Lawyer
Cooper, Samuel	Military	Military	—
Corse, Montgomery D.	Banker	Military	Banker
Cox, William R.	Lawyer-Planter	Military	Lawyer-Businessman
Craige, Francis B.	Lawyer	Congressman	Lawyer
Craigmiles, John H.	Banker	Commissary Agent	Banker
Crawford, Martin J.	Farmer-Lawyer	Congressman	Lawyer-Judge
Crenshaw, William G.	Merchant	Diplomat-Industrialist	Industrialist
Crittenden, George B.	Lawyer-Military	Military	Librarian
Crockett, John W.	Lawyer	Congressman	Lawyer
Cruikshank, Marcus H.	Lawyer-Editor	Congressman	Editor
Crump, William W.	Lawyer	Sub-Cabinet	Lawyer
Cumming, Alfred	Military	Military	Farmer

Name	Prewar	Wartime	Postwar
Currin, David M.	Lawyer	Congressman	*
Curry, Jabez L. M.	Lawyer	Congressman	College President-Diplomat
Dabney, Robert L.	Minister-Educator	Minister-Educator	Minister-Educator
Daniel, John M.	Journalist	Journalist	*
Daniel, Junius	Military-Planter	Military	*
Darden, Stephen H.	Farmer-Politician	Congressman	State Politician
Dargan, Edmund S.	Lawyer	Congressman	Lawyer
Davidson, Allen T.	Lawyer-Banker	Congressman	Lawyer
Davis, George	Lawyer	Congressman-Senator	Lawyer
Davis, Jefferson	Lawyer-Planter	President	Planter-Businessman
Davis, Joseph R.	Lawyer-Farmer	Military	Lawyer-Farmer
Davis, Nicholas, Jr.	Planter-Lawyer	Congressman	Lawyer
Davis, Reuben	Lawyer	Congressman	Lawyer-State Politician
Davis, Varina H.	Homemaker	First Lady	Writer
Davis, William G. M.	Lawyer-Businessman	Military	Lawyer-Planter
Dawkins, James B.	Farmer-Lawyer	Congressman-Judge	Lawyer-Judge
Deas, Zachariah C.	Cotton Broker	Military	Cotton Broker
DeBow, James D. B.	Editor-Educator	Editor	Editor
DeClouet, Alexander	Lawyer-Planter	Congressman	State Politician
deFontaine, Felix G.	Journalist	Journalist	Journalist

Name	Prewar	Wartime	Postwar
De Jarnette, Daniel C.	Farmer	Congressman	Farmer
De Leon, David C.	Military-Physician	Military-Physician	Physician
De Leon, Edwin	Editor-Diplomat	Diplomat	Writer
Devine, Thomas J.	Lawyer	Diplomat	Lawyer
DeWitt, William H.	Lawyer-Educator	Congressman	Lawyer
Dibrell, George G.	Lawyer	Military	Farmer-Businessman
Dickinson, James S.	Lawyer	Congressman	Lawyer
Doles, George P.	Merchant	Military	*
Donelson, Daniel S.	Planter	Military	*
Dortch, William T.	Planter-Lawyer	Senator	Farmer-Lawyer
Duke, Basil C.	Physician	Physician	Physician
Duke, Basil W.	Lawyer	Military	Lawyer-Writer
Dupré, Lucius Jacques	Lawyer	Congressman	Lawyer
Early, Jubal A.	Lawyer-Military	Military	Lawyer
Echols, John	Lawyer	Military	Lawyer-Businessman
Echols, Joseph H.	Minister-Planter-Lawyer-College President	Congressman	Lawyer-Minister
Ector, Matthew D.	Lawyer	Military	Lawyer-Judge
Elliott, John M.	Lawyer	Congressman	Judge
Elliott, Stephen	Minister-Educator	Bishop-Religious Leader	Religious Leader
Ellis, John W.	Lawyer-Politician	Governor	*

Name	Prewar	Wartime	Postwar
Elzey, Arnold	Military	Military	Farmer
Evans, Augusta J.	Novelist	Novelist-Nurse	Novelist
Evans, Clement A.	Lawyer	Military	Minister-Writer
Ewell, Richard S.	Military-College President	Military	Farmer
Ewing, George	Lawyer-Planter	Congressman	Farmer
Fagan, James F.	Banker-State Politician	Military	Farmer-Politician
Farrow, James	Lawyer-Editor	Congressman	State Politician
Fearn, Thomas	Physician	Congressman	*
Featherston, Winfield S.	Lawyer	Military	Lawyer-Politician
Ferguson, Samuel W.	Military	Military	Lawyer-Engineer
Field, Charles W.	Military-Educator	Military	Military-Government Official
Finley, Jesse J.	Lawyer	Military-Judge	Lawyer-State Politician
Flanagin, Harris	Lawyer	Governor	Lawyer
Foote, Henry S.	Lawyer-Planter	Congressman	Lawyer
Ford, Samuel H.	Minister	Congressman	Minister
Forman, Thomas M.	Farmer	Congressman	Farmer
Forney, John H.	Military	Military	Planter-Engineer
Forrest, Nathan B.	Planter-Businessman	Military	Planter
Forsyth, John	Lawyer-Editor	Mayor	Editor
Foster, Thomas J.	Planter-Manufacturer	Congressman	—

Name	Prewar	Wartime	Postwar
Freeman, Thomas W.	Lawyer	Congressman	*
French, Samuel G.	Military-Planter	Military	Planter-Businessman
Fry, Birkett D.	Lawyer-Businessman	Military	Industrialist
Fuller, Thomas C.	Lawyer	Congressman	Lawyer
Funsten, David	Lawyer	Congressman	Lawyer
Furman, James C.	Minister-Educator	Religious Leader	Minister-Educator
Gaither, Burgess S.	Lawyer	Congressman	Lawyer
Gardenhire, Erasmus	Lawyer	Congressman	Lawyer-State Politician
Gardner, Franklin	Military	Military	Planter
Garland, Augustus H.	Lawyer	Congressman-Senator	Lawyer
Garland, Landon C.	Educator-College President	Educator-College President	Educator
Garland, Rufus K.	Lawyer-Farmer-Preacher	Congressman	Lawyer-Preacher
Garnett, Muscoe R. H.	Lawyer-Planter	Congressman	*
Gartrell, Lucius J.	Lawyer	Congressman-Military	Lawyer
Gentry, Meredith P.	Lawyer-Politician	Congressman	Farmer
Gholson, Samuel J.	Lawyer	Military	Lawyer
Gholson, Thomas S.	Lawyer-Businessman	Congressman	Merchant
Gibson, Randall L.	Planter	Military	Planter-Lawyer
Gilmer, Francis M.	Industrialist-Planter	Presidential Advisor	Banker-Industrialist
Gilmer, Jeremy F. F.	Military-Engineer	Military-Engineer	Engineer-Businessman

Name	Prewar	Wartime	Postwar
Gilmer, John A.	Lawyer-Politician	Congressman	Lawyer
Gist, States R.	Lawyer	Military	*
Goode, John, Jr.	Lawyer	Congressman	Lawyer
Gordon, James B.	Merchant-Farmer	Military	*
Gordon, John B.	Lawyer	Military	Politician-Businessman
Gorgas, Josiah	Military	Military	Industrialist-Educator
Govan, Daniel C.	Planter	Military	Planter
Gracie, Archibald, Jr.	Merchant-Military	Military	*
Graham, Malcolm D.	Lawyer	Congressman-Judge	Lawyer
Graham, William A.	Lawyer	Senator	Writer-Historian
Gray, Henry	Lawyer	Congressman	Lawyer-State Politician
Gray, Peter W.	Lawyer	Congressman	Lawyer
Green, Thomas	Lawyer	Military	*
Greenhow, Rose O.	Hostess	Intelligence Agent	*
Gregg, John	Lawyer	Congressman-Military	*
Gregg, Maxcy	Lawyer-Scientist	Military	*
Gregg, William	Manufacturer	Manufacturer-Financier	Manufacturer
Grimes, Bryan	Planter	Military	Planter
Hale, Stephen F.	Lawyer-Planter	Congressman	*
Hampton, Wade	Planter-Lawyer	Military	Planter-Politician

Name	Prewar	Wartime	Postwar
Hanly, Thomas B.	Lawyer-Farmer	Congressman	State Politician
Hardee, William J.	Military-Educator	Military	Planter-Businessman
Hardinge, Belle B.	Student	Intelligence Agent	Actress-Writer
Harris, Isham G.	Lawyer	Governor	Politician
Harris, Nathaniel H.	Lawyer	Military	Lawyer-Businessman
Harris, Thomas A.	Lawyer-Journalist	Military	Journalist-Businessman
Harris, Wiley P.	Lawyer	Congressman	Lawyer
Harrison, James T.	Lawyer	Congressman	Scientist
Harrison, Thomas	Lawyer	Military	Judge-Lawyer
Hartridge, Julian	Lawyer	Military	Lawyer-Politician
Hatcher, Robert A.	Lawyer	Congressman	Lawyer
Hawes, James M.	Military	Military	Merchant
Hawes, Richard	Lawyer-Politician	Governor	Lawyer-Judge
Haynes, Landon C.	Lawyer-Politician	Senator	Lawyer
Hays, Harry T.	Lawyer	Military	Lawyer
Hébert, Louis	Military-Engineer-Planter	Military	Planter-Editor
Hébert, Paul O.	Military-Engineer	Military	Engineer-State Politician
Heiskell, Joseph B.	Lawyer-Editor	Congressman	Lawyer
Helm, Benjamin H.	Lawyer	Military	*
Hemphill, John	Lawyer	Congressman	*

Name	Prewar	Wartime	Postwar
Henry, Gustavus A.	Lawyer	Senator	Lawyer
Herbert, Caleb C.	Farmer	Congressman	Farmer
Heth, Henry	Military	Military	Businessman-Engineer
Hill, Ambrose P.	Military	Military	*
Hill, Benjamin H.	Lawyer	Senator	Lawyer
Hill, Benjamin J.	Merchant	Military	Merchant-Lawyer
Hill, Daniel H.	Military-Educator	Military	College President-Journalist
Hilton, Robert B.	Lawyer-Journalist	Congressman	Lawyer
Hindman, Thomas C.	Planter-Lawyer	Military	Planter-State Politician
Hodge, Benjamin L.	Farmer-Lawyer-Merchant	Congressman-Judge	*
Hodge, George B.	Lawyer	Congressman-Military	Lawyer
Hoke, Robert F.	Manufacturer	Military	Businessman
Holcombe, James P.	Educator	Congressman	Educator
Holden, William W.	Editor	Editor-Politician	Editor-Politician
Holder, William D.	Planter	Congressman	Farmer
Holliday, Frederick W.M.	Lawyer	Congressman	Lawyer-Farmer
Hollins, George N.	Military	Military	Court Officer
Holmes, Theophilus H.	Military	Military	Farmer
Holt, Hines	Lawyer	Congressman	Lawyer
Holtzclaw, James T.	Lawyer	Military	State Politician

Name	Prewar	Wartime	Postwar
Hood, John B.	Military	Military	Merchant
Hotchkiss, Jebediah	Educator	Military-Topographer	Educator-Engineer
Hotze, Henry	Journalist	Journalist-Diplomat	Journalist
House, John F.	Lawyer	Congressman-Judge	Politician
Hubbard, David	Lawyer-Industrialist	Bureaucrat	Businessman
Huger, Benjamin	Military	Military	Farmer
Hume, Thomas	Educator	Minister	Educator-College President
Humes, William Y. C.	Lawyer	Military	Lawyer
Humphreys, Benjamin G.	Lawyer-Planter	Military	Planter-Businessman
Hunter, Robert M. T.	Lawyer-Planter-Politician	Cabinet-Senator	Politician
Hunton, Eppa	Lawyer	Military	Lawyer
Hurst, David W.	Lawyer	Judge	Lawyer
Huse, Caleb	Military-Educator	Government Agent	Educator
Ingram, Porter	Lawyer-Planter	Congressman	Lawyer
Iverson, Alfred, Jr.	Military-Railroad Contractor	Military	Businessman-Planter
Jackson, Claiborne F.	Businessman-Banker	Governor	*
Jackson, Henry R.	Lawyer	Military-Judge	Lawyer-Businessman
Jackson, John K.	Lawyer	Military	Lawyer
Jackson, Thomas J.	Military-Educator	Military	*
Jackson, William H.	Military	Military	Planter-Businessman

Name	Prewar	Wartime	Postwar
Jackson, William L.	Lawyer	Military	Lawyer
Jemison, Robert, Jr.	Planter-Businessman	Senator	Businessman-Philanthropist
Jenkins, Albert G.	Farmer	Congressman-Military	*
Jenkins, Charles J.	Lawyer	Judge	Politician
Jenkins, Micah	Educator	Military	*
Johnson, Bushrod R.	Military-Educator	Military	Educator
Johnson, Edward	Military	Military	Farmer
Johnson, George W.	Lawyer	Governor	*
Johnson, Herschel V.	Planter-Lawyer	Senator	Lawyer
Johnson, Robert W.	Lawyer-Editor	Senator	Lawyer
Johnson, Thomas	Merchant	Congressman	Merchant
Johnson, Waldo P.	Lawyer	Senator	Lawyer
Johnson, Albert S.	Military	Military	*
Johnston, George D.	Lawyer	Military	Lawyer-Educator
Johnston, Joseph E.	Military	Military	Businessman
Johnston, Robert	Lawyer	Congressman	Lawyer-Judge
Johnston, Robert D.	Student	Military	Lawyer-Editor-Banker
Johnston, William P.	Lawyer	Military (aide)	College President
Jones, David R.	Military	Military	*
Jones, George W.	Laborer-Politician	Congressman	Businessman

Name	Prewar	Wartime	Postwar
Jones, Henry C.	Lawyer	Manufacturer	Lawyer
Jones, John B.	Writer-Editor	Sub-Cabinet	Writer
Jones, Joseph	Educator	Physician	Educator-Physician
Jones, Robert M.	Farmer-Businessman	Congressman	Farmer
Jones, Samuel	Military	Military	Farmer-Government Official
Jones, Thomas M.	Lawyer	Congressman	Lawyer
Jones, William G.	Lawyer	Judge	Lawyer
Jordan, Thomas	Military	Military	Editor
Kean, Robert G. H.	Lawyer	Sub-Cabinet	Lawyer
Keeble, Edwin A.	Lawyer-Planter-Editor	Congressman	Lawyer
Keitt, Lawrence M.	Lawyer	Congressman	*
Kell, John M.	Military	Military	Farmer
Kelly, John H.	Student	Military	*
Kemper, James L.	Lawyer	Military	Lawyer-Farmer
Kenan, Augustus H.	Lawyer	Congressman	Lawyer
Kenan, Oren R.	Planter	Congressman	Lawyer
Kenner, Duncan F.	Lawyer-Planter	Congressman-Diplomat	Businessman
Kershaw, Joseph B.	Lawyer	Military	Local Politician
Keyes, Wade, Jr.	Lawyer	Sub-Cabinet	Lawyer
Lamar, Gazaway B.	Banker-Financier	Banker	Businessman

Name	Prewar	Wartime	Postwar
Lamar, Lucius Q. C.	Lawyer-Planter-Politician	Diplomat-Judge	Educator-National Politician
Lamkin, John T.	Lawyer-Farmer	Congressman	Lawyer
Lander, William	Lawyer-Farmer	Congressman	Lawyer
Lane, James H.	Educator	Military	Educator
Law, Evander M.	Lawyer-Educator	Military	Planter-Businesman-Educator
Lawton, Alexander R.	Lawyer-Railroad President	Military-Sub-Cabinet	Lawyer
Leach, James M.	Lawyer	Congressman	State Politician
Leach, James T.	Physician-Farmer	Congressman	Farmer
Lee, Fitzhugh	Military-Educator	Military	Farmer-Politician
Lee, George W. C.	Military-Engineer	Military	Educator-College President
Lee, Robert E.	Military	Military	College President
Lee, Stephen D.	Military	Military	Politician-College President
Lee, William H. F.	Military	Military	Planter
Lester, George N.	Lawyer	Congressman	Lawyer
Letcher, John	Lawyer-Editor-Politician	Governor	Lawyer
Lewis, David P.	Lawyer-Planter	Congressman-Judge	Lawyer
Lewis, David W.	Lawyer-Planter	Congressman	Politician-College President
Lewis, John W.	Farmer-Physician-Preacher-Manufacturer	Congressman-Manufacturer	*
Lewis, Joseph H.	Lawyer-Farmer	Military	Lawyer-Farmer
Logan, George W.	Lawyer-Farmer	Congressman	Editor-Businessman

Name	Prewar	Wartime	Postwar
Lomax, Lunsford L.	Military	Military	Farmer-College President
Long, Armistead L.	Military	Military	Engineer
Longstreet, James	Military	Military	Businessman
Loring, William W.	Military-Lawyer	Military	Banker-Military
Lovell, Mansfield	Military-Businessman	Military	Engineer-Planter
Lowrey, Mark P.	Laborer-Clergyman	Military	Clergyman-Educator
Lubbock, Francis R.	Rancher-Politician	Governor	Businessman
Lynch, Patrick N.	Clergyman-Bishop	Bishop	Bishop
Lyon, Francis S.	Lawyer	Congressman	State Politician
Lyons, James	Lawyer	Congressman	Lawyer
McCallum, James	Lawyer	Congressman	Businessman
McCausland, John	Educator	Military	Farmer
McCaw, James B.	Physician-Educator	Physician	Physician-Educator
McCown, John P.	Military	Military	Educator-Farmer
McDowell, Thomas D.	Planter-Lawyer	Congressman	Lawyer
MacFarland, William H.	Lawyer-Financier	Congressman	Lawyer
McGeehee, Edward	Planter-Businessman	Businessman	Planter
McGowan, Samuel,	Lawyer-Politician	Military	Lawyer-Politician
McGrath, Andrew G.	Lawyer	Governor-Judge	Lawyer
McGuire, Hunter H.	Physician-Educator	Military-Physician	Physician-Planter

Name	Prewar	Wartime	Postwar
Machen, Willis B.	Farmer-Merchant-Manufacturer	Congressman	Manufacturer
Mackall, William W.	Military	Military	Farmer
McLaws, Lafayette	Military	Military	Businessman
McLean, James R.	Lawyer-Farmer	Congressman	Lawyer
McMullen, Fayette	Farmer-Laborer	Congressman	Farmer
McQueen, John	Planter-Lawyer	Congressman	Farmer
McRae, Colin J.	Businessman	Government Financial Agent	Planter
McRae, John J.	Lawyer-Editor-Businessman	Congressman	Planter
McTyeire, Holland N.	Clergyman	Bishop-Editor	College President
MacWillie, Malcolm H.	Lawyer	Congressman	—
Maffitt, John N.	Military	Military	Farmer
Magruder, John B.	Military	Military	Lecturer
Mahone, William	Engineer	Military	Businessman
Mallet, John W.	Educator	Scientist	Educator-Scientist
Mallory, Stephen R.	Lawyer-Politician	Cabinet	Lawyer
Maney, George E.	Lawyer	Military	Railroad President
Manigault, Arthur M.	Merchant-Planter	Military	Planter
Manly, Basil	Clergyman-Educator	Clergyman	Clergyman
Mann, Ambrose D.	Lawyer-Politician	Diplomat	Journalist
Marmaduke, John S.	Military	Military	Businessman

Name	Prewar	Wartime	Postwar
Marshall, Henry	Farmer	Congressman	*
Marshall, Humphrey	Lawyer-Planter	Military-Congressman	Lawyer
Martin, Augustus M.	Clergyman-Bishop	Bishop	Bishop
Martin, James G.	Military	Military	Lawyer
Martin, John M.	Planter	Congressman	Railroad Promoter
Martin, William T.	Lawyer	Military	Businessman
Mason, James M.	Lawyer	Congressman-Diplomat	Farmer
Maury, Dabney H.	Military-Educator	Military	Educator
Maury, Matthew F.	Military-Scientist	Military-Scientist-Diplomat	Educator
Maxey, Samuel B.	Military-Lawyer	Military	Lawyer
Maxwell, Augustus E.	Lawyer-Politician	Congressman	Lawyer-Railroad President
Memminger, Christopher G.	Lawyer	Cabinet	Lawyer-Manufacturer
Menees, Thomas	Physician-Investor	Congressman	Physician-Educator
Merrick, Edwin T.	Lawyer-Planter	Judge	Lawyer
Miles, William P.	Educator-Lawyer	Congressman	Planter-College President
Miller, Samuel A.	Lawyer-Businessman	Congressman	Lawyer
Milton, John	Lawyer-Farmer	Governor	*
Mitchel, Charles B.	Physician	Congressman	*
Monroe, Thomas B.	Lawyer-Educator	Congressman	*
Montague, Robert L.	Lawyer	Congressman	Lawyer-Judge

Name	Prewar	Wartime	Postwar
Moore, Andrew B.	Lawyer	Governor	Lawyer
Moore, James W.	Lawyer	Congressman	Lawyer
Moore, John C.	Military-Educator	Military	Educator
Moore, Samuel P.	Military-Physician	Cabinet	Farmer-Educator
Moore, Thomas O.	Planter	Governor	Planter
Morehead, John M.	Businessman-Politician	Congressman	Businessman
Morgan, John H.	Merchant-Manufacturer	Congressman	*
Morgan, John T.	Lawyer	Military	National Politician
Morgan, Simpson H.	Lawyer-Farmer	Congressman	*
Morris, William S.	Businessman-Physician	Chief of Military Telegraph	—
Morton, Jackson C.	Planter-Manufacturer	Congressman	Businessman
Munnerlyn, Charles J.	Planter	Congressman	Railroad Business
Murrah, Pendleton	Lawyer	Governor	*
Murray, John P.	Lawyer	Congressman	Lawyer
Myers, Abraham C.	Military	Military	—
Newsom, Ella K.	Homemaker	Hospital Administrator	Government Official
Nicholls, Francis R.	Lawyer	Military	Lawyer-Planter
Nisbet, Engenius A.	Lawyer	Congressman	Writer-Lecturer
Northrop, Lucius B.	Military Physician	Commissary General	Farmer
Norton, Nimrod L.	Farmer	Congressman	Farmer

Name	Prewar	Wartime	Postwar
Ochiltree, William B.	Lawyer	Congressman	Lawyer
Oldham, Williamson S.	Lawyer-Politician	Congressman	Photographer-Writer
O'Neal, Edward A.	Lawyer	Military	State Politician
Orr, James L.	Lawyer-Politician	Congressman	Politician-Diplomat
Orr, John A.	Lawyer	Congressman	Lawyer
Ould, Robert	Lawyer	Sub-Cabinet	Lawyer
Oury, Granville H.	Lawyer-Farmer	Congressman	Lawyer
Owens, James B.	Planter	Congressman	Planter
Page, Richard L.	Military	Military	Educator
Palmer, Benjamin M.	Clergyman-Educator-Editor	Chaplain	Clergyman
Parsons, Mosby M.	Lawyer	Military	Adventurer-Military
Payne, William H. F.	Lawyer	Military	Lawyer
Pearson, Richmond M.	Lawyer	Judge	Lawyer-Judge
Pegram, John	Military	Military	*
Pemberton, John L.	Military	Military	Farmer
Pender, William D.	Military	Military	*
Pendleton, William N.	Educator-Clergyman	Military	Clergyman
Perkins, John, Jr.	Lawyer-Planter	Congressman	Planter
Perry, Edward A.	Lawyer	Military	Lawyer-Businessman
Pettigrew, James J.	Lawyer	Military	*

Name	Prewar	Wartime	Postwar
Pettus, Edmund W.	Lawyer	Military	Lawyer-Politician
Pettus, John J.	Lawyer	Governor	*
Peyton, Robert L. Y.	Lawyer-Planter	Congressman	*
Phelan, James	Lawyer-Journalist	Congressman-Judge	Lawyer
Pickens, Francis W.	Planter-Lawyer	Governor	Planter
Pickett, George E.	Military	Military	Insurance Business
Pickett, John T.	Lawyer-Diplomat	Diplomat	Lawyer
Pierce, George F.	Educator-Minister	Bishop	Minister
de Polignac, Camille A.J.M.	Military	Military	Engineer-Military
Polk, Leonidas	Clergyman-Bishop	Military	*
Polk, Lucius E.	Planter	Military	Planter
Pollard, Edward A.	Journalist	Journalist	Journalist
Pope, Joseph D.	Lawyer	Bureaucrat	Lawyer-Educator
Porcher, Francis P.	Physician	Surgeon	Physician-Surgeon
Power, John L.	Printer-Editor	State Bureaucrat-Printer	Journalist-Printer
Pratt, Daniel	Laborer-Industrialist	Businessman	Businessman
Preston, John S.	Lawyer-Planter	Military	Philanthropist
Preston, Walter	Lawyer-Planter	Congressman	Lawyer
Preston, William	Lawyer	Military Diplomat	Lawyer
Preston, William B.	Lawyer-Businessman	Congressman	*

Name	Prewar	Wartime	Postwar
Price, Sterling	Farmer-Politician	Military	Adventurer
Pryor, Roger A.	Journalist	Congressman-Military	Lawyer
Pugh, James L.	Lawyer	Congressman	Lawyer
Puryear, Richard C.	Planter	Congressman	Planter
Quintard, Charles T.	Physician-Clergyman	Chaplain-Physician	Bishop-Educator
Quintero, Juan	Lawyer	Diplomat	State Government Official
Rains, Gabriel J.	Military	Military	Military
Rains, George W.	Military-Industrialist	Bureaucrat	Educator-Businessman
Ralls, John P.	Physician	Congressman	Physician
Ramsay, James G.	Physician-Farmer	Congressman	Physician
Ramseur, Stephen D.	Military	Military	*
Randolph, George W.	Lawyer	Cabinet	*
Ransom, Matt W.	Lawyer-Planter	Military	Lawyer-Planter
Ransom, Robert, Jr.	Military	Military	Farmer-Engineer
Read, Henry E.	Lawyer-Politician	Congressman	Merchant
Reade, Edwin G.	Farmer-Lawyer	Congressman	Lawyer-Banker
Reagan, John H.	Farmer-Lawyer	Cabinet	Lawyer
Rector, Henry M.	Farmer-Lawyer	Governor	Planter
Reynolds, Thomas C.	Lawyer	Governor	Politician
Rhett, Robert B.	Planter-Lawyer	Congressman-Editor	Planter

Name	Prewar	Wartime	Postwar
Ripley, Roswell S.	Military-Educator-Businessman	Military	Businessman
Rives, Alfred L.	Engineer	Bureaucrat	Engineer
Rives, William C.	Planter-Lawyer	Congressman	Writer
Roberts, Oran M.	Lawyer-Farmer	Judge	Lawyer-Educator
Robertson, Jerome B.	Physician-Military	Military	Physician-Businessman
Robinson, Cornelius	Commission Merchant	Congressman	Planter
Roddey, Philip D.	Businessman	Military	Businessman
Rodes, Robert E.	Teacher-Engineer	Military	*
Rogers, Samuel St. G.	Lawyer-Planter	Congressman	Planter
Ross, Lawrence S.	Indian Fighter	Military	Educator-College President
Rosser, Thomas L.	Student	Military	Railroad Engineer
Royston, Grandison D.	Lawyer	Congressman	Lawyer
Ruffin, Thomas	Lawyer-Farmer	Statesman	Lawyer
Ruffin, Thomas	Lawyer-Politician	Congressman	*
Russell, Charles W.	Lawyer	Congressman	Lawyer-Author
Rust, Albert	Lawyer-Planter	Congressman-Military	Lawyer-Politician
St. John, Isaac M.	Engineer	Bureaucrat	Engineer
Sale, John B.	Lawyer	Military (Staff)	Lawyer
Sanderson, John P.	Planter-Lawyer	Congressman	Planter
Scott, Robert E.	Lawyer-Farmer	Congressman	*

Name	Prewar	Wartime	Postwar
Seddon, James A.	Lawyer-Planter	Cabinet	Businessman
Semmes, Raphael	Military	Military	Lawyer-Editor
Semmes, Thomas J.	Lawyer	Congressman	Lawyer-Educator
Sexton, Franklin B.	Lawyer-Farmer	Congressman	Lawyer
Shelby, Joseph O.	Businessman-Planter	General	Farmer
Shelby, Charles M.	Businessman	General	Lawyer-Businessman
Shewmake, John T.	Lawyer	Congressman	Lawyer
Shorter, John G.	Lawyer	Congressman-Governor	Lawyer
Shoup, Francis A.	Military-Lawyer	Military	Minister-Educator
Simms, William E.	Lawyer	Congressman	Farmer
Simpson, William D.	Lawyer	Congressman	Lawyer
Sims, Frederick W.	Editor-Businessman	Bureaucrat	Businessman-Editor
Singleton, Ortho R.	Lawyer-Planter	Congressman	Lawyer
Slaughter, James E.	Military	Military	Engineer
Slidell, John	Lawyer-Businessman	Diplomat	*
Smith, Charles H.	Lawyer	Writer	Writer
Smith, Edmund K.	Military	Military	Educator
Smith, Gustavus W.	Engineer-Military	Military	Businessman
Smith, James A.	Military	Military	Educator
Smith, James M.	Lawyer	Congressman	Lawyer

Name	Prewar	Wartime	Postwar
Smith, Martin L.	Military	Military	Engineer
Smith, Robert H.	Lawyer	Congressman	Lawyer
Smith, William	Lawyer	Military-Governor-Congressman	Farmer
Smith, William E.	Lawyer-Planter	Congressman	Lawyer
Smith, William N. H.	Lawyer	Congressman	Lawyer
Smith, William R.	Lawyer-Editor	Congressman	Lawyer-Educator
Snead, Thomas L.	Editor	Congressman	Lawyer-Editor
Sorrel, Gilbert M.	Businessman	Military	Businessman
Soulé, Pierre	Lawyer	Diplomat	Lawyer
Sparrow, Edward	Lawyer-Planter	Congressman	Lawyer
Staples, Waller R.	Lawyer	Congressman	Lawyer
Stephens, Alexander H.	Lawyer	Vice-President	Lawyer
Stephens, Linton	Lawyer	State Legislator	Lawyer
Steuart, George H.	Military	Military	Farmer
Stevens, Walter H.	Military	Military	Engineer
Stevenson, Carter L.	Military	Military	Engineer
Stewart, Alexander P.	Educator	Military	Educator
Strickland, Hardy	Farmer	Congressman	Farmer
Stuart, James E. B.	Military	Military	*
Swain, David L.	Educator	Educator	Educator
Swan, William G.	Businessman-Editor	Congressman	Businessman-Lawyer

Name	Prewar	Wartime	Postwar
Taliaferro, William B.	Lawyer-Planter	Military	Planter
Tappan, James C.	Lawyer	Military	Lawyer
Tattnall, Josiah	Military (Navy)	Military (Navy)	*
Taylor, Richard	Planter	Military	Writer
Terry, William	Lawyer-Editor	Military	Lawyer
Thomas, Edward L.	Planter	Military	Planter
Thomas, James H.	Lawyer-Farmer	Congressman	Lawyer
Thomas, John J.	Planter	Congressman	Businessman
Thomason, Hugh F.	Lawyer	Congressman	Lawyer
Thompson, Jacob	Lawyer	Diplomat	Planter
Thompson, John R.	Editor-Lawyer	Diplomat-Editor	Editor
Thornwell, James H.	Minister	Minister-Editor	*
Tibbs, William H.	Businessman-Farmer	Congressman	Businessman
Tift, Nelson	Businessman-Editor	Businessman	Businessman
Tompkins, Sally L.	Philanthropist	Nurse	Philanthropist
Toombs, Robert A.	Lawyer-Planter	Congressman-Military-Cabinet	Lawyer
Trenholm, George A.	Businessman	Cabinet	Businessman
Trimble, Isaac R.	Engineer	Military	Engineer
Triplett, George W.	Businessman-Farmer	Congressman	Farmer
Trippe, Robert P.	Lawyer	Congressman	Lawyer

Name	Prewar	Wartime	Postwar
Tucker, John R.	Military (Navy)	Military (Navy)	Businessman
Turner, Joseph A.	Editor-Lawyer	Editor-Businessman	*
Turner, Josiah, Jr.	Lawyer	Congressman	Businessman-Editor
Tyler, John	Lawyer	Congressman	*
Vance, Zebulon B.	Lawyer	Governor	Lawyer
Van Dorn, Earl	Military	Military	*
Venable, Abraham W.	Lawyer	Congressman	Lawyer
Verot, Jean Pierre Augustin M.	Clergyman	Clergyman	Clergyman
Vest, George G.	Lawyer	Congressman	Lawyer
Villeré, Charles J.	Lawyer-Planter	Congressman	Planter
Wadley, William M.	Businessman	Bureaucrat	Businessman
Walker, James A.	Lawyer	Military	Lawyer
Walker, John G.	Military	Military	Businessman
Walker, Leroy P.	Lawyer	Cabinet-Military	Lawyer
Walker, Reuben L.	Farmer	Military	Farmer-Businessman
Walker, Richard W.	Lawyer-Planter	Congressman	Lawyer
Walker, William H. T.	Military	Military	*
Walthall, Edward C.	Lawyer	Military	Lawyer
Ward, George T.	Businessman-Planter	Congressman	*
Ware, Horace	Businessman	Businessman	Businessman

Name	Prewar	Wartime	Postwar
Warren, Edward	Physician	Physician	Physician
Watie, Stand	Farmer-Editor	Military	Farmer-Businessman
Watkins, W. W.	Lawyer	Congressman	Lawyer
Watson, John W. C.	Lawyer	Congressman	Lawyer
Watterson, Henry	Editor	Editor	Editor
Watts, Thomas H.	Lawyer	Cabinet-Governor	Lawyer
Waul, Thomas N.	Lawyer	Congressman-Military	Lawyer
Welsh, Israel	Lawyer	Congressman	Lawyer
Wharton, John A.	Lawyer	Military	*
Wheeler, Joseph	Military	Military	Lawyer-Military
White, Daniel P.	Physician-Businessman	Congressman	Businessman
Whitfield, Robert H.	Lawyer-Farmer	Congressman	*
Whiting, William H. C.	Military	Military	*
Wickham, Williams C.	Lawyer-Planter	Congressman-Military	Businessman
Wigfall, Louis T.	Lawyer	Congressman	Lawyer
Wilcox, Cadmus M.	Military	Military	Government
Wilcox, John A.	Lawyer	Congressman	*
Wilkes, John	Businessman-Military(Navy)	Businessman	Businessman
Wilkes, Peter S.	Farmer-Lawyer	Congressman	Lawyer
Wilkinson, John	Military(Navy)	Businessman-Military(Navy)	Businessman-Military(Navy)

Name	Prewar	Wartime	Postwar
Williams, James	Businessman-Editor	Diplomat	*
Williams, John S.	Lawyer-Rancher	Military	Farmer
Williams, Thomas H.	Physician-Military	Physician	Physician
Wilson, William S.	Lawyer	Congressman	*
Winder, John H.	Military	Military	*
Wise, Henry A.	Lawyer	Military	Lawyer
Withers, Jones M.	Lawyer-Businessman	Military	Businessman-Editor
Withers, Thomas J.	Lawyer-Planter	Congressman	*
Witherspoon, James H.	Farmer	Congressman	*
Wofford, William T.	Lawyer-Planter	Military	Planter
Wood, John T.	Military	Military	Businessman
Worth, Jonathan	Businessman-Planter	State Legislator	Lawyer
Wright, Ambrose R.	Lawyer-Planter	Military	Lawyer
Wright, Augustus, R.	Lawyer-Planter	Congressman	Lawyer
Wright, John V.	Lawyer-Planter	Congressman-Judge	Government
Wright, Marcus J.	Businessman	Military	Editor
Wright, William B.	Lawyer	Congressman	Lawyer
Yancey, William L.	Lawyer-Planter	Congressman-Diplomat	*
Yandell, David W.	Physician	Physician	Physician
Young, Pierce M. B.	Educator	Military	Planter-Diplomat
Young, William H.	Student	Military	Lawyer

appendix III / *Religious Affiliation*

Most of the Confederate leaders had strong religious ties. The Episcopal church had the oldest tradition in the Southeast. But, by the end of the eighteenth century, the Presbyterian church, especially in the Scots-Irish settlements of the Piedmont, had the largest church membership in the South. At the beginning of the nineteenth century, the Methodist and Methodist-Episcopal churches, which had been associated with the Episcopal church, began to flourish in the newer settlements of the Southwest. At the same time, the Baptists separated from the Presbyterians and soon were competing with the Methodists on the southwestern frontier. By the 1820s, various fundamentalist sects, including the Campbellite Christian church, were competing with the established churches of the southwest. In 1860, the Baptist and Methodist churches held at least two-thirds of the church membership of the South. The Catholic church flourished within the German and English settlements in Maryland and Kentucky, the French settlements in Louisiana, and the urban settlements of Charleston and Mobile, but it had less than 10 percent of the Southern church membership on the eve of the Civil War. Jews lived in Savannah and Charleston in the late seventeenth century, but their numbers were very small in the antebellum South.

BAPTIST

Ashcraft, Thomas
Ayer, Lewis M., Jr.
Barksdale, William E.
Battle, Cullen A.
Brown, Joseph E.
Chilton, William P.
Cooper, Douglas H.
Crawford, Martin J.
Curry, Jabez L. M.
Dargan, Edmund S.
Davis, Reuben
Ford, Samuel H.
Furman, James C.
Gordon, John B.
Hale, Stephen F.
Harrison, James T.

Harrison, Thomas
Hartridge, Julian
Hatcher, Robert A.
Hill, Ambrose P.
Hume, Thomas
Logan, George W.
Lowry, Mark P.
Manly, Basil
Montague, Robert
Newsom, Ella K.
Shorter, John G.
Smith, James M.
Thomas, John J.
Watts, Thomas H.
Waul, Thomas N.
Wright, Augustus R.

CHRISTIAN

Burnett, Henry C.

Gardenhire, E. L.

EPISCOPALIAN

Anderson, Joseph R.
Anderson, Richard H.
Armistead, Lewis A.
Ashe, Thomas S.
Ashe, William S.
Barnwell, Robert W.
Peale, Richard L. T.
Bee, Hamilton P.
Bledsoe, Albert T.
Boggs, William R.
Bonham, Milledge L.
Boyce, William W.
Bragg, Braxton
Bratton, John
Brooke, John M.
Buchanan, Franklin
Buckner, Simon B.
Burnett, Theodore L.
Cabell, William L.
Cantey, James
Carter, John C.
Cheves, Landon
Clay, Clement C.
Clayton, Alexander M.
Clayton, Henry D.
Cleburne, Patrick R.
Conner, James
Conrad, Charles M.
Cooper, Samuel
Corse, Montgomery D.
Cox, William R.
Craigmiles, John H.
Crenshaw, William G.
Crump, William W.
Cumming, Alfred
Daniel, John M.
Davis, George
Davis, Jefferson
Davis, Varina H.
Davis, William G. M.
Deas, Zachariah C.

De Bow, James D. B.
Duke, Basil C.
Duke, Basil W.
Early, Jubal A.
Echols, John
Elliott, Stephen
Ellis, John W.
Ewell, Richard S.
Ferguson, Samuel W.
Foote, Henry S.
Forney, John H.
Fry, Birckett D.
Garnett, Ruscoe R. H.
Gholson, Thomas S.
Goode, John, Jr.
Gordon, James B.
Gorgas, Josiah
Govan, Daniel C.
Gracie, Archibald, Jr.
Gregg, Maxcy
Gregg, William
Hampton, Wade
Hardee, William J.
Hardinge, Belle B.
Hawes, James M.
Hawes, Richard
Heth, Henry
Hoke, Robert F.
Hood, John B.
Hubbard, David
Humes, William Y. C.
Hunter, Robert M. T.
Jackson, William H.
Jenkins, Micah
Johnson, Edward
Johnston, Albert S.
Johnston, Joseph E.
Johnston, William P.
Jones, John B.
Jones, Thomas M.
Kean, Robert G. H.

Lander, William
Lane, James H.
Lee, Fitzhugh
Lee, George W. C.
Lee, Robert E.
Lee, William H. F.
Loring, William W.
Lyon, Francis S.
MacFarland, William H.
McGowan, Samuel
McGuire, Hunter H.
McQueen, John
Magrath, Andrew G.
Mahone, William
Mallet, John W.
Mallory, Stephen R.
Manigault, Arthur M.
Martin, James G.
Mason, James M.
Maury, Dabney H.
Maury, Matthew F.
Maxwell, Augustus E.
Memminger, Christopher G.
Miles, William P.
Morgan, John II.
Ochiltree, William B.
Pegram, John
Pender, William D.

Pendleton, William N.
Pettigrew, James J.
Polk, Leonidas
Polk, Lucius E.
Pollard, Edward A.
Pope, Joseph D.
Pugh, James L.
Quintard, Charles T.
Randolph, George W.
Ruffin, Thomas
Shoup, Francis A.
Smith, Edmund K.
Stuart, James E. B.
Taliaferro, William B.
Taylor, Richard
Thompson, Jacob
Thompson, John R.
Tompkins, Sallie L.
Toombs, Robert A.
Tyler, John
Walthall, Edward C.
Ward, George T.
Warren, Edward
Wheeler, Joseph
Wigfall, Louis T.
Wilkes, John
Wright, John V.
Wright, Marcus J.

JEWISH

Benjamin, Judah P.
De Leon, David C.

De Leon, Edwin
Myers, Abraham C.

METHODIST

Akin, Warren
Allen, William W.
Anderson, George T.
Atkins, John D. C.
Barksdale, Ethelbert
Colquitt, Alfred H.
Dibrell, George G.
Echols, Joseph H.
Evans, Augusta J.
Evans, Clement A.
Garland, Landon C.
Garland, Rufus K.
Gilmer, Francis M.
Gist, States R.
Hill, Benjamin H.

House, John F.
Ingram, Porter
Jemison, Robert, Jr.,
Jones, Henry C.
Kenan, Augustus H.
Keyes, Wade, Jr.
Lamar, Lucius Q.C.
McTyeire, Holland N.
Merrick, Edwin T.
Morgan, John T.
Munnerlyn, Charles J.
O'Neal, Edward A.
Reagan, John H.
Robinson, Cornelius
Ross, Lawrence S.

Rust, Albert
Sexton, Franklin B.
Shelley, Charles M.
Thomas, Edward L.

Turner, Joseph A.
Williams, John S.
Wofford, William T.

METHODIST-EPISCOPAL

Bell, Hiram P.
Capers, Ellison
Clopton, David
Davidson, Allen T.
DeWitt, William H.
Holden, William W.
Holtzclaw, James T.

Maffitt, John N.
Menees, Thomas
Murray, John P.
Pierce, George F.
Ralls, John P.
Trippe, Robert P.

PRESBYTERIAN

Alcorn, James L.
Alexander, Edward P.
Allen, Henry W.
Anderson, Clifford
Archer, James J.
Avery, William W.
Baker, James M.
Barringer, Rufus
Barry, William T. S.
Bocock, Thomas S.
Boteler, Alexander R.
Bowen, John S.
Bragg, Thomas
Breckinridge, John C.
Breckinridge, Robert J.
Brown, Albert G.
Campbell, John A.
Campbell, Josiah A. P.
Caruthers, Robert L.
Chambers, Henry C.
Chesnut, James, Jr.
Clapp, Jeremiah W.
Clingman, Thomas L.
Cobb, Howell
Cobb, Thomas R. R.
Cruikshank, Marcus H.
Dabney, Robert L.
Donelson, Daniel S.
Finley, Jesse J.
Forrest, Nathan B.
Forsyth, John

Fuller, Thomas C.
Gilmer, John A.
Graham, William A.
Green, Thomas
Heiskell, Joseph B.
Hemphill, John
Hill, Daniel H.
Hindman, Thomas C.
Holcombe, James P.
Holliday, Frederick W. M.
Hotchkiss, Jedediah
Iverson, Alfred, Jr.
Jackson, Thomas J.
Jackson, William L.
Jenkins, Albert G.
Jenkins, Charles J.
Johnson, Herschel V.
Johnston, George D.
Johnston, Robert D.
Jones, Joseph
Jones, Samuel
Law, Evander M.
Letcher, John
McCallum, James
McDowell, Thomas D. S.
McLean, James R.
McRae, Colin J.
McRae, John J.
Marshall, Henry
Mitchel, Charles B.
Moore, Andrew B.

Morehead, John M.
Nisbet, Eugenius A.
Orr, James L.
Orr, Jehu A.
Palmer, Benjamin M.
Perry, Edward A.
Pettus, Edmund W.
Pettus, John J.
Power, John L.
Preston, John S.
Preston, William B.
Price, Sterling
Pryor, Roger A.
Ramsay, James G.
Ramseur, Stephen D.
Royston, Grandison D.
Simpson, William D.
Slaughter, James E.
Smith, William N. H.
Sorrel, Gilbert M.

Stephens, Alexander H.
Stephens, Linton
Stewart, Alexander P.
Swain, David L.
Thornwell, James H.
Vance, Zebulon B.
Van Dorn, Earl
Venable, Abraham W.
Vest, George G.
Walker, Leroy P.
Walker, Richard W.
Watson, John W. C.
Wharton, John A.
Wise, Henry A.
Withers, Jones M.
Witherspoon, James H.
Wright, William B.
Yancey, William L.
Young, Pierce M. B.

QUAKER

Johnson, Bushrod R.
Kershaw, Joseph B.

Pemberton, John L.

ROMAN CATHOLIC

Baker, Alpheus
Beauregard, Pierre G. T.
Carroll, David W.
DeClouet, Alexander
deFontaine, Felix G.
Devine, Thomas J.
Gardner, Franklin
Greenhow, Rose O.
Hays, Harry T.
Hébert, Louis
Hébert, Paul O.
Longstreet, James
Lynch, Patrick N.
Martin, Augustus M.
Nicholls, Francis R.
Northrop, Lucius B.

Ould, Robert
Perkins, John, Jr.
Preston, William
Quintero, Juan
Semmes, Raphael
Semmes, Thomas J.
Singleton, Ortho R.
Smith, William R.
Soulé, Pierre
Sparrow, Edward
Stevens, Walter H.
Verot, Jean Pierre Augustin M.
Villeré, Charles J.
Walker, John G.
Watterson, Henry
Whiting, William H. C.

appendix **IV** / *Education*

Educational levels present problems of categorization. Most of these Confederate leaders had some form of pre-University education, though some notable exceptions exist. Common schools or public grammar schools existed throughout the South, but many of these leaders either had home tutors for university preparation, or attended private schools. Few public secondary schools existed. What were commonly called colleges were actually private secondary schools. Many of these leaders attended university for only a short period of time and did not bother to take degrees. Therefore attendance rather than graduation has been used to illustrate the level of education of these Confederate leaders.

Categories: 1. Public school — primary or secondary
2. Private school — tutor, primary, and secondary (college)
3. Southern university
4. Northern university
5. United States Military Academy
6. Law school
7. Medical school
8. Graduate education (before the War this did not go above the M.A. level).
9. No information

	1	*2*	*3*	*4*	*5*	*6*	*7*	*8*	*9*
Name	*PUS*	*PRS*	*SoU*	*NoU*	*USMA*	*LAW*	*MED*	*GRAD*	*NI*
Adams, Daniel W.		X	X						
Adams, John		X			X				
Adams, William W.	X								
Akin, Warren	X								

Name	1 PUS	2 PRS	3 SoU	4 NoU	5 USMA	6 LAW	7 MED	8 GRAD	9 NI
Alcorn, James L.		X							
Alexander, Edward P.		X			X				
Alexander, Peter W.		X	X						
Allen, Henry W.		X		X					
Allen, William W.		X		X					
Anderson, Clifford	X								
Anderson, George T.		X	X						
Anderson, James P.		X		X		X			
Anderson, Joseph R.		X			X				
Anderson, Richard H.		X			X				
Anderson, Robert H.		X			X				
Archer, James J.		X		X					
Armistead, Lewis A.		X			X				
Armstrong, Frank C.		X		X					
Arrington, Archibald H.		X							
Ashby, Turner		X							
Ashcraft, Thomas	X								
Ashe, Thomas S.		X	X						
Ashe, William S.		X							
Atkins, John D. C.		X	X						
Avery, William W.		X	X						
Ayer, Lewis M., Jr.		X	X	X		X			
Bagby, George		X					X		
Baker, Alpheus		X							
Baker, James M.		X	X						
Baker, Laurence S.		X			X				
Baldwin, John B.		X	X						
Barksdale, Ethelbert	X								
Barksdale, William E.	X	X							
Barnwell, Robert W.		X	X	X				X	
Barringer, Rufus		X	X						
Barron, Samuel									X
Barry, William T. S.		X		X					
Bartow, Francis S.		X	X						
Bass, Nathan	X								
Bate, William B.		X				X			
Batson, Felix I.									X
Battle, Cullen A.		X	X						
Baylor, John R.									X
Beale, Richard L. T.		X		X		X			
Beauregard, Pierre G. T.		X			X				

Name	*1* PUS	*2* PRS	*3* SoU	*4* NoU	*5* USMA	*6* LAW	*7* MED	*8* GRAD	*9* NI
Bee, Hamilton P.		X							
Bell, Casper W.		X	X			X			
Bell, Hiram P.		X							
Benjamin, Judah P.	X			X					
Benning, Henry L.		X	X						
Blandford, Mark H.		X	X						
Bledsoe, Albert T.				X	X				
Bocock, Thomas S.		X	X						
Boggs, William R.		X			X				
Bonham, Milledge L.		X	X						
Boteler, Alexander R.		X		X					
Boudinot, Elias C.									X
Bowen, John S.		X			X				
Boyce, William W.		X				X			
Bradford, Alexander B.									X
Bradley, Benjamin F.		X	X						
Bragg, Braxton		X			X				
Bragg, Thomas		X							
Branch, Anthony M.		X	X						
Bratton, John		X	X				X		
Breckinridge, John C.		X		X		X			
Breckinridge, Robert J.		X	X						
Bridgers, Robert R.		X	X						
Brockenbrough, John W.		X	X			X			
Brooke, John M.		X			X				
Brooke, Walker		X	X						
Brown, Albert G.		X							
Brown, John C.		X							
Brown, Joseph E.	X			X		X			
Browne, William M.									X
Bruce, Eli M.	X								
Bruce, Horatio W.		X							
Bryan, Goode		X			X				
Buchanan, Franklin									X
Buckner, Simon B.		X			X				
Bulloch, James D.		X							
Burnett, Henry C.		X							
Burnett, Theodore L.		X	X						
Burton, James H.									X
Butler, Matthew C.		X	X						
Cabell, William L.		X			X				

Name	1 PUS	2 PRS	3 SoU	4 NoU	5 USMA	6 LAW	7 MED	8 GRAD	9 NI
Callahan, Samuel B.									X
Campbell, Alexander W.		X	X			X			
Campbell, John A.		X	X		X				
Campbell, Josiah A. P.		X	X						
Cantey, James		X	X						
Capers, Ellison		X	X						
Caperton, Allen T.		X		X					
Carroll, David W.		X	X						
Carter, John C.		X	X			X			
Caruthers, Robert L.		X							
Chalmers, James R.		X	X						
Chambers, Henry C.		X		X					
Chambliss, John R., Sr.	X								
Cheatham, Benjamin F.		X							
Chesnut, James, Jr.		X		X					
Cheves, Langdon		X	X		X				
Chilton, Robert H.		X			X				
Chilton, William P.									X
Chisholm, John J.		X					X		
Chrisman, James S.	X								
Churchill, Thomas J.		X				X			
Clanton, James H.		X	X						
Clapp, Jeremiah W.		X	X						
Clark, Charles									X
Clark, Henry T.		X	X					X	
Clark, John B.	X								
Clark, William W.									X
Clark, Willis G.				X					
Clay, Clement C.		X	X			X			
Clayton, Alexander M.									X
Clayton, Henry D.		X	X						
Clayton, Philip		X	X						
Cleburne, Patrick R.	X								
Clingman, Thomas L.		X	X						
Clopton, David		X							
Clusky, Michael W.									X
Cobb, Howell		X	X						
Cobb, Thomas R. R.		X	X						
Cockrell, Francis M.		X							
Collier, Charles F.	X		X	X		X			
Colquitt, Alfred H.		X		X					

Name	1 PUS	2 PRS	3 SoU	4 NoU	5 USMA	6 LAW	7 MED	8 GRAD	9 NI
Colston, Raleigh E.		X	X						
Colyar, Arthur St. C.	X								
Conner, James		X	X						
Conrad, Charles M.		X							
Conrow, Aaron H.									X
Cooke, John E.									X
Cooke, John R.		X	X	X					
Cooke, William M.		X	X						
Cooper, Charles P.									X
Cooper, Douglas H.		X	X						
Cooper, Samuel		X			X				
Corse, Montgomery D.		X							
Cox, William R.		X	X			X			
Craige, Francis B.		X	X						
Craigmiles, John H.									X
Crawford, Martin J.		X							
Crenshaw, William G.									X
Crittenden, George B.		X	X		X	X			
Crockett, John W.	X								
Cruikshank, Marcus H.	X								
Crump, William W.		X	X						
Cumming, Alfred		X			X				
Currin, David M.	X		X						
Curry, Jabez L. M.		X	X	X		X			
Dabney, Robert L.		X	X					X	
Daniel, John M.	X								
Daniel, Junius		X			X				
Darden, Stephen H.									X
Dargan, Edmund S.	X								
Davidson, Allen T.		X							
Davis, George		X	X						
Davis, Jefferson		X	X		X				
Davis, Joseph R.		X		X					
Davis, Nicholas, Jr.		X	X						
Davis, Reuben	X								
Davis, Varina H.		X							
Davis, William G. M.	X								
Dawkins, James B.	X		X						
Deas, Zachariah C.		X							
DeBow, James D. B.	X		X						
DeClouet, Alexander		X	X						

Name	1 PUS	2 PRS	3 SoU	4 NoU	5 USMA	6 LAW	7 MED	8 GRAD	9 NI
deFontaine, Felix G.		X							
De Jarnette, Daniel C.		X		X					
De Leon, David C.		X	X				X		
De Leon, Edwin		X	X						
Devine, Thomas J.		X				X			
DeWitt, William H.		X							
Dibrell, George G.		X							
Dickinson, James S.		X				X			
Doles, George P.	X								
Donelson, Daniel S.		X			X				
Dortch, William T.		X							
Duke, Basil C.		X							
Duke, Basil W.		X	X			X			
Dupré, Lucius J.		X	X			X			
Early, Jubal A.		X			X				
Echols, John		X	X	X		X			
Echols, Joseph H.	X								
Ector, Matthew D.		X							
Elliott, John M.		X							
Elliott, Stephen		X	X						
Ellis, John W.		X	X						
Elzey, Arnold		X			X				
Evans, Augusta J.		X							
Evans, Clement A.		X				X			
Ewell, Richard S.		X			X				
Ewing, George	X								
Fagan, James F.	X								
Farrow, James	X								
Fearn, Thomas		X	X				X		
Featherston, Winfield S.	X								
Ferguson, Samuel W.		X			X				
Field, Charles W.		X			X				
Finley, Jesse J.		X							
Flanagin, Harris		X							
Foote, Henry S.		X	X						
Ford, Samuel H.	X		X						
Forman, Thomas M.									X
Forney, John H.		X			X				
Forrest, Nathan B.	X								
Forsyth, John		X		X					
Foster, Thomas J.									X

Name	1 PUS	2 PRS	3 SoU	4 NoU	5 USMA	6 LAW	7 MED	8 GRAD	9 NI
Freeman, Thomas W.	X								
French, Samuel G.		X			X				
Fry, Birkett D.		X	X		X				
Fuller, Thomas C.		X	X			X			
Funsten, David		X		X					
Furman, James C.		X	X						
Gaither, Burgess S.		X	X						
Gardenhire, Erasmus L.		X							
Gardner, Franklin		X			X				
Garland, Augustus H.		X	X						
Garland, Landon C.		X	X						
Garland, Rufus K.	X								
Garnett, Muscoe R. H.		X	X						
Gartrell, Lucius J.		X	X						
Gentry, Meredith P.	X								
Gholson, Samuel J.	X								
Gholson, Thomas S.		X	X						
Gibson, Randall L.		X		X		X			
Gilmer, Francis M.	X								
Gilmer, Jeremy F. F.		X			X				
Gilmer, John A.		X							
Gist, States R.		X	X	X		X			
Goode, John, Jr.		X				X			
Gordon, James B.		X							
Gordon, John B.		X	X						
Gorgas, Josiah		X			X				
Govan, Daniel C.		X	X						
Gracie, Archibald, Jr.		X			X				
Graham, Malcolm D.		X	X						
Graham, William A.		X	X						
Gray, Henry		X	X						
Gray, Peter W.	X								
Green, Thomas		X	X						
Greenhow, Rose O.									X
Gregg, John		X							
Gregg, Maxcy		X	X						
Gregg, William	X								
Grimes, Bryan		X	X						
Hale, Stephen F.		X	X			X			
Hampton, Wade		X	X						
Hanly, Thomas B.	X								

Name	1 PUS	2 PRS	3 SoU	4 NoU	5 USMA	6 LAW	7 MED	8 GRAD	9 NI
Hardee, William J.		X			X				
Hardinge, Belle B.		X							
Harris, Isham G.		X							
Harris, Nathaniel H.		X	X						
Harris, Thomas A.		X			X				
Harris, Wiley P.		X	X			X			
Harrison, James T.		X	X						
Harrison, Thomas	X								
Hartridge, Julian		X		X		X			
Hatcher, Robert A.		X							
Hawes, James M.		X			X				
Hawes, Richard		X	X						
Haynes, Landon C.		X	X						
Hays, Harry T.		X	X						
Hébert, Louis		X	X		X				
Hébert, Paul O.		X	X		X				
Heiskell, Joseph B.		X	X						
Helm, Benjamin H.		X			X				
Hemphill, John		X		X					
Henry, Gustavus A.		X	X						
Herbert, Caleb C.	X								
Heth, Henry		X	X		X				
Hill, Ambrose P.		X			X				
Hill, Benjamin H.		X	X						
Hill, Benjamin J.	X								
Hill, Daniel H.		X			X				
Hilton, Robert B.	X								
Hindman, Thomas C.		X		X					
Hodge, Benjamin L.	X								
Hodge, George B.		X			X				
Hoke, Robert F.		X							
Holcombe, James P.		X		X		X			
Holden, William W.	X								
Holder, William D.	X								
Holliday, Frederick W. M.		X		X		X			
Hollins, George N.	X								
Holmes, Theophilus H.		X			X				
Holt, Hines		X	X						
Holtzclaw, James T.		X							
Hood, John B.		X			X				
Hotchkiss, Jedediah	X								

Name	1 PUS	2 PRS	3 SoU	4 NoU	5 USMA	6 LAW	7 MED	8 GRAD	9 NI
Hotze, Henry									X
House, John F.		X	X			X			
Hubbard, David	X								
Huger, Benjamin		X			X				
Hume, Thomas		X	X						
Humes, William Y. C.		X	X						
Humphreys, Benjamin G.		X			X				
Hunter, Robert M. T.		X	X			X			
Hunton, Eppa		X							
Hurst, David W.		X							
Huse, Caleb		X			X				
Ingram, Porter		X		X					
Iverson, Alfred, Jr.		X							
Jackson, Claiborne F.	X								
Jackson, Henry R.		X		X					
Jackson, John K.		X	X						
Jackson, Thomas J.		X			X				
Jackson, William H.		X			X				
Jackson, William L.	X								
Jemison, Robert, Jr.		X	X			X			
Jenkins, Albert G.		X		X		X			
Jenkins, Charles J.		X		X					
Jenkins, Micah		X	X						
Johnson, Bushrod R.		X			X				
Johnson, Edward		X			X				
Johnson, George W.		X				X			
Johnson, Herschel V.		X	X						
Johnson, Robert W.		X		X		X			
Johnson, Thomas	X								
Johnson, Waldo P.		X							
Johnston, Albert S.		X			X				
Johnston, George D.		X				X			
Johnston, Joseph E.		X			X				
Johnston, Robert	X								
Johnston, Robert D.		X	X			X			
Johnston, William P.		X		X		X			
Jones, David R.		X			X				
Jones, George W.	X								
Jones, Henry C.		X							
Jones, John B.	X								
Jones, Joseph		X		X			X		

Name	1 PUS	2 PRS	3 SoU	4 NoU	5 USMA	6 LAW	7 MED	8 GRAD	9 NI
Jones, Robert M.									X
Jones, Samuel		X			X				
Jones, Thomas M.		X	X						
Jones, William G.		X	X						
Jordan, Thomas		X			X				
Kean, Robert G. H.		X	X					X	
Keeble, Edwin A.		X	X						
Keitt, Lawrence M.		X	X						
Kell, John M.		X			X				
Kelly, John H.		X			X				
Kemper, James L.		X	X					X	
Kenan, Augustus H.	X								
Kenan, Oren R.		X							
Kenner, Duncan F.		X		X					
Kershaw, Joseph B.		X							
Keyes, Wade, Jr.		X	X						
Lamar, Gazaway B.	X								
Lamar, Lucius Q. C.		X							
Lamkin, John T.	X								
Lander, William		X							
Lane, James H.		X	X						
Law, Evander M.		X	X						
Lawton, Alexander R.		X		X	X	X			
Leach, James M.		X			X				
Leach, James T.	X					X			
Lee, Fitzhugh		X			X				
Lee, George W. C.		X			X				
Lee, Robert E.		X			X				
Lee, Stephen D.		X			X				
Lee, William H. F.		X		X					
Lester, George N.	X								
Letcher, John		X	X						
Lewis, David P.									X
Lewis, David W.		X	X						
Lewis, John W.		X							
Lewis, Joseph H.		X							
Logan, George W.	X								
Lomax, Lunsford L.		X			X				
Long, Armistead L.		X			X				
Longstreet, James		X			X				
Loring, William W.		X	X						

Name	1 PUS	2 PRS	3 SoU	4 NoU	5 USMA	6 LAW	7 MED	8 GRAD	9 NI
Lovell, Mansfield		X			X				
Lowrey, Mark P.	X								
Lubbock, Francis R.	X								
Lynch, Patrick N.								X	
Lyon, Francis S.	X								
Lyons, James		X	X						
McCallum, James	X								
McCausland, John		X	X						
McCaw, James B.			X				X		
McCown, John P.		X			X				
McDowell, Thomas D.		X	X						
MacFarland, William H.		X	X						
McGeehee, Edward	X								
McGowan, Samuel		X	X						
McGuire, Hunter H.		X		X			X		
Machen, Willis B.		X							
Mackall, William W.		X			X				
McLaws, Lafayette		X			X				
McLean, James R.	X								
McMullen, Fayette		X							
McQueen, John		X	X						
McRae, Colin J.		X							
McRae, John J.		X		X					
McTyeire, Holland N.		X	X						
MacWillie, Malcolm H.									X
Maffitt, John N.	X								
Magrath, Andrew G.		X	X	X		X			
Magruder, John B.		X			X				
Mahone, William		X	X						
Mallet, John W.				X				X	
Mallory, Stephen R.		X							
Maney, George E.		X							
Manigault, Arthur M.		X	X						
Manly, Basil		X	X						
Mann, Ambrose D.		X			X				
Marmaduke, John S.		X			X				
Marshall, Henry				X					
Marshall, Humphrey		X			X				
Martin, Augustus M.									X
Martin, James G.		X			X				
Martin, John M.	X		X						

Name	1 PUS	2 PRS	3 SoU	4 NoU	5 USMA	6 LAW	7 MED	8 GRAD	9 NI
Martin, William T.		X							
Mason, James M.				X		X			
Maury, Dabney H.		X			X				
Maury, Matthew F.		X							
Maxey, Samuel B.		X			X				
Maxwell, Augustus E.		X	X						
Memminger, Christopher G.	X	X	X						
Menees, Thomas		X					X		
Merrick, Edwin T.		X							
Miles, William P.		X	X					X	
Miller, Samuel A.	X			X					
Milton, John		X							
Mitchel, Charles B.		X					X		
Monroe, Thomas B.	X								
Montague, Robert L.		X	X						
Moore, Andrew B.		X							
Moore, John C.		X			X				
Moore, John W.	X								
Moore, Samuel P.		X	X				X		
Moore, Thomas O.	X								
Morehead, John M.		X	X						
Morgan, John H.		X	X						
Morgan, John T.		X							
Morgan, Simpson H.	X								
Morris, William S.	X								
Morton, Jackson C.		X	X						
Munnerlyn, Charles J.		X							
Murrah, Pendleton	X								
Murray, John P.	X								
Myers, Abraham C.		X			X				
Newsom, Ella K.	X								
Nicholls, Francis R.		X			X	X			
Nisbet, Eugenius A.		X	X						
Northrop, Lucius B.		X		X	X		X		
Norton, Nimrod L.		X							
Ochiltree, William B.	X								
Oldham, Williamson S.	X								
O'Neal, Edward A.		X							
Orr, James L.		X	X						
Orr, Jehu A.		X	X	X					
Ould, Robert		X	X						

Name	1 PUS	2 PRS	3 SoU	4 NoU	5 USMA	6 LAW	7 MED	8 GRAD	9 NI
Oury, Granville H.	X								
Owens, James B.		X						X	
Page, Richard L.		X			X				
Palmer, Benjamin M.		X	X					X	
Parsons, Mosby M.		X							
Payne, William H. F.		X	X						
Pearson, Richmond M.		X	X						
Pegram, John		X			X				
Pemberton, John L.		X			X				
Pender, William D.		X			X				
Pendleton, William N.		X			X				
Perkins, John, Jr.		X		X		X			
Perry, Edward A.		X		X					
Pettigrew, James J.		X	X						
Pettus, Edmund W.		X							
Pettus, John J.	X								
Peyton, Robert L. Y.		X		X		X			
Phelan, James	X								
Pickens, Francis W.		X	X						
Pickett, George E.		X							
Pickett, John T.		X			X				
Pierce, George F.		X	X					X	
de Polignac, Camille A.J.M.									X
Polk, Leonidas		X			X				
Polk, Lucius E.		X	X						
Pollard, Edward A.		X				X			
Pope, Joseph D.		X	X						
Porcher, Francis P.		X	X				X		
Power, John L.	X								
Pratt, Daniel	X								
Preston, John S.		X	X	X		X			
Preston, Walter		X	X	X					
Preston, William		X				X			
Preston, William B.		X	X			X			
Price, Sterling		X	X						
Pryor, Roger A.		X	X						
Pugh, James L.		X							
Puryear, Richard C.	X								
Quintard, Charles T.		X		X			X	X	
Quintero, Juan	X								
Rains, Gabriel J.		X			X				

Name	1 PUS	2 PRS	3 SoU	4 NoU	5 USMA	6 LAW	7 MED	8 GRAD	9 NI
Rains, George W.		X			X				
Ralls, John P.		X					X		
Ramsey, James G.	X								
Ramseur, Stephen D.		X	X		X				
Randolph, George W.		X	X	X					
Ransom, Matt W.		X	X						
Ransom, Robert, Jr.		X			X				
Read, Henry E.	X								
Reade, Edwin G.	X								
Reagan, John H.		X							
Rector, Henry M.	X								
Reynolds, Thomas C.		X	X					X	
Rhett, Robert B.	X								
Ripley, Roswell S.		X			X				
Rives, Alfred L.		X	X					X	
Rives, William C.		X	X						
Roberts, Oran M.		X	X						
Robertson, Jerome B.		X					X		
Robinson, Cornelius		X	X						
Roddey, Philip D.	X								
Rodes, Robert E.		X	X						
Rogers, Samuel St. G.									X
Ross, Lawrence S.	X		X						
Rosser, Thomas L.		X			X				
Royston, Grandison D.		X							
Ruffin, Thomas		X		X					
Ruffin, Thomas		X	X						
Russell, Charles W.		X		X					
Rust, Albert	X								
St. John, Isaac M.		X		X				X	
Sale, John B.		X	X						
Sanderson, John P.				X					
Scott, Robert E.		X	X						
Seddon, James A.		X	X						
Semmes, Raphael		X			X				
Semmes, Thomas J.		X	X			X			
Sexton, Franklin B.		X							
Shelby, Joseph O.		X	X						
Shelley, Charles M.	X								
Shewmake, John T.				X					
Shorter, John G.		X	X						

Name	1 PUS	2 PRS	3 SoU	4 NoU	5 USMA	6 LAW	7 MED	8 GRAD	9 NI
Shoup, Francis A.		X			X				
Simms, William E.		X	X						
Simpson, William D.		X	X			X			
Sims, Frederick W.									X
Singleton, Ortho R.		X							
Slaughter, James E.		X	X						
Slidell, John		X		X					
Smith, Charles H.		X	X						
Smith, Edmund K.		X			X				
Smith, Gustavus W.		X			X				
Smith, James A.		X			X				
Smith, James M.	X								
Smith, Martin L.		X			X				
Smith, Robert H.		X			X				
Smith, William		X							
Smith, William E.									X
Smith, William N. H.		X		X		X			
Smith, William R.			X						
Snead, Thomas L.		X	X						
Sorrel, Gilbert M.	X								
Soulé, Pierre									X
Sparrow, Edward				X					
Staples, Waller R.		X	X						
Stephens, Alexander H.	X	X	X						
Stephens, Linton		X	X						
Steuart, George H.		X			X				
Stevens, Walter H.		X			X				
Stevenson, Carter L.		X			X				
Stewart, Alexander P.		X			X				
Strickland, Hardy									X
Stuart, James E. B.		X			X				
Swain, David L.	X		X						
Swan, William G.									X
Taliaferro, William B.		X	X			X			
Tappan, James C.		X		X					
Tattnall, Josiah		X							
Taylor, Richard		X		X					
Terry, William		X	X						
Thomas, Edward L.		X	X						
Thomas, James H.		X							
Thomas, John J.									X

Name	1 PUS	2 PRS	3 SoU	4 NoU	5 USMA	6 LAW	7 MED	8 GRAD	9 NI
Thomason, Hugh F.	X								
Thompson, Jacob		X	X						
Thompson, John R.		X				X			
Thornwell, James H.		X	X					X	
Tibbs, William H.									X
Tift, Nelson	X								
Tompkins, Sally L.		X							
Toombs, Robert A.		X	X	X		X			
Trenholm, George A.		X							
Trimble, Isaac R.		X			X				
Triplett, George W.									X
Trippe, Robert P.		X	X						
Tucker, John R.									X
Turner, Joseph A.		X	X						
Turner, Josiah, Jr.		X	X						
Tyler, John		X	X						
Vance, Zebulon B.						X			
Van Dorn, Earl		X			X				
Venable, Abraham W.		X		X					
Verot, Jean Pierre Augustin M.								X	
Vest, George G.		X	X						
Villeré, Charles J.		X	X						
Wadley, William M.	X								
Walker, James A.		X	X						
Walker, John G.		X							
Walker, Leroy P.		X	X						
Walker, Reuben L.		X	X						
Walker, Richard W.		X		X					
Walker, William H. T.		X			X				
Walthall, Edward C.		X							
Ward, George T.		X	X						
Ware, Horace	X								
Warren, Edward		X	X				X		
Watie, Stand		X							
Watkins, W. W.									X
Watson, John W. C.		X				X			
Watterson, Henry		X							
Watts, Thomas H.		X	X						
Waul, Thomas N.		X	X						
Welsh, Israel									X

Name	1 PUS	2 PRS	3 SoU	4 NoU	5 USMA	6 LAW	7 MED	8 GRAD	9 NI
Wharton, John A.		X	X						
Wheeler, Joseph		X			X				
White, Daniel P.		X	X						
Whitfield, Robert H.									X
Whiting, William H. C.		X			X				
Wickham, Williams C.		X	X						
Wigfall, Louis T.		X	X						
Wilcox, Cadmus M.		X			X				
Wilcox, John A.	X								
Wilkes, John		X			X				
Wilkes, Peter S.									X
Wilkinson, John		X							
Williams, James									X
Williams, John S.		X		X				X	
Williams, Thomas H.			X						
Wilson, William S.									X
Winder, John S.		X			X				
Wise, Henry A.		X		X					
Withers, Jones M.		X			X				
Withers, Thomas J.		X	X						
Witherspoon, James H.			X						
Wofford, William T.		X	X						
Wood, John T.									X
Worth, Jonathan		X							
Wright, Ambrose R.		X							
Wright, Augustus R.			X			X			
Wright, John V.									X
Wright, Marcus J.		X							
Wright, William B.									X
Yancey, William L.		X		X					
Yandell, David W.		X					X		
Young, Pierce M. B.		X			X				
Young, William H.		X	X						

Prewar and Postwar Political Party Affiliation

The political designation represents the party an individual usually supported or the party through which he sought public office. Often, prewar career military personnel neither voted nor ran for political office; these have been classified as having had no party affiliation. Some leaders switched parties during their prewar careers, and they have been given multiple party designations. For example, during the nullification crisis and the subsequent bank war, Democrats switched to the Whig party. In the last decade before the war, the Whig party collapsed, and some politicians switched to the Democrats, while a few remained diehard Whigs. No parties existed in the South during the Civil War. After the war, the vast majority of former Confederate leaders either became Democrats or refused to participate in political life. Only a few joined the Republican party.

(X) designates prewar party affiliation or support, and (Y) designates postwar party affiliation or support. An (*) means that the leader died during the Civil War.

Categories: 1 Democratic Party (Dem.)
               2 Whig Party (Whig)
               3 American Party (Amer.)
               4 Whig-Democrat (W-D)
               5 No Party Affiliation or Political Activity (NoP)
               6 Party Unknown (PUn)
               7 Republican Party (Rep.)

Name	1 Dem.	2 Whig	3 Amer.	4 W-D	5 NoP	6 PUn	7 Rep.
Adams, Daniel W.						XY	
Adams, John						X*	
Adams, William W.	Y	X					
Akin, Warren		X			Y		
Alcorn, James L.		X					Y
Alexander, Edward P.	Y				X		
Alexander, Peter W.	Y	X					
Allen, Henry W.	X					Y	
Allen, William W.	Y					X	
Anderson, Clifford	Y	X					
Anderson, George T.	Y				X		
Anderson, James P.	X				Y		
Anderson, Joseph R.				X	Y		
Anderson, Richard H.					Y	X	
Anderson, Robert H.	Y					X	
Archer, James J.						X*	
Armistead, Lewis A.						X*	
Armstrong, Frank C.	Y					X	
Arrington, Archibald H.	X						Y
Ashby, Turner						X*	
Ashcraft, Thomas				X	Y		
Ashe, Thomas S.	Y	X					
Ashe, William S.	X					*	
Atkins, John D. C.	XY						
Avery, William W.	X					*	
Ayer, Lewis M., Jr.	X				Y		
Bagby, George W.	XY						
Baker, Alpheus	X					Y	
Baker, James M.	Y	X					
Baker, Laurence S.					Y	X	
Baldwin, John B.	Y	X					
Barksdale, Ethelbert	XY						
Barksdale, William E.	X					*	
Barnwell, Robert W.	X				Y		
Barringer, Rufus				X			Y
Barron, Samuel					Y	X	
Barry, William T. S.	X				Y		
Bartow, Francis S.		X	X			*	
Bass, Nathan	X					Y	
Bate, William B.	XY						

Name	1 Dem.	2 Whig	3 Amer.	4 W-D	5 NoP	6 PUn	7 Rep.
Batson, Felix I.	X				Y		
Battle, Cullen A.	XY						
Baylor, John R.	X					Y	
Beale, Richard L. T.	XY						
Beauregard, Pierre G. T.	Y				X		
Bee, Hamilton P.	X				Y		
Bell, Casper W.	Y			X			
Bell, Hiram P.	Y	X					
Benjamin, Judah P.				X	Y		
Benning, Henry L.	X				Y		
Blandford, Mark H.	Y					X	
Bledsoe, Albert T.	X				Y		
Bocock, Thomas S.	XY						
Boggs, William R.					Y	X	
Bonham, Milledge L.	XY						
Boteler, Alexander R.		X	X				Y
Boudinot, Elias C.	XY						
Bowen, John S.						X*	
Boyce, William W.	X				Y		
Bradford, Alexander B.		X			Y		
Bradley, Benjamin F.	XY						
Bragg, Braxton	Y				X		
Bragg, Thomas	XY						
Branch, Anthony M.	XY						
Bratton, John	XY						
Breckinridge, John C.	XY						
Breckinridge, Robert J.	XY						
Bridgers, Robert R.	X				Y		
Brockenbrough, John W.	X				Y		
Brooke, John M.					XY		
Brooke, Walker				X	Y		
Brown, Albert G.	X				Y		
Brown, John C.	Y	X					
Brown, Joseph E.	XY						Y
Browne, William M.	X				Y		
Bruce, Eli M.	X					Y	
Bruce, Horatio W.	Y	X	X				
Bryan, Goode	X				Y		
Buchanan, Franklin					Y	X	
Buckner, Simon B.	XY						

Name	1 Dem.	2 Whig	3 Amer.	4 W-D	5 NoP	6 PUn	7 Rep.
Bulloch, James D.					XY		
Burnett, Henry C.	X				Y		
Burnett, Theodore L.		X			Y		
Burton, James H.						XY	
Butler, Matthew C.	XY						
Cabell, William L.	XY						
Callahan, Samuel B.					Y	X	
Campbell, Alexander W.	XY						
Campbell, John A.	XY						
Campbell, Josiah A. P.	XY						
Cantey, James	X				Y		
Capers, Ellison	XY						
Caperton, Allen T.	Y			X			
Carroll, David W.	XY						
Carter, John C.						X*	
Caruthers, Robert L.		X			Y		
Chalmers, James R.	XY						Y
Chambers, Henry C.	XY						
Chambliss, John R., Sr.		X				Y	
Cheatham, Benjamin F.	XY						
Chesnut, James, Jr.	XY						
Cheves, Langdon	X					*	
Chilton, Robert H.					Y	X	
Chilton, William P.				X	Y		
Chisholm, John J.					Y	X	
Chrisman, James S.	XY						
Churchill, Thomas J.	Y	X					
Clanton, James H.	XY						
Clapp, Jeremiah W.	Y			X			
Clark, Charles	Y			X			
Clark, Henry T.	X				Y		
Clark, John B.	X				Y		
Clark, William W.						XY	
Clark, Willis G.	XY						
Clay, Clement C.	X				Y		
Clayton, Alexander M.	X				Y		
Clayton, Henry D.	XY						
Clayton, Philip	X						Y
Cleburne, Patrick R.	X					*	
Clingman, Thomas L.	Y			X			

Name	1 Dem.	2 Whig	3 Amer.	4 W-D	5 NoP	6 PUn	7 Rep.
Clopton, David	XY						
Clusky, Michael W.	XY						
Cobb, Howell	XY						
Cobb, Thomas R. R.	X					*	
Cockrell, Francis M.	XY						
Collier, Charles F.	X					Y	
Cloquitt, Alfred H.	XY						
Colston, Raleigh E.					Y	X	
Colyar, Arthur St. C.	Y			X			
Conner, James	XY						
Conrad, Charles M.	X	X				Y	
Conrow, Aaron H.	X				Y		
Cooke, John E.	X					Y	
Cooke, John R.	Y					X	
Cooke, William M.	X					*	
Cooper, Charles P.	XY						
Cooper, Douglas H.	X				Y		
Cooper, Samuel	X				Y		
Corse, Montgomery D.					Y	X	
Cox, William R.	XY						
Craige, Francis B.	X					Y	
Craigmiles, John H.						XY	
Crawford, Martin J.	XY						
Crenshaw, William G.	X					Y	
Crittenden, George B.		X			Y		
Crockett, John W.		X			Y		
Cruikshank, Marcus H.		X			Y		
Crump, William W.	XY						
Cumming, Alfred					Y	X	
Currin, David M.	X					*	
Curry, Jabez L. M.	XY						
Dabney, Robert L.					Y	X	
Daniel, John M.	X					*	
Daniel, Junius	X					*	
Darden, Stephen H.	XY						
Dargan, Edmund S.	X					Y	
Davidson, Allen T.		X				Y	
Davis, George		X			Y		
Davis, Jefferson	X				Y		
Davis, Joseph R.	X					Y	

Name	1 Dem.	2 Whig	3 Amer.	4 W-D	5 NoP	6 PUn	7 Rep.
Davis, Nicholas, Jr.		X					Y
Davis, Reuben	Y			X			
Davis, Varina H.	X				Y		
Davis, William G. M.		X			Y		
Dawkins, James B.						XY	
Deas, Zachariah C.	X				Y		
DeBow, James D. B.	XY						
DeClouet, Alexander				X	Y		
deFontaine, Felix G.	XY						
De Jarnette, Daniel C.	X				Y		
De Leon, David C.					Y	X	
De Leon, Edwin	X				Y		
Devine, Thomas J.	XY						
DeWitt, William H.	Y	X					
Dibrell, George W.	Y	X					
Dickinson, James S.	X					Y	
Doles, George P.						X*	
Donelson, Daniel S.	X					*	
Dortch, William T.	XY						
Duke, Basil C.	Y	X					
Duke, Basil W.	XY						
Dupré, Lucius J.		X				Y	
Early, Jubal A.		X			Y		
Echols, John	XY						
Echols, Joseph H.	X				Y		
Ector, Matthew D.	XY						
Elliott, John M.	XY						
Elliott, Stephen	X				Y		
Ellis, John W.	X					*	
Elzey, Arnold					XY		
Evans, Augusta J.	X				Y		
Evans, Clement A.	X				Y		
Ewell, Richard S.					XY		
Ewing, George		X			Y		
Fagan, James F.		X					Y
Farrow, James	X						Y
Fearn, Thomas	X					*	
Featherston, Winfield S.	XY						
Ferguson, Samuel W.	XY						
Field, Charles W.					X	Y	

Name	1 Dem.	2 Whig	3 Amer.	4 W-D	5 NoP	6 PUn	7 Rep.
Finley, Jesse J.	Y	X					
Flanagin, Harris	XY						
Foote, Henry S.		X					Y
Ford, Samuel H.						XY	
Forman, Thomas M.	X					Y	
Forney, John H.	X				Y		
Forrest, Nathan B.	XY						
Forsyth, John	XY						
Foster, Thomas J.	Y	X					
Freeman, Thomas W.	X					Y	
French, Samuel G.					Y	X	
Fry, Birkett D.					XY		
Fuller, Thomas C.	Y	X					
Funsten, David						XY	
Furman, James C.	X				Y		
Gaither, Burgess S.		X			Y		
Gardenhire, Erasmus L.	XY						
Gardner, Franklin	X				Y		
Garland, Augustus H.	Y	X					
Garland, Landon C.		X			Y		
Garland, Rufus K.				X	Y		
Garnett, Muscoe R. H.	X					*	
Gartrell, Lucius J.	Y			X			
Gentry, Meredith P.		X	X		Y		
Gholson, Samuel J.	XY						
Gholson, Thomas S.		X			Y		
Gibson, Randall L.	XY						
Gilmer, Francis M.	X					Y	
Gilmer, Jeremy F. F.					XY		
Gilmer, John A.		X	X		Y		
Gist, States R.	X					*	
Goode, John, Jr.	XY						
Gordon, James B.	X					*	
Gordon, John B.	Y			X			
Gorgas, Josiah	X				Y		
Govan, Daniel C.	X				Y		
Gracie, Archibald, Jr.					X	*	
Graham, Malcolm D.	X				Y		
Graham, William A.	Y	X					
Gray, Henry	Y			X			

Name	1 Dem.	2 Whig	3 Amer.	4 W-D	5 NoP	6 PUn	7 Rep.
Gray, Peter W.	XY						
Green, Thomas	X					*	
Greenhow, Rose O.						X*	
Gregg, John						X*	
Gregg, Maxcy	X					*	
Gregg, William	X				Y		
Grimes, Bryan		X			Y		
Hale, Stephen F.		X				*	
Hampton, Wade	XY						
Hanly, Thomas B.	XY						
Hardee, William J.					XY		
Hardinge, Belle B.					Y	X	
Harris, Isham G.	XY						
Harris, Nathaniel H.					Y	X	
Harris, Thomas A.	X					Y	
Harris, Wiley P.	X					Y	
Harrison, James T.	XY						
Harrison, Thomas	XY						
Hartridge, Julian	XY						
Hatcher, Robert A.	XY						
Hawes, James M.					XY		
Hawes, Richard	Y	X					
Haynes, Landon C.	X				Y		
Hays, Harry T.	Y	X					
Hébert, Louis	X				Y		
Hébert, Paul O.	XY						
Heiskell, Joseph B.	Y	X					
Helm, Benjamin H.				X		*	
Hemphill, John	X					*	
Henry, Gustavus A.		X			Y		
Herbert, Caleb C.	X				Y		
Heth, Henry					X	Y	
Hill, Ambrose P.					X	*	
Hill, Benjamin H.	Y	X	X				
Hill, Benjamin J.					Y	X	
Hill, Daniel H.					XY		
Hilton, Robert B.	X					Y	
Hindman, Thomas C.	X				Y		
Hodge, Benjamin L.		X				*	
Hodge, George B.	Y			X			

Name	1 Dem.	2 Whig	3 Amer.	4 W-D	5 NoP	6 PUn	7 Rep.
Hoke, Robert F.	X				Y		
Holcombe, James P.	X				Y		
Holden, William W.				X			Y
Holder, William D.		X				Y	
Holliday, Frederick W. M.	XY						
Hollins, George N.					Y	X	
Holmes, Theophilus H.					XY		
Holt, Hines		X	X		Y		
Holtzclaw, James T.	XY						
Hood, John B.					XY		
Hotchkiss, Jebediah					Y	X	
Hotze, Henry					Y	X	
House, John F.	Y	X					
Hubbard, David	X				Y		
Huger, Benjamin					XY		
Hume, Thomas	X				Y		
Humes, William Y. C.						XY	
Humphreys, Benjamin G.	Y	X					
Hunter, Robert M. T.	XY	X		X			
Hunton, Eppa	XY						
Hurst, David W.		X				Y	
Huse, Caleb					Y	X	
Ingram, Porter	X				Y		
Iverson, Alfred, Jr.	X				Y		
Jackson, Claiborne F.	X					*	
Jackson, Henry R.	XY						
Jackson, John K.					Y	X	
Jackson, Thomas J.	X					*	
Jackson, William H.	Y	X					
Jackson, William L.	XY						
Jemison, Robert, Jr.	Y	X					
Jenkins, Albert G.	X					*	
Jenkins, Charles J.	Y	X					
Jenkins, Micah	X					*	
Johnson, Bushrod R.					XY		
Johnson, Edward					XY		
Johnson, George W.	X					*	
Johnson, Herschel V.	XY						
Johnson, Robert W.	X				Y		
Johnson, Thomas					Y	X	

Name	1 Dem.	2 Whig	3 Amer.	4 W-D	5 NoP	6 PUn	7 Rep.
Johnson, Waldo P.	X					Y	
Johnston, Albert S.	X					*	
Johnston, George D.	XY						
Johnston, Joseph E.	XY						
Johnston, Robert ⁞	X					Y	
Johnston, Robert D.	X				Y		
Johnston, William P.				X	Y		
Jones, David R.					X	*	
Jones, George W.	XY						
Jones, Henry C.	XY						
Jones, John B.	X				Y		
Jones, Joseph					Y	X	
Jones, Robert M.						XY	
Jones, Samuel					XY		
Jones, Thomas M.	XY						
Jones, William G.				X		Y	
Jordan, Thomas					XY		
Kean, Robert G. H.	XY						
Keeble, Edwin A.	X				Y		
Keitt, Lawrence M.	X					*	
Kell, John M.					XY		
Kelly, John H.					X	*	
Kemper, James L.	Y					X	
Kenan, Augustus H.		X			Y		
Kenan, Oren R.	XY						
Kenner, Duncan F.	Y	X					
Kershaw, Joseph B.	XY						
Keyes, Wade, Jr.	X					Y	
Lamar, Gazaway B.					Y	X	
Lamar, Lucius Q. C.	XY						
Lamkin, John T.		X			Y		
Lander, William	X				Y		
Lane, James H.	X				Y		
Law, Evander M.	X				Y		
Lawton, Alexander R.	XY						
Leach, James M.	Y	X	X				
Leach, James T.		X					Y
Lee, Fitzhugh	XY						
Lee, George W. C.					XY		
Lee, Robert E.		X			Y		

Name	1 Dem.	2 Whig	3 Amer.	4 W-D	5 NoP	6 PUn	7 Rep.
Lee, Stephen D.	XY						
Lee, William H. F.	XY						
Lester, George N.	XY						
Letcher, John	XY						
Lewis, David P.	X						Y
Lewis, David W.				X	Y		
Lewis, John W.	X				Y		
Lewis, Joseph H.	Y			X			
Logan, George W.		X					Y
Lomax, Lunsford L.					XY		
Long, Armistead L.					XY		
Longstreet, James					X		Y
Loring, William W.	XY						
Lovell, Mansfield					XY		
Lowrey, Mark P.					Y	X	
Lubbock, Francis R.	XY						
Lynch, Patrick N.					XY		
Lyon, Francis S.	Y			X			
Lyons, James		X				Y	
McCallum, James	Y	X					
McCausland, John					Y	X	
McCaw, James B.					Y	X	
McCown, John P.					XY		
McDowell, Thomas. D.				X		Y	
MacFarland, William H.	Y	X					
McGeehee, Edward					Y	X	
McGowan, Samuel	XY						
McGuire, Hunter H.					Y	X	
Machen, Willis B.	XY						
Mackall, William W.					XY		
McLaws, Lafayette					XY		
McLean, James R.	X						Y
McMullen, Fayette	XY						
McQueen, John	X				Y		
McRae, Colin J.	X				Y		
McRae, John J.	X				Y		
McTyeire, Holland N.					Y	X	
MacWillie, Malcolm H.						XY	
Maffitt, John N.					XY		
Magrath, Andrew G.	X				Y		

Name	1 Dem.	2 Whig	3 Amer.	4 W-D	5 NoP	6 PUn	7 Rep.
Magruder, John B.					XY		
Mahone, William	X						Y
Mallet, John W.					Y	X	
Mallory, Stephen R.	X				Y		
Maney, George E.						X	Y
Manigault, Arthur M.	XY						
Manly, Basil					XY		
Mann, Ambrose D.	X	X			Y		
Marmaduke, John S.	XY						
Marshall, Henry						X*	
Marshall, Humphrey		X	X		Y		
Martin, Augustus M.					XY		
Martin, James G.					X	Y	
Martin, John M.	X					Y	
Martin, William T.	Y	X					
Mason, James M.	X				Y		
Maury, Dabney H.	Y				X		
Maury, Matthew F.					XY		
Maxey, Samuel B.	Y			X			
Maxwell, Augustus E.	XY						
Memminger, Christopher G.	X				Y		
Menees, Thomas	X				Y		
Merrick, Edwin T.		X				Y	
Miles, William P.	X				Y		
Miller, Samuel A.						XY	
Milton, John	X					*	
Mitchel, Charles B.	X					*	
Monroe, Thomas B.	X				Y		
Montague, Robert L.	XY						
Moore, Andrew B.				X	Y		
Moore, John C.					XY		
Moore, James W.	X					Y	
Moore, Samuel P.					XY		
Moore, Thomas O.	X				Y		
Morehead, John M.	X	X			Y		
Morgan, John H.					X	*	
Morgan, John T.	XY						
Morgan, Simpson H.						X*	
Morris, William S.						XY	
Morton, Jackson C.					Y	X	

Name	1 Dem.	2 Whig	3 Amer.	4 W-D	5 NoP	6 PUn	7 Rep.
Munnerlyn, Charles J.					XY		
Murrah, Pendleton	X				Y		
Murray, John P.	X					Y	
Myers, Abraham C.					XY		
Newsom, Ella K.					XY		
Nicholls, Francis R.	XY						
Nisbet, Eugenius A.		X	X		Y		
Northrop, Lucius B.					XY		
Norton, Nimrod L.						XY	
Ochiltree, William B.		X			Y		
Oldham, Williamson S.	X				Y		
O'Neal, Edward A.	XY						
Orr, James L.	XY						Y
Orr, Jehu A.	XY						
Ould, Robert	X				Y		
Oury, Granville H.	XY						
Owens, James B.	X					Y	
Page, Richard L.					XY		
Palmer, Benjamin M.	X				Y		
Parsons, Mosby M.					Y	X	
Payne, William H. F.	XY						
Pearson, Richmond M.		X					Y
Pegram, John					X	*	
Pemberton, John L.	X				Y		
Pender, William D.					X	*	
Pendleton, William N.	X				Y		
Perkins, John, Jr.	X				Y		
Perry, Edward A.	XY						
Pettigrew, James J.	X					*	
Pettus, Edmund W.	XY						
Pettus, John J.	X				Y		
Peyton, Robert L. Y.	X					*	
Phelan, James	X				Y		
Pickens, Francis W.	X				Y		
Pickett, George E.					Y	X	
Pickett, John T.	X				Y		
Pierce, George F.					Y	X	
de Polignac, Camille A.J.M.					XY		
Polk, Leonidas	X	X				*	
Polk, Lucius E.	XY						

Name	1 Dem.	2 Whig	3 Amer.	4 W-D	5 NoP	6 PUn	7 Rep.
Pollard, Edward A.	X				Y		
Pope, Joseph D.	X				Y		
Porcher, Francis P.					XY		
Power, John L.	Y					X	
Pratt, Daniel					Y	X	
Preston, John S.	X				Y		
Preston, Walter		X			Y		
Preston, William	Y			X			
Preston, William B.		X				*	
Price, Sterling	X				Y		
Pryor, Roger A.	XY						
Pugh, James L.	Y			X			
Puryear, Richard C.		X	X				Y
Quintard, Charles T.					XY		
Quintero, Juan					X	Y	
Rains, Gabriel J.					XY		
Rains, George W.					XY		
Ralls, John P.	XY						
Ramsay, James G.		X					Y
Ramseur, Stephen D.					X	*	
Randolph, George W.	X				Y		
Ransom, Matt W.	Y			X			
Ransom, Robert, Jr.					XY		
Read, Henry E.					Y	X	
Reade, Edwin G.		X	X				Y
Reagan, John H.	XY						
Rector, Henry M.	XY						
Reynolds, Thomas C.	XY						
Rhett, Robert B.	XY						
Ripley, Roswell S.					XY		
Rives, Alfred L.	X				Y		
Rives, William C.	X	X			Y		
Roberts, Oran M.	XY						
Robertson, Jerome B.					XY		
Robinson, Cornelius	X				Y		
Roddey, Philip D.					Y	X	
Rodes, Robert E.					Y	*	
Rogers, Samuel St. G.					Y	X	
Ross, Lawrence S.	XY						
Rosser, Thomas L.					XY		

Name	1 Dem.	2 Whig	3 Amer.	4 W-D	5 NoP	6 PUn	7 Rep.
Royston, Grandison D.	XY						
Ruffin, Thomas	X				Y		
Ruffin, Thomas	X					*	
Russell, Charles W.	X				Y		
Rust, Albert	X						Y
St. John, Isaac M.					Y	X	
Sale, John B.					Y	X	
Sanderson, John P.	X					Y	
Scott, Robert E.		X				*	
Seddon, James A.	X				Y		
Semmes, Raphael	X				Y		
Semmes, Thomas J.	X				Y		
Sexton, Franklin B.	XY						
Shelby, Joseph O.	X				Y		
Shelley, Charles M.	XY						
Shewmake, John T.						XY	
Shorter, John G.	X				Y		
Shoup, Francis A.					XY		
Simms, William E.	X				Y		
Simpson, William D.	XY						
Sims, Frederick W.					Y	X	
Singleton, Ortho R.	XY						
Slaughter, James E.					Y	X	
Slidell, John	X				Y		
Smith, Charles H.	X				Y		
Smith, Edmund K.	X				Y		
Smith, Gustavus W.	X				Y		
Smith, James A.					XY		
Smith, James M.	XY						
Smith, Martin L.					XY		
Smith, Robert H.		X					Y
Smith, William	XY						
Smith, William E.	Y	X					
Smith, William N. H.	Y	X					
Smith, William R.	Y			X			
Snead, Thomas L.	X				Y		
Sorrel, Gilbert M.					Y	X	
Soulé, Pierre	X				Y		
Sparrow, Edward		X			Y		
Staples, Waller R.	Y	X					

Name	1 Dem.	2 Whig	3 Amer.	4 W-D	5 NoP	6 PUn	7 Rep.
Stephens, Alexander H.	Y	X					
Stephens, Linton	Y	X					
Steuart, George H.					XY		
Stevens, Walter H.					XY		
Stevenson, Carter L.					XY		
Stewart, Alexander P.		X			Y		
Strickland, Hardy	X					Y	
Stuart, James E. B.					X	*	
Swain, David L.		X			Y		
Swan, William G.				X		Y	
Taliaferro, William B.	XY						
Tappan, James C.	XY						
Tattnall, Josiah					Y	X	
Taylor, Richard				X	Y		
Terry, William	XY						
Thomas, Edward L.	Y					X	
Thomas, James H.	X				Y		
Thomas, John J.						XY	
Thomason, Hugh F.	XY		X				
Thompson, Jacob	X				Y		
Thompson, John R.		X			Y		
Thornwell, James H.	X					*	
Tibbs, William H.		X				Y	
Tift, Nelson	Y					X	
Tompkins, Sally L.					XY		
Toombs, Robert A.	Y			X			
Trenholm, George A.	XY						
Trimble, Isaac R.					XY		
Triplett, George W.		X				Y	
Trippe, Robert P.	Y	X					
Tucker, John R.					Y	X	
Turner, Joseph A.	XY						
Turner, Josiah, Jr.	Y	X					Y
Tyler, John		X				*	
Vance, Zebulon B.	Y			X			
Van Dorn, Earl					X	*	
Venable, Abraham W.	X				Y		
Verot, Jean Pierre Augustin M.					XY		
Vest, George G.	XY						

Name	1 Dem.	2 Whig	3 Amer.	4 W-D	5 NoP	6 PUn	7 Rep.
Villeré, Charles J.	X					Y	
Wadley, William M.					Y	X	
Walker, James A.	XY						Y
Walker, John G.					Y	X	
Walker, Leroy P.	XY						
Walker, Reuben L.					Y	X	
Walker, Richard W.		X			Y		
Walker, William H. T.	X					*	
Walthall, Edward C.	XY						
Ward, George T.		X				*	
Ware, Horace					Y	X	
Warren, Edward		X			Y		
Watie, Stand					Y	X	
Watkins, W. W.						XY	
Watson, John W. C.	Y	X					
Watterson, Henry	XY						
Watts, Thomas H.	Y	X	X				
Waul, Thomas N.	X				Y		
Welsh, Israel	X				Y		
Wharton, John A.	X					*	
Wheeler, Joseph	XY						
White, Daniel P.	X				Y		
Whitfield, Robert H.						XY	
Whiting, William H. C.					X	*	
Wickham, Williams C.	Y	X					
Wigfall, Louis T.	X				Y		
Wilcox, Cadmus M.	X				Y		
Wilcox, John A.		X				*	
Wilkes, John					XY		
Wilkes, Peter S.	X					Y	
Wilkinson, John					XY		
Williams, James				X	Y		
Williams, John S.	Y	X					
Williams, Thomas H.					Y	X	
Wilson, William S.	X					Y	
Winder, John S.					X	*	
Wise, Henry A.	X				Y		
Withers, Jones M	XY		X				
Withers, Thomas J.	X				Y		
Witherspoon, James H.	X					Y	

Name	1 Dem.	2 Whig	3 Amer.	4 W-D	5 NoP	6 PUn	7 Rep.
Wofford, William T.	XY						
Wood, John T.					Y	X	
Worth, Jonathan		X					Y
Wright, Ambrose R.	XY		X				
Wright, Augustus R.				X	Y		
Wright, John V.	XY						
Wright, Marcus J.		X			Y		
Wright, William B.	X					Y	
Yancey, William L.	X					*	
Yandell, David W.					Y	X	
Young, Pierce M. B.	XY						
Young, William H.					Y	X	

Bibliography

Abel, Annie Heloise, *The American Indian as Participant in the Civil War* (Cleveland, Ohio, 1919).

———, *The American Indian as Slaveholder and Secessionist* (2 vols., Cleveland, Ohio, 1919).

Alderman, Edwin Anderson, and Gordon, Armistead Churchill, *Jabez L. M. Curry* (New York, 1911).

Ambler, Charles W. (ed.), *Correspondence of Robert M. T. Hunter* (New York, 1925).

———, *Sectionalism in Virginia, 1776-1861* (New York, 1964).

American Mercury, 1925.

Amnesty Petitions, Confederacy (National Archives), Record Group #94.

Anderson, Mabel Washbourne, *Life of General Stand Watie* (Pryor, Okla., 1915).

Andrews, J. Cutler, *The South Reports the Civil War* (Princeton, N.J., 1970).

Appleton's Cyclopedia of American Biography (6 vols., New York, 1887-1889).

Armes, Ethel Marie, *The Story of Coal and Iron in Alabama* (Birmingham, Ala., 1910).

Arnett, Ethel Stephens, *Greensboro* (Chapel Hill, N.C., 1955).

Arthur, S. C., and deKernion, G.C.H., *Old Families of Louisiana* (New Orleans, 1931).

Ashe, Samuel A'Court, *Cyclopedia of Eminent and Representative Men of the Carolinas of the Nineteenth Century* (2 vols., Madison, Wisc., 1892).

———, *George Davis, Attorney General of the Confederate States* (Raleigh, N.C., 1916).

———. *History of North Carolina*, II. Spartanburg, S.C., 1971.

Atkinson, George W. (ed.) *Bench and Bar of West Virginia*. Charleston, W. Va., 1919.

Atlanta Constitution. July 27, 1830.

"Autobiography of General Patton Anderson." *Southern Historical Society Papers*, XXIV (1904).

"Autobiography of William Woods Holden." *Historical Papers of Trinity College*, III, 1911.

Bagby, George W. *The Old Virginia Gentleman*. New York, 1911.

Barksdale, John A. *Barksdale Family History and Geneology*. San Rafael, Calif., 1940.

Barnes, William H. *A History of The Congress in the United States, 1875-1877*. New York, 1878.

Barrett, John Gilchrist. *The Civil War in North Carolina*. Chapel Hill, N.C., 1963.

Basso, Hamilton. *Beauregard*. New York, 1933.

Battey, George. *A History of Rome and Floyd County*. Atlanta, 1922.

Bay, William V. N. *Reminiscences of the Bench and Bar of Missouri*. St. Louis, Mo., 1878.

Beale, Richard Lee Turbeville. *History of the Ninth Virginia Cavalry*. Richmond, 1899.

Beaty, John O. *John Esten Cooke, Virginian*. New York, 1922.

Bell, Hiram Parks. *Men and Things*. Atlanta, Ga., 1907.

Bench and Bar of Missouri Cities. St. Louis, 1884.

Bettersworth, John K. *Mississippi in the Confederacy*. Baton Rouge, La., 1961.

Biographical and Historical Memoirs of Eastern Arkansas. Chicago, 1890.

Biographical and Historical Memoirs of Louisiana. Chicago, 1892.

Biographical and Historical Memoirs of Mississippi. Chicago, 1891.

Biographical Cyclopedia of Representative Men of Maryland and D.C., The, Baltimore, Md., 1879.

Biographical Directory of the American Congress. Washington, D.C., 1947.

Biographical Encyclopedia of Kentucky of Dead and Living Men of the Nineteenth Century. Cincinnati, Ohio, 1878.

Bivins, John F. "Life and Character of Jacob Thompson." *Publications of the Historical Society of Trinity College*. 1898.

Black, Robert C. *The Railroads of the Confederacy*. Chapel Hill, N.C., 1952.

Bladen County, North Carolina, Abstracts of Wills. Elizabethtown, N.C., 1962.

Blake, Nelson Morehouse. *William Mahone of Virginia*. Richmond, Va., 1935.

Blied, Benjamin J. *Catholics in the Civil War*. Milwaukee, Wis., 1945.

Boggs, William R. *Military Reminiscences of General William R. Boggs*. Durham, N.C., 1913.

Boney, F. N. *John Letcher of Virginia*. Tuscaloosa, Ala., 1966

Boutwell, George S. *Reminiscences*. 2 vols., New York, 1902.

Boyd, Belle. *Belle Boyd in Camp and Prison*. New York, 1968.

Boyd, Hazel Mason (comp.) *Some Marriages in Montgomery County, Kentucky Before 1864*. Mount Sterling, Ky., 1901.

Bragg, Jefferson Davis. *Louisiana in the Confederacy*. Baton Rouge, La., 1941.

Brantley, Rabun Lee. *Georgia Journalism of the Civil War Period*. Nashville, Tenn., 1925.

Brawley, James S. *The Rowan Story*. Salisbury, N.C., 1953.

Bridges, Hal. *Lee's Maverick General*. New York, 1961.

Brooks, Ulysses Robert. *Butler and His Cavalry in the War of Secession*. Columbia, S.C., 1909.

————. *South Carolina Bench and Bar*. Columbia, S.C., 1908.

Brown, John Henry. *Indian Wars and Pioneers of Texas*. Austin, Tex., n.d.

Bryan, T. Conn. *Confederate Georgia*. Athens, Ga., 1953.

Burrage, Walter L., and Kelly, Howard A. (eds.) *American Medical Biographies*. Baltimore, Md., 1920.

Burt, Jesse C. *Nashville: Its Life and Times*. Nashville, Tenn., 1959.

Bushong, Millard Kessler. *Old Jube*. Boyce, Va., 1955.

Caldwell, Joshua William. *Sketches of the Bench and Bar of Tennessee*. Knoxville, Tenn., 1898.

Calhoun, Robert Dabney. "A History of Concordia Parish, Louisiana." *Louisiana Historical Quarterly*, XV (1932).

————. "The John Perkins Family of Northeast Louisiana." *Louisiana Historical Quarterly*, XIX (1936).

Callahan, James M. *Diplomatic History of the Confederacy*. Baltimore, Md., 1901.

Candler, Allen D., and Evans, Clement Anselm (eds.), *Cyclopedia of Georgia*. 3 vols. Atlanta, Ga., 1906.

Capers, Henry D. *The Life and Times of C. G. Memminger*. Richmond, Va., 1893.

Capers, Walter Branham. *The Soldier-Bishop Ellison Capers*. New York, 1912.

Cate, Wirt Armistead. *Lucius Q. C. Lamar*. New York, 1969.

Catherwood, T. B. (ed.) *Life of William M. Wadley*. Savannah, Ga., 1885.

Cauthen, Charles Edward. *South Carolina Goes to War, 1861-1865*. Chapel Hill, N.C., 1950.

Charleston *News and Courier*, August 1881; December 1890.

Chitwood, Oliver P. *John Tyler: Champion of the Old South*. New York, 1939.

Christian, William Asbury. *Richmond, Her Past and Present*. Richmond, Va., 1912.

Clark, Walter (ed.) *Histories of the Several Regiments and Battalions from North Carolina in the Great War, 1861-1865*. 5 vols. Raleigh, N.C., 1901.

Clayton, William W. *History of Davidson County, Tennessee*. Philadelphia, 1880.

Clift, G. Glenn. *Governors of Kentucky*. Cynthiana, Ky., 1942.

———— (comp.) *Kentucky Marriages* 1797-1865. Baltimore, Md., 1966.

Collins, Lewis. *Historical Sketches of Kentucky*. 2 vols., Covington, Ky., 1882.

Conerly, Luke Ward. *Pike County, Mississippi*. Nashville, Tenn., 1909.

Confederate Veteran. 40 vols., Nashville, Tenn., 1893-1932.

Connelley, William E., and Coulter, E. Merton, *History of Kentucky*. 5 vols., Chicago, 1922.

Connelly, Thomas Lawrence. *Army of the Heartland*. Baton Rouge, La., 1967.

————. *Autumn of Glory*. Baton Rouge, La., 1971.

————, and Jones, Archer. *The Politics of Command* Baton Rouge, La., 1973.

Conner, Henry G. *John Archibald Campbell*. New York, 1920.

Conner, R. W. D. *North Carolina Biography*. 6 vols., Chicago, 1919.

Conrad, Howard L. (ed.) *Encyclopedia of the History of Missouri*. 8 vols., New York, 1901.

Cook, Anna Maria Green. *History of Baldwin County, Georgia*. Anderson, S.C., 1925.

Cook, Harvey T. *The Life and Work of James Clement Furman*. Greenville, S.C., 1926.

Cooper, William J. "A Reassessment of Jefferson Davis as War Leader: The Case from Atlanta to Nashville." *Journal of Southern History*, XXXVI (1970).

"Correspondence of Thomas R. Cobb." *Southern History Association Publications*, XI (1907).

Couper, William. *One Hundred Years at V. M. I.* Richmond, Va., 1939.

Cowles, William H. *The Life and Services of James B. Gordon.* n.p., n.d.

Cox, William Ruffin. *Address on the Life and Services of General James H. Lane, Army of Northern Virginia.* Richmond, Va., 1908.

Crawford, Clifton E. *History of Bladen County.* Elizabethtown, N.C., 1957.

Cullop, Charles P. *Confederate Propaganda in Europe.* Coral Gables, Fla., 1969.

Culver, Emma Beale. "Thomas Hill Watts: A Statesman of the Old Regime." *Alabama Historical Society Transactions*, IV (1903).

Cummings, Charles M. *The Curious Career of Bushrod Rust Johnson.* Rutherford, N.J., 1971.

Cunningham, Horace Herndon. *Doctors in Gray.* Baton Rouge, La., 1958.

Cunyus, Lucy J. *History of Bartow County.* Cartersville, Ga., 1933.

Curry, Roy L. "James A. Seddon, A Southern Prototype." *Virginia Magazine of History and Biography*, LXII (1950).

Dale, Edward E. (ed.) *Cherokee Cavaliers.* Norman, Okla., 1939.

Daniell, L. E. (comp.) *Personnel of the Texas State Government.* Austin, Tex., 1887.

Davidson, Chalmers Gaston. *The Last Foray.* Columbia, S.C., 1971.

Davis, Burke. *Jeb Stuart: The Last Cavalier.* New York, 1957.

Davis, Charles Shepard. *Colin J. McRae: Confederate Financial Agent.* Tuscaloosa, Ala., 1961.

Davis, Reuben. *Recollections of Mississippi and Mississippians.* New York, 1889.

Davis, William C. *Breckenridge: Statesman, Soldier, Symbol.* Baton Rouge, La., 1973.

Davis, William W. *The Civil War and Reconstruction in Florida.* New York, 1913.

Denman, Charles Phillips. *The Secession Movement in Alabama.* Montgomery, Ala., 1933.

Dew, Charles R. *Ironmaker to the Confederacy.* New Haven, Conn., 1966.

Dinwiddie County. Richmond, Va., 1942.

Dorsey, Sarah A. *Recollections of Henry Watkins Allen.* New Orleans, La., 1866.

Douglas, Henry Kyd. *I Rode with Stonewall.* Chapel Hill, N.C., 1940.

Dowd, Clement. *Life of Zebulon B. Vance.* Charlotte, N.C., 1897.

Dowd, Jerome. *Sketches of Prominent Living North Carolinians.* Raleigh, N.C., 1888.

Downs, Winfield S. (ed.) *Encyclopedia of American Biography.* 32 vols., New York, 1934-1960.

Dubose, John Witherspoon. *The Life and Times of William Lowndes Yancey.* 2 vols., New York, 1942.

Dufour, Charles L. *Nine Men in Gray.* Garden City, N.Y., 1963.

Duke, Basil William. *Reminiscences of Basil William Duke.* New York, 1911.

Duncan, George W. "John Archibald Campbell." *Transactions of the Alabama Historical Society*, V (1904).

Durden, Robert. *The Gray and the Black: Confederate Debate on Emancipation.* Durham, N.C., 1973.

Durham, Walter T. *The Great Leap Westward.* Gallatin, Tex., 1969.

Durkin, Joseph T. *Stephen R. Mallory: Confederate Navy Chief.* Chapel Hill, N.C., 1954.

Dyer, John Percy. *"Fightin' Joe" Wheeler*. Baton Rouge, La., 1941.

———. *The Gallant Hood*. Indianapolis, Ind., 1950.

Early, Jubal A. *Autobiographical Sketch and Narrative of the War Between the States*. Philadelphia, 1912.

Easby-Smith, Anne. *William Russell Smith of Alabama*. Philadelphia, 1931.

East Tennessee, Historical and Biographical. Chattanooga, Tenn., 1893.

Eckenrode, Hamilton James, and Conrad, Bryan. *James Longstreet*. Chapel Hill, N.C., 1936.

Eliot, Ellsworth. *West Point in the Confederacy*. New Haven, Conn., 1905.

———. *Yale in the Civil War*. New Haven, Conn., 1932.

Estill, Mary S. (ed.) "Diary of a Confederate Congressman, 1862-1863." *Southwestern Historical Quarterly*, XXXIX (1935-1936).

Ettinger, Amos Aschbach. *The Mission of Pierre Soulé to Spain, 1853-1855*. New Haven, Conn., 1932.

Evans, Clement A. (ed.) *Confederate Military History*, 12 vols., Atlanta, 1899.

Fahner, Alvin A. "William 'Extra Billy' Smith, Governor of Virginia, 1864-1865." *Virginia Magazine of History and Biography*, LXXIV (1966).

Farish, Thomas Edwin. *History of Arizona*. 8 vols., Phoenix, Ariz., 1915.

Faunt, Joan Reynolds, and May, John Amasa. *South Carolina Secedes*. Columbia, S.C., 1960.

———, and Reynolds, Emily Bellinger. *Biographical Directory of the Senate of the State of South Carolina, 1776-1964*. Columbia, S.C., 1964.

Felt, Jeremy P. "Lucius B. Northrop and the Confederate Subsistence Department." *Virginia Magazine of History and Biography*, LXIX (1961).

Felton, Rebecca, *Memoirs of Georgia Politics*. Atlanta, 1913.

Fidler, William Percy. *Augusta Jane Evans Wilson, 1835-1900*. Tuscaloosa, Ala., 1951.

Fitzgerald, Oscar Penn. *Bishop George F. Pierce*. Nashville, Tenn., 1896.

Fleming, Walter Lynwood. *Civil War and Reconstruction in Alabama*. New York, 1905.

Flippin, Percy Scott. *Herschel V. Johnson of Georgia*. Richmond, Va., 1931.

Florida Law Journal, XXIII, 1949.

Foote, Henry Stuart. *War of the Rebellion*. New York, 1885.

Fortier, Alcee. *A History of Louisiana*. 2 vols., New York, 1904.

Freeman, Douglas Southal. *Lee's Lieutenants*. 3 vols., New York, 1942-1945.

———. *Robert E. Lee: A Biography*. 4 vols., New York, 1934-1935.

French, Edwin Malcolm Chase. *Senator George G. Vest*. Boston, 1930.

French, Samuel Gibbs. *Two Wars: An Autobiography*. Nashville, Tenn., 1901.

Gaines, William H. *Biographical Register of Members, Virginia State Convention of 1861*. Richmond, 1969.

Gandrud, Pauline Jones. *Marriage Records of Greene County, Alabama, 1823-1860*. Memphis, Tenn., 1969.

Gannon, Michael V. *Rebel Bishop: The Life and Era of Augustin Verot*. Milwaukee, Wis., 1964.

Garnett, James Mercer. "Biographical Sketch of Honorable Muscoe Russell Hunter Garnett." *William and Mary Quarterly*, XVIII (1909).

Garrard, Annie W. "John W. Ellis." M.A. Thesis, Duke University, 1930.

Garrett, William. *Reminiscences of Public Men in Alabama*. Atlanta, Ga., 1872.

Ginther, James E. "Alias Bill Arp." *Georgia Review*, IV (1950).

Goff, Richard D. *Confederate Supply*. Durham, N.C., 1969.

Gonzales, John E. "Henry Stuart Foote: Confederate Congressman and Exile." *Civil War History*, XI (1963).

Goode, John. *Recollections of a Lifetime*. New York, 1906.

Govan, Gilbert Eaton, and Livingood, James W. *A Different Valor*. Indianapolis, Ind., 1950.

Green, John W. *Law and Lawyers*. Jackson, Tenn., 1950.

Griffin, Clarence W. *History of Old Tryon and Rutherford Counties*. Asheville, N.C., 1937.

Groene, Bertram H. *Ante-Bellum Tallahassee*. Tallahassee, Fla., 1971.

Guerry, Moultrie. *Men Who Made Sewanee*. Sewanee, Tenn., 1932.

Hale, William T., and Merritt, David L. *A History of Tennessee and Tennesseans*. 8 vols., Chicago, 1913.

Hallum, John. *Biographical and Pictorial History of Arkansas*. Albany, N.Y., 1887.

Hamilton, Joseph Gregoire deRoulhac (ed.) *Correspondence of Jonathan Worth*. Raleigh, N.C., 1909.

————. *Reconstruction in North Carolina*. New York, 1914.

Hamlin, Percy Gatling. *"Old Bald Head."* Strasburg, Va., 1940.

Handy, Joseph Breckinridge. *A Genealogical Compilation of the Wilson Family*. New York, 1897.

Hardy, John. *Selma: Her Institutions and Her Men*. Selma, Ala., 1879.

Harris, William Charles. *Leroy Pope Walker, Confederate Secretary of War*. Tuscaloosa, Ala., 1962.

Harris, W. M. *From the Diary of General Nat H. Harris*. Duncansby, Miss., 1901.

Hartje, Robert George. *Van Dorn*. Nashville, Tenn., 1967.

Hatton, Roy O. "Prince Camille de Polignac and the American Civil War, 1863-1865." *Louisiana Studies*, III (1964).

Hay, Thomas Robinson. "Lucius B. Northrop: Commissary General of the Confederacy." *Civil War History*, IX (1963).

Haymond, Henry. *History of Harrison County, West Virginia*. Morgantown, W. Va., 1910.

Haynesworth, Hugh C. *Haynesworth, Furman and Allied Families*. Sumter, S.C., 1942.

Heitman, Francis Bernard. *Historical Register and Dictionary of the United States Army*. 2 vols., Washington, D.C., 1903.

Hempstead, Fay. *Historical Review of Arkansas*. 4 vols., Chicago, 1911.

Henderson, Harry McCarry. *Texas in the Confederacy*. San Antonio, Tex., 1955.

Henry, Robert Selph. *"First with the Most" Forrest*. Jackson, Tenn., 1969.

Hill, Benjamin Harvey, Jr. *Senator Benjamin Harvey Hill of Georgia: His Life, Speeches, and Writing*. Atlanta, Ga., 1891.

Hill, Louise Biles. *Joseph E. Brown and the Confederacy*. Chapel Hill, N.C., 1939.

History of Cass and Bates County, Missouri. St. Joseph, Mo., 1883.

History of the Baptist Denomination in Georgia. Atlanta, Ga., 1881.

History of Ray County, Missouri. St. Louis, Mo., 1881.

History of Spartanburg County, A. Spartanburg, S.C., 1940.

Horton, Louise. *Samuel Bell Maxey*. Austin, Tex., 1974.

Huff, Lawrence. "Joseph Addison Turner's Role in Georgia Politics, 1851-1860." *Georgia Historical Quarterly*, L (1966).

————. "Joseph Addison Turner: Southern Editor During the Civil War." *Journal of Southern History*, XXIX (1963).

Hughs, Nathaniel Cheairs. *General William J. Hardee*. Baton Rouge, La., 1965.

Hughs, Robert W. *Editors of the Past*. Richmond, Va., 1897.

Hurlburt, J. S. *History of the Rebellion in Bradley County*. Indianapolis, Ind., 1866.

Huse, Caleb. *The Suppliers of the Confederate Army*. Boston, 1904.

Jemison, E. Grove. *Historic Tales of Talladega*. Montgomery, Ala., 1959.

Johnson, Augusta Phillips. *A Century of Wayne County, Kentucky*. Louisville, Ky., 1939.

Johnson, Ludwell H. *Red River Campaign*. Baltimore, Md., 1958.

Johnson, Robert U., and Buel, Clarence C. (eds.) *Battles and Leaders of the Civil War*. 4 vols., New York, 1956.

Johnson, Sidney Smith. *Texans Who Wore the Gray*. Tyler, Tex., 1907.

Johnson, Thomas Cary. *Life and Letters of Robert Lewis Dabney*. Richmond, Va., 1906.

Johnston, Frederick (comp.) *Memorials of Old Virginia Clerks*. Lynchburg, Va., 1888.

Jones, Archer W. *Confederate Strategy from Shiloh to Vicksburg*. Baton Rouge, La., 1961.

————. "Some Aspects of George W. Randolph's Service as Confederate Secretary of War." *Journal of Southern History*, XXVI (1960).

Jones, Samuel. *The Siege of Charleston*. New York, 1911.

Journal of the Confederate Congress. 7 vols., Washington, D.C., 1904-1905.

Kell, John McIntosh. *Recollections of a Naval Life*. Washington, D.C., 1900.

Kelly, Howard A., and Burrage, Walter L. (eds.) *American Medical Biographies*. Baltimore, Md., 1920.

Kerby, Robert L. *The Confederate Invasion of New Mexico and Arizona*. Los Angeles, 1958.

————. *Kirby Smith's Confederacy: The Trans-Mississippi South, 1863-1865*. New York, 1972.

King, Alma Dexter. "The Political Career of William Simpson Oldham." *Southwestern Historical Quarterly*, XXXIII (1929).

King, Alvy L. *Louis T. Wigfall*. Baton Rouge, La., 1970.

King, Joseph L. *Dr. William Bagby*. Richmond, Va., 1927.

Kirkland, Edward Chase. *The Peacemakers of 1864*. New York, 1927.

Kirkland, T. J., and Kennedy, R. M. *Historic Camden*. Columbia, S.C., 1926.

Kirkpatrick, Arthur R. "Missouri's Delegation to the Confederate Congress." *Civil War History*, V (1957).

Kirwin, Albert D. *John J. Crittenden: The Struggle for the Union*. Lexington, Ky., 1962.

Klein, Maury. *Edward Porter Alexander*. Athens, Ga., 1971.

Knight, Lucian Lamar. *A Standard History of Georgia and Georgians*. New York, 1917.

Konkle, Burton Alva. *John Motley Morehead and the Development of North Carolina, 1796-1866*. Spartanburg, S.C., 1971.

Lee, Charles Robert. *The Confederate Constitutions*. Chapel Hill, N.C., 1963.

Lee, Susan Pendleton. *Memoirs of William Nelson Pendleton, D.D.* Philadelphia, 1893.

Levin H. (ed.) *The Lawyers and Lawmakers of Kentucky*. Chicago, 1897.

Lewis, William Draper. *Great American Lawyers*. 8 vols., Philadelphia, 1907-1909.

Lindsley, John Berrien (ed.) *Military Annals of Tennessee, Confederate*. Nashville, Tenn., 1886.

Longstreet, James. *From Manassas to Appomattox*. New York, 1896.

Lonn, Ella. *Foreigners in the Confederacy*. Chapel Hill, N.C., 1940.

Loring, William Wing. *A Confederate Soldier in Egypt*. New York, 1884.

Lowe, Marshall, and Scott, Gary. *Green County Historical Factbook*. Greensburg, Ky., 1970.

Lubbock, Percy. *Six Decades in Texas: The Memoirs of Francis R. Lubbock*. Austin, Tex., 1968.

Lynch, James Daniel. *The Bench and Bar of Mississippi*. New York, 1881.

———. *The Bench and Bar of Texas*. St. Louis, Mo., 1885.

Maccosson, Isaac Frederick. *"Marse Henry."* New York, 1951.

MacKall, William Wann. *A Son's Recollections of His Father*. New York, 1930.

Maddex, Jack. *The Reconstruction of Edward A. Pollard*. Chapel Hill, N.C., 1974.

———. *The Virginia Conservatives*. Chapel Hill, N.C., 1970.

Maffitt, Emma Martin. *The Life and Services of John Newland Maffitt*. New York, 1906.

Makers of America, Florida Edition. 2 vols., Atlanta, Ga., 1909.

Marshall, Park. *William B. Bate*. Nashville, Tenn., 1908.

Mason, Virginia. *The Public Life and Diplomatic Correspondence of James M. Mason*. Roanoke, Va., 1903.

Massey, Mary Elizabeth. *Bonnet Brigades*. New York, 1966.

Mathes, J. Harvey. *The Old Guard in Gray*. Memphis, Tenn., 1897.

McCormick, John G. "Personnel of the Convention of 1861." *James Sprunt Studies in History and Political Science*. Chapel Hill, N.C., 1900.

McDonald, Archie P. (ed.) *Make Me a Map of the Valley: The Civil War Journal of Stonewall Jackson's Topographer*. Dallas, Tex., 1973.

McGrady, Edward. *Cyclopedia of Eminent and Representative Men of the Carolinas of the Nineteenth Century*, II. Madison, Wis., 1892.

———. "Gregg's South Carolina Brigade." *Southern Historical Society Papers*, XIII (1909).

McGregor, James C. *The Disruption of Virginia*. New York, 1922.

McLemore, Richard A. *A History of Mississippi Baptists, 1780-1970*. Jackson, Miss., 1971.

McLure, Mary Lillia. *Louisiana Leaders*. Shreveport, La., 1935.

McMurtry, R. Gerald. *Ben Hardin Helm*. Chicago, 1943.

McWhiney, Grady. *Braxton Bragg and Confederate Defeat*. New York, 1973.

Meade, Robert D. *Judah P. Benjamin*. Chicago, 1944.

Memories of Northwest Louisiana. Nashville, Tenn., n.d.

Meriwether, Colyar. *Raphael Semmes*. Philadelphia, 1913.

Mitchell, Broadus. *William Gregg*. Chapel Hill, N.C., 1928.

Monaghan, James. *Civil War on the Western Border, 1854-1865*. Boston, 1955.

Montgomery, Horace. *Howell Cobb's Confederate Career*. Tuscaloosa, Ala., 1959.

Moore, Avery C. *Destiny's Soldier*. San Francisco, 1958.

Moore, John Preston (ed.) *The Letters of A. Dudley Mann to Jefferson Davis, 1869-1889*. Tuscaloosa, Ala., 1960.

———. "Pierre Soulé: Southern Expansionist and Promoter." *Journal of Southern History*, XXI (1950).

Morgan, James Appleton. *A History of the Family of Morgan*. New York, 1902.

Morrison, James L. (ed.) *Memoirs of Henry Heth*. Westport, Conn., 1973.

Morton, Frederick O. (ed.) *A History of Monroe County, West Virginia*. Baltimore, 1974.

Myers, Robert Manson. *The Children of Pride*. New Haven, Conn., 1972.

Nash, Charles Edward. *Biographical Sketches of Generals Pat Cleburne and Thomas C. Hindman*. Little Rock, Ark., 1898.

Natchez *Democrat*. October 24, 1883.

National Cyclopedia of American Biography, LI, 5th ed., (1969).

Nevins, Allan. *Statesmanship of the Civil War*. New York, 1947.

Newberry, Farrar. *A Life of Mr. Garland of Arkansas*. Arkadelphia, Ark., 1908.

New Orleans *Daily Picayune*. 1892.

Nichols, James L. *Confederate Engineers*. Tuscaloosa, Ala., 1957.

Noll, Arthur Howard. *Doctor Quintard*. Sewanee, Tenn., 1905.

———. *History of the Church in the Diocese of Tennessee*. New York, 1900.

Northen, William J. (ed.) *Men of Mark in Georgia*. 6 vols., Atlanta, Ga., 1911.

Nuermberger, Ruth Ketring. *The Clays of Alabama*. Lexington, Ky., 1958.

O'Flaherty, Daniel. *General J. Shelby, Undefeated Rebel*. Chapel Hill, N.C., 1954.

O'Neal, John B. *Biographical Sketches of the Bench and Bar of South Carolina*. 2 vols., Columbia, S.C., 1859.

Orr, John A. "Life of Honorable James T. Harrison." *Publications of the Mississippi Historical Society*, VIII (1904).

Ott, Eloise Robinson, and Chazel, Louis Hickman. *Ocali County*. Ocala, Fla., 1966.

Owen, Thomas McAdory. *History of Alabama and Dictionary of Alabama Biography*. 4 vols., Chicago, 1921.

Owens, Hubert Bond. *Georgia's Painting Prelate*. Athens, Ga., 1945.

Owsley, Frank Lawrence. *King Cotton Diplomacy*. Chicago, 1925.

Palmer, Benjamin Morgan. *Life and Letters of James Henry Thornwell*. Richmond, Va., 1875.

Parks, Joseph Howard. *General Edmund Kirby Smith*. Baton Rouge, La., 1954.

————. *General Leonidas Polk*. Baton Rouge, La., 1962.

Patrick, Rembert W. *Jefferson Davis and His Cabinet*. Baton Rouge, La., 1944.

Patton, James Welch. *Unionism and Reconstruction in Tennessee*. Chapel Hill, N.C., 1934.

Pearce, Haywood Jefferson. *Benjamin H. Hill, Secession and Reconstruction*. Chicago, 1928.

Peele, William J. (comp.) *Lives of Distinguished North Carolinians*. Raleigh, N.C., 1898.

Pemberton, John Clifford. *Pemberton, Defender of Vicksburg*. Chapel Hill, N.C., 1942.

Pereya, Lillian A. *James Lusk Alcorn*. Baton Rouge, La., 1966.

Perman, Michael. *Reunion Without Compromise*. Cambridge, England, 1973.

Perrin, William Henry (ed.) *Southwest Louisiana Biographical and Historical*. New Orleans, 1891.

Peyton, John L. *History of Augusta County, Virginia*. Bridgewater, Va., 1953.

Phillips, Ulrich B. *Robert Toombs*. New York, 1913.

Pickett, LaSalle C. *The Heart of a Soldier as Revealed in the Intimate Letters of General George E. Pickett*. Boston, 1928.

Pilcher, James E. *The Surgeon-Generals of the United States Army*. Carlisle, Pa., 1905.

Polk, William Harrison. *Polk Family and Kinsmen*. Louisville, Ky., 1912.

Polk, William N. *Leonidas Polk*. 2 vols., New York, 1893.

Potter, Davis. *Lincoln and His Party in the Secession Crisis*. New Haven, Conn., 1941.

Proctor, Ben H. *Not Without Honor*. Austin, Tex., 1962.

Pryor, John P. *History of Forrest's Campaign*. New Orleans, 1868.

Purdue, Howell, and Purdue, Elizabeth. *Pat Cleburne, Confederate General*. Hillsboro, Tex., 1973.

Rainwater, Percy. *Mississippi, Storm Center of Secession, 1856-1861*. Baton Rouge, La., 1938.

Ramsdell, Charles W. *Behind the Lines in the Southern Confederacy*. Baton Rouge, La., 1944.

————. *Reconstruction in Texas*. New York, 1910.

Ranck, James B. *Albert Gallatin Brown*. New York, 1937.

Raper, Horace W. "William Woods Holden; a Political Biography." Ph.D. dissertation, University of North Carolina, 1951.

Reagan, John H. *Memoirs*. New York, 1906.

Register, Alvaretta K. (comp.) *The Kenan Family and Some Allied Families*. Statesboro, Ga., 1967.

Rerick, Rowland H. *Memoirs of Florida*. 2 vols., Atlanta, Ga., 1902.

Reynolds, Donald E. *Editors Make War*. Nashville, Tenn., 1970.

Rice, Madeleine H. *American Catholic Opinion and the Slavery Controversy*. New York, 1944.

Richard, J. Fraise. *The Florence Nightingale of the Confederate Army*. New York, 1914.

Riley, Benjamin Franklin. *Makers and Romance of Alabama History.* n.p., 1915.

Roberts, Walter Adolphe. *Semmes of the Alabama.* Indianapolis, Ind., 1938.

Robinson, William Morris. *The Confederate Privateers.* New Haven, Conn., 1928.

———. *Justice in Grey.* Cambridge, Mass., 1941.

Rochelle, James Henry. *Life of Rear Admiral John Randolph Tucker.* Washington, D.C., 1903.

Rogers, Mary Nixon. *A History of Brazoria County, Texas.* n.p., 1958.

Roland, Charles P. *Albert Sidney Johnston: Soldier of Three Republics.* Austin, Tex., 1964.

Ross. Ishbel. *First Lady of the South.* New York, 1958.

———. *Rebel Rose.* New York, 1954.

Rowland, Dunbar. *Biographical Guide to the Mississippi Hall of Fame.* Jackson, Miss., 1935.

———. *Courts, Judges, and Lawyers of Mississippi, 1798-1935.* Jackson, Miss., 1935.

———. *History of Mississippi.* 2 vols., Chicago, 1925.

Rumple, Jethro. *A History of Rowan County.* Salisbury, N.C., 1881.

Russell, Charles Wells. *Roebuck.* Baltimore, Md., 1868.

Ryle, Walter. *Missouri: Union or Secession.* Nashville, Tenn., 1931.

Sanger, Donald B., and Hay, Thomas R. *James Longstreet.* 2 vols., Baton Rouge, La., 1952.

Sarrafian, Mary K. *The Harrison Family of Texas.* Waco, Tex., 1966.

Scharf, John Thomas. *History of the Confederate Navy.* New York, 1887.

———. *History of St. Louis, . . . Including Biographical Sketches of Representative Men.* 2 vols., Philadelphia, 1883.

Schneck, Martin. *Up Came Hill.* Harrisburg, Pa., 1958.

Scott, Mary Wingfield. *Houses of Old Richmond.* Richmond, Va., 1941.

Sears, Louis Martin. *John Slidell.* Durham, N.C., 1925.

Seitz, Don C. *Braxton Bragg.* Columbia, S.C., 1924.

Shalhope, Robert. *Sterling Price.* Columbia, Mo., 1971.

Shaw, Arthur Marvin. *William Preston Johnson: A Transitional Figure of the Confederacy.* Baton Rouge, La., 1943.

Shawkey, Morris Purdy. *West Virginia.* 5 vols., New York, 1928.

Sherrill, William Lander. *Annals of Lincoln County, North Carolina.* Baltimore, Md., 1967.

Shinn, Josiah H. *Pioneers and Makers of Arkansas.* n.p., 1908.

Sillers, F.W. *History of Bolivar County.* Jackson, Miss., 1948.

Silver, James Wesley. *Confederate Morale and Church Propaganda.* Tuscaloosa, Ala., 1957.

———. *Mississippi in the Confederacy.* 2 vols., Baton Rouge, La., 1961.

Simms, Henry Harrison. *Life of Robert M. T. Hunter.* Richmond, Va., 1935.

Simpkins, Francis Butler, and Patton, James Welch. *Women in the Confederacy.* Richmond, Va., 1936.

Simpson, Amos E., and Cassidy, Vincent H. *Henry Watkins Allen*. Baton Rouge, La., 1964.

Simpson, Harold B. (ed.) *Texas in the War, 1861-1865*. Hillsboro, Tex., 1965.

Sims, Carlton C. (ed.) *A History of Rutherford County*. Murfreesboro, N.C., 1947.

Skipper, Otis Clark. *J.D.B. DeBow, Magazinist of the Old South*. Athens, Ga., 1958.

Slaughter, Philip. *History of Bristol Parish*. Richmond, Va., 1846.

Smith, Florie Carter. *The History of Oglethorpe County, Georgia*. Washington, Ga., 1970.

Smith, Margaret Vowell. *Virginia, 1492-1892*. Washington, D.C., 1893.

Smith, William Russell. *The History and Debates of the Convention of the People of Alabama*. Montgomery, Ala., 1861.

Snow, William Parker. *Southern Generals, Their Lives and Campaigns*. New York, 1866.

Sobel, Robert (ed.) *Biographical Directory of the United States Cabinet*. Westport, Conn., 1971.

Sona, Guy McClure, and Sona, Ruth Wells. *Marriage Records of Cole County, Missouri*. Jefferson City, Mo., 1964.

Sorrel, Gilbert Moxley. *Recollections of a Confederate Staff Officer*. New York, 1905.

South Carolina Historical and Genealogical Magazine, II.

Southern Bivouac. I-V (1883-1887).

Southern History Association Publications. 15 vols., Richmond, Va., 1876-1915.

South in the Building of the Nation, The. 12 vols., Richmond, Va., 1909-1913.

Speer, William S. (comp.) *Biographical Directory of the Tennessee General Assembly*. Nashville, Tenn., 1968.

————. *Sketches of Prominent Tennesseans*. Nashville, Tenn., 1888.

Spencer, J. H. *A History of Kentucky Baptists from 1769 to 1885*. 2 vols., Cincinnati, Ohio, 1885.

Standard, William D. *Columbus, Georgia in the Confederacy*. New York, 1954.

Starling, Edmund L. *History of Henderson County, Kentucky*. Henderson, Ky., 1887.

Sterx, H. E. *Partners in Rebellion: Alabama Women in the Civil War*. Rutherford, N.J., 1970.

Stewart, G.J.D. (ed.) *The History of the Bench and Bar of Missouri*. St. Louis, Mo., 1898.

Stewart, George W. *Pickett's Charge*. Boston, 1959.

Stickles, Arndt Mathias. *Simon Bolivar Buckner*. Chapel Hill, N.C., 1940.

Stockard, Sallie W. *History of Guilford County, North Carolina*. Knoxville, Tenn., 1902.

Strode, Hudson, *Jefferson Davis*. 3 vols., New York, 1955-1964.

Stubbs, Elizabeth Saunders Blair. *Early Settlers in Alabama*. Baltimore, Md., 1969.

Summers, Lewis Preston. *History of Southwest Virginia*. Baltimore, Md., 1966.

Swiggett, Howard. *The Rebel Raider: A Life of John Hunt Morgan*. Garden City, N.Y., 1937.

Tankersley, Allen P. *John B. Gordon: A Study in Gallantry*. Atlanta, Ga., 1955.

Tarrant, S.F.H. *Honorable Daniel Pratt: A Biography*. Richmond, Va., 1904.

Taylor, Richard. *Destruction and Reconstruction*. New York, 1879.

Tebeau, Charlton W. *A History of Florida*. Coral Gables, Fla., 1971.

Telfair, Nancy. *A History of Columbus, Georgia*. Columbus, Ga., 1929.

Temple, Oliver M. *Notable Men of Tennessee from 1833 to 1875*. New York, 1912.

Temple, Sarah B. *The First Hundred Years: A Short History of Cobb County, in Georgia*. Atlanta, Ga., 1935.

Tennessee Historical Quarterly. 12 (1953).

Thomas, Davis Yancey. *Arkansas and Its People, A History, 1541-1930*. 4 vols., New York, 1930.

———. *Arkansas in War and Reconstruction, 1861-1874*. Little Rock, Ark., 1926.

Thomas, Henry W. *A History of the Doles-Cook Brigade*. Atlanta, Ga., 1903.

Thompson, Robert Luther. *Wiring a Continent*. New York, 1972.

Thompson, Samuel Bernard. *Confederate Purchasing Operations Abroad*. Chapel Hill, N.C., 1935.

Thompson, William Y. *Robert Toombs of Georgia*. Baton Rouge, La., 1966.

Tilghman, Oswald. *History of Talbot County, Maryland*. 2 vols., Baltimore, Md., 1915.

Todd, Richard Cecil. *Confederate Finance*. Athens, Ga., 1954.

Tucker, Glenn. *Zeb Vance, Champion of Personal Freedom*. Indianapolis, Ind., 1966.

Turner, Joseph Addison. *Autobiography of the "Countryman."* Atlanta, Ga., 1943.

Tyler, Lyon. *Encyclopedia of Virginia Biography*. 5 vols., New York, 1915.

———. *Men of Mark in Virginia*. 5 vols., Washington, D.C., 1906-1909.

University of North Carolina Magazine, 1-29 (1857-1906).

Vandiver, Frank E. (ed.) *Confederate Blockade Running Through Bermuda*. Austin, Tex., 1947.

———. *Jubal's Raid*. Baton Rouge, La., 1960.

———. *Mighty Stonewall*. New York, 1957.

———. *Ploughshares into Swords*. Austin, Tex., 1952.

Venable, Austin L. "The Public Career of William Lowndes Yancey." *Alabama Review*, XVI (1963).

Venable, Elizabeth M. *The Venables of Virginia*. n.p., 1925.

Von Abele, Rudolph. *Alexander H. Stephens*. Westport, Conn., 1971.

Waddell, James D. *Biographical Sketch of Linton Stephens*. Atlanta, Ga., 1879.

Wakelyn, Jon L. *The Politics of a Literary Man*. Westport, Conn., 1973.

Walker, Charles Duy. *Biographical Sketches of the Graduates and Eleves of the Virginia Military Institute*. Philadelphia, 1875.

Walker, C. Irvine. *The Life of General Richard Heron Anderson*. Charleston, S.C., 1917.

Wall, Joseph Frazier. *Henry Watterson, Reconstructed Rebel*. New York, 1956.

Wardlow, Joseph G. (comp.) *Genealogy of the Witherspoon Family*. Yorkville, S.C., 1910.

War of the Rebellion: A Compilation of the Official Records of the Union and Confederate Armies. 73 vols., Washington, D.C., 1880-1901.

Warner, Ezra J. *Generals in Gray*. Baton Rouge, La., 1959.

———, and Yearns, W. Buck. *Biographical Register of the Confederate Congress*. Baton Rouge, La., 1975.

Warren, Edward. *A Doctor's Experiences in Three Continents*. Baltimore, Md., 1885.

Wellman, Manley Wade. *Giant in Gray*. New York, 1949.

Wessels, William L. *Born to Be a Soldier: The Military Career of William Wing Loring.* Fort Worth, Tex., 1972.

Wheeler, John H. *Historical Sketches of North Carolina.* 2 vols., Baltimore, Md., 1964.

————. *Reminiscences and Memoirs of North Carolina.* Columbus, Ohio, 1884.

White, Laura A. *Robert Barnwell Rhett: Father of Secession.* New York, 1931.

Who's Who in America, 1905, 1912, 1913.

Wiley, Bell J. (ed.) *Letters of Warren Aiken, Confederate Congressman.* Westport, Conn., 1975.

Williams, Frances Leigh. *Matthew Fontaine Maury.* New Brunswick, N.J., 1963.

Williams, T. Harry. *Napoleon in Gray.* Baton Rouge, La., 1955.

Williamson, Joel. *After Slavery.* Chapel Hill, N.C., 1965.

Wilson, Harold. "Basil Manly, Apologist for Slavocracy." *Alabama Review*, XV (1962).

Wingfield, Marshall. *General A. P. Stewart, His Life and Letters.* Memphis, Tenn., 1954.

————. *A History of Caroline County, Virginia.* Baltimore, Md., 1969.

Winters, John D. *The Civil War in Louisiana.* Baton Rouge, La., 1963.

Wise, Barton H. *The Life of Henry A. Wise of Virginia.* New York, 1899.

Woods, Thomas H. "A Sketch of the Mississippi Secession Convention of 1861—Its Membership and Work." *Publications of the Mississippi Historical Society*, VI (1902).

Woodward, Comer Vann. *Origins of the New South.* Baton Rouge, La., 1951.

Wooldridge, John. *History of Nashville.* Nashville, Tenn., 1890.

Woolfolk, Sarah V. "Five Men Called Scalawags." *Alabama Review*, XVII (1964).

Wright, Marcus J. *General Officers of the Confederate Army.* New York, 1911.

————. *Texas in the War.* Hillsboro, Tex., 1965.

Yearns, Wilfred Buck. *The Confederate Congress.* Athens, Ga., 1960.

Young, Jesse B. *The Battle of Gettysburg.* New York, 1913.

Younger, Edward (ed.) *Inside the Confederate Government: The Diary of Robert Garlick Hill Kean.* New York, 1957.

Zuber, Richard L. *Jonathan Worth: A Biography of a Southern Unionist.* Chapel Hill, N.C., 1965.

Index

About the Author

Jon L. Wakelyn, an associate professor of history and a dean at Catholic University, is a specialist in Southern history and the Civil War and Reconstruction era. Among his other publications is *The Politics of a Literary Man.*

About the Advisory Editor

Frank E. Vandiver, provost and Harris Masterson Jr. Professor of History at Rice University, is one of the leading scholars of the Civil War and American military history.